THE BUICK
A COMPLETE HISTORY

FOURTH EDITION

The first edition published in 1980 soon became the accepted standard work on Buick and acknowledged
by historians and the Buick Motor Division as the only complete history of the marque.
The original edition has now been amended and updated.

THE BU

UICK

A COMPLETE HISTORY

BY TERRY B. DUNHAM AND LAWRENCE R. GUSTIN
WITH THE STAFF OF AUTOMOBILE QUARTERLY

90TH ANNIVERSARY EDITION

AN AUTOMOBILE QUARTERLY LIBRARY SERIES BOOK

for
Jeanne
and
Rose Mary

FOURTH EDITION

Typesetting by The Kutztown Publishing Co. Inc., Kutztown, Pennsylvania
Color separations by Lincoln Graphics Inc., Cherry Hill, New Jersey,
American Color Corp., Santa Ana, California, and South China Printing Co. Hong Kong
Printing and binding by South China Printing Co., Hong Kong

AUTOMOBILE QUARTERLY PUBLICATIONS

Publishing Director: JONATHAN A. STEIN
Associate Editor: JOHN A. HEILIG
Art Director: MICHAEL PARDO
Associate Art Director: JEAN SEIBERT

•

BUICK BOOK STAFF
Editor: BEVERLY RAE KIMES
Design: THEODORE R.F. HALL

•

Founding Editor and Publisher
L. SCOTT BAILEY

ABOUT AUTOMOBILE QUARTERLY

Automobile Quarterly was founded in 1962 as The Connoisseur's Magazine of Motoring Today, Yesterday and Tomorrow. In 1971 the magazine established its Library Series book division with the publication of the encyclopedia, *The American Car Since 1775*. Subsequent marque histories published in the Library Series include: *Cadillac: Standard of the World* by Maurice D. Hendry; *Corvette: America's Star-Spangled Sports Car* by Karl Ludvigsen; *Ferrari, The Man, The Machines* edited by Stan Grayson; *The Cars That Henry Ford Built* by Beverly Rae Kimes; *Kaiser-Frazer: The Last Onslaught on Detroit* by Richard M. Langworth; *The Golden Anniversary of the Lincoln Motorcar* by Beverly Rae Kimes; *Mustang! The Complete History of America's Pioneer Ponycar* by Gary Witzenburg; *Oldsmobile: The First Seventy-Five Years* by Beverly Rae Kimes and Richard M. Langworth; *Opel: Wheels to the World* by Karl Ludvigsen and Paul Frere; *Packard: A History of the Motor Car and the Company* edited by Beverly Rae Kimes; *Porsche: Excellence Was Expected* by Karl Ludvigsen; *Packard: The Pride* by J.M. Fenster; *The Alfa Romeo Tradition* by Griffith Borgeson; *Mercury Cougar 1967-1987* by Gary Witzenburg. *Camaro!* by Gary Witzenburg. The first book in Automobile Quarterly's new Restoration Guide Series is *The Complete Corvette Restoration & Technical Guide, Volume I, 1953-1962* by Noland Adams. *Volume II, 1963-1967* has been added. The Translated Edition Series was inaugurated with *BMW: A History* by Halwart Schrader, translated and adapted by Ron Wakefield. Additional books include Automobile Quarterly's *World of Cars; Great Cars & Grand Marques* edited by Beverly Rae Kimes; Automobile Quarterly's *Complete Handbook of Automobile Hobbies* edited by Beverly Rae Kimes; *The Best of Corvette News* edited by Karl Ludvigsen; *Corvette: A Piece of the Action* by William L. Mitchell and Allan Girdler; and *The Motor Car in Art*, by John Zolomij.

PREFACE

It was not just Buick.

"We're going down to The Buick," people in Flint would say. "The Buick" was a widely used colloquial expression, no doubt perpetuated because people looked upon building Buicks as something special. And it was—and is.

A plumbing inventor named David Dunbar Buick founded the company. A carriage manufacturer named William C. Durant promoted it. Later a red-headed former spark plug executive named Harlow Curtice saved it. And the cast of characters contributing to the Buick's history is perhaps more stellar than that of any automobile company in America, as a glance through the index of this volume will indicate.

In 1908 Buick was the number one producer of automobiles in the United States, and that year it provided the base for what would become the world's largest industrial corporation. And when General Motors was in trouble a decade later it was the strength of Buick which largely contributed to the corporation's survival.

In the history of the American automobile industry, there is no more dramatic and significant a chapter than that of the motorcar from Flint.

All this makes rather surprising the fact that Buick has never before been the subject of a full-length history, although perhaps it was the immensity of the task which until now has prevented a book of this scope to be published. Certainly a mention of the background surrounding this volume lends credence to that view.

More than a decade of research, interviews and documentation is represented between these two covers.

Since a dark night in 1957, when a modified 1937 Dodge coupe he was driving was soundly beaten in a drag race by a stock 1937 Buick Century sedan, Terry B. Dunham has been an enthusiast of the Buick and a student of its history. Soon thereafter he began gathering together what today is a most impressive archive of Buick lore, and during the late Sixties he began a campaign to search out and interview engineers, designers, executives and others who contributed to Buick history. In 1975 he suggested the idea for this book to *Automobile Quarterly*. Further research was conducted not only from coast to coast in the United States and across the border in Canada, but in England as well. Terry retired from General Motors in 1992 after 29 years of service.

A native of Flint, Michigan, Buick's headquarters city, Lawrence R. Gustin was a member of the staff of *The Flint Journal* and was long a writer on Buick and Flint history. In 1976 he produced *The Flint Journal Picture History of Flint* and in 1978 he edited the newspaper's Buick 75th Anniversary edition. Four years earlier he wrote *Billy Durant: Creator of General Motors*, the first full-length biography of Buick's early promoter, which won two national awards for historical writing and research. Some of the material used in *The Buick: A Complete History* was originally gathered for the Durant biography and recognition should be given particularly to the late Catherine L. Durant, widow of William C. Durant, and to Aristo Scrobogna, Durant's last personal secretary, both of whom were interviewed at length and provided the first access allowed any writer to the Durant papers. Larry wrote his sections of *The Buick: A Complete History* at Durant's personal desk, which is now in his home. The desk was given to him by the Durant estate after the death of Catherine Durant in 1974. Larry, whose grandfather, T.E. Irving, came to Flint from England in 1928 to work in Buick's foundry (and was later a wood patternmaker there), joined Buick in 1984 as manager of internal communications and started *Inside Buick* magazine. He became Buick's manager of news relations in 1987.

The author of the early and modern sections of this book, chapters one through six and 14 through 20 (and Appendix Seven), is Larry Gustin. Terry Dunham is responsible for the middle Buick period, chapters seven through thirteen, as well as most chapters in the appendices. The authors thank John Heilig of *Automobile Quarterly* for his work on this edition.

Because both authors, as well as the staff of *Automobile Quarterly*, were deeply involved in the research effort which resulted in this book, the contributions of those whose helped will be acknowledged on behalf of all.

Very special thanks should be given first to John W. Burnside, retired customer relations manager for Buick. His knowledge of Buick history is vast. In addition to reading the manuscript for accuracy, offering suggestions, providing specific information and photographs for a number of chapters, and delivering hundreds of pages of Buick production and sales statistics, he generously responded to every request with his time and his enthusiasm throughout this project.

Among the pioneers of Buick history who provided their recollections of the early days were Fred G. Hoelzle, who began his career at Buick when David Buick was still there, and Loren Hodge, the last surviving member of the original Buick racing team. Charles Stewart Mott was interviewed at length shortly before his death in 1973.

More recently, David Dunbar Buick II, grandson of Buick's founder, was interviewed at his home in Detroit. Charles E. Hulse of Flint supplied notes, information and advice from his original research into Buick's early years. Walter L. Marr III, grandson of Buick's first chief engineer, provided photos, old letters and clippings, and checked early chapters for accuracy about his grandfather. Mrs. Edward E. Hays, the daughter of Walter Marr, provided additional assistance.

Automotive historian George S. May made available a copy of Mrs. Alanson P. Brush's unpublished account of her husband's years at Buick. And Richard Scharchburg, General Motors Institute professor and curator of the

GMI Alumni Archives, which now contain the papers of William C. Durant and early Buick documents and photographs, provided further materials for the pioneer and middle years.

The Flint Journal, which has best chronicled Buick's history, permitted the use of the vast collections of clippings and other materials on file. *The Flint Journal*'s chief librarian, David W. Larzelere, provided research assistance. The manuscript, "An Industrial History of Flint," by a former *Journal* reporter and librarian, Frank Rodolf, was particularly helpful.

Numerous of the men responsible for the engineering of the Buick motorcar provided reminiscences and technical data. Charles Chayne and Adolph Braun were interviewed on several occasions regarding their experiences. Grateful acknowledgement should be made, too, to John Dolza, Jack Crouter, Clifford Studaker and Charles D. Holton—and to Joseph D. Turley, who not only consented to numerous interviews but also checked all chapters relating to the many years of his Buick career.

Among General Motors and Buick designers who contributed to the research for this book were Ned Nickles, William L. Mitchell, Frank Hershey, Charles M. Jordan, David R. Holls, David I. Clark, Jerry Hirshberg, William Porter and Wayne Kady—and Hermann C. Brunn chronicled his Brunn & Company days with Buick.

General Managers of Buick who were interviewed or contributed information include Ivan L. Wiles, Robert L. Kessler, Lee N. Mays, George R. Elges, Donald H. McPherson, Lloyd E. Reuss, Donald E. Hackworth and Edward H. Mertz. Further assistance was provided by these Buick and General Motors officials and employees: Gerald H. Rideout, Anthony W. DeLorenzo, Mary Gainey Turnbull, Waldo McNaught, Helen Turi, Thomas L. Pond, David Hudgens, Conn L. Clifford, Darwin E. Allen, R.S. O'Connell, William J. Schiffel, Dennis D. Duford.

Howard Clark offered reminiscences of his early proving ground work with Buick, and Walter Herndon of his automatic transmission development days. For their recollections of Harlow Curtice, gratitude to his longtime secretary, Alice Dewey, and to his daughter, Mrs. Catherine Horner—and for memories of William F. Hufstader, appreciation to his secretary of many years, Mrs. Helen Robinson.

Background on Buick sales activities, especially during the B.O.P. era, was provided by the late Albert H. Belfie, former general sales manager for Buick in Flint. With regard to the Howard Automobile Company in California, Phil Hall, C.F. Theilman, Mrs. Leslie Fenton (widow of C.S. Howard) and Mrs. Louise Howard offered reminiscences. In England, Russell Johns and Frank Dodd provided recollections of Lendrum & Hartman. Charles Murray, Stan Wellesley and Graham Bennett offered later information on the firm.

The help of the following Buick enthusiasts and automobile historians is also gratefully acknowledged: Gerry Fauth, and his son G. Gregory Fauth, for access to their Buick history collection; David Norton and Vern Bethel, for their innovative research into Buick's presence in England and Canada, respectively; the late Peter Helck and Charles Betts, for their expertise about Buick racing; Bob Trueax and Ronald Weidner for their knowledge of Buick Estate Wagon history; David Ware Chambers, for his documentation on the Buick six-cylinder years to 1930. Providing additional research assistance on varied subjects relating to Buick were Wayne Bouvé, Gary Hinkle, Bob Pipkin, Michael Rosen, Kenneth Amrhein, Michael Sedgwick, Nettie Seabrooks, Robert S. Gustin, Mr. and Mrs. Roy Scharfenburg, David W. Roman, Lisa Orrison, Eric Buick and Michael W.R. Davis.

The more than five hundred historic photographs which appear in this book are the result of a formidable search. Many are rare and never before published. And many people helped to get them. Acknowledgment for specific photographs appears at the conclusion of this volume, but appreciation should be extended to those thus far not mentioned here who assisted to generously in this effort: the late Henry Austin Clark Jr., of the Long Island Automotive Museum; G.N. Georgano of the National Motor Museum at Beaulieu; Philip C. Kwiatkowski and Merle Perry of the Alfred P. Sloan Museum; Mary Jacobs of the Product Information Department of Buick Motor Division; Floyd Joliet of General Motors Staff Operations; James A. Wren of the Motor Vehicle Manufacturers Association; the staff of the Kansas State Historical Society; and the archives of the Indianapolis Motor Speedway Corporation. And for their personal collections: William Browning, John A. Conde, Howard and Shelby Applegate, Jerry Pfafflin, George Dammann, Leonard J. Peterson, Barry Edmonds, Bruce Edwards.

The color portfolios herein are from *Automobile Quarterly*'s car portrait collection and, with the exception of a very few transparencies already on file, were commissioned especially for this book. For their talent and help, many thanks to photographers Rick Lenz, Roy Query, William L. Bailey, Gary D. Smith and David Franklin.

Lastly, mention should be made of the organizations devoted to the marque: the Buick Club of America and the McLaughlin-Buick Club of Canada. Many of the people who contributed to this book are members of these fine clubs, and have been acknowledged individually. Specific information about the clubs is included in the Notes and Photo Credits section of this book. But a salute is appropriate here to their members, for their ardent dedication to the preservation and restoration of the motorcars, for their steadfast efforts to perpetuate the history—and for personifying the spirit which made a project as awesome as this one such a pleasure to pursue.

CONTENTS

Chapter One

THE BUICK IN THE BEGINNING

Buick. Once the name belonged to a Scotsman, David Dunbar Buick, whose ancestors had changed it from the original "Buik." Later, Billy Durant, who made David's last name famous on thousands of automobiles, worried that people might pronounce it "Booick." But Durant, for a time, liked unusual names for his cars. He thought Buick had a nice ring to it. And it does seem so today, especially after it has been stamped on more than 32 million cars over nine decades.

But Buick is more than just a name for one of the few automobiles that has survived through the many crises of nine decades. In the history of the American automobile, the story of Buick is one of the most dramatic and important chapters. Henry Ford and his Model T have become associated in the public mind as the man and machine that almost singlehandedly put America on power-driven wheels. That common perception is somewhat overstated. Henry Ford, by producing in great numbers one car as reliable and inexpensive as possible, brought the automobile to a vast and virgin market. But the promoter of the Buick had a good idea, too. He went for variety rather than low price and relative simplicity, and in doing so made Buick the foundation of the largest industrial corporation in the history of the world—General Motors.

That promoter was William C. Durant. Even back in 1908, when Henry Ford was getting his Model T ready for market, Durant was considered by many of his contemporaries in the business to be the leading figure in the American automobile industry. Once, Durant attempted to buy out Ford—and may have come closer than is generally believed.

In 1940, Chris Sinsabaugh, who as a newspaperman had covered the automobile industry from its inception, reflected that "barring the initial success of Olds, which had begun to bog down toward the end of the first decade of the century, Buick was the first real success of the automobile industry and did more to promote the industry's well-being, in terms of public education, engineering advancement, and manufacturing progress than perhaps any other company."

The story of the Buick automobile begins obscurely enough, with the Scotsman, David Buick, who was, by trade, a plumbing inventor and manufacturer. With the assistance of others in Detroit, he developed a fine engine but was unable to follow through by bringing his horseless carriage to market.

The scene soon shifted sixty miles to the north, to Flint, Michigan, in 1903 a carriage-making community of 14,000 people. There, a normally conservative wagon maker, James H. Whiting, tried to make a success of David Buick's automobile, only to see the fledgling firm nearly go bankrupt. And then, with the entry of the irrepressible Billy Durant on the scene, Buick became a remarkable success. Durant, like Whiting a manufacturer of horse-drawn vehicles in Flint, took over the Buick company, promoted it into the number one producer of U.S. automobiles within four years and used that success to create General Motors. In the process, he probably saved the Oldsmobile, Cadillac and Pontiac (then Oakland) companies, as well as Buick, from extinction—and later he developed the Chevrolet.

None of this did much for David Dunbar Buick, however. Although his name has been carried on millions of automobiles, the bare facts of David Buick's automotive career are harsh.

He started the Buick Motor Company but instead of making a fortune, he lost one. By 1908, when the Buick company claimed the number one position in the industry, David Buick was no longer there. And in old age he was so poor he could afford neither a telephone nor a Buick.

David Buick has often been described as a tinkerer, dreamer, poor businessman. One contemporary called him a crank. More recently a historian wrote: "Seldom has history produced such an unrecalled—or misrecalled—man."

Those assessments seem fair enough. An objective look at David Buick's life would lead an impartial observer to believe he should have done better. Obviously, some important elements of personality were missing. Things just seemed to slip away from him.

And, somehow, that seems surprising. Some good things can be said about David Buick. He had shown, in the beginning, that he could be a successful businessman. And he demonstrated the strength of character to see his ideas through to completion.

In the plumbing business, Buick was an inventor with talent and

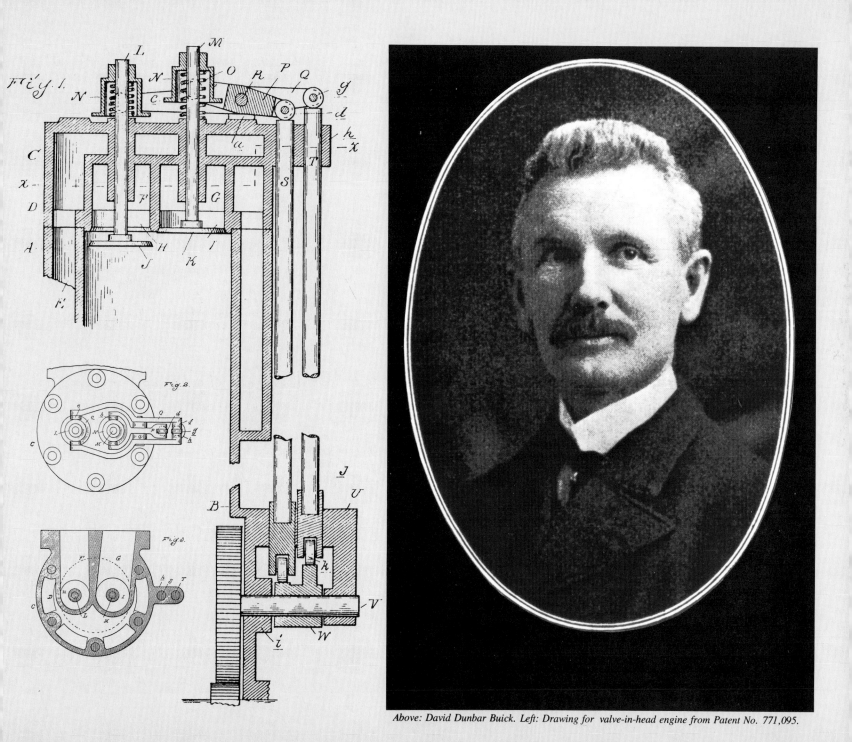

Above: David Dunbar Buick. Left: Drawing for valve-in-head engine from Patent No. 771,095.

Green Street in Arbroath, Scotland, where David Buick was born about halfway up block on left, September 19, 1854. Note decorations for Queen Elizabeth II's 1953 coronation but buildings may date back a century. His birth record is at top right. Buick and his second wife, Margaret, are pictured above right.

president of a profitable firm. When he became involved with gasoline engines, he led a small group of engineers who made a significant breakthrough in engine design. Even though continually running out of money, he had enough faith in his product to stay with it until the Buick automobile was finally a manufacturing success—even though it took others to get it there.

And ultimately, decades later, when it had all gotten away from him and he was an obscure instructor at the Detroit School of Trades, he refused to complain about what might have been. Bruce Catton, later to become renowned as a Civil War historian, interviewed Buick for a Detroit newspaper in April 1928. He found a seventy-four-year-old man with grey hair, a slight frame and a deeply lined face, but bright and cheerful eyes.

"I'm not worrying," the old man told Catton. "The failure is the man who stays down when he falls—the man who sits and worries about what happened yesterday, instead of jumping up and figuring what he's going to do today and tomorrow. That's what success is—looking ahead to tomorrow."

The undramatic early life of David Buick can be told quickly because it is known only in outline. He was born September 17th, 1854, at 26 Green Street in Arbroath, Scotland. His father, Alexander, was a joiner by trade. The family moved to the United States

when David was two, eventually settling in Detroit.

His father died when he was five (his mother, who remarried, operated a Detroit candy store for years). David delivered papers, he worked on a farm. At fifteen he went to work for the Alexander Manufacturing Company, Detroit, which made plumbing fixtures. Eventually he became a foreman there. At some time during this period he reportedly also worked in the James Flower & Brothers Manufacturing Company as an apprentice machinist. Henry Ford was an apprentice at that company in 1880.

In 1882, Buick and an old schoolmate, William Sherwood, took over the Alexander business when it failed. By all accounts, they were successful. Buick himself is credited with thirteen inventions between 1881 and 1889 for such things as a lawn sprinkler, valves, water closets, bathtubs and a flushing device. Perhaps his greatest plumbing achievement was devising a way to fix enamel to cast iron, helping make possible today's white bathroom and kitchen fixtures.

In the late Nineteenth Century, the Buick & Sherwood Manufacturing Company at Champlain and Meldrum streets in Detroit was prospering, and it would seem that the partners could have become wealthy merely by doing business as usual.* But Buick was more interested in making things work than in making money—apparently unable to figure out a way to do both at the same time. When he discovered the gasoline internal combustion engine, which was already making noises in a few shops around Detroit, he became obsessed with it.

"I had one horse-drawn dray to take my goods to town, but I needed another," Buick told Bruce Catton in 1928. "I couldn't afford a new team, although I got my second dray on credit; and I got to thinking about making an engine that would move the dray without horses."

Buick's interest in moving a wagon without horses for his personal needs may have been a factor, but more likely he was just plain fascinated with engines. His inventive mind must have railed finally at the thought of building only better bathtubs and toilets.

Buick said his enthusiasm for engines began in 1895 which, if true, was pretty close to the beginning of big things in Detroit. Motor pioneer Charles B. King began advertising as a manufacturer of gasoline engines in Detroit late that year. In March of 1896, King became the first person to drive an automobile in public there. Later in 1896, Henry Ford completed and tested his first automobile.

Buick was so delighted with the possibilities of the gasoline engine that at age forty-five he decided it was time for a career change. Buick & Sherwood** was sold to the Standard Sanitary Manufacturing Company of Pittsburgh for $100,000 in 1899, though Buick retained some stock for a time. Buick then organized a firm with the vigorous name of Buick Auto-Vim and Power Company. Its purpose was to manufacture gasoline engines for the farm and for marine use. In this venture he was soon working with a five-foot-six mechanical genius named Walter Lorenzo Marr, and the company turned to experiments with an automobile. (Buick himself was only five-five-and-a-half and weighed 120 pounds, a grandson recalls.)

Walter Marr would become so important in the early development of the Buick automobile that his early life is worth relating in detail. He was born in 1865 in Lexington, in Michigan's Thumb, the son of George Ernest and Sarah Ashelford Marr. His father died when he was six. He served an apprenticeship with John Walker & Sons, an

A few portraits of David Buick survive. Among them are these (above) from his grandson's album. William Sherwood, Buick's plumbing partner, is pictured below with family members.

---

*Buick was president, Sherwood vice-president and A.B. Babcock secretary and treasurer of the firm, which billed itself as "manufacturers and dealers in sanitary specialties" on its stationery, which was also decorated with a drawing of a toilet.

**According to Roy Scharfenberg, whose wife is William Sherwood's granddaughter, Sherwood became angry at David Buick's constant fiddling with gasoline engines and finally said, "Dave, you either get down to work or get out." Scharfenberg said there was no love lost between Sherwood and Buick. After ending his relationship with Buick, Sherwood founded the Sherwood Brass Company in 1903. Still in existence in Detroit, it was sold to Lear-Siegler in 1970.

engineering firm in East Tawas, Michigan, in 1882. He worked for a Saginaw sawmill and steamboat engineering company, Wickes Brothers, from 1887 to 1896, and in 1888 he built a one-cylinder engine designed by his plant superintendent. For a period of three months, the engine was the subject of a number of experiments with different carburetors and gave Marr a valuable early lesson in power-plant design and construction.

Even more than David Buick, as soon as Marr became involved with gasoline engines, he couldn't leave them alone. After departing Saginaw, he opened a bicycle shop on Grand River at Second in Detroit which, he recalled decades later, was close to a shop operated by Henry Ford. Marr used a variety of gasoline engines to drive machinery for the manufacture of bicycles.

With his background in, and continued use of, gasoline engines of various types, Marr said he was able to make a successful four-cylinder gasoline motor wagon, perfecting it in 1898. He evidently had a lot of trouble with it at first. "When you took it out it would start on four cylinders and you would get home on one; then you'd take the head off and pick out the pieces," he told one interviewer. He told another that Henry Ford had tried to help him solve an ignition problem.

In 1934, Marr was interviewed by Charles E. Hulse of Flint. According to unpublished notes based on that interview still held by Hulse, Marr said he finally put a spark advance device (the first in the country) on the car and the trouble was over. The same day, Ford saw Marr's vehicle come up the street and make a smooth stop, which was unusual. The next morning Ford was waiting to ask Marr what he had done to improve the performance.

Marr told another interviewer that most of the weight—the engine and water cooler—was in the back and the car would rear up on occasion. Marr and Ford discussed the spark problem and Marr concluded he needed a faster spark, and so developed the spark advance.

It would appear that Marr built at least three motor vehicles between 1898 and 1900. One was the four-cylinder car; another a motor-powered tricycle, and a third a one-cylinder car with three-point suspension, underslung springs, special chassis and forty-four-inch buggy wheels. This last vehicle is the one in which, Marr said, he and his wife, the former Abbie Farrar of Saginaw, were photographed. There is also some conjecture—though it is by no means certain—that this was the first automobile to be called a Buick.

Exactly in what order he built these vehicles is unclear, for he told the story of his early career in different ways to different chroniclers, and the evidence suggests he was not always entirely accurate in his recollections. This makes a precise recounting of this part of his

career difficult, for often he is the only source of information.

In 1899, Marr said, he sold his bicycle shop and went to work for the Detroit Shipbuilding Company. He said he first met David Buick when Buick was a commodore in the Detroit Yacht Club and Marr was working with some friends on a motor for a speedboat, while in the shipbuilder's employ. While they were tinkering with the engine, Buick strolled by, watched Marr at work and perceived the man's ability at once, hiring him on the spot. Marr told Hulse that a man from Canada named Murray, who also worked for Buick, put a motor in a boat and it did not work, so Buick fired him and made

Walter Lorenzo Marr, photographed with his racing cycle and his medals.

Marr foreman at Buick Auto-Vim and Power Company for three months and manager for one year. He once said he built the first marine motors for David Buick, including one that beat everything in the twenty-four-foot class on the Detroit River, but that he could not get Buick interested in automobiles.

Whether Marr helped Buick design the conventional L-head engine the latter began sporadically manufacturing is one of the many uncertainties of this thinly recorded period. It would seem that some work on it must have been done by Buick and his son, Thomas. But the evidence strongly suggests that Marr was largely responsible for the automobile being built at the turn of the century (1899 to 1901) at Buick's shop in a barn behind his home on Meldrum.* On several occasions, Marr said he built the first Buick.

---

*For the record, David Buick lived at 373 Meldrum; Buick & Sherwood was at Meldrum and Champlain; Buick Auto-Vim and Power Company was at 39 Beaubien in 1901; Buick Manufacturing Company was at 416-418 Howard Street in 1902 and 1903. Walter Marr's home was at 397 Howard. The block numbers have since been changed. David Buick retained his family home in Detroit until 1905, when he and his first wife Caroline and their family moved to 406 Stevens Street in Flint.

From the Marr family scrapbook, proud owner Walter Marr at his bicycle shop on Grand River at Second in Detroit which, Marr said, was close to the shop of Henry Ford.

In 1903, Hugh Dolnar (real name Horace Arnold) wrote in *Cycle and Automobile Trade Journal*: "In 1900, while with the Buick concern, Marr built his second motor wagon, driven by a single-cylinder, 4-inch bore by 5-inch stroke, horizontal, water-cooled, jump-spark ignition. The first wagon [the four-cylinder vehicle] had a speed-change arrangement of constantly meshed gearing, friction clutch engaged; the second wagon had a chain transmission, and in the motor Marr was the first of the group of Detroit experimenters in automobile origination to use the jump spark."

If Dolnar in 1903 was accurately quoting information he obviously got from Marr, then Marr had changed the story somewhat by the 1930's, when he was quoted in speeches and by Hulse. In the Thirties, Marr indicated that it was the four-cylinder car, not the one-cylinder, which had the first spark advance, and also that he built the one-cylinder car before his association with David Buick. (But, almost in the same breath, if Hulse's notes are accurate, he called this car the first Buick, possibly meaning that he had started it before being associated with Buick, but completed it after he joined Buick; or that he built it before his later association with the Buick Motor Company in Flint.)

In 1934, a Chattanooga, Tennessee newspaper reported this reminiscence from a Marr speech: "Mr. Marr never managed to get Mr. Buick into the shop but once. They went for a ride in the Buick car. The vibrator stuck, stalling the car. Buick was disgusted. A street car was passing and he boarded it."

Although there is little reference to it elsewhere, Marr told Hulse he quit Buick over this incident, told him to get another man. It is generally known that Marr worked for Buick twice, but Hulse said Marr told him he worked for Buick at least three times, and another interview corroborates.

Both Buick and Marr were known for their quick tempers. Buick was said to be a rough-talking man, "always chewing tobacco," as one acquaintance remembered; "a crank, and a hard man to do business with," recalled another, Detroit businessman John C. Lodge. Marr, though he had a wry wit, was allegedly even more mercurial, as his employment of 1899 to 1904 would suggest.

One of their splits, apparently growing out of the above incident, is documented in a letter, dated March 25th, 1901, from David Buick to Marr: "After considering the conversation we had the other day, and wherein you offered your resignation, I have concluded that it is best for both parties to accept the same, and to take effect at once. You will please turn over the keys, and such other articles that you may have to Mr. Sherwood, and oblige."

On April 5th, also on stationery of the Buick & Sherwood Manufacturing Company, David Buick offered to sell to Marr "the

Buick (seated) and Marr, the only photo known to exist of them together.

Automobile, known as the Buick Automobile, for the sum of $300." He also made available some engines under experimentation, including patterns to make them, a delivery wagon body, two new carriage bodies and one runabout body, for an additional $1500. Apparently Buick was by this time strapped for cash.

Until recently, no one knew whether Marr had taken Buick up on the offer. But another letter, found in Marr's papers and donated not long ago to the Sloan Museum in Flint by a Marr grandson, Richard Marr, answers that question. Dated August 16th, more than four months after Buick's original offer, and signed by David Buick, it states: "In consideration of the sum of Two Hundred and Twenty-five Dollars ($225.00) cash paid me this day, I hereby transfer and assign to Walter L. Marr all my right (sic), title and interest in the Automobile known as the Buick automobile."

The first Buick had been sold—and at "below list." By waiting,

Prices subject to change without notice, and all quotations, unless otherwise agreed, subject to prompt acceptance. All orders and contracts subject to our approval if accepted by a salesman or a selling agent, also subject to strikes, accidents and causes beyond our control.

D. D. BUICK, Prest.
.HERWOOD, Vice Prest   A.D. BABCOCK, Secy & Treas.

Detroit, Mich March 25, 1901.

Mr. Walter Marr,

Detroit, Mich

Dear Sir:--

After considering the conversation that we had the other day, and wherein you offered your resignation, I have concluded that it is best for both parties to accept the same, and to take effect at once.

You will please turn over the keys, and such other articles that you may have to Mr. Sherwood, and oblige,

Yours very truly,

D. D. Buick

The two men were frequently at odds, as this letter from 1901 indicates.

Marr had pushed the price down by $75 on a car he may have built with Buick financing. If this was the buggy-wheeled vehicle, then Marr had either built it with Buick's money while working for Buick, as Dolnar's article suggests, or Buick had somehow gotten title to it from Marr after Marr began working for him.

Charles Hulse says he believes it was the same car, and that this is the car in the photograph with Marr and his wife. Therefore this photo would be of the first Buick, so named by David Buick in his two letters to Marr. However, Marr's grandson, Walter L. Marr III, says he believes it is not the same car, that Marr bought a different vehicle from Buick in 1901, and that the car in the photograph is one Marr built in Cleveland. "But then, Hulse interviewed my grandfather, and I didn't," he said. In any case, the car sold to Marr was the last car David Buick would sell for two years.

Immediately after leaving his Buick job, Marr wrote to an old friend, Charles G. Annesley, who was employed by the Buffalo Gasolene Motor Company in Buffalo, New York. On March 28th, Annesley replied:

> *My dear Walter:*
> *I was awfully surprised to hear that you had left the Buick concern, as I thought that you were getting along so nicely. . . .*
> *We have all the help we require at present, but perhaps we will put a good hustling salesman on the road a little later on.*
> *My boy, shake the dust of a slow old Detroit off your feet, and go east with some good responsible house where your abilities will be appreciated. What the devil do you think would have become of me if I had stayed there? Here I have the very nicest of a company, good salary, and stock in the concern.*

Annesley also added this classic comment: "What is poor old Ford doing? I feel so sorry for him. He is a good man and perfectly capable, and yet cannot get out of the hole just because he won't leave Detroit."

There is something else interesting about that letter. Annesley had bought Henry Ford's first horseless carriage, the 1896 quadricycle; therefore, the letter was from the first buyer of a Ford to the first buyer of a Buick.

Marr quickly took a job with Ransom Eli Olds' factory in Detroit. He has said he helped build the first two curved-dash Oldsmobiles, but Hulse, owner of a 1901 Olds and an expert on Olds history, insists that Marr did not join Olds until after production started again in April 1901, after the famous March fire at Olds. Possibly he built the first two curved-dash vehicles after production restarted. In any case, he was there only a few weeks. He quit, he said, because he learned that a strike was about to be called, and not believing in strikes, he didn't want to be embroiled in it. By May he was gone from Olds. He was out of work six weeks.

Then Marr latched onto a job perfecting a bicycle motor for the Detroit Brass, Iron and Novelty Company, but was not there long. He was still experimenting with the car he had bought—or bought back—from David Buick and once, he told Hulse, he was arrested in it for speeding in Detroit. In court, the judge asked the officer how fast Marr was going. "He was doing 16 miles an hour with plenty to spare," the officer replied. The judge said that any man who could make a car that could go 16 miles per hour could probably spare $16, which Marr was fined.

Still in 1901, Marr learned that someone in Cleveland, Ohio wanted to build a car. He told Hulse he gave his wife all his money except a dollar, and told her he was going to Cleveland to build automobiles

Marr with his wife in the "Cleveland" car (left) which may be the first Buick; and with Will Starling (at left in right photo) in Marr's earlier 4-cylinder car.

"and won't be back until I do." He paid a dollar for boat fare to Cleveland, and was hired on arrival and given a $6 advance in pay.

He soon returned to Detroit, got the original car (the Buick, apparently) and took it to Cleveland to use as a model for a car to be built there. (Walter Marr III says Marr and his wife were photographed in the buggy-wheeled car in Cleveland, which would seem to further strengthen, though not prove, Hulse's contention that this was the car bought from David Buick.) The Cleveland firm was the American Motor Carriage Company, and Marr was chief designer and superintendent.

The first American was on the road by December 1901, a one-cylinder job with jump-spark ignition and a carburetor of Marr's own design. As usual, Marr and his employers were soon at odds, so in 1902 Marr demanded $100 in payment for his work and his original car back, and was soon back in Detroit.

Meanwhile, David Buick was struggling along in Detroit. In 1902 he reorganized the Buick Auto-Vim and Power Company as the Buick Manufacturing Company, and the evidence suggests that he and Marr had another short-lived working relationship that year. Marr told another interviewer that he worked for David Buick three times, and each time Buick's company had a different name (Buick Auto-Vim and Power, Buick Manufacturing and Buick Motor). And he told Hulse he went to work for Buick again after returning from Cleveland, at a time Buick was building stationary motors.

At that time the company was having carburetor troubles, and one day Marr was in the basement and had a carburetor running "on the gas." Buick asked what he was doing. Marr explained that the carburetors were leaky and he was trying to find the trouble. Buick intimated that Marr was wasting Buick's money, so after a few words, Marr left Buick again.*

Now Marr found a job with J.P. Schneider, a Detroit automobile dealer, beginning construction on a new motor wagon that had its first run on Christmas night of 1902. This one-cylinder vehicle was so satisfactory—it underwent a successful road test of 1000 miles in January or February of 1903—that Marr formed the Marr Autocar Company in early 1903, entering into a contract with the Fauber Manufacturing Company of Elgin, Illinois to construct the first 100 vehicles.

Buick, meanwhile, had hired another talented machinist, Eugene C. Richard (pronounced RICH-ard not ri-SHARD, family members and acquaintances insist, despite his French beginnings). Richard was born in the province of Savoy, France, April 8th, 1867, and had learned about engines in Philadelphia and also worked on early

---

*Later, when they decided to team up again in 1904, Marr suggested that the two of them, because they were both rather quick-tempered, agree that in any further dispute they wait until the next day to settle it "when reasoning power had returned to both," according to Hulse's notes.

Oldsmobiles.

Somehow, among these three men—David Buick, Walter Marr and Eugene Richard—the Buick company hit upon a new idea in engine design: the "valve-in-head" engine. It was an important development. With its valves directly over the pistons (unlike the L-head engine in general use at the time), the Buick powerplant had a more compact combustion chamber and a faster fuel-burn rate. It was, in essence, a more efficient machine. And because it was so efficient, it developed more horsepower than other engines its size. Eventually the entire industry would make use of its principle, although not before the Buick engine developed a reputation for power and performance which helped the company survive in those desperate early years.

But who invented it? Marr said he did. In a 1936 interview with Sam Adkins of the *Chattanooga Free Press*, he explained that "I made the valve-in-head device first because it was the easiest way to make a motorcycle engine." On still another occasion, Marr claimed the invention and said the valves were first put in the head because, owing to the way the motor had been built, they could not be put in anywhere else. The discovery, he said, came by accident.

On the other hand, the valve-in-head engine was patented by Richard. Patent No. 771,095 covered, among other features, "the combination of the cylinder-head, of induction and deduction valves, having their stems extending through said head."

Charles Hulse, who in addition to interviewing Marr has talked to relatives of Richard and researched old documents during his more than forty years of interest in the automotive pioneering era, gives most of the credit to Richard. Hulse says Richard probably started to work for Buick Auto-Vim and Power Company as a machinist in March or April of 1901, after the Olds fire and after Marr's first departure from Buick. At the same time, according to Hulse, Richard was also working part-time for the Peerless Motor Company and the Kneeland Crystal Creamery, both in Lansing.

On February 18th, 1902, Richard filed for a patent on the valve-in-head engine, and assigned the patent to the Buick Manufacturing Company. On December 7th, 1903, he filed another patent for a stationary engine and assigned it to Mrs. Sarah Kneeland. Mrs. Kneeland was the wife of Charles Kneeland who that year sold the creamery and started the Kneeland Manufacturing Company which built gasoline engines for some years. On January 11th, 1904, Richard filed for a patent on a carburetor and assigned it to the Buick Motor Company, which by this time had moved to Flint.

According to Hulse, Richard remembered that steam engines in his native Europe had used the valve-in-head feature for years, and he merely applied the principle to gasoline engines.

Eugene C. Richard (above). The barn (below) behind David Buick's home on Meldrum in Detroit where first Buick was said to have been built. Inset is a heavily retouched photo of first Flint Buick shown on Page 34.

D. D. BUICK, Prest.

Wm. SHERWOOD, Vice Prest.   A. D. BABCOCK, Secy. & Treas.

BUICK & SHERWOOD MFG CO.

SANITARY SPECIALTIES

Detroit, Mich. April 5, 1901.

Mr. Walter Marr,
                City.

Dear Sir:--

        We will sell you the Automobile, known as the Buick Automobile for the sum of $300.00. We will also sell you all engines with the exception of the following:

                One known as Stegmeyer's engine
                One known as the Noeker Engine
                One known as The Double Ended Carriage engine and
                three of the four Cycles.

        This also includes all patterns, which we have on hand for making these engines, also deliver wagon body, two new carriage bodies, and one runabout body, for the sum of $1,500, making a total of Automobile, engines, patterns, etc., of $1800.

        This option is good for thirty days.

                                Yours very truly,

                                J. D. Buick Bros.

First known mention of the Buick automobile is this April 5, 1901, letter (above) from David Buick offering to sell "the Buick Automobile" to Walter Marr. Agreement (below) in August 1901 indicates Marr bought it for $75 less than the asking price.

AGREEMENT
. . . .

        In consideration of the sum of Two Hundred and Twenty-five Dollars ($225.00) cash paid me this day, I hereby transfer and assign to Walter L. Marr all my right, title and interest in the Automobile known as the Buick Automobile.

Dated this 26th day of August 1901.

                Signed   D. D. Buick Bros.

Accepted,

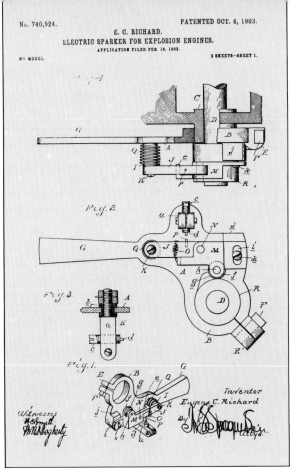

No. 740,924.   PATENTED OCT. 6, 1903.

E. C. RICHARD.

ELECTRIC SPARKER FOR EXPLOSION ENGINES.

APPLICATION FILED FEB. 18, 1903.

NO MODEL.   2 SHEETS—SHEET 1.

Fig. 2

Fig. 3

Fig. 1

Witnesses   Inventor
                                        Eugene C. Richard
                                        By his Attys.

No. 771,096.

UNITED STAT

EUGENE C. RICHARD, OF DE
BUICK MOTOR COMPANY,
TION OF MICHIGAN.

CARBURETE

SPECIFICATION forming part o

Application filed Ja

To all whom it may concern:

Be it known that I, EUGENE C. RICHAR
citizen of the United States, residing at
troit, in the county of Wayne and State
Michigan, have invented certain new and
ful Improvements in Carbureters, of which
following is a specification, reference be
had therein to the accompanying drawing

The invention relates to carbureters, and
more particular reference to a construction
tended for use in explosion-engines.

The invention consists in the peculiar c
struction, arrangement, and combination
parts, as hereinafter set forth.

In the drawings, Figure 1 is a longitud
section, partly in elevation. Fig. 2 is a cr
section, and Fig. 3 is a plan.

A is a receptacle for the oil, provided w
an inlet-conduit B, which is controlled b
valve C, attached to a float D within the re
ceptacle, the arrangement being designed
maintain substantially constant level of
within the receptacle.

E is an outlet-conduit from the receptac
which connects with a vertical nozzle F,
ing a controlling needle-valve G.

H is a plug-valve in the nozzle above
needle-valve G and adapted to variably
strict the passage in the nozzle.

I is an air-conduit into which the end of
nozzle F is directed, said conduit leading
the inner valve of the explosion-engine.
lower end of this conduit I is connected
a horizontally-extending casing J, having
inlet-tube K, through which air may be
mitted into the casing and thence into the
duit I.

L is a funnel-shaped tube arranged w
the tube K, connected at its lower end
an oil conduit or chamber M, leading to
valve H and communicating with a port
said valve. This port a connects with a
b, which forms the connecting-passage i
nozzle F.

N is a valve-stem for the valve H, w
passes out through the casing and is con
ed with a gear-segment O. This seg
meshes with a complementary segmen

Although the precise "authorship" of the valve-in-head engine remains

In 1921, Benjamin Briscoe, Jr. wrote that, in his opinion, the industry owed to Richard "the original proper application of the overhead valve principle." Briscoe had been a longtime business supplier and friend of David Buick's, and his Briscoe Manufacturing Company was ideally positioned to be aware of what was going on in what Briscoe aptly called the "incubating" automobile industry in Detroit.

Briscoe was well acquainted with Richard's inventive work and, indeed, four days after Briscoe became the financial angel in a reorganization of Buick in May of 1903, Richard was signed to a contract as "designer and inventor and head of the drafting department."

Briscoe had started his sheet metal business with a few hundred

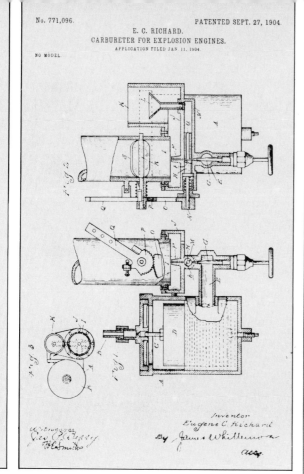

spute, Eugene Richard's inventiveness does not, as these patents prove.

dollars in 1888 but had almost lost it during a Detroit financial crisis in 1901. Somehow he persuaded J.P. Morgan to invest $100,000 in the firm, a gesture Briscoe found so surprising that he quickly cashed the check in New York before the financier could change his mind. With the money, he bought sophisticated equipment so he could manufacture something more complex than his staple, which was garbage cans. No sooner was he ready for advanced business than he was visited by Ransom Olds, who was getting his curved-dash into significant production and wanted Briscoe to provide the "coolers" (radiators) for that car. Briscoe landed a contract for producing 4400 of them and was soon making sheet metal parts for an increasing number of other manufacturers. Within two or three years, Briscoe had 1200 employees and the firm was making big profits.

FIRSTS IN PRINT

Word of Buick's existence slipped into the press in small news items and then a few advertisements. On May 21, 1903, *Motor World* reported, under "Recent Incorporations," this item datelined Detroit: "Buick Motor Company, under Michigan laws, to manufacture automobiles, automobile equipment, power machinery, etc., capital $100,000. Incorporators: David D. Buick, Thomas D. Buick and Emil D. Moessner." On September 24, 1903, the same publication reported Buick was moving to a 200 x 65-foot brick building in Flint. Also in September, the first known Buick advertisement (top) was published in *Cycle and Automobile Trade Journal*. Note the Detroit address. The same publication ran Buick's first known ad to feature a car (below) in October 1904. On November 3, 1904, *Motor Age* provided first news of a Buick dealership, H.L. Palmer of Cleveland, "opening a repair shop and sales room" on Euclid Avenue near Dodge Street "where he will make a specialty of handling the Buick car, built by the Flint Wagon Works. . . ." And on September 28, 1905, *Motor Way* said "Buick Motor Company of Flint contemplates the establishment of an agency and warehouse in London, England. . . ." Billy Durant's expansive imagination was clearly at work.

Briscoe had known David Buick since the 1890's and had appreciated the fact that Buick had given him thousands of dollars worth of work in the plumbing supply days. To Briscoe, Buick was not only a business associate, but a friend and "generally a fine chap." And Briscoe was somewhat impressed with people who built automobiles. As he later wrote:

"No man in those days . . . would have gone into the automobile business if he had been a hard-boiled conservative businessman. It took a man of pioneering instinct, an idealist [and] of an adventurous nature."

By 1902, Buick was in debt to Briscoe for a few hundred dollars for supplies, but Briscoe made little effort to be repaid. He told his collector to visit Buick periodically, but to put on no pressure. One day the collector told Briscoe that Buick wished him to visit the Buick factory.

Briscoe proceeded to the plant on Howard Street near Twelfth, where David Buick explained he had invested most of his money in a design for a new automobile. Briscoe had been planning his first horseless carriage purchase and by the time they finished talking, Briscoe had worked out a deal to buy the incomplete car and advance Buick enough money to finish it. Buick said that would take $650. As the weeks rolled on, however, Briscoe discovered more than twice that sum was needed. But finally, early in 1903, the car was finished and Briscoe took delivery. Buick was given permission to borrow the vehicle when necessary to use as a demonstrator to help get the financial backing needed to put it into production.

In a letter to the editor of *The Automobile* magazine in 1915, Briscoe provided a description of this car. He called it Buick No. 1, although it was the second car to be called a Buick, the first having been sold to Marr.

"I recall that the motor had exceptionally large valves, was a single cylinder motor of about 4 x 5, as I now recall, and did develop by brake test about 26 horsepower, which was quite marvelous at that time for that size motor; in fact, would be a good performance even for today. . . . I used the car for some months and I guess I discovered most of the bugs that were in it. Anyway, I was a part of the experimental department, and as such had many strenuous experiences."

Briscoe's firm supplied all of the sheet metal and machined small parts for the car. Research by Hulse indicates that it was registered as "the Bewick" in Detroit on January 24th, 1904, shortly after Detroit passed a city ordinance, in advance of the state, requiring that cars be registered. It was then owned by Briscoe and assigned numer 365.

While awaiting completion of the Buick early in 1903, Briscoe had

decided to become more than a supplier for the fledgling Detroit automobile industry. He became bitten by the bug: "When a man became infested by the automobile germ, it was as though he had a disease," Briscoe once wrote, referring to David Buick. "It has to run its course."

Studying the mechanics of the car as Buick and Richard worked on it, Briscoe made up his mind to become an automobile manufacturer. Initially he thought of teaming up with Buick, but was concerned about his incessant spending and the meager results it brought. One day he discussed this with Jonathan D. Maxwell, the mechanical chief of the short-lived Northern Automobile Company of Detroit, and asked Maxwell to take a look at the Buick and give him his opinion.

Maxwell returned without saying anything pro or con about the Buick car, but instead suggested that he and Briscoe go into the automobile business together. His credentials were impressive. Maxwell had collaborated with the Apperson brothers and Elwood Haynes in Indiana, and had helped Ransom Olds develop the curved-dash Oldsmobile. Comparatively, David Buick must have seemed to Briscoe to be an inept amateur. On July 4th, 1903, Briscoe and Maxwell signed a contract to enter the automobile manufacturing field together and the Maxwell-Briscoe Motor Company was formed.

There was one problem left. And that was for Briscoe to disengage himself from David Buick.

In the spring of 1903, Buick and Briscoe had worked out an arrangement whereby Buick was provided additional cash. Briscoe had agreed to lend $1,500 more if Buick restructured the Buick Manufacturing Company. The firm was duly incorporated on May 19, 1903, as the Buick Motor Company, with $100,000 in capital stock.* Of this Briscoe held $99,700, Buick receiving the remaining $300. It was an unusual contract under which Buick, as president, was given the option of repaying what he owed Briscoe—about $3,500—and receiving in return all of the stock—or, failing that, relinquishing control of the Buick Motor Company to Briscoe by September 1903. All Briscoe really wanted now was his money back, but he figured that if Buick couldn't pay, at least he would have the Buick shop which Maxwell could use as a nucleus for a factory to produce the Maxwell car. Knowing Buick as he did, Briscoe must have assumed he would end up with the shop.

There is more than one account of what happened next. Briscoe's version is that he learned from a salesman that a company in Flint,

_____

*Above arrangement per Briscoe. Incorporation papers notarized 5/12/03 and recorded 5/19/03 show D. Buick with 9,499 shares, T. Buick with 500 and Emil D. Moessner, Briscoe's son-in-law, with one. Briscoe's name does not appear.

Above: Benjamin Briscoe, traveling abroad. Below: This photo from the May 18, 1904, Flint Journal *is believed by researcher Charles Hulse to be of Detroit-built Buick No. 2, the "Briscoe Buick."*

the Flint Wagon Works, wanted to get into the car manufacturing business. According to this story, Briscoe, believing this would be a good opportunity to unload the Buick company, grabbed his brother Frank, who assisted him in the Briscoe business, and together they headed north. While in Flint that very day, they sold the Buick firm to the Flint Wagon Works in principle, though negotiations continued between David Buick and the Flint interests for several months. In the meantime Ben Briscoe went off to France to study the manufacture of radiators.

Another version is that Frank Briscoe learned of the Flint firm's interest from Dwight T. Stone, a young real estate agent in that town who was related by marriage to the Briscoes.

In either case, negotiations with the Flint Wagon Works were at once serious. Wrote Ben Briscoe: "They [the Flint Wagon Works directors] came to Detroit in a few days and although there were some discouraging moments during the negotiations and the attempted trial runs of the car, I could see that nothing but some unexpected turn in events could 'unsell them.' "

Briscoe traveled to Europe with the final details still unsettled, but was telephoned by David Buick immediately on his return in September—the deadline month for Buick to settle his account or lose control of his company. Meeting with Briscoe at the Russel House in Detroit, Buick said agreement had been reached with the "Flint people" and asked that Briscoe's stock be delivered to them. He then paid Briscoe what he owed him, plus interest and a bonus of an unreported amount. Briscoe wrote that this "justified my high opinion of his integrity."

Briscoe, however, was concerned that Buick had not made such a good deal for himself. Part of Buick's contract with the Flint Wagon Works interests stated that he would get his stock in the reorganized company only when his debts had been paid, either by himself personally or out of the dividends on his stock. Buick explained that the bank financing the deal had insisted on that clause. Briscoe regarded it warily. He was convinced, correctly, that Buick would be unlikely to raise the amount of his debts personally. Further, he did not believe it likely that dividends from the stock would pay the obligations in the foreseeable future.

For David Buick, the move to Flint would only delay by a few years his departure from the company he had struggled to build. But for the Buick Motor Company, and for Flint, the change in location would produce results so dramatic that they could not be imagined.

In 1921, Briscoe himself was sufficiently struck by what had happened in less than two decades that he called the chain of events "so fraught with romance that it made the Arabian Nights tales look commonplace."

23

Chapter Two

MOVE UP TO FLINT

Flint, Michigan had survived several previous economic dislocations and could have faced another early in the Twentieth Century had not its dominant carriage industry been transformed into automobile manufacturing. The city had started as a trading post in 1819 when an Indian trader named Jacob Smith set up shop at a shallow crossing of the Flint River. It was a strategic spot because Indians traveling from northern Michigan to trade furs could canoe no further south on the river than the site of Flint before having to hike sixty miles overland to the trading center of Detroit. By setting up business at this spot, Smith could trade without competition and save the Indians the walk.

Still, Flint did not become a true settlement until 1830, five years after Smith's death, when John and Polly Todd established a tavern there. When, a few years later, the Indian trail was widened by a government road hacked through the woods and swamps from Detroit to Flint, and a land office was set up in Flint, settlers began to arrive in large numbers.

North of Flint along the river were large stands of pine, the one natural resource in addition to the small river and the Indian trail which gave Flint a chance to build an economy. But the lumbering industry did not really begin to move until Henry Howland Crapo arrived by sleigh in January of 1856. Crapo (it's pronounced with a long "a"), a versatile businessman from the old whaling port of New Bedford, Massachusetts, was sent to inspect timber land bought by several New Bedford investors. Instead of looking and leaving, Crapo decided he would have to stay and build and operate lumber

mills if the investors were to get a satisfactory return.

Within three years Crapo had several successful mills in operation. Within four he was mayor of Flint. Two years later he was a state senator, and in two more years the governor of Michigan. He was reelected. More than a century after his death in 1869, Crapo was still regarded as one of Flint's most important historical figures. He built Flint's economy, as governor he visited with President Abraham Lincoln several times during the Civil War, he constructed a railroad which opened Flint commerce to a railhead to the south— and he was the grandfather of William Crapo "Billy" Durant, who in the next century would save the Buick Motor Company and found General Motors.

By the 1880's the timber had been depleted and Flint's lumbering business was in the doldrums. It became clear that the town's citizens would have to look for other work. William A. Paterson had opened a carriage shop in 1869 and had gained a reputation for quality craftsmanship. Other men began to get interested in this field.

One was James H. Whiting, born in Torrington, Connecticut on May 12th, 1842, who journeyed to Flint after serving in the Civil War. For some years he ran a hardware business. In 1882 he took over as manager of the Begole, Fox & Company lumber mills on the city's west side and was given the mission of converting the firm from a processor of raw material into a manufacturer of finished wooden products. Whiting did this successfully; the Flint Wagon Works, the town's first incorporated business, was established that year.

Flint began to prosper as a center of production of horse-drawn carriages. Paterson had low production but fine quality. Whiting's company initially concentrated on farm wagon manufacture but eventually moved into carriages. It also made its own wheels and axles.

Then there was Crapo's grandson, William Crapo Durant. Durant was born December 8th, 1861 at 40 Springfield in Boston. He was the second child and only son of Rebecca Crapo, Henry Crapo's favorite of ten daughters, and her husband, William Clark Durant. Rebecca's husband was a Boston bank clerk and—according to Henry Crapo— was also both a stock speculator and a drunk. Crapo loved his small grandson, "Willie," who first visited the Crapos in Flint when he was only eighteen months old, but he had no regard for the father. Crapo's contempt for William Clark Durant may have hastened the split between Rebecca and her husband, though Durant's drinking and carousing were largely responsible. By 1871, two years after Henry Crapo's death, Rebecca had moved to Flint with son Billy and daughter Rosa. William Clark Durant occasionally visited Flint but was no longer part of the family.

Young Durant grew up in Flint, quit school at seventeen, though

Page preceding: Before the Buick came to town, Saginaw Street in downtown Flint, Michigan, in a photograph taken sometime during the summer of 1903.
Above: The house at the corner of Church and West Second in Flint owned by Rebecca Crapo Durant. Below: Rebecca's son, the young Billy Durant.

he was a better than average student, and went to work as a laborer in his late grandfather's lumber yard. Later he sold patent medicine, cigars and insurance. At one time he was the popularly elected manager of a local baseball team, and he also played cornet in the cigar company's band. A fellow cornet player was John A.C. Menton who, in 1911, when Durant was becoming Flint's leading capitalist, was elected the only socialist mayor in the city's history.

In 1886, in a characteristically dramatic way, Durant, like James H. Whiting and William A. Paterson before him, got into the business of making horse-drawn vehicles. One day in September, he caught a ride in a friend's new two-wheeled road cart. He was so impressed with the way the vehicle's patented spring suspension cushioned the bumps that he checked a local dealer and learned the carts were being made by the Coldwater Road Cart Company in Coldwater, Michigan, 110 miles away.

That night Durant took the train to Coldwater. The next day he arranged to buy the rights to the business for $1500—he would figure out how to borrow the money later—and was suddenly a manufacturer . . . on paper. He went to a small Flint bank, borrowed $2000 on a ninety-day renewable note, and talked a friend (Josiah Dallas Dort, a partner in Whiting's former hardware enterprise) into becoming an equal partner for $1000. Then Durant headed for a state fair in Wisconsin with the only road cart he had procured from Coldwater.

It was a memorable trip. Durant talked the judges into giving his cart a blue ribbon—hence the beginning of the "Famous Blue Ribbon Line" of vehicles—and took orders for 600 carts before he had built one. Durant had no way of manufacturing the carts to fill the orders, but solved that by getting Paterson to build them for him at wholesale. He then sold them for nearly twice what he paid Paterson. Within a few months the Flint Road Cart Company was beginning to prosper.

The deal with Paterson couldn't last—the old carriage maker would eventually find some of Durant's customers and tell them they could buy Flint Road Cart Company vehicles cheaper by dealing directly with him. So Durant and Dort took over an idle Flint cotton mill and hired their own workers.

Among the laborers Durant and Dort took on was a former farm hand named Charles W. Nash, to whom Durant had taken an immediate liking after spotting him at work in the W.C. Pierce hardware store in Flint. Nash started in the blacksmith shop and then stuffed buggy cushions but soon worked into a position of authority, eventually becoming general superintendent. Nash would someday do better, becoming general manager of Buick in 1910 and president of Buick and General Motors in 1912.

In 1895 the Flint Road Cart Company was renamed the Durant-

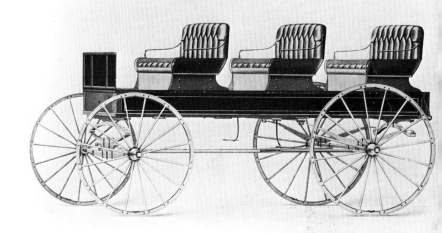

No. 266 Blue Ribbon Depot Wagon

In the Durant-Dort offices, from the left, Dallas Dort, Billy Durant, Charles Bonbright, Fred A. Aldrich. Above: One of the company products.

The Flint Wagon Works, the company that brought Buick to town, and the front page of the Daily Journal, *announcing the Buick's arrival.*

THE FLINT DAILY JOURNAL.

TWENTY-FIRST YEAR—NO. 163   FLINT, MICHIGAN, FRIDAY, SEPTEMBER 11, 1903.   SINGLE COPY TWO CENTS.

NEW INDUSTRY FOR FLINT

Buick Motor Company of Detroit Is to Be Moved to This City

Concern Will Employ At Least 100 Men At the Outset.

Ground Was Broken This Morning For Erection of a Substantial Brick Building 64x100 Feet, Located Near Wagon Works Plant.

SHOERS FEASTED !

CROWDS ARE LARGE

DAVISON MEN RELEASED

FINE BANQUET AT THE DRYDEN

FOR OLDER MEMBERS

PLAY FOR A PURSE

IN SOUTHERN CAMP

CAUGHT IN SAGINAW

COULDN'T GET IN FIVE IN ONE WEEK

BY U. S. INSPECTOR

Dort Carriage Company. By the turn of the century it was the largest volume producer of horse-drawn vehicles in the United States, if not the world, though Studebaker, with higher-priced carriages, had higher profits. The affable Dort was the company's administrator, Nash took care of the manufacturing operations and Durant, as treasurer, opened a network of sales dealerships across the country. As Dort later said, Durant was the firm's "leading force and genius."

Durant had a few simple rules for selling. One was to find a product so good it could sell itself. He believed he had that with the snappy road cart, and later with carriages which could be sold at lower prices than his competitors. Another rule was to assume that the customer was smarter than the salesman and to listen to him. Durant was a good listener, he had a dazzling smile, he was not a backslapper, he was extremely soft-spoken. Somehow this combination of traits co-mingled in a personality which inspired trust and confidence. Judging from his effect on other people, Billy Durant had lots of charisma.

Durant liked selling partly because he enjoyed any challenge. In the 1890's he went head-to-head with trusts which were attempting to take over such vehicle suppliers as manufacturers of linseed oil, varnish, axles and wheels. Durant won most of these battles by, in some cases, putting in long-range volume orders with companies at pretrust prices and, in others, simply by purchasing supplier companies and moving them to Flint. Clustered around the city soon were numerous wheel, axle, varnish, seat and top manufacturers wholly owned by Durant-Dort. The Durant-Dort Carriage Company has sometimes been called the General Motors of the buggy era. By controlling supplier costs through ownership of supplier firms, the company effectively undercut the prices charged by other carriage enterprises which had to pay trust prices for components.

One of Durant's ideas was to start a separate company to produce an extremely low-priced buggy. He hired A.B.C. (Alexander Brunell Cullen) Hardy, manager of the Davison Road Cart Company near Flint, to manage it. The firm was immediately profitable and when Dort left the Durant-Dort Carriage Company briefly to take his ill wife to Arizona—he returned in 1901 after her death—Hardy was installed as president.

In 1901, while David Buick and Walter Marr were tinkering with the first Buick automobile in Detroit, Flint was prospering as a carriage town and seemingly giving little thought to the horseless carriage. One man, Circuit Judge Charles H. Wisner, had built a cumbersome automotive machine in Flint as early as 1898, but it was usually in the shop. A doctor, Hiram H. Bardwell, assembled a kit car in 1901. But men like Durant, Dort and Nash were disdainful of that contraption called an automobile. When Durant's daughter Margery went for a ride in a Panhard in 1902, he severely criticized her for taking a foolish risk.

However, two of Flint's carriage leaders were becoming interested. One was A.B.C. Hardy, who quit the Durant-Dort Carriage Company in 1901 because he was exhausted by the pressures of fighting the trusts alongside Durant. With his wife, he took an extended trip to Europe and became fascinated with the advanced automobiles of France. Returning home, Hardy advised his former carriage partners to get into the automobile business if they wanted to survive. They showed no interest, so Hardy started his own automobile company in Flint. He built fifty-two low-priced Hardy Flint Roadsters between 1901 and late 1903, thus becoming the city's first automobile manufacturer.

The other Flint carriage maker now intrigued with automobiles was James H. Whiting, the conservative sixty-year-old manager of the Flint Wagon Works. Occasionally, when he went to a carriage convention in New York, he would steal over to an automobile show, look at the cars and sometimes even take up the manufacturers on their offers of free rides. Back in Flint, he would visit Hardy at his small automobile factory, watch him work and listen to his ideas.

Whiting accepted Hardy's theory that the horseless carriage would eventually make the horse-drawn variety obsolete. If Flint in general, and the Flint Wagon Works in particular, were to prosper, this was surely a new field to carefully consider. Whiting had a vehicle plant and a little money. If he could just get a good engine man, he thought, it should be a simple matter to make the conversion. And so, when he learned that the Buick Motor Company was for sale, and had what was purported to be a high-quality engine design, he persuaded the other directors of the Flint Wagon Works to join him in buying the firm and moving it to Flint.

On September 11th, 1903, the front page of *The Flint Journal* prominently displayed an article headlined "New Industry for Flint: Buick Motor Company of Detroit Is to Be Moved to This City." Another article on the same page reported that the Michigan Master Horse Shoers Association, meeting in Flint, had called for the creation of a state college of horse shoeing. It was a case of two transportation eras meeting in passing.

The Journal noted that the Buick company would be largely owned by the stockholders of the Flint Wagon Works, but would be a separate corporation. The capital stock was $50,000—"every dollar of which is paid in"—and the company was expected to have at least 100 skilled mechanics and machinists at the start. Ground had been broken that morning for a substantial brick building opposite the main Flint Wagon Works structure on Kearsley Street on the city's west side. The new company had purchased the machinery, patents, drawings, patterns and "good will" of the Buick Motor Company and the entire operation of the Detroit concern would soon be in Flint.

In making the announcement, Whiting said that the company would produce stationary and marine engines, automobile engines, transmissions, carburetors and spark plugs. No mention was made of automobile manufacture. The newspaper article noted there had been rumors in recent weeks that the Wagon Works was considering this, but that when Whiting was asked, "he smiled pleasantly and suggested that for the present the engines and accessories would be built by the new factory and that the broader opportunity was one for further consideration."

Observed *The Journal*: "The announcement that this new enterprise is in the hands of such successful, conservative and prudent businessmen as the stockholders of the Flint Wagon Works is at once a guarantee to the people of Flint that an industry of importance has been added to the manufacturing interests of the town and there is every reason to believe that the new company will grow very rapidly . . . ."

Since the Flint Wagon Works dealt regularly with farmers in the sale of wagons, since the Buick firm had built engines for the farm, and since Whiting was considered a conservative businessman, it is logical to assume that he wanted Buick primarily to build stationary engines for farm use. But given his interest in the automobile, and his concern about the horseless carriage as a threat to his horse-drawn carriage business, Whiting was probably interested in pursuing automobile manufacture from the beginning.

According to Flint sources, Whiting and his associates bought the Buick company with $10,000 borrowed from the Union Trust & Savings Bank of Flint, but the loan was not made for an automobile concern. Banks were simply not providing funds for automobile manufacture at that time. Instead, the loan was made to the sound and successful Flint Wagon Works and was guaranteed by the personal signatures of its five directors.

Details of this period are given in an unpublished manuscript, *An Industrial History of Flint*, compiled by Frank Rodolf when he was a librarian at *The Flint Journal* in the 1940's. Some of the material derived from earlier news clippings, some from personal interviews. The manuscript states that the $10,000 note was for a year, longer than usually allowed; L.H. Bridgman, who discounted it at the bank, recalled that a special effort was made to grant the time extension. Bridgman also remembered vividly the signatures of James H. Whiting, Charles M. Begole (son of former Michigan governor Josiah Begole), George L. Walker, William S. Ballenger and Charles

A. Cumings.

Just in case Whiting was wavering on whether Buick should become a producer of automobiles, *The Journal* tried to give him an editorial nudge the day after his announcement, to wit: "Flint is the most natural center for the manufacture of autos in the whole country. It is the vehicle city of the United States and in order to maintain this name by which it is known from ocean to ocean there must be developed factories here for the manufacture of automobiles."

Without naming A.B.C. Hardy's company, the editorial further commented that "the automobile plant already in operation here is turning out a very superior machine and is building up a good reputation which can be drawn on as time proceeds." But not, unfortunately, for long. On October 24th, *The Journal* reported that the Association of Licensed Automobile Manufacturers, the organization which controlled the Selden patent and which was attempting to control the industry, had forced Hardy out of business and filed suit against the Ford Motor Company. Neither Hardy nor Ford had ALAM licenses to produce automobiles. Ford was to take the Association to court and eventually break its hold on the industry, but in the fall of 1903, Hardy was not up to such a court fight. Indeed, with only fifty-two low-priced cars built in more than two years, his business must have been only marginally profitable, if that.

During that same fall of 1903, work proceeded on the Buick plant,

originally one story but designed so that second and third floors could be added later (which they were). On December 5th the plant was in business. On December 11th, *The Journal* noted, the factory had twenty-five employees—mostly from Flint, a few from Detroit—and about five engines of three-quarter to thirteen horsepower had been made. Work was starting, the story said, on "a huge double-cylinder auto engine." The first three recorded employees were Arthur C. Mason, who moved to Flint about December 1st from Cadillac in Detroit to superintend the transfer of the machinery between the two cities; Thomas Clint, as machine shop foreman; and William Beacraft, in charge of engine assembly (a job he held until his retirement in 1925). Beacraft, a Salvation Army major, is also remembered for setting up factory religious meetings and recreational programs during the noon hours.

A Buick Motor Company catalogue printed in Flint, apparently the first although undated, was devoted almost exclusively to stationary and marine engines. "Known All Over The World," the cover said, a slogan illustrated with a drawing of Uncle Sam pulling a portable engine "on truck" over a globe. Inside, the copy extolled the virtues of the Buick powerplants: " . . . all parts are made with jigs or templates, and are enterchangeable (sic) . . . all the moving parts are made of the best steel and hardened . . . . We use the jump spark and not the mechanical spark, the former being much more simple, and

James H. Whiting, who moved Buick to Flint; the first Buick factory, with the two upper stories which were added later. On the page opposite is the office staff of Buick in 1903, photographed at the home of a Mrs. Beckman where many early employees took room and board.

not so liable to get out of order and give trouble . . . the cams for the inlet valve, exhaust valve, and contact breaker are all in one piece, and there is only one way this can go, no matter how the gearing is meshed. When the cam is put back in place the valves are bound to open and close at the proper time. It does not require any readjustment. This we consider a very strong point in our engine."

The stationary Buick engine was a two-cycle (two horsepower on skids, four on truck), the marine a four-cycle (one horsepower at 600 rpm)—the latter to be placed "as low in the bow of the boat as possible . . . to have the gasoline below the mixer, as we use a pump for pumping the gasoline in place of the gravity system," the former adaptable to a myriad of uses among which Buick suggested grain elevators, creameries, cheese factories, blacksmith shops, wood sawing, coffee roasters, sausage machinery, railway hand cars and "to take the place of Wind Mills."

According to the catalogue, every Buick stationary and marine engine was tested under heavy load for several days before shipment. That this proved successful for the reliability of the product was demonstrated in the letters of commendation which arrived in Flint from satisfied users. Of his stationary engine, one Will Wood of Clinton, Michigan said he was "proud of the little chap, and like[d] to show my friends what a dandy engine I have." And from Detroit, Albert Stegmeyer wrote to ask about stepping up to a higher horsepower Buick marine engine since he was expanding his business—"I discontinued the bath house, remodeling it into a Gasoline Launch Livery, which will hold twenty launches"—and he had noticed "something always the matter" with boats powered by engines other than Buick's; "I consider your gasoline engine the best there is on the Detroit river." Testimonial letters such as these were published in the catalogue.

Comparatively, the Buick automobile engine was given short shrift, just three of the thirty pages, which advised of the availability of two versions: a single cylinder of five-by-six bore and stroke developing six to ten horsepower at 580 rpm and selling for $150 complete with spark plug and carburetor, and the "double cylinder opposed end type" of twelve horsepower at 800 rpm for which no price was given.

There was the occasional half-page advertisement in the trade press, i.e., "Are You Successful? You Will Be If You Use This Engine In The Construction Of Your Car. Need You Wait?," in *Cycle and Automobile Trade Journal*. As for the automobile, it was not mentioned at all in the catalogue, but shortly after its printing, a small, four-page folder was produced to announce that a Buick Model "B" automobile was on the market—although the back page of the folder was still devoted to the stationary engine. At this point,

obviously, the Buick emphasis remained steadfastly dedicated to the provedly profitable.

Some Buick histories state that sixteen cars were built in Flint in 1903. In truth, there were none. Probably the only Buick produced that year was the one owned by Ben Briscoe, built in Detroit. There is no substantial evidence that David Buick had built more than two cars, the one sold to Marr and the one sold to Briscoe, by the start of 1904.

On January 25th, 1904, *The Journal* reported that "The Buick Motor Company of Detroit has filed notice of dissolution, all the property having been sold and transferred to James H. Whiting, trustee, of Flint. The new company will be known as the Buick Motor Company of Flint. The company will have capital stock of $75,000 with $37,000 paid in." The official incorporation date was January 30th, and the $75,000 capitalization represented an increase of $25,000 over the figure as announced in September. David Buick and his son Thomas were alloted 1500 shares between them although, as noted earlier, some sources claim they would not receive the stock until its dividends had paid their debts. Other large stockholders included Whiting, president, 1505 shares; Begole, vice-president, 1000; Walker, director, 725; Ballenger, treasurer, 707. The officers were the same as those of the Flint Wagon Works, with the addition of David Buick as secretary of the motor company.

In the center is Miss Ethel Lobbdell, behind her (with big moustache) is William Beacraft; to her right (back row), Thomas D. Clint, Arthur Mason.

THE BUICK MOTOR COMPANY

MANUFACTURERS OF

AUTOMOBILES, STATIONARY, MARINE and AUTOMOBILE GAS and GASOLINE ENGINES

TRANSMISSION GEARS, SPARK PLUGS, CARBURETERS, ETC.

Flint, Mich. _____ **Jan. 8th,** ____190__ **4**

Mr. Walter R. Marr,

    C/o J. P. Schneider,

        Jefferson & Bates

           Detroit, Mich.

Friend Marr:-

        I have just learned that you have severed your

connections with the Reed Manufacturing Company. If you have

not succeeded in obtaining a position would be pleased to have

you call at my home on Sunday afternoon or call me up on the

phone, East 120.

           Yours truly,

                  The Buick Motor Co.

               Per D.D.Buick
                      Per M.

Below: Half-page ad in Cycle and Automobile Trade Journal, *July 1904.*
Page opposite, clockwise: Portable on truck, cover illustration, marine engine, two-cylinder automobile engine, from the first Flint catalogue.

The Buick 12 H. P. Motor

We also Manufacture Transmissions of Planetary and Sliding Gear Type ✧ ✧ ✧

ARE
YOU SUCCESSFUL ?
YOU
WILL BE
IF YOU USE THIS
ENGINE
IN
THE CONSTRUCTION
OF YOUR CARS
NEED

YOU WAIT?
LET US KNOW YOUR
REQUIREMENTS

THE BUICK MOTOR CO., Manufacturers of Automobile, Stationary and Marine Engines

---

Eugene Richard did not move to Flint with David Buick. Instead he stayed for a time with the companies he worked for in Lansing.* But in April 1904, David Buick was rejoined by Walter Marr. According to one version of what happened, Buick had met his old employee by chance in Detroit and learned of his dissatisfaction with the way the Marr Autocar Company was going. Some sources state that firm failed because of a fire; Rodolf reports that Marr was primarily upset because he felt his investors "wanted all the money." Both versions could be true. The Fauber Manufacturing Company's building at Elgin was burned out in a $325,000 fire which destroyed fourteen Marr Autocars (ten had been shipped only a few days before) and was not rebuilt. But this happened August 11th, 1904, after Marr had already returned to Buick. The beginnings and endings of things did not always occur tidily in this early period of automobile history; the fact that Marr had returned to Buick did not necessarily mean that the Marr Autocar was yet dead. But if Marr's departure did not kill off the Autocar, the fire of 1904 did.

Marr, in fact, did not go directly from the Marr Autocar Company back to Buick.

Letters in the possession of his grandson Walter Marr III reveal that Marr worked instead for the automobile department of the Reid Manufacturing Company, which built the Wolverine Touring Car, beginning December 1st, 1903, when he was hired at thirty dollars per week "until further notice." On January 5th, 1904, Marr was sent a check for sixty dollars and a letter notifying him that "we will not require your services after tonight." The letter continued: "Beg to advise, that work which you have done is satisfactory. If we can be of any assistance to you in getting another position, we will be very glad to do so."

Three days later, Marr received a warm letter:

> Friend Marr:—
> I have just learned that you have severed your connections with the Reed (sic) Manufacturing Company. If you have not succeeded in obtaining a position would be pleased to have you call at my home on Sunday afternoon or call me up on the phone, East 120.
>
>   Yours truly,
>   D.D. Buick

---

*Richard in 1905 began living in Flint, apparently working part-time for Buick and part-time for the Peerless Motor Company in Lansing. By 1908 he was again a full-time Buick employee, and was an engineer on special projects until 1930. He died in 1938.

KNOWN
ALL OVER
THE WORLD

THE BUICK MOTOR COMPANY
FLINT MICH. U.S.A.

Marr and Buick were teamed up again and Marr went to work immediately improving the two-cylinder valve-in-head engine. Between them, they persuaded Whiting that it was time to build an automobile.

As Beacraft remembered at his retirement, the engine was ready for installation in a vehicle on May 27th, 1904. By the first week in July, the first Flint Buick was chugging around the grounds of the Flint Wagon Works. On July 9th, *The Journal* enthused that "one of the new Buick autos was on the streets this afternoon and attracted considerable favorable attention. The machine was not wholly completed but from its speed it looks as though the Buick will cut quite a figure in the auto world when the company gets to turning them out in greater numbers."

That same day two men wearing dusters and caps drove the car from the plant with a special mission in mind. At the wheel was Marr. His passenger was Buick's son Thomas. Their automobile was little more than a chassis and bench buggy seat, on which the men sat looking high over the radiator. There were no fenders, no body. The vehicle had heavy wooden-spoke wheels, a square fuel-water tank in front of the passengers and a two-cylinder engine hidden somewhere under the seat.

Marr and Tom Buick left Flint's Sherman House at 1:15 p.m., heading on a 90-mile route to Detroit via Lapeer. *The Flint Daily News* said they spent the night in Lapeer due to a "hot box" (rear wheel bearing) failure. They arrived in Detroit Sunday, July 10th, "the distance from Pontiac to Birmingham being covered in 10 minutes," *The Journal* said. They bought car license No. 1024 Monday and headed back to Flint Tuesday.

Marr decided to see how fast he could go. Driving in a steady rain through the small towns of Pontiac, Oxford and Lapeer—"the roads were deep in mud every mile of the way," he recalled—Marr was able to average more than thirty miles an hour. "I did the driving and Buick was kept busy wiping the mud off my goggles."

In one town they were challenged to a race by an electric car but the Buick "showed them the way." "We went so fast at another time," Marr said, "that we could not see the village six-mile-an-hour sign." He did not explain whether a local constable had pointed this out to him. "At one place, going down a hill, I saw a bump at a bridge too late to slow up. When I hit it, I threw on all the power and landed over it safely in the road. Buick was just taking a chew of tobacco, and a lump of mud as large as a baseball hit him square in the face, filling his mouth completely. We were plastered with mud from head to foot when we reached Flint."

The trip was a little longer in distance than planned, Marr having missed a turn at Lapeer. But the 115 miles had been covered in 217

Left: Walter Marr and passenger Tom Buick photographed on East First Street in Flint, after trip to Detroit and back in first Flint Buick. Above: Later that same day, in front of the Buick plant. Below: Marr behind the wheel of the first production Buick, designated Model B.

Begole and Whiting in back, Marr and Tom Buick in front, first Model B

minutes and that, he said, was "a record."*

Marr was so excited about the performance of the vehicle that instead of heading back to the factory, he drove it directly downtown and stopped in front of the office of *The Flint Journal*. "The machine made the run without a skip," he told a reporter. "It reached here in the best of condition. We took the hills handily with our high-speed gear and the machine sounded like a locomotive. It simply climbed." A freelance photographer, Charles R. Quay, took a picture of the mud-encrusted men and car as a crowd gathered.

The reporter was suitably impressed. He tapped out this lead for the following day's editions: "Bespattered with flying real estate from every county they had touched, but with the knowledge that they had made a 'record,' Tom Buick and W.L. Marr, of the Buick Motor Works, who left for Detroit on Saturday to give the first automobile turned out by that concern a trial on the road, returned to the city late yesterday afternoon. The test of the machine was eminently satisfactory, and, in fact, exceeded expectations."

According to Charles Hulse's 1934 interview with Marr, the happy ending of that trip was exceedingly important because Whiting had

*Some early Buick histories state that when Briscoe sold Buick to the Flint Wagon Works, Briscoe's Buick made the trip to Flint on a demonstration run. There is no known contemporary confirmation of this, and the story may be an inaccurate version of the test run described above.

initially expressed doubts about Marr's suggestion that the Buick company was ready to build automobiles, but finally said he would think about it if he could drive an experimental model to Detroit and back successfully. When Marr arrived back in Flint, and exclaimed to the Flint Wagon Works directors, "Well, here we are," they had replied, "So are we," and the money for initial production was quickly found.

It is said that the success of that test sold at least seventeen cars before a complete one was built. A Flint doctor, Herbert H. Hills, was permitted to drive the test car several times and received the first delivery of a new Model B. Although he had been seventeenth in line for one of the cars, according to his diary, he took delivery August 13th, 1904, having climbed to the top of the list after agreeing to allow his vehicle to be used as a demonstrator. Hills said he drove his Buick for four years, and sold it to a Buick superintendent, George Weber, who drove it three more years and then tore it down to sell the parts.

There is some conflict here as to the car itself and the precise date of its delivery. Hugh Dolnar, writing in *Cycle and Automobile Trade Journal*, said that the July 9th-12th test car, fitted with a body, was the vehicle delivered to Hills, and that the date was July 27th, 1904, not August 13th. Dolnar wrote his article on September 16th and 17th, immediately after talking to Hills in Flint.

Noted Dolnar: "Dr. Hills has driven this car almost the whole time, day and night, over the very hilly and sandy country about Flint, and has had no repairs, except a split gasoline pipe, this day, Sept. 16, and believes he has the best car in the world."

Up to that date, Dolnar wrote, sixteen Buicks had been shipped to purchasers, and orders for eleven others were on the books. The plant, he said, could produce a car a day. Dolnar was fairly ecstatic about the Buick. The factory, he continued, "is equipped with the best machinery made by the best American tool builders." And on September 17th, Dolnar was given a ride by Tom Buick and found the car "thoroughly responsive; had more power everywhere than could be used . . . this was a ride to be remembered." The engine was not quite silent, "but makes no more noise than is desirable" and "we could accelerate on any hill slope we met without beginning to call on the motor for full-charge work."

He continued: "At first, Buick drove with some decent regard for law and prudence, but the road was hard, the clear air was intoxicating, and after one request to 'push her' up one steep hill, which the car mounted at 25 miles speed, Buick began to be proud of his mount and drive for fun. Later in the day he was fined $12 for fast driving. The Beak considerably informing him it would be more next time."

Dolnar said that the side-entrance tonneau body was designed by

David Buick, ''who conceived the happy idea of hinging the side entrance door in front. This gives two distinct advantages, first, a good substantial door hinge, and second, in connection with the full-length running board, the swinging of the door to the front gives the easiest possible entrance to the tonneau seats.'' (This wasn't the first magazine report on the Flint-built Buick. *The Automobile* on July 30, 1904, carried a brief article and the first published use of the photo on page 34 of Marr and Tom Buick in the stripped car.)

Dolnar went on: "The tonneau is a 'solid job,' that is, not detachable. The upholstering is the best grade of 'machine buff' leather. The standard body color will be indigo blue, with yellow running gear, any colored leather . . .

"The car simply ran to perfection, and is extremely easy, especially in sharp side crooks of the road wheel ruts, and has very little bounce over short road depressions. The writer never went so fast on a rough, hilly road. The rear brakes were not connected and what braking was done was with the reverse. But the brake was not used. The car flew down the hills and flew up the hills, all the same rate, and the engine purred and the wind whistled past and the soft September sun smiled benignly on the fine farms we ran by, and it was all delightful.''

Albert B. Calver, an assembler at the Flint Wagon Works, adjacent to Buick in 1904, recalled in a 1953 interview with Bob Bennett of the *Flint News-Advertiser* that he had helped build the wooden body for the first Flint Buick.

"They just came in and told us one day that we were going to work on the Buick. They gave us some blueprints to go by, but a lot of the design had to be made up as we went along. Whenever we got stuck, we just did things the way we had done with the buggies. Sounds funny to say that we lined up the wheels with a old pine yardstick and the frame with a piece of string, but that's the way we did it—same as we'd lined up thousands of buggies."

The frame and chassis were made of huge angle irons. The axles and springs were shipped across town from the Armstrong Spring and Axle Company. Said Calver: "There was no such thing as welding, so all the parts had to be joined with rivets. And none of the bolts we used were cut to size. We just went around to the barrel and hunted around for bolts we thought might fit. If they were too long, we just cut them off.

"The biggest job, though, was getting the motor to fit into the frame. When we got the frame done, the motor was just too big. We spent some long hours with cold chisels hacking away at those angle irons to make room for the motor. When we finally finished getting the frame and motor together, we had to carry it all over to the old Buick motor plant by hand. It was just across the street, but it was a job.''

Dr. Herbert H. Hills and his Model B, the first production Buick sold.

With Buicks in production in the fall of 1904, it would seem that Whiting should have been highly pleased. But the elderly businessman was instead deeply worried. In order to get the Buick into production, the small amount of capital had been quickly depleted. Rodolf reported that not only had the firm exhausted the $37,500, but it owed $25,000 each to three Flint banks. This was a large percentage of the capital of those banks in 1904. Even the farm engines, for which Cumings and others had obtained large orders, were not forthcoming. When David Buick and Walter Marr worked on an automobile, they thought of nothing else.

Whiting, from outward appearances on the verge of success, could see it all about to fall apart. What was necessary for Buick, he decided, was a younger man to run the business. Plus something that the Buick firm had always needed—more money.

In the fall of 1904, James Whiting, bound by train for a carriage convention in Chicago, discussed his problems with Fred A. Aldrich, secretary of Flint's largest coachbuilding firm, the Durant-Dort Carriage Company. Aldrich said he might have an answer. The man he had in mind for the job didn't like cars much, and he was in New York at the moment. But if Whiting and Aldrich could get him interested, there was no one who could get things moving faster than Aldrich's boss—the energetic supersalesman Billy Durant.

Chapter Three

BILLY DURANT TAKES OVER

In the late summer of 1904, the future of the Buick Motor Company was riding with Billy Durant as he headed home on the train from New York to Flint. For about three years Durant had been an absentee partner in the Durant-Dort Carriage Company, living in New York partly because of his fascination with the stock market, partly perhaps because of his growing estrangement from his wife, Clara. He had even tried to resign from the carriage company, but the directors had turned him down.

Now the slight, five-foot-eight "king" of Flint's carriage industry was to take a look at what James Whiting had bought, and now wanted someone else to manage, the Buick Motor Company. Durant knew enough about automobiles to have a distaste for them. He had once taken a ride in Judge Charles Wisner's homemade car, the first built in Flint, and they'd had to push it over crosswalks. He had been a passenger in the steam Mobile of his cousin, W.C. Orrell, and its sounds had irritated him. He may have even taken a spin with a Flint acquaintance, Arthur Jerome Eddy, who was married to Orrell's sister Lucy and who had driven between Chicago and Boston and written a book, *Two Thousand Miles on an Automobile*, about the adventure.

Nevertheless, in the summer of 1904, Durant was still an unreconstructed carriage man. Automobiles, he felt, were noisy, foul-smelling and generally obnoxious to both horses and humans, not to mention carriage manufacturers. While Hardy and Whiting had become deeply involved in automobiles, Durant had been busily trying to organize a holding company of carriage manufacturers. He could make a good case for such a combine on paper, but the carriage makers were too independent to pay much attention.

Arriving in Flint, Durant discussed the Buick situation with Whiting. On September 4th, 1904, he was given his first ride in a Buick by Dr. Herbert Hills, who recalled the episode a half-century later: "We started off with Durant and me in the front seat, and Mrs. Durant and their daughter in the rear. We drove out E. Kearsley Street, then one of the few paved streets in Flint, and Durant kept firing questions at me about how the car ran and if I liked it or not. We didn't talk about anything else the whole time."

Durant was becoming interested, but told Whiting he wanted to borrow a car for awhile so he could try it himself. For weeks, it is said, Durant personally tested the Buick, taking it through mud, up and down hills and over all manner of rough terrain to satisfy himself of the car's power and durability. The more he tested the Buick, and the more he thought about its potential, the more excited Durant became about its prospects. There were a number of good reasons for his interest. One was that the high-performance Buick was, like any good horseless carriage, a "self-seller" like the little road cart which had started him on his way to fortune less than twenty years earlier. Another was that if automobiles could perform this well, the carriage business was clearly in some danger.

Yet another factor was that Durant felt a strong loyalty to Flint—a trait evidenced many times in his career—and the possibility was real that the failure of Buick could cripple the local economy. Further, there was the fact that influential Flint residents, many of them his friends, some his relatives, were turning to him for help. And, moreover, the stockholders of Buick were so concerned about the company's future that they were willing to turn over controlling interest to him. Probably the clincher was that the Durant-Dort Carriage Company had a large, idle factory at Jackson, Michigan, which had housed the Imperial Wheel Company before Durant-Dort moved that enterprise to Flint. It was a readily available building in which to expand Buick production.

For about six weeks, Durant hesitated, possibly to sweeten the deal for his takeover, probably to consider all of the ramifications. The company was, after all—in Durant's words—"practically insolvent." Finally, one day in October, Durant and Whiting drove a Buick around Flint, then pulled up in front of Whiting's house on East Kearsley Street and sat and talked in the car for more than an hour. When Whiting walked into the house, he announced to his family, with some relief: "Billy's sold."

On November 1st, 1904, the Buick Motor Company directors took a series of actions. Durant was elected to the board. Typically, he declined the presidency, though it was understood he now held con-

trol. Whiting resigned as Buick president to devote more time, it was said, to the Flint Wagon Works, and Charles L. Begole was elected to succeed him. Buick capital stock was increased from $75,000 to $300,000, with plans announced for a projected quick increase to $500,000. It was also agreed that Buick assembly would be moved to the factory in Jackson and production greatly expanded.

The same day all this was revealed, the owners of the Flint Gas Light Company announced they were selling out to other interests for $325,000. Of this sum, a large amount was reportedly invested in the new Buick stock issue. It is interesting to note that the gas light company's directors were largely friends and relatives of Durant, who had once been that firm's treasurer.

On November 19th, Buick capital stock was jumped, as planned, to $500,000, of which Durant received $325,000 worth as his individual property. The remainder was divided among the other stockholders. Durant then transferred $101,000 of his shares to Whiting and $22,000 to Begole in exchange for their management in Jackson and Flint. (This caused a fuss in 1911 when Ballenger and others filed a claim protesting they didn't know Whiting was "making any secret profit" while representing Buick stockholders in the deal. Whiting and Durant responded that there was no secret deal in the November 19, 1904, stock agreement and that Durant approached Whiting and Begole in December when he decided he needed their help.) Durant turned over most or all of his remaining Buick stock to Durant-Dort because, he said, he was promoting Buick on the carriage company's time. He was also taking over the plant it owned in Jackson and involving other Durant-Dort officers in the Buick venture.

While all of these maneuverings were going on, the Buick factory in Flint was slowly turning out the first production Buicks, as well as press releases to the various automobile publications about the new

Page preceding: Dealer driveaway of Model C Buicks in Jackson during 1905. Below: The photo Durant ordered to be taken in Flint, November 1904.

cars. The emphasis, of course, was on the Buick's engine, the valve-in-head two-cylinder of 4.5 by 5 bore and stroke for a piston displacement of 159 cubic inches and horsepower of 15 at 900 rpm, 21.0 at 1230 rpm—though these figures would be superseded and some considerable contretemps would result.

The rest of the Buick was noncontroversial—very much in the prevailing mode of American "light touring automobile" design. It featured chain drive, a cone clutch, a two-speed planetary gearset ("transmission . . . of the sun-and-planet type," as Buick press releases put it). Ignition was jump spark, the carburetor float feed, the radiator a continuous coil with fins and water circulation by gear-driven pump. Lubrication was accomplished by a "seven-feed, gear-driven, mechanically operated oiler, with an individual pump for each bearing" and an automatic sight feed on the dash. The frame was angle iron with cross supports for strength. The suspension consisted of long thirty-six-inch three-quarter elliptic springs in front, forty-inch half elliptics in the rear. The drive was right hand, the steering wheel tilted (a feature Marr had included on his Marr Autocar). The wooden five-passenger side entrance tonneau body was finished in dark blue with brass trimming around the seats and on the dashboard. The vehicle complete weighed 1,675 pounds, its price was $950. It was designated the Model B.

Buick production had not begun until after the first Flint-built car had completed its test run to Detroit and back in early July 1904. On one official Buick production list, the oft-quoted figure of sixteen cars for 1903 is footnoted "16 cars set up as 1903 per W.E. McNaught." Waldo McNaught, Buick public relations director during the 1950's, once told the writer he had no official documents to back up that figure, but pulled it from early unofficial Buick histories. There is no question as to its inaccuracy. The fact that Buick did not begin producing cars in Flint until 1904 is clear from contemporary newspaper articles, from Hugh Dolnar's magazine articles, from early interviews of Walter L. Marr, and from early Buick catalogues.

How many Buicks were built in 1904? The generally accepted number is 37—the total listed for 1904 in the 1908 Buick catalog and in most official lists. Most were probably Model Bs, but opinion ranges from all 37 as Model Bs to some Model Cs included late in the model year and possibly some Bs with C characteristics. Details in Appendix Seven. The earliest Bs had 83-inch wheelbases, engines with pushrods on the bottom (instead of top) and narrow (rather than wide) brass moldings on the front of the hood.

Specific numbers were not the concern that year in any case. As plant foreman William Beacraft recalled: "Our first thought then was whether we could sell the cars when we made them, but this soon

Above: The Koehler-entered Model B at Eagle Rock hill climb, November 1904.
Below: Advertisement from Cycle and Automobile Trade Journal, *January 1905.*

reversed itself to: How can we get them out fast enough to supply the demand? In those days we were so busy that I used to sleep in the shop, but we never could keep up with the demand."

In November 1904 a Buick agency was opened in Cleveland. *Motor Age*, in announcing this, described Buick as "a little machine that has attracted an immense amount of attention in the past few weeks owing to its high power and low price." Some of this attention stemmed from Dolnar's published observations regarding a test he personally witnessed in which the Buick valve-in-head engine produced 22 horsepower at 924 revolutions per minute by brake test. That was considered unbelievable, so his editors sent him back for another look. This time, in December 1904, he witnessed the following results: 23 horsepower at 1152 rpm, 26.4 horsepower at 1320 rpm, and then 29 horsepower at 1320 rpm.

In its 1905 catalogue, Buick made much of the notion that Dolnar's original report had "startled the whole mechanical world" and raised doubts about the accuracy of both Buick's claims and Dolnar's reporting. It pointed out that the second series of demonstrations witnessed by Dolnar had erased those doubts, producing an average of 27.7 horsepower in three tests, whereas Buick claimed a mere twenty-two. And in some cases one less, as for the half-page advertisement published in various trade magazines in October 1904: "In a class by itself. Actual 21 Brake Horse Power on the stand. Experienced Drivers can get the same on the road."

In his own autobiographical notes, written decades later, Durant said he hired a motor expert to study Buick's engine in the face of the widespread doubts about its power. The expert told Buick factory superintendent Arthur C. Mason that the engine was unsound, extremely dangerous and "quite likely to explode," as Durant's notes relate. "In fact, I would suggest the purchase of a bushel basket with every one sold in order to be able to pick up the pieces."

To which Mason reportedly reacted by starting the engine, placing his head alongside it, and replying: "If it explodes, I might as well go with it."

The story sounds like one that probably improved with age, but there was no doubt that Buick's engine was something of a phenomenon. Durant wrote: "Power, the achievement of Mason's long experiments and hard work, became synonymous with Buick. We played on that one item: Power! Power to outclimb, power to outspeed anything on wheels in our class. With Buick we sold the assurance that the power to perform was there. Power sold Buick and made it what it is today."

Buick's boast that it had the most powerful engine in its class was soon competition tested. On Thanksgiving Day, 1904, one of the several dozen Model B's then in existence was entered by H.J.

Koehler (Buick agent for New York and New Jersey) in a major hill climbing contest against stiff foreign and American competition at Eagle Rock, near Newark, New Jersey. *Motor World*, one of the leading automotive publications, reported: "In the class for cars between $850 and $1250, the new Buick car made its initial appearance, and in a twinkling stamped itself a wonder. It easily carried off the first honors in its class by a wide margin, cutting the record from 4:13½ to 2:18-2/5. The clean cut and business like appearance of the car and its quiet running caused much favorable comment."

Durant did not like to spend money advertising, so the free publicity for winning a hillclimb was something to remember. He had the article reprinted in his 1905 catalogue, noting that "the car which made this phenomenal record was not specially built or geared for hillclimbing or for racing; it was a regular stock model, taken from the garage of our Newark agent, and was driven by a gentleman who is in no sense a professional, while many of the cars in this contest were specifically built or specially geared and driven by factory experts." (The first known race involving a Buick was on August 27, 1904, when Marr finished third behind a Ford and a Franklin in a five-miler at Grosse Pointe, Michigan.)

Before the year was out, another Buick, this one stripped to the chassis, won its class in the first Race to the Clouds up Mt. Washington in New Hampshire, driven by a man named Chase.

With these victories, Durant was sold. He had some details to attend to at the moment, but once he found time he would develop a Buick racing team that would gather trophies—and headlines—across the country.

As Buick supervisors worked to get the Jackson plant ready late in 1904, Durant turned his attention to his first loves—promoting and selling. The first thing he sold was Buick's potential to its creditors. A number of them were hounding the company for delivery of pre-sold stationary engines and payment for supplies. Durant explained that if they called their debts, Buick could be forced into bankruptcy and the creditors wouldn't collect much. But he could see big things ahead for the firm. If they would hold off, Buick would soon be on its feet and able to pay its debts. Apparently Durant's name and selling job worked. The creditors agreed to wait.

On November 3, 1904, just two days after he took control, Durant staged a Buick spectacle in downtown Flint. He lined up all the Buicks he could find—including two apparently not quite yet finished—and paraded them through the city "with tooting bugles . . (creating) a great deal of attention and much favorable comment," as *The Daily News* reported. The eight motorcars were lined up at Flint's main thoroughfare, Saginaw Street, long enough for Charles Quay to take the photograph on page 40.

Moving quickly, Durant went to New York late in November 1904 and negotiated membership in the Association of Licensed Automobile Manufacturers after proving Buick had purchased Pope-Robinson and its Selden license. Discussing this, *The Motor World* of November 24, 1904, accurately saw Buick as "probably the most notable accession the industry has had in recent years" because of its "capital, largely increased facilities and in the accession of men whose names are synonymous with success in the big Michigan centres. . . ."

Both Durant and David Buick showed up at the New York Auto Show in January 1905 with a complete car ("indigo blue and yellow") and chassis. *The Motor World* noted "Mr. Buick . . . very generally and in a very nice way explains why he certainly is getting more horsepower than engines of similar size." *Horseless Age* found Durant "in the restaurant, presiding over the finished car of his firm . . . he believed that (people at the show) really understood the mechanism and construction of cars and appreciated the honest efforts made to give them a reliable and desirable machine at a fair price."

Page opposite: 1905 Model C. Above and below: Rare sequential series of photos of another '05 C showing hazards of motoring on roads of the day.

But the New York event was of more significance than Buick's first appearance at an auto show. Several weeks after it ended that January, his wife Clara, still boasting of her husband's work despite their cooling relationship, wrote to a friend: "William has just returned from the auto show in New York, where he sold 1,108 machines. The Buick is certainly a success."

In 1886, Durant had sold 600 road carts before he had built one. Now, if Clara's letter is accurate, he had sold more than a thousand Buicks before the company had built forty. Durant's reputation as a supersalesman was secure. As Walter Chrysler later wrote, "He could charm a bird right down out of a tree."

The move to Jackson was a quick solution to Buick's need for assembly space, but it was a makeshift and an unsatisfactory one. Not only were the Flint-based stockholders unhappy with the decision to assemble cars outside their city—they accepted it only because of economic realities—but Durant found it inconvenient and expensive to ship bodies, wheels, springs, engines and transmissions from Flint to Jackson.

Reportedly he tried to interest investors in both Jackson and Bay City, Michigan in building a large new Buick factory. There were good reasons for this. Jackson was twice as large as Flint at the beginning of the century, had a good deal of industry and was a major railroad junction. Bay City had the advantage of excellent port facilities on Lake Huron. But businessmen in neither city offered encouragement, or cash, to lure Buick. And it seems unlikely that Durant really strongly considered any place but Flint anyway. That was where his financial backing, and his supplier plants, were. Talk-

ing about Jackson and Bay City was probably no more than a feint to get more money from Flint investors. In the 1890's he had made a similar move, incidentally, announcing that he was taking his carriage firm to Saginaw, in an apparent effort to wring some concession out of Flint. It had worked then, and it worked this time.

Durant offered to consolidate Buick in Flint if capitalization could be raised to $1.5 million so that a suitable plant could be built. He already had a site—the 220-acre Hamilton farm just north of the city which was already partially in use for some of the Durant-Dort Carriage Company subsidiaries and supplier firms. He had often talked of it as a center for manufacturing, what would today be called an industrial park.

The Flint financial community again came through. Although banking institutions were not generally buying industrial stocks under their own names in those days, the directors of three Flint banks joined personally in making commitments for more Buick shares. One of them, Genesee County Savings Bank, had a special account begun with funds from the sale of some outdated equipment and periodically fattened when old debts were paid after having been written off. The bank used that account for the $20,000 it invested in the Buick company. In total, $80,000 of Buick stock was acquired by Flint banks, for which they received $100,000 in shares, including a twenty-five percent bonus of common stock. (Genesee Bank at last report still held some of this stock, which had grown in value to $8,-000,000.)

One of the 1905 agreements, still preserved, notes that the subscription was being made "with the understanding that the Buick

Page opposite: Two strange 1905 Model Cs, in unusual white paint, the one at right with a rare two-seat body style. Above: D.J. Powers and family in a 1906 or '07 Model F. Above right: A Model C in England, 1905, probably the first Buick overseas, with William C. Orrell, a cousin of Durant; Clark C. Hyatt standing. Below: Buick two-cylinder engine from 1905.

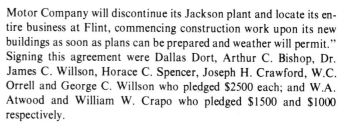

Motor Company will discontinue its Jackson plant and locate its entire business at Flint, commencing construction work upon its new buildings as soon as plans can be prepared and weather will permit." Signing this agreement were Dallas Dort, Arthur C. Bishop, Dr. James C. Willson, Horace C. Spencer, Joseph H. Crawford, W.C. Orrell and George C. Willson who pledged $2500 each; and W.A. Atwood and William W. Crapo who pledged $1500 and $1000 respectively.

Dr. Willson was Durant's uncle, with whom he and his mother and sister had lived when they first moved to Flint; W.W. Crapo was also his uncle (Henry Crapo's only son and a prominent lawyer and Massachusetts congressman); George Willson and Orrell were his cousins; Dallas Dort was his carriage partner, and Bishop was a close friend and financial backer whom Durant would later place on the board of General Motors.

With money pledged, Durant got Buick's stock formally increased to $1.5 million on September 11th, 1905. The company's attorney, John J. Carton of Flint, later wrote of his difficulty in finding enough equity to justify the increase. He totted up all Buick's assets and was still $60,000 short. So he merely assigned a $60,000 value to the "ownership of invention of combustion engine construction not patented for business reasons." It was a rather intangible asset—Carton said he managed to get it approved because he was "very well acquainted" in Michigan's capital of Lansing—and in the next session of the Legislature a law was passed prohibiting such listings in the future. Thereafter, however, Buick was home free. Durant had no trouble getting the capitalization boosted to $2.6 million on June

45

Above: Rare photo of Billy Durant (in the light-colored cap) in a Buick (a Model F) during the 1906 Glidden Tour. Durant's car was disqualified for helping another driver and a photo (below) found in the Walter Marr Collection now in the GMI Archives appears to capture the violation. The No. 30 Buick is pulling another car from a ditch and Durant (in cap) can be seen at the tow rope. Opposite, from the top: Walter Marr and a Model D on the 1906 Glidden; H.J. Koehler in a 1906 Model G; Koehler in a 1907 Model G.

12th, 1907. By then the company was worth every penny. But Carton's assistance exemplified two important factors regarding Flint in this automotive pioneering era: the unusual number of talented and well-connected men there, and how effectively Durant made use of their abilities. Carton was at the time one of the state's foremost Republican leaders, having been speaker of the state House in 1901 and 1903. He would serve as president of a state constitutional convention in 1907-1908. For a number of years, he would be the attorney for both Buick and Durant.

Durant later boasted that he sold $500,000 worth of stock in Buick, all of it in Flint, in forty-eight hours. Most of the buyers, he said, "had never ridden in an automobile." While it has been pointed out that he sold most of the issue to persons he knew well, the fact that those who knew him best had such confidence in his abilities is a tribute to Durant's reputation at that time.

Not all of the money for Buick's expansion came from Flint. Durant traveled around Michigan and to nearby states to get further funds. But the small city of 14,000 people had invested in Buick to a remarkable degree, much of the money having originated in the lumbering industry thirty years before.

That Durant had placed practically all of the economic power in Flint behind Buick is evident from the stockholder lists. Whiting and the Flint Wagon Works still held major blocks of stock. Among other big investors was the Durant-Dort Carriage Company, which bought $100,000 worth. (Durant-Dort became almost a holding company for automobile firms backed by Durant, starting with Buick.) One of the pioneer Flint builders of carriage bodies, William F. Stewart, invested in Buick, as did William A. Paterson, the oldest of Flint's major carriage builders. Both Stewart and Paterson served for a time on the Buick board, alongside representatives of Durant-Dort and Flint Wagon Works. Stewart's W.F. Stewart Company built a factory on the Hamilton farm which became a body-building subsidiary for Buick. Paterson, however, eventually went his own way, producing the Paterson automobile which survived until 1923, two years after Paterson's death.

While Durant was pulling the economic forces in Flint together, Buick was finally getting into significant production in Jackson. Seven hundred fifty cars were built in 1905, all of them the new Model C. Only eight American companies had a higher production that year. Although the major components were shipped from Flint, apparently all the cars were assembled at Jackson. Durant himself moved to Jackson, living for a time at the Otsego Hotel and setting up a headquarters at the factory. The second Buick catalogue lists Jackson as the home of Buick. Durant's factory manager there was H. George Field, a former Detroit architect who later went into the

Left: The Buick Motor Company, this photograph identified on the back in 1908 as "first General Motors plant." Right: The Buick office building, also from 1908.

electric car business and then returned to architecture after the Jackson operations of Buick were essentially ended. As Buick's sales manager, Durant named Charles Van Horn (or Van Horne), a veteran of the bicycle industry who would remain with the company about a year. W.L. Hibbard, who had been manager of the Chicago office of Studebaker, was the assistant sales manager.

In some early advertisements, the 1905 Buick was referred to as a Model B, though the designation was soon changed to Model C. One of these early ads touts the Buick as "The Car of Quality" and hopefully adds, "Agents wanted everywhere." One of the early agents, the Pence Automobile Company of Fargo, North Dakota, noted in a letter to a customer, "We have a machine called the Buick which is new to the Automobile world this year which develops 22 h.p. and with the finish they put on their bodies is the best high-powered proposition on the market."

The Model C Buick was changed only in detail from the 1904 Model B. There were a few new features, such as a foot-operated service brake and an extra-cost cape cart top that could be fitted with side curtains and celluloid windshield. The reliable two-cylinder valve-in-head engine had the same specifications as in 1904, although its 22 horsepower was now said to be developed at 1200 rpm. The Buick catalogue boasted that the car "embodies every feature and every advantage of the best foreign and American inventions; has every desirable feature in the simplest form to meet the requirements of American and foreign road conditions, and in addition has many individual features possessed by no other car. It has more speed, more power, more room and style and less vibration, and makes less noise and trouble than any other car in its class on the market." On

the West Coast, one Buick dealer placed a full-page newspaper advertisement which simply said, in large type, "Jesse James would have never been caught if there had been a Buick in those days."

Among other changes, the engine pushrods were on the top, wheelbase was 85 or 87 inches and the price had risen to $1,200. The body was painted royal blue, the wheels ivory, the name "Buick" was boldly stamped on the steel running boards later in the model year. Durant came up with a slogan: "We do with two cylinders what others try to do with four." This was short-lived, however, for by May 1906 Buick had introduced its own four-cylinder engine.

Meanwhile, Buicks were beginning to make big news on the racing and hill climbing circuits. In a single issue of *The Flint Journal*, September 15th, 1905, three victories were announced:

"At the Readville track at Boston on Saturday the Buick automobile established a new world's five-mile record for two-cylinder machines, covering the distance in 6 minutes and 19-3/5 seconds."

"At Newark, N.J., on Saturday, the Buick carried off all the speed honors in sight, establishing the track record for one mile, 1 minute and 2 seconds; defeating the Pope-Hartford whose time was 1 minute and 16 seconds, and the Wayne, whose time was 1 minute and 17 seconds."

"In the six-mile free-for-all race at Newark on Saturday, the Buick also was the winner . . . defeating the Knox and Locomobile; and the Flint machine likewise cleaned up on the Knox and Reo in the three-mile race, covering the distance in 4 minutes and 16 seconds. The Knox made the three miles in 4 minutes and 33 seconds, and the Reo in 5 minutes and 25 seconds."

Above: Although the track was a makeshift, all early Buick production car chassis were given a test run before return to the plant for fitting of bodies and final trim.

In 1905, a young man named Bob Burman from the small town of Imlay City near Flint graduated from test driver to race driver.

As an early Buick employee, William H. Washer, recalled, Buick used to borrow Burman from the Flint Wagon Works to paint engines. After a while, Burman became an engine tester.

"One time an engine bearing froze during a test," Washer reminisced. "Burman asked what to do and I told him he'd have to chisel off the bearing cap. He did, but he also accidentally put a chisel mark in the crankshaft bearing. Mr. Mason, the superintendent, came along and noticed the damaged crankshaft. He asked Bob who had done it and Bob admitted he had. 'Go to the time office,' Mr. Mason said, 'You're all through. Your money will be waiting for you.'"

Burman later got a job as chief tester of the Jackson Automobile Company, but Durant hired him back as a Buick tester and racer. Recalled Washer: "I remember that when Burman raced for Buick he came to the engine plant and told Mr. Mason—who had fired him—just how he wanted the cams ground on a racing engine."

Before his death in a racing accident in Corona, California, in 1916, Burman had become Buick's greatest racing driver—surpassing, in most judgments, the ability of legendary teammate Louis Chevrolet. The title of "world speed king" formerly held by Barney Oldfield belonged to him as well.

While production increased at Jackson, Durant raced ahead with the plans for Flint. With his new-found money, he began construction of a factory on Flint's North Side that was huge for the period. Boasting fourteen acres under roof, it was said to be the largest automobile plant in the world. A number of factories were claimed to be that during this period, but if Durant's wasn't the biggest, his plans for it were gargantuan. He fully intended to be the world's largest producer of automobiles, just as he had been number one in carriage production with the Durant-Dort Carriage Company.

In Durant's busy mind, he could envision gathering automobile component firms in Flint to supply Buick, just as he had brought axle, varnish and wheel companies to town to supply his buggies. His first move in this direction came in 1905. On June 4th he sent a letter to Utica, New York, addressed to Charles Stewart Mott, president of the Weston-Mott Company, producer of axles for Buick and other automobile companies.

Durant wrote: "Would you entertain a proposition of removing or establishing a branch factory at Flint, Michigan, provided the business of three or four large concerns was assured for a term of years? Flint is in the center of the automobile industry, a progressive city, good people, with conditions for manufacturing, ideal."*

Mott replied that he would not be interested in setting up a branch in Flint because it could not be easily managed at such long range. He would, however, consider moving the whole business to Flint, given the right proposal.

---

*The typist put her initials, C.L., at the bottom of the letter. Catherine Lederer, a schoolgirl twenty-five years Durant's junior, was Durant's personal secretary in Jackson in 1905. In 1908, one day after his divorce from his first wife Clara became final, Durant married Catherine in New York City. Catherine Durant lived until 1974 and supplied author Lawrence Gustin with original Durant material, including the first release ever of her husband's autobiographical notes, for his 1973 biography, *Billy Durant: Creator of General Motors*, and also used in this book.

The Buick Motor Company and how it grew. During 1907 the men who put Buick engines together gathered outside the plant on West Kearsley for a group portrait.

On Labor Day weekend, 1905, Durant and Dort showed up in Utica and accompanied Mott, his partner William G. Doolittle, and their wives, on the train to Flint. They arrived on September 2nd.

Mott later wrote: "My first impression of Flint was that it was a small country town with about 15,000 population and a lot of good, progressive people wanting to make it a fine city. . . . W.C. Durant was the spark plug with great ideas and very loyal to Flint. Dort was a fine man and Flint's No. 1 citizen. Always ready to help make Flint grow and become a better place in which to live."

Durant had put together a package that Mott could hardly refuse. Flint investors would give Weston-Mott $100,000 in new capital and a factory site next to Buick. Durant would give Mott an exclusive contract to make axles for Buick, yet still allow him to sell to other

suppliers. The new Buick and Weston-Mott factories were completed in the summer of 1906 and Mott moved his family to Flint on February 1st, 1907.*

---

*Mott would later become Flint's great philanthropist. (His partner, Doolittle, died within a year.) In 1908 forty-nine percent of Weston-Mott stock was exchanged for General Motors stock. Mott exchanged the other fifty-one percent in 1913, again for GM stock. A mayor of Flint three times, he built a personal fortune once estimated at more than $800 million, and turned much of it over to the Mott Foundation, which through the years has pumped millions of dollars into Flint education and recreational programs and parks, and more recently into downtown redevelopment, and other programs across the country. Mott was ninety-seven years old when he died in 1973. He had been a director of General Motors for sixty years.

As the men who built Buicks produced more of them, it was necessary to augment the office staff whose job was paperwork and promotion, this photo circa 1910.

Just how far Buick had come in one year, from late 1904 to late 1905, is evident in Mott's actions. In 1904, Mott had required Buick to pay in advance for axles, so shaky was the company's reputation. In 1905, Mott was willing to close his Utica plant and move his entire operation to Flint to serve Buick.

And Durant's negotiations with Mott also suggest something of the importance of Dallas Dort, president of the Durant-Dort Carriage Company, in key decisions involving Buick. Durant had first written to Mott from Jackson, but had directed him to reply to the Durant-Dort headquarters building in Flint, where Dort opened the mail. (The headquarters building, still standing, is now a Michigan historical landmark, listed on the National Register of Historic Places and a National Historical Landmark. More than the

headquarters of Durant-Dort, the building is closely associated with the birth of General Motors. The bringing together of Buick and Weston-Mott was the first major move to tie industries together in what would later evolve into GM, although Weston-Mott was not one of the original principals in GM.) Durant is correctly credited as the man who promoted Buick into a success and founded General Motors. Dort, in the background, was probably more fully involved than can ever be documented.

Ground was broken for the new Flint Buick factory on November 1st, 1905. On December 16th, *The Flint Journal* reported that the Charles A. Moses Construction Company of Chicago, the general contractor, was making great progress because of "remarkable weather and competent workmen." The transformation of the

51

From the top: The Model H, Model S and Model K built during 1907.
Page opposite: The Model 5 touring car produced the following year.

property was, according to the article, "quite remarkable, considering the fact that but little over a month ago a person could see oak scrubs by the score growing on the site of what is to be one of the greatest automobile factories in the world."

As the new Buick and Weston-Mott factories rose together on the Hamilton farm north of Flint, Buick production continued to increase in Jackson in 1906. Indeed, Buick's volume virtually doubled that year as 1400 units were produced. And, for the first time, these "units" included more than one model.

The Model C, according to brochures and press releases, was continued but this was merely a stock-clearing exercise for the 1905 model. New for 1906 was the Model F which was basically the C with a few updating features and was clearly that model's successor. The front end of the F was new, with a radiator that allowed all water to be recirculated, eliminating the large water storage tank, and for $1250 the acetylene headlamps and oil side and taillights were now included. Also included was an extra set of dry cells. A companion car, the two-seater Model G roadster, was available at $1150. Its mechanical specifications the same as the Model F, it was described by the company as "one of the handsomest cars ever put on the market, and it is built especially for people who want style and power." But not many of them, for only 193 were produced.

Garnering more attention was the brand-new Model D, Buick's first four-cylinder automobile. "A hurriedly finished example," as *The Automobile* said, had been given the place of honor on the Buick stand at the New York Automobile Show in January, but it was not until May of 1906 that the car was formally introduced. (Official records show that the car was considered a 1907 model.) The Model D represented several departures from Buick engineering practice thus far, and prevailing American practice as well.

Its 235-cubic-inch 30 hp engine (4¼ by 4½ bore/stroke dimensions) was a T-head design with opposed intake and exhaust valves and in *Motor Age*'s words, "most of the earmarks characteristic of four-cylinder, vertical, four-cycle, water cooled motors." Of special note, however, was the in-unit housing of the motor crankshaft, multiple disc clutch and three-speed sliding gear transmission. Similar to the design of the Stevens-Duryea, St. Louis and Dorris (with three-point suspension), and the Mora (with a continuous support along the side frame pieces), the Buick version used five-point suspension, and did it neatly. As *The Automobile* noted, "the disposition of the flywheel in front of the engine and the housing of the disc clutch and its actuating mechanism and of the change speed in a continuous aluminum case gives the car a clean and unusual appearance. The entire power plant and gear set is so disposed on the frame that alignment is constant." The crankcase was provided two long arms integrally cast at the front end and bolted to the pressed steel side frame members; at the back the transmission was loosely attached to a dropped cross frame member, with stiff helical springs interposed. Shaft drive was employed, suspension was semi-elliptic front and rear; the wheelbase was 102 inches as compared to the 87 inches (raised to 89 for 1907) of the Models F and G. The price of the Model D, complete with top, storm front, gas and oil lamps, horn and a set of tools, was $2500. The production total was 523.

The Buick catalogue now used the slogan, "Our customers are our best salesmen"—and boasted: "Three competing manufacturers have recently purchased Buick cars for the apparent purpose of studying the secret of their phenomenal power, and their unusual accessibility to all working parts."

What the catalogue did not mention, of course, were any of the Buick's foibles. Like every other automobile being manufactured during those dawning days of the industry, the Buick had its weaknesses. As Harry Shiland discovered.

Shiland was among the country's earliest automobile dealers, his business in Worcester, Massachusetts dating to about 1900. He had added Buick to his line after seeing one at the New York Automobile Show in January of 1905, according to Frank Rodolf. When his foreman took the Buick for a drive, several unpleasant things happened—the chain broke, the transmission froze and the carburetor acted up.

Shiland took a look, had repairs made, and discovered that once the problems were solved, the Buick had the fastest acceleration, the most power, of any car he had ever seen. He was so delighted with it that he challenged owners of other vehicles to a race but found no takers. Before he knew it, he was selling Buicks faster than he could get them. But he had to have every one of them overhauled first.

Finally he visited Durant in Jackson to see if he could get faster delivery, and also to find out what was going wrong. "You aren't selling cars to mechanics," he chided. "Cars have to be foolproof for the average doctor or lawyer or businessman to want them."

Durant was interested in a man who seemed so knowledgeable, and who was so direct. He kept Shiland in Jackson for two days and had him inspect the plant. Shiland suggested a number of changes. One was to switch chain manufacturers. Another was to use the Kingston adjustable carburetor in place of the Buick variety which had to be taken apart to adjust.

Durant bought the ideas, and also hired Shiland, who soon succeeded Charles Van Horn as Buick's sales manager. Remaining with the company until 1910, Shiland proved to be a valuable acquisition. Not only did he help set up a nationwide system of sales branches, but he also fought continually to improve Buick quality.

In 1906, for example, Durant decided to equip Buick connecting rods with steel bushings, instead of the usual bronze, because he felt they were quieter. Shiland protested, to no avail. However, that year both Durant and Shiland, with drivers, entered cars in the publicity-gathering Glidden Tour through New England. The Buicks failed to finish. Durant was disqualified for stopping to help another driver: Shiland's car broke down because the new steel bushings failed. Both men were disconsolate with the results, but as Shiland later pointed out, at least he had discovered the problem with the bushings—and proved it to Durant—before many cars had been equipped with them.

One of Shiland's first duties for Durant was to establish a sales branch in Chicago. Already, by 1906, 100 Buick agencies had been set up. In a letter that year, Durant boasted of these dealerships and also that Buick, building fifteen to seventeen automobiles a day, was an enormous success because "we are manufacturing a machine of rare merit at a very reasonable price; our motor being conceded by all gas engine experts to be one of the greatest improvements in gas engine practice ever designed."

What Durant preached in his catalogue, Buick practiced on the race tracks of America. Chief engineer Walter Marr was now driving in hill climbs and winning with some regularity. A Buick piloted by H.J. Koehler won a 100-mile race at Yonkers, New York, with an

average speed of 47.8 mph. Another Buick won a 100-mile free-for-all at the Empire City Track in New York City.

In 1906, a Model F Buick was the only car to complete a 1000-mile relay run from Chicago to New York, sponsored by the *Chicago American and Examiner*. According to one contemporary published account: "The only drawbacks in the entire trip were the stretches of bad road . . . rendered well nigh impassable by the rainstorms. . . . In the few places where the roads were good the Buick was run at its highest speed, the Warner auto-meter recording from 35 to 40 miles per hour. Even when the roads were full of chuckholes and the car hit only the high places, half the time off the ground, the speed registered 20 to 25 miles. There was a constant bumping, and if it were not for gripping a handrail fastened to the front seat, the passengers in the tonneau would have been thrown out many times. Yet through all this struggle of a thousand miles, the Buick never failed to move forward."

Boasted the company in a press release: "The phenomenal success of the Buick is the wonder and talk wherever the run is discussed, and that is from one end of the country to the other, for the Hearst chain of newspapers has reported it from point to point and the Associated Press has given it universal publicity."

Soon Buick was calling the Model F "Old Faithful," a title it used on a booklet of specifications for that model it published in 1907. "As a doctor's car," the company stated regarding its reliability, "there is no automobile manufactured that will prove anywhere near its equal." The tag stuck. For decades after, Buick was often referred to as "the doctor's car."

Walter Marr, in addition to being a competition enthusiast, was a perfectionist. He continually experimented with new engines, often assisted by David Buick, who was still on the payroll although maintaining such a low profile as to be almost invisible. Marr even mixed his own fuels, looking for just the right combination to increase performance. His assistants complained that they practically had to take an engine away from him to put it into production because he was incessantly trying to improve it.

Assisting Marr, in addition to David Buick, was Enos A. DeWaters. DeWaters was Marr's assistant from 1905 to 1913 and chief engineer until mid-1929 when Dutch Bower succeeded him. Before joining Buick in January 1905, he had worked on the Thomas Flyer in Buffalo, New York in 1903, and on the Cadillac in Detroit in 1904.

With the new Flint Buick factory in production, Buick assembled more than three times as many cars in 1907 as in 1906. Its total of 4641 was second only to Ford's 14,887. And there were more Buick models than ever now. The old reliable two-cylinder touring car, introduced as the Model B in 1904, continued as the Model C in 1905 and the Model F in 1906, was retained as the Model F for 1907. Unchanged except for two more inches in wheelbase and the addition of a belly pan to hide the engine and transmission, it was still by far the sales leader, a total of 3465 being delivered. The Model G runabout, also largely unchanged, had a production run of 535.

It was in the four-cylinder line that Buick offered proliferation for 1907. There were four models in all, comprising two body styles and two transmissions. The touring car was available as the Model D (sliding gear transmission, 523 units built) and the Model H (two-speed planetary transmission, 36 units built). A roadster could be had as the Model S (sliding gear transmission, 69 units built) or the Model K (planetary transmission, 13 units built). Given the choice, Durant's customers were obviously not as enamoured of the planetary system as Henry Ford's customers would have no choice but to be. Buick's four-cylinder models were priced from $1750 to $2500.

And by now Durant had worked out a deal with R. Samuel McLaughlin that saw the beginning of Buick's sales of engines and other components to Canada's largest carriage company. It hadn't been easy.

McLaughlin, son of Robert McLaughlin who had founded the

Page opposite: "Vehicle City," circa 1908, after the Buick came to town. Above: Outside of the real estate office of Gillespie & VanWagoner in Flint, the office staff poses with its first company car, an '08 Model F.

McLaughlin Carriage Company in Oshawa, Ontario, had known Durant from carriage days. But when he traveled to Jackson in 1905 it was for the purpose of buying two cars from the Jackson Automobile Company, the ultimate aim being an alliance with an American company to enter into the automobile business in Canada. While there, McLaughlin met Durant, who suggested that if the Jackson car didn't work out, maybe he would be interested in the Buick.

McLaughlin liked the Buick better than the Jackson, but couldn't reach financial terms with Durant. They parted friends, but McLaughlin decided to return to Oshawa and build his own car. As it happened, his engineer became ill, and so McLaughlin and Durant got together again, and this time the deal was done. During 1908, 154 McLaughlin cars were built in Canada with Buick engines. This was the forerunner of McLaughlin-Buick, which eventually became General Motors of Canada. Sam McLaughlin was still chairman of GM of Canada at his death in 1972. He was 100 years old.

Another new personality on the Buick scene was William H. Little, an ironic name for he was a giant of a man. He had been building the Orient Buckboard car in Waltham, Massachusetts, and was named Buick general manager after the company's return to Flint. Little was something of a character. Once, he became so irritated at running out of upholstery tacks that he ordered three carloads. Some of them were said to still be around decades later.

Little also liked to skid his car around on the pavement before

The team that Durant built, Bob Burman is pictured fourth from the left; the two moustachioed fellows in the center are Louis and Art Chevrolet, respectively.

parking it at the curb in front of Flint's Dresden Hotel when he went there for lunch. Mott recalled that one day he skidded more violently than he intended and the curb took off all four wheels.

On still another occasion, after being ordered to develop new brakes for the Buick, Little took Durant on a test run to show him how they operated. As Richard Crabb relates the story, when Little hit the brakes, they locked, and his boss tumbled from the back seat into the front and then out onto the ground. Durant got up, brushed himself off and said, mildly, "Well, you certainly got some brakes, Bill." Little, shaken, asked Durant to get back in and he would take him back to the factory. To which Durant replied, "No thanks, I'll walk."

If Little was becoming colorful, Durant was becoming legendary. When he breezed into town, things jumped. He was "The Man," and

the citizens of Flint marveled at the way he put thousands of dollars together and turned farms into factories with little more, it seemed, than a wave of the hand. Durant never seemed to sleep. He would still be conducting business in his office after midnight, yet he was at work again at 7:00 a.m. the next day. And sometimes, in between, he sandwiched in an all-night poker game at the Bryant House, a hotel in town.

Durant looked at the broad picture, selling stock, getting money, creating an organization, bringing in suppliers, putting together new companies. Often a new firm would not even carry his name among the organizers, but if you looked carefully, you could find a close Durant associate in a key position. One example was Michigan Motor Castings Company, built near Buick and incorporated in 1907 with $50,000 capitalization. Although at first Buick had no financial

Shown in the racing car with which he competed in Lowell, Massachusetts in 1908 is "Wild" Bob Burman, this Buick racer based on the 1908 Model D chassis.

interest in it, and Durant was not on the board, the firm's secretary was Arnold H. Goss, who was secretary of Buick and a close ally of Durant's. Within a few years the plant was producing 100 tons of castings a day for Buick, and eventually it was taken over for Buick by General Motors.

By the end of 1907, the Buick Motor Company under Durant was ready for big things. In the three years since he had taken control, he had raised the corporation's capital from $75,000—actually from the brink of bankruptcy—to $2.6 million, had increased annual production from thirty-seven cars to nearly five thousand, and had moved Buick to Jackson and then back to Flint, housing it in one of the world's finest factories. He had begun to supply McLaughlin in Canada, and had started to assemble what would soon be the best racing team in the country. Furthermore, he had quickly put together

the best network of automobile dealerships and displays in the country. That last had been easy. His Durant-Dort Carriage Company had a national dealer system built by Durant himself. By simply turning its outlets into Buick dealerships too, he was able to make Buick the most widely displayed automobile in the United States.

And while Durant established dealerships, Shiland set up a network of sales districts and branch warehouses to help distribute both cars and parts. Among the early successful distributors were Charles Howard in San Francisco, Harry Pence in Minneapolis, C.C. Coddington in the Carolinas and Richard H. Collins (who would succeed Shiland as Buick sales manager in 1910) in Kansas City.

Financing, production, distribution, sales and racing—Buick was forging ahead on all fronts. And most of this was entirely due to Billy

The Model 10 of 1908. At the wheel in the center photo is George Mason who, at age fifteen, taught Buick owners how to drive in North Dakota.

Durant, who had turned up his nose at automobiles only a few years before. What was happening, what was about to happen, showed that sheer genius was at work here. Durant was living up to his reputation as a promoter and the greatest supersalesman of them all, and he was also proving something else: He was one of the greatest organizers of all time. Durant has been scorned as an administrator. The truth is, administering a going concern bored him. Putting things together was the fun part, and nobody had more fun putting businesses together than Durant. The fun was just beginning.

At the New York Automobile Show in November 1907, Buick unveiled another new model. It was small. It was cute. And it was priced at only $900. It was the Model 10. *Motor World* called it the "sensation" of the show ["as might naturally be expected," Buick said] and predicted it would be the first car produced by a member of the Association of Licensed Automobile Manufacturers to provide "real opposition to some of the low-priced . . . unlicensed cars," a veiled reference to Ford.

The Model 10, described by Buick as "a gentlemen's light four-cylinder roadster," was set on an 88-inch wheelbase. It was powered by a new 3¾ by 3¾, 165-cubic-inch 22.5 hp engine of valve-in-head design which had apparently evolved out of one of Durant's ongoing efforts to make some use of the Jackson factory, which he had promised Flint investors he would phase out as a Buick site. Durant had brought to Jackson a naval armaments engineer named Janney, who had designed large coastal defense guns and other naval weapons. The Janney Motor Company was organized at Jackson to produce a light four-cylinder engine and reportedly two models were designed and two samples of each built. However the motor was not quite satisfactory and within a few months the whole business was apparently absorbed by Buick in an exchange of stock. Walter Marr and Enos DeWaters redesigned the motor, which found its way into the Model 10.

The Model 10 in essence selected some of its specifications from among the contemporary Buick fours, others from the two-cylinder cars. Ignition was by jump spark, lubrication a gear-driven force-feed; the clutch was a cone, and the transmission two-speed planetary. Suspension was semi-elliptic in front, full elliptic in the rear; drive was by shaft and bevel gear to a divided rear axle.

The car's popularity stemmed from its ease of control, smooth engine, eventual racing success and its price tag. For $900 a customer received a vehicle equipped with acetylene headlights, oil side and tail lamps and a bulb horn. The three-passenger car, called the "White Streak" because it was finished in an off-white color known as Buick gray, also had lots of brass and attractive lines. Almost half of the 1908 Buicks—4002 of them—were Model 10's. Some historians believe Durant would have more successfully challenged Ford's Model T, introduced late in 1908, had he marketed only the Model 10. History would record, however, that Durant's vision of producing models in various price ranges would ultimately prevail in the industry.

The latter part of 1907 and the early months of 1908 were not good times to sell automobiles. There was a financial panic in '07, and a cold, rainy spring dampened buyer interest the following year.

Durant, ever the gambler, decided to ignore all of this and ordered his factories to produce at full tilt. He juggled bills from suppliers, including Weston-Mott, and forced the suppliers to extend credit. New Buicks were being stored in fields, warehouses and even barns. Fortunately for Durant and his suppliers, the recession was a short one. And when people began to buy cars again in the early summer of 1908, Buick was the only automaker with plenty on hand.

C.S. Mott, ever the conservative, sounded almost incredulous telling the writer about this when he was in his late nineties, shortly before his death: "He was one hell of a gambler. To this day, I don't know how he was able to handle it financially, but he did it."

Mott also recalled Durant as the great salesman. Once, he said, he was traveling with him from Flint to Utica, and they stopped in Detroit to change trains. Because there was a little more than an hour layover, they walked to a nearby Buick dealership, where Durant learned the man in charge was having trouble closing a few deals. He got the name of one of the prospects, asked Mott to wait for him in the showroom, and returned with a sale in time to rejoin Mott and make the train connection.

Durant was pushing his Buick factories hard. In mid-January of 1908 a night shift was added. By the end of February, three shifts were operating seven days a week building engines in the original Buick plant on West Kearsley, feeding car assemblers in Flint and Jackson, who were also working overtime. In March 1908, some 2100 men were turning out fifty cars a day and Durant announced he would hire 350 more workers by May to increase output to eighty a day. Freight trains thirty cars long filled with Buicks were leaving Flint regularly for Kansas City, St. Louis and other points. In June, Buick built a record 1409 cars in Flint and 245 in Jackson. In November, Buick announced it would need 1000 more workers and even then could not fill its back orders until the following July.

In 1908, it appears, Durant fulfilled his goal of being the world's leading producer of automobiles. Buick built 8820 cars that year, more than the next two largest producers—Ford (6181) and Cadillac (2380)—combined, according to the most commonly cited figures. Although some sources quote a 10,202 production for Ford in 1908, this figure is probably for the fiscal or model year, rather than the calendar year. Ford did not introduce the famous Model T until very late in 1908, and Buick had been stockpiling its Model 10 and other cars since late 1907. Buick's claim of being the number one automobile builder and seller for calendar year 1908 is probably accurate.

As plant production increased rapidly, thousands of workers poured into Flint. The number of factory wage earners rose from 4500 in 1908 to 10,200 in 1909 to 15,000 in 1910. The pretty little Nineteenth Century city was suddenly a boom town. Workers camped in tents along the Flint River, up to a thousand of them and their families at a time. People lived in tarpaper shacks, chicken coops, even piano crates. Beds were rented to day workers for the night, and night workers for the day—the same beds. Home owners converted attics and basements into apartments and quickly filled them. In 1910 seven square miles were added to the city. Four schools were built. The small downtown section of Flint was jammed, sidewalks and saloons, on Buick pay nights.

In 1909 a newspaper reporter from Detroit came to Flint, looked around in amazement and filed this report: "One must see for himself; one must get into the atmosphere of the tremendous undertakings; one must himself walk over the literal miles of factories in process of construction before one begins to grasp the immensity of the manufacturing undertaking that has made Flint, next to Detroit, the automobile center of the world. . . . Whence has Durant this ability to use his boyhood village as a commercial center for the country? Oh, ask something easy. Who knows anything about the springs of genius?"

Buick as an economic force almost overshadowed Buick as a product. In 1908, the Model 10 was the big product news, of course, but the old reliable, the Model F, was holding its own, with 3281 produced. That car and its companion Model G, of which 219 were built, remained much the same, though they were spruced up with a new hood, fender and cowl design. Rear springs were now full elliptic, brakes were improved by increasing drum size to fourteen inches and providing a lining of "camel's hair felt, which can be renewed at a very slight expense when necessary"—and the wheelbase was extended to ninety-two inches. "The change in the location of the spark and carburetor control levers to the top of the steering wheel and on an immovable sector will be found a great convenience," Buick said. *Motor Age* was less delicate and noted that the relocation eliminated "molesting the tilting feature of the column."

Models K and H were dropped, but the latter was replaced by another top-of-the-line touring car, the Model 5. It featured a new Buick four, with opposed valves, cylinders cast in pairs and quite large water jackets. The crankcase was aluminum, the crankshaft

nickel steel. With 4⅝ by 5-inch bore/stroke dimensions, the Model 5's displacement was 336 cubic inches; developed horsepower was cited as 34.2. Suspension was semi-elliptic all around, the clutch a leather faced cone, transmission the three-speed sliding gear, the wheelbase 108 inches. The price of the Model 5 was listed as $2500. Buick built 402 of them. The Model S was continued, but dropped a whopping $750 in price (to $1750), and the Model D, at the same price, was $100 less expensive than the year previous. Buick produced 373 of the former, 543 of the latter.

All of the activity of 1908 was the last straw for David Dunbar Buick. "There wasn't an executive in the place that ever knew what time it was," he complained. "We worked until we had the day's job done and were ready for tomorrow and then we went home—and not until then." Obviously, Buick did not find any of this appealing.

The Buick family's status in the company continued to slide. David had relinquished the manager's title to Durant February 13, 1906. Thomas had quit in a personality clash with Durant, according to his son (and David Buick's grandson), David Dunbar Buick II, who was the last living member with the Buick name. "Grandpa was quiet, a dreamer," David Buick II told the writer. "My father was aggressive, very domineering. But their relationship was closer than father and son." (David Buick II died in April 1988.)

Family money troubles were evident in a long unpaid bill for $92.58 from John Carton to David Buick for legal services tied to an auto accident involving a Buick daughter. Durant wrote Carton March 14th, 1906: "Mr. Buick wishes me to say that until a few moments ago this was more money than he had in the world. He dislikes very much to make this admission . . ." A check was enclosed. At that time, Buick may have gained control of some of his stock. He may have invested some in his son's brass foundry. Thomas was now supplying Buick with most of its brass.

At one point during 1908, David Buick's number of shares of Buick stock had increased to three hundred. By the end of that year, however, he had severed his ties with the Buick Motor Company. The most often repeated account is that Buick had sold his stock to Durant for $100,000, though there is some indication he held some Buick shares for awhile, eventually being forced to sell them as his later business enterprises fell through. However, David II says his father contended at the time of David Buick's death in 1929 that stock that should have been given to David, and never was, would have then been worth $115 million—and that David did not receive a $10,000 annual salary that had been promised in a verbal agreement. David II says he has no supporting evidence, only family stories. "My father was very bitter about this, but Grandpa never seemed to be," he said.

Opposite: Arthur C. Mason at the wheel of a Model 10 on a Western tour in 1908. Above: In 1910 Bob Burman posed in a mock race against an airplane at Daytona Beach.

In 1980, when this manuscript was being written, there was at least one man still living who had worked at Buick when David Buick was still with the company. Fred G. Hoelzle, aged ninety-two, of Flint, roomed with the family of Eugene Richard from 1905, when Richard returned to Buick, to 1907. Of David Buick, Hoelzle remembers: "He never seemed to fit himself in with others. Nobody seemed to take to him. I think he was most interested in finances. He was quiet and we didn't see him very often. Finally, he just kind of faded away. Nobody seemed to notice."

David's first wife Caroline died about 1912, and he lived for several years with Thomas' family before he and his second wife, Margaret, were married. Tom lost his brass foundry when Buick could not pay its bills (apparently in the crisis of 1910), according to David II. He lost his fancy $75,000 house (to which he had made $100,000 in improvements) in Grosse Ile after living there only three years. Tom's first wife, Georgiana Stephens, daughter of a Manistee music teacher, whom he had met in Flint when she lived with an uncle, died of cancer. "We never seemed to have any money after Grosse Ile, and we must have been tossed out of apartments thirteen times for non-payment of rent," David II recalls. "It drove my mother to the hospital with migraines."

David Buick's later investments—a questionable oil venture in California, risky land deals during a Florida boom—always went sour. At one time he and Tom tried manufacturing their patented carburetors. In 1921 he surfaced as president of Lorraine Motors in Grand Rapids; in 1923 he was in Walden, New York with a car called the Dunbar which never went beyond a single prototype. By 1928, when Bruce Catton found him at the Detroit School of Trades, David Buick was broke. As he grew more feeble, he was placed at the school's information desk, "a thin, bent little man, peering through heavy glasses," a newspaper reported.

According to David II, embarrassment to GM by the disclosure of David's plight caused him to lose this job, though again this may only be a family story. One night in 1929, he was planning to join a family gathering at son Winton's place, but Margaret called, saying he was ill. Tom rushed to his apartment and took him to Harper Hospital in Detroit. An operation for a bowel obstruction revealed cancer. A few days later he contracted pneumonia (David II says a nurse left a window open); he died, at age seventy-four, on March 5th, 1929. Surviving besides his wife and sons Thomas and Winton (twenty years younger) were daughters Mrs. James (Mabel) Coyle and Mrs. F.O. (Francis) Patterson, and a half-sister. He was buried in Woodmere Cemetery in Detroit.

Thomas was a Fuller Brush salesman when he died in 1942. The man who had given Hugh Dolnar his first Buick ride never drove a car in the memory of his son. David II, who owned several Buicks, worked twenty-five years as a clerk at Chrysler.

The year of David Buick's departure from the Buick company found the man who had been its savior in the most productive period of his remarkable life. He was about to give Buick its major role in automotive history. In 1908, Billy Durant, with Buick as his ace, incorporated a company he called General Motors.

Chapter Four

BUICK PLUS DURANT EQUALS GM

If nothing else had happened, William C. Durant's promotion of the Buick Motor Company into a major industry and Henry Ford's introduction of the Model T would have made 1908 a memorable year for the U.S. automobile industry.

But something else did happen. And what was going on in hotel coffee shops and suites, and in private offices in Flint, Detroit and New York, unknown to the public, was to have a profound effect not only within the auto industry, but on world business history.

As Durant recalled several decades later, it began on May 15th, 1908, while Durant was dining with his daughter Margery in Flint. The telephone rang. Benjamin Briscoe was on the line.

Briscoe: "Hello, Billy, I have a most important matter to discuss with you and want you to take the first train to Chicago."

Durant: "What's the big idea, Ben?"

Briscoe: "Don't ask me to explain; it's the biggest thing in the country. There's millions in it. Can you come?"

Durant: "Impossible, too busy, sorry. But I can see you here. Why don't you take the 10 o'clock Grand Trunk arriving at 7 o'clock tomorrow morning. I will meet you at the station and we will have breakfast together."

This was the same Ben Briscoe who had backed David Buick in Detroit and had been instrumental in the sale of Buick to James Whiting and the other Flint Wagon Works directors in 1903. But on this day, according to Durant's autobiographical notes, Briscoe was talking about a deal that would lead, within a few months, to the for-

mation of General Motors.

Before events had run their course, there would be summit meetings, arranged by Briscoe, among the three major figures of Michigan automobile history: Durant, Ford and Ransom Eli Olds, who had preceded them both in early experiments with horseless carriages and in significant production of automobiles. Olds had been building and driving steam-powered vehicles in 1887, when Durant was just getting under way with his horse-drawn road cart. He had been building curved dash Oldsmobiles by the hundreds in 1901. In 1904 he had walked out of the Olds Motor Works in a management dispute and by 1908 was in charge of the Reo Motor Car Company of Lansing, Michigan. The name was derived from his initials.

When Durant's widow, Catherine, made her husband's autobiography, letters and other papers available for the first time in 1972, new information came to light on the events leading to the creation of General Motors. Still, Durant in his notes was sometimes wrong on specific details.

The eminent automotive historian George S. May believes Briscoe's initial contact with Durant was some months earlier than Durant remembered. In his research on Olds, May found notes indicating that early discussions may have begun late in 1907 and that specific consolidation talks took place on January 17th, 1908 in Detroit, on January 24th-25th in New York, on May 11th in New York, and in New York again at the end of May.

But whatever the date, it is apparent that the first meeting took place in Flint. The morning after the phone conversation, Briscoe arrived on the train from Chicago. He was met by Durant and they had breakfast at the Dresden Hotel downtown. Then they adjourned to Durant's office at Buick. Briscoe's big news was that George W. Perkins, a partner in J. P. Morgan and Company and a financial backer of Maxwell-Briscoe, was exploring the possibility of a large merger of automobile companies.

Briscoe's ideas were grandiose. His first thought was to call a meeting of about twenty leading companies, but Durant immediately saw that this would be chaotic. He suggested that Briscoe consider a merger of a few companies in the medium-priced field, naming Ford, Buick, Reo and Maxwell-Briscoe.

"I suggested he first see Henry Ford, who was in the limelight, liked publicity and unless he could lead the procession would not play," Durant wrote. Briscoe set out to see what he could do.

In Lansing, he found Olds receptive. In Detroit, Ford said he was willing to discuss it. A few weeks later, Briscoe got them together in the old Penobscot Building in Detroit. Durant related: "In the public reception room were gathered the principals, their close associates

and advisers. The room was small, no place to discuss business. I sensed, unless we ran to cover, plenty of undesirable publicity in the offing. As I had commodious quarters in the [old] Pontchartrain Hotel, and as the luncheon hour was approaching, I suggested that we separate and meet in my room as soon as convenient. I had the unexpected pleasure of entertaining the entire party until mid-afternoon."

So the four leading personalities in the business were closeted together in a hotel suite, discussing such delicate matters as the relative values of their four companies. When Briscoe got to the point, and urged that the four put together some plan to present to Perkins, there were a few moments of embarrassed silence. Finally, Durant plunged in: "If we put a value of $10 million on Ford, would Ford consider $6 million a reasonable figure for Reo?"

Ford said he didn't have the slightest idea of the value of Reo. Durant pushed on. If Ford were worth $10 million, and Reo $6 million, would a value of $5 million for Maxwell-Briscoe seem reasonable? The question seemed to irritate Briscoe. What about Buick, he asked? Durant was as noncommital as the others. He replied that the report of the appraisers and auditors and the "conditions and terms of the agreement" would be his answer.

But at least Durant had gotten the four to talk about important issues. There were questions among them about how a consolidated company would be managed, about who would be in control. It was Briscoe's idea that a central committee should rule on all operating policies. He suggested that the purchasing, engineering, advertising and sales departments of the companies be combined.

Durant said he thought that too complicated. All he wanted, he said, was a holding company. What he did not want was any interference in the internal operations of the companies.

"Ho, ho," said Briscoe. "Durant is for states' rights. I am for a union."

About the only decision to come out of the meeting was to get together again, when Briscoe could arrange a date with the Morgan interests. This meeting, apparently the one dated by Olds as January 24th-25th, 1908, took place in New York, in the law offices of Ward, Hayden and Satterlee. Herbert L. Satterlee was a son-in-law of J. Pierpont Morgan and Briscoe felt obligated to use him as the attorney through which discussions would continue. Ford had suggested another attorney, Job Hedges, and Briscoe later wrote that the plan may have held Ford's interest had Hedges been used.

During the two days of conferences, questions were raised about which firms had what percentages of the market, about the advantages of consolidations, about any objections there might be to a consolidation. Durant reported that Ford had one major objection: that the tendency of consolidations was to increase prices. He "was in favor of keeping prices down to the lowest possible point, giving to the multitude the benefit of cheap transportation."

By preserving that message, Durant was paying high tribute to Henry Ford, whom he came to admire greatly in the years to follow. In a speech once Durant said that Ford had "done more for America than any other man—more for the world."

In one of several meetings with Satterlee, Ford finally came to the point, as far as he was concerned. He wasn't interested in getting stock in any consolidation—what he wanted was cash. Some accounts note that Ford mentioned a figure of $3 million for his company for starters, but Durant said this was not true. Ford wanted cash, but he wouldn't say how much. Olds is also supposed to have said he wanted money too. The two men had met in advance and concluded they would rather sell out and retire than become involved in some complicated stock deal.

This attitude surprised Satterlee. No one had said anything to him about the manufacturers wanting money to unload their companies.

Page preceding: Billy Durant, romantic adventurer, determined entrepreneur.

The idea was for them to pool their stock. Satterlee took Durant into an adjoining room. What was going on here? Durant said it was all news to him and suggested that he talk to Briscoe.

Wrote Durant: "Briscoe, when questioned, said that Mr. Ford had correctly stated the case, but that he had shown such an interest as the matter progressed that Briscoe, whether rightly or wrongly, inferred that Mr. Ford had changed his mind and would go along with the others. Mr. Satterlee was quite put out and after giving the matter a few moments' thought, went back into the other room and very diplomatically stated that there had been a misunderstanding, but that the matter of finance was entirely up to the bankers, and when they had perfected their plans, another meeting would be called."

This, apparently, was the end of the involvement of Ford and Olds in the consolidation talks, although Durant's notes indicate they may have been in a few more discussions. In effect, the proposal was now primarily a matter among only Buick, Maxwell-Briscoe and some Morgan partners.

For a few weeks, a consolidation appeared to be at hand. The original name was to be United Motors. On July 1st, 1908, Ward, Hayden and Satterlee notified Buick's attorney, John J. Carton, that "the certificate for incorporation of United Motors Co." had been filed and that unless something unforeseen were to arise, its stock would be ready for issue within a few days.

Obviously something did arise, for two days later Durant, though still optimistic, wrote to Carton: "Had a long hot session with our friends in New York yesterday and was pretty nearly used up at the finish. If you think it is an easy matter to get money from New York capitalists to finance a motor car proposition in Michigan, you have another guess coming. Notwithstanding the fact that quoted rates are very low, money is hard to get owing to a somewhat unaccountable feeling of uneasiness and a general distrust of the automobile proposition."

In the midst of continuing talks, Perkins suggested that the consolidation's name be changed from United Motors to the International Motor Car Company. Durant had no problem with that. And Perkins, in a conversation with Durant on a train, appeared to

From the left: Billy Durant in a sidewalk conference with J. Dallas Dort in 1908 during GM organization; Albert Champion; Alanson Brush with his Brush Runabout.

A 1909 Model 10 Tourabout. Below: E.L. Sapp in 1923 driving his 1908 Model 10, showing 100,000 miles, at Flint en route to California. At left of Sapp is Arthur Case, said to be its designer. Opposite page: 1909 Model 17 and 1910 Model F.

buy Durant's holding company idea. Still, the Morgan partners hesitated. In late July, Durant was asked to meet with Francis Lynde Stetson, J.P. Morgan's most trusted attorney. It was a disastrous meeting. Durant and John Carton had prepared for the consolidation by drawing up an agreement, to be signed by Buick stockholders, authorizing Durant to act for them in any exchange of stock between Buick and the planned new company. The exchange was to be on the same terms for them as it would be for Durant. Every share of Buick stock, according to Durant, was endorsed under this agreement.

Stetson didn't like the arrangement and suggested that the Buick stockholders execute a new set of papers. He said he needed better title. Durant replied that "the stockholders had confidence in me and that the matter was entirely in my hands." He felt that Stetson's position was arrogant and suggestive of something improper by Durant. "Up to that time, I was what you might say 'quite warm' for the merger, but after my interview with Mr. Stetson, I am frank to say I cooled off 'slightly.' "

On July 29th, Carton wrote Stetson that Durant's arrangement regarding Buick stock was, it seemed to him, "a perfectly plain transaction" and declined to change it.

As the kings of Wall Street finance, the Morgans were not accustomed to their directives being treated in such a cavalier fashion, especially by some upstart industrialist from the Midwest. In addition to this, the Morgans were incensed to read an article in *The New*

York Times on July 31st, 1908 that said "the first big combination in the automobile world is now in the making" and reporting, accurately, some of the details, including the fact that several members of the Morgan company were among the underwriters. Although no source was cited for the information, the Morgans reputedly felt it was leaked by Durant. (This was unlikely, since Durant had continually refused to discuss rumors of a consolidation with the press.)

Briscoe, arriving in New York after a trip, had the misfortune in timing to visit the Morgan people just after the article appeared. He was stunned by their anger. On August 4th he wrote Durant saying he was surprised to find the situation with the Morgans "in somewhat of a chaotic state" and couldn't understand why they were upset. "It has always appeared to me," he observed, "that one of the surest ways to get publicity is to deny things, or to refuse to confirm or deny them, and this has been too much our attitude in regard to the publication of this matter."

Briscoe also sympathized with Durant in his disagreement with Stetson on the stock issue and suggested "it would be possible for you and myself, and perhaps one or two others that we could attach to us, to take hold of this matter and work it out without waiting on anybody. We have both concluded that a million dollars in cash would be enough to finance the proposition and I will eat my shoes if we can't raise a million dollars between us."

Briscoe soon learned, however, that when the Morgans invested heavily in a company, they also exerted control. And once they had concluded they could not work with Durant, they were opposed to letting Briscoe make his own deal with the Buick leader. What the Morgans did not count on was that Durant didn't need them and that he could produce a consolidation without Maxwell-Briscoe, Reo or Ford. During the summer of 1908, while he was heavily embroiled with Briscoe and the others, he had found time to make a midnight trip to Lansing and talk to the owners of Ransom Olds' original creation, the Olds Motor Works. The Olds firm had gone downhill after its founder's departure, but at least it was a company which seemed willing to do business with Durant. At the end of August 1908, when it became obvious that Durant and the Morgans would not get together, Herbert Satterlee asked Durant what he would do.

In Durant's words: "I told him that I had come to New York several months earlier, and had been led to believe that the consolidation sponsored by the Morgan firm was being seriously considered and had so informed my people; that the Buick stock had been deposited and if released could never again be collected in the same form—nor would I have the courage, or care, to make another attempt. I must have a consolidation.

"Mr. Satterlee said, 'Mr. Durant, you only have the Buick, how can you have a consolidation?' I replied that I would have no difficulty in securing another company, as a matter of fact I had one in mind at the moment—the Olds Motor Works of Lansing, Michigan.

Hot-rodding the Buick, officially and unofficially. Above: A backyard sporting conversion on a 1909 Model 16 chassis in New Jersey. Below: A 1909 Buick translated into a Marquette-Buick. Page opposite: Trying out a 1909 Model 10 runabout on the Buick test track (above); Louis Chevrolet road testing a Model 16 chassis during 1909 (below).

The company—one of the oldest in the business—was controlled by Mr. S.L. Smith of Detroit, and was being operated by his sons, Fred and Angus Smith, whom I knew intimately. While the company was not a success, I believed it had possibilities. Mr. Henry Russel, vice-president of the Michigan Central Railroad, a great friend of Mr. Smith, was president of the Olds Motor Works. I was acquainted with Mr. Russel and said I would wire him immediately asking if he would meet me in Lansing the following Saturday, mentioning the fact that I would like to discuss a possible merger of Olds and Buick, which I did.

"Satterlee asked about the capitalization and how the common stock was to be issued. I told him I had in the Buick organization a competent engineer, by the name of Walter Marr, with whom I had worked closely for several years; that the engineering success of the Buick was due largely to his efforts; that he was a crank on carburetors and had taken numerous patents; that he was very fond of me, had named his only son after me, and I was quite sure he would set aside for my use a sufficient number of patents and applications against which the common stock could be issued."

Durant learned that Perkins wanted to reserve the name of International Motor Car Company for his own use. Therefore, he looked over a list of names that had been previously prepared when the group had been considering a combination "and when we came to General Motors I selected that name and as of that moment the General Motors Company came into being."

Not quite. Durant first went to Lansing and found that the Smiths and Russel would agree to the merger. Then he discussed with Satterlee the filing of incorporation papers. On September 10th, 1908, Durant received a letter from Ward, Hayden and Satterlee stating that "we find it impractical to use the 'International Motor Company' . . . we might use the 'United Motors Company' were it not for the fact that there is already a 'United Motors Car Company' in that state [New Jersey]. We suggest the name, 'General Motors Company,' which we have ascertained can be used . . . "

Curtis R. Hatheway, a young attorney with the law firm, filed articles of incorporation for the General Motors Company of New Jersey with the New Jersey secretary of state's office on September 16th, 1908. Unlike Michigan, New Jersey placed almost no restrictions on the activities of a firm incorporated in that state. Now General Motors was born.

The company's capital stock was listed as only $2000 and the names of the incorporators, chosen by Durant, were generally unknown so as not to attract attention. These incorporators—George E. Daniels, Benjamin Marcuse and Arthur W. Britton—met on September 22nd and elected themselves interim directors, with Daniels as president. Durant, working behind the scenes, gave the firm a rather healthy increase in capitalization on September 28th—from $2000 to $12.5 million in twelve days.

On that date, in a sham of a meeting, Daniels announced that a man named W.C. Durant "is present and is prepared to make a business proposition to the company." Durant, the minutes show, said he was advised that General Motors had been incorporated and that, among other things, was planning to build automobiles. Since that was the case, he thought the company might be interested in buying the Buick Motor Company.

It was not surprising that the company was. General Motors was so interested, in fact, that it bought Buick for about $3.75 million, that figure, except for $1500, being provided in an exchange of stock on September 29th, 1908.* The price was remarkably low, but since Durant was selling it to himself, it didn't matter much.

Ten days later, General Motors had new officers. William M. Eaton, onetime manager of the gas light company in Jackson, Michigan and in 1908 an officer with a Wall Street investment firm, was named president. Durant had probably known him from the 1880's, when Durant was an officer in the Flint Gas Light Company. (One list prepared by a GM official notes that Eaton had actually succeeded Begole as Buick president on November 3rd, 1905, but if this is true, it has been entirely forgotten by historians, and by Buick.) The other new GM officers were Durant, vice-president, and Hatheway, secretary. The company immediately bought the W.F. Stewart body plant next to Buick in Flint for $240,000 and leased it to Buick.

Then, on November 12th, General Motors purchased all of the common stock of the Olds Motor Works for a little more than $3 million, all of it (except $17,279 cash) in an exchange of stock. On that day, Olds leaders Fred Smith and Henry Russel were named to the GM board, replacing Daniels and Marcuse. Britton, the third member of the original GM directors, had been dropped October 20th.

There's a famous story about how Durant helped Oldsmobile become immediately solvent by permitting that company to sell a slightly larger version of the Model 10, the hottest-selling Buick of the moment.

This is how Durant describes it: "I sent to the Oldsmobile factory by truck one of these [Model 10] bodies in the white, following with my engineer and production manager. Arriving at the plant, I had the

---

*Officially, General Motors bought from Durant 18,870 shares of Buick common stock and 1130 of Buick preferred at $150 a share, payable two-thirds in GM preferred and one-third common.

Buicks from 1910. The Model 41 limousine and "White Streak" Model 10 behind; Model 19 and 10 touring cars in center; Model 17 touring and 16-17 chassis at right.

body placed on two ordinary saw horses and asked the plant manager if there was a cross-cut saw. When it was produced, I asked to have the body cut lengthwise from front to rear and crosswise in the center from side to side (bodies at that time were made of wood), giving me an opportunity to widen and lengthen the body, changing the size and appearance completely. When finished it was a handsome creation, painted and trimmed to meet the Oldsmobile standard and priced to the trade at $1200 [$200 more than the Model 10]. This gave to Oldsmobile dealers a very handsome small car without interfering in any way with the Buick Model 10. A happy solution to the problem—placing the Oldsmobile Division of General Motors immediately on a profitable basis."

While Durant was in the process of creating General Motors, he was still hard at work developing Buick's sales organization. According to a previously unpublished fragment of his autobiographical notes, his original hometown of Boston was the center of his sales activities. He wrote: "The great Buick Motor sales organization was created in Boston, and it is, in every sense of the word, a great sales organization pioneered by a great salesman. Modesty prevents mentioning the name.

"It required the best part of two years to lay the foundation and to establish branches and distributors in twenty-seven principal cities in the United States including Boston, New York, Philadelphia, Pittsburgh, Cleveland, Cincinnati, Chicago, Kansas City, Omaha, Minneapolis, St. Louis, Atlanta, Denver, Salt Lake, Portland, San Francisco, Los Angeles, and Dallas, each one of which I personally visited with my field force. To assist me in this task, I delegated Bill Meade as my chief of staff and C.L. Peden as my architect and contractor."*

One day, apparently in 1908, Durant was in the Buick salesroom in Boston, getting it in order, when, he wrote, "a gentleman appeared on the scene with a very neat gadget that had much merit. The gadget was well designed and showed good taste. I thought that anyone who could produce that kind of device might do other worthwhile things as well."

Durant never explained what the device was, but he identified the man as Albert Champion, whose name was already on the Champion spark plug and whose initials would eventually form the name of AC Spark Plug Division of General Motors.

Champion, who had a thick French accent, told Durant that he made magnetoes and spark plugs in his shop. Durant replied that Buick did not use magnetoes but was having difficulty finding a spark

The Model 19 of 1910, on display at the New York Automobile Show.

plug suited to the needs of its high performance engine: "[I told him we] had been able to find only one plug in the country that answered our purpose—the Rajah, made in Bloomfield, New Jersey, for which we were paying 35 cents each. If he were quite sure he could make a plug that would answer our purpose, I suggested that we go to Flint, and if he liked the place and the layout, I would start an experimental plant, and if he could make good, I would give him an interest in the business. He had never been to Flint, and knew nothing of the Buick or the plans I had for the future."

Durant offered Champion $2000 for his small business. Champion was willing to accept, but a few days later mentioned that his backers, a family named Stranahan, would not sell the Champion company name. Answered Durant: "I'm not interested in the name. I'm interested in spark plugs." To which Champion replied: "I am very much interested in the name—that's my name."

Although Durant did not succeed in getting clear title to the name

*The story of the Durant distribution system for Buick and how it evolved through subsequent decades is told in the Appendices.

Above, right and left: The Model 19 of 1910. Below left: The 1910 Model 7, one of eighty-five built. Below right: The 1910 Model 16 with "tourabout" style seating.

Champion, he did lure Albert Champion to Flint. According to his notes, he paid the Stranahans $2000 for the right to take the man, if not the name, and also entered into an arrangement with them to open a Buick dealership in Boston. Durant wrote: "Very promptly, thereafter, the firm of Stranahan & Eldridge was organized. A retail store on Commonwealth Avenue was opened and I think most of the $2000 paid to Mr. Stranahan came back.

"As soon as I could arrange it, I took Albert Champion to Flint, found a small building near my office, and put him to work. While I was busy with the Buick sales organization—traveling all over the

72

Above left: 1910 Model 41 limousine. Above right: 1910 Model 17 touring car. Below left: Model 14 prototype, 1910. Below right: 1910 Model 16 toy tonneau.

country—Champion was busy with his spark plug experimental work. It was some time before Champion could produce a plug equal to the Rajah, but he finally succeeded in submitting to our engineers a spark plug of real merit, and after passing the severest test, was accepted and made a part of the Buick equipment. The price paid the

Champion Department was 25 cents, a saving of 10 cents each. It was not long before the Buick was using 1000 spark plugs a day, a saving on this item alone of $100 a day.

"I sent for Champion ... congratulated him on his splendid success and reminded him that we had never discussed what his in-

The "surrey" body style of the Model 10 from 1910.

terest was to be if he made good, that up to that time he had only received living expenses, that I intended to organize [a spark plug] division of General Motors with paid up capital of $100,000, and that he was to have a quarter interest of $25,000, and asked him how he would like to have the stock issued. He said that a man by the name of [Albert] Schmidt had come with him from Boston, had been very helpful and he would like him to have $7500, the balance of $17,500 to himself."

The $7500 made Schmidt wealthy within a decade.

Champion, born in Paris April 2nd, 1878, had been a world bicycle racing champion who had turned to automobile racing, almost losing a leg in an accident, before meeting Durant. In Flint, his firm—which for a time worked out of a corner of the Buick complex—was at first known as Champion Ignition Company, organized October 26th, 1908, a little more than a month after General Motors was incorporated. A few years later, to avoid a possible lawsuit with the Champion Spark Plug Company over use of the name, Champion Ignition became AC Spark Plug—a name that became famous because of Durant and Buick.

Of all the colorful characters who prospered through their association with Durant and Buick, Albert Champion was probably the most flamboyant. He had a monumental temper, which showed itself almost daily as he walked through his factory, firing employees for any reason—then complaining when the victims were not at work the next day. After awhile, an associate followed Champion around,

rehiring employees as fast as the boss fired them.

Champion also had a reputation as "a lady's man," which is confirmed by Irene Champion, the widow of his brother, Prosper Champion. Mrs. Champion still lives in Flint.*

Durant's new General Motors Company had managed to incorporate and take control of Buick and Oldsmobile stock almost without public notice. Although rumor articles had appeared in various newspapers since May of 1908, solid reports that General Motors had been formed did not reach the newspapers until the end of December. And as late as December 28th, when *The Flint Journal* asked Durant about consolidation reports, he replied that "there was nothing in regard to the matter which he could give out for publication."

But by the start of 1909, Durant was ready to move in a big way. His vision told him there was a vast market for automobiles, and that the only way he could be sure of filling that market would be to have a wide variety of models. The best way to get them was to buy a lot of companies, he figured, and the best way to buy them would be to exchange their stock for stock in General Motors.

He wrote: "I figured if I could acquire a few more companies like the Buick, I would have control of the greatest industry in this country. A great opportunity, no time to lose, I must get busy. I felt confident, because of the hazardous nature of the automobile business, that if money in sufficient quantity could be obtained, a reasonable number of good companies could be induced to sell out or become members of a central organization that would provide engineering and patent protection and minimize the hazards which were constantly developing."

In an incredible burst of energy, Durant in eighteen months

---

*Albert Champion died on October 28th, 1927, a few moments after he collapsed into the arms of a friend in the banquet room of a hotel in Paris, France. He and his second wife Edna, an attractive former chorus girl, had traveled there for the automobile show.

His brother, Prosper, claimed in lawsuits that Albert's death came an hour after a former prizefighter had struck him. Albert had caught the man with Champion's wife, according to Prosper's widow. "They had a fight and he hit Albert and Albert collapsed on the floor in front of the fireplace," she told a *Flint Journal* reporter.

Some years later the ex-prizefighter, attempting to claim part of the Champion fortune, said in court testimony that after Albert Champion's death, he entered into a common-law relationship with Edna Champion. Edna's relatives claimed, however, that he beat her and she hired guards to keep him away. According to one report, as Edna Champion lay dying, the ex-prizefighter "flourishing a gun, broke through a glass-paned door, shouting hysterically that his love was being kept prisoner. The guards beat him off and hurled him into the street." Six months later, the ex-prizefighter was himself dead, his death attributed in part to the beating he had taken that night.

negotiated the purchase of, or a substantial interest in, the following firms and plants for General Motors.

Buick Motor Company, Flint
W.F. Stewart Company's Plant 4, Flint
Olds Motor Works, Lansing
Seagar Engine Works, Lansing
Oakland Motor Car Company, Pontiac
Marquette Motor Company, Saginaw
Cadillac Motor Company, Detroit
Michigan Motor Castings Company, Flint
Randolph Truck Company, Flint
Champion Ignition Company (AC), Flint
Reliance Motor Truck Company, Owosso
Rainier Motor Company, Saginaw
Welch Motor Car Company, Pontiac
Welch-Detroit Company, Detroit
Jackson-Church-Wilcox Company, Jackson
Michigan Auto Parts Company, Detroit
Rapid Motor Vehicle Company, Pontiac
Cartercar Company, Pontiac
Ewing Automobile Company, Geneva (Ohio)
Elmore Manufacturing Company, Clyde (Ohio)
Dow Rim Company, New York City
Northway Motor & Manufacturing Company, Detroit
Bedford Motors Company, London (Ontario)
National Motor Cab Company
Novelty Incandescent Lamp Company
Heany Lamp Companies (Heany Company, Heany Lamp Company, Heany Electric Company, Tipless Lamp Company)
Brown-Lipe-Chapin Company, Syracuse (New York)
Oak Park Power Company, Flint

Some of these companies were not worth much. And Durant had blundered badly in purchasing the Heany companies, because he was buying into a lawsuit. John Albert Heany's cloudy patent rights to electric lightbulbs were voided and the eventual loss to General Motors was estimated at more than $12 million. (Some historians believe Durant saw the Heany problems and bought the companies anyway as part of an elaborate stock-watering deal.)

But in putting under one umbrella Buick, Oldsmobile, Cadillac, Oakland (forerunner of Pontiac), AC Spark Plug, and several truck companies which would later become GMC Truck & Coach Division, Durant had formed the nucleus of today's General Motors Corporation. And he would provide the one major missing element, Chevrolet, a few years later.

The "toy tonneau" body style of the Model 10 of 1910.

None of his moves in 1908 and 1909 would have been possible had Durant not taken the forlorn Buick Motor Company of 1904 and turned it into a giant.

Durant didn't get all of the companies he went after. He made a pass at the E.R. Thomas Company of Buffalo, New York, which had earned a permanent place in automotive history in 1908 when one of its Thomas Flyers won "The Great Race" from New York to Paris. Perhaps if he had been successful in buying it, the Thomas would have survived to this day.

Another company, however, undoubtedly did better because Durant was unsuccessful in his efforts: the Ford Motor Company.

In 1908, during the consolidation talks, Ford had indicated he wanted to sell. Whether indeed he did at that time—or if Olds did either—remains open to speculation. Their participation might have been more in the nature of a fact-finding mission to learn firsthand what was going on. Obviously, the Briscoe-Durant plan, if effected, promised to have major repercussions in the industry in which both were prominent figures.

In 1909, however, Ford was dealt a blow when he lost a round in his long—and eventually successful—court fight against paying royalties to the ALAM, administrators of the Selden patent. On September 15th, a New York District Court judge ruled that Ford had infringed the patent. The date is interesting because confidential General Motors board minutes show that on October 26th, 1909—less than six weeks later—GM's board gave Durant authority to

On a ranch in Kansas, the surrey or tourabout version of the 1910 Model 10.

purchase Ford if financing could be arranged.

According to Durant, Ford's position that he would be willing to sell out had been "generally understood" from the time the Briscoe-led consolidation talks had failed in the summer of 1908. But Durant was so tied up with his initial effort to gather companies together under GM, and in the expansion of Buick, that it was not until well into 1909 that he began to seriously pursue the Ford Motor Company.

Durant and James C. Couzens, Ford's business manager, spent one Sunday looking over the Ford plant, then Durant told Couzens he would like to buy. If Ford were agreeable to a discussion, Couzens was invited to have him meet with Durant in New York prepared to close the deal.

Couzens and Ford went to New York but Ford became ill, so Couzens went alone to see Durant. According to Durant, Couzens made the following statement: "Mr. Ford is very much concerned about the Selden patent suit and its outcome . . . . Mr. Ford will sell the Ford Motor Company for $8 million, giving me [Couzens] the privilege of purchasing twenty-five percent of the company's stock as part compensation for my many years of service . . . the balance of the purchase price, $6 million, to be paid as follows: $2 million at time of sale, the remaining $4 million at five percent interest due on or before three years."

Durant was agreeable and the next day met with officials of the National City Bank of New York to ask for a loan of $2 million. He said the bankers were encouraging but told him the loan would have to be authorized by the bank's board and loan committee.

On October 26th, 1909, the GM board gave Durant authority to buy Ford if financing could be arranged. However, a few days later, Durant was reached by an officer of the bank at his Buick office at Flint. The message was that the bank had been criticized recently for a large loan to a copper company and the committee was afraid to invest heavily in an automobile company. In general, banks at this time still regarded the auto industry as a speculative and shaky investment.

"I made no further attempt to secure the $2 million and notified Mr. Ford that the purchase could not be financed at the present time," Durant wrote.

Only two years later, Durant noted, Couzens told him that Ford's earnings were up to $35 million a year. Durant said his banker friends never forgave themselves for turning down the loan request but that he himself had few regrets.

"I never would have built up that business the way Ford did," he wrote.*

While Durant bounced around the country, trading stock and making multi-million-dollar deals, the Buick factories in Flint were producing at an ever-increasing rate. From 8820 cars in 1908, production increased to 14,606 in 1909—though Ford with the Model T moved back into first place in the industry.

Again, the Model 10 was the big seller, with 8100 built. There was little need to change a winner—and so it remained pretty much the same, with four inches added to its wheelbase (for 92 inches) and a toy tonneau (with a single-unit body and real doors) added to its available body styles.

The rarest 1909 Buick was the Model 6A, of which only six were built. Although it used the same 336 engine as the Model 5 (which was dropped for 1909), it was a far different car—a sporty roadster

---

*The real seriousness of Henry Ford in this entire episode is open to some interpretation. Conceivably Ford was so discouraged by the initial court defeat in the Selden patent case as to briefly consider selling out to General Motors. Henry Ford could be as impulsive as he was stubborn. The success of the Model T, and his almost religious belief in what the car represented and what it would mean to the "common man," tend to make incredible his giving deep consideration to giving it all up. His paternal interest in his company was of epic proportion. Earlier he had expressed fears that his factory manager, Walter E. Flanders, a formidable personality, might overwhelm him in the operation of his own firm. Walter Flanders hadn't remained with Ford long. Whether Ford was playing in his gestures to Durant is speculative too. What he was really doing, what he really felt, he took to his grave. Two things are certain, Henry Ford was mercurial. Henry Ford was wily.

Left: Runabout version of the 1910 Model 10; Right: Rare photo of the first GM Building, 127 Woodward, Detroit.

on a 113-inch wheelbase and carrying a claimed horsepower rating of 50, and a $2750 price tag. The other four-cylinder engine was now 318 cubic inches and powered the Model 16 roadster (née the Model S, 497 built) and the Model 17 touring car (née the Model D, 2003 built). The Models 16 and 17 had 112-inch wheelbases. All three (Models 6A, 16 and 17) cars shared the three-speed selective transmission and cone clutch. The planetary transmission favored by the Model 10 was retained as well in the carryover two-cylinder, 159-cubic-inch Models F and G, of which 4000 units were built, including a delivery truck body version. This was the first production Buick truck, it lasted only one season, and no separate production numbers were kept—it was simply a Model F variant.

Buick did not provide motoring journals with much new copy this year; Durant was otherwise occupied and Buicks were being sold as fast as they could be built anyway. One item that did make the publications was a report that Buicks would be built in England. In 1909, Buick began shipping chassis to Bedford Motors, Limited, of London, where British coachwork was added, and the result named Bedford Buick. The firm's name would become General Motors (Europe), Limited in 1912, but until 1914 would handle only Buicks. It would be combined with General Motors Export in 1918.

There was also a published rumor in 1909 that a new model to be designated the 14, to be known as the Buick Buggyabout and to sell for $450 ("more or less"), was on the horizon. It was, but a little further off than suspected, not to be produced until late 1910.

The Buggyabout, according to some students of Buick history, was the idea of Alanson P. Brush, one of the many talented automotive pioneers who worked awhile for the company. Not much has been published about Brush's career at Buick,* but according to his widow's unpublished biography, her husband was brought to Flint from Oakland in Pontiac by Durant to fill in for Walter Marr, who was seriously ill with tuberculosis. "Mr. Durant's methods did not lead to quiet and orderly change," Mrs. Brush wrote. "One week we had been living in Pontiac. The next found us in a Flint hotel, trying to adjust ourselves to a new way of living. Speed was the order of the day. New factory buildings were going up overnight. They seemed to spring up like mushrooms, and in an unbelievable short time, cars were being turned out from them."

The Brushes finally bought an old colonial house on Liberty Street in Flint and Brush found himself immediately busy because of Marr's absence. Durant was available only on "fleeting visits," Mrs. Brush wrote, so her husband dealt primarily with the general manager, "Big

*Master machinist Henry Martyn Leland, the father of the Cadillac, considered Brush the outstanding automotive engine expert in the country in the early years of the Twentieth Century. But in 1905 Brush left his job as Cadillac chief engineer after a dispute with Leland, then developed the small Brush Runabout which was manufactured by Frank Briscoe, and thereafter went on to careers at Oakland, Buick and eventually Marmon.

Bill" Little. Mrs. Brush found Little to be an "odd character," with a puckish sense of humor and a flair for practical jokes, but a man who also had unbounded enthusiasm, ability to work hard and a devoted loyalty to Durant. The Brush family also became close socially to the Charles Stewart Motts.

Often Brush, Mott and Little would gather in the Brush home to discuss proposed changes for the next Buick model. Wrote Mrs. Brush: "My husband had incorporated several new ideas in his Oakland car design, which had so demonstrated their desirability that when he proposed them for the Buick, there was little argument. A case in point was the substitution of alloyed steel in place of the old case-hardened soft steel for their transmission gears. Buick's old

case-hardened gears had been giving them much trouble. This change went through with little opposition .... I cannot vouch for all the changes Al made in the Buick cars, but I listened to much talk of gears, of oiling systems, of four-door cars, of pinion mountings, and other similar expressions." Mrs. Brush did not mention the Buggyabout, nor the exact year Brush arrived at Buick, though it was probably 1909.

The next year, 1910, would be a most unsettling one for Alanson Brush and Buick because of Durant's financial problems, but from a production standpoint it was a most successful one. Buick built 30,-525 cars that year. There has been some debate among historians as to whether production really was that high, but a recently discovered model breakdown produced by Buick's engineering department supports the figure: 11,000 Model 10's, 6002 Model 17's, 4000 Model F's, 4000 Model 19's, 2252 Model 16's, 2048 Model 14's (about which more details will follow), 1098 Model 2 (or 2-A) trucks, 85 Model 7 (or 7-A) seven-passenger touring cars, and 40 Model 41 limousines. The Model 41, Buick's new top-of-the-line prestige car, featured the company's first closed body. The rear compartment shrouded its occupants comfortably and completely, but the driver's area, typically, was protected only by storm curtains. The Model 41 also featured a speaking tube and imported goatskin upholstery.

Buick also made a real venture into the manufacture of commercial vehicles in 1910, its Model 2-A truck being adapted to a variety of styles. In a collection of 1910 truck photos in Buick's engineering department are a "paddy wagon" used by the New York Society for the Prevention of Cruelty to Children; an "Old English Motor Bus" used as a courtesy car by the Plaza Hotel in New York City, and one example of a whole fleet of Buick trucks ordered by *The Saturday Evening Post*. The trucks were even used for racing. Author George H. Dammann notes that, late in 1910, one of them won the commercial class in a Fort Lee, New Jersey hill climb. During this period Buick was formidably aggressive in promotion of its commercial line, writing dozens of letters to its truck customers in solicitation of testimonials. Their responses were routinely used in advertising, and the letters themselves remained in a bound volume in the records of the Engineering Department for decades. The trucks themselves were either photographed by Buick, or their photographs solicited, and published in numerous brochures and catalogues to demonstrate their wide variety of commercial uses.

Perhaps the most unusual Buick vehicle, however, was a conversion of a Model 10—used as an ice sled in Nome, Alaska, as Dammann has noted. Not a snowmobile, it had runners both front and rear, with traction provided by spikes on the standard rear wheels. (A Buick snowmobile had been put together in 1906 by one Virgil D. White, using a Model G as its base.)

Engineering changes to the more usual Buicks were minimal, the most noteworthy the adoption of a vertical tube radiator, practically the entire industry deciding in its favor in 1910. The Model 10 was provided better cooling, too, by the substitution of its gear pump by a centrifugal type. Facilities were now available in Flint for the lapping of pistons before final testing, which produced a better fit and finish of those parts. Driving gears were connected direct to the timing gears instead of the idler. And the magneto was revised to produce a more intense spark at slow engine speeds, so the car could run as slowly on the magneto as on the battery.

In the heat of production, there was still occasionally time for

Buick embarks upon commercial vehicle production. Page opposite: This official factory photograph of a 1910-1911 Model 2-A refers to the body style as a "Furniture Wagon" and indicates its price as $1160. Above: The Model 2-A entered in the Commercial Vehicle Reliability Run sponsored by the Chicago Evening American in 1910. Below: One of a fleet of Buick light trucks, with special covered body, purchased that year for delivery of two of the most popular magazines in America.

whimsy. On March 17th, 1910, R. Samuel McLaughlin in Canada wrote to William H. Little in Flint that one of his "boys" had enjoyed a novel experience that morning while testing a Model 10 chassis supplied to the Canadian auto builder by Buick. When he pushed the reverse pedal, the car shot ahead; when he put on the "slow speed ahead," the car reversed. Wrote McLaughlin: "This would be a dandy type of car for a hilly country where there would be danger of the carburetor running dry. It would beat out the Elmore in that respect. It seems that the boys in the [Weston-Mott] axle plant got the bevel gear on the wrong side."

Little replied six days later, explaining that McLaughlin had inadvertently received the new Model 10 "Female" car. He continued: "This is a new model we are getting out and it was not intended that you should receive one at this time. We call it a 'Female' car because it does just the opposite of what you expect it will (my stenographer glared at me when I said this) .... Upon the same theory you should put the water in the gasoline tank and the gasoline in the radiator. You will also probably find hair-pins scattered all over it every morning, or you probably would if Allen had been driving it the night before ... "

Little, who went on in this vein at some length, sent a copy of the letter to Charles Stewart Mott: "I trust my explanation of the trouble meets with your approval; if not I would be glad to make any changes you may suggest."

Whether Mott added any comment is not recorded, but Mott attached a reminiscence of his own to the letter: "Do you remember back in 1908 and 1909 when Buick was building their first . . . Model 10? It had a tool box on the platform to the rear of the front seat. Then they got the idea of putting a single dickey seat on top of this tool box for an extra charge of $50. Well do I remember the reaction of Dallas Dort who had been building buggies to sell at three for $100. And here was Buick getting the price of one and one-half buggies for one single little seat—some difference in values."

In retrospect the most noteworthy factor about the 1910 Buick line was that it marked the last appearance of the venerable Model F, which traced its lineage all the way back to the Model B of 1904. It had been a good run.

First-hand impressions from the period about the two-cylinder Buicks are almost unanimous in their praise. In fact, the only caviling discovered in published reports appeared in *The Autocar* in response to a query of a reader for information on how the Buick performed. "The worst part about it seems to be the carburetter," J.A. Smith grumbled. "This has an adjustable jet working something after the style of that fitted in the sight feed of a Dubrulle lubricator, screwed up or down from the bottom of the mixing chamber; there is also an adjustable air, and if these two are not set exact it will not pull."

More typical was the report of another owner: "It has given me every satisfaction, and I have never had a mechanical stop of any description. I look after the car entirely myself, and find it a very easy matter to do without the help of a mechanic. It has plenty of speed, and can maintain an average of well over the legal limit, and is capable of doing over forty miles an hour on the flat. I have kept a careful record as regards petrol consumption, and find that I can average twenty-eight miles to the gallon. The car is most simple to drive, the control is easy, and I certainly like the epicyclic gears, as they are very effective and give absolutely no trouble whatever. The engine is so flexible and smooth in running that when travelling on top speed one can hardly hear the car running. As a hill-climber I really think for a light car it is extraordinary, and I have really often myself been astonished at the steep hills this little car has negotiated on top speed. The oiling arrangements are very simple and effective. Every part of the mechanism is very accessible, and any little adjustment that might be required can be done without the least trouble. In conclusion, I would say that I am very pleased indeed with my little Buick, and would not change it for any other car."

And perhaps even more telling was the performance revealed with a satisfied grin by A.G. Southworth, manager of the Buick branch in New York City: "Three Buicks purchased three and a half years ago to carry U.S. mail between Torrance and Roswell, New Mexico, have run 110,000 miles each, covering 110 miles a day on an average of 300 days a year—they are still in active service, with the probability that they will round out five years in Uncle Sam's employment."

Unfortunately, this same probability did not appear to exist for Billy Durant's control over General Motors.

The decision by a bank late in 1909 to reject Durant's request to borrow $2 million to buy Ford may have been an early indication of what was about to happen to Durant's new empire. Also late that year, a speaker at a convention of bankers warned that many auto companies were not properly financed, that money was being spent recklessly, and that if bankers were not careful in their investments, an industrial and financial panic might occur.

Perhaps the speaker was not talking directly about Durant. But he might have been. (Benjamin Briscoe had not yet put together his disastrous United States Motor Company.) Durant had combined thirty-odd companies under General Motors, based largely on Buick's profits and his own confidence. And since he did not believe in having a large central staff, he had no real control over the financial operations of the individual firms. As a holding company, GM held stock but did not itself engage in manufacturing.

Not all financial analysts were disturbed by Durant's methods of operation. One stock market newsletter pointed out in 1909 that General Motors "is well named, for they deal largely in generalities with the public" but added, "That the management of the company is in capable hands is not questioned by anyone. The prominent figure is Mr. W.C. Durant, and while actual information is hard to get, the unbounded confidence in Mr. Durant displayed by those in close touch with him goes far toward maintaining a value for the stock, which would not be possible in many other corporations with the same dearth of definite information. It looks good."

Durant, sensing tight money days ahead as a result of the warning to bankers, began a fight to build confidence in his company that was reminiscent of his head-on battle with the carriage trusts of the 1890's. In March 1910 he sent a letter to stockholders pointing out that "valuable properties have recently been acquired" and that "General Motors securities are valuable to hold as a permanent investment." (At that time, GM had authorized capital of $40 million in common stock, with $15 million outstanding, and $20 million in preferred stock, with $8.5 million outstanding.) That same month he floated a million-dollar stock issue to build a new Buick engine plant in Flint. Buick employees were reported to have subscribed to $122,-000 of it by mid-March, and the rest was said to have been sold in the next three days. Half was raised in Flint and the remainder in Detroit, Cincinnati and New York.

Durant wrote an article in a GM publication emphasizing that "the automobile is here to stay" and reported that the appraised value of Buick alone was $17.4 million. He sent a letter to holders of GM preferred, seeking their help in creating a holding pool to control the stock for fifteen months, explaining that it was selling at too low a price because of actions by brokers acting "for their own personal gain."

Durant even did the forbidden, publishing a list of production figures of all companies in the Association of Licensed Automobile Manufacturers, showing Buick was number one and Cadillac number two. (Ford, it must be remembered, was not an ALAM member.) The ALAM in turn censured Durant, concluding that GM had published the list—its publisher had not been identified—not only because Buick and Cadillac were the leaders, but because "the names of all General Motors concerns were printed . . . in heavy type."

Durant could not have cared less that the other ALAM members considered their production figures confidential. He was trying to build public confidence in General Motors, and he did not like paying royalties to the ALAM any more than Henry Ford did, though unlike Ford he paid them. (For a time, though, Durant didn't pay them either. In 1908 when Carton told him the Selden patent was

The assembly line of the Buick Motor Company, photographed during 1910.

meaningless, he stopped submitting royalties on each car sold. The ALAM sued, and Durant countersued, claiming conspiracy in restraint of trade. But when a court—later overruled—upheld the Selden patent in 1909 in the Ford case, he reportedly gave in and sent an estimated $1 million in back royalties. According to William Greenleaf in *Monopoly on Wheels*, Durant—who had brought Buick into the ALAM by acquiring the Pope-Robinson license in 1904—probably received a portion of the $1 million back for GM in the form of dividends paid by the ALAM.)

Despite Durant's efforts to bolster confidence in GM, despite the fact that GM's sales volume increased from $29 million in 1909 to $49.4 million in 1910, the tight money crunch hit General Motors in the spring of 1910. The daily money flow needed to do business was cut off. There was no cash to buy supplies or pay workers. Quite abruptly, Buick, Cadillac, Oldsmobile and other GM companies had to close shop.

In New York, GM's creditors met, determined that Buick alone owed between $6.7 million and $7.7 million, and named a committee of creditors to try to "effect a reorganization of management and a restriction of enthusiasm."

Durant was beside himself with fury and a sense of helplessness. "By May 1st, our bank loans were all called and we were deprived of every dollar of working capital—the life-blood of our institution—which brought about the complete stoppage of our business with a loss to us of more than $60,000 a day."

Durant hit the road, traveling around the country, looking for operating money. He got a Detroit bank to lend $500,000 to meet a Cadillac payroll. In Boston, Harry K. Noyes, who managed that Buick district, sent cash to Flint in suitcases for fear the banks would

"When the day is done at the Buicks" reads the caption of this 1910 photograph of the Flint complex; the Weston-Mott building is in the foreground at the left.

seize it if sent through regular channels.

Wrote Durant: "I tried the large financial institutions. I tried the life insurance companies. I tried the men who were known to possess large fortunes—but while I was considered an excellent salesman and had a wonderful proposition to offer, my efforts in that direction were to no avail. I admit that it was discouraging but as I never had what might be called 'a soft job' in my life, and my experience had taught me that 'the tougher the job the harder you must work,' I kept right on looking for the money."

Still, Durant could maintain a wry sense of humor. A.B.C. Hardy, the pioneer Flint auto manufacturer who had rejoined Durant at General Motors, traveled for a time with him and Arnold Goss in their search for money. Hardy told this anecdote: "The train stopped in Elkhart, Indiana, in a pouring rainstorm. Far down the dark and dismal street shone one electric sign—BANK. Durant shook Goss, who was dozing dejectedly in a corner. 'Wake up, Goss,' said Durant. 'There's one we missed.' "

By September, almost everyone except Durant had given up hope of finding a money source to keep GM from receivership. But one of Durant's associates, J.H. McClement, advised him that he had ex-

plored the financing problem with the firm of Lee, Higginson & Company of Boston. This outfit, said McClement, might be able to put together a group to provide enough money to save GM.

After several weeks of negotiations, the Boston firm and J. & W. Seligman & Company, New York agreed to underwrite up to $20 million worth of six percent notes, although only $15 million was actually issued. In effect, they offered a loan of $15 million.

The terms have generally been characterized as severe. In return, the bankers required a commission of $4.1 million in preferred stock and $2 million in common stock, at par value. They required a blanket mortgage of GM's Michigan properties. And, according to some sources, GM actually received only $12.75 million and thus would have to repay $2.25 million it did not receive. According to Durant's figures, the worth of the stock given the bankers was actually $21.6 million and GM received only $12.25 million, giving the bankers a total compensation of $9.3 million.

In addition to the compensation, the bankers also insisted on control of General Motors, a voting trust at least for the five-year term of the loan. Durant was aghast: "The $15 million loan . . . had outrageous terms which I was forced to accept to save my 'baby,' born

Workers by the thousands were brought to Flint during this period of rapid expansion at Buick; many of them lived in tarpaper shacks surrounding the factory.

and raised by me, the result of hectic years of night and day work and diligent applications . . . and listen to this—it took seven months to secure the money at the frightful price paid for it to start the wheels in motion and put thousands of men back to work. This having been accomplished, we notified our dealers that we were again doing business as usual, and the first week we received orders for 13,886 Buick cars having a money value of $13,886,000.''

Durant was still a vice-president of General Motors but no longer in control. The bankers who were had no interest in Durant's ideas. He sat back sullenly and watched them chop away at the company he had created. Finally Durant decided not to participate any longer. "With no idea of being disloyal, it seemed to me that it would be better to let the new group handle the business to suit themselves and if I ever expected to regain control of General Motors, which I certainly intended to do, I should have a company of my own, run in my own way. In other words, another one-man institution, but taking a leaf from Henry Ford's book—No bankers.''

By then, Durant was already talking to a former Buick race driver, Louis Chevrolet, about starting a new automobile company.

With Durant's departure—temporarily—from an active role in the company he had founded, it is perhaps appropriate to recall the words of Oldsmobile's Fred Smith, published in *Detroit Saturday Night* in 1928: "Durant saw the possibilities of a strong combination earlier and more clearly than anyone else in or out of the industry, and he put it over; a feat more staggering at the time than can be easily appreciated today. In spite of frequent and earnest scraps with W.C., I had at least the intelligence to see in him the strongest and most courageous individual then in the business and the master salesman of all time. No man ever lived who could sell such a variety of commodities in so short a space of time, cigars, buggies, automobiles, ideas and himself, believing wholeheartedly in his wares and in the last item especially . . . . It would be a poorly-posted analyst who failed to list W.C. Durant as the most picturesque, spectacular and aggressive figure in the chronicles of American automobiledom. He certainly made some capital mistakes . . . but the man who makes no mistakes rarely makes anything at all on a large scale.''

For the first time since November 1st, 1904, the man who had built Buick was no longer in charge of its destiny. Buick's fate was in the hands of the bankers who now controlled General Motors.

83

Chapter Five

NASH AND CHRYSLER AND BUICK

In his autobiography, General Motors chairman Alfred P. Sloan, Jr. observed, "it was no accident that Buick remained the mainstay of General Motors through its early years. It had the management of stars."

The stars in the years immediately following Durant's 1910 withdrawal were Charles W. Nash and Walter P. Chrysler.

Nash had watched Durant's promotion of Buick from a ringside seat as vice-president and general manager of the Durant-Dort Carriage Company in Flint. But both Nash and Dallas Dort were still wedded to carriages, and despite Durant-Dort's financial interest in Buick, they were content to stay with their carriage business, which had its best year in 1906.

In fact, one day that year Nash and Dort went to see Durant, hoping to talk him into becoming more actively involved again with the carriage firm. Summoned into his house, they found Durant vigorously pumping the player piano and singing. When he stopped, and the two started to broach the subject of carriages, Durant instead began to talk enthusiastically about the future of Buick. The scene struck Nash, who turned to Dort and said, "Dallas, I think Billy has gone crazy."

But in the fall of 1910, when the bankers were looking for a new manager for Buick, they reached the conclusion, on Durant's recommendation, that Nash was their man. They could hardly have done better. Nash was a born leader, a good businessman and, unlike Durant, conservative, practical and deeply concerned that money not

be spent unnecessarily. His temperament was just what the bankers were looking for.

Nash's respect for money ran deep, from an unusually deprived childhood. "I never was born—I just sprung up and grew," he commented once in a letter. It just seemed that way. Nash was born January 28th, 1864 to D.L. and Anna Caldwell Nash, in DeKalb County, Illinois. They separated when he was six, and since neither apparently wanted their son, a court appointed a guardian, farmer Robert Lapworth near Flint, to care for him. Under the guardianship, Charles was expected to do farm chores and receive room and board—and, at age twenty-one, a new suit of clothes and a hundred dollars in cash.

Nash couldn't wait that long. At age twelve, he slipped away from the Lapworth house, walked fifteen miles to another farm and got a job for pay. Later he raised sheep there and joined a nearby farmer as a contractor for compressing and baling hay. He married a farmer's daughter, Jessie Halleck. When her health declined, Nash moved into nearby Flint to be close to medical assistance and got a job as a clerk with the W.C. Pierce hardware store. That's where Durant first noticed him, and hired him as a dollar-a-day laborer in the Flint Road Cart Company. Durant noted in a 1942 letter to Nash that "I remember so well meeting you in the hardware store, at which time I was very much interested in you. . . . I suggested that you come over to the factory and you promptly accepted."

Nash started in the company's blacksmith shop. He had been there only a few days when he suggested it would be a good idea to buy a mechanical hammer which, he pointed out, would cost only about $35 and could do more hammering in a day than he could in a month. Nash soon was transferred into the upholstery department, where he stuffed cushions for buggy seats. He was strong, and the work was not far removed from baling hay, and his personal production was higher than the other laborers. They grumbled that he made them look bad. Nash responded that he needed the money, and worked all the harder.

Within a year, Nash was superintendent and soon became a general superintendent and eventually vice-president and general manager as the Flint Road Cart Company evolved into the thriving Durant-Dort Carriage Company. He drove his first horseless carriage in 1897, an imported electric, and later said this was the beginning of his interest in automobiles. But there was no indication Nash was willing to leave the carriage industry until his appointment as general manager of Buick on September 9th, 1910, the day Durant resigned from that post.

Other administrative changes were also being made. In 1910, Richard Collins, formerly the Kansas City Buick distributor, became

Page preceding: A 1911 Model 21 touring car on Buick's test hill. Above: Charles W. Nash at his desk at Buick in Flint. Below: Nash's daughter Ruth was among Flint's earliest women drivers; here she is in a Model 10, the baby beside her is William Rowen. Page opposite, above: Among the Buick officials in the group photo are—first row, seated, from the left, purchasing agent Edward J. Copeland, consulting engineer Walter Marr, works manager Walter P. Chrysler, president Charles W. Nash, and sales manager Richard H. Collins. Machine plant superintendent Cady Durham is the shortest man in the second row; chief engineer Enos DeWaters is on the far left in the third row, and motor department manager William Beacraft is in fifth row center, with chauffeur's cap and big moustache.

Buick's general sales manager when Harry E. Shiland was transferred to the managership of General Motors' Saginaw plants. Collins brought with him Fred W.A. Vesper as assistant sales manager and advertising man. Vesper was well known in Flint, having sold thousands of Durant-Dort carriages. And he would be credited with the initial coining of Buick's most famous advertising slogan: "When Better Automobiles Are Built, Buick Will Build Them."

James J. Storrow, briefly president of General Motors after the bankers took over, felt that while Nash could handle Buick's major administrative decisions, he could use an experienced manufacturing man to help him run the factory, a vastly more complex operation than the carriage business. And he had a candidate in mind. Storrow was not only interim president of General Motors but also a director of the American Locomotive Company. That firm had a new assistant works manager of its Pittsburgh plant who had transformed the factory into a moneymaker for the first time in years. His name was Walter P. Chrysler.

Storrow brought Chrysler to New York, told him of the prospect of going to Flint and arranged for Nash and Chrysler to meet. The two sat down to lunch in the Fort Pitt Hotel in downtown Pittsburgh. Chrysler felt that Nash was cool at first, carefully studying the man Storrow wanted as Buick's works manager. After lunch, upon discovering they both smoked the same brand of cigars, they became better acquainted.

Nash extended an invitation to visit Buick. Arriving in Flint, machinist Chrysler was astonished to find much of the work being done with wood. The workmen shaped poplar boards in steam kilns to make the car bodies, and at this, Chrysler later noted, they were "admirably skillful." He was not nearly as impressed with the way they worked with metal.

"I became excitedly eager, and thought, 'What a job I could do here, if I were boss,' " he wrote.

The bargaining period was short. Chrysler told Nash he was making $12,000 a year at American Locomotive. Nash said he could offer only $6000. Chrysler accepted at once. He wanted to get into the automobile business.

Chrysler had shown an intense early interest in machines. A native of Kansas, son of an engineer on the Kansas & Pacific Railroad, he had made a working railroad model and his own apprentice machine tools as a youth; and, as an adult, when he bought his first car, a Locomobile, he spent months tearing it apart and rebuilding it before ever learning how to drive. His main interest was in how the machinery worked.

Within about a year after Durant's departure, the Nash-Chrysler

team was in place, and ready to make its own impact on Buick. The timing was fortunate, for in the immediate aftermath of his leaving, Buick had lost the momentum of the Durant years. Instead of vying with Ford for number one, Buick struggled through 1911 with a production of only 13,389 cars, falling from second place to fifth, behind Ford, Studebaker, Willys-Overland and Maxwell. In 1911, Henry Ford was reaching full stride, producing nearly 70,000 Model T's that year to dominate the industry.

In the general confusion of Buick's change in management, a strange decision was made—to drop the Model 10, Buick's most popular car, of which 11,000 had been built the previous year. Some historians state this was a decision of the bankers who wanted to build larger cars. Others have written that the bankers wanted to be builders of prestige cars, wanted to cater to the "carriage trade," their theory being that a customer might buy a Ford first but eventually would want to step up to a Buick.

Maybe so, but this does not seem entirely borne out by Buick's

Above: Buick executives photographed in 1911, identified in caption on opposite page. Below: President Taft in a 1911 Model 21 in Detroit. Left: Portrait of Chief Engineer Enos A. De Waters.

The Model 14, or Buggyabout, which arrived late in 1910 as a 1911 model.

1911 offerings. In fact, the company replaced the Model 10 with a Model 32 roadster and Model 33 touring which used the same 22.5 hp four-cylinder engine that had powered the Model 10. The roadster's wheelbase was only 90 inches (the touring's was a hundred), compared with the 92-inch wheelbase of the old Model 10. The Model 32 was smaller and lighter than the car it replaced and, at $800, was priced $200 less.

It seems more likely to speculate that if ulterior motives were involved, they were those of the new management wishing to separate itself from the management decisions of Durant, and by doing so eliminated the most successful model Durant had ever introduced.

Whatever the reason for the decision, it was apparently an unwise one.

The Model 32 roadster was not even Buick's smallest car of the year. For the Buggyabout finally made its appearance, late in 1910 as a 1911 model, and it was, as rumored two years before, designated Model 14. (There was a slight variant, the 14B, with the fuel tank at the rear instead of under the seat.) This brief, and belated, experiment to challenge in the low-priced field had a 79-inch wheelbase and its own 127-cubic-inch two-cylinder 14.2 hp motor. Last of the two-cylinder Buick passenger cars, it weighed only 1425 pounds but its "more or less $450" price tag had risen to $550. Production totaled 2048 units late in 1910 and 1252 in 1911 before the Buggyabout was dropped.

These models aside, there was indeed a push for more puissant cars, and no fewer than five different four-cylinder engines powered the other 1911 Buicks. In addition to the old Model 10 engine in the Models 32 and 33, there was a new 201-cubic-inch powerplant with four-inch-square bore/stroke dimensions and 25.6 horsepower in the Model 26 roadster and Model 27 touring. The older 255-cubic-inch four was used in the Model 21 touring, and a 318-cubic-inch engine powered the Model 38 roadster and Model 39 touring, big cars with 116-inch wheelbases replacing the former Models 16 and 17. Another new engine version, the largest Buick had yet built, was a 338-cubic-inch four in the Model 41 limousine.

If that wasn't sufficient model proliferation, Buick's two-cylinder Model 2-A delivery trucks were fitted with a variety of bodies by specialist coachbuilders—and, in Canada, McLaughlin was building McLaughlin-Buicks totally different in styling from the Flint cars.

But for all the new models and the additions of inches to wheelbase and cubic inches to horsepower, the Buicks retained their essential character; they were refined, they were not really changed. An automatic high-speed clutch release was fitted to the models with planetary transmissions, and on the larger cars full-elliptic rear springs gave way to three-quarter elliptics. A centrifugal water pump was given the bigger Buicks too, as well as a new dual ignition system. A plunger pump replaced the former gear pump, and a foot accelerator was now fitted. The cone clutch had given way to a multiple disc, and the selective transmission was refined to be less noisy on intermediate gears. The frame was kicked up more over the rear axle so the drive could be more straight-line. Diagonal struts or radius rods were another improvement. All in all, it was business as usual—if a little confusing amidst the welter of various models—in Buick's product line, with the hope that business as usual would soon be reflected in the sales figures.

Buick recovered somewhat in 1912, building 19,812 cars to nose out Maxwell for fourth place. The Nash-Chrysler team effectively streamlined operations by reducing the number of models and engines. There were three touring cars (Models 29, 35 and 43) and three roadsters (the 28, 34 and 36). Gone were the little Buggyabout and the big Model 41 limousine, though that seven-passenger car was succeeded as Buick's largest by the five-passenger Model 43, Buick's most expensive 1912 car at $1725.

Again, there were engineering refinements, guides being provided the pushrods, grease cups fitted to the pivot pins of all rocker arms, and spark plugs more conveniently secured in the cylinders at an angle of 45 degrees instead of horizontally. Brakes were redesigned, the externals for service and operated by a pedal, the internals emergencies operated by hand lever. Grease cups were added to spring shackles, steering knuckles, clutch and brake mechanisms and all outboard bearings. The gearshift lever moved inside the body.

The venerable planetary transmission (Models 34 and 35) gave way to a three-speed selective sliding gear, the shifting lever neatly enclosed in a steel casing with only its handle visible. Foot accelerators were provided these cars, and the horn was incorporated "in the mud apron between the frame and running board in an ingenious manner." The motor, clutch and transmission were now built in unit; the cone clutch was back, replacing the multiple disc.

By now Buick engineers were busy at work on a new six-cylinder engine, but it wouldn't be ready for production for two years. The important news at Buick in 1912, besides the teaming of Nash, Chrysler and Walter Marr, was not experimentation, but that Buick had turned around. GM's most important property was on its way back. Not in a dramatic fashion, not yet, but it had survived and production was increasing.*

---

*The company was getting better at copywriting too. Its immortal slogan which initially had read "When Better Automobiles Are Made, Buick Will Build Them" was refined in 1912 to the more effective "When Better Cars Are Built, Buick Will Build Them." The word "Cars" was changed back to "Automobiles" the following year, and that was that—for decades.

One reason for the increased production was Chrysler's practical methods of speeding things up. He observed that workmen were finishing chassis as they had in the carriage industry—sandpapering the frames, painting them with a primary coat rich with putty that would not dry for twelve hours, sandpapering again, and then adding a finishing coat of varnish that would take twelve more hours to dry. Chrysler cut out the sandpapering and glazing coat, which was treating metal as if it were wood, and this cut production time on that phase from four days to two. To those craftsmen who complained, he pointed out that the hidden portion of the chassis would be caked with road mud the first day it was used.

Within six months Chrysler figured a way to dry two coats of paint in just half a day, and those minor changes alone increased production from forty-five Buicks a day to seventy-five. Chrysler credited Chet Smith, his production manager, with helping make the changes.

When Chrysler arrived at Buick, the chassis room of about 70-by-600 foot dimensions had a roof supported by a forest of wooden posts no more than twenty feet apart. Chrysler had the roof supported by stouter trusses, taking out many of the posts that were in every workman's way.

According to Chrysler, Buick may have pioneered a rudimentary form of mass production. Chassis were supported on tables while axles, springs and wheels were attached. Then a chain hoist was used to lift the chassis from the tables and onto a pair of tracks made of two-by-fours. The chassis were then pushed along by hand, while men added the fenders, gas tanks and finally the bodies. Buick also developed a method of squirting paint, using air pressure. With one improvement after another, production soared to 200 cars a day.

After Buick developed its line, according to Chrysler, Henry Ford went to work and developed the first chain conveyor in the industry, providing a true mass production system that the rest of the industry copied. Buick employee Fred Hoelzle, who was interviewed at age ninety-two for this book, stated that Ford and Buick shared manufacturing ideas. Hoelzle knew all of the early Buick leaders. He remembered that Billy Durant used to pull up a wooden box, sit down on it and chat with the workers; that Charles Nash was sometimes gruff, but a good businessman who quickly learned manufacturing; and that he (Hoelzle) occasionally drank beer with Walter Chrysler, who was always interested in improving production.

Hoelzle swapped manufacturing ideas with Henry Ford, occasionally having dinner with the manufacturer during trips to Dearborn. Hoelzle built the first Buick assembly line, putting wheels on carts and installing tracks of channel iron to push them around on. Once, he picked up an idea at a tool show for running engines under block test on "city gas" (a purer form of manufactured gas) instead

Above left: 1911 Model 41 limousine. Above right: 1911 Model 38 roadster. Below left: 1911 Model 21 touring. Below right: 1911 Model 32 roadster.

of the gasoline which created dangerous fumes and almost daily caused workers to be overcome. Hoelzle talked Buick into trying city gas, a practice adopted after tests showed that this did not injure the engines. He shared the idea with Henry Ford, who put it into use immediately. Soon the use of city gas instead of gasoline for fueling engines under factory test became practically universal.

While Chrysler was digging into production problems, Walter

Marr's active role in Buick was coming to a close. The main problem was his fragile health. According to some reports, in 1912 he was convinced he was about to die (a premature concern; he lived until 1941). On a trip that year, he discovered a beautiful place to retire, Signal Mountain, near Chattanooga, Tennessee. And there he built what was described as one of the most beautiful homes in the South.

Marr's departure from Buick was gradual. Much of his routine

Above: 1911 Model 2-A truck, and a special-built depot wagon body on a 2-A chassis of the same vintage. Below: 1911 Model 26 roadster and 27 touring.

work was taken over by his assistant Enos A. DeWaters, increasingly so as his absence became longer. Finally one day Chrysler asked DeWaters why he still signed letters under the title assistant chief engineer. He replied that no one had told him he was chief. Chrysler responded, "Well, I'm telling you now." In those informal days, that is how such things were often done.

Marr remained a consulting engineer for Buick until 1923. New models were brought to him at Signal Mountain for inspection and he went to Flint whenever he felt it necessary. Leo W. Goossen, an extraordinary young car and engine designer, spent a good deal of time with Marr at Signal Mountain shortly after Marr moved there. Goossen, a native of Kalamazoo, Michigan, had started as a record clerk at Buick, them moved into experimental work after Marr and DeWaters became aware of his drawings of automobile components.

Once, Marr assigned Goossen to design an experimental four-cylinder side-valve engine, of which two prototypes were made. He also designed a V-12 engine, and two were built and installed in Buicks. One of the two cars, a 1915 model, is still in the possession of Marr's grandson Walter L. Marr III, who plans to preserve the car for his children. Goossen also designed a V-6. One prototype was built and installed in a car—nearly a half century before the famous Buick V-6 of 1962. Goossen left Buick in 1919 for health reasons and later went on to a lengthy, varied and monumental career as a race car designer.

In 1914, Marr designed the Marr Cyclecar, which was an effort by Buick to develop an unusually inexpensive vehicle. Unlike most vehicles of the cyclecar genre, which were virtually four-wheeled motorcycles, the Marr Cyclecar had a small water-cooled engine and was as substantial as a regular automobile, but narrow, so that the only passenger seat was directly behind the driver's seat. One Buick expert says Buick decided not to manufacture the car primarily because it would have cost nearly as much to produce as the small regular Buick. Only one Marr Cyclecar was made, and it is on display at the Sloan Museum today.

Apparently about this time, Marr also became more interested in aviation. In 1910, during a ten-month rest in Denver, Marr had experimented with aircraft, and had returned to Buick with a patent on a new type of rudder control. He tried it out on Flint's first airplane, the Flint Flyer, at a field north of the Buick plant, with Bob Burman at the controls. That year, Burman got the plane four or five feet off the ground on one occasion, but hit a rail fence on another try, and repairing the plane required more money than the skeptical backers would produce. Marr apparently engaged in some other aircraft activities in 1914 and later, though details of his specific work in this

field are sketchy. After World War I, however, he did donate to Chattanooga that city's first airfield, Marr Field.

DeWaters, Marr's successor at Buick, was born in Kalamazoo County in 1874 and graduated from Kalamazoo College in 1899. He received an engineering degree at the University of Michigan in 1903. After working at several other auto firms, he began at Buick in Jackson in 1905 and went on to Flint on Thanksgiving Day in 1906 as Buick discontinued, for a time, its Jackson operations. DeWaters was chief engineer until 1929 and a consultant for two years thereafter. He died in 1962 at age eighty-eight.

There were other men who gave the Buick organization some stability in this transitional post-1910 period. One was Cady B. Durham. Durham, son of a blacksmith at Seneca Falls, New York, quit school at thirteen to become an apprentice mechanic. He spent eight years learning his trade with the Payne Engine Works in Elmira, then decided his goal would be to work for every company in the United States requiring his skill. He didn't achieve that lofty ambition because he found a home at Buick in Flint, becoming assistant superintendent of Buick Factory 11 in 1909.

Chrysler, quickly recognizing Durham's talents, promoted him to superintendent in 1912. Later he became general master mechanic (1916), works manager (1919) and assistant general manager (1920). Eventually (1929) he moved to the staff of Alfred P. Sloan, Jr. when Sloan was GM president.

During his twenty years at Buick, Durham's personality as well as his ability made a lasting impression. Extremely popular with the workmen, Durham claimed he could call virtually every one of them by their first names. "Cady," as everyone called him, never lost touch with his workers and mingled with them at every opportunity. His picturesque speech and his explosive spontaneity became something of a legend in Flint.

Once, during a testimonial for Durham, it was said "he has the reputation among Buick's employees of being able to step in and operate any machine in the factories." That wasn't too surprising: He had designed many of them. Durham gave much of his time and money to local charities, helped foreign-born Buick workers in their studies for American citizenship, and supported English language classes for them.*

*Buick's need for workers brought a large number of foreign-born people to Flint and many had difficulty with the English language. Genesee County, of which Flint is the largest city, had 5400 foreign-born in 1900; by 1920 that number had grown to 18,600. One area of Flint became known as a "Little Europe" with many languages and native customs. Although a few blacks had worked for Buick from its beginning in Flint in late 1903, it was not until shortly after World War I that hundreds of blacks from the South moved to Flint to work at Buick and other local automobile factories.

While Nash and Chrysler were bringing Buick back into a powerful position following the crisis of 1910, Billy Durant was working miracles of his own. A brief review of the early history of Chevrolet is important in a Buick history, for Chevrolet was created largely with the help of former Buick employees. Indeed, the beginnings of Buick and Chevrolet bear a remarkable resemblance because Durant was using much of the same formula, and in some cases the same men and buildings, he had used to build Buick a few years earlier. And the results of his new endeavor would have a large impact on Buick, Charles Nash and Walter Chrysler—not to mention General Motors.

Both Buick and Chevrolet companies had their beginnings in Detroit, but neither became successful until their moves to Flint. Both were financed with the help of the Durant-Dort Carriage Company, and both grew after Durant took over operations of James H. Whiting. Both David Buick and Louis Chevrolet were not long with the companies bearing their names, yet both names remain famous because Durant—ironically much less well known today—promoted those automobiles into successes.

Durant, who retained his title of vice-president of General Motors though no longer in control, late in 1910 told Louis Chevrolet, Buick's former racing star, that "we're going to need a car." Durant provided the money, Louis the car.

The first few Chevrolets were built in 1911 under Louis Chevrolet's direction in Detroit, probably far fewer than the 2999 production figure generally cited. Durant hadn't been satisfied with the large and expensive car Chevrolet had developed, so he started another automobile company in Flint, the Little Motor Car Company. It was named for Big Bill Little, who had been Buick's Flint factories manager under Durant. Next Durant organized the Mason Motor Company, operated by none other than Arthur C. Mason, who had been in charge of engine production when Buick had first started up in Flint.

James Whiting, getting on in years, wanted to retire, so Whiting, Charles M. Begole (like Whiting a former Buick president) and William S. Ballenger (one of the original Buick stockholders in Flint), sold the Flint Wagon Works to Durant. Whiting had been building an automobile called the Whiting at the wagon works, but neither automobile nor wagon production was faring well. Juggling his players, Durant soon sent Bill Little to Detroit to help Louis Chevrolet get production going on the Chevrolet; at the same time he brought in A.B.C. Hardy, his former associate at Durant-Dort and GM (and Flint's first automobile manufacturer) to get the Little automobile into production at the Flint Wagon Works. In 1913 the Mason Motor Company moved out of its corner of the wagon works

Page opposite: 1912 Model 34 roadster. Above: 1912 Model 35 touring. Below: 1912 Model 29 touring. Production of these cars totaled 13,450.

Buick artwork of the period, exemplified by a catalogue cover from 1912.

and into the nearby factory originally built for Buick in 1903.

Now Arthur Mason was back where he had started in Flint, except he was building engines for Chevrolet instead of for Buick.

Other plans were in motion. In addition to creating Chevrolet, Little and Mason Motor, Durant also incorporated two other com-

panies in this highly active 1911-1913 period. They were Sterling Motor Company of Detroit, of which Dallas Dort, Durant, Little and Curtis Hatheway were among the directors, and Republic Motors Company of Delaware, which was planned as a holding company for Durant-backed firms—in effect, a new General Motors.

Dort was supposed to be a major figure in Republic, but for some reason he hesitated. Perhaps he was too conservative to go along with Durant's seemingly reckless plans. In a series of complicated maneuvers, Durant suddenly dropped the Republic idea and soon the Little name from his Flint automobile, then used the Chevrolet name for both his holding company and his manufacturing operations (though Mason Motor retained a separate identity for a few years). For a time, Durant concentrated his Chevrolet production in Flint; the Chevrolet is more an outgrowth of the Little Motor Car Company of Flint than of the Chevrolet Motor Company of Detroit.

In 1913, Louis Chevrolet left, ostensibly because he was angered that Durant had dumped the large car of his dreams. The last straw, however, was that Durant kept complaining about the way Louis smoked. As Durant's widow Catherine recalled: "I don't think it was so much that he was smoking, but the way he did it. Louis would have a cigarette hanging on his lower lip and it used to annoy Willie to tears." Durant, an ex-cigar smoker and salesman, suggested to Chevrolet that if a gentleman had to smoke, it should be cigars. To which Louis replied: "I sold you my car and I sold you my name, but I'm not going to sell myself to you. I'm going to smoke my cigarettes as much as I want. And I'm getting out."

Between 1911 and 1915, Durant nursed his latest baby, Chevrolet, into a respectable automobile company. Now he was about to take dead aim on his target from the beginning: to get General Motors back from the bankers.

If Nash, Chrysler and the bankers knew this was coming, they gave no sign of it. Very likely, they were thinking of other things. Nash was elected president of General Motors and Buick on December 10th, 1912, succeeding Thomas Neal, a Detroit paint manufacturer, who had served from February 16th, 1911. And Chrysler was learning all there was to know about the automobile business, and loving every minute of it as Buick became stronger and stronger.

In 1913, Buick production continued to rise, reaching 26,666 units, despite management's decision that the electric self-starter—offered on Cadillac in 1912 and on some other cars in 1913—was not yet perfected and therefore not fit for a Buick.

Buick's 1913 cars included three touring models (the 25, 31 and 40), two roadsters (the 24 and 30) and two trucks (the models 3 and 4). None used the six-cylinder engine still under development. The two-cylinder was finally retired even from the truck line, so all Buick cars and trucks now had four-cylinder power.

The most popular Buick of 1913 was the Model 31 five-passenger touring priced at $1285, of which 10,000 were produced. Second in production was the smaller Model 25 touring (105-inch wheelbase as opposed to 108 of the Model 31) of which 8150 were built. Priced at $1050, this car used the old Model 10 engine. Its companion Model 24 roadster (2850 were produced at $950) was Buick's least expensive car of the year. Electric side and taillamps were combined with oil lights and gas headlights on the Models 30 and 31.

The Model 30 was described rather redundantly as "a new type of roadster . . . with a body of distinctly roadster type. . . . The snappy lines of the body are effectively supplemented by the dip and curve of the mudguards." The top-of-the-line Model 40, on a 115-inch wheelbase and selling for $1650, was noteworthy, Buick said, for the generous use of its upholstery, "deep and rich . . . it has been extended up to and over the end of the body and the door, the leather extending a short distance down the outside, thus adding to both the comfort and the appearance of the car."

This was perhaps the first year in which Buick laid special emphasis on style, and gave a nod to the feminine side of its following. In an article given to *The Los Angeles Times* in its April 11th, 1913 edition, Buick claimed that the enclosed gearshift which it had pioneered the year before "meant absolute protection to skirts from the levers, that in operation had more than once torn and stained milady's dress." And now Buick had again "met the requirements of Dame Fashion by adding an extra step to the 1913 Buick Model 31 touring car. The step [which may have been an accoutrement added by the trendy L.A. dealer] is placed between the usual running board and the ground, to accommodate purely the requirements of the follower of the fashion which points to tight skirts—frocks in fact of the design so commonly referred to as the 'hobble'."

A little further up north, however, Buick distributor C.S. Howard paid tribute to the marque's more traditional virtues in a large advertisement showing a whimsical dragon of "the Cretaceous Period," with text reference to what had happened to the prehistoric beast and a bit of promotional doggerel singularly appropriate to San Francisco: "If a quake should come and bury us / And a million years had pass'd / And then a club of scientists / Would dig us out at last, / Among the things they'd find intact / Is a Buick car—you bet / For no one ever, ever has / Worn out a Buick yet."

In the commercial end of its business, although Buick built only 461 Model 4 and 199 Model 3 trucks, the company used considerable space in its catalogue to rationalize the offering of an L-head engine in the truck line, while boasting at the same time of the valve-in-head feature of its passenger car engines.

The Buick house organ, with graphics similar to The Saturday Evening Post.

"We want to state that we still maintain and guarantee that the Buick overhead valve motor will produce more speed and more power than any other type of motor manufactured and our position is not in any way modified by the fact that we produce in the Buick truck a motor of another type," the catalogue explained, noting that

Above: Louis Chevrolet in a 1914 Model B-25 touring car. Below: Louis in a Buick racer. The "cigarette hanging on his lower lip . . . used to annoy Willie to tears," according to Durant's widow, and was among the reasons that the Chevrolet/Durant partnership was abruptly terminated.

the L-head engine "utilizing our large valve construction and employing special timing" produced "extraordinary lugging power at low speeds" while losing some "snap" at higher speeds. The absence of high speeds would actually be an advantage to the buyer, Buick reasoned, using the interesting argument that the buyer of a truck usually hired someone else to operate it: The driver would not be tempted to speed and abuse the vehicle, and therefore the owner's in-

vestment would be protected. The two truck models used the same four-cylinder 141-cubic-inch engine of 14.4 horsepower.

The argument may have been logical but the L-head engine was dropped the following year.

Under the Nash-Chrysler leadership, Buick had a big year in 1914. The Delco system of electric self-starting and lighting had been finally perfected in the judgment of Buick management and was introduced as standard equipment on all 1914 models. In its catalogue Buick stated, somewhat pompously:

"A year ago, when untried, unproved self-starters were being bolted onto many an excellent car in any available place—a source of bitter disappointment in thousands of cases—the Buick management took a firm stand. It announced that no self-starter would be incorporated into any Buick car until a starter had been found as good as the Buick car itself.

"Such a starter is the Delco and the Delco installation in the Buick is something you may rely upon as a fulfillment of the Buick ideals, which means 'uninterrupted use of his investment' to every Buick owner. All this at a cost which makes the self-starting, automatically lighted Buick of 1914 the greatest motor car value offered this season."

There were other Buick innovations this year. The steering wheel was moved from the right side to the left, with controls moved to the center. In her unpublished biography of her husband, Mrs. Alanson P. Brush wrote: "To move the driver's seat from the right hand side to the left seemed so radical a change at first as to bring protests. Drivers always sat on the right hand side. This let them watch the edge of the road; if you sat on the left side you might run over the edge, into the ditch. So they argued. It was hard to convince them that more important than the edge of the road was the car coming toward them. . . . Al supervised the building of a sample left-hand-drive car. It did not take many demonstrations to prove the advantage of this change."

Brush's work on the left-hand-drive system in 1913, for the 1914 model year, was apparently his last major contribution to Buick. Some of his innovations had not always been successful. Mrs. Brush remembered accompanying her husband on one trip east after there was a flood of complaints about malfunctions in the Buick oiling system. Brush had made a change that required a much lighter grade of oil than previously, but the new cars had been sent out without instructions as to the type of oil: "Al found that the sales organization had made no plans for correcting the situation, so he decided to do something himself. We made a tour of six or seven of the biggest eastern dealers, explaining and correcting the oversight. The trip was made entirely at Al's own expense, but it seemed well worthwhile.

The dealers seemed deeply appreciative of Al's efforts and spoke with enthusiasm of the improvements he had made in the Buick cars."

Although Mrs. Brush's account seems the most substantial in existence about her husband's Buick career, his name is still remembered by some antique Buick owners. One, Greg Fauth, a student of Buick history in Flint, says oldtimers have told him that Brush brought the multiple-disc clutch idea with him from Oakland to Buick. The problem with the oiling system mentioned by Mrs. Brush gives antique Buick owners, particularly of 1911-1913 models, trouble to this day, according to Fauth, and Brush's "one-way" approach (through pump to engine never to return) tended to over-lubricate the Buicks of that period, and the bearings of these cars leaked an inordinate amount of oil. "Brush was always seeking to reduce friction, so he always over-lubricated," said Fauth.

Like others who had money tied to Buick, Brush lost most of his "snug little fortune," as his widow put it, in the financial crisis of 1910, but luckily continued to get royalties from his patents that were in use at Cadillac, Oakland and Buick, plus a comfortable income from the Brush Runabout.

By 1913 it became apparent to Brush that his future would not be with Buick. His patron Durant had lost control. Mrs. Brush wrote that there were rumors Walter Marr had made a miraculous recovery and was about to return. Perhaps Brush believed, correctly, that whether this was true or not, the post of chief engineer would never be his. He couldn't have helped noticing that Chrysler leaned more to DeWaters than to himself in Marr's absences. Possibly some of the technical problems had not endeared him to Buick management in the Nash-Chrysler regime. Although Brush served as a Buick engineer at Durant's insistence, his official title was as a consultant to General Motors. After leaving Buick, Brush negotiated a new contract with GM and was soon doing consulting work for a number of firms, most of them directly or indirectly concerned with building automobiles.

For Buick in 1914, the most important development was that it moved into production on its six-cylinder engine, offering it on the Model B-55, a five-passenger car on a 130-inch wheelbase selling for $1985 ($2135 in the West). Like other Buick engines, the valve-in-head six had its cylinders cast in pairs. The 331-cubic-inch powerplant had an SAE horsepower rating of 33.75, and developed 48 hp by brake test. Buick built 2045 of these cars.

There was a little sorting out among Buick fours. The B-36 and B-37 roadster and touring, which succeeded the former 30 and 31 models, had a new size engine, replacing the four-inch-square motor of the year before with a long-stroke unit (3.75 by 5, the same dimensions as the six, 220.9 cubic inches and 35 bhp under brake test).

Above: Governor George H. Hodges (center, rear seat) and state officials in the 1913 Model 31, which left Hutchinson (Kansas) at 5:01 a.m. and checked in at the Kansas City Star office at 4:24 p.m., averaging 37.5 mph for 303 miles. Below: Custom coupe body on a 1913 Model 31 chassis.

There was also a four-inch increase in the wheelbases, which now measured 112 inches. The smaller 105-inch-wheelbase four, now B-24 and B-25, retained basically the old Model 10 engine, with 3.75-inch bore and stroke, 165.8 cubic inches and brake tests now showing it to develop 28 horsepower. Mechanically, there were new rocker arms and camshaft rods with ball joints working in oil-soaked, felt-lined sockets, a quieter proposition—and the exhaust manifold, in-

stead of passing along the cylinders below the intake manifold, ran above them for better accessibility. Lubrication was revised to a splash system of the constant level variety with oil circulated by a gear-driven pump operated by bevel gearing from the rear end of the camshaft. Rear axles were now of the three-quarter floating type, much lighter and stronger than previously. On the larger fours (and the six), the fuel tank was removed to the rear of the chassis and hung from brackets attached to the frame. On the B-24 and B-25, however, it remained under the seat.

The most noticeable changes to Buicks for 1914 were outside, however. *The Automobile*'s reporter even suggested that it was only by lifting the hood that one could be sure it was a Buick: "In its new dress many a veteran motorist who can name any machine at a glance will fail to recognize the Buicks at first glance." That was something of an exaggeration since the new Buick look was simply a little streamlining of lines and a roundness added to the hood and radiator of the large fours and six. "Besides, they are up to the minute in design," enthused *Motor Age*, its editors extolling the fact that "the running boards are clear, having no battery boxes or other attachments on them." Also new in 1914 was a coupe, the Model B-38, Buick's first mass-produced enclosed car, if one considers a production run of fifty mass produced. Buick's largest volume car was the B-25: 13,446 built for the domestic market.

Buick got its production up to 32,889 in 1914, finally topping the claimed 1910 record. And if the innovations and production record were not enough good news, a Buick dealer in Argentina, Johnson Martin, claimed in 1914 to be the first person to drive a car across South America after he took a 1912 Model 28 from Buenos Aires over the Andes to Santiago, Chile. Buick was becoming ever more a world car. The factory shipped 1544 Model B-25 chassis overseas. Most went to England where Bedford bodies were mounted, but some were sent to the Abadal Company of Barcelona, Spain, where

custom bodies were added for the European trade, an arrangement which continued on a small scale from 1913 to 1922.

Walter Chrysler had made things happen at Buick, trimming waste, requiring work schedules, building efficiency, improving production. But he was still making only $6000 a year. He went to see Nash.

"Charlie, I want $25,000 a year," Chrysler announced. Nash almost screamed in protest. Chrysler threatened to quit. Nash and Storrow conferred. Finally Storrow told Chrysler he could have the $25,000. To which Chrysler replied thanks, then added he would be back for an additional $25,000 increase the next year.

Despite the salary fuss, Chrysler and Nash were, as Chrysler once wrote, "the best, warmest kind of friends. We became friends, in fact, for life. Charlie is a grand man."

Chrysler proved he was well worth his salary. In 1915, Buick production rose to 43,946 (although Maxwell's 44,000 took fourth place in the industry). There were three touring models (C-25, C-37 and C-55), three roadsters (C-24, C-36 and C-54), plus export versions of the C-24 and C-25 with right-hand drive, one truck (the C-4) and an export version of it. The most popular model (19,080 units built) was the C-25, its price cut a hundred dollars (to $950), an inch added to its wheelbase (for 106) and its engine still the Model 10's, the last year this unit was manufactured. There were two six-cylinder cars, the C-55, now boosted to seven-passenger capacity with the addition of two jumpseats, and its companion C-54 roadster. The six developed 55 hp by brake test this year, but even more significantly its price was dramatically lowered, $335 from 1914—to $1650.

Mechanical alterations were few, a lengthening of pistons, for example, to provide a greater bearing surface and to reduce piston slap, tungsten steel valves instead of nickel-steel because they resisted pitting and were more durable. Cantilever springs were tried on the six this season, concealed door hinges previously used only on the six were added to the four, and a "rain-vision ventilating windshield" was introduced throughout the line.

So minimal were the changes to Buick during this era that reporters were hard put to write the full-length stories on the new cars required by their editors. One enterprising journalist came up with this: "Though it is not new the Buick method for supporting the front end of the torque stay is worthy of study since it is the same in effect as a ball and socket, but much simpler and cheaper to make. The torque tube is forked like many others, but instead of linking the fork end to solid pins on the chassis, it is attached to a ring that swivels upon vertical pivots. This gives a perfect universality of movement to the torque tube and so to the axle to which it is attached." The following year he changed the description a little because the feature was "worthy of continued study."

Staying with a good thing was obviously the Buick way. In 1915 Buick built more trucks for export (748) than it did for home consumption (645), largely because World War I had begun in Europe. In London, the Red Cross—after having a number of chassis tested—chose Buick for its ambulances. The Buick ambulance would see much action during the war years.

Buicks were seeing action in lots of places by now. *The Buick Bulletin*, the large-format house organ the company began in 1912, routinely published photographs and reports of the cars and celebrities and competition: a victory in a hill climb in South Africa, winning a tug-of-war with an elephant, a trek through New Zealand, the Sultan of Johore and his Buick in the Far East, General John J. Pershing and his flag-bedecked official staff car.

Nash and Chrysler did not really have time to enjoy Buick's success of 1915, for unusual things were happening behind the scenes. Durant was making his move. He had conceived and developed General Motors, and he wanted it back. Nothing motivated him more than the memory of how the bankers had humiliated him, taken his company, chopped off some of the divisions and shunned his ideas.

It was true that Buick and General Motors had grown during his absence: GM produced net profits of nearly $15 million in fiscal 1915 compared with $10.2 million in 1910. But some people, even within GM's top administration, believed the corporation would have done better with Durant than with the conservative bankers. After all, much more growth might have been expected in a largely virgin American market, even against the competition of Ford's Model T. Durant supporters could point out that General Motors had produced twenty-one percent of the country's automobiles in 1910, the year Durant left, but only 8.5 percent by 1915.

The Durant faction felt there was no way he would have allowed

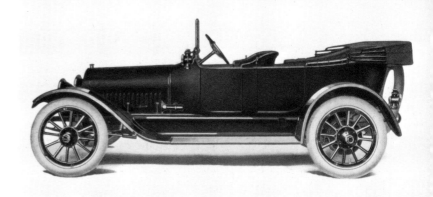

Page opposite: 1913 Model 30 roadster and 1913 Model 25 touring car. Above: 1914 Model B-55 seven-passenger and Model B-37 five-passenger touring cars. Below: A 1914 Model B-38 with enclosed coupe coachwork.

Ford to so overwhelmingly dominate the low-priced end of the market. One unnamed General Motors vice-president, quoted by Lawrence H. Seltzer in *A Financial History of the American Automobile Industry*, remarked: "The bankers were too skeptical about the future of the automobile industry. They were chiefly interested in trying to realize savings, so they closed down some plants, concentrating in others. They didn't take advantage of the opportunities. Under Durant, the company might have had a little financial difficulty now and then, but it would have grown much faster and its earnings would have been much greater."

In building Chevrolet, Durant had made some major financial alliances. One was with Louis G. Kaufman, president of the Chatham & Phenix Bank of New York, and the other was with Pierre S. du Pont, president of E.I. du Pont de Nemours & Company of Wilmington, Delaware. Kaufman had invested heavily in Chevrolet and later said he got Pierre du Pont interested in supporting Durant's move to get control of GM. Another story is that Durant learned Du Pont company treasurer John J. Raskob had bought 500 shares of GM stock in 1914 and cultivated Raskob's support for Durant's drive to gain control.

However it happened, Durant found himself in position to start buying GM stock in great amounts, secretly, on the open market. Almost without notice, the price of GM stock began to rise rapidly.

Durant had timed his move well. The last $2.5 million of the 1910 loan to General Motors of $15 million was to be paid October 1st, 1915, at which time the five-year voting trust held by the bankers would expire, and a new board of directors would be nominated to be presented at the stockholders meeting in November.

Durant was driven in his obsession to take control now. He called on relatives, old friends, former business associates for support. A.B.C. Hardy said that A.M. Bentley of Owosso, near Flint, brought in briefcases filled with GM stock certificates and turned them over to Durant without asking for a receipt. Bentley had originally procured the stock from Durant when GM took over Bentley's Reliance Motor Truck Company, which the bankers had dissolved.

As the board of directors meeting of September 16th approached, Durant held forth in a suite of three rooms in New York's Belmont Hotel, using wall phones in each room to buy GM stock from

Below: Walter Marr (far right) with his patented rudder and Flint's first plane, the 1910 Flint Flyer. Right: Walter Chrysler, Walter Marr and Charles Nash (third, fourth and fifth from the left, respectively) look over the Marr Cyclecar. Marr is shown in the tandem two-seater in the photograph below, taken in 1914.

brokers around the country. As the stock price soared—it rose from $82 in January of 1915 to $558 in December—Durant pulled the strings. His frantic activities are indicated in two telegrams he sent to his cousin, George Crapo Willson, in Flint. One, on August 22nd, says, "Don't sell any part of your holdings. I will protect if necessary." The other, on September 1st: "Hold every share you have regardless of price changes."

Contrary to some historical accounts, GM's board was not totally in the dark about Durant's plans. Durant himself had pleaded with Nash to join him in his drive. He told Nash he could retain the presidency; all Durant wanted was the vice-presidency—and control. In the first two weeks of September, Durant and Kaufman met several times with GM's banker interests. Three days before the September 16th meeting, Albert Strauss of the bankers' board was convinced enough of Durant's voting strength to offer a motion at a GM Finance Committee meeting that Durant be given an opportunity to express his views on company policy at the directors meeting. It was adopted unanimously.

Reportedly, Durant and James J. Storrow met on the morning of

Above left: Buick from 1915 (a '16 prototype) in which a Marr experimental V-12 was installed. Below: Elderly Marr and son Walter with a Model C.

Marr and family in the 1916 Buick prototype with V-12 engine that still exists. Below: Model C-4 chassis of 1915. Jitney bus coachwork by W.S. Seaman.

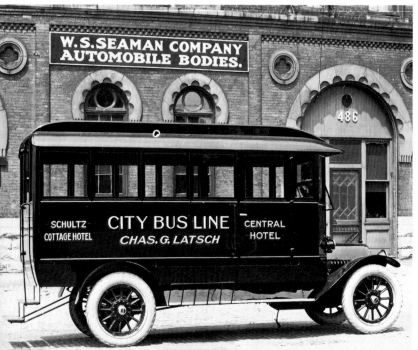

the 16th, and Storrow said he hoped there would be no quarrel at the board meeting. Durant replied that there was no need of any quarrel because "I'm in control of General Motors today."

The meeting was scheduled for 2:00 p.m. on September 16th, 1915 in Room 282 of the Belmont Hotel. However, apparently, the big show was going on elsewhere. A previously unpublished letter in Durant's papers from a GM director, J.H. McClement (who had helped Durant arrange the banker loan in 1910) to Dr. Edwin R. Campbell (Durant's son-in-law) dated September 20th, 1915 states:

"My letter of September 15th gave you full information up to the meeting of Directors, which was held on Thursday, the 16th. This meeting was called for two o'clock. I had to forego lunch in order to be on time and appeared in a room at the Hotel Belmont where Messrs. Neal, Murphy, Mott, Tilney, Wertheim and several other of the non-important ones [GM directors] were waiting for a quorum.

"So I concluded to go down stairs and have my lunch, and I took plenty of time, as it appeared that we would be delayed for some time.

"In the meantime, Mr. Wertheim tried to 'pump me' as to my position, stating that Mr. Durant had represented that with my influence and support, he had control, and if Mr. Durant got control, Mr. Nash would not serve as President.

"I answered that no plan had been put up to me, either by Mr. Durant or Mr. Storrow, and that I was very much in the dark as to what was going on, and that he had better exercise patience until some definite plan was proposed. That Mr. Durant had informed me that he had control, and that I believed Mr. Durant to be truthful, and if he did have control there would be no contest, and it would only be a question of compromise.

"After waiting for half an hour, I suggested that we send down and get a pack of cards and play auction bridge, while waiting for the powers that be to return and inform us of the result of their deliberations. This was done, Mr. Wertheim and I playing against Messrs. Mott and Tilney.

"About 5:30 Mr. Durant appeared and we invited him into the game. At about six o'clock Messrs. Storrow and Nash appeared and there was a regular love feast.

"The meeting was then held and Mr. Nash proposed the 50 percent dividend, and complimented Mr. Durant as being the essential factor in reaching an agreement by the sacrifices he had made.

"Mr. Storrow explained that new interests had purchased large amounts of stock, which accounted for its advance, and he regretted very much that some of the Directors serving would have to be dropped. That an agreement had been made for a Proxy Committee and for a new Board consisting of 17 members, which in all human probability would go through."

What had happened was that Pierre du Pont had joined the meeting "downtown" with Kaufman, Durant, Storrow, Nash and some of the other members of the bankers' board. Du Pont had expected that Durant and Kaufman would be in complete control, but the bankers had balked at caving in and there was a deadlock. Finally, at Storrow's urging, du Pont agreed to name three directors not connected with either faction. Perhaps more important to the stockholders was another agreement that day—to declare a cash dividend of fifty percent on the common stock—$50 a share on stock which had sold for $25 two years earlier. Durant remarked later in the meeting that he believed the board was justified in paying the dividend, a move he said he had previously felt would be unwise.

Minutes of that GM board meeting, though failing to show the dramatics of the day, reveal that Nash said the harmonious agreement resulted from the "broad view" taken by Durant. Durant is quoted as saying that all sides had made concessions, and that Storrow and Nash were directly responsible for bringing about agreement after so many days of unsuccessful negotiations.

Most historical accounts indicate that Durant regained control of GM at this meeting, but that is not exactly true. If du Pont could be counted on as a Durant ally, then Durant held the balance of power; but Durant could not be sure that du Pont and the three directors he had named would always fully support him. Durant was now a major force in GM again, but Storrow and some of the other bankers were still on board.

Without a pause to reflect on what he had accomplished, Durant continued his drive for complete control of General Motors. In late 1915 he privately, and then publicly, offered to trade five shares of Chevrolet stock for one share of GM. On December 23rd, he startled the financial world by announcing that Chevrolet stockholders had voted to increase Chevrolet's capital stock from $20 million to $80 million, and that the $60 million increase was voted in order to purchase controlling interest in GM.

Tiny Chevrolet trying to buy General Motors? New York newspapers, using such phrases as Jonah swallowing the whale, and the tail wagging the dog, saw the plan as one of the most audacious in the history of American finance. Some expressed belief that Durant could not bring it off. Indeed, eight General Motors directors, rallying around Nash and the bankers, suggested to the stockholders in January 1916 that a new three-year voting trust be established, clearly an anti-Durant proposal. Signing it were James J. Storrow, Albert Strauss, Samuel F. Pryor, Albert H. Wiggin, Thomas Neal, Charles H. Sabin, Emory Clark and Charles Stewart Mott. (Mott had earlier been an associate of Durant, and would years later extol Durant's impact on Flint and GM, but said he always tried to support policies he felt were best for the corporation, instead of personalities.)

Perhaps significantly, GM president Nash did not sign the proposal, nor would he publicly support it, though his heart was with the bankers. Nash was in torment. He had worked well with the bankers' board, and he knew that if Durant got complete control, Durant would run the show, even if he retained the presidency. Yet Nash could hardly oppose the man who had given him his first job in the carriage business, and later helped put him in charge of Buick.

In early 1916, Nash messaged Durant in answer to a query that he did not want to serve as a member of a new voting trust "as I do not want to get mixed up in any way with this scrap." Early in March, replying to another message from Durant, Nash said he did not want his name used by advocates of the proposed voting trust "as stockholders would think I was trying to insure my job. I do not want this impression to prevail as I am fast becoming discouraged and losing interest in the whole proposition."

By April 1916, Nash had decided to resign. Durant's son-in-law, Dr. Campbell, advised Durant that Nash's resignation would not matter as long as he could retain the services of Walter Chrysler at Buick. In mid-May Durant announced that he was in control of a majority of the General Motors voting stock, that Chevrolet owned 450,000 of the 825,589 shares outstanding.

On June 1st, 1916, the official date of Nash's resignation, Durant was elected president for the first time of General Motors, the company he had founded in 1908.

His victory this time was complete. Even Pierre du Pont offered to resign, though Durant turned him down. Storrow did not even attend the June 1st board meeting, and he and several other bankers retired from the board.

But Storrow was an immediate problem. For a time he backed a plan under which Nash and Chrysler would join him in buying the Packard Motor Car Company. When that fell through, Storrow backed Nash in his purchase, in July of 1916, of the Thomas B. Jeffery Company of Kenosha, Wisconsin, which became the Nash Motors Company (a predecessor of American Motors Corporation).

Durant could accept the loss of Nash, but Chrysler was another matter. His job of rebuilding Buick had been masterful. But Chrysler and Nash had become fast friends, and Storrow had given him his chance at the Buick job. Now they had gone elsewhere, and Durant was informed that Chrysler felt obliged to go with them.

Durant knew well what his first job as GM president would be. He immediately left New York for Flint. He had to get to Buick at once and talk to Walter Chrysler.

Chapter Six

DURANT COMES BACK ...BRIEFLY

When Buick general manager Walter P. Chrysler arrived at his office one morning in June of 1916 and found Billy Durant at his doorstep, two of the automotive industry's great personalities were set to engage in one of the most noteworthy conversations in Buick history.

The visitor, Durant, had an iron will softened with great personal charm; he was a man who had been king in both the carriage and the automobile industries, and who against all odds had taken on the bankers who had yanked General Motors from him, and sent them packing.

His host, Chrysler, had a will as strong as Durant's. His creative impulses were not the equal and he was often more blunt than charming in his speech. But Chrysler was a practical manufacturing man, as Durant was not. And he was generally willing to gamble his career on what he thought was right.

Durant felt he would have to handle Chrysler carefully—his recollection decades later was that Chrysler had decided to leave Buick in 1916, though Chrysler recalled that he had decided to stay even before his meeting with Durant. But neither man at the time was assured of the other's position.

They exchanged courtesies, then sat down between Chrysler's rolltop desk and a long table. Durant felt comfortable. This had been his office from 1906 to 1910. From it, he had directed some of the maneuvers that had led to the development of General Motors.

Durant said he told Chrysler that "he occupied a position of great responsibility . . . that I trusted him implicitly and planned to make the Buick division the pivotal part of a very large institution, and that I needed his organization without interruption.

"I talked with him about the responsibility toward the men who believed in him and who had come with him . . . . I used every argument that I was possessed of having to do with the future of the good men who he had secured as a part of his organization. When I had exhausted every argument, in his usual direct manner came the following:

" 'What is your proposition? What have you to offer?'

"In reply, quite as promptly, I made the following proposition:

" 'I will execute a three-year contract with you dating today, giving you $10,000 a month in cash and at the end of each year $500,000 in cash or, if you prefer, $500,000 in General Motors stock, based on the price of the stock today. In other words, if you take the stock, you are to have whatever value General Motors has obtained as the result of the organization, which . . . is to be of your selection without interference.' "

Chrysler was stunned. This was far beyond anything he had expected. He accepted, with one condition:

"I don't want any other boss but you. If you feel that anything is going wrong, if you don't like some action of mine, you just come to me. Just have one channel between Flint and Detroit: from me to you. Full authority is what I want."

Chrysler recalled Durant's reaction:

"He was beaming at me then. I saw him touch his fingers lightly to the table top for emphasis. 'It's a deal,' he said."

It may have been a deal, but Chrysler and Durant were both forceful men, and clashes were inevitable. Chrysler, who was elected president of Buick shortly after his meeting with Durant, had been in office only about three months when the first major one occurred.

Richard Collins, who had left Buick and gone to Detroit to work more closely with Durant, walked into Chrysler's office one day and announced that he had bought Buick's Detroit branch from Durant. Chrysler said that was not true; Chrysler ran Buick. Then he stormed to Durant's Detroit office, reiterated that they had an agreement to the effect that Chrysler made such decisions as who owned Buick's Detroit branch, and got Durant to back down.

Such clashes became more frequent. Chrysler pleaded with Durant to leave the Buick organization alone. He would be willing to carry out Durant's policies, if he only knew what they were. Durant laughed at the thought.

"I believe in changing the policies just as often as my office door opens and closes," he replied.

Said Chrysler: "You and I can never get along."

Page preceding: Practice drill with Buick ambulance during World War I. From the top: 1916 funeral car on a D-4 chassis; 1917 D-46 coupe; 1919 H-47 sedan. Page opposite: 1916 D-44 (right), '18 E-44 (left) roadsters.

But as he later wrote: "That's the kind of fellow he was though; we'd fight, and then he'd want to raise my salary. The automobile industry owes more to Durant than it has yet acknowledged. In some ways, he has been its greatest man."

Between the arguments, Buick managed to build some cars. And all of them, the company said in its 1916 new car announcement, would have six-cylinder engines. *The Automobile* took this as "somewhat of a surprise" and *Motor Age* puzzled about the decision in view of the fact "that the Buick company introduced its six-cylinder model so short a time . . . ago and that the popularity of its four-cylinder car has been so great." But nonetheless, Buick officially produced only sixes for 1916.* Whether this was Chrysler's idea, or Durant's, whether they agreed on it, or disagreed, is problematical. But the Buick rationale, as released to the press, was further standardization of parts, assembly line efficiency, and cost-savings that would make possible a reduction in price of the large six to the $1500 range.

The new small six would be brought in at $985. Its 224-cubic-inch 45 hp engine had a 3¼ by 4½ bore and stroke, compared to the 331-cubic-inch 55 hp six's 3¾ by 5—and at first reporters thought there were considerable variations between the two. But closer inspection revealed the difference essentially to be the block casting of cylinders on the small engine as opposed to the pair-casting of the large, and as one journalist noted, "really, the block casting of the small motor is three pairs joined together, as both motors have crankshafts with four bearings." Birds of a feather actually.

New this year was the use of bronze bushings in the pistons for added life of both wrist pins and pistons. Improved, too, was the Marvel carburetor, used in conjunction with an aluminum manifold branched so as to insure an even supply to each cylinder. A more noteworthy improvement, however, was the clutch. The old coupling, which even a friendly Buick observer allowed was "a little liable to rattle," was replaced by a clutch shaft fashioned of a single piece of steel integral with the constant mesh pinion of the gearset. An entirely new design, the clutch featured a very light aluminum center cone and three small springs arranged in a circle instead of the usual heavy single spring. Adjustment promised to be infinitely simpler now. And an interlocking device on the gearshift prevented the simultaneous engagement of two gears by "improper or careless handling of the gearshift lever." Cantilever rear springs were used on both sixes.

---

*The word "officially" is important. A D-34 roadster, D-35 touring, various export models, the D-4 truck and miscellaneous chassis would be built during the 1916 model year with four-cylinder engines. Buick just didn't mention them much, preferring the promotional cachet of going six all the way.

Wheelbases of the two lines were 115 and 130 respectively, which was viewed as "not much difference in size," but provided for two more passengers in the big six touring car. The small six would accommodate only five. There was both a big and small six roadster, but only the latter six was given closed body styles, a sedan and coupe, rather pricey at $1875 and $1350. What Buick was doing was obvious. It was following the crowd. The "light six" automobile was the industry's newest bandwagon.

In the fall of 1916, Durant reorganized the General Motors Company as the General Motors Corporation, turning the various GM companies, including Buick, into divisions. He replaced the bankers leaving the GM board with the general managers of his car and truck divisions. (The following year, in September 1917, during a reorganization of Buick, Durant himself finally became president of Buick, the nameplate he had promoted from obscurity to fame. He was president for sixty minutes. Chrysler, who had been Buick president since 1916, was reelected president at the end of the hour.)

Because of restrictions on the use of steel and other materials as the United States geared up for World War I, Buick production slid to 115,267 in calendar 1917, and Flint surprised the press again.* The small six had been a smash hit during its introductory year (73,827 of the touring car alone were sold), but Buick nonetheless decided to take a step off the bandwagon. A Buick four was back, officially, an indication, *The Automobile* said, that "there is a big demand for a moderate-priced vehicle of this type." Or that the door to Durant's office had opened and closed.

*Production totals in 1917-1918 vary, because of some confusion as to model introduction dates. Calendar-year U.S. totals are used in the text. For the model years, Buick produced only 55,578 for 1917, but 128,632 for 1918, not including Canada.

The new four had a 3⅜-inch bore, a 4¾-inch stroke and, as the press marveled, "is a high efficiency type, as is seen from the output of 35 hp from a displacement of 170 cubic inches. This is close to 1 hp for every 5 cu. in. displacement." The only variance from traditional Buick practice in this four was the detachable cylinder head; on all other Buicks the valves remained mounted in cages directly in the head. Regarding the chassis, the only departure was the use of semi-elliptic springs instead of cantilever. The wheelbase was 106 inches with "plenty of room for five passengers" and the prices were an attractive $665 for touring and $650 for roadster. Buick sixes were continued unchanged. Flint was preoccupied with other matters by now.

That year, Buick joined the war effort as Chrysler, according to his autobiography, negotiated in three hours a contract with the War Department for the production of up to 3000 Liberty aero engines.

As Chrysler tells it, there were some dramatics to the move into war work. He recalled taking rolls of blueprints from the War Department to Flint, turning his own offices into a drafting room and beginning a marathon schedule of planning and drawing. Cots were brought into the offices and, during one stretch, Chrysler did not go home for two weeks.

When it came to tooling the plant for the Liberty engine, he turned to his master mechanic, K.T. Keller, who eventually became the head of Chrysler Corporation. Chrysler had first noticed Keller when the latter was a member of the GM central office staff, spending most of his time working with Cadillac. He saw in him a man with the same love of machinery that dominated his own life. Later, when Keller moved to other automobile companies, Chrysler kept track of his career and eventually hired him away from the Cole Motor Car Company in Indianapolis. Eventually was not too long, for Keller was Buick's master mechanic before age thirty. He is credited by

Chrysler with moving Buick quickly into war production.

Buick turned out 1338 Liberty engines, mostly twelve-cylinder units though a few were eights; 1.2 million three-inch mortar shells, 1.2 million mortar bases, 1.05 million shell casings, 397,000 cartridge containers, 13,500 trucks and 11,000 sets of truck axles.

Some of the war work was for the British government, including power and driving units for military tractors. Buick even tried its hand at building military tanks for Britain, though only a few experimental models were produced.* Largely because of Buick's production, GM received a gracious note of thanks from Winston Churchill, then minister of munitions. Durant read the letter at a Flint dinner in his (Durant's) honor, then said he would send a cable of reply, offering Churchill good wishes and sincere thanks from Flint, "the birthplace of the General Motors Corporation, the pride of every Flint citizen, everyone without exception interested in the development, progress, ideals and standards of that organization."

Probably the most famous single unit produced by Buick and used during World War I was an ambulance. It looked like a small house or garage attached to a Buick chassis. This machine served the Allied wounded from 1914 to 1917, was captured by the Germans and later retaken by American forces in 1918. The battered vehicle was then awarded the Croix de Guerre by the French government and later it was returned to the United States and placed in the Red Cross museum in Washington.

Because of the military effort, Buick automobile production fell to 77,691 in calendar 1918, and for the first time, Chevrolet production topped Buick's. By the time of the armistice, regular car production was reduced to thirty units a day. Model lines had been simplified. The little six was dropped for '18, and the two sixes which remained used a 242-cubic-inch engine in two model lines differing only in wheelbase, 118 and 124 inches. Detail improvements to the four included a gear-type oil circulating pump to replace the former plunger type, an oil sight on dashboard, an ammeter, a longer control lever "making the car more convenient from the driver's standpoint," a narrower instrument board, trim rails circling the body, seats that were lower and with higher backs, linoleum on the floor in place of rubber, and mohair for the top rather than the cloth fabric used

---

*According to one published account, Walter Marr was called from his home on Signal Mountain for consultation with other leading engineers of the United States and England who were seeking a satisfactory tank for the bomb-torn terrain of European battlefields. He is said to have worked seven straight days, with less than two hours of sleep a night, on an idea for a tank which was approved by Thomas A. Edison and other engineers. The tank parts were then cast and tried out over the immense coal piles in the yards of the Buick factory.

Left: Fitting the camshafts to one of the 1338 Liberty aero engines built by Buick during the war. Above: The Buick test sheds in Flint for the Liberty.

previously. A more streamlined body and slanting windshield made the four-cylinder roadster a racier proposition, and the removable side posts in Buick's most expensive car (the $2175 six sedan) have since led some historians to refer to it as Buick's first "hardtop convertible."

Also notable in 1918 was the sale of the McLaughlin firm to General Motors, although the Canadian Buicks were still called McLaughlins.

The years 1918 and 1919 were big ones for General Motors. In May 1918 the assets of Chevrolet were sold to GM, though Chevrolet continued to exist as a separate holding company for a few years, its function being to hold the controlling block of General Motors stock. At the end of 1918, GM also bought United Motors, a group of supplier firms headed by Alfred P. Sloan, Jr., who became a GM vice-president and director. United Motors had earlier been put together by Durant, with Sloan placed in charge.

Durant remained Durant. He launched what proved to be a calamitous experiment in farm tractor production, which eventually produced a $33 million loss but at least got the Janesville, Wisconsin factories which eventually were used for Chevrolet. Though tractors were a disaster, another Durant idea, investing in a fledgling refrigerator company, was for years a spectacular success—until GM divested itself of Frigidaire in 1979. The name Frigidaire was Durant's idea, too.

As General Motors president, Durant worked with John J. Raskob, a du Pont man and chairman of the GM Finance Committee after the du Pont company invested heavily in GM, in a $25-million postwar expansion program. The corporation, plunging boldly ahead in many directions, created General Motors Acceptance Corporation, designed to finance sales of GM products; developed housing construction companies to build homes for GM workers in Flint, Detroit, Lansing and other cities, and invested large sums in tire, die casting and other manufacturing firms.

During this big expansion, GM made such significant purchases as a sixty-percent interest in the Fisher Body Corporation, the world's largest producer of automobile bodies, and completed buying Charles F. Kettering's companies, including the Dayton Wright Airplane Company in Dayton, Ohio. This brought the inventor of the automobile self-starter fully into the GM fold.

Other major moves included purchase of the Interstate Motor

109

Company of Muncie, Indiana, where the Sheridan car was produced in 1920-1921, and the beginning of work on the General Motors Building (originally the Durant Building) in Detroit, which was to be the world's largest office structure.

Buick prospered along with the rest of the corporation. Production rose to 119,310 in calendar 1919, good for third place behind Ford and Chevrolet, even though Buick again had curtailed its lineup. The 1919 Buicks were designated Series H and all models shared the 242-cubic-inch six-cylinder engine. The in-again/out-again four-cylinder car was out again. Body styles were reduced to five- and seven-

passenger versions of the sedan and touring, a three-passenger roadster and a coupe for four. Still unwinding from the rigors of its military production, and aware that one of the positive benefits of World War I was the public realization of the efficacy of the motorcar, Buick was aware it could sell anything on wheels it built—and consequently kept things as simple as possible.

Internally, however, things were far from simple at General Motors. The clashes between Durant and Chrysler were becoming more bitter.

On one occasion, Dallas Dort announced at a meeting of the Flint Chamber of Commerce that his former carriage partner had just sent a telegram authorizing construction of a $6 million GM plant to build frames for Buick at Flint. In the audience, in contrast to the cheering around him, Chrysler reacted angrily. He stated that GM would not build a frame plant in Flint so long as he was at Buick. One reason he gave was that Flint did not have enough facilities to house the workers already attracted to that city.

The next day, at a GM board meeting in Detroit, Chrysler attacked Durant about the announcement, calling the way it was handled unfair and the decision itself uneconomical. He said he could immediately save GM $1.5 million a year by entering into a new frame contract with the A.O. Smith Company of Milwaukee. A few weeks later he proved it, reaching agreement with the firm. According to Chrysler, the resulting economy was $1.75 million in comparison with the prices GM paid for frames the year before.

Still, Chrysler knew his time with Buick was about up. "Billy was nice to me after that, as nice as only Billy Durant knows how to be, but I felt—indeed, I knew—he could not forgive me for my heated opposition."

They argued about many things. Chrysler complained that Durant paid too much for the Janesville Machine Company for his tractor project. He was concerned about other investments he didn't like. "Billy Durant says he did not like some of them either, but at the time I was arguing with Billy," he wrote. Chrysler claimed Buick was making about half of GM's profits but the corporation was spending much faster than Buick could earn.

Finally, Chrysler told Durant: "Now, Billy, I'm done." Despite attempts by Sloan and others to get him to change his mind, Chrysler could not be dissuaded from leaving. Durant said he paid Chrysler $10 million for the stock he had received in lieu of cash during his three-year contract. It was enough to bankroll what became the Chrysler Corporation a few years later.

Chrysler was followed as Buick president by Harry H. Bassett, who had joined the company in 1916 after C.S. Mott's Weston-Mott Company was consolidated with Buick. When Durant had named

Left: Testing a tank for the British behind the Buick factory. Above: Buick ambulance in France. Below: Armored car by Buick in New York.

Walter Chrysler president of Buick in 1916, Bassett succeeded him as general manager. Now, on January 13th, 1920, Bassett—age forty-four—became Buick's chief and a General Motors vice-president.

Bassett had started in business as an office boy in the Remington Arms Company factory in Ilion, New York. As he rose in that company he was placed in the department of time study and costs—where he learned how to figure to the hundredth of a cent the exact cost of each part manufactured in the plant. When Weston-Mott was still at Utica (New York), C.S. Mott hired Bassett to become assistant superintendent of that automobile axles factory.

In accepting the job, Bassett was leaving a plant employing 2400 people for one employing about 600. But within six months, he was in complete charge of the manufacturing operations. With the move of Weston-Mott to Flint in 1906-1907 at Durant's invitation, Bassett went to that city as works manager. By 1913, Weston-Mott was one of the largest builders of automobile axles in the country, and Bassett was its general manager. Three years later, in 1916, he was elected vice-president as well. That was the year the adjacent Buick Motor Company took over Weston-Mott and in so doing acquired its future top executive.*

Before his sudden death in 1926, Bassett made a mark as a fair and able leader. He also campaigned for construction of a greatly expanded Flint hospital, Hurley Hospital; laid the groundwork for an organization pledged to work for improvements in the city and led the effort which resulted in the construction of General Motors Institute in Flint.

Of Bassett, Sloan once remarked: "Any reference to GM is not complete without mentioning Harry Bassett and his organization at Buick. There was much uncertainty as to the future of the industry in 1919. The confidence in the future of the Buick gave confidence in GM. Again in 1920, Mr. Bassett and Buick stepped in to renew that confidence."

Confidence was a valuable commodity at General Motors in 1920,

---

*In addition to Bassett, other former Weston-Mott employees were moving into key positions at Buick. C.J. Ross, who had started with Weston-Mott in 1904 as a toolmaker and later became its general superintendent, was named general superintendent of the entire Buick complex in 1919, a post he retained until his retirement ten years later. Harvey Mallery, who had begun as Weston-Mott comptroller in 1907, became special auditor at Buick in 1920, a year in which he was elected a GM vice-president, and was named Buick comptroller in 1921. He also retired in 1929. (Ross' successor in '29 was Loron C. Kurtz, also a onetime Weston-Mott employee; Mallery was succeeded by Robert T. Longway, who had been Buick divisional comptroller for years and whose name is enshrined at Flint's Longway Planetarium.) The most famous Weston-Mott employee of them all, Charles Stewart Mott, became Sloan's chief of the advisory staff at the GM corporate level.

for everything began to go wrong. By the end of 1919 GM was, as Raskob pointed out, eight times as large as it was in 1915 when Durant had reasserted his influence in the corporation. But in 1920 the postwar boom came to a halt, and the United States was suddenly in a sharp recession. Automobile sales began to drop rapidly, and dealers were suddenly overstocked.

The corporation, in the midst of its mushrooming, was overextended and short on cash. In a plan developed by Raskob, GM had launched a drive in January to raise $85 million to help finance the expansion program, a plan which included issuing new stock and new debentures. But in five months, only $12 million was brought in. Seeking other avenues, Raskob and Pierre du Pont persuaded J.P. Morgan and Company to become a new partner in GM by forming a syndicate to distribute 1.4 million of the new shares to raise $28 million quickly. Durant and the Morgans had no love for each other, their animosity apparently going back to the ill-fated International Motor Car Company plan of 1908 when they dropped their backing of Durant. But the Morgans could do business with du Pont, and Durant saw the desperate need for new money, so the deal was made.

Durant later contended that this was the beginning of the end for him, though he didn't know it at the time. He claimed that the Morgan representative who became a member of the GM board un-

der the plan, Edward Stettinius, was responsible for the Morgan company dumping 125,000 shares of GM stock on the market at a time GM was trying to stabilize the price by purchasing stock.

Durant was furious. He called Stettinius into his office, according to documents in Durant's papers, and in the presence of Pierre du Pont and John J. Raskob confronted him with the information that the sale of the stock had been traced to him. He asked for an explanation. According to a statement "dictated by Mr. W.C. Durant in the presence of Mr. Stettinius," Durant, who referred to himself in the third person, amplified: "Mr. Stettinius' excuse was that he believed the stock could be repurchased at a lower price but agreed that the [stock-buying] syndicate would support the price [of the stock] at $20 a share. This Mr. Stettinius failed to do, as evidenced by purchase slips at a meeting two or three days later, showing the purchase by Mr. Durant and his friends at less than $20 a share."

According to the statement, Durant told Stettinius that he felt the stock sale was "almost a betrayal of trust" and that it led directly to his personal disaster, his loss of more than $90 million.

Durant apparently never got over that feeling. In a letter sent January 19th, 1973 to the writer, Durant's widow Catherine wrote: "There was never any doubt in my husband's mind that the collapse of GM stock was artificially created . . . that without the connivance

Left: Buick assembly line in 1919. Below: C.S. Mott (second from left, back row), Walter Chrysler and John J. Raskob (fifth and seventh); in the front row, Pierre S. du Pont is fifth from the left; next to him from the left, Billy Durant, A.B.C. Hardy and J. Amory Haskell. Right: Portrait of Harry Bassett.

of some of them [members of the stock syndicate], it could not have happened. He felt that it was engineering by Raskob and Stettinius. When in 1945 Edward Stettinius, Jr. was prominently connected with the writing of the United Nations Charter and was mentioned daily in the newspapers, in discussing the organization one evening at the dinner table Mr. Durant, always a man of peace, asked: 'I wonder if that nice young man knows what his father did to me.' ''

Mrs. Durant, who died in January 1974, added this postscript: "By this letter I don't intend to exonerate my husband entirely for his downfall—merely to acquaint you of my memories."

Durant, however, never wrote a studied report of his version of his downfall at GM in 1920. Stettinius was later quoted as saying he sold the GM stock "for the account of the syndicate" and that the bankers made no money on the transaction, though this does not answer Durant's charge that the action undermined his financial position.

The essential fact was that Durant was buying GM stock not only through a syndicate managed by the Morgans, and supported by GM

leadership, but also outside the syndicate. Durant could not recover from the continual decline of the price of GM stock through 1920. Ever the optimist, he was buying heavily as the price fell, and he was urging old friends to do so likewise. His motives are not entirely clear. He may have been trying to support the corporation, or make a big profit when the price went up, or regain total control from the du Ponts and the Morgans, or crush market short-sellers, or corner the market (which he almost did).

Stock could be bought on a ten percent margin at the time, and as the price continued downward, his friends began to ask him for financial assistance to bail themselves out. No matter how much trouble he was in, Durant was loyal to his friends. And so when these friends who had bought stock on his advice said they were facing ruin, Durant took the stock off their hands.

As he became more preoccupied with his financial problems, the criticism of his leadership began to mount. Durant had been responsible for Walter Chrysler leaving. Durant was responsible for factory

Left: The Buick factory, photographed May 1921. Above: Transport by train in 1915, by barge in 1918. Below: Trucking Buicks during 1923.

inventories getting out of hand. Durant was responsible for the fact that the car divisions, except for Buick and Cadillac, were in poor shape because of inadequate engineering and testing. Durant was always on the phone with his brokers.

Finally it fell apart. In an all-night meeting on November 18th, 1920, the Morgan partners, Raskob, du Pont and Durant reached an agreement: Durant would resign as president of General Motors. The Morgans and du Ponts would raise enough money to make a cash offer for all of Durant's indebtedness. Durant would be left with some money.

The man who had built Buick, Chevrolet and General Motors was gone for good from all three. He would make a spectacular comeback in the 1920's with Durant Motors and its subsidiaries, and become a lion of Wall Street, but eventually his companies would fail, his stock brokers would sell him out. He would lose heavily in the Great Depression of 1929 and declare bankruptcy in 1936.

In his last working years, Durant could be found behind the counter at North Flint Recreation, a bowling alley he established in the shadow of the huge Flint Buick complex he had created decades earlier. Durant opened a small restaurant too, and one Flint car dealer liked to take his salesmen there so, as he put it, the founder of General Motors could sell them a hamburger.

Durant was unbroken. His was not a bowling alley, but a classy bowling establishment with a wholesome atmosphere for all members of a family. He had plans to start a chain of them across the country. And he loved to sit in his restaurant (the first drive-in eating establishment in Flint) with the manager, and talk to her about the new equipment they would buy. Occasionally he would bring his aide, Aristo Scrobogna, in from the East and have him cook spaghetti for Charles Stewart Mott and other old auto leaders in private dinners at the place. One day he threw a breakfast for the bowling alley's pinboys. He told one interviewer: "I haven't a dollar, but I'm happy and I'm carrying on because I can't stop. There's more to life than money."

Of Durant, John J. Carton, his old personal lawyer, once told historian Arthur Pound: "Billy never thought that GM would become the big manufacturer it did. What he desired, most of all, were large stock issues in which he, from an inside position, could dicker and trade. After Billy left Durant-Dort for Buick there were always too many yes men around him for his own good. Dallas Dort and Charlie Nash and Fred Aldrich and the rest of them in Durant-Dort could bring Billy down to earth. Away from them he just soared, high, wide and handsome."

The recession's effect on General Motors was more apparent in 1921 statistics than in those for 1920, for the latter year had started

strongly. Buick produced 115,176 cars in 1920, only 82,930 in 1921.*
Yet the health of the entire industry was such that while in 1920
Buick was only fourth in sales (behind Ford, Dodge and Chevrolet),
the lower figure the year following was good enough for second place.
Indeed, Alfred P. Sloan, Jr. has written that in 1921 Buick and
Cadillac were the only GM cars that were making any money.

In this period, Sloan reminisced, "It was Buick that made any kind
of General Motors car line worth talking about." He felt this so
strongly that in 1921 he wrote to Pierre du Pont: "It is far better that
the rest of General Motors be scrapped than any chances taken with
Buick's earning power."

The evidence strongly suggests that Buick, the financial rock on
which Durant founded General Motors in 1908, remained the financial rock that pulled GM through the disaster of 1920-1921, until
Sloan's strong new management techniques could build GM into
what has become the largest manufacturing empire in history.

The 1920-1921 years did not produce many revisions in the Buick
product. "Old Prices, Slight Changes" was one appropriate press
headline for the 1920 line. Most significant that year were the stiffer
springs on heavier body styles "to prevent contact of the bumpers
and the frame when traveling over rough roads" and the nice idea of
an adjustment stop on the steering gear to allow for more than one
turning radius. Nineteen twenty-two brought revisions which, according to J. Edward Schipper in *Automotive Industries*, "appear to
be based upon reports of service departments to provide greater wear
and increased accessibility and convenience for the owner and service
station." Quietness, too, was another aim in such detail refinements
as larger piston pins and a more positive method of anchoring them,
a stiffer support for the pump shaft bearing, the reaming of all bearings after bolting to the crankcase. Since these improvements could

---

*Interestingly, some of these cars were built outside of Michigan. This was
the result of the railroad car shortage at the time and the clever idea that Win
Stephens of the Pence Automobile Company in Minneapolis came up with.
He decided to get his Buicks unassembled—the bodies arriving from their
original source; frames from theirs; wheels, tires and other items from
theirs—because obviously he could get more Buicks that way, whole
automobiles requiring considerably more space in a rail car than their component parts neatly stacked. In a large Pence warehouse in north Minneapolis,
and with the assistance of only one man from Flint, the cars were put together.
It worked, and within a year Minneapolis was assembling seventy-five cars a
day for the use of the Pence company and for other areas such as Salt Lake
City, Portland and Seattle. Meantime Buick had decided the idea was good
but the location was too far north, so all the assembly line machinery was
shipped to St. Louis, Missouri and set up in a plant there. Buick then shipped
enough material to build 1000 cars, delivering 700 of them to dealers in the
Midwest and West, 300 to Pence if Stephens agreed to supervise their
assembly, which he did, shipping the cars back to Minneapolis by rail.

*Above: 1920 K-49 touring and K-50 sedan. Below: 1921 Model 21-46 coupe.
Right: Commercial cars from 1922; the sport touring Model 22-55 of 1922.*

Same Remarkable Buick Values Found in New Special Delivery

Open Body with Cab Complete $840

Canopy Top with Screen Sides Complete $875

Canopy Top Delivery Complete $855

Combination Passenger and Express Complete $935

As in the case of the passenger models, the Buick Special Delivery has been redesigned to make it better and more efficient in every department of motoring service. These changes include virtually all the important units of the car. The bodies have also been improved in appearance and in construction.

Any one of the six body styles is generous in its roominess and is finished and equipped throughout with the best of materials and workmanship.

And combined with the good qualities of the Buick chassis, each is genuinely economical from every standpoint.

All prices f. o. b. Flint, Michigan

Ask about the G. M. A. C. Purchase Plan which provides for Deferred Payments

Buick Motor Company, Flint, Michigan

Division of General Motors Corporation
Pioneer Builders of Valve-in-Head Motor Cars
Branches in All Principal Cities—Dealers Everywhere

not be seen, Buick provided a few more that could, styling the cars with a narrower, higher radiator and raising the cowl a couple of inches for the straight-line effect. Essentially the cars were the same otherwise, save for their designations which were K series for 1920, 21 series for 1921.

An interesting road test of a new 1920 Buick appeared in the British magazine *The Motor* in March of that year and offers a valuable first-hand impression of what owning a Buick in that era meant. "At the present time one can feel that the various parts of the chassis have not quite taken upon themselves a working finish and there is a suggestion of stiffness which will, doubtless, disappear after a few hundred miles have been covered," the magazine commented. "The springs, for instance are at present rather stiff. This is a good fault, as it means that the machine has been carried out to close limits and no slackness will be in evidence for some time to come .... In town the flexibility of the six-cylinder overhead valved engine is a very praiseworthy characteristic. In the thickest traffic it appears possible to pick up from practically a walking pace without easing the clutch, and this without any indication of unwillingness on the part of the engine."

Further, *The Motor* said, Buick obviously had in mind "the type of motorist who has to look after his own car. All grease cups and adjustments are accessibly situated. Lubrication of chassis parts is a comparatively simple matter and, in addition, the grease retainers are made of such a size that the supply is sufficient for several hundreds of miles on the road. In place of milled edges to afford a grip on the movable part of the cups, a neat flat projection is provided, so that no matter how greasy the operator's hands may become, he can always get a grip to screw the cup tight."

And in conclusion, and verifying that Flint had indeed solved the problem, *The Motor* mentioned, "There is another feature about the Buick which is worthy of note. The clutch and gearbox unit displays no trace of that annoying looseness which is to be found on a number of American productions. One can distinctly feel the invisible gate when changing gear, so that there is practically no risk of a noisy or faulty change being made. Altogether . . . an excellent all-purpose vehicle."

For 1922 Buick offered a new excellent, all-purpose vehicle. "Buick Comes to Bat with Its Four" was one trade magazine headline, in what—if memory serves—was its third inning in six years. Although this time the four was back apparently because dealers had clamored for it.

As one reporter noted, Buick dealers were "a powerful and well established body" and to withhold a car they very much wanted to sell "might involve in time if not immediately a division of allegiance."

Above: Sales manager Ed Strong, with the millionth Buick built, a 1923 Model 23-55 Sport Touring. Below: From the left, motor plant manager William Beacraft, research engineer Eugene C. Richard (who patented valve-in-head engine), superintendent C.J. Ross, assistant chief engineer F.A. "Dutch" Bower, chief engineer Enos DeWaters. Right: 1923 Model 23-44 roadster.

That being a possibility unwanted in Flint, a four was provided, "as tight a little competitor as any dealer could wish in the almost-a-thousand-dollar class."

Again the engine was a 170-cubic-inch unit (3⅜ by 4¾ bore and stroke) with 35 to 40 brake horsepower claimed—and a wheelbase of 109 inches, three more than Buick's last four. Other than refinements which had occurred in the meantime to the six and which could be incorporated, the new four was basically similar to the old four. Its oiling system was combination pressure and splash, cooling water circulated by pump, a Marvel carburetor was standard (and provided now with a new automatic heating system interconnected with the throttle so that heat supplied would vary with engine speed), the clutch multiple disc, drive Hotchkiss type, springs semi-elliptics all around.

Distinctions the new Buick offered from the norm of fours in its price class included a turning radius of an admirable thirty-six feet despite its longer wheelbase, a weight above the ton mark which meant durability in those days, and a new tire size (31x4 straight-sided cord "built to Buick specifications") which promised more pleasant riding qualities than the usual 31x3½.

There was a certain cockiness now to Buick advertising, both from Flint and the field. "Just count the Buicks Saturday at the Big Game," one 1922 ad read. "In driving to the Stanford Stadium make a mental note of the popularity of the Buick. You'll see them by the thousands performing like the champion University of California football team. Always in the lead."

By 1923 the postwar depression was over, replaced by the first boom of the Roaring Twenties. Buick was more ready than ever. Nothing fundamentally was changed but there were refinements throughout: a new foundry practice of "chilling" the cylinder bore for a harder casting, longer connecting rods, longer pistons, a new and larger crankshaft used together with connecting rod and main bearings of hard babbitt, revised rear spring hanger positions to eliminate rebound and side sway, a lower body suspension and a new top to eliminate noise in six-cylinder closed cars, rounded-edge window frames and "anti-rattler catches" on windows, a longer gearshift lever, a windshield wiper, a transmission lock "which will reduce theft insurance rate by twenty percent."

The new Buicks had new lines, a sleeker look—and perhaps most significant, an across-the-board reduction in price tag. The price-leading six-cylinder five-passenger touring car in 1922, for example, sold for $1525, $1395 after New Year's Day of '22; in '23 the same but improved car sold for $1195. Buick produced 45,227 of them, and 47 for export.

Twenty-five units of another 1923 model, the seven-passenger six-

cylinder touring, were shipped overseas too. One of them became famous. It was bought by writer/traveler Lowell Thomas and driven on a widely reported trip to Afghanistan. He claimed he and his entourage were the first outsiders to penetrate that country in an automobile.

Meanwhile the Buick four was winning signal honors in Japan as the lowest gasoline consumer (18.08 mpg) amongst a dozen American entries undergoing tests conducted by the military there. Indeed, only three cars in the entire competition used less fuel than the Buick, all of them of much less horsepower, one of them a little two-cylinder "Jinrickashawette."

At the other end of the Buick lineup was the return of the roadster on the big chassis, the "Special 6-54"—introduced in 1916 but not built since that year. It came back with a vengeance. On April 17th, 1923, racing driver Joe Nikrent—timed officially by the AAA with the celebrated Fred Wagner acting as starter—stormed across the dry lake near Muroc, California in a mildly tweaked example of the

model and hit 108.24 mph.

"Buick does not intend to again enter the racing game . . .," advertising demurred. "This performance was just another little demonstration to call attention to the fact that the 1923 Buick is the greatest Buick ever built . . ."

There were more of them built too. Buick was in robust health, topping the 200,000 production mark for the first time. The precise figure was 201,572 cars and trucks (like many other manufacturers Buick would discontinue commercial vehicle production hereafter). Only Ford and Chevrolet outproduced Buick in 1923.

In 1923, too, Buick built its one-millionth car. It was an appropriate year for such a milestone, emphasizing the staying power of a marque now approaching its twentieth birthday, a marque which had itself given birth to General Motors in 1908 and had meant so much to GM's survival in 1920-1921. Now Buick and General Motors had turned the corner. The future of David Buick's dream and Billy Durant's effort certainly looked secure.

Chapter Seven

BUILDING TO A SILVER ANNIVERSARY

"Unprecedented," Harry Bassett said. That was how he saw it: August 1st, 1923, when Buick Day was celebrated. It wasn't an anniversary, nothing like that—nothing more really than the introduction of the new Buick line for 1924—but it had been played up rather more enthusiastically than usual. Two thousand dealers across the country had rushed to their local newspaper offices with full-page advertisements in hand telling all about the new Buicks. There was a lot to tell.

They had four-wheel brakes. The idea of providing stopping power at each corner of an automobile was scarcely new, of course, but the idea of providing it in a mass-produced American automobile was. Rickenbacker had been first with the announcement, followed quickly by Packard—and now Buick. Cadillac and Oakland, among others, were expected to join in momentarily. Expected, too, was some adverse reaction to the concept—and it came, via Studebaker for example in a concerted advertising campaign declaring four-wheel braking to be unsafe. Still, it was an idea whose time had assuredly come and, as Buick noted, "when it is realized that the brakes now used on the front wheels are exactly the same type of construction that has been used for years on the rear wheels, it is readily seen that Buick is making no experiment in their adoption of four-wheel brakes."

Two and a half years of research and development which, one reporter noted, "carried the engineers to Europe for investigation of the many curious braking layouts to be found only over there," and 150,000 miles of road testing, preceded the Buick announcement.

The Buick system was a simple one, with both front and rear brakes of the external contracting type and interchangeable on all four wheels. Except for the universal joints necessary to permit the deflection of the front wheels in steering, the Buick brakes were applied in exactly the same way as conventional outside brakes on the rear wheels only.

An interesting design feature was the anchoring of the bands to their spiders so as to give a three-quarter wrap when moving forward. A single-acting brake, with the band anchored at one end, had long been viewed as undesirable; when brake pressure was applied, it tended to wrap itself more tightly around the drum, and when the drum turned in the opposite direction to unwrap. Conversely, a band anchored in the middle was equally effective in both directions, but more effort was required to secure the same retarding effect as with a single-acting band. The Buick three-quarter-point anchor had the virtual effectiveness of a full-wrapping brake when rolling forward, and since rolling backward seldom required full braking power, no safety factor was compromised. It seemed to work well.

The Autocar, in its road test of one of the new Buicks, noted the prejudice against contracting bands (difficulty in adjustment and exposure in full to mud) and the advantages (better contact with more of the drum) vis-à-vis the expanding shoe principle which was more popular in Europe. "During the course of the test, which was in very evil weather," the report concluded, "the car was taken as much as possible down side lanes which were inches deep in sticky clay or chalk mud, the result being that the whole of the brake gear was bathed in mud. It was quite definite that there were no bad results, and that the wheels were as free at the end of the time as they had been at the beginning, while there seemed at no time to be any suggestion of binding. The power of the brakes is undoubted and, by reason of the leverage chosen and the compensation of the rear and front sets, it does not need great effort to apply the bands to their full extent. . . . the stopping power is all that could be required, and this fact immensely increases the capability of the car." *The Autocar* was left only to cavil that Buick's brakes "are not so neat and possibly are more difficult to keep clean" than the expanding shoe variety.

Caviling aside, four-wheel brakes were only one part of the Buick story for 1924. Equally significant from a promotional point of view—particularly since the anti-four-wheel-brake propaganda initially put the company on the defensive—was the 1924 Buick as a whole. Without changing any fundamental aspect of its character, the new Buick was, for the most part, exactly that. New.

The venerable four-cylinder engine remained much the same—and the reason for that was apparent the year following—but the six was given a quarter-inch increase in stroke (for 255 cubic inches), larger

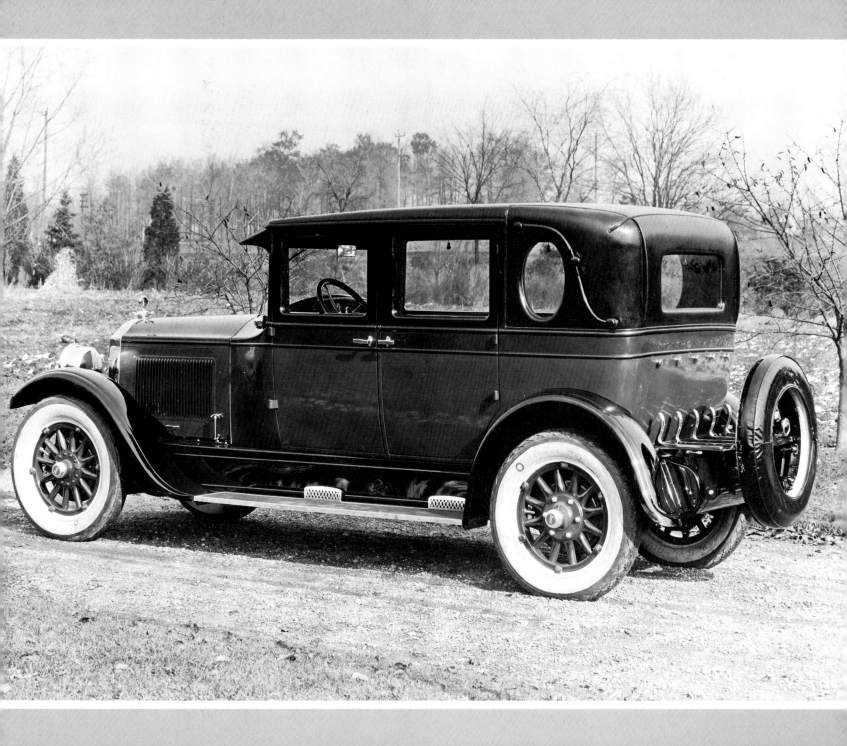

Page preceding: 1926 Master Six Brougham Sedan. Above: Showroom display of new 1924 models in a Wisconsin dealership. Below: 1924 Model 24-48.

Six-Cylinder Four-Passenger Coupe
The Standard of Comparison

THE new and roomy four-passenger, six-cylinder Buick Coupe is everywhere finding marked favor among women. Its impressive grace and beauty, its luxurious appointments and its general tone of richness and elegance exert an irresistible appeal. This appeal is further heightened by the greater certainty of control and safety contributed by the proved Buick four-wheel brakes and the greater smoothness and flexibility of its more powerful Buick valve-in-head engine. These are among the many advanced mechanical features that make this coupe the ideal car for women who delight in doing their own driving.

WHEN BETTER AUTOMOBILES ARE BUILT, BUICK WILL BUILD THE

BUICK MOTOR COMPANY, FLINT, MICHIGAN
Division of General Motors Corporation
Pioneer Builders of Valve-in-Head Motor Cars · Branches in All Principal Cities—Dealers Everywhere

valves (this made possible by the engine's now detachable head), higher compression, redesigned intake passages, larger crankshaft, a new Marvel carburetor (with full exhaust heat control regulated by the throttle opening and also controlled manually from the dash), a full pressure lubrication system (with a drilled crankshaft to carry oil to all connecting rod bearings). It had been quite a design overhaul, and the result was about fifty percent more power: 70 bhp at 2800 rpm.

The cars were bigger on the outside, and interiors were more roomy. Frames and axles were strengthened to accommodate the new brakes on both four- and six-cylinder models. And both cars were given a fresh appeal in styling, a new high radiator contour, high crowned fenders, smoother and longer lines to the body, a sharp edge at the hood. The look was especially effective in closed cars, among them the town car bearing, as was widely said at the time, "a degree of luxurious finish remarkable to a car selling under $3000."

Automobile Topics noted that the new Buick line as a whole offered "the purchaser a more aristocratic body than has heretofore been included in the Buick lineup"—and at an increase in price ($50-$130) which the *Automobile Trade Journal* found "surprisingly small" in consideration of the improvements and refinements received. Some 171,561 of the new cars would be built, fewer than the model year previous but still the second best ever thus far in Buick's history, and accomplished in a year when design changes were both more numerous and more pronounced—and thus more potentially time-consuming on the assembly line—than Buick had experienced since its earliest days.

The Buick was selling spectacularly well, better than many cars beneath its price range, superlatively more than cars above it. There was only one problem. The new car looked rather like a Packard. Obviously this did not bother Buick dealers or customers. But it bothered Packard.

For months there were rumors that a lawsuit for design infringement would be initiated at East Grand Boulevard in Detroit where Packard people couldn't help but notice the radiator design similarity. Apparently, Packard president Alvan Macauley's sense of noblesse oblige prevailed. As was pointedly said in the press, "whether no action was taken because no infringement was discovered by the Packard company . . . or because it believes imitation to be the sincerest form of flattery, has not been disclosed." What Packard said in a few advertisements was, "When prettier cars are built, Packard will build them."

Sales figures aside, this was not the sort of public exposure that benefited Buick, and the adverse publicity did the marque's image no good. But it was also a matter easily fixed.

A subtle redefinition of the Buick look for 1925 resolved the matter to Flint's satisfaction, and Packard returned to its own advertising slogan about asking the man who owns one. Buick had important news "unexpectedly disclosed" now which tended to obliterate any notions of plagiarism still wafting about in any case.

It was a new six, to replace the Buick fours. (They were truly gone now; it would be a half century before Buick would again build a four-cylinder car.) Set on a 114-5/16-inch wheelbase and given eight body styles, the new Buick six was called the Standard. Its 3 by 4½-inch 191-cubic-inch motor developed 50 hp at 2800 rpm, and with an unusually flat torque curve (120 lb/ft at 1600 rpm) provided for hefty pulling power at low speeds. The ratio of rear axle torque to weight was substantially the same as the bigger Buick six, which meant that the new six was practically its performing equal. It promised to be a winner, and it didn't disappoint.

Lest Flint be accused of neglecting its other six, Buick renamed it the Master and provided roomier bodies. Wheelbases increased in 1924 to 124″, and 128″ continued. Buick proceeded to build as many of both Standard and Master series cars as it possibly could: 192,100 of them. Buick was roaring with the Twenties.

Goldfish gulping and flagpole sitting were but two of the more inane bits of foolishness the decade prompted. The publicity stunt—and the wackier the better—had come of age. Who thought up most of them is generally unrecorded, and deservedly so. The author of Buick's version merits recognition, however, though he is unfortunately unknown. Buick's stunt had a certain patina of the bizarre, but it made good sense too, and was great promotion: the sending of a 1925 touring car around the world—without a driver. The idea was to demonstrate the worldwide dealer and service network of Buick and General Motors.

Leaving New York by boat in December 1924, the car returned in about six months with nearly 20,000 miles on its odometer and having covered that many miles on water. Each dealer or distributor along the way was responsible for delivering the "Around the World" Buick to its next stop. The log book carried inside it was signed by the dignitaries of many lands, and the Buick was ceremonially photographed in front of the Sphinx and pyramids of Egypt. After circling the globe it continued to tour the United States in the same way, driven by each dealer to the next, until its mileage ran into the hundreds of thousands. The car had passed through Flint June 19th on its way to New York near the end of its first lap of the world. Already 600 dealers had driven it.

Six weeks later, on July 31st, 1925, the new Buick line for 1926 was introduced. It was the beginning of the end of an era.

No one in Flint recognized it. From executive to file clerk to

Above: Jack Dempsey with his new 1924 Model 24-54 Sport Roadster. Below: Ad from February 1924; note the last sentence mention of four-wheel brakes.

The Six-Cylinder Five-Passenger Brougham Sedan
The Standard of Comparison

BUICK establishes a new style in motor cars with its five-passenger Brougham Sedan. Built both for luxurious touring and general family service, its design is of exclusive Buick origin. Its rich and comfortable upholstery and the unique accommodation it provides for a full size steamer trunk are refinements that women will particularly appreciate. Greater power and greater driving safety with its new Buick valve-in-head motor and the proved Buick four-wheel brakes are important among the many other features of this distinctive car.

WHEN BETTER AUTOMOBILES ARE BUILT, BUICK WILL BUILD THEM

BUICK MOTOR COMPANY, FLINT, MICHIGAN
Division of General Motors Corporation
Pioneer Builders of Valve-in-Head Motor Cars   Branches in All Principal Cities — Dealers Everywhere

assembly line worker, everyone was much too busy seeing that production records were set and congratulating themselves when sales figures arrived from the dealer network. The 1926 Buicks would go down in the record books as among the most important ever introduced by the company. The 266,753 cars produced during 1926 would represent the company's greatest calendar production year since it all began. What could go wrong with everything going so right?

Complacency reigned in Flint.

The period following World War I had brought a new sophistication to the automobile. Self-starters, reliable electrical equipment, enclosed bodies, four-wheel brakes, stoplights, automatic windshield wipers, engine vibration dampers and a host of other engineering advances and convenience features had rendered motoring both practical and pleasurable. The headache that was once part and parcel of motorcar ownership had largely gone away. America had been put solidly on wheels. And manufacturers were learning yearly of new ways to get more and more of those wheels on the road.

Market saturation had never before been a problem. The number of cars sold was dictated more by the capacity of the factories building them than it was by the number of people willing and ready to purchase them. That there might be too many cars and not enough purchasers wasn't considered—until the mid-Twenties brought ominous warnings from some industry observers that a saturation point might one day be reached. Nonsense, said the manufacturers, these people are alarmists, they're silly Cassandras. During the first week of February 1926, Harry Bassett, in an interview published by Dow, Jones & Company, was quoted as seeing "no reason to apprehend overstocking of dealers this year." Instead, trade publication headlines carried such news as "Buick October Shipments Break All Monthly Marks," "Buick to Produce 1200 Cars per Day," "Buick Maintaining a Heavy Schedule," "Buick . . . 31,000 Cars Ahead of 1924 Output," "Buick Approaching Maximum Production," "Buick Handles 86,422 Carloads," "Buick Shipments Far Ahead of Last Year."

But with more and more cars being produced, it followed that competition among manufacturers would be keener too. And with more and more cars available, it followed that prospective purchasers could become more choosey. With the practical requirements of a motorcar met, they could begin demanding better performance, better styling, better value. Or, at the very least, they would opt for those motorcars which best provided those qualities. This really was no time for complacency. That it was pervasive at Flint was simply because the people managing Buick were, after all, only human.

The first choice of space at the national automobile shows in New York and Chicago traditionally was awarded to the member of the National Automobile Chamber of Commerce boasting the largest dollar volume of sales the year preceding. Buick had won it in 1919. In 1926 the company did again, for the eighth straight year.

"Again Buick Has Built a Better Automobile," the ads would headline. "To be as Good as Buick a car would need to have . . . " And there was no doubting that the line for 1926 was a very marketable one. In a prosperous year, it hit the target straight on. More than fifteen thousand customer orders for the new cars were written by dealers on the first day of the public showing. Telegrams to Flint with order increases followed, and many distributors thereafter personally traveled to the factory to request additional allotments.

There were a number of reasons for the ready public acceptance of the new Buick line. The cars were well styled, had good performance—and, perhaps most important, were introduced with price reductions ranging from fifty to five hundred dollars over the year previous. In the face of an expanding automobile market, this last was an especial boon. For a lot of people, it changed the question of "can I afford to buy a car" to "how can I afford not to buy a Buick at those low prices?"

From the little two-passenger Standard Six coupe to the big seven-passenger Master Six sedan, there were sixteen Buicks in all, six in the Standard line, ten in the Master series. Engine improvements represented their most significant advances. With a slight increase in bore, Buick was able to raise the horsepower in both the Standard and Master powerplants, the eight percent displacement increase resulting in a sixteen percent jump in horsepower. Standard engines were now 207 cubic inches and 60 hp, Masters were 274 cubic inches and 75 hp, with torque increasing to 140 and 178 ft/lb respectively. Performance for the new Standards was a 70 mph maximum and 16-18 mpg, for the new Masters it was 75 mph and 14-16 mpg. Mention of this was frequently advertised.

Advertised too was the addition of an air filter, the new unit designed to start intake air spinning as it entered the air cleaner and then use centrifugal force to separate two substances of different specific gravities: air and dust. After a 4000-mile drive at the new General Motors proving grounds in Milford, a test car with the new filter collected some 3.62 ounces of abrasive dirt. Metal mesh and cotton fabric comprising 450 square inches made up the filters. Mounted behind the air cleaners were new Marvel carburetors. New intake manifolding to provide more efficiency was developed for the new carburetion.

Filtering the air wasn't Buick's only new idea. Developed too were

Page opposite: Buicks for 1925, the Master Six coupe, the Standard Six coach, the Master Six Brougham Sedan, respectively. Above: Buick at the New York Automobile Show in 1925. Below: The "three-seated combination utility passenger and baggage body called the 'Beverly' " built on a '25 Master Six chassis by the Cotton Body Company in Boston, Massachusetts.

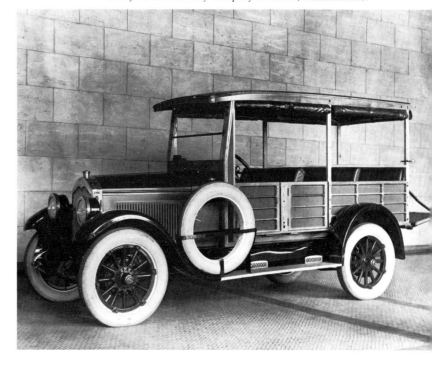

A Buick 1925 Master Six, Model 49, in Moscow's Red Square at the finish of a Leningrad-to-Moscow endurance and reliability run it won in 1925 (see pg. 413). Buicks for 1926: below, Pete De Paolo (at the wheel) and Tommy Milton with the Master Six Sport Touring on the boards at Charlotte (N.C.) Speedway. Above right: The Master Six seven-passenger sedan and the Master Six Sport Touring. Below right: Advertising the 1926 Buicks.

WHEN BETTER AUTOMOBILES ARE BUILT, BUICK WILL BUILD THEM

With its 75 horsepower, 75 mile-an-hour performance, the Better Buick is as different from the usual car as June from December. Undiscovered pleasures in motoring—undiscovered economy in ownership are now found in the Better Buick.

- - *The Better Buick* - -

The Better Buick

new gas and oil filters to further improve the "sealed chassis" concept. The oil filters, mounted on the firewall, incorporated a device with a handle, a quick check feature to determine whether the unit was operating properly or was plugged. Turning the handle allowed oil to exit from a hole on the face of the filter indicating everything was copacetic. If the filter had become plugged, the oil would be rerouted by a check valve back into the engine to assure proper lubrication. It was claimed that at a speed of twenty miles an hour, the entire oil supply was filtered every five minutes. The gasoline strainer, as Buick called its new fuel filter, used a fine gauge copper screen inside a glass bowl which was to be removed and cleaned every few thousand miles.

With the power improvements for 1926, Buick engineers deemed it wise to strengthen the multiple disc clutch pack as well as other driveline componentry. Transmission gears were beefed up, together with axles and frames. The water pump was a freshly designed unit with only one packing nut. The former combination starter and generator was dropped in favor of a separate two-unit system. The gearshift control lever was lengthened to make "shifting possible with the tips of your fingers." Headlamps were of the dual-beam type controlled by a switch in the center of the steering wheel. Mounted on a tie bar running across the front of the radiator, they had a new look and the practical advantage of not deviating in aim or alignment in the event of a minor front-end collision. For the first time, hubcaps, gasoline filler caps and crankshaft cover plugs were aluminum stampings instead of nickel-plated brass.

The opening of the new proving grounds would prove a godsend to every test engineer in every division within General Motors, and Buick was quick to capitalize on the new facility. Its Milford location had been chosen for reasons of its central proximity, twenty-five miles from Oakland and Pontiac offices, forty miles from Buick, Cadillac and Chevrolet, and fifty miles from Oldsmobile. With a 35 mph speed limit prevailing in Michigan at that time, it took the men from Flint about an hour and a half to drive the distance in the morning, about the same on the return trip that evening. Though sometimes they remained at the proving grounds longer than that.

The steady, high speed driving afforded by the new GM track would locate for engineers the source of numerous problems being reported from the field. One example, in Buick's case, was valve head burning. Rain or shine, day and night, test drivers ran at speed, as many as twenty and thirty Buicks on the track at one time, the fastest models in front as the leaders and to break wind resistance for the smaller, slower cars behind them. Wide open throttle, with ten to fifteen feet clearance between each car, it was an automotive "crack the whip," the idea being to put miles on the vehicles as quickly as possible and to fail the engines with the valve head problem. Drivers averaged five hundred miles a shift; when they ran low on gasoline, they pulled off, refueled, checked their oil and went right back on the track at full throttle again.

It must have been something to see. As one of the test drivers, Howard Clark, described it, "You had only about enough clearance to see the tailpipe of the guy in front of you. If he failed a valve and the head burned off, all you could see was a steady stream of black smoke pouring out the tailpipe. He would then pull to the side of the road, the line would close up, and the wrecker would come and haul him away."

Testing for the valve problem began in the latter part of 1926, continued into the early months of 1927 and was ultimately corrected in time for the 1929 anniversary year cars. It was Buick engineer John Foster who discovered the failures were being caused by inadequate cylinder head cooling at the exhaust port seats. As heat built up, the exhaust valves began to pound in their seats, eventually burning the head off. When this happened, the molten steel head of the burned off valve would be forced through the top of the piston and down into the oil pan. Foster corrected the problem by redesigning the water passages in the head for better valve cooling.

Being a test driver in the mid-1920's was always interesting but it wasn't always fun. Buick's foreman at Milford believed that if his drivers became too comfortable during testing, they might fall asleep and accidents would follow. As a result, no matter what the season, no Buick test vehicle ever had a heater installed. Michigan's winters are not temperate, of course, and Buick's drivers were not at all anxious to freeze while on duty. There was a solution. Located in one of the garages at the track was an emergency fire truck with a good supply of kerosene lanterns. When the chill winds blew, many a Buick driver would be seen sneaking away from the fire truck, lantern in hand. It would be placed on the floorboard of the test car, under a blanket covering the driver's legs. No Buick driver ever froze. No Buick driver ever fell asleep. And no fires were ever reported.

Not from the lanterns anyway. But the unexpected remained the rule. Howard Clark recalled one testing day when the glass jar on the bottom of his vacuum fuel tank loosened causing gasoline to drip on the cherry red hot exhaust manifold. He noticed something was wrong when flames began shooting up around the steering column mast jacket. He stopped immediately and made good use of his fire extinguisher.

Although engine refinements were the most marked changes to Buicks for 1926, attention had been given the car throughout. The edges of the radiator shell were rounded for a more modern look.
Zerk fittings were installed at all lubrication spots on the chassis to

Above: The 1927 Standard Model 26 coupe; the 1927 Master Six Sport Roadst

for nine consecutive years Buick has been first in volume of sales among all the members of the National Automobile Chamber of Commerce. Only a very superior motor car could have established its leadership so conclusively.

THE GREATEST BUICK EVER BUILT
WHEN BETTER AUTOMOBILES ARE BUILT   BUICK WILL BUILD THEM

with accessory windshield. Below: Advertising in 1927 (left), '28 (right).

JUNE 1928

BUICK
One of the Good Things of Life

A motor car may be only a motor car—*but a Buick is a Buick*—one of the good things of life to every man or woman fortunate enough to possess one.

The difference between Buick and ordinary cars is the difference between the superlative and the commonplace; and that difference is apparent in every phase of Buick design.

You'll find it in the smarter, more distinctive lines of Buick bodies by Fisher—in the matchless riding comfort of Buick's Lovejoy hydraulic shock absorbers and cantilever springs—and above all, in the vibrationless performance of Buick's famous Valve-in-Head six-cylinder engine.

Decide now to enjoy this finer kind of motoring . . . make your next car a Buick.

WHEN BETTER AUTOMOBILES ARE BUILT...BUICK WILL BUILD THEM

allow easier maintenance and longer life at friction points. Brake linings were one-piece construction instead of two. New body mounts gave additional support to closed cars, and seats were more comfortable in all models. Door locks were integral with new bar-type door handles. Two belt moldings, one above and the other below the door handles, were featured on all cars.

"All records for attendance and enthusiasm went by the boards when unprecedented crowds of motor fans fairly mobbed the local Buick dealer's headquarters in an attempt to get a look at the new 1926 models." Thus did one reporter enthusiastically sum up what happened in his town when the new Buicks arrived. Pretty much the same thing occurred in most showrooms throughout the country. Nineteen twenty-six was, as mentioned, a record-breaking year. It was decisive, too, for another reason, one infinitely sadder and, for Buick, most unfortunate. Harry Bassett died on October 17th.

His death was a shock. On September 22nd, he had left New York with Cadillac president Lawrence P. Fisher on a business trip to Europe. A bad cold interrupted his annual visit to the Paris Salon, but he thought little more about it. When the cold didn't improve, he checked into the American hospital at Neuilly. He died there four days later of bronchial pneumonia. He was only fifty-one years old. "A popular leader among his own associates and a splendid type of all-round man," the press said. He was keenly mourned. He would be very much missed.

His successor was announced by Alfred P. Sloan, Jr. six weeks later. The choice was perhaps a logical one: Edward Thomas Strong. "One of the upstanding figures of the industry," *Automobile Topics* remarked. And all the trade magazines recounted how this son of an Imlay City blacksmith had studied farm machinery as a boy, went to work after his high school graduation for McCormick Harvester setting up its machinery in the field initially, then selling it, traveling his territory in a Buick he bought in 1908 in Lapeer. His career with the Flint company began a few years after that, and in 1916 he became Buick's general sales manager. On June 1st, 1926, he had celebrated his tenth anniversary in that position, and it was noted then that "under Strong's guidance, the Company has sold 1,360,259 Buick cars or 84 percent of all the Company has ever manufactured." Now it was reported that Buick dealers "are rejoiced" at Strong's selection as the company's new president and general manager. "He has the marked advantage of having worked up through the branches and into the factory, so that the problems of the retailer are an old and familiar story to him," the press said. "In addition he is personally acquainted with the Buick dealers far and wide, possesses their confidence and has played an important part in the upbuilding of the organization to the point where it is one of the most cohesive, as well as one of the most prosperous, in the industry."

But managing sales for a company and managing a company are two different things entirely. As Buick's president, Ed Strong would not prove nearly as effective as he had as its sales manager. He would now be making decisions regarding Buick's future products. Charged with managing their sales was C.W. Churchill, former general sales manager and general manager for Winton in Cleveland and a member of the Buick sales staff in Flint since 1921. For the first six months in his new job, he had rather an easy time of it.

The Buicks for 1927 had been introduced, as traditional, during mid-summer of 1926, before Harry Bassett's death. They were very well received. It seemed like business as usual in Flint.

It is interesting to reflect upon the public image of Buick during this turning-point period in its history. Even the press seemed to share Flint's complacency. The report regarding the new cars in the July 31st, 1926 issue of *Automobile Topics* is representative, if a bit ponderous: "In the resourcefulness and sureness of stride that has enabled it to show a clean pair of heels to a considerable portion of the automobile industry, year after year, the Buick Motor Co. has inspired a great deal of admiration and some soreness of heart. Its annual announcements are awaited with the keenest interest, and despite an unflagging fidelity to one line of policy through many years, it is usually credited in advance with purposes most radical and upsetting to the trade. This year has proved no exception to the rule, for again the Company has been credited by rumor with intentions quite foreign to the probabilities, and again it has done the most obvious and profitable thing in the world. It has built a better Buick. But the statement seriously understates the fact and if left without qualification would literally spoil the story of the 'greatest Buick ever built,' as its makers term the 1927 product."

There followed some several dozen paragraphs extolling the features which made the 1927 Buick the greatest ever. Chief among these was an engine that was "Vibrationless Beyond Belief," the phrase credited to a report from the engineering department though probably it was coined a few doors down in advertising and sales. Hyperbole notwithstanding, it was aptly descriptive.

Engineering had developed a much heavier flywheel, new motor mounts, a counterbalanced crankshaft and a torsional balancer intended to "counteract periods of vibration." The latter was an interesting device. Mounted on the second crankshaft throw and lubricated by the crankshaft oiling system, it was completely enclosed in the crankcase and designed to last the entire life of the engine. Its principle was simple. During each power stroke the crankshaft twists in the direction of the rotation of the crankshaft and at the end of the power stroke unwinds suddenly, this winding

and unwinding being termed torsional vibration. At certain engine speeds, the rhythm of the power impulses increases this vibration—just as the properly timed movements of a child on a swing causes the swing to soar higher and higher—and such vibration could cause bearings to rattle violently and break the crankshaft. The Buick device was a forerunner of the harmonic balancer and was very effective—although it did impose a penalty. The heavier components required in the drivetrain made the car less responsive. Performance suffered noticeably.

Although changed barely noticeably in body design, the new Buicks were offered in a strikingly new range of paint colors. Even then the press was referring to 1927 as "the polychrome year of automobile history." A winged Gothic Goddess radiator cap replaced the motometer on the sport roadster and touring Models 24 and 25 and the 128-inch wheelbase cars. A one-piece windshield was introduced to, and cowl ventilators featured on, all open cars. Closed bodies used the Fisher windshield which opened to allow entry of fresh air. Speedometers were now located directly in front of the driver.

To increase rigidity, an additional cross member located in back of the rear engine mounts was provided Buick frames. All Standard Series cars, as well as Master sedan Models 40, 47 and 48, had their fuel gauges mounted on the gas tank. All remaining Buicks had them more conveniently located on the dashboard. Indirect lighting of dashboards was provided the entire Buick line.

A vacuum ventilator was added to the engines. It had no moving parts, consisting of a funnel which channeled air past an opening in the crankcase, thus creating a suction to pull out unwanted vapors, lessening the chance for formation of diluted lubricating oil and preventing offensive odors from entering the passenger compartment. With the new ventilator, Buick claimed it was now possible to change oil only four times a year. In conjunction with it, a thermostat was introduced to the Buick's cooling system. Both the ventilator and thermostat were developed by Buick engineer Walter Geise.

Meantime other Buick engineers had turned their attention to another matter. Though the new Buick engine might be Vibrationless Beyond Belief, it remained Noisier Than Desirable. Valve train commotion was excessive, customers were complaining, and dealership mechanics were responding by adjusting valve clearances closer than those called for by Engineering. This mitigated the noise, but had a negative side effect. With the closer clearances, both intake and exhaust valves were burning at a rate which made Buick fear for its reliability image.

Otto Berry (a college engineering instructor before coming to Buick), Otto Burkhardt (a mathematician), and a man identified as

November 1927: Ed Strong (hat in hand, arms folded) looking pleased as the body is lowered onto the chassis of a milestone Buick, the two-millionth car in its history.

"Richards" and "the oldest engineer in the department" (doubtless Eugene Richard who had worked with David Buick and Marr on the first Buick) were assigned to the task. Working together, they discovered the noise was arriving at a point when the valve was closing, but they did not know if part of the valve train, lifter, pushrod, or perhaps the valve itself was causing it. No sophisticated instrumentation was available for pinpointing the source; the only thing they could do was eliminate one phenomenon at a time until there was only one left.

Burkhardt and Richard finally realized the noise was the result of the pushrods deflecting when the valves closed. It was an unusual situation since it was almost impossible to discern any difference between the opening and closing profiles on the camshaft, yet the closing profile had to be associated with the problem in some manner. Further testing convinced them that the noise they were trying to eliminate was directly related to the camshaft itself.

131

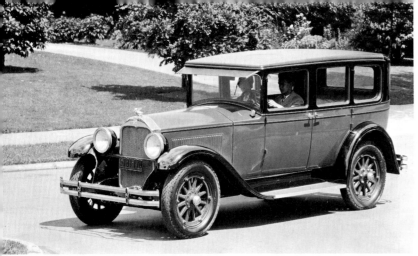

Buicks for 1928: Above: The Master Six Model 28-47 sedan. Below: The Standard Six Model 28-20 coach. Page opposite: Master Six Model 28-58 coupe (left) and Master Six Model 28-50 seven-passenger sedan (right).

A recent arrival in the department at the time was a young Italian engineering graduate named John Dolza. He barely spoke English. He was assigned to drafting prints for the sheet metal of what would become Buick's model line for 1929. Accustomed as he was to the Italian carrozzeria school of design, the forthcoming Buick's styling distressed him, but he was new, he didn't speak the language well, and he didn't wish to be "insulting"—so he said nothing, and looked around at every available opportunity for something else to do.

When he saw the problem camshaft he thought he had found his chance. He offered to help. It was not the sort of suggestion that was appreciated from an apprentice engineer, and development continued for the next three months without him. Dolza had a strong calculus and dynamics background, and near the end of the preliminary work he looked at the calculations and concluded the camshaft as designed would not work. He offered to draw up a layout using its specifications to check the profile and was given the go-ahead. When assistant chief engineer Ferdinand A. "Dutch" Bower saw the result, he nearly went through the roof: "Who in the hell designed that?" The specifications had called for a cam profile with a dip right in the middle of the cam lobes. It won't work, Bower said. Dolza replied that he didn't think so either, and offered to redesign the cam. Bower said that if he could come up with something workable, an engineering job away from his tedious drafting board would be his.

That was all the incentive Dolza needed. He completed his engineering drawings in short order. Bower approved his camshaft design, it was built and tested—and worked. It entered production with the first 1928 cars, and Dolza never again was relegated to drafting prints for the sheet metal of forthcoming Buicks.

His next assignment, in fact, was another noise problem, this one air cleaner resonance, or colloquially, engine roar. Again, since no sound analyzers were available, the work of locating and correcting the problem had to be done by ear. Dolza developed a new air cleaner with a spiral path and strategically located slots on the spiral so that a sound wave at its peak would meet another sound wave at the valley and they would effectively cancel each other out. The idea worked well. But, for some reason, the test engineer responsible for the overall project did not want the design for Buick. Instead it was given to AC Spark Plug Division, and AC in turn produced the silencers and sold them to Nash, a curious turn of events.

GM Research in Detroit found out what had happened and raised a fuss—but that didn't solve Buick's air cleaner resonance problem. Subsequently, a chemist who was also well trained in acoustics at GM Research, Ernie Wilson, came up with a solution even simpler than the Dolza spiral design: a series of resonance chambers, a princi-

ple upon which Buick engineer John Foster had experimented earlier.

Buick production for calendar year 1927 totaled 255,160 cars or 8.7 percent of industry production, 1.7 percent better than the year previous. The total units produced represented a four percent decrease over 1926, but the industrywide decline was twenty-two percent—attributable, everyone said, to a temporary downturn in the economy.

There was nothing to worry about in Flint, Buick president Strong decided and, during the summer of 1927, he introduced the new Buicks for '28 with a special flair—using the latest electronics marvel, radio. "The hook-up is the largest ever assembled by any manufacturer for commercial purposes and, in fact, the largest ever used in commercial exploitation except that employed in the Dempsey-Sharkey fight which was arranged by a newspaper syndicate," the press said. "It is the first time an automobile manufacturer has used radio in this way. Dealers in all parts of the Country are prepared to cash in on the scheme by installing radio receivers in their showrooms and inviting the public to come in for the double purpose of looking over the new line and enjoying the music."

The music was selected by S.F. Rothafel, "famed impressario of the Roxy Theatre," and performed by Arthur Pryor's band, Anna Case, and the orchestra of the St. Francis Hotel in San Francisco. Whether it met with favor by the public has not been documented. The new Buicks did not, comparatively. Buick production for calendar year 1928 would slip again, to 221,758 units, a thirteen percent decrease. Industrywide, there was an increase, of thirty percent. Buick's share of the market fell to 5.8 percent.

There were improvements in the cars, to be sure. Cylinder heads incorporated a spherical combustion chamber for more power and to decrease the chances of detonation. Frames were of the double-drop type with deeper side channels and reinforced between upper and lower flanges at the engine cross member and spring trunnions. Additional strength had been provided by large flanges on the front engine cross member, brake shaft and rear kick-up cross members. Standard for the first time were Lovejoy hydraulic shock absorbers on both front and rear of all models.

A radiator emblem was now standard too, and the gas gauge was mounted on the instrument board throughout the line. Water temperature gauges were dashboard-mounted as well, and radiator capacity was increased. A special triangular method of bracing for the radiator was designed. All open cars utilized forward folding windshields, improved tops which were narrowed at the front, natural wood bows with nickeled hinges, form-fitting cushions and leather trim. Nickel finish was used on radiators, lamps, windshields, hand brake levers and hood fasteners. Closed bodies had clear vision fronts, a feature realized through use of narrow windshield and front door posts and narrower windshield top bars.

But one of the most interesting changes to the new Buicks was a reversion to the norm. Previously, Buick had used a gearshift pattern which was unconventional, placing low gear where high usually was, second where reverse would normally be found, high in the normal low position and reverse in the place usually occupied by second. For 1928 Buick adopted the standard SAE shift pattern, although the company did make available a conversion kit for traditionalists who preferred to shift their Buicks as they always had. Perhaps one of the reasons for the change was to make things easier for the hordes of former drivers of other American cars whom the people in Flint confidently expected might be likely to step up to a Buick in 1928. Given the sales figures for the year, the effort was really not necessary.

Still Ed Strong was not particularly concerned. One bad year did not have to signal a trend. Nineteen twenty-nine was coming, Buick's silver anniversary year. And Buick had a special anniversary car to celebrate it. With brand-new styling.

A lot of people would say it looked pregnant.

Chapter Eight

BUICK GOES TO AN EIGHT

Among the reasons the Buicks for 1928 had fallen from public favor were simply that they were not as good-looking, did not perform as well and could not deliver the fuel economy of much of their competition. This problem was compounded for 1929. The new Buicks were even better at not being very good.

The promotional opportunity of the marque's silver anniversary was largely wasted. These were obviously not cars to celebrate. Their bulging side panels, with a look more obstetric than aesthetic, provided little visual appeal; the Buick's performance on the road was more ponderous, and reports from owners of big series models that fuel consumption was in the ten-to-twelve-mile-a-gallon range were hardly welcomed in Flint.

The Standard and Master designations were dropped, replaced by model numbers 116 and 121, denoting wheelbase length. For the first time, all engines were equipped with a fuel pump and, in another first for Buick, color options were made available on all models. Marvel carburetors and Delco-Remy ignition were used throughout. Closed cars had slanting non-glare windshields, adjustable front seats, double electric windshield wipers and side cowl ventilators.

Automobile production industrywide increased twenty percent during calendar 1929. But there were twenty-five thousand fewer cars from Flint than in 1928. (Total production was 196,104 units.) Buick's share of the market slipped from 5.8 to 4.3 percent, and Hudson-Essex slipped in behind Chevrolet and Ford for third place in sales. Buick moved down to fourth. It was clearly time to begin worrying in Flint.

Quality had been a Buick hallmark for years now. The car was frequently viewed as a Cadillac or Packard equal with a more attractive price tag. The attention to quality had its own price tag, of course, and as year passed year Buicks had become steadily more costly. This was not detrimental during the Twenties when the country's economy was seemingly in a never-to-end boom period, and people had more money every year to spend. But the exercise in fantasy optimism that was the Roaring Twenties was to end with a crash, and marketing parameters throughout the industry would have to be rethought.

This would be difficult for Buick. Complacency and conservatism tend to perpetuate themselves, and in the spring of 1929 when ill health forced chief engineer Enos A. DeWaters to give up his post and Dutch Bower was appointed to fill it, the road down which Buick would continue to proceed seemed clear. Ferdinand A. Bower was the embodiment of the Buick that was. A native of Oil City, Pennsylvania, he had been in Flint since 1908 when he became an engineer for Weston-Mott and stayed on after the axle company was taken over by Buick a few years later. Dutch Bower's philosophy was, basically, that quality should be pursued regardless of cost and things shouldn't be changed unless irrevocably necessary. Hence the ever-increasing price tags of Buicks. And hence the car's retention of such features as mechanical brakes and composite bodies after other members of the General Motors family had switched to hydraulics and all-steel. Because DeWaters' health had been failing for several years previous, Bower had been de facto chief engineer prior to his official title. But once he had that, he became even more resolute regarding what he thought was best for Buick. And he convinced Buick president Strong that he was right.

There were some at Buick—younger people mostly—who believed a restructuring of the Buick price lines was advisable. They were overruled. Instead—like Oakland with its Pontiac, Cadillac with its LaSalle, Oldsmobile with its Viking—Buick made the decision to market another car in a lesser price range. It was called the Marquette. History would call it a mistake.

The Marquette was a johnny-come-lately among GM companion cars—the Pontiac, the LaSalle and the Viking having preceded it into the marketplace. It was destined for the 1930 model year—and was perhaps more unakin its parent marque than any of the others. As an internal memorandum from the engineering department summed it up, "The Marquette engine is the 'L' head type which means the valves are at the side, giving an 'L' shape combustion chamber. [It was virtually a carbon copy of the Oldsmobile flathead six.] This type of engine while not as efficient as the Buick Over-Head Valve type lends itself to lighter and more economical manufacture and is in

Page preceding: 1929 Series 121 sedan being serviced at Marysville, California garage. Above: Series 121 Buicks for 1929 being introduced by Wisconsin dealership.

general use in practically all makes of cars except those equipped with ohv and Knight engines. Standard engineering practice makes it possible to build cars more economically and of less weight than specialized designs as used by Buick, but with the same careful engineering and manufacturing the Marquette cars are outstanding for performance, durability, speed, appearance, and riding comfort."

This smacked rather of rationalization, or at least a studied indifference or lack of enthusiasm toward the new car by the men assigned the task of designing it. Buick engineers were little enamoured of the Marquette's Hotchkiss drive, semi-floating rear axle and single plate clutch (compared to the Buick's torque tube, three-quarter floating axle and multiple disc clutch).

The Marquette was offered in six body styles—Model 30 two-door sedan, Model 34 sport roadster, Model 35 phaeton, Model 36 business coupe and 36S special coupe, Model 37 four-door sedan— and was rushed into production on June 1st, 1929, almost two months before the scheduled introduction of the new Buick line. The extra time, it was thought, would be well used to acquaint America with this brand-new car from Flint.

Buick really tried. The company bombarded automobile publications with news of the Marquette, and it would appear the press was more favorably disposed toward the car than anyone at Flint: "powerful reinforcement for the Buick line," "advances the company into the most active sector of the competitive struggle," "greatly widens the outlook of the Buick dealers." That there was nothing radical about the vehicle was conceded by reporters, though they didn't happen to notice—or mention anyway—that the car's body design, like its engine, was practically carbon copied from Oldsmobile as well. (One reporter, in fact, noted that "it would do very well in looks as a small edition of the Cadillac.") Its only really distinctive feature was the seven-degree forward and down slope of its windshield, which was designed to reduce glare.

More widely touted was the Marquette performance: "unusual acceleration and get-away . . . rugged power, tremendous hill climbing ability and flashing speed." What this translated to statistically was a 212.8-cubic-inch engine developing 67.5 hp at 3000 rpm moving a Marquette from 5 to 25 mph in 8.8 seconds, from 10 to 60 mph in 31.0 seconds, and having a claimed top speed approaching 70 mph. In a promotion stunt, a stock Marquette sedan was taken from Death Valley to Pikes Peak: "Seven hundred and seventy-eight miles in 40 hours and 45 minutes! From the lowest point in America to the highest accessible point. From the blistering temperature of . . . desert to the perpetual winter above the snow line! Through a cloudburst without faltering! A 21-mile climb up Pikes Peak in an hour and 20 minutes. An average speed of 50 miles an hour across the

Buicks for 1929. Page opposite: Model 29-46S Sport Coupe (left) and Model 29-57 Four-Door Sedan (right). This page, from the top: Model 29-51 Sport Sedan; Model 29-48 Coupe, introduced at mid-model year, shown with accessory wire wheels; and the Model 29-44 Sport Roadster.

Above and below: From 1930, the Model 30-47 sedan and Model 30-68 coupe. Page opposite: Advertising the Marquette in Canada and on the Continent.

desert!''

But neither the overused exclamation points, nor the reassuring reports from owners that Marquettes were averaging from 19 to 20 mpg, could hide from Buick dealers the fact that the car they were selling was more Lansing than Flint. And selling an Oldsmobile derivative was anathema to a Buick man. Buick dealers were a proud lot.

Admittedly, the American motoring public was not overwhelmed by the Marquette either, although the stock market crash four months after the car's introduction may have been partly responsible for that. In any case, after only 35,007 units were built, the car was summarily dropped—and Buick's account ledger recorded as a loss the cost of the 4000 special Marquette service signs which had been sent out into the field to be posted next to Authorized Buick Service logos.

Meanwhile, in Flint, the Buick was fixed. The line for 1930 was perhaps the most remedial ever built by the company—a case of undoing what had been done. Performance and acceleration were improved; both engines were bored out an eighth-of-an-inch, for 80.5 hp now for the Series 40, 99 hp for the Series 50 and 60. Transmissions were quieter thanks to a new method of cutting gears. Fuel tank capacity was increased three gallons (for nineteen on the Series 40, twenty-two on the 50 and 60); two inches were added to the 40's wheelbase (118 inches), three inches to the 50 and 60 (124 and 132 inches respectively). The cars had been lowered two inches, sported new wheels, hubs and hub caps, improved clutches and mufflers. A thermostatically controlled shutter was added to the radiator both to aid in engine warm-up and to improve front appearance.

But most important, the new Buick didn't look pregnant anymore. In response to what had to have been a frantic phone call from Flint, Fisher Body came up with a fast solution: a beltline molding running from front to rear and continuing around the back of the car at the lower edge of the rear window. That a simple belt could so improve the Buick look might seem surprising—to anyone perhaps except a fashion designer—but there was no doubting that the new car was at least publicly acceptable.

For calendar year 1930 Buick took back its third-place position in the industry. Fewer cars were produced than the year before, a total of 119,277 units, though this was 41,936 more cars than fourth-place ranking Pontiac. Buick's percentage of the total industry remained stable at 4.3 percent.

In November 1930, C.W. Churchill came away from a meeting with his regional managers and stated that Buick was looking for good business conditions in the early months of 1931. In January Ed Strong issued a public statement: "Judging from the fact that our

December reports are decidedly favorable, and taking into consideration the stabilizing influence which the resumption of plant operations in various lines of industry will have upon the Country as a whole, it appears to me that one big veil of the depression finally has been lifted. We are looking forward to Spring with renewed interest and the facts as shown in these first sales reports of the new year would seem to indicate a definite trend upward."

It was a typical announcement of the period. No one, it would appear, could see—or wanted to—what lay just ahead.

The big thing Buick was looking ahead to now was a new engine.

Just after the introduction of the 1930 line, and before the stock market crash, the decision was made to think in eights as a possible new image and sales builder for the marque. Dutch Bower was asked to investigate, and he passed the assignment along to his protégé, John Dolza.

By this time Studebaker had introduced a nicely designed straight-eight L-head engine. Hudson had one too. And Packard's Standard Eight was on the market. Dolza and his team proceeded to analyze all three.

The Packard found the least favor, its babbitt bearings, especially for the rods, being a weak point. Prevailing theory then was to place a sixteenth-inch of babbitt on the main and rod bearings, machine them well, polish the crankshaft to a fine finish, and give the whole system a good supply of oil. However, oil filters at the time were rather crude and, if used at all, were relatively ineffective. For any kind of reliability, the bearings had to be designed with plenty of surface area, and Buick Engineering thought Packard had skimped too much on that point. Hudson interested Buick because it used an F-head, a cross between ohv and L-head design, the intake valves mounted as overhead, the exhaust valves as flathead.

After two months of dynamometer and proving ground testing, Dolza discussed his findings with Dutch Bower. It was Dolza's feeling that, with regard to a possible Buick straight-eight, certain features from Studebaker, a very little from Packard and nothing from Hudson might be effectively incorporated. And, of course, continuation of ohv design was one of his major suggestions. Bower talked with Buick management, GM Research and people at the GM corporate level. A few days later he asked Dolza to bring his reports and exhibits to the GM proving grounds for a meeting. It was to be one of the most important in the history of Buick.

Attending the meeting that fall morning were Charles Kettering, the Fisher brothers, Alfred P. Sloan, Jr., corporate engineer C.E. Wilson, and Ed Strong. Bower opened the meeting and then turned it over to Dolza for the formal presentation. Numerous charts, graphs, exhibits and data compilations later, he offered a recommendation: that Buick immediately begin to engineer its own ohv straight-eight engine for production.

Kettering was impressed, but he suggested that before actual design work was started, a Studebaker eight should be installed in an experimental Buick for further testing. This brought Bower immediately to his feet. The Studebaker powerplant was much too long for installation in a Buick car, he argued; the project would be difficult with little actual engineering benefit resulting. If a straight-eight was to be considered, it should be a Buick straight-eight installed in a Buick car. Bower won. The decision was made.

Because of his initial investigations, Dolza was Bower's—and the obvious—choice for development work on the new project. But he was only twenty-seven years old, and men in Buick Engineering who were his senior both in age and experience thought the assignment should be theirs. There were many eyebrows raised. And a few toes stepped on. But Dolza got the job.

With three layout men and a student engineer, he went downstairs in the engineering building to a dynamometer room. The door was locked. Bower wanted absolute secrecy. Security rules were to be strictly enforced. This was to be a priority project.

Above: 1930 Series 50 Model 30-57 Four-Door Sedan, featuring optional demountable wood spoke wheels. Below: 1930 Series 40 Model 30-47 sedan.

Shortly after initial design work had begun, Bower was stricken with a serious strep infection necessitating a short leave of absence. Before he left, he gave Dolza a firm order: to design the new engine with dimensions allowing it to fit in the same engine compartment as Buick's current six-cylinder. Dolza shook his head. This was a mistake and he knew it. It would make his work much more difficult; he did not require much additional room, only an inch; he desperately wanted to increase the bearing area. But Dutch Bower was a stubborn man.

The initial drawings were shown to a recuperating Bower at his home. Since time was critical, and his boss was contagious, Dolza

Among the sportier Buicks for 1930 in the Series 60 line. Above: Model 30-64C DeLuxe or Country Club Coupe. Below: Model 30-64 Sport Roadster.

stood at the opposite end of the room and explained the drawings. How well he could see them ten feet away is questionable, but from his bed Bower made a quick decision: "Go ahead and build it."

Buick did it almost as quickly as Bower said it. Castings were made, bearings were poured, crankshafts were machined. Within a few weeks the first prototype was completed and mounted on a dynamometer. Fuel and oil lines were connected, a batter hooked up. The engine was cranked. It sputtered to life. The next few days were spent running the engine in and making minor adjustments. When Bower returned to work, a full dynamometer load had not yet been tried. No one really knew what the engine was capable of.

Bower decided it was time to find out. He approached the engine and opened the throttle. A short while later, he smiled. "John," he said, "you did a good job. Now design two more engines."

While Dolza did that, testing continued on the prototype. This resulted in a cam bearing failure when a camshaft journal scrubbed against a valve lifter causing enough heat to be generated to melt the babbitt. Bower was furious. He believed in the tried and true. His favorite expression was "beef it up." When the failure occurred, he immediately ordered a change from babbitt to bronze. Bronze cam bearings had been used successfully in Buick's six-cylinder engines, and Bower saw no reason to change, especially in the face of failure.

Dolza argued that the failure had been accidental, that by slightly relocating the valve lifter which had scrubbed the cam journal the problem would not recur. The engine had been designed with closer tolerances than the six, requiring force-feed lubrication to carry sufficient lubricating oil to the cam bearings. With the mediocre oil filters then available, he and his associates were afraid that the oil would become contaminated after a few thousand miles of driving and carry enough dirt to the close-toleranced cam bearings to seize them. But Dutch Bower was chief engineer.

For nearly a month development work shifted to the change in cam bearing composition material. Blueprints were altered, specifications revised. Though continuing experiments with bronze cam bearings were not encouraging, Buick's first production straight-eights would have them. But when failure rates in subsequent tests remained high, the drawings were again revised, production machining was changed back to accept the originally specified material, and a running change was made to babbitted cam bearings.

Meantime some interesting engine destruction tests had been carried out to compare engine life of the new Buick eight to the old Buick six as well as the eight from Packard. Two 1930 Buick sixes were sent to the proving grounds to put up twenty-five miles at 65 mph, followed by twenty-five miles at wide open throttle, then back to twenty-five miles at 65—for as long as they could. The first car went 2857 miles before the balancer broke and two rod bearings failed. The second put up 3972 miles before it burned out all the rod bearings.

In twenty-five-mile segments at 70 mph, alternating with the same distance at wide-open throttle, a new 1931 Buick straight-eight without an oil temperature regulator was driven 5094 miles before all its rod bearings burned out. The same model equipped with an oil temperature regulator motored in cycles of twenty-five miles at 65 mph, twenty-five at 70 and five miles at wide-open throttle for 7952 miles before burning out its numbers one and three rods.

Then a Packard Model 733 with oil temperature regulator was

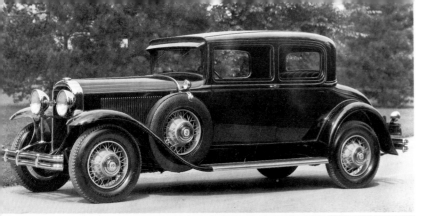

Buicks for 1930, from the top: Model 30-68 Coupe, Model 30-40 Two-Door Sedan and Model 30-46S Sport Coupe. Page opposite: Model 30-45 Phaeton in the service of the police department in Oakland (California), with officer Frank C. Hughes pointing out the aperture in the bullet-proof windshield "through which rifle may be fired . . . with comparative safety."

driven through the same sequence. Number one rod bearing failed after 2431 miles. A complete new set of rod bearings was installed, and the Packard sent out again. This time it made it to 2819 miles before rod bearing failure occurred.

Buick decided it had built its straight-eight strong enough.

The overall testing of the new 1931 Buicks prior to production was impressive: 616,627 miles for the engines, 903,397 for the front axles, 868,884 for the rear axles, 745,293 for the clutches, 823,432 for the transmissions, 677,007 for the steering gears, 705,797 for the frames, 635,995 for the bodies. Buick wanted to make certain the rest of the car was worthy of the new engines.

Interestingly, although no good engineering reason suggested itself for the limitation of making the powerplant to fit in the physical space formerly occupied by the six, no particular harm was done. This was the first time that an engine at Buick had to be designed with such thin bearing surfaces but satisfactory bearing life was found to be possible with the addition of the external oil cooler.

The three versions of the Buick straight-eight were the 8-50 (2⅞ by 4½, 220.7 cubic inches, 77 hp at 3200 rpm), the 8-60 (3-1/16 by 4⅝, 272.6 cubic inches, 90 hp at 3000 rpm) and the 8-80 and 8-90 (3-5/16 by 5, 344.8 cubic inches, 104 hp at 2800 rpm). Maximum car speed for the smallest was 69.25 mph, for the biggest, 75.75 mph.

The decision to go to a straight-eight had been a pragmatic one. The limit in size, smoothness and efficiency of a six had been reached, Buick Engineering felt. The cachet of adopting a new Buick engine throughout its line would be good in the marketplace, Sales believed. So there was agreement all around on the straight-eight. That three different versions of it were developed, however, resulted in some dissension. Obviously with profits down and the nation's economy in a turmoil, cost cutting measures were indicated. But frugality had seldom been considered during the Twenties, and old schools of thought die hard especially when good times are seen just around the schoolyard corner.

Still, Dolza and others in the engineering, manufacturing and purchasing departments wanted to make the three engines as interchangeable as possible. Dutch Bower said no. Ed Strong and the management group agreed with him. There would be enough production and sales to warrant the tooling. It all added up to a very large and unnecessary expense, one made at a time when Buick could ill afford it.

But at least Buick had some brand-new cars. And a lot to shout about. "A Milestone in Buick History," "1931—A History Making Year," "Buick Is the First Large Producer to Adopt Eight Cylinder Engines Exclusively," the ads said. Synchromesh was introduced on all Buicks—on the Series 50, however, as a mid-model-year running

change—but other manufacturers already had it, so Buick didn't talk much about it. Styling remained basically the same, and not much was said about that either. All attention was devoted to the brand-new straight-eight—and the fact that Buick was introducing it with price tags only twenty-five dollars higher than the year previous. A

$1025-$1095 range for the Series 50, $1285-$1335 for the 60, $1285-$1335 for the 80 and 90.

That was a lot of money in 1931, a lot of money a lot of people didn't have. Buick sales slumped to 90,873, Plymouth built four thousand more of its lower-priced cars and took the third spot in the industry away from Flint.

The only good Buick news that year came by way of Indianapolis and courtesy of a redhead named Phil Shafer. He was a General Motors employee, an Indy 500 enthusiast and a competitor there since the early Twenties, his best finish a third in a Miller in '25. With the advent of the Buick straight-eight, Red Shafer decided to build his own car for the 500, using the new powerplant (the 272-cubic-inch size) from Flint. He named the result the Shafer 8, qualified it for the '31 Memorial Day classic at 105.103 mph, started in twenty-third position and worked his way up to a respectable twelfth place finish.*

Buick was meantime working its way down. In 1932 its new car registrations fell fifty-five percent, to 49,708 units. People were buying those cars they could afford—the lower-priced automobiles of other manufacturers were the only ones doing well at all. Buick slumped to seventh place in the industry. It was an awful period.

Buick had thought a little magic might be helpful, and for 1932 had introduced Wizard Control as its most widely touted new feature. It combined the free-wheeling then in vogue and what the engineering department called a power clutch. The latter operated automatically with the accelerator pedal and a control button conveniently located nearly flush with the floorboard to the lower left of the clutch pedal; with the engine running, it was possible to put the car in motion from standstill, shift gears and free-wheel by simply using the gas pedal.

The mechanism consisted of a simple vacuum cylinder connected to the intake manifold through a control valve and a selector valve. The dual control valve comprised a brass valve body and two chrome-plated plunger sliding valves. The selector valve consisted of a brass valve body, three chrome-plated plunger sliding valves and one chrome-plated oscillating barrel valve which also contained a ball check valve. The power clutch and piston assembly—rubber

*There was no Buick racing per se during this period; the factory did not, like Studebaker for example, field an Indy team. Nonetheless, Buick was modestly represented in the 500 via independently built specials using Buick engines. The Butcher Brothers Special in which Harry Butcher placed fourteenth in 1930 had a 332-cubic-inch Buick six engine, and Butcher installed a Buick eight for 1931 but completed only six laps before he crashed the car. In the 1932 Indy 500 Shafer improved on his '31 finish by one position, finishing eleventh. In 1933 Stubby Stubblefield drove a Buick-engined Shafer 8 to a fifth-place finish in the 500, and Shafer won the last of the road racing classics held in Elgin, Illinois. In the 1934 Indianapolis 500, two Buick-engined Shafer 8's were fielded, Al Miller finishing sixth; Shafer was forced out with a broken cam drive after 130 laps. In '35 Stubblefield was killed tragically while practicing for the 500, and in the race Cliff Bergere drove another of the Shafer cars (the Victor Gasket Special), completed 196 laps, then ran out of gas but was awarded a thirteenth-place finish. Although Shafer's Indianapolis adventure was an independent one, Buick was cooperative in supplying engines and parts. Charles Chayne had become personally interested in Shafer.

Buicks for 1931, from the top: Series 50 Model 56 Business Coupe, Series 90 Model 96 Coupe, Series 50 Model 50 Two-Door Sedan. Right: Ed Strong (at the wheel) and general sales manager C.W. Churchill in the Series 90 Model 94 Sport Roadster at Strong's home in Flint.

diaphragm type, clamped between two steel shells—was mounted at the rear of the transmission. Intake manifold, dual control valve, selector valve and power cylinder assembly were all interconnected with brass tubing and rubber couplings. The rubber diaphragm of the power cylinder was directly connected through mechanical linkage to the clutch release mechanism.

By depressing the "Wizard Control Button" and releasing the accelerator, vacuum flowed from the engine to the power cylinder and the clutch disengaged. Gearshifting could then be accomplished without manually depressing the clutch. After the transmission had been shifted into the desired gear, merely pressing on the accelerator pedal caused the clutch to once again engage. Successive shifts could be performed by keeping the button depressed and releasing the accelerator pedal. At speed, free-wheeling was available with the same operation; if the engine stalled during free-wheeling it was automatically recranked for starting because, with the engine vacuum lost, the clutch would automatically engage.

It was an interesting system albeit one with some problems. In one episode at the proving grounds, the power clutch failed to disengage in a test car approaching its parking stall and a very close call with the garage wall resulted. Nonetheless, Wizard Control was featured on Buicks through 1934; for 1935 it would be replaced with another interesting power device: power brakes.

Wizard Control, of course, provided automotive journalists with all sorts of stylistic turns of phrase to describe it, and it would appear that not one variation on the theme of "Black Art" was missed. Less attention was paid in the press to another innovation Buick was trying, and probably everyone at Flint was just as glad. It was a ride regulator system. By means of an operating lever attached to the steering column, the driver could move a complicated series of linkages which changed the valving in each individual shock absorber, thus regulating the oil flow between the rebound and compression cylinders in the shocks. Adjustment in ride stiffness was said to be possible while the car was in motion and was intended to provide better ride and control as the road surface changed. The steering column lever was graduated from one for a smooth road on up to six for a really rough one. But apparently the system was just too complicated and expensive to be worth the effort, and the idea was dropped the year following.

There were other changes for '32. Hood doors replaced the cut-out slots which had served as Buick ventilation louvers since 1907. Windshields tilted back a few degrees to give the cars a slightly more rakish look. Horns moved outside the car to a position just below the headlights, cowl lights disappeared, parking lights were now mounted on the fenders.

Mechanically, only the Series 50 engine changed, bored out to 2-5/16ths inches for 230.4 cubic inches and 78.5 hp at 3200 rpm. Wheelbases of the Series 80 and 90 were increased to 126 and 134 in-ches respectively. Twenty-six models—compared with twenty-one for 1931—were offered in the four series.

Perhaps the reporter for *Automobile Topics* unwittingly said it best: "The base price of $935 is the lowest at which any six- or eight-cylinder Buick has ever been sold. It is $90 lower than the 1931 base price. The topmost price, on the other hand, is $2055, or $20 above the 1931 top. Hence, notwithstanding the inclusion of five additional models in the string the price range is increased but $110." His

Phil "Red" Shafer with his mechanic Charles Cariens at the Indianapolis 500 in 1931. Right: Shafer adjusting the valves on one of his Buick-powered cars.

The 1932 Series 90 Model 91 Club Sedan for five passengers. The total Buick production of this body style for the model year was 2238 units.

arithmetic was questionable at best, but the real point in the throes of the Great Depression was whether this was really the time to raise prices at all.

A year later, in reporting the new Buicks for 1933, *Automobile Topics* would note that prices had been held steady on about half the models and "the remainder are not strictly comparative, hence, their higher prices are deceptive."

For 1933, in addition to "deceptive" higher prices, Buicks had longer wheelbases (119, 127, 130 and 138 inches for the Series 50, 60, 80 and 90 respectively), bodies wider by an inch-and-a-half and lower by about an inch-and-a-quarter, and Fisher "no-draft" ventilation was introduced. There were fewer Buicks than the year before (twenty models), and fewer of them sold.

If 1931 had been bad for Buick and 1932 worse, 1933 plunged headlong to the superlative. The company produced only 40,621 cars, a mere 2.6 percent of an industry total which had seen an increase of nearly 450,000 cars over the year previous. It was a disaster, and no one in Flint knew exactly what to do—or even what had happened.

One reporter described the new Buicks as having "conservatively avoided radicalisms." It was a telling statement—and the crux of a Buick dilemma. It was a pleasant way of saying the marque had become old-fashioned. Since the mid-Twenties, with each succeeding model year, the Buick had become a little bigger and a little more expensive—in seven years the car had gained 1200 pounds and increased about $500 in price. It was clearly not a very marketable proposition for the Threadbare Thirties.

Moreover, a problem precipitated in the Twenties was continuing to divert attention away from the more pressing matters at hand. The Swan Intake Manifold Case was still in court.

On September 17th, 1921, John W. Swan, founder of the Swan Carburetor Company of Cleveland, had applied to the United States Patent Office for a patent covering an improved design for an automobile intake manifold. Swan had discovered that air/fuel flow through an intake manifold could be enhanced by rounding the passageways within the manifold especially at the points where it was angled for a corner. On April 28th, 1925, and later on July 25th,

The 1932 Series 60 Model 66 Business Coupe for two passengers. The total Buick production of this body style for the model year was 636 units.

1927, patents were issued to cover his designs, and on November 9th, 1926 Swan had entered into an agreement with General Motors which granted the corporation use of the new design for a royalty payment of approximately fifteen cents per car. The Swan manifold henceforth appeared on Buick, Pontiac, Oldsmobile, Oakland and Chevrolet cars, and royalties were duly paid awhile. Then abruptly GM stopped the payments claiming "misrepresentation" in the contract. Swan sued—not only General Motors, but Chrysler and Nash among other licensees. Since the design had been used on more than 802,000 of its vehicles, Buick became deeply involved in GM defense testimony. Engineers were routinely called away from their jobs to appear in court—and the case was a protracted one. Its final conclusion was not resolved until the mid-Thirties, and Swan was eventually awarded more than $715,000 by GM alone.

But Buick's problems did not end in the courtroom or with its cars during this period. The entire organization was in turmoil because, in effect, Buick had been taken away from Buick. GM took it.

The colossus that was General Motors could not escape the Great Depression. Its very size was some protection, and the financial controls and operating methods set up after Billy Durant's second—and irrevocable—departure would be effective in saving the corporation from unmitigated disaster. Still, GM was in trouble. It was operating at less than thirty percent of capacity. Sales in the United States and Canada had dropped seventy-two percent between 1929 and 1932. Profits had fallen from $248,000,000 to $165,000 during those same years.

Cost cutting within the corporation took on the patina of a religion. Work was coordinated in purchasing, design, production and sales. Interchangeability of parts was increased, and the number of bodies decreased to just three basic types. Wage and salary reductions were rife, so were employee cutbacks. People with ten to fifteen years seniority sat at their desks frequently knowing that the next cutback would mean their jobs.

In his book *My Years with General Motors*, Alfred P. Sloan, Jr. describes what is probably the least understood of all the cost-cutting measures of the period, the formation of the B.O.P.: "The most dif-

Below: Buick advertising for 1932 (left) and 1933 (right). Above: 1933 Model 87 Four-Door Sedan and 88C Convertible Phaeton. Page opposite: 1933 Model 57 sedan.

ficult economies to get were in commercial or selling expense and here we took the most drastic measures of reorganization. In March 1932 the Operations Committee, after a three-day session, adopted a radical revision of the product policy of 1921. The decision was taken to deconsolidate the manufacturing of Chevrolet and Pontiac and place them under Mr. Knudsen's jurisdiction. A similar consolidation was ordered between Buick and Oldsmobile. On the sales end the activities of Buick, Olds and Pontiac were consolidated in a single new sales company, B.O.P., and dealers were given more than one new car to sell. In effect, from a management point of view, General Motors . . . was reduced from five to three car divisions."

The B.O.P. was conceived by Bill Bless at Pontiac who in turn took the idea to R.H. Grant, vice-president in charge of sales for GM. Grant developed it further within his department, and then sold Alfred P. Sloan, Jr. on the concept.

Of the three car lines—Buick, Olds and Pontiac—Buick had the strongest dealer organization, even though Buick was suffering greater sales losses than the other two. Basically the B.O.P. idea was to combine the sales organizations of the three divisions using the Buick dealer group as an anchor to help stabilize the losses of all three sales groups. When a dealer failed, the B.O.P. would prevent the reinstallation of a new single-line dealer; instead the franchise would be awarded to the nearest surviving GM dealer, giving him another car to sell and, theoretically, a better chance to weather the storm himself. In addition, and in theory, the B.O.P. would also prevent wide-scale layoffs within the separate GM sales divisions. In actuality, however, these occurred during the consolidation, and many GM zone offices around the country closed as the B.O.P took effect and the three lines moved into one office location. These same retrenchments took place at regional levels, and there were no longer separate divisional managers as there had been.

That the B.O.P. was a disaster for Buick has been a widely held belief among both old-time Buick dealers and Buick historians. But to lay the blame for the Buick decline of 1932-1933 to the B.O.P. is to find a convenient scapegoat. The fact was that Buick was in trouble, B.O.P. or no B.O.P. Buick dealers had traditionally been among the most capable and loyal automobile retailers within General Motors, and during the good years they had come to expect extraordinarily fine and extremely marketable cars from Flint. When Buicks became less than that, and with the B.O.P. prospect of Buick dealers having to sell a better designed General Motors car alongside their own, obviously disenchantment would set in—and remain for the duration of the B.O.P. program. For all the broadsides directed against it, however, there is considerable argument to be made that the B.O.P. not only did not devastate Buick but it was a course which served to

keep the division, as well as General Motors itself, afloat during an extremely troubled period.

Meantime Ed Strong retired. Oakland (Pontiac) president Irving J. Reuter wound up with the job of directing Buick during the B.O.P. A longtime veteran of General Motors, the former president of Olds Motor Works, and the man who had directed the development of Adam Opel AG in Germany, Reuter's job now was an unsavory one. The "directing" part of it amounted to little more than extensive cost-cutting and wholesale layoffs of Buick personnel in Flint. Upon his arrival, a "welcome to Flint dinner" was planned in his honor, but by the time it was held many of the guests asked to sit at the head table with Reuter had already been fired by him.

What would happen next was anyone's guess. Buick's production of 40,621 cars during 1933 marked the first time since 1915 that the company had built less than 43,000 cars. By the mid-Twenties Buick had been geared up to produce 260,000 cars in a single year. The sales organization had been developed to sell them. Now it all was in shambles. Independent companies experiencing a production and sales slide similar to Buick's were being forced to the wall so quickly by this time that automotive trade journals could barely keep pace. Obituaries became their stock in trade. Some wondered if one would have to be written for Buick.

A miracle was needed at Buick. It arrived on October 23rd, 1933. Buick's miracle was Harlow Herbert Curtice.

Chapter Nine

ENTER HARLOW CURTICE

He was born in Petrieville, Michigan, a few miles from Eaton Rapids, on August 15th, 1893, the second son of Marion Joel and Mary Ellen Eckhart Curtice. His father was a commission merchant dealing in carload lots of fruit, and as a schoolboy he attended to those, and kept his father's books as well. His first job, in 1912, was at the Horner Woolen Mills in Eaton Rapids, initially in the yarn room, then as a shipping clerk, later an outside salesman. Early on he discovered a copy of an old prayer written by a Scottish preacher in the Highlands: "Oh Lord, guide us a' right for we are verra verra determined." That was Harlow Curtice.

Finding his future limited at the mills, the determined young man enrolled at Ferris Institute in Big Rapids, financing his two-year business course there with work as a short order cook at the Blue Front Cafe. When he graduated in February 1914, his old employer helped him find a job. One of the Horner daughters had married the company manager of the Standard Rule Company, producers of steel tape measures. He would work there. The company was in Flint, Michigan.

The job paid fifteen dollars a week, and young Curtice moved into a three-dollar-a-week boarding house. It was run by a maiden lady named Anna E. Kelleher, whose residents would come to be known as the Kelleher Klan. They were an estimable group. She managed the house for nearly three decades, and when she died in 1942, all of her pall bearers were former boarders: Harlow Curtice, Dutch Bower, Walter W. Bacon (assistant treasurer of Buick, later governor of Delaware), Taine G. McDougal (director of spark plug

engineering for AC) and assorted doctors and attorneys.

Harlow Curtice was out of work within a few months after he arrived in Flint. The Standard Rule Company was sold, and he began searching the classifieds. "Wanted—A high grade young man for office position requiring some bookkeeping experience," read one blind ad appearing in the April 23rd issue of the Flint *Daily Journal*. "A fine opportunity for the right applicant. Frank Swan, 404 Harrison." He answered it. Swan, no relation to John Swan, was head of the Free Factory Employment Agency, working on behalf of AC Spark Plug Division. He sent Curtice over to see AC's comptroller. What is your ambition, the comptroller asked the young man. "Your job within a year," Harlow Curtice replied.

It was as a bookkeeper working on a high stool in a tiny office that he was hired. But he didn't stay on that stool long. "Some of these accountant fellows just sit and look at pieces of paper," John Lee Pratt would remember years later. "That young red-headed fellow started going down in the plant and found out what determined costs. He had to learn the technical side of the business and he went out and learned it." And on his own time. Pratt, then a member of the General Motors presidential staff, was impressed. A year passed, and Harlow Curtice was made the company comptroller, replacing the man who had hired him. He had just turned twenty-one. He was the youngest executive in the automobile industry.

During the First World War, Curtice served in France, ironically in a post supplying equipment for horse-drawn military units. He left the army with the rank of private first class. Back home at AC, his rise through the ranks was rather more rapid. By 1923 he had added the position of assistant general manager, and four years later a vice-presidency was his. In between he had met a young girl from Sherman, Texas named Dorothy Biggs. She was charmed by his dapper good looks, that shock of red hair, his fair complexion, his ear-to-ear smile, and the appealing way he blushed so easily. They were married May 5th, 1927, honeymooned in Europe and were in Paris the day Charles Lindbergh landed with the *Spirit of St. Louis*, the plane, incidentally, having been fitted with AC spark plugs for the flight. Three daughters were born to the Curtices, Mary Leila, Dorothy Anne and Catherine Dale.

Though Curtice would treasure the hours he spent with his wife and daughters, there would not be too many of them. "My family would like to see more of me," he said once, "but there's a lot of work to be done." On another occasion, when a news conference he was holding was running past schedule and an aide reminded him of that fact, he replied, "I never run out of time." That was Harlow Curtice too. Always so much work to do, always he found the time to do it. "Workaholic" is a relatively new term in the lexicon. It could have

Page preceding: Harlow Curtice, the man who would save Buick. Above: 1934 Series 40 Model 48 Two-Door Touring Sedan and Model 41 Four-Door Touring Sedan.

been invented to describe Harlow Curtice.

In 1929, two years after the death of Albert Champion, Harlow Curtice was made the president of AC. He immediately expanded the product line of the company to include oil pumps, oil filters, speedometers, fuel pumps. This diversification helped AC to stabilize employment during the early hard years of the Depression, and indeed AC's employment rolls actually increased *after* the stock market crash, a fact in which Curtice took great personal pride. "Do it the hard way" was his motto. Almost invariably, as his long career would demonstrate, it was the right way.

Curtice was also fond of saying, "you never stand still in this business. You either go up or down." Two verities presented themselves at this time. One was the direction in which Curtice was heading, the other the direction of AC's neighbor in Flint. At Buick, engineering department workers were being asked to take a month's vacation without pay in order to keep layoffs at a minimum. At GM headquarters, there was dark talk of dropping Buick from the corporation.

Fortunately, Buick had a friend at General Motors. Executive vice-president William Knudsen wanted to save the division and he thought he knew the man who could handle the job. Other members of the board were not quite so certain. That red-haired fellow over at AC was a little young, just forty years old, to handle a task so formidable and, moreover, he had no automobile manufacturing ex-

perience. Knudsen was steadfast. "Vait and see," said the "Great Dane" of General Motors.

The job offer to head Buick came to Curtice in one of two ways. The less likely version has Knudsen traveling to Flint to talk to him personally. The more likely has Curtice visiting Detroit, and it happened like this. In mid-1933 Curtice was phoned by his old friend, GM director John Pratt, who asked him to drop by the next time he was in Detroit. A few days later, upon arriving in Pratt's office, Curtice discovered that it was not his friend who wished to see him and he was ushered into the office of the man who did. Knudsen was sitting at his desk, wearing his usual black derby hat, and the two men talked. The GM/B.O.P. structure was to be abolished the following New Year's Day, Knudsen explained, and would Curtice be willing to pick up the pieces of Buick and put them back together again? Apparently Curtice agreed on the spot. It would have been very like him, in any case, to decide without hesitation to give up the presidency of a company in robust good health and take on the challenge of a company whose illness seemed terminal. Curtice left Knudsen's office as Buick's new president.

The only thing that changed in the months ahead was the date the appointment would be effective. Dissolution of the complicated B.O.P. program was not a matter easily kept secret, and when news of it leaked out, Curtice was told his move to Buick would be set for October 23rd. At AC everyone knew something was happening, but not precisely what. In mid-October, when the name of Buick's new president was announced, the AC offices went wild.

Alice Dewey was Curtice's secretary, originally hired by Albert Champion as his secretary and transferred to Curtice when Champion traveled to France shortly before his death. She had quickly become Curtice's right arm. "Will I go too?" she shouted. "You sure do," her boss replied.

Few transfers of power could have been more welcome in Flint. With the arrival of Curtice, I.J. Reuter retired. His regime had not been a pleasant one for Flint. His had been a thankless job. He had been part of the "purge" and had led the "wrecking crew," as dealers termed the B.O.P. Buick had lost talented personnel during those days, and morale hit rock bottom. The Buick organization was fragmented now, diversity among its departments was rampant. Production blamed problems on engineering, engineering saw styling as its nemesis, and so on down the line.

Curtice dug in. As he had during his earliest days at AC, he spent long hours in the plants, familiarizing himself with every aspect of the company's procedures. He got to know the people and sized them up, determined to fit the right man into the right spot in the organization, determined too to keep as many of the men already there as possible. And he went after and rehired some of the managers who had been dismissed during the B.O.P. purge.

He thought on his feet, and made quick decisions. He was an exceptional administrator. He drove his people hard, but no one harder than himself. Some would later call him a martinet, and perhaps he was that. But he was more a motivator, demanding and being sanguinely given the proverbial 110 percent of an employee's efforts.

Red Curtice—only his close friends called him by his nickname—was one with his people. The pomposity that frequently accompanies positions of high authority was not his way. He was the roll-up-the-shirtsleeves sort. He was a fair man to work for. And he never carried a grudge.

One day Curtice called his assistant manufacturing manager to his office and chewed him out royally. It was a particularly vociferous performance, and even Alice Dewey was a little embarrassed to have been a witness. But later that evening Curtice was found sitting in that same manager's office, chair tipped back, feet on the man's desk. "This has been one hell of a day, hasn't it?" he remarked.

One of Curtice's earliest—and wisest—personnel decisions upon assuming the helm of Buick was his appointment of William F. Hufstader as general sales manager. Five years Curtice's junior, Hufstader was born in Jersey City, New Jersey, attended Denison University and began his career in the automobile business with Pierce-Arrow. After serving in the Army Quartermaster Corps dur-

ing World War I, he moved to Flint as publicity director for the Flint Chamber of Commerce in 1920 and then became something of a gypsy for the remainder of the decade: 1922 with Dort; 1923 as sales manager for Mason, the truck division of the Durant company; 1925 as Minneapolis district manager for the Graham Brothers, later that year as executive assistant to Ray Graham in Detroit; 1926 as district manager in Seattle for Dodge; 1927, same title, same company, but in St. Louis; 1928 as used car manager for Dodge in Detroit.

On March 1st, 1929, Hufstader returned to Flint as Buick's used car manager—but he didn't stay long. Next he was B.O.P. regional sales manager in Chicago, and the final days of the B.O.P. found him in Detroit working up Buick sales promotional materials. His return to Flint, as number two man to Curtice and as general sales manager for Buick, became effective the same day the Curtice appointment did, October 23rd. Doubtless Hufstader couldn't have been more pleased. Now he would stay put . . . for the next fifteen years.

His widely varied experience worked to Buick's advantage. He was a great "dealers' man"—he understood their problems, he talked their language, he was a terrific salesman himself. A handsome man with a big booming voice and a stunning command of the English language, Hufstader was a fine public speaker—something Curtice initially was not. Flint people recall an early managerial meeting Curtice called; it did not go well. Curtice's ideas were sound, he just hadn't been able to put them across effectively. Gradually, he became better at it, until finally he could hold the attention of an audience for an hour with no more than eight words on the back of an envelope to guide him.

Whether Hufstader's influence was responsible for this is an unknown. But the two men complemented each other extremely well. Curtice was close to all his managers, but especially so with Hufstader. Red Curtice and Bill Hufstader. They made a great team, one of the finest the industry has ever known.

Curtice saw the Buick problem as concentrated on three fronts, and he attacked them all immediately. First, before anything really constructive could be accomplished, he had to eliminate the infighting among departments. This he did with good humor and the simple expedient of effecting congenial internal communication among department heads, with everyone encouraged to participate in the formulation of every major decision and the working out of every major problem. In a word, teamwork returned to Buick.

Next Curtice looked at the car. The Buick reputation for reliability, durability and fine engineering remained intact. The downhill slide had been the result of the car having grown too heavy and its price tag having been increased too far above its logical market. With Depression dollars few and far between, it was clear in any case that a lower-priced, good-performing smaller car was needed. And Curtice was determined that Buick would have one. It was, he knew, a makeshift solution, but success with it would put Buick into a better market and profit position and would afford the luxury of the time needed to reengineer and restyle the complete Buick line.

Two obstacles had to be tackled. The first was the Marquette experience, still lingering in the minds of many—the new smaller Buick had to be a Buick, one which could trade on the marque's traditional engineering reputation, something the Marquette had not been able to do. The second obstacle was the GM Finance Committee. Harlow Curtice could not build the car without its approval.

This was a battle he very nearly lost. The committee, during an early discussion meeting, seemed reluctant to consider a smaller Buick as doing anything other than lessening the quality reputation of the car. Curtice was becoming edgy. Finally, Alfred P. Sloan, Jr., chairman of the group, called a halt to the bantering and asked that each member in turn express his own thoughts on the subject. It has been said that important moments in history are sometimes influenced by the seemingly insignificant. On this day circumstance placed Flint's great industrialist, C.S. Mott, in the chair to which Sloan first turned. Mott's words were these: "If Mr. Curtice is to be criticized, and I think he should be criticized, the criticism is that this car should have been put into production a year or two ago and, if it is not put into production now, the Buick business will diminish, and its production and reputation will be passed by other automobile builders." Mott's words carried the day. Harlow Curtice breathed easier. He didn't mind being criticized at all, and he didn't bother to mention that as president of AC at the time it would have been logistically difficult for him to have put the new Buick into production a year or two before.

Curtice's third frontal assault was the B.O.P. which he viewed as the "greatest mistake ever made by GM." That was moot, of course, but B.O.P. administrators had managed to eliminate Buick personnel from upper echelon positions in the organization with the result that Buick dealers, believing correctly that they were not being adequately represented within General Motors, had become increasingly disconsolate. B.O.P. was, derisively, "Bo-Peep" to them, and their morale couldn't have been lower. During the phaseout, it was originally intended by the corporation that Pontiac would continue to control the distribution and sales system for Buick. Harlow Curtice would have none of that.

In mid-1934 he invited Harry Klingler, chief of Pontiac (and pun intended), to his office for a chat. Curtice came straight to the point; he wanted the sales and distribution for his car. Klingler was equally

adamant, he liked things the way they were—and why not? The Buick was one of the Pontiac's principal competitors; a more felicitous position couldn't be imagined than Pontiac controlling the distribution of its rival. The argument was a long and heated one, and neither man gave ground. So Curtice went to the directors of General Motors, made an earnest appeal and got his way. By November of 1934, Buick was once again whole, with Curtice in charge of the complete operation and Buick's factory sales organization back in the business of handling its own car.

This was one of the most significant steps Curtice would make in putting Buick back on the road to recovery. And it was apparent immediately. Dealers hadn't been given a competitive car. Many of them were losing their shirts. But more odious to them than either of those unpleasant realities was the hated B.O.P. or, as one dealer remarked to a Flint-bound distributor, "Tell Red that if the B.O.P. couldn't get us, we should be able to withstand anything."

Once Curtice received his approval from GM, Buick began an extensive recruiting and training program to develop its own field organization. And this was not the only company rebuilding project that was begun. The GM Finance Committee, after acting favorably on the smaller Buick proposal, approved an expenditure of some $8,-105,632 for tooling up for the new model and for plant expansion and modernization, two areas which had been neglected during the sales skid. Over $500,000 was spent on the engine assembly plant, $750,-000 on the drop forge facility, and more than $2.5 million went into expansion of the transmission plant. It was the greatest updating of Buick manufacturing facilities since 1925. In addition Curtice asked for and received an additional $4,675,475 to begin long-range tooling for the 1936 cars.

Meantime the 1934 Buicks had been introduced, on December 27th, 1933, just two months after Curtice took charge. He could do little more than nod in their direction and send them out to be sold. In appearance they were little changed, the vent doors along the sides of the hood, however, having given way to a series of narrow horizontal louvers running the length of the hood. The big news was underneath: independent suspension (knee action) in the front, and a ride stabilizer in the rear.

The new suspension system, developed by the GM Technical Section, had been tested by Buick engineers and drivers at Milford. The only significant problem encountered was the limited service life of the rubber bushings, a matter quickly seen to. Even prestigious Rolls-Royce was impressed and approached General Motors about purchasing patent rights. Arrangements were worked out, and the following year the new Rolls-Royce Phantom III used both GM's independent front suspension and ride stabilizer. In the Buick, the latter was mounted just ahead of the rear frame cross member and across the rear end of the frame. It contributed, as its name suggested, to a much more stable ride under difficult road conditions and helped to control body sway and lean under adverse circumstances. "When bumps become ridges and ridges disappear" was how Buick advertising phrased it.

A Bendix power vacuum booster was added to the four-wheel mechanical brakes, and an accelerator-operated switch to engage the starter motor—this to become a popular Buick feature in the years following—was introduced. Safety glass windshields and vent windows were standard equipment on all 1934 Buicks, with safety glass all around provided in the Series 90, and available optionally in the Series 50 and 60, at prices ranging from $9.75 to $20.00.

Model 91 Club Sedan for 1934; the screened cowl ventilator for 1934.

Above, from the left: Harlow Curtice shaking hands with Dutch Bower, as Bill Hufstader looks on, and the first Series 40 car comes off the line in May 1934. Below: Curtice with R.S. McLaughlin during 1935.

While the industry tendency in general was moving toward lightness and economy, Curtice's predecessors at Buick had handed him a vehicle both heavier and longer, together with some new engines. The Series 50 was given a 235-cubic-inch engine developing 88 hp at 3200 rpm. The Series 60 had grown an inch in wheelbase to 128, and had a new engine too, 278 cubic inches, 100 hp. The Series 90 remained the same in both wheelbase and engine, though horsepower was increased to 116.

But the only number Harlow Curtice was thinking about now was 40—the designation for the new smaller Buick. A glance at the 1934 line indicated how desperately it was needed. To get the new car into production as quickly as possible required the cooperation of Chevrolet, then using the body which the new series would require, and Fisher Body, the division building it. Of course, GM Art & Colour would be involved too—and that meant Harley Earl.

Harley Earl was a giant of a man, six feet four, and well built. Lawrence Fisher, then head of Cadillac, had met him in 1925 at the Earl Carriage Works in Los Angeles, and talked him into coming to Detroit the following year to work on a design which eventually became the LaSalle and which led ultimately to Earl's establishment of GM's styling organization. Both Earl and Curtice were moving fast and up when they met in 1934.

Legend surrounds that first meeting, though Harley Earl's brother has confirmed the story to be true. Curtice asked Earl what kind of car he drove. Earl said a Cadillac. Curtice replied, "Then how about designing me a Buick you would like to own yourself?" Already image was important to Curtice; he was weary of Buicks for old men and bankers. He wanted something he could sell to the likes of a dashing Harley Earl. The two men established an immediate affinity, and their close association worked immeasurably to Buick's benefit. Earl knew he could count on a much freer hand with Curtice and Buick than he could with other GM divisions, and in years to come he offered Buick designs which were outstanding for their time. He styled the industry's first experimental design car, the Y-Job, around a 1937 Buick chassis, Buick built it for him in 1938 at Flint, and the Y-Job thereafter became a significant factor in Buick styling for years to come.

But now, in 1934, the pressing matter was the Buick 40. Harley Earl came through for Curtice, and so did everyone else. The Series 40 was rushed through engineering and styling and raced headlong into production. From approval to assembly line was a short six months. The car was introduced May 12th, 1934. It was the shot in the arm Buick needed.

With 182 inches overall on a 117-inch wheelbase, the new car was 550 pounds lighter than the lightest predecessor Buick—and it was price tagged at an attractive $795-$925. Its 233-cubic-inch engine developed 93 hp at 3200 rpm—and factory performance figures revealed an 85 mph top and acceleration from 10-60 of 21.0 seconds. It was a nice package but not one without its problems.

For reasons of cost cutting and high speed production, the connecting rod cap on the new engines was split on an angle rather than a horizontal plane. This proved a disaster in the field. After about 10,000 miles, the capscrews holding the rod cap to its assembly would loosen, the pressure placed on the capscrews by the split-angled connecting rod caps being directly responsible. Buick found itself looking at big trouble. As capscrews loosened and rods failed, many complete engine blocks were being destroyed. For those cars already sold, a repair campaign—a special locking bolt and nut for dealer installation—was inaugurated. To solve the problem in production, John Dolza, then working on a special transmission assignment, was called back by Dutch Bower, and he made a running change to the more conventional rod cap cut on a horizontal plane.

Together with that revision, Buick began using two large nickel steel heat-treated bolts for retaining caps to rods. The high percentage of earlier failures had been expensive both in terms of cost to repair field failures and in terms of Buick's reliability image. To ascertain that it would not happen again, the engineering department took several cars equipped with the new rods to the proving grounds and drove them day and night, with stops only for driver changes and replenishment of gas, oil and water. Segmented into two laps at sixty miles an hour, followed by two more at seventy and the final two at wide open throttle, the total distance covered was 15,000 miles, nearly double that to which any other car had been subjected under similar conditions. When the engines were torn down and checked afterwards, bearings and rod nuts were found to be in good condition. Bower was satisfied: "It gave us a mighty big factor of safety in our engines."

More important, the Series 40 gave Buick dealers a car they could sell. It was mainly responsible for pulling Buick sales to 63,067 for calendar year 1934, an almost fifty percent increase over 1933. And most important of all, it gave Harlow Curtice breathing time.

By the spring of 1934, Curtice had things moving along pretty well. The Series 40 was in the works, the final remnants of the B.O.P. were soon to be removed from his organization, Harley Earl was at work on new designs for his 1936 cars, and his division was pulling in the direction he wanted it to. It was now time to turn to the dealer organization. With Hufstader and Bower, he traveled the entire country by train getting to know the major dealers and distributors personally, learning their problems firsthand. He took his wife and mother along on several of these trips—deftly combining being a

good family man with being a good businessman—and the two women fit into the group well, joining in the poker games with Curtice and his associates between train stops.

Curtice and Hufstader were fully aware that if Buick was ever to regain its former status, it would have to be with a much stronger dealer organization. The great dualing patterns (one GM dealer handling more than one GM franchise) established during the days of the B.O.P. had to be reversed. Dealers handling only the Buick franchise now numbered just sixty-seven. Buick's two top men were fine salesmen themselves fortunately. They had quite a selling job to do; convincing a dealer of the great future ahead with Buick as his only line was no mean task. But Curtice and Hufstader were good at it.

Meantime the Buicks to be sold for model year 1935 were prepared and introduced. This was a study in moderation. "Four lines of motor cars are announced by the Buick Motor Company for 1935," the press release of December 15th, 1934 stated, "covering the broad range from the low medium to the high medium price fields and offering the largest variety of body types in the history of the Buick organization." Not much enthusiasm there.

But at a sales meeting in the Knickerbocker Hotel in Chicago on January 25th, 1935, Dutch Bower was excited: "In the past year Buick has had a great revolution. You know that for the past five or six years Buick has been kicked around and has not been going places. Once we had a wonderful sale of cars and built 250,000 or more cars per year. The sales have been dropping off until 1933 they fell to 42,000 cars. Now this past year things have turned about. We have a live wire at the head of Buick. This man Curtice is a go-getter. He has his fingers in everything . . . "

The subdued announcement and Bower's focus upon Curtice rather than the cars suggests that the 1935 line was a marking-time gesture between the entrance of Curtice and the introduction of the first all-Curtice cars. And Buick would have to wait until 1936 for that.

Something had to be sold in the interim, however, and the 1935's represented little more than carryovers from 1934. Many people today, in fact, believe the only changes were in the serial numbers. There were a few more. An automatic choke, for example, was added throughout the line. A higher 22:1 steering gear ratio was introduced to the Series 60, together with a rear-seat center armrest in the 60 closed cars. There were new colors and trims available in all lines, and a special heavy girder frame was devised for all convertibles. The horns mounted alongside the grille looked a little different too.

Most attention had been given the Series 40 which Dutch Bower admitted to the salesmen had not been "one thousand percent perfect," but without it in 1934 Buick would surely have been "out on a limb," and with the refinements for 1935, "it is a real Buick car and you do not have to be ashamed to go out and sell it." What he was saying, simply, was that the bugs had been worked out. Stromberg dual downdraft carburetors replaced the previous and troublesome Marvel units. A ball clutch release bearing, improved clutch throwout linkage, a glovebox door lock, two windshield wipers and a convertible coupe body style were new; scoring valve lifters, timing chain wear and excessive muffler noise were seen to, and some minor handling problems were corrected. The result was "the finest handling, best performing job Buick had ever built," according to Bower.

One thing the new Buicks didn't have, which would be a short-lived vogue on other GM cars, were center-hinged door posts, what have since come to be known as "suicide doors." Bower assured Buick salesmen that Buick doors "will always be hinged on the front posts, the same as at present." Interestingly, the remark drew strong applause from his audience.

Two further things the new Buicks didn't have—and less commendably—were a turret top and hydraulic brakes. Bower acknowledged the advantages of the former, noting its use by Chevrolet, Pontiac and Oldsmobile and "as time goes by you will probably see it on Buick and Cadillac."

About the latter, he was adamant: "Now the difference between hydraulic and mechanical brakes is simply . . . in the means of applying brakes, that is the hook-up between the brake and the brake pedal. Buick uses the cable hook-up which means that we have a steel cable running from the brake to the brake pedal. These cables are securely fastened with steel pins which are locked in place with cotter pins. On the hydraulic brakes they have a tube with a rubber hose on one end filled with oil. Now there is the real difference between hydraulic brakes and mechanical. One has a steel cable to operate the brake and the other has a tube with a rubber hose filled with oil. There is not much mystery when you throw these things on the table and analyze them. We can talk about safety in our brake hook-up and if we place our steel cable on the table and show how it is hooked up, against the tube and rubber hose, I am sure we can put up a very convincing argument to the customers and we should have very little sales resistance."

Bower admitted Buick had been experimenting with hydraulic brakes for the past three years, had been unsatisfied with their operation, but "when we do succeed in working them out to where we feel absolutely sure about them, and *if the sales department demands them*, we will be glad to put them on our cars." The emphasis has been added. Obviously Bower was being pressured by Buick and its sales organization; obviously too he was not prepared to let go of his mechanical brakes one moment sooner than he absolutely had to.

Only the fellow building Ford V-8's in Dearborn was more stubborn.

Other mechanical matters were looked to. A carburetion problem, for example, worked out by Buick's fine carburetion engineer, Adolph Braun. Zenith carburetors utilizing a horizontal needle and seat arrangement had been in use successfully at Ford but for some reason they had a tendency to stick on the Buick. Braun discovered that the horizontal set-up was more susceptible to dirt than the previous vertical needles. The field problems being reported were apparently directly related to the improper filtering of fuel. His tests had shown that the carburetor would digest a particle up to .002 but nothing larger. The AC fuel pump then being supplied had a #80 mesh screen filter but it was still passing through dirt particles large enough to cause flooding and sticking at the needle and seat. Zenith had designed a small-edge-type fuel filter which would mount on a plate inside the fuel pump. It was a good filter and more than adequate to correct the condition. Braun went to AC and asked to have that filter installed in future Buick pumps. AC wasn't happy about the change but cooperated. Two years later, however, AC designed a new pump which omitted the filter; Buick refused to accept it.

Another problem Braun attacked was corrosion in the float bowls, brought to his attention by Dutch Bower when his personal car became plagued with watered fuel corroding the carburetor. Braun had read an engineering article about a Dycramate finish which would retard rusting. He talked to the people at Marvel, then supplying some Buick carburetors, and asked if they were familiar with the process. They were and described the details to him. Within a week Braun had ordered both Marvel and Stromberg to begin supplying the new finish; within two weeks both suppliers were providing castings coated with it. Looking back, Braun remembered with a smile how much easier it was to get things done in those days. He hadn't even had to go through purchasing personnel for approval.

The Buicks for 1935 saw a slight increase in price and a somewhat larger decrease in sales: 53,249 units, a reduction of some 17,760 cars from 1934 figures. Curtice expected this and was unconcerned. The cars were not really "new"—and toward the end of the model year were advertised virtually not at all.

Everyone now was gearing up for the 1936 line. Promotion of it was paramount. In February 1935 the first issue of *The Buick Magazine*, successor to *The Buick Bulletin*, appeared. A direct-mail publication, it would be sent to Buick purchasers and provided a soft-sell approach. More important was the matter of advertising.

"When we looked over the sketches for our 1936 product, we felt that perhaps it deserved a little advertising," Curtice later joked. A classic understatement. He had planned a zesty campaign for the new Buicks from the beginning. AC's advertising had been handled by

Erwin Wasey & Company during Curtice's spark plug days, and he had been impressed with the capabilities of the account executive, Arthur Kudner. When he decided Buick advertising, then handled by Campbell-Ewald, should be opened to competition, Curtice had Kudner in the back of his mind. Erwin Wasey and several other agencies bid for the Buick business but when Kudner decided to organize his own firm Curtice quickly offered him the account. It was a decision he never regretted.

Curtice brought Kudner and his men right into the Buick offices,

kept no secrets from them, treated them as an integral part of the Buick team. They were there for some nine months before their first ads appeared. This close collaboration—most unusual in the industry—paid off. Art Kudner and his group were fired up. Eye-catching and provocative headlines like "Hot? It's a Ball of Fire," "Up Where We Hardly Belong," and "Ever Hear the One About the Farmer's Daughter?" followed—and some of the most imaginative automobile advertising of the period.

Selling the dealers continued. In early 1935, Gus Southworth of

The "shot in the arm Buick needed" and Curtice introduced, these sedans and coupes being among the 2752 Series 40 cars and chassis destined for export in 1934.

Glidden Buick Corporation in New York, the largest Buick dealer in the country, was invited to Flint for a sneak preview of the 1936 line. He liked what he saw, increased his initial order by 500 cars, returned to New York, and immediately canceled all his other franchises. Thereafter, many other dealers joined Southworth in deciding to handle Buicks only. From the low of sixty-seven in March of 1934, Buick's exclusive dealer body grew to 317 by the end of 1935, an improvement of 473 percent. The total number of dealers selling the Buick line, which had plummeted from 2609 outlets in September of 1927 to 2095 in September 1932, climbed back to 2520 by December 1935. Curtice, of course, liked the exclusive Buick dealers best, they would be responsible for retailing 41.4 percent of Buick's sales in 1935. By the end of 1936, total dealer outlets would rise to 2658 and the greatest increase would be in the exclusive dealer figures, now at 998 franchises retailing 61.7 percent of the total sales.*

In August of 1935 the first 1936 pilot models were ready. On Monday morning the 19th, Buick called together all national field service personnel for a look. Later that month dealers and district managers were brought in for the big showing. As Alice Dewey remembered, "The dealers who came into Flint were all in agreement: 'This car is going to make us great!' "

Harlow Curtice was practically beside himself. "I am not a man of easy enthusiasms," he told the crowd before unveiling the cars. "I have to be shown. Even then, it's my instinct to discount the showing a little. Some people have pointed me out as the man who believed that if the truth were known, Paul Revere's horse ran away with him. I mention these things to you because I want you to keep that in mind when I talk about the 1936 Buick cars. In other words, I want you to keep remembering that these automobiles had to be phenomenally good for me to feel the way I do about them."

And then he talked of the '36 cars taking Buick out of the utility and into the "smart style class, to point up and at the same time extend its appeal, to make it a youth car as well as a dependable car, to endow it with flashing, thrilling performance with no sacrifice of basic durability or economy."

Gingerly combining revival sermon and pragmatic lecture, Curtice

*The Buick dealer organization was to hit its prewar peak in June of 1941 when a total of 3038 dealers sold the line, 1783 of them exclusively, the latter responsible for 81.4 percent of Buick's total sales. The time given by Curtice and Hufstader to wooing dealers away from the dual General Motors franchises of B.O.P. days had been well spent. That program, together with Curtice's weaning of the Buick distribution system from the independents to whom Billy Durant had entrusted Buick sales and dealership control—that story is told in the appendices—were two very vital factors in his Buick re-
juvenation plan.

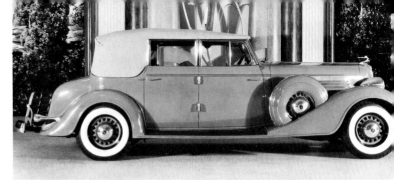

Above: Buicks for 1935, the Model 98C Convertible Phaeton of which only forty-three were built for the U.S. and for export—and the popular Series 40 Model 48 Two-Door Touring Sedan, of which more than 5000 were produced.

explained the Buick situation: "Probably the seat of our troubles lay in this fact. In 1927 the price brackets within which Buick worked represented twenty-eight percent of the total car market. We got the lion's share of that percentage and it gave us a good business. But by 1933 that picture had radically changed. Those same price brackets embraced only four percent of the market. It's easy to see that if we got all the business within that minor percentage we still wouldn't have satisfactory sales. Then we made the first move to climb out. We produced the Series 40, as the first rung up the ladder. It wasn't everything that we might have wished, so we bettered it in 1935. I

Below: Two brand-new 1935 Series 60 Buicks being delivered in Hollywood to Paramount Studios director John Cromwell and his wife. The Model 66C Convertible Coupe is his, and the Model 68C Convertible Phaeton is hers.

don't need to tell you men how much that able car has helped to start us on our way up.

"Sometimes I look at the job we've been working on here at the factory during the last year and a half as a sort of industrial iceberg. The biggest fact about an iceberg, you know, is that no matter how much of it looms above water, seven-eighths of it is submerged. That's the way it has seemed to me our work has appeared. At no time in Buick history has there been so much and so widespread an alteration going on as in the last few months. You have all seen signs of it. But about seven-eighths of it didn't show, wasn't ready to show

until now.

"The target of all that work . . . was the 1936 program. We didn't propose merely to bring out new models. What we undertook to do was to effect so consequential and comprehensive a change in our whole business, in product, distribution, manufacturing, advertising, and sales, that 1936 would thereafter shine out in Buick history like a beacon. We're ready to launch that program now."

Was Buick ever! The curtain was raised revealing the new car; the applause from the dealers was thunderous; probably more than any other moment in his career, this was the one Harlow Curtice would savor for the rest of his life.

"Buick's The Buy" became the first Kudner advertising theme— and a lot of people bought. Production of 1936 models would total 168,596 units, a 317-percent increase over 1935. And Buick would outsell Pontiac and move into sixth place in the industry.

Perhaps Buick dealers anticipated all this. The new cars were given names as well as numbers—Special (40), Century (60), Roadmaster (80), Limited (90)—and were officially announced September 28th. But a good many potential customers saw them in August. Following the dealer meeting, a massive driveaway was launched, Buick placing a sack lunch in the glove compartment of each car so dealers would not have to tarry long from the road. Specials on the way to California clocked 90.5 mph. Century models on the way to New York broke a hundred. For weeks afterwards, dealers talked about their drives home, and many could even call up the memory decades later. These were, they all agreed, super cars.

The new generation small engine had been introduced with the 1934 Series 40; it was continued with refinements. The old 235.3-, 278.1- and 344.8-cubic-inch engines used in the 1935 Series 50, 60 and 90 were dropped, however, and replaced with a new 320.2-cubic-inch unit with a 5.45 to one compression ratio and 120 horsepower. Weight had been considerably reduced, from 1008 pounds in 1935 to a trim 843 for the new engine. It utilized a larger bore and shorter stroke design, reducing the height of the unit as well as its piston travel. Larger valves had been installed and the old oil temperature regulator done away with. Buick claimed a decrease in valve train noise too, advertising it with decals on the rocker arm cover of each engine reading, "Buick Silent Oil Cushioned Valve In Head Eight." Whereas the Series 40 had previously been the strong road performer, now it was the Series 60 Century, with the new engine and smart small body.

One of Buick's major advancements for 1936 was piston design. Complementing his tenets regarding hydraulic braking, Dutch Bower had been reluctant to discard the reliable cast iron, tin-plated piston for the more modern and lighter weight aluminum version.

ROADMASTER!

This Roadmaster, $1255
Series 80 six-passenger
Sedan - 120-horsepower,
111-inch wheelbase —
Fenderwells extra. All Buick prices include
Safety Glass throughout as standard equipment

STYLED FOR A PARTY, BUT POWERED FOR A THRILL !

THIS high-powered, well-mannered, dazzlingly smart series eighty Buick is Roadmaster by nature as by name.

On take-off it can sink you a full inch back into the cushions with its instant sweep.

At speed on the open road it can swing that speedometer needle miles higher than any sensible man will normally want to travel.

Idling or full-out, its engine is hushed as a country snowfall.

There is literally nothing like its spectacular performance in all your past

YOU CAN AFFORD THE NEW BUICK
List prices $765 to $1945 at
range from Flint, Mich.

Subject to change without notice. Standard and special accessories groups on all models at extra cost. *Convenient GMAC time payment plan*

You'll hear this enthusiastic verdict repeated at the Automobile Shows:

"BUICK'S THE BUY!"

Every one of the new Buicks — the Special, Century, Roadmaster, or Limited — handles with the feather-balance of a fly-rod—in any one a 100-pound woman can drive all day long without strain.

Every one slows down to swift stoppage from speed under tiptoe-pressure

driving experience — and nothing approaching it today, except in the other members of that stellar quartet which has so dramatically set America talking Buick.

Every one has the same integrity of manufacture and materials—steadiness, stability, safety engineered to last through the years.

But even in such notable company, the Roadmaster eminently deserves its name. Just slip behind the wheel—drive it a mile —and you'll know why.

Buick 8
FIRST OF THE GENERAL MOTORS CARS

Among the many good ideas Harlow Curtice had for getting Buick back onto its feet was putting some zip into Buick advertising, and he hired Art Kudner to do it. Curtice had become aware of Kudner's talents during his spark plug days, when the advertising account for AC was being handled by Erwin Wasey & Company; Art Kudner was one of that firm's account executives. By the time Curtice came to Buick, Kudner had decided to start his own advertising agency—and Buick quickly became one of his first accounts. The zip that Kudner added to Buick promotion is well indicated in these advertisements for the 1936 model line.

164

"THE CAR THAT SKIPPED THE AWKWARD AGE !"

The ROADMASTER, series 80 six-passenger sedan pictured above has 120 horsepower, carries a list price of $1255 at Flint, Mich.* fenderwells extra
All Buick prices include safety glass throughout as standard equipment

THEY'RE a critical lot, those old-time Buick owners, and it means a very great deal that you see them going around now with their faces wreathed in smiles.

They have watched and wondered while car styles evolved through what seemed to be abrupt and painful stages—hoping for a streamlined car they could call beautiful, and mean it!

Then came the 1936 Buick—and streamlining blossomed forth full mature, satisfying, all trace of awkwardness gone, all ungracefulness artfully avoided!

Nowhere in the long sleek winning loveliness of this great car is there a single instance of straining for effect.

Nowhere, from tapered fender to tasteful interior, is there a suggestion of the inept hand, the groping taste.

Buick style is the welcome style of experienced artists, demonstrated again and again in that deft repetition of the fundamental motif which is the foundation of all true beauty.

Buick style is streamline style and gives full benefit of air-slipping efficiency; yet no hard angularities spoil this flowing grace, no harsh demands of function make this form unbeautiful!

But why should we tell you that Buick is beautiful as well as big— lovely to look upon as well as luxurious to ride in? Your own eyes bear grateful witness.

And for once the size of your purse puts no limit on the style you may enjoy. Buy any Buick — and you buy a car that has skipped the awkward age.

★ *$765 to $1945 are the list prices of the new Buicks at Flint, Michigan, subject to change without notice. Standard and special accessories groups at extra cost. Convenient new* **GMAC 6% TIME PAYMENT PLAN**

WHEN BETTER AUTOMOBILES ARE BUILT BUICK WILL BUILD THEM

Buick 8
FIRST OF THE GENERAL MOTORS CARS

HEADSTART to HAPPINESS!

Now's the time and here's the car to make your dreams come true . . . The Buick CENTURY Series 60 Convertible Coupe, $1135 list at Flint, Mich.

YOU know a straight white road where the new leaves wait to whisper in the breeze of your passing.

You know a pretty girl with laughter-ready lips, and an eagerness to taste the fresh caress of a soft spring night upon her cheek.

Take your pretty girl, and on that moon-washed road let the Century tell its own sweet-voiced story of power and steadiness and even-keeled comfort.

Feel the surge of its take-off, the smoothness of its swing into speed. Sample the nerveless firmness of its tiptoe hydrau-

lics, its instant responsiveness to your hands on the wheel. Test the perfect balance of it, unspoiled by jerk, shiver, strain or rubbery jumpiness—and find a motoring thrill that needs no touch of hazard to give it spice.

Not long since the winds were howling and the roads were glazed with ice. Now you have spring nights, clear roads, a headstart to the happiness that should be yours this summer in a Buick Century.

Isn't this the time to see this brilliant new Buick—and drive it—and decide to have one for your own?

NO OTHER CAR IN THE WORLD HAS ALL THESE FEATURES

Valve-in-Head Straight-Eight Engine . . . Anolite Pistons . . . Sealed Chassis . . . Luxurious "Turret Top" Body by Fisher with Fisher No Draft Ventilation . . . Tiptoe Hydraulic Brakes . . . Knee-Action Comfort and Safety . . . Torque-Tube Drive . . . Automatic Starting, Spark and Heat Control . . . Built-in Luggage Compartments . . . Front-End Ride Stabilizer

$765 to $1945 are list prices of the new Buicks at Flint, Mich. Standard and special accessories groups at extra cost

Buick **8**
A GENERAL MOTORS PRODUCT

★ ★ ★ ★ WHEN BETTER AUTOMOBILES ARE BUILT, BUICK WILL BUILD THEM ★ ★ ★ ★

WHEN WE DESIGNED FOR 1936 WE THREW AWAY ALL THE OLD DIMENS...

The Buick Limited, Series 90 four-door six passenger sedan — 120 horsepower, 138 inch wheelbase — list price at Flint. $1695

All Buick prices include safety plate glass throughout at standard equipment

WE started with a lot of experience and a clean sheet of paper when we designed the great roomy Buick Limited for 1936.

We wanted something more than a surface refinement here and there.

We deliberately set ourselves to produce the finest Buicks ever built for the fine car market—new in sparkling, streamlined beauty, new in elbow-room, leg-room, headroom comfort, new in flashing phenomenal performance, new in exuberant power.

Only one thing in the new Buick Limited is old—sound, durable, dependable Buick *quality*.

On this solid foundation we have built these sensational new-dimension cars.

Viewing them at the curb, you will

call them smartly and modernly low. Their width is more than their height.

Yet inside, the smartly tailored roof arches far above your head. There is generous space for six or eight full-grown passengers.

And perhaps the greatest surprise of all is their fingertip lightness of control, their silky mobility, their tiptoe braking, their easy obedience to a hundred pound woman at the wheel.

Come see and try these magnificently poised Buick Limiteds.

One ride and you'll know that your motor car dollar buys more than it ever did before.

NO OTHER CAR IN THE WORLD HAS ALL THESE FEATURES

Valve-in-Head Straight-Eight Engine, giving safe, sure take-off of engine of equal displacement and compression

Anolite Pistons, durable, long-lasting, 50% lighter, increase bearing life 150%

Sealed Chassis, keeps dirt and water from all moving parts, protects from wear and strain

Luxurious "Turret Top" Body by Fisher, with No Draft Ventilation—the smart, safe, stronger body built

Automatic Starting, Spark and Heat Control, for convenience, efficiency, economy

Built-in Luggage Compartments, to add ample capacity for necessary luggage

Ride Stabilizer, for elimination of side sway at speed or on curves

YOU CAN AFFORD THE NEW BUICK

List prices $765 to $1995 at range from Flint, Mich. These prices are subject to change without notice. Standard and special accessories groups on all models at extra cost.

Convenient GMAC time payment plan

Buick **8**
FIRST OF THE GENERAL MOTORS CARS

READY FOR ANYTHING AS THEY COME OFF THE L...

WHAT A PAL FOR YOUR VAC...

IN the whirring vastness of the Buick factory a gleaming new car lordly and complete rolls off the far-ranging assembly line.

There is water in the radiator, lubricant in the transmission, gas in the tank—that Buick is ready to go.

And it needs no five-hundred-mile vacation of engine-coddling—no days of crawling along behind the procession to tune it up or "wear it in."

That whole marvelously wrought and marvelously serviceable mechanism is fit and sensitive as a master's fiddle, ready for whatever you want to give it as soon as it leaves the plant and hits the road.

When you do point its eager beauty down the highway, what a fresh experience, what an exhilarating thrill it gives you!

The great tide of power that comes pouring from that valve-in-head straight-eight Buick engine in oil-cushioned silence carries you like a conqueror on its crest.

The car travels with incredible "road-sense," taking curve without weave or sway, hill without labor, control without hitch or fault—all in firm, steady, luxurious ease.

Whether you touch throttle or the big soft-action hydraulics, the positive response you get tells you *this* is the car built especially for you!

NO OTHER CAR IN THE WORLD HAS ALL THESE FEATURES

VALVE-IN-HEAD STRAIGHT-EIGHT ENGINE gives more power per unit of fuel than any other type of engine of equal displacement and compression

ANOLITE PISTONS, durable, long-lasting, 50% lighter, increase bearing life 150% from all moving parts, protects from wear and strain

LUXURIOUS "TURRET-TOP" BODY BY FISHER with No Draft Ventilation the smartest, safest, strongest body built

TIPTOE HYDRAULIC BRAKES, giving safe, straight-line stops under lightest pressure

TORQUE-TUBE DRIVE, for steadier, more stable roadability

AUTOMATIC STARTING, SPARK AND HEAT CONTROL, for convenience, efficiency, economy

BUILT-IN LUGGAGE COMPARTMENTS, add ample capacity for necessary luggage

FRONT-END RIDE STABILIZER, for elimination of side-sway at speed or on curves

SAFETY GLASS, standard equipment throughout at no extra cost

$765 to $1995 are the list prices of the new Buicks at Flint, Mich., subject to change without notice. Standard and special accessories groups on all models at extra cost.

MONTHLY PAYMENTS TO FIT YOUR PURSE! Ask about the General Motors installment plan

Buick **8**
A GENERAL MOTORS PRODUCT

★ ★ ★ ★ WHEN BETTER AUTOMOBILES ARE BUILT, BUICK WILL BUILD THEM ★ ★ ★ ★

In Hollywood, actor Ralph Morgan, his collie, his 1936 Roadmaster sedan.

Chrysler Corporation and other manufacturers then using the aluminum design were experiencing high piston wear factors, and replacement of pistons and rings was often necessary after as little as 12,000-15,000 miles. Bower preferred to wait further development.

It arrived: an aluminum piston fifty percent lighter than cast iron and coated with an anodic treatment after the piston was ground, thus providing an oxidized surface which was slightly porous and much harder. Its porosity allowed oil to adhere to the surface area of the piston thus giving a much greater lubricating property between piston and cylinder wall. The scuffing and scoring when an engine was new or cold, which had been such a problem with aluminum pistons before, was eliminated. A few production Cadillacs had featured the process, but that company's use of it had been very limited.

Buick called its new pistons Anolite, a word which coded to "An" (anodic treatment), "o" (the new oil properties) and "lite" (lighter piston weight). It was claimed the new process provided a greater piston life and allowed substantial weight and strain to be taken off the connecting rod bearings, increasing their life as much as 150 percent. Piston and connecting rod assemblies now weighed 3.86 pounds

as against 5.43 in 1935.

Engines using the new pistons were run in high speed tests at the proving grounds for more than 40,000 miles without a significant increase in oil consumption or excessive piston wear. In another check of the process, two cars—with four cast iron pistons and four Anolite pistons each—were driven 2700 miles at 45 mph on dusty gravel roads. The subsequent engine teardown showed both piston types to have worn equally: .0067. Even Dutch Bower was convinced now.

The new pistons, of course, contributed principally to the engine weight reduction, and this in turn contributed in large measure to the dramatically improved performance. Buick would claim internally that the new Century was capable of an honest 95 mph, but it didn't take customers long to discover they could push their Series 60 cars to a hundred and beyond.

Dutch Bower had to bite his tongue every time he talked about them, but Buick now offered hydraulic brakes. The system was a conventional one—cast iron drums, a master cylinder and wheel cylinders—though Bower did brag that Buick's brakes would run three times as far between adjustments as power-brake-equipped cars offered the year before. Brake linings had been carefully selected for long life and Buick cautioned its field people not to mix them with earlier lining parts stock or other brands. Special equipment had been installed at the assembly plant for bleeding the new brake system and to insure no air remained in the lines. The emergency brake lever was located under the cowl and operated through cables on the rear wheels.

Buick bodies were not shared with either Oldsmobile or Pontiac, the "suicide doors" of both making that impossible. Trunk design differed as well. All this was expensive, but it was worth it. Exclusivity always has panache. Front and rear seats were wider, interior design and trim materials were improved, bodies were more completely insulated and heavier dash mats were used to aid in reducing noise levels. The former cardboard sun visors were cloth covered, and the radiator grille was die cast rather than steel stamped.

Body styles were cut from twenty-five to fourteen and this with the fewer engines Buick now used, combined to save millions of dollars in tooling. Manifolds, clutches and fans were reduced from four to two; batteries, distributors, starter motors and mufflers from three to two; three sets of engine mountings replaced four, and there were only seven different rear springs against a former sixteen. The list went on and on. Another very smart move by Curtice.

Fuel economy was enhanced. The Series 40 Special, though slightly heavier, remained a good 15 mpg. The Century 60 was capable of 14.2 mpg at 50 mph, the Series 90 Limited was 12.6 as compared to 11.0 in 1935. Oil mileage was nearly doubled in all series.

Clutches were improved in both size and smoothness of operation. The discs and a newly designed pressure plate were said to give soft, smooth pedal action, positive control of cushioning engagement, and long life. A completely new transmission was designed and built at Buick for the larger series cars. Lighter than the previous year's version, it provided quieter operation and smoother shifting. All bearings were ball and roller, there were no bronze bushings.

Rear leaf springs were designed and mounted in such a way as to offset the loading. Because the rear end of the spring had to travel further when absorbing loads, it was nine inches longer than the front. Front springs and shock absorbers were more flexible and the stabilizer bar, mounted on the rear suspension when knee action was first installed at Buick, was relocated on the front suspension for better rideability and control. Frames were lighter, yet stiffer.

Series 40 cars had a wheelbase of 118 inches; the 60 was 122; the 80, 131; the 90, 138. Gear ratios were 4.44 on the 40; 3.90, 4.22 and 4.55 respectively on the larger cars.

All in all, the 1936 cars represented a gargantuan undertaking from all quarters in the Buick organization. And Harley Earl over at Art & Colour had contributed handsomely too. Everyone everywhere said the new Buicks had style.

Early 1936 saw a major engineering change at Buick—not in the car but in the man who would henceforth head the department. Dutch Bower was transferred to Opel in Germany. Whether this might have been the result of Curtice's disenchantment with Bower's penchant not to consider an engineering advance a reality until it was without-shadow-of-doubt proven is speculative—but Bower proceeded to do a fine job reorganizing the Opel engineering department . . . and Buick received the services of a top-notch new chief engineer. His name was Charles A. Chayne.

Born in Harrisburg, Pennsylvania in 1898, Chayne was perhaps the best educated engineer in Buick's history thus far, attending Harvard and the Massachusetts Institute of Technology, graduating from the latter in 1919. He worked briefly for the National Advisory Committee for Aeronautics, returned to his alma mater to teach until 1926, that year went to work for Lycoming, and the year following became an engine designer for Marmon. He joined Buick in 1930 as supervisor in charge of the engine area, and was promoted to assistant chief engineer under Bower in November 1933.

Chayne's promotion to the top job in the engineering department was consequential. Now Buick had a heady triumvirate—Curtice, Hufstader and Chayne—and one which would remain intact until 1948. With the Chayne appointment, John Dolza took over as assistant chief engineer.

Despite his work schedule during those busy months Curtice, an

The 1936 Special Series 40 Model 46 Business Coupe for two passengers.

avid fight fan, managed to keep up with what was happening in the boxing world—and turned it into Buick's advantage. Having earlier taken an interest in the career of a boxer named Joe Louis, he saw to it that Buick had the radio rights to live coverage broadcast from ringside when Louis, a young heavyweight contender, met Max Baer, the former heavyweight champ, in September 1935. To call the fight, he wanted someone impartial who could deliver an accurate and rapid-fire commentary, and the man selected after numerous auditions was Clem McCarthy. Radio people scoffed, McCarthy was an expert at announcing horse races—but could a turf man properly handle a boxing match? Yes, indeed, he could. "Authority and vividness etched in exciting vocal lines" was the rather cumbersome way one reviewer described the style of "Buick Mac." In that fight, Louis, McCarthy and Buick all came out winners. Telegrams and letters of thanks poured into Flint afterwards. They were put in a big pile on top of Curtice's desk.

What Harlow Curtice had accomplished in a short space of time was nothing short of phenomenal. It was almost otherworldly. The Flint fates were smiling on the northside car builders once again. Buick had been saved. And Harlow Curtice had just begun.

The Buick—

COLOR PORTFOLIO I

Page preceding: 1910 Model 10 Toy Tonneau \ Above left: 1905 Model C Touring \ Above right: 1907 Model F Touring
Below: 1906 Model G Runabout \ Right: 1911 Model 14 Roadster

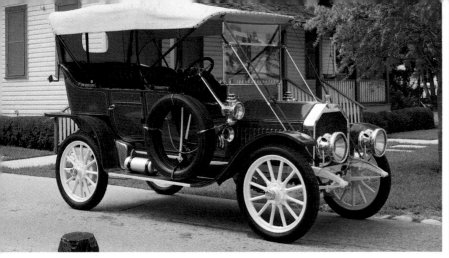

Above left: 1909 Model 17 Touring | Above right: 1913 Buick-Zinn Racer | Below: 1909 Model 10 Surrey | Right: 1910 Marquette-Buick Race Car

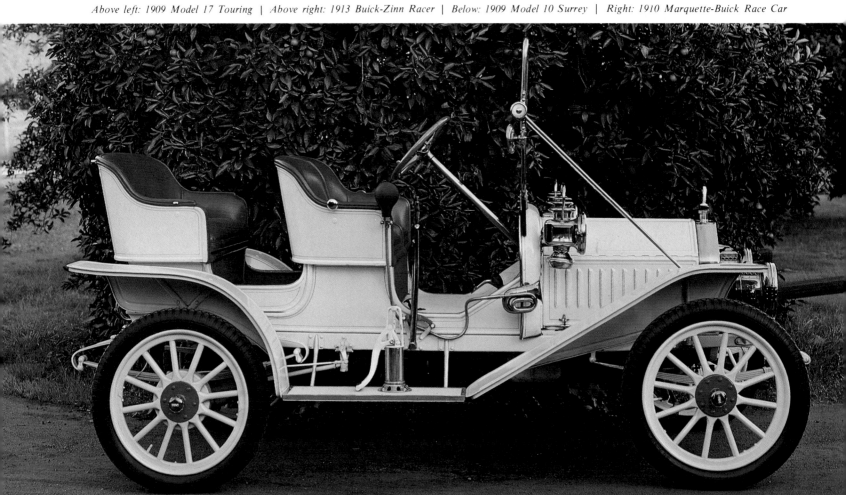

Left: 1911 Model 26 Runabout | Above: 1912 Model 36 Roadster | Below: 1913 Model 31 Touring

Left: 1913 Model 30 Roadster | Above: 1915 Model C-36 Roadster | Below: 1917 Model D-45 Touring

Left: 1918 Model E-45 Touring | Above: 1919 Model H-49 Touring
Below: 1920 Model K-45 Touring

Left: 1921 Model 21-45 Touring | *Above: 1922 Roadster, English body, coachbuilder unknown*
Below: 1923 Model 23-41 Touring Sedan

Left: 1924 Model 24-51 Brougham Touring Sedan | Above: 1925 Standard Series Model 25-25 Touring
Below: 1926 Standard Series Model 26-26 Coupe

Above: 1927 Master Series Model 27-55 DeLuxe Sport Touring | Below: 1927 Master Series Model 27-58 Coupe

Above: 1928 Standard Series Model 28-26S Country Club Coupe | Below: 1928 Master Series Model 28-58 Coupe

*Above: 1929 Series 116 Model 29-20 Two-Door Sedan \ Below: 1930 Marquette Model 30-36 Business Coupe
Right: 1930 Series 60 Model 30-64C DeLuxe Coupe*

Left: 1930 Series 40 Model 30-44 Sport Roadster | Above: 1931 Series 50 Model 54 Sport Roadster
Below: 1932 Series 90 Model 91 Club Sedan

Above: 1932 Series 90 Model 96C Convertible Coupe
Below: 1933 Series 50 Model 58 Victoria Coupe

Above: 1934 Series 60 Model 68C Convertible Phaeton \ Below: 1935 Series 40 Model 46C Convertible Coupe
Page following: 1936 Century Model 61 Four-Door Sedan

OWNER & PHOTOGRAPHER CREDITS

1910 Model 10 Toy Tonneau
Yesterday's Wheels Collection
Photograph by Roy Query

1905 Model C Touring
Owner: Alton Walker
Photograph by Rick Lenz

1907 Model F Touring
Owner: John Jonigian
Photograph by Rick Lenz

1906 Model G Runabout
Owner: Jack Garrison
Photograph by Rick Lenz

1911 Model 14 Roadster
Owner: Earl Van Antwerp
Photograph by Rick Lenz

1909 Model 10 Surrey
Owner: Neil Vaughn
Photograph by Rick Lenz

1909 Model 17 Touring
Owner: Stanley W. Kahn
Photograph by Roy Query

1913 Buick-Zinn Racer
Owner: George M. Nutting
Photograph by Roy Query

1910 Marquette-Buick
Harrah's Automobile Collection
Photograph by Rick Lenz

1911 Model 26 Runabout
Owner: Greg Fauth
Photograph by William L. Bailey

1912 Model 36 Roadster
Owner: Maynard O. Hall
Photograph by Rick Lenz

1913 Model 31 Touring
Owner: Tom Hinsch
Photograph by Rick Lenz

1913 Model 30 Roadster
Owner: B. Plez Nance
Photograph by Rick Lenz

1915 Model C-36 Roadster
Owner: Robert Scott
Photograph by Rick Lenz

1917 Model D-45 Touring
Owner: Lee Hanks, Jr.
Photograph by Roy Query

1918 Model E-45 Touring
Owner: Raymond LaPorte
Photograph by Rick Lenz

1919 Model H-49 Touring
Owner: Jack H. Knowlden
Photograph by Rick Lenz

1920 Model K-45 Touring
Owner: Nelson C. Vout
Photograph by William L. Bailey

1921 Model 21-45 Touring
Owner: Ronald W. Cook
Photograph by William L. Bailey

1922 Roadster with English body
Owner: Frank A. Kleptz
Photograph by Rick Lenz

1923 Model 23-41 Touring Sedan
Owner: R.L. Green
Photograph by Rick Lenz

1924 Model 24-51 Brougham Touring Sedan
Owner: Lou Staller
Photograph by Stan Grayson

1925 Standard Series Model 25-25 Touring
C & C Antique Auto Museum
Photograph by Roy Query

1926 Standard Series Model 26-26 Coupe
Owner: Gordon Dennis
Photograph by Rick Lenz

1927 Master Series Model 27-55 DeLuxe Sport Touring
Owner: Robert J. Hadden
Photograph by Rick Lenz

1927 Master Series Model 27-58 Coupe
C & C Antique Auto Museum
Photograph by Roy Query

1928 Standard Series Model 28-26S Country Club Coupe
Owner: Joseph Kotlar
Photograph by Dan Carter

1928 Master Series Model 28-58 Coupe
Owner: Al Lipp
Photograph by Rick Lenz

1929 Series 116 Model 29-20 Two-Door Sedan
Owner: Paul Smock
Photograph by Rick Lenz

1930 Marquette Model 30-36 Business Coupe
Owner: Richard Loveday
Photograph by Rick Lenz

1930 Series 60 Model 30-64C DeLuxe Coupe
Owner: Steve Javorek
Photograph by Roy Query

1930 Series 40 Model 30-44 Sport Roadster
Owner: Guy B. Bennett, Jr.
Photograph by Roy Query

1931 Series 50 Model 54 Sport Roadster
Owner: Don Allen
Photograph by Rick Lenz

1932 Series 90 Model 91 Club Sedan
Owner: David Crow
Photograph by Rick Lenz

1932 Series 90 Model 96C Convertible Coupe
Owners: Carter and Betty Taylor
Photograph by Roy Query

1933 Series 50 Model 58 Victoria Coupe
Owner: Larry J. Havens
Photograph by Rick Lenz

1934 Series 60 Model 68C Convertible Phaeton
Owner: Steve Qua
Photograph by Rick Lenz

1935 Series 40 Model 46C Convertible Coupe
Owner: Ray Lawson
Photograph by William L. Bailey

1936 Century Model 61 Four-Door Sedan
Owner: Bob Zaitlin
Photograph by Rick Lenz

Chapter Ten

SHIFTING INTO SECOND

Harlow Curtice was fond of metaphor. Had he been asked to render his performance for '36 figuratively, he might have said that he jammed the gearshift lever of his Buick machinery into low, pushed throttle to floorboard, and pulled Buick out of the ditch and back onto the road. What he was going to do next was obvious. For '37 he was going to shift into second.

By November of 1935 it had become apparent that the '36 cars were going to be a strong sales success. October had seen Buick deliver 14,164 units, the largest single month's business in more than five years. Total sales through November 20th were 73,470 cars, vis-à-vis 64,889 for the same period the year before. The 4479 Buicks delivered during the second ten days of November broke a record that had been standing since 1926. By the end of that month, Buick had built and shipped more than 30,000 of the new 1936 cars and had on hand the largest bank of unfilled dealer car orders in a half decade. Production was raised to 800 cars a day to meet the demand.

But Curtice knew that at least part of the sales success was due to an external factor, the rapidly improving economy of the country which benefited all industry. Now his worry was overconfidence. In late 1935, with records being broken virtually every day, Curtice told his people, "The uphill pull is yet to come, sure to come."

As the first 1937 cars were driven off the assembly line, Hufstader urged Buick dealers to clean and polish their showrooms and to reduce used car inventories "by vigorous selling and the advertising of special sales. Use any means within your power to get speedy action, for you'll need floor space for the new trade-ins."

The success story of '36 had to be repeated. If it wasn't, the industry would buzz with talk of "fluke" and "flash in the pan"—and Buick would be back where it had been before Curtice. How to convey this to his dealers, how to combine verve with caution, how to say congratulations for '36 without suggesting a slowdown of effort for '37, how to avoid any semblance that resting on laurels could even be pondered—all this concerned Curtice as he prepared his remarks to his dealers for new car announcement week in Flint.

He was enthusiastic, to be sure, he was congratulatory as well—but he was pragmatic too, and he made special note of the role of General Motors in Buick affairs. That was good politics. It has been said—and accurately—that without the attention and assistance of GM, Buick might easily have proceeded from nadir to oblivion in 1933. Curtice was anxious that his dealers recognize the close GM/Buick liaison. And if the VIP's at corporate level obtained a copy of his speech? Well, that wouldn't hurt either.

"Buick enjoys a special relation with General Motors . . .," he said. "We were the first unit in the parent corporation. We were for years the producer of the greatest dollar sales. We had our troublous period and now we're starting in to make good all over again in a big way. General Motors has pride in that as well as we have. I know it is the popular impression that each year General Motors picks out a pet division to be the recipient of its special attention. It was widely said that Buick was the fortunate division this year. That may or may not be true, but I want to venture the assurance now that Buick will *always* be a 'pet' division with the corporation so long as it deserves to be. I say this in acknowledgment of the greater contributions General Motors has made to our 1937 program, in every particular of sound, generous and enthusiastic cooperation. When you have seen all phases of that program, you will see what I mean by our special relation. Don't forget that. It is valuable to you. It is one of the strongest weapons in our whole armory."

Among the "musts" for the 1937 product that Curtice laid before Chayne's engineering department were "better styling . . . bigger, stronger, quieter . . . better value." No mean task, since the steel and rubber industries had raised costs to Buick by about ten percent, but to the credit of the engineers, they gave Curtice the car he wanted and still held the price consistent with 1936. Indeed, assistant chief engineer Dolza was to say in later years that Buick reached its quality peak in 1937.

The atmosphere in the engineering department was different now. Dutch Bower had been known as "Mr. Quality" at Buick, but he had come to be called "Mr. Driver" too. Nights, holidays and Sundays were common hours for engineers to work under Bower, and he demanded results. Life under Chayne would be easier, there would be

Page preceding: The 1937 assembly line in Flint. Above: Alfred P. Sloan, Jr. extends congratulations to Harlow Curtice on the 1937 Buick line. Below: A 1938 Buick chassis is explained to San Francisco auto editors.

less tension—engineering in quality could be accomplished more amenably. Chayne was a much more polished individual than Bower had been, and a better engineer. He was more organized, spoke well before a group, got his points across with much more facility. All this worked to the advantage of Buick—and its cars.

The 1937 models were introduced on October 24th, 1936. They had a new longer look with pointed hoods, headlights and fenderlights—and there were more of them, twenty-two models, increased from fifteen in 1936.

With a quarter-inch added to its stroke (from 3⅞ to 4⅛ inches), the Series 40 engine was increased in displacement from 233 cubic inches to 248, and was now 100 hp at 3200 rpm. It had a new block, crankshaft and rods, and a higher compression ratio of 5.7 to one. A stiffer flywheel housing was introduced to the Series 40 to reduce the amount of shock transmitted through the torque tube. Previously, the transmission had been known to jump out of gear, which could be irritating.

A reworked crankshaft and main bearings were given to the larger series engines. And all Buick engines now used aluminum rocker arm shaft brackets for a much quieter valve train noise level during normal operating temperatures and the colder warm-up period.

The new Series 40 would accelerate from 10-60 mph in 19.2 seconds, which was faster than the 1936 Century. But the 1937 Century was faster too, improving its 10-60 time from 19.6 to 18.5. Top speed for the Series 40 was listed at 90 mph; it was 101 for the Series 60, 91 for the Series 80 and 88 for the Series 90.

All 1937 Buicks had larger gas tanks, improved generators, running board radio antennas, stabilizer bars front and rear, and a thermal circuit breaker in the lighting circuit to eliminate the need for fuses. The new radio antenna had resulted from a special Buick engineering project indicating that the running board itself could be used as an antenna if properly insulated from the body.

The same engineering group responsible for that discovery was responsible as well for testing radio receiver selectivity, sensitivity and fidelity. RCA, Zenith and Columbia were among the units evaluated. Early radio development in the industry had placed the speaker on the firewall of the car with the result that sound reproduction was hampered, noise was excessive, and when the volume level was good for the driver it was concomitantly bad for anyone riding in the back seat. To solve this, Buick engineered a combination radio/speaker unit and, with considerable logistic difficulty, managed to mount it in the center of the dashboard. Buick was one of the first in the industry—perhaps *the* first—to go to a center dash location with its radio.

New to '37 Buicks, too, was the "Aerobat" carburetor. Employing an aircraft principal, it was designed to allow more favorable and consistent operation under demanding conditions. The change involved the re-engineering of the center location of the fuel nozzle in the carburetor bowl to provide a uniform flow of fuel to the cylinders. The metering system would function on any grade, it would not flood when parked on a steep hill, it eliminated the tendency to stall on fast stops, provided smoother acceleration at low speeds, made hot engine and hot weather starting easier. In the past Buick had, for the most part, used only one source of supply for its carburetors. In 1937 two sources would be used, and there is an interesting story as to why.

In 1936 Adolph Braun was preparing to go to bed one evening when the phone rang. The caller identified himself as William Knudsen and Braun thought he was the victim of a joke. Why would a corporation official as high up as Knudsen be calling the Buick carburetion engineer at this time of night? Braun told the caller to quit kidding and almost hung up on him. But it was Knudsen—and he was calling to warn Braun that Buick would soon be without carburetors because Stromberg, then the division's only carburetor supplier, was set to go out on strike the following day. Knudsen suggested Carter as a quick substitute, Braun countered with Marvel—and Marvel it was. That company was quickly contacted. Buick was able to maintain production, but just barely, and thereafter was always careful to maintain two sources of carburetor supply.

The strike, however, was not the only carburetion problem Buick experienced on the 1937 cars. The last two or three months of production saw carburetor float levels being set too high. Dealers were forced to reset frequently to get reasonable performance. The situation was not really corrected until the introduction of the 1938 cars when Buick insisted upon a higher level of quality control from the suppliers. As Chayne himself said, "It was just plain hell to keep those things coming through consistently."

Late in 1936 the UAW sitdown strikes hit Flint. One of the Fisher Body plants in the city was among the first struck, immediately causing a problem on the Buick assembly line. Attempts were made to shut down Buick too. Reports of union organizers running through the assembly facilities with baseball bats to make sure everyone was out of the plant are still remembered by Buick old-timers.*

Less turbulent, but significant as well, was the advent for 1937 of all-steel body construction. Used on the Series 40 and 60 cars, these bodies were the result of a cooperative venture between Buick and Fisher body engineers. Automotive body construction had been the subject of numerous professional engineering seminars since the

---

* However, the focus of the famous sitdown strike which led to recognition of the UAW was at Chevrolet and Fisher in Flint, not at Buick.

Above, from the left: Charlie Chayne and William S. Knudsen look at the "knee action" of the 1937 Buick with Flint banker A.G. Bishop. Below: Curtice and Sloan talk things over at Buick sales banquet, September '37.

early 1930's. Composite (wood and steel combination) and all-steel were the choices available to body builders, and the choice made was largely based on the particular requirements of the car and the general market in which it was expected to sell. There were advantages and disadvantages to each type.

It was really a matter of economics. The all-steel body adapted best to volume production, where its per-unit cost was less than the composite. The composite body was cheaper per unit to produce in low-volume or luxury class cars. Thus Buick decided to go with all steel for its Specials and Centurys, retaining for its Roadmasters and Limiteds the "time-proven custom wood and steel construction."

Initial work with all-steel construction had shown a greater factor of noise, both when the car was being driven and when its doors were closed, than did the composite body. That "tinny" sound was clearly heard by the quality-conscious "pride of work ethic" engineers who were working with the problem. The wooden body main sills of composite construction were recognized as good sound insulators between the floor pan and the body walls and were highly effective in keeping chassis and floor vibrations from reaching the passenger compartment. Another composite body advantage was the ability of wood to render the noise of a door being closed solid and substantial rather than a clatter of metal. Body designers had felt that so long as these noticeable differences existed between the two body types, it would not be wise to use the all-steel body on higher quality cars.

As the state of the art progressed, however, different means of sound deadening were found which soon brought the all-steel body to a level very nearly matching that of the composite body in quietness. In addition, it had been discovered that much of the noise with early steel construction was arriving in the body from the chassis. That problem was eliminated in the 1937 Specials and Centurys with a new I-beam frame, a version more rigid than Buick frames of years past. Further, large and resilient rubber shims were inserted between body and frame at all points of connection to further aid in reducing the areas in which noise could be introduced into the body.

Structurally, the new Series 40 and 60 bodies were composed of steel outer panels reinforced by a framework of steel stampings within, all joined together into one assembly by welding. Body sills and pillars were hollow box sections formed by welding stamped steel channel sections together. For additional strength, the inner body panels were ribbed, but as lightly as possible to keep total body weight down.

Buick customers received some real advantages from these new body designs. Maximum body width had been increased 2⅞ inches over 1936, seat width three inches in front and an inch and a half in the rear. The height of the car had been reduced more than an inch,

the floor level more than two inches, providing greater headroom inside. Door openings were higher, and on four-door sedans, the rear doors were wider for easier passenger access. There was increased leg room in the rear, and trunk space was augmented as well.

Given the trend toward streamlining in all modes of transportation, Fisher Body had come up with a new "fastback" trunk line for General Motors in 1937. At Buick it was called "Plain Back," which described it well, a trunk design flowing in one unbroken line from roof to lower body panel. The design was first available on the two- and four-door sedans and was expanded later in the year to convertible sedans. The traditional hump-back was continued and termed "Trunk Back." Either style was available to the purchaser. The "Plain Back" was very popular on the 1937 cars, but it quickly lost its appeal. (It would be phased out with a special handful of limited production cars built during the 1940 model year.) The reason was simple. The public liked streamlining so long as it was practical. The "Plain Back" afforded twelve cubic feet of trunk space, the "Trunk Back" offered fourteen. Granted, 1936 Series 40 and 60 models had provided only nine cubic feet of trunk space, three less than the 1937 "Plain Back," but when customers discovered they would get two more with a little hump, they overwhelmingly concluded they would rather have room for another suitcase than be chic.

Coupe bodies for the Series 40 and 60 were improved too. The area behind the front seat had been lengthened and two opera seats added so passengers could be accommodated with sufficient leg room and head clearance. When the opera seats were folded flush with the body compartment, a generous storage space resulted. Since the body was longer in '37, two rear-quarter windows were added. In 1936 convertible coupes and closed coupes were available only with sidemounts since adequate room did not exist in the trunk to store the spare tires. For 1937 the extra wheel and tire was carried in a compartment below the rumble seat, with access through a separate door in the rear just below the rumble seat door lid.

New rear-quarter window ventilators had been designed for the Series 40 and 60 four-door sedans. The entire window was hinged on vertical pivots near its front edge and swung outward at the rear when opened. The pivots were designed with sufficient friction to hold the window in whatever position was desired and the window was locked with a simple T-handle fastener.

The bodies for Series 80 and 90 Roadmasters and Limiteds were, comparatively, little changed. New instrument panels were, however, featured in all 1937 Buicks. Instruments were grouped to the left directly in front of the driver, gloveboxes were moved to the right of the dash (necessary because of the center-of-dash availability of a radio), and an ash tray was standard equipment. A "severely plain

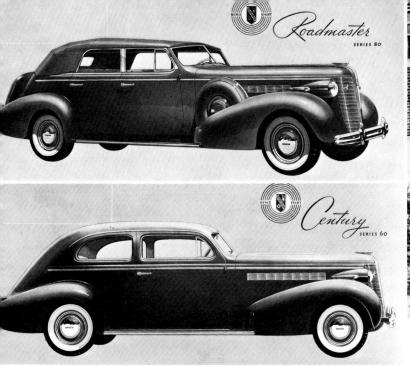

Roadmaster SERIES 80

Century SERIES 60

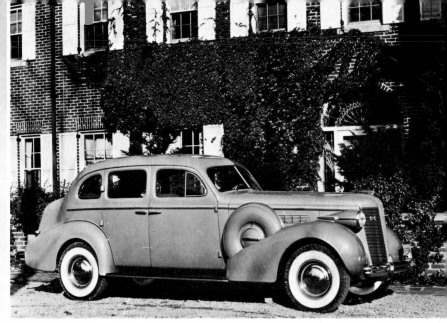

Left: For 1937, the Roadmaster Model 80C Four-Door Phaeton and the Century Model 64 Touring Sedan. Above: Model 61 Century sedan with Trunk Back for 1937. Below: The '37 Special 46C Convertible Coupe.

style" designed to add "dignity and refinement" was Buick's description for upholstery and trim. Several Bedford cords and taupe mohair fabrics in various shades of brown and grey were available, together with red, blue, green, grey, tan and black leather. Rear-compartment ash trays were located in the front seatback on four-door sedans, on two-doors at the front edge of both rear armrests.

New garnish moldings on the door windows were attached with a concealed fastener, eliminating the oval-headed screws and washers formerly used. Clutch and brake pedal seals were of the rubber bellows type, replacing the former felt, which gave a more positive sealing area and reduced the possibility of dust and engine fumes entering the passenger compartment. Drip moldings ran from the beltline at the front over all large windows to the rear quarter on all closed car bodies. There was new body hardware throughout.

And if all these cars didn't offer everything desired—and you knew someone—you could get another Buick. Harlow Curtice, for example, had a Century convertible coupe built with special trim and the initials H.H.C. on the center of the front door. Another Century convertible coupe with a high compression head and special axle was delivered to a man named Landell. Other cars were provided with special paint, and several Series 40's were assembled with Series 90 trim.

In calendar year 1936 Buick produced 179,533 cars, 4.9 percent of the total industry figure. In calendar year 1937 Buick built 227,038 cars which translated to 5.8 percent. Obviously Buick had been no fluke, no flash in the pan. And now the company had its 1938 models which have since become among the most prized, the most respected and the most sought after of Buicks ever built.

Styling changes for '38 comprised a couple of quick sleight of hand tricks: a simple widening of the horizontal bar spacing in the grille and a redesign of hubcaps into a scallop look. But the effect was smashing, one of the subtlest yet most successful facelifts ever applied to an American automobile.

The biggest changes were in engineering, and these were literally among the biggest ever to come out of Buick: "Torque Free Springing," "Dynaflash Engine," "Self Shifter."* That the company feared some competitive reprisal with the introduction of these advances was indicated at the dealer meeting when Hufstader cautioned, "Four wheel brakes went through a period of controversy. Knee-Action was subjected to a competitive smearing campaign. Competitors will be no less alert, will in fact be literally driven by necessity to point a finger of suspicion at our new ride and engineering developments at Buick, which means that we must be prepared and constant-

ly vigilant. . . ."

There were other refinements throughout, which were modest enough to escape the ire of the competition but worthy enough to be noticed. From ten to forty-seven pounds had been trimmed from the 1938 cars, largely through the use of new frames. The same battery was used on all series and was now located on the frame at the right side of the engine. It was insulated with a metal shield for protection from engine heat and directed a cooling stream of air over the battery from the front of the engine compartment. Differential bearing failure reported by a few owners of 1936 and 1937 cars was corrected with a high spherical roller differential side bearing with better self-aligning characteristics than the ball bearings previously used and capable of carrying considerably greater stresses and loads.

The emergency brake lever assembly, with a design change to the ratchet mechanism teeth and a revised mechanical arm linkage, proved more efficient and easily operable. Clutch chatter, a problem in '37, was solved with a new facing material. An interesting option was a trunk-mounted radio—a first for Buick—which took up valuable luggage space but some Series 90 buyers had apparently implied they preferred that to having control of the radio up front in the chauffeur's compartment. Doubtless this re-engineering for the carriage trade hadn't concerned chief engineer Chayne much.

What did was the new rear coil spring suspension. This was his personal pride, the first radical engineering change he introduced to Buick after being appointed to his new post. The original drawings had been done on a sketch pad at the IMA Auditorium in Flint, probably during the announcement meeting for the 1936 cars. Between speeches, Chayne had been talking with Vern Mathews about what might be done to eliminate leaf springs and had sketched his ideas for Mathews "almost exactly as the suspension went into production." Buick claimed an industry first with the design. Most other manufacturers would eventually follow.

The semi-elliptic leaf spring to support the rear axle and provide springing for rear suspension components had become pretty much an industry standard. But it had inherent problems too, and no one believed it was the final answer to a comfortable ride. Because the springs supported the rear axle and transmitted torque to the frame, they had to be heavily designed to bear those stresses. The Buick ride had always been a better-than-average one principally through the use of the torque tube which absorbed much of the stress of the springs. But the semi-elliptic spring had to be periodically lubricated to prevent squeaks, and that was a bother. And before anything like coil springs could be considered, shock absorbers had to advance to the point where the additional demands placed upon them by the new suspension system could be handled. The shock absorbers finally

*The fascinating story behind the "Self Shifter" is told in the Appendices.

supplied by Delco to Buick for the 1938 cars were fully four times as large as the conventional rear shock absorbers used previously.

One of Chayne's major concerns was that the public, with no past experience to draw upon concerning four-wheel coil springs, would conclude that Buick now had an independent rear suspension, and that was a rumor he didn't want circulated. Buick engineers had experimented extensively at the proving grounds with 1937 production models and experimental 1938 cars converted to i.r.s., and they had not liked what they found. In Germany, Mercedes had been using an independent rear suspension system for years, especially on its race cars—but Buick had been informed that due to the problems encountered the company would be giving it up and returning to a solid rear axle. This only reinforced Buick thoughts on the subject.

The difficulties Buick had encountered with its early i.r.s. experiments were many. Camber would change radically under some driving conditions. When the car was rocked, both rear wheels would rock with it—or if the supporting linkage was changed so both rear wheels would remain at right angles when simultaneously rolling over a bump, the camber would go wild and the sides of the tires would scrub on the road. All these difficulties had introduced a series of terrific handling problems, and engineering attempts in compensating for them had not been successful.

For a long time Buick engineers had been unable to find a system which—in Chayne's words—would "not waggle its tail when it went down the road, give a snakey feeling when you rode in the back seat, and not be of such expensive construction that it would be prohibitive for production." Chayne's concern regarding expense was the cost to install the two necessary universal joints on each half of the axle to get power from the differential and out to the wheels. So i.r.s was out; fighting its problems was less desirable than opting instead for the solid rear axle with its simplicity, proven dependability and economical construction.

So far as Buick was then able to determine, no other automaker in this country was about to come out with an i.r.s. system on a production car. Chayne had a feeling that Packard "was about to use some trick suspension stuff" with a transverse radius rod, as Buick had earlier done, but he also heard that Packard was having some trouble making springs and shackles strong enough to use the radius rod without wrecking the frame.

Stiffening up rear suspension for special demands placed on the car was going to be a new experience for Buick field people. In the past, if a customer wanted a stiffer spring for pulling a trailer or for more load-carrying capacity, new spring leaves could be added. Now complete spring assemblies with stiffer spring rates would have to be used. But, it was pointed out, special application springs would be

Above: The 1938 Roadmaster Model 81 Touring Sedan, without sidemounts, a rarity. Below: The Special Convertible Coupe, Model 46C, for 1938; the top-of-the-line Limited Model 90 Four-Door Touring Sedan for 1938.

available from normal replacement parts stock.

Buick engineers had decided to remove the rear stabilizer on 1938 cars and substitute a radius rod. By doing this, they were able to change the roll center of the rear suspension and control the amount of body roll in a tight corner. The noticeable difference in handling would come in a hard fast turn in which the body would both roll and swing to one side at the same time. The new radius rod was not designed to control roll so much as it was body sway, and it was body swinging which gave such an out-of-control sensation especially to rear seat passengers. With the elimination of the rear stabilizer, entirely leaving the roll on the outside wheel in a hard corner, the car was better balanced.

Semi-elliptic springs and a radius rod, Buick found, made for a fight in the action of the spring itself. And there was plenty of fight, indeed, because with the suspension radius rods installed on 1937 test cars, the mounting brackets for the rod were ripped away from the frame during an overnight test run. Cadillac was using the radius rod on its leaf spring, and Buick had attempted to duplicate it. When the Buick test cars performed so dismally, the engineers acquired a standard production 1937 Cadillac to see what they were doing wrong. At the end of a day's testing on the Belgian block road at the track, the Cadillac's rods and brackets were dragging on the ground. Buick engineers concluded that their counterparts at Cadillac didn't test cars very severely.

With Buick's new coil springs, attempts to soften up the ride were no longer required, in fact it became necessary to find ways to stiffen it up! Another benefit was the life of the springs themselves, the coils would last some three times as long as semi-elliptics.

To check handling characteristics of the new rear suspension under emergency conditions, Buick hired an independent test and camera crew to drive one of the cars with coil springs installed and a dynamite cap wired to a rear tire. When the tire was blown at 70 mph, the car was so easily brought to a stop it was thought at first the cap had failed to detonate. The rear tires under blow-out conditions would whip over far enough to hit the wheel house from about 50 mph on up. But the wheelhouse would not be hit as hard; the new system simply did not swing as far sideways under emergency conditions as the old semi-elliptics had.

But a new Series 60 Century did hit something: 103 mph, as clocked by Buick. Horsepower of the two Buick engines had been increased from 100 to 130 for 1937 to 107 and 141 for 1938. And with no corresponding increase in fuel consumption. The reason was a mouthful to say—the new "Turbulator Pistons" in the "Dynaflash Eight" engines—and it had all come about rather inadvertently.

A mechanic working in a dealership, while rebuilding the engine in his personal Buick, had fastened some slugs to the top of the pistons before reinstalling them. Driving the car afterwards, he was convinced he had increased the horsepower, and showed the pistons to a Buick field man. The idea subsequently found its way to the experimental section in Flint.

It appeared at first that the power improvement had been the result of an increase in compression ratio since the combustion chamber had been diminished. But that was not in fact what had happened. The slugs had effectively changed the shape of the combustion chamber making it more efficient. When Buick engineers figured that out, they became immediately interested.

Development of the new "turbulator"—sometimes called the "bump top"—piston design was assigned to Joseph D. Turlay.

Buicks for 1938 along Riverside Drive in Memphis, Tennessee. From the left: Special Model 48 Two-Door Touring Sedan, Special Series 40 chassis, Special Model

Turlay, who had come to Buick in January of 1929 as a draftsman, had worked in the engine test area, in the automatic transmission development group with John Dolza, and on both crankshafts and cylinder heads for the second generation Buick straight-eights. The 1935 cars featured valve mechanisms and camshafts designed by Turlay and for many years thereafter engines from Buick used Turlay's cam ideas. Later he would be responsible for such advances as the experimental narrow vee developed just after World War II, the experimental XP-300 engine and the Buick aluminum engine, the first V-8 in 1953 and the V-6 of the early 1960's—and when he retired it was stated that he had set a record for the number of patents granted to him while employed at Buick.

Turlay's experiments with the pistons showed him that when he located the bump away from the spark plug there was a "quench area" near the cylinder head on the far side of the piston. It was another way of achieving what was called "volume control," then an ongoing program within GM. In general terms, research was trying to discover combustion chamber designs which would allow the use of higher compression ratios without a severe spark rap problem.

The venerable L-head engine of the industry's early days basically used a flat-top piston and a uniform and flat combustion chamber. At low speeds and with only moderate loads, the engine would pre-ignite and spark knock badly. Through the years, manufacturers tried varying combustion chamber configurations and spark plug placements to alleviate the problem. By the mid-1930's, there was no real consistency in L-head design.

Car makers using ohv designs confined themselves generally to the same conventional chamber with rounded edges. No one had found anything to be gained by modifications attempting to obtain a chill-

ur-Door Sport Sedan, Special Model 41 Four-Door Touring Sedan. Above: The Art Kudner theme for advertising the top-of-the-line Series 90 Limited for 1938.

ing section in the combustion chamber until Chevrolet introduced its first ohv six in 1929, which was basically an L-head chamber developed so that an ohv design could be used. But Chevrolet's next move was a complicated casting with a warped surface and some real progress was made.

Using ultra high speed photography, it was found that as the flame progressed in its journey across the chamber, the speed of the burning accelerated. As the flame burned, it compressed the air/fuel charge just ahead of it and raised the temperature of the mixture not yet burned. Naturally, the higher the temperature of the unburned fuel still in the chamber, the easier it became for the flame wave to suddenly ignite it. As a result, the velocity picture of the burn in the chamber increased dramatically just as the burn neared its end. If the heat could be reduced so this last part of the burn would be less violent and abrupt, detonation or "spark rap" would be greatly reduced or eliminated.

Combustion chambers were designed with thinner walls to ease the passage of heat out of the chamber and into the water jacket. Along with this, some attention was paid to the total distance the flame had to travel on the L-head engine from the spark plug to the furthest point in the combustion chamber. During the early 1930's a Chevrolet engineer named Taub developed a combustion chamber placing intake and exhaust valves at different angles in the head and changing chamber shape into a slight warp effect.

This was progress, but Buick did not like the substantial increase it meant in the expense of making a head. A double machine operation was necessary for valve placement, and the complicated head casting shape was difficult to control consistently in production. There was a warping tendency, and valve seat trouble developed easily. But Buick respected the design sufficiently to want to investigate further.

It became the Buick intent to change combustion chamber shape by utilizing piston design alone. However, with the decreased clearance realized with a domed piston—between the piston's high point in cylinder travel and the position of the valves when fully extended— it was immediately realized that the new domed pistons would have to clear the valve with both piston and valves in their extreme extended positions, so that if a valve stuck open the piston would not hit it and ruin the cylinder head.

The shape upon which Turlay finally settled was the product of cut and try until he got a definite increase in usable compression ratio. The new pistons did not cause an increase in piston side thrust—and, strangely enough, Buick was not entirely certain exactly what the flame travel pattern was when the mixture was ignited in the different combustion chamber which resulted. All Buick engineers really knew for certain was that flame travel was now so rapid that detonation

was reduced. For the same amount of spark rap which had been built into the 1937 cars—and a small amount was commercially acceptable—Buick engineers now had a higher usable compression ratio for 1938.

In 1937 scored pistons due to excessive heat build-up had been a vexation, due to the fuel-air mixtures blowing by the upper compression rings and removing the lubricating oil off the cylinder wall. This had occurred to a minor extent in normal service driving but now promised to be greatly magnified with the new style pistons. Some unusual dynamometer readings on the first test engines had been revealed. With only two or three full-power runs, power would suddenly fall off badly. Investigations immediately pointed to piston ring failure and premature ring life expectancy. No piston rings commercially available were able to hold the increased combustion chamber pressures. After running at full power, the rings were so badly damaged they looked as though knurling tools had been run over them.

As a solution, Buick went to a new type of Perfect Circle compression ring in the top groove of the piston, made of a special iron alloy, given a special heat treatment, and using a new shape for the ring itself. At first glance, it looked like the old Buick taper ring, but it was twisted and black in color, the latter due to a chemical coating which acted in a manner similar to a hypoid lubricant.

And an additional modification to minimize piston heat build-up was discovered. By machining a small groove into the piston a "heat dam" was created which kept some of the heat of combustion in the piston dome and away from the top compression ring, thus lengthening its life considerably.

Some competitors could advertise compression ratios as high as the Buick's, but as chief engineer Chayne put it, "Compression ratio doesn't mean a damned thing, it is what you get out of it." What he meant was that Buick had been able to create a higher mean effective pressure in its engines than had the competition with an old-style design using the same compression ratio. The new design pistons were providing Buick a mean effective pressure of 127 on the big series engine, 121 on the small series. No competitive engine of which Buick was aware could come within seven points of the smaller figure; most were in the neighborhood of 115 or below. Unfortunately, much of this, Buick realized, would be lost on the public. Advertising a high compression ratio was advantageous, but there was little likelihood the average customer would completely understand the full significance of the Buick piston advancement.

Interestingly, radical departure from conventional combustion chamber design that it was, it was not patented. About halfway through development, Buick had discovered that engineers at the

Ethyl Corporation, under the direction of Frank Elliott, had been working along almost the same lines and had reached almost the same conclusions. The two groups decided to cooperate and leave the patents open. Apparently the decision was not an agonizing one. According to Chayne, Buick engineers were "damned sure that [this] did not represent the ultimate shape for a piston." And they would continue to experiment.

Actually, there was more to this development than compression ratio increase. If the cylinder head of a 1937 car with the old-style pistons was planed off to raise the compression, and if the driver used one of the few high octane fuels commercially available to keep spark rap down, then the 1937 engine could be made to duplicate the power of the 1938. However, it would be extremely rough running, especially on full throttle acceleration up to 50 or 60 mph, due entirely to the rate of burning of the fuel mixture in the combustion chambers. With the new pistons and combustion chamber design, a lower octane fuel could be used, the compression could still be raised, smoother burning would result when the mixture was fired, and there was no engine roughness. All the experimentation Turlay had done with the piston domes was designed to get the combustion chamber shape desired. It was then that the shape of the head was changed to obtain the desired compression ratio. The whole key to the picture lay in the improved burning rates for the fuel/air mixtures which resulted.

During the late 1930's Buick drivers at the proving grounds used to run what were called exhaust checks. A piece of flexible tubing was connected in place of the muffler and then routed out and under the left running board to be secured about the level of the driver's door handle. The driver would then run the car at full throttle to check for high speed miss by listening to the exhaust note roaring in his ear. The 1938 engines were tested in just this way.

"This is a fighting year," Harlow Curtice had said at new-car introduction time. "Two years of sales success can dull the memory of hard sledding. We must not forget the sales hunger which spurred us to our first great advance." It was a fighting year, but what would be fought was a recession.

Comparatively, Buick fared very well. Calendar 1938 production was 173,905 cars, a decrease of twenty-three percent over the 1937 record. But the industrywide decrease was forty-nine percent. And Buick's market percentage had increased, from 5.8 to 8.8 percent. That was healthy, and so was Buick's stalwart move into fourth place in the industry, behind Chevrolet, Ford and Plymouth.

Obviously the company was anxious for 1939 and a better year. Model changeover was completed in record time, just ten days. At the dealer announcement meeting, Curtice and Hufstader arranged

Probably because the Milford facilities were preempted by other of the GM divisions, Buick rented the Packard proving ground at Utica and a Packard towing dynamometer to test its new '38 Special Touring Sedan.

Buick brochure cover for 1939; Below, chief engineer Charlie Chayne with a Buick Roadmaster, the official pace car for the 1939 Indianapolis 500.

to have an airplane parked on stage, with the numerals 200,000 painted on its wings. That was the sales goal, and it would prove to be passed or missed depending upon viewpoint. Total worldwide sales would be 208,000, though "only" 198,000 would be sold in the United States. Probably only Curtice was really disappointed in that.

Really rarin' to go was Art Kudner, and he gave Buick dealers an inkling why in explaining the need for courage in advertising: "Maybe I can give you an example of what I mean by this. Let's suppose an oil company has a new gasoline to put on the market. Let's say the feature of this new gasoline is that it vaporizes quickly—that it fires with a kick. Now with all that flood of advertising being done on gasoline, I don't think this new gasoline would be much of a sensation if it were advertised in the conventional fashion simply as 'the gas with a kick.' I don't think anybody would get very excited about that.

"But there is a way that gas could be advertised that would make people wake up and talk about it. It's simply a different approach. But it would take courage, and courage in advertising is rarer than you think. All you would have to do to make that new gasoline instantly known, and to have people discussing it, would be to put up some giant billboards or buy some pages in publications. All you would have to say in that space would be one sentence. That sentence would be this:

WHAT THIS COUNTRY NEEDS
IS
A GOOD KICK IN THE GAS!

"You get the point. It is simply this: if Buick advertising has been effective in helping you move cars, part of the reason for it is that the executives here at the plant have the nerve to let us say something interesting."

Well, perhaps not quite as interesting as "a good kick in the gas," but such Kudner-created headlines as "Tail Doesn't Wag Car—And That's News!," "Just Look What You're Missing, Mister," and "Ever Want to Go Fly a Kite?," continued to represent an imaginatively fresh approach to advertising that no other manufacturer matched. Kudner was a master.

The Buicks he advertised for 1939 were somewhat different from the solid ideas of 1938. Wheelbases remained the same, save for the Series 40 which was two inches shorter. A sun roof called the Sunshine Turret Top was introduced on the 41, 48 and 61 Series sedans. It was built by Fisher Body and used also by Cadillac and LaSalle. Sidemount covers slipped on the tires and were designed to fit outside the fender wells on the Series 40 and 60, those cars also being provided a 26.8 percent increase in windshield glass area. Nineteen thirty-eight had seen the last of Buick's rumble seats; the 1939's used opera seats behind the front seats, and jump seats in the 90 and 90L Limiteds. Parking lights on the front fenders became optional.

An industry first was Buick's introduction of turn signals as standard equipment. The signal was at the rear of the car only, a red plastic lens in the emblem mounted in the center of the trunk, operated by a switch on the gearshift lever. The gearshift lever itself had been moved, from off the floorboards and onto the steering column and it was renamed "Handi-shift." Which initially it wasn't. Originally engineered to carry 5/16-inch steel control rods to move the linkage, the rods had been reduced, due to cost-cutting, to only a quarter-inch in diameter in production. When cold weather came, thickening the transmission lubricant and increasing the shifting effort necessary to change gears, the smaller rods buckled and had to be changed in most cases.

Buick's first pushbutton radios, introduced for '39, caused a little static in the beginning, though not the usual kind. The interference came from Motorola, the people there deciding to take legal action because Buick was designing them out of the market. However, in their installation packages, the Motorola engineers used a static collector which was covered by a patent issued to Buick electrical engineer Harry Doane. The suit was nicely settled out of court. Buick agreed to let Motorola use the static collector. Motorola agreed not to sue Buick.

For 1939 the front stabilizer was located ahead of the front wheel centerline instead of behind it. Optional rear axle ratios were available in the Series 40 (3.6, 3.9 and 4.4) and Series 60 (3.4, 3.6 and 3.9) to tailor performance to individual requirements. There was no change in either engine or transmission when an optional ratio was specified.

But there were some engine refinements for 1939. Stromberg and Carter (replacing Marvel) were now the carburetion suppliers, and both provided a new integral automatic choke. Air cleaners of a simpler and more effective design were installed, and for the first time the Series 40 used a horizontal type. On all series, a new rubber support pad assembly secured the rear of the engine on a new transverse cross member. The transmission support for the Series 40 and 60 was thought to be unnecessary due to a new rear axle design and so was eliminated. A completely new transmission was developed for the Series 40, shorter, lighter and more rigid than the 1938 variety.

Clutches were improved in the Series 40 and 60, with the number of moving parts in the pressure plate assemblies being reduced from forty-one to only nine. The fastback trunk design was fading away, but still available in the Series 80 Roadmaster four-door sedan and four-door convertible sedan on special order.

Regarding the styling of the 1939 cars, it was a matter of liking it or not. Even today enthusiasts seldom take a middle position. What Buick had attempted to do was think European. The front end and grille had been patterned after the designs of several highly successful Continental racing cars which, according to Buick engineering, "had been built for years with a minimum of wind resistance and a maximum of visability." The streamlining idea was reaching its zenith.

For better vision, a narrower front door hinge pillar, wider and higher windshield, and larger front windows were used. The divider bar on the rear window was removed and the window was now of a one-piece flat design. The Series 40 and 60 could be ordered with what was called a "rocker panel trim strip." It was narrower than the usual standard running board and covered with stainless steel molding.

Another stainless steel molding began at the radiator grille, followed the vee of the radiator shell and continued along the center of the hood ending at the cowl. The body belt molding, also stainless, was narrower and a different shape from '38, extending along the side of the hood and up to the radiator shell. Stamped into the molding at the front end of the hood was the series name.

Standard on the Series 60, 80 and 90—and optional on the 40—was another stainless steel molding used to surround windshield and rear window glasses. Hubcaps were new, and so was a monogram mounted on the radiator shell center strip near the top of the molding. Front fender lamps were new too. Inside door and window crank handles, the steering wheel and other appointments used a new ruby-colored lumarith (cellulose acetate) in their construction.

Instrument panels had been completely redesigned. The dash contour was convex from the bottom of the windshield to the bottom edge of the panel, and instruments were now mounted in a horizontal plane. Garnish moldings on the Series 40 were now walnut finish, on the Series 60 mahogany. This same finish was continued on the Series 80 and 90 but these cars also had new mahogany trim panels below, inset with a new medallion. Garnish moldings on all convertibles were chromed. There was a new trunk emblem.

The cars were well received upon introduction and it looked like the beginning of a good and solid year. Unfortunately . . .

As advance planning was completed for the 1939 models, Harlow Curtice had issued a directive to Chayne and his engineers: "There must be a ten percent reduction in the cost of every piece in the 1939 automobile." And Curtice wasn't kidding.

The recession had curtailed the Buick business in the 1938 model year, and a good deal of the corporation's money had previously been spent in helping Buick back onto the road to recovery. Thus it seemed

compartment. With a body having sufficient strength to support itself there is no apparent reason to carrying the extra length of frame back of the rear axle. Extension of frames beyond this point is merely a carry-over from the first days of the automobile when support was needed for the rear end of the leaf type spring. The use of torque free coil rear springs has now eliminated this support, and the rear portion of the frame has been proven to be unnecessary."

All this had the sound of rationale mixed with equal parts wishful thinking. There was more to it than that. Indeed, the first experimental bodies had been tested extensively at the proving grounds. Trunks had been loaded with sandbags to simulate the weight of luggage and spare tires. Cars had been pounded over the Belgian block section of the track time and again. No apparent problems. The short frames were okayed for production. And then began the nightmare.

Two Buick men took one of the first production cars to Detroit for a meeting of corporation executives. Afterwards they returned to the car to find someone had parked closely behind them: Maneuvering out, they nudged the bumper of the car parked to the rear. Scarcely an uncommon occurrence. But arriving at their destination, the men couldn't get out of the car. The slight impact had been just enough to spring the body, and the doors would not open.

Shortly after this, a Michigan farmer loaded the trunk of his new '39 with potatoes and headed for home. He didn't make it. The entire trunk floor collapsed around the rear axle. It was not a pretty sight.

Dealers and Buick field personnel bombarded Flint with similar woeful tales. "It was darn tough to get those reports," Chayne remembered. It was even tougher getting a solution worked out. Fisher Body was asked to add supports to strengthen the body of the car—and did. But even that did not work. Production bodies simply were not coming up to the strength and expectations of the pre-production prototypes.

Tests were immediately ordered, and several cars were backed into a concrete wall to check for damage. What all this proved—almost whimsically—was that it was less expensive to repair a rear-damaged car without frame extensions than one which had them.

Buick was, in truth, dragging its feet. Finally, General Motors president Knudsen sent his engineering vice-president, O.E. Hunt, up to Buick for a weekend to see about getting necessary changes instituted as quickly as possible. Within a matter of days all Buicks coming off the assembly lines had full-length frames installed.

But something had to be done about the vehicles already built and shipped to dealers. Buick engineering developed a twenty-four-inch angle iron extension to be bolted between frame and body and shipped them around the country. It was a massive recall campaign. One dealer in Denver alone modified more than 230 cars.

a good time for Buick to cut all unnecessary expenses and show an extra strong divisional profit when the books were closed at the end of the 1939 model year. Engineering didn't like the economy measure idea at all. But Curtice was the boss.

When the time came for the cost reduction to be applied to the frames for the small series 1939 cars, there were two choices. The frames could be either lightened or shortened; the latter was chosen.

In April of 1938 the Technical Data Section of the Engineering Department prepared a report for Art Kudner so he could begin to plan the features for the 1939 Buick advertising campaign: "The frames for the Series 40 and 60 have been completely redesigned and now terminate just back of the rear axle centerline," it read. "With slight changes the body has been strengthened sufficiently to carry the gasoline tank and whatever luggage may be carried in the trunk

Buicks for 1939. Page opposite, from the top: Special Model 46C and Century 66C Convertible Coupes, Roadmaster Model 81 Touring Sedan. Above: Testing the Special.

Meantime in showrooms from coast to coast, Buick dealers watched helplessly as customers got down on their hands and knees to check for themselves what kind of frame the displayed car had. The short-framed versions became known as the "Bob-Tailed Buicks"—a cute phrase, a ghastly blunder.

Another problem was driveshaft vibration. Series 40 and 60 cars utilized a two-piece driveshaft with a U-joint in the center, which was found to be the cause of the vibration, and an attempt at correction was made by the installation of a bearing support. Cadillac had been similarly plagued and corrected by lengthening the output shaft from the transmission and shortening the driveshaft the same measure. Both the Cadillac and Buick solutions were the same geometrically, but the Buick change did not provide the necessary stability and the drivelines in these two series resonated easily. Also, with sidemounts,

the front doors on Series 40 cars didn't open at all well . . .

But for as troublesome as all this was, it should be noted that what must have seemed to people in Flint as the "Buick plague of '39" was confined largely to the Series 40 and 60. The 80 and 90 emerged relatively unscathed. And the whole thing did not seem to have caused Buick untoward reputation damage. Sales were in the 200,000-unit range, and Buick remained solidly in fourth place in the industry.

Muttering something to himself about being penny-wise and pound-foolish, Harlow Curtice perhaps looked upon 1939—as enthusiasts do today—as a transitional twelve months from the pacesetting of 1938 to the solid modernity of 1940. Transitions are frequently fraught with difficulty. In any case, Harlow Curtice was now convinced it was time to shift his Buick machine into high.

209

Chapter Eleven

GOING CUSTOM WITH BRUNN

The 1940 model year at Buick was to be one of the most interesting the company would ever know. It would mark the first time since 1926 that Buick registrations passed the 233,000 mark. The Estate Wagon was introduced, together with the all-new Super line. Phasing out of such now-démodé accoutrements to the motorcar as the side-mounted spare and the running board had begun. The new Sunshine Turret Top was continued from 1939 in Century and Special touring sedans. Under Art Kudner, Buick advertising hit its highest peak yet. Everywhere you looked around Flint, something new and exciting was being offered or tried at Buick.

Characteristically, as good a year as 1940 was for the marque, it proved not quite good enough for Harlow Curtice. He was aiming higher—and for '40 had set his sights on third place in sales and a market penetration of ten percent. Neither of those goals would be his that year—nor did another idea he had work out exactly as he planned. It was a case of what the poet Robert Burns once referred to as "best laid schemes."

For 1940 a Series 80 had been added to the 90 previously offered in the Buicks designated as Limited, which augmented the marque's prestige line nicely. But, more significantly, Harlow Curtice decided to go even above top-of-the-line. He decided to go custom.

This was not conceived as a massive reordering of Buick priorities, it was a very small tick of the clock around company corridors. The image-conscious Curtice viewed the custom body program as a low-volume and low-key fillip, a super-prestige-gathering adjunct to the overall Buick scheme of things. He still had a very hard time of it.

First, he approached Cadillac and Fleetwood/Fisher, asking if they would cooperate in supplying a series of custom bodies to be mounted on Buick chassis. The answer was a resounding "no"—which might have been expected. Buick's Limiteds were already making inroads into the luxury-class territory which Cadillac regarded as its private preserve in General Motors. No further competition from Flint was desired, thank you. Curtice accepted Cadillac's decision politely—and thought again. In September of 1939 he summoned assistant chief engineer Edward T. Ragsdale into his office, gave him direct responsibility for the program (chief engineer Chayne would not be involved) and over the next few weeks the two men tossed around alternatives. Ultimately, Ragsdale was instructed to contact Brunn & Company of Buffalo, New York to get something going. Brunn was enthusiastic.

To place the Brunn reaction to the Buick proposal in perspective, a little history is necessary. The Brunn family had arrived in the United States from Bavaria in 1848, eventually settling in Buffalo. The Brunn Carriage Manufacturing Company arrived a short time later, founded by Henry Brunn—and in 1890 his nephew, Hermann A. Brunn, began as an apprentice woodworker there at age sixteen. Thereafter the young Brunn studied at the Andrew J. Johnson Carriage School on the Bowery in New York and then spent about a decade traveling the East and adding to his experience in jobs for a number of coachbuilders: Andrew J. Joyce Carriage Company in Washington (supplier of coaches to the White House and other prominent customers in the D.C. area); the New Haven Carriage Company in Connecticut (where he worked on the body for the Columbia Electric that Hiram Percy Maxim designed for Colonel Albert Pope); William Hooker Atwood, also in New Haven (reputed to be the top man in the country on designing carriage interiors); and the renowned H.H. Babcock Company in Watertown, New York.

Returning to Buffalo and rejoining Brunn Carriage, Hermann Brunn soon found that financial disagreements made staying there not congenial, so he borrowed money from friends and in 1908 crossed Main Street and established Brunn & Company in direct competition to his Uncle Henry. There were Brunns on both sides of the street now, but whereas Henry Brunn was carriage oriented, Hermann Brunn was happy to cater to the horseless trade, and his business grew rapidly.

Initially his work was largely on foreign chassis, but two cars designed for the actress Leslie Carter on the Thomas Flyer brought a good deal of publicity to the company and many new orders which resulted in expansion into larger quarters a few blocks east and an enviable reputation in the coachbuilding field by the 1920's. Work on Pierce-Arrow, Stearns-Knight, Reo and Cadillac (prior to the ac-

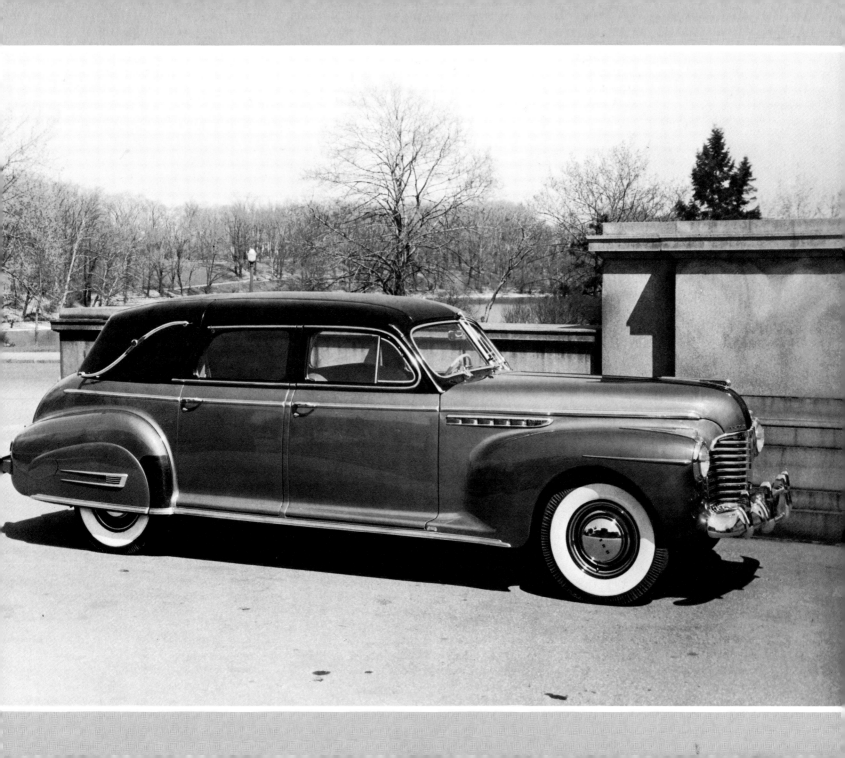

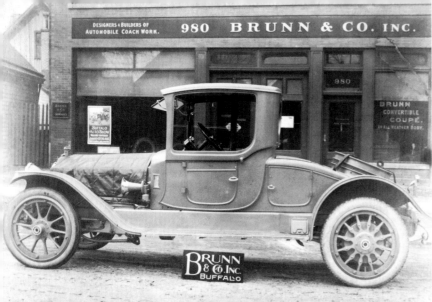

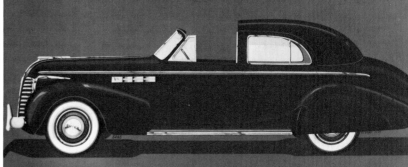

Page preceding: The 1941 Brunn Buick built for the McCormick family. Left: A Brunn-bodied Packard Twin Six in front of the showroom in Buffalo, and Hermann C. Brunn during his Buick days. Above and below: The Townmaster by Brunn of 1940—in actuality, in rendering and in an advertisement from National Geographic. Page opposite: The Brunn convertible which followed.

Custom Built FOR CUSTOM SERVICE

Available now on special order is the custom-built Buick pictured here, the 1940 Buick Townmaster Sedan.

With bodywork by Brunn, the chassis is the standard ROADMASTER chassis with all 1940 Buick features, including the 141-horsepower straight-eight engine, electrically balanced *after* assembly; coil springs

on all four wheels; and the s ing torque-tube drive and Buick frame.

Interior trim and appointmer subject to your taste through variety of upholstery options. ard equipment includes rem top for the chauffeur's compar speaking phone, center arm the three-passenger rear sea ing window behind the drive built-in heater.

At $3895*, delivered at Flin plete except for transportation on rail rates, state and loca (if any), the Townmaster is value on its quality and fine

*Price subject to chan without notice.

"Best buy's *Buick*

EXEMPLAR OF GENERAL MOTORS V

quisition of Fleetwood by General Motors) chassis had been profitable, but most lucrative to Brunn was the relationship to Lincoln. The company designed many of Henry Ford's personal cars and during the late Twenties was delivering eighteen and nineteen custom bodies a month to Dearborn, with Lincoln asking for still more. The stock market crash put a crimp in all this, of course, layoffs followed (peak employment had been 175 workers) and from 1930 Brunn began losing money.

Previously famed for convertibles, phaetons and especially town cars, in 1936 Brunn came up with a touring cabriolet design which was marketed with some success to Lincoln and Packard, and Edsel Ford asked for a few custom Zephyrs, but by now the Brunn business was largely relegated to the modification of existing bodies into custom cars for the occasional individual client. Scarcely stimulating work. Nor very profitable.

Small wonder then that the invitation from Buick was so avidly received in Buffalo. Employment at Brunn was but fifty people, Hermann A. Brunn was ailing, his son was running the company. "I responded with great haste," Hermann C. Brunn recalls. "I was met at the Michigan Central Depot in Detroit by a Buick driver and was driven to Flint to meet Mr. Ragsdale. Time has not dimmed my memory to the extent that I have forgotten the enthusiasm with which I responded to that call." The Buick program just might turn into a Lincoln-like windfall.

The details were worked out with Ed Ragsdale, who had suggested Brunn to Curtice, remembering the company's quality work from his early days in the Pierce-Arrow drafting department. Although Curtice and Brunn were not to meet regarding the project, it was Curtice nonetheless who dictated its parameters. First on the agenda was a town car, on the 126-inch-wheelbase Roadmaster chassis.

Brunn returned to his drafting board and proceeded to revise the Roadmaster four-door sedan, sectioning the roof just behind the driver, with provision for roof panels over the driving compartment (to be stored in the header behind the driver's seat) and a two-piece sliding divider window separating the driver/passenger compartment. The roof sectioning made necessary relocation of the radio antenna to the rear of the left front fender, stock 1940 Buick fender skirts would be used, Brunn's rendering was completed in December of '39, and the first car shortly thereafter.

Ed Ragsdale later recounted: "The car had black top grain cowhide from the belt up [better described as black straight Landau leather] and the lower body sheet metal was Brewster Green. It was shown in 1940 at the GM exhibit at the Waldorf during the National Automobile Show at the old Palace. The car had quite an enthusiastic reception but unfortunately the price tag [$3750] proved

a deterrent to sales."

Undeterred, however, was the Buick resolve regarding its custom body adventure. The Brunn Buick was officially named the Town Master,* and its official introductory date was February 18th, 1940. Hermann C. Brunn remembers that week in New York well. On Saturday he was summoned to Art Kudner's hotel suite to discuss the program. Unfortunately, Kudner was a football fan, there was a big Notre Dame game being broadcast that day, and whenever the custom car conversation seemed to be getting somewhere, a critical play would develop and Kudner would hush up Brunn, lean forward and turn all his attention to the game. It was the first of Brunn's many frustrations in this adventure.

Next, Brunn was asked to see what he could come up with in the way of a custom convertible, again in the Roadmaster series. Back to the drawing board he went, and the result this time was a convertible coupe colored grey, with a beautiful sweeping red spear beginning at the front sides of the hood, running in a widening arc down the doors just to the bottom of the quarter panels in front of the rear fenders, and swinging up again to finish at a point above and at the middle of the rear fender line. The spears were to be a specially cast and polished aluminum molding designed and fabricated at Brunn, the red leather interior and top boot were to be custom, the fender skirts standard. (The spear, however, would be altered somewhat, and the fender skirts eliminated, in the actual car.)

The rendering was completed July 17th, 1940 and work on the car began immediately. As with the Town Master, Buick shipped the body via rail from Flint to Buffalo where it was modified as per the approved rendering and then reshipped by rail back to Flint for

*For years it has been assumed the Town Master was lost to history. It was known to have been delivered to Art Kudner after the New York show introduction but thereafter its trail turned cold. Recently, however, the car turned up in the hands of an Eastern collector. Apparently, it had been sold to a member of the Eli Lily Drug Company family and had become a part of the estate.

213

mounting on the chassis. This done, everyone took a good look, decided it was too mild a custom and that something more radical along the lines of the Town Master was preferred. However, Buick did accept the car; its ultimate fate is unknown today.

By now the 1940 model year was nearing its end. The pilot Brunn cars had, of course, been completed too late for inclusion in any 1940 Buick sales catalogues, though the Town Master was advertised in *National Geographic, MoToR* and *The Buick Magazine.* If the program was to be continued, decisions had to be made quickly so

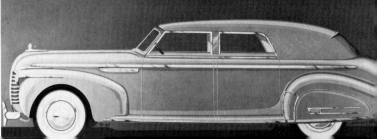

that the cars could be properly announced, promoted and produced for the 1941 model year.

Based on what he had seen thus far, Curtice gave the go-ahead, but with a few new wrinkles. Ragsdale called Brunn in Buffalo with the news: "Mr. Curtice has the idea that he would like to have some custom cars again but this time on our Limited Series chassis. We would like you to develop a program for our 1941 cars using the larger Limited, and body designs similar to the program you had with Lincoln."

Page opposite: Buick styling prototype photos given Brunn to work up 1941 Brunn program; note bombsight hood ornament not to appear in production until after World War II. Left, from the top: Renderings for All Weather Cabriolet, All Weather Brougham and two versions of Convertible Phaeton. Above and below: Clear Vision Brougham, Formal Sedan, Touring Cabriolet.

This time the complete car would be shipped to Buffalo, not simply the body, and this time Brunn was provided prototype photographs of the 1941 Limited to use in developing his renderings. There were seven, the first completed March 21st, 1940, the remaining six the following month. As designated in Buffalo, they were:

1. The All Weather Cabriolet. This was to be a town car using the 139-inch-wheelbase Limited four-door sedan with divider window, landau irons in place of the usual rear quarter windows, and a solid top over the passengers.

2. The All Weather Brougham. Also using the Limited four-door sedan body with divider window, this town car would retain the rear quarter windows.

3. The Convertible Phaeton. Aluminum body side moldings similar to those used on the 1940 Brunn Roadmaster convertible were to be featured in this version.

4. The Convertible Phaeton. The same car as above but minus the aluminum body side moldings.

5. The Clear Vision Brougham. Similar to cars one and two, this style would utilize modified window pillar posts (made of stainless steel, and thinner than stock) in the rear quarter windows and would provide for a better field of vision for those riding in the passenger compartment.

6. The Formal Sedan. Using the same four-door body, this style would display no spears on the fender skirts and the rear-quarter windows would be closed in.

7. The Touring Cabiolet. This was to be a four-door sedan with top solid over the driver and a folding top over the rear-seat passenger area.

The renderings received in Flint, Buick management decided to go with four Brunn cars for '41. The renderings were passed along to the company's promotion artists to be redrawn in full-color for the catalogue. (Something would be lost in the translation, according to Hermann Brunn.) And the names of the styles were changed. Now they were called the Custom Brougham and the Custom Town Car (these were two versions of Brunn's All Weather Cabriolet, the former with, the latter without, landau bars), the Custom Phaeton (Brunn's Convertible Phaeton without side molding) and the Custom Landau (Brunn's Touring Cabriolet).

"Available on special order only . . . equipped virtually according to your own specifications" was the way Buick copywriters made known the Brunn offerings in the seven-page special section inserted in the back of the 1941 spiral-bound catalogue for the Limited Series. The listing of appointments was indeed impressive: rear-seat personalized radio, hand-cut stainless steel initials for passenger compartment doors, numerous color choices for plastic interior trim

parts, an illuminated mirror in the rear quarter of the passenger compartment, color-keyed door handles and window cranks, deep-nap sheepskin rugs dyed to match upholstery for the rear passenger floor. A lap robe of the same material as the upholstery was also available; a customer could request an electric clock in the trim panel on the back of the front seat, or have special pillows made from a covering fabric matching the car's interior; handmade wooden panels could be installed below the quarter windows at both sides of the rear seat and a pair of matching carpet-covered hassocks to serve as foot rests could be provided. All this was, in a word, lush.

Or as Bill Hufstader told Buick dealers in Flint for the pre-announcement preview of the 1941 cars, "the sky is the absolute limit for luxury of finish and appointment." The official announcement of the 1941 line came and went. A few orders trickled into Buffalo for the special-bodied cars, a very few. And, in fact, the first 1941 Buick Brunn built wasn't even one of the catalogued Limiteds. It was a special Roadmaster Convertible Coupe ordered by Buick for display in the 1941 New York Automobile Show held in October of 1940.

A writer from *The New Yorker* was impressed. "Up on the mezzanine I ran across a Buick Roadmaster Convertible," he wrote, "that seemed to me to forecast a whole new range of ideas in color styles; its body, by Brunn, is painted a rich cinnamon brown, and along each side there is a streak of yellow in the shape of a shallow V. [The Brunn aluminum molding was back.] The sides of the body, back to each door are cut away in a smaller V whose contour follows the streak of color. The upholstery is tan cord, trimmed with leather. Built only on order it will cost you about $3500." That price figure was probably the result of the reporter's query.

The second 1941 Brunn was ordered by Colonel LeRoy Berdeau of Chicago and Palm Beach, Florida. It was Brunn's All Weather Cabriolet with landau irons. Although this style had been pictured in both the Brunn renderings and the Buick catalogue with spears on the fender skirts, these were deleted for the Berdeau car. It was painted grey, with a black leather top, and an exquisite powder blue interior. Completed in mid-January of 1941, Brunn sent the car over to Klepfer Brothers, the Buick dealership in Buffalo, for two days of display before shipping it to Colonel Berdeau in Florida.

The next '41 Brunn was ordered by the famous McCormick family of Chicago, and it was the Buick-designated Custom Landau, painted a medium grey, its leather top folding down into the rear deck for motoring in the sunshine, the spears installed on the fender skirts, and the interior done in Bedford cloth.

This third '41 Brunn Buick was also the last.

By now Cadillac had complained. So had Fisher Body. Both took their grievances directly to GM corporate management, and

Above: Brunn convertible renderings from '40 and '41, and the Brunn show convertible that impressed The New Yorker. *Below: The Touring Cabriolet built for the McCormick family. Right: The version for Colonel Berdeau.*

management in turn issued a directive to Harlow Curtice which, freely translated, told him to stop fooling around in a market in which he didn't belong and with a car body that, heaven forbid, wasn't even built by General Motors. Curtice had been halted in very few of his projects since being named head of Buick, and the experience was a new one for him. But he knew when to quit. Ragsdale was again called to Curtice's office and instructed to communicate the bad news to Buffalo.

It was a terrible blow to Brunn. Buick tried to soften it by advising the coachbuilder that, although official support had to be withdrawn, Brunn was free to develop whatever business he could on his own with the Buick dealer body. But for a company that had been losing money since 1930, that was impossible. The end of the Buick project really meant the end of the line for Brunn & Company. In mid-1941

Hermann C. Brunn closed the doors of his proud family company. Still in his early thirties, he initially took a job designing jigs and fixtures for a shock absorber manufacturer. In 1943 he was hired by Henry Ford II and remained with the Ford Motor Company until his retirement in the early 1970's, working with the design and interior styling departments at Mercury.

Only five Brunn Buicks had been built. Only one, the Town Master, is known to exist today. In the early Seventies, Flint historian Clarence Young summed up the adventure well: "Curtice came up with a startling idea in 1939, Buicks with special bodies by Brunn. The coachbuilder agreed but a frown sifted down through the corporation and the prestige Buick concept fell through the floorboards."

It was a most unfortunate fall.

Chapter Twelve

THEN...
THE SHIFT
INTO HIGH

If the Brunn caper and Cadillac's testy reaction to it addled Harlow Curtice in 1940, it was a minor irritation comparatively. The Buick frame problem of the year previous had created near paranoia before being resolved on February 1st, 1939. At the Flint announcement meeting for the 1940 cars, reference was made to it no less than four times.

"No gains without pains," Curtice said as he opened the meeting, then cheerfully mixing his metaphors, added, "As a very small fly may spoil a very large cup of coffee, an unexpected factor that entered the picture for a very brief time threatened to cloud its whole appeal," although thanks to a fine dealer effort the car had ultimately "met the test and held the line under competitive fire." But it had been a very close call.

Not wishing to repeat the experience, Buick decided to play it safe in 1940, offering a "traditional car" with the proven engineering of straight-eight engine, torque tube drive and sealed chassis. "Try all things," Curtice said, "hold fast that which is good." To be certain the new models would live up to established guidelines, they were subjected to a stricter-than-usual pre-production testing program. In May of 1939, as plans were being made final, Curtice called a meeting of his manufacturing and engineering staffs. It was not too late to change designs and specifications, he commented. If anyone could think of anything that might help, now was the time to bring it up. Out of that meeting came still further detail refinements.

In total, the 1940 cars were put through almost three million miles of cross-country testing, a program virtually without parallel in

Buick history. Curtice, although still vitally interested in cost reduction and expense control, had loosened the financial grip on his engineers. Less encumbered, they had been able to engineer quality in, potential problems out. During the last week in June 1939, Curtice personally drove one car from each of the series over the roads of Michigan, Ohio and Pennsylvania to prove to himself the new Buicks were everything they should be. Convinced they were, he set a 240,000-unit sales target, a twenty percent increase over model year 1939. He was sure it could be easily met.

One of the principal reasons for his confidence was the plethora of Buicks being offered for 1940, the additions placing Buick squarely in the middle of market segments in which it had not been able to compete before. There were now five series instead of four, and the Limited was expanded for the first time into two lines (the Series 80 on a 133-inch wheelbase and the 90 on 140 inches). Buick knew which cars were its real profit makers. However, the company was also attuned, perhaps more so than any other manufacturer in America at the time, to the fact that the prestige, reputation and impression of those cars at the upper end of the line would have great influence and sales impact on the volume desired from the lower series. Buick wanted the Limited to demonstrate that Buick ownership was synonymous with quality, good taste, social acceptance and value. A new Limited catalogue was produced—the most beautiful piece of artwork thus far in Buick history—and available models numbered nine, three of them with the last of the fastback trunk design, available only on special order. Even more special than these, of course, were the proposed new Brunn custom designs. Harlow Curtice really liked the idea of prestige Buicks.

But paramount to the fortunes of the company, of course, were its bread-and-butter cars—and for the demanding owner in the medium-price field, Buick offered a brand-new line: the Super, numerically the Series 50. Sharing its 248-cubic-inch engine and 121-inch wheelbase with the Special and its body with the Roadmaster, the Super was available at introduction as a four-door touring sedan and a sport coupe with full rear seat. During the model year the series would be expanded to include the new Estate Wagon, a convertible coupe and convertible sedan, the latter two styles also being added to the Roadmaster series. Sales manager Hufstader predicted that the Supers would ignite a "super sales bonfire." He was right. Dealers couldn't get enough of the cars.

The 1940 Buicks could be divided into three groups—the Specials and the Centurys, the Supers and the Roadmasters, and the Limiteds—and Art Kudner promoted them all with a vengeance, in an advertising campaign that put "its best foot forward" and was Buick's best ever.

4 MILLIONTH
BUICK
Owned and Displayed by
GLIDDEN BUICK CORP.

BUICK'S LARGEST DEALER
FOR 31 YEARS

AND NEW YORK'S OLDEST
AND LARGEST NEW AND
USED CAR DEALERS

TO DATE THIS YEAR BUICK HAS DELIVERED
MORE NEW CARS IN NEW YORK COUNTY THAN
ANY OTHER MAKER OF CARS IN ANY PRICE CLASS

Page preceding: Alfred P. Sloan, Jr. congratulates Glidden's Arthur Lee Newton, November 1940. Above left: At an engineering conference in 1940, from the left, J.G. Hammond, Verner Mathews, H. Smith, Charlie Chayne, Harlow Curtice, O.W. Young. Above right: A production record is set May 28th, 1940, as Curtice (with big grin) looks on. Below, from the left: Hufstader with Harry E. Shiland (Buick's first sales manager); Art Kudner with Charles F. Kettering; Adolph Braun.

The Special and Century featured bodies of the six-window or slab-side type, with three windows on each side—two in the doors, the third in the rear quarter panel. Two annoyances from '39 were fixed in '40 on the Specials. A slight wheelbase increase meant that the doors on sidemount-equipped cars would now open fully, and a dual diaphragm fuel pump assisted the vacuum wiper motor in keeping Series 40 windshields clear.

Interior plastic decorative trim was white this year and there were plastic inlays in doors and window handles on all series above the Special. On both Special and Century four-door sedans, the rear door locking mechanisms had been redesigned so that when locked from the inside the remote control door latch rods were disconnected,

making it impossible for a child to open the door while the car was in motion. The sport coupe in the Special series now carried a full-width rear seat which was removable to provide additional luggage-carrying capacity.

Fabrics for the Special interiors consisted of a new Bedford cloth and low-pile mohair with a herringbone design, and two-tone broadcloth as an extra-cost option. The Century was available with a tan or grey Bedford cloth, the same material as used in the Limiteds.

Super and Roadmaster bodies were of the four-window type and were mounted farther forward on the chassis than the Special and Century series. With very short external cowls, the hood tops extended back close to the windshield and cowl ventilator. Front fenders flowed all the way to the leading edges of the front doors. The width of these new bodies, combined with their front-seat width, made running boards unnecessary and Buick took them off. Super interiors were trimmed in a new two-tone tan Bedford cord, Roadmasters in either grey or tan. Two-tone paint combinations were available on both lines as well.

The Limited Series 80 featured a six-passenger body, while the 90 offered accommodations for either six or eight. Body construction of the Limited remained composite type, and its interiors were available in tan or grey Bedford cloth, leathers, broadcloth and tan or grey cloths with new two-tone patterns. Dome lights were operated by an automatic switch on the right rear door doorpost—and by a manual switch on the left pillar post on the Series 90, a manual switch in the lefthand arm rest on the 80. All Limiteds had heaters and defrosters as standard equipment.

As had been the Buick custom for many years, all series shared the same front end grille treatment. New sheet metal with the headlights molded into the fenders carried on the streamlining tradition, and the front grille horizontal bar spacing was made wider to provide better air flow over the radiator core and reduce the possibility of overheating. Mounted just above the headlamps, streamlined chrome parking lights were wired into the directional system to give turn indication from the front of the car as well as the rear.

Hood-opening pull handles—designated "Louve-Lock"—were located on both sides of the split hood, with the series name embossed on them in easily-read letters. This identification would be carried over into 1941 and 1942, which delighted certain wily members of the Buick sales organization. Discovering early on that they could be interchanged with little difficulty, more than one Buick salesman was known to have put Special hood pulls on his Century demonstrator, providing a prospect with Series 60 performance in what he (the unsuspecting potential customer) thought was a Series 40 Buick.

Engine-turned dash panels and glove compartment doors enhanced the interiors of 1940 Buicks. Not retained from 1939 was the steering column locking-type ignition switch because of a clearance problem between the new instrument panel and the mast jacket. Buick now mounted all closed car radio antennas in the center of the windshield header with a knob for raising and lowering inside the car, an arrangement that would endure until the end of 1953 production. Telescoping vacuum-operated power antennas were mounted on the left front fenders of all radio-equipped open cars.

Underneath all this was what chief engineer Chayne called "the stiffest frames ever put under cars of comparable size." Front suspension remained the same basic design used since 1934, but on all series save the Limited the entire suspension assembly was rotated backward four degrees. This meant that when a front wheel hit a bump, it retreated slightly, the most noticeable benefit being a lowering of shock and noise transmitted into the passenger compartment. Bearings of a compressed fabric design at the inner ends of the lower control arms were self-lubricating and self-sealing—and, unfortunately, short in service life. The Limited's suspension used sealed, threaded type bearings for protection against sticking due to misalignment, and more positive caster put additional "feel" into the steering. On all series below the Limited, both front and rear stabilizers were installed to eliminate any sensation of oversteer. Two stabilizers were deemed unnecessary in the Limited due to weight distribution, center of gravity location and rear suspension geometry.

Carburetors were redesigned, and intake and exhaust manifolds were new with no gaskets between exhaust manifold and head, this permitting—at least in theory—the manifold to slide more easily as it expanded and contracted with heat. Cooling was improved with new radiator designs and a pressure cap of seven p.s.i. The Special and Super engine used an oil pump capable of twenty-five percent greater capacity than previous, and all 1940 engines were subjected to a new "assembly balancing" technique in which the units were assembled complete with clutches and then checked for running balance on a special machine.

The metal sliding Sunshine Turret top was available on Special two- and four-door touring sedans and on the Century four-door sedan. Sealed beam headlamps came to Buick in 1940—and an unusual new model arrived, a taxicab. Designated the 41-T, it was a Special complete with heavy duty brakes and clutch and a red warning light on the dash to warn the driver when the rear door was open. Several hundred of these Buick taxis were sold to major fleet accounts throughout the country.

The most interesting new Buick for 1940, however, was introduced mid-year. Art Kudner called it the Estate Wagon, which sounded classier than the prosaic "station." The suggestion for it came from Hollywood in mid-1938 during a dealer visit to the West Coast made by Curtice, Hufstader, Kudner and Harley Earl. Film director Norman McLeod and his wife Bunny had invited the group to their home for dinner, and had gaily strung Buick banners all through the house—but there wasn't a Buick in the garage. Why not? someone asked. "You don't build a station wagon and I need one," Bunny McLeod answered. Harlow Curtice considered that a personal challenge.

On the Super Chief heading back to Michigan, Harley Earl got out his drawing pad and before the train pulled into the Flint station he had sketched what would be Buick's first production station wagon. Pontiac, Chevrolet and Oldsmobile were offering the body style already, but not since an open-bodied affair in the 1920's had Buick contemplated such a car. Once having made up his mind, however, Harlow Curtice lost no time. Nor would he forget to give credit where it was due. The prototype would be a special present to Bunny McLeod.*

The Estate Wagon project was assigned to assistant chief engineer Ed Ragsdale. Ragsdale enlisted the help of Frank Short, an engineer with Buick since 1920 who had worked variously as a draftsman and in trim assembly on open cars and who would become Buick's head station wagon engineer. Because a run of only 500 cars—on the Super chassis and to sell for $1242—was projected to test market reaction, Fisher Body wasn't particularly interested. Nor would Cadillac or Fleetwood complain in this instance about Buick's looking outside General Motors for a coachbuilding source to produce the complicated wooden bodies. Cadillac didn't build a station wagon. Finding someone to do it for Buick was Ragsdale's and Short's first job.

The Biehl Body Company of Reading, Pennsylvania was selected. The firm's history dated back to 1877 when George Biehl and five associates founded Biehl's Wagon Works; Biehl's son Earl was now active in the company. While serving in the First World War, Earl Biehl had become friends with a Buick man—it always helps to know someone on the inside—and it was this Buick friend who suggested the Biehl company for the prototype which became Bunny McLeod's car. Curtice was so impressed with the result that Biehl was contracted for the 1940 production run.

Only the floorpans and cowl assembles were shipped to Biehl by rail. Biehl built the bodies, mounted them and shipped them back to Buick where they were wired, trimmed and sent to the assembly line.

The first Estate Wagons after Bunny McLeod's went to Harley Earl and Harlow Curtice, with a third set up for patterns to be used in the event the decision was made to carry the car into the 1941 model year. That decision was made and, Biehl being unable to supply in the production volume now needed, Buick turned instead to the Hercules Body Company of Evansville, Indiana for coachwork. Again, Cadillac did not object. Buick continued with Hercules through 1948.

Raw wood for the bodies arrived in Evansville from Canada. Large shapers would work the wood into the necessary panels, and the panels were then soaked in a highly toxic material called wood life, a preservative against rot and termites. Completed bodies were subsequently shipped back to Buick by rail, four to a box car. By 1941 the floor, rear compartment pan, windshield opening and all metal hardware was being purchased by Buick from Fisher Body in what was called a package. In this same package were sill plates, front door glasses, door regulators and windshield trim. All this made the job a good deal easier in Flint than it had been with the first Biehl-produced cars.

Still, there were difficulties. For example, in 1941 Buick contracted with a wood supplier in Canada for hard maple, but was shipped soft wood by mistake. It did not hold the varnish properly and deteriorated with alarming speed. Estate Wagons leaked water initially, especially in the tailgate area—and body fit, specifically door alignment, was a continuing problem. This worried Curtice. He was a perpetual visitor to the engineering department to see for himself if the cars were coming through any better.

Problems aside, the Buick Estate Wagon was a snappy-looking vehicle, and it caught on, nowhere more than in Hollywood where the idea had been conceived in the first place. Movie stars, directors and film studios took to it enthusiastically, and it was their acceptance of the Estate Wagon which played a major role in the decision to continue with the car as a regular production model. Hollywood glamour was good for Buick. Curtice knew that.

In mid-1940, while traveling on the West Coast with distributor Charles Howard and his staff, Harlow Curtice was informed from New York that he had been elected a vice-president of General Motors. It was a cause for celebration, and a congratulatory dinner was hastily arranged in his honor. Meantime, in Flint, there was another cause for celebration. On May 28th, 1940, the figure 250,117 was ceremonially painted on the windshield of a Buick as it rolled off the assembly line. The company had just exceeded its all-time model year production total of 250,116 cars, established in 1928. Although Harlow Curtice had set his sights for an even grander year for Buick—third place in sales, a market penetration of ten percent—which was not quite realized, there was no doubting the robust good health the marque now enjoyed. An average one hundred Buicks per dealer point were being sold—no other manufacturer in the industry could claim this—and Buick dealers were far and away the most

---

*And it was a special Estate Wagon, with a little metallic bunny to decorate the side of the car and chrome letters on the rear door spelling out "Bunny Bar Ranch," the latter rather appropriately since the vehicle would later be pressed into service by the McLeods as a mobile cocktail lounge during closing hours of the usual ones. The Buick engineers working on Mrs. McLeod's vehicle called it "the bunny hop car." It was presented to her at the Coconut Grove nightclub in Hollywood, Curtice having had it shipped via enclosed rail car to the West Coast with special instructions to Hollywood dealer Phil Hall that it be kept under wraps until the dealer meeting at which it would be unveiled. Bunny McLeod was invited to that meeting, called up on stage by Curtice, thanked for her inadvertent suggestion which led to the building of the car and then given its keys. She was so delighted she cried. She used her Estate Wagon for a number of years, until one day lending it to a friend who never bothered to return it. What happened to it subsequently is not known.

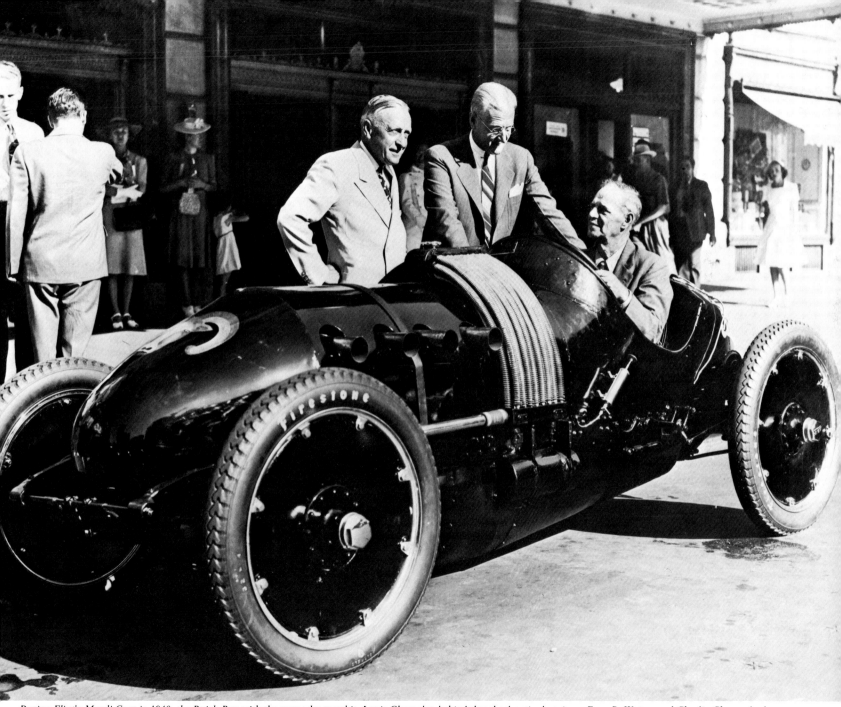

During Flint's Mardi Gras in 1940, the Buick Bug with the man who raced it, Louis Chevrolet, behind the wheel; retired engineer Enos DeWaters and Charlie Chayne look on.

profitable in America.

In 1940 Buick had accomplished what Hufstader liked to call a "buttoning up job" with its cars. But for 1941 Buick would have a whole new set of clothes. Some ten million dollars was spent on product development of the '41 line, and on expansion of plant facilities—bringing to a cool sixty million the dollars allotted to Buick for product and production since the arrival of Curtice. They had been well spent.

The Special, Century and Limited models all received new bodies for 1941. But it was the Limited which was Buick's special pride—and Cadillac's nemesis. With the strength of its volume and tooling base, Buick hit the luxury market with a vengeance, and with "the first stylish and distinctively modern car ever produced in the large car field, a car in which the designers had the courage to admit that there is a difference between the terms 'conservative' and 'old-fashioned'."

Because of their low-volume production, among other factors, luxury cars tended to change more slowly than vehicles in the less rarified strata of the marketplace. With the strength of his middle-range base behind him, and his awareness of the value of prestige rub-off, however, Curtice decided to surprise the industry with a fresh-looking luxury car. An indicator of the interest Buick had in all this was the fact that Hufstader personally asked every dealer with customers in the high-priced market to have a Limited demonstrator

The Special Model 46S Sport Coupe of 1940, with accessory front bumper guard.

in service. Another indicator, of course, was the Brunn program. Although, as earlier related, Cadillac objected loud and long to the Brunn cars, there was not an awful lot GM's top division could do about the regular production top-of-the-line Buicks. They happened virtually before Cadillac noticed. Harlow Curtice had deftly taken his car into the luxury car class almost sub rosa. Only when made aware of what he had done could Cadillac complain. And by that time the damage was done.

The floorline of the new Limited was as low as the shorter wheelbase series, running boards were of concealed built-in design, and the exterior molding treatment emphasized the long low lines of the car. Inside, garnish moldings were chrome finished with grained trim panels, grain-finished moldings optional to harmonize with trim panels if desired. The Limited limousine had a new divider assembly utilizing an electric power window operated by pushbuttons in the vanity case of the rear-seat armrests. In jumpseat-equipped cars, the backs of the auxiliary seats were trimmed with chrome so that when folded into the divider they provided a stylish and attractive look to the front seatback. The Series 80 Limited was discontinued; all prestige Buicks were the long-wheelbase Series 90.

A new fresh air impact heater was provided. The main heater, mounted under the right front seat, provided heat directly to the front compartment, and to the rear via ducts leading to grilles at each side of the division board. Air for the system was supplied from a large tube running from the heater forward to a screened opening beside the radiator core. Suspension for the Series 90 was simplified to the smaller series type, with the unfortunate result that the front shock absorbers weren't equal to the Limited's task, and ride quality suffered some. But the car looked great.

The big engineering news for 1941 was the introduction of Compound Carburetion and 10 mm spark plugs. The resulting big-engine 165 hp Buicks were the highest-powered standard production automobiles built in America. Moreover, as Curtice told his dealers, Buick customers could now expect better mileage at speeds over 40 mph with the 1941 big series engine than had been provided on the 1940 small series car.

Late 1939 had seen the first experimental dual carburetion setups being tested at the proving grounds. The manifolding for the device was the work of Joe Turlay. Adolph Braun was responsible for working out the final carburetor details, and it was Braun who invented and patented the progressive linkage the system used.

Experimentation with carburetion and fuel injection had been ongoing at Buick since the early Thirties. One car, called "the flying bathtub" and using a big series engine and multiple carburetors, reached a top speed of about 116 mph. In another program Braun utilized eight single-barrel carburetors to feed an engine. Apparently, multiple carburetion development within General Motors was predominantly a Buick project.

Compound Carburetion became a reality mainly because chief engineer Chayne liked advances which could easily be worked into the assembly line or, as he said, something he could "build under the table and not spend a lot of money." It was his hope that Turlay could somehow use two regular two-barrel carburetors on a single intake manifold, though Turlay's first thought was to rig a single-barrel carburetor to each port.

Since two intake valves fed off each intake port of the straight-eight, Turlay took two of the biggest double-barrel carburetors available from Buick and fabricated a manifold which allowed each barrel to feed the two valves. He then made some power runs but was disappointed in the results. Working for months on the project in his spare time, he tried everything, testing what he came up with in the dynamometer room, checking out the results at the end of each day. "Let's see what the hell we can get out of it" was his guiding maxim. One of his first changes in the experimental manifolds involved balancing tubes running from the front of the engine to the back. He then tried tubes with no connecting runners between them. Next came the installation of little connecting tubes between the runners. This last showed promise, both on the dynamometer and at the proving grounds. Now in the "99% perspiration" phase of his work, Turlay kept at it until he developed a system with balance pipes as large as the manifold branches, the efficiency of which surprised even him. Fuel distribution and breathing were both improved, resulting in better fuel economy and a considerable gain in power.

The exhaust manifolds designed for the carburetors were very successful too. A two-section unit was developed, the forward piece carrying off the gases from the front four cylinders, the rear section from the rear four. Both flanges for the exhaust manifold were bolted to a Y pipe which then carried the exhaust to a single muffler.

The help of performance and racing people around the country was enlisted throughout. Indianapolis veteran Wilbur Shaw was personally acquainted with Chayne (who had been behind the wheel of the Buick that paced the '39 500) and was given one of the first built. After trying his unit out, Shaw returned to Flint and told the chief engineer he could sell as many of them as he could get—a terrific endorsement from a respected race driver.

All this "back-door" success finally attracted Curtice's attention. He decided it would add further sparkle to the glitter of the 1941 line and told Chayne to prepare the system for production. Initially, the decision was made to offer Compound Carburetion as standard equipment only on the convertible models. That suited the engineers just fine. They wanted the opportunity for further testing before across-the-board installation. The later decision to extend Compound Carburetion as standard equipment to all series above the Special and Super was not greeted warmly in Engineering.

Braun was on a cross-country trip with a test car on his way to Colorado and Arizona when he was advised that the sales department wanted to expand "CC" to the Series 40 optionally and Series 50 as standard. He "screamed"—but it did him no good. It was Braun's fear that multiple carburetion had been insufficiently tested to ensure trouble-free operation and, most important, no work had been done on calibration for the small series carburetors nor had the manifolds been designed for the small series engine. Nonetheless, it was rushed through to production.

On both large and small engines, Compound Carburetion used two double-barrel carburetors, either Carter or Stromberg. The outside runner of the manifold was connected to the outside barrel of both carburetors and fed cylinders 1, 2, 7 and 8; the inside runner connected to the inside barrel and fed cylinders 3, 4, 5 and 6. Thus either the front or rear carburetor could feed to all eight cylinders.

The front carburetor was complete with all systems, float, main metering, acceleration, power bypass, idling, starter switch and automatic choke. The rear carburetor had only a float, idle and main metering system. Both carburetors were slightly smaller than the single units used previously.

The 1940 Super Model 56S Sport Coupe, photographed at New York auto show.

Buicks for 1940. Above: The first Estate Wagon. Below: Century Model 66C. Page opposite, above and below: Century Model 66C and Special Model 41C. The convertible coupe photographs are from Hollywood films of this period, Dennis Morgan talking to pilot in scene from Flight Angels *at below right.*

When the engine idled up to about 22 mph on part trottle, the idle systems of both carburetors were in operation. A damper valve assembly was placed between the rear carburetor and the intake manifold, its purpose to govern the operation of the rear carburetor, preventing the engine from operating too lean at lower speeds and eliminating any flat spot or hesitation. Since the butterflies in the valve were not a tight fit, the idling system of the rear carburetor would function even with the valve closed. The throttle linkage for both carburetors was hooked to a pickup lever on the firewall. With the car in third gear and a speed of approximately 75 mph on part throttle, only the front carburetor and the idle system of the rear carburetor were in operation. At full throttle, the pickup lever engaged the linkage for the rear carburetor, the added air flow past the damper valve in the rear carburetor opened the valve and the rear unit was brought into full operation. Both carburetors were now feeding equally. If the accelerator pedal was fully depressed at low speeds, only the front carburetor was operational until manifold vacuum was sufficiently high to open the damper valve. The system was somewhat difficult to keep in correct adjustment, and many mechanics did not understand it. However, it did work extremely well in high power situations. During World War II many owners would install a metal plate underneath the base of the rear carburetor to block it off in an attempt to increase gasoline mileage.

In addition to dual carburetion, Buick had further increased horsepower through the use of a thinner .015 head gasket coated on both sides with lacquer to prevent leakage. Turlay claimed he had a near racing-valve timing on the camshafts released for production. The cars operated so well, once the bugs were eliminated, and gained such a solid performance reputation, there was some discussion at the corporate level that perhaps Buick was overdoing it in light of the usual Flint and General Motors traditions. Chayne and William Knudsen were talking one day about Buick products in general, and Chayne happened to remark that Buick no longer built a truck. "No, you don't," was the GM president's instant response. "You build a goddamm racing car!"

While Compound Carburetion may have had a few field development problems after introduction, there were two other areas which proved even more troublesome. Ten millimeter spark plugs and engine oil filters—both products of Curtice's alma mater, AC—were serious and costly errors for Buick.

It was the contention of AC that the smaller spark plug it had developed had an infinite heat range and would be more effective than stock 14 mm plugs under hard operating conditions. AC's chief engineer undertook quite a selling job on Curtice, and with Chayne's approval the decision was made to go to the smaller plug for 1941 production. (Cadillac, LaSalle, Packard and Chevrolet had considered it too.)

Joe Turlay was against the small plug from the beginning, though for reasons quite different from those which turned out to be the cause of the problem. He did not believe the plug was strong enough mechanically, nor as good as AC said it was. He told Chayne about this, but the decision stood, and he was instructed to modify the production cylinder heads to accept the smaller plugs. Fortunately for Buick, Joe Turlay was a very cautious engineer. Instead of changing the coring inside the head, he simply revised the machining operation on the outside for the plug and plug recess. He was certain Buick would ultimately be forced to revert to the larger plugs, and the change he made would allow a simple production modification and quick field repair without the expense of a new cylinder head when that eventuality occurred.

It was not long before 1941 Buick owners began queuing up in front of dealerships throughout the country complaining of fouled up plugs and rough running engines. But instead of breaking down under hard operation as Turlay had feared, what happened was just the opposite. AC was using an aluminum oxide insulator which could easily take the high temperatures of high speed driving—which had apparently been the conditions under which it was tested—but was very prone to fouling at low speeds. Chicago was one of the first areas of the country to report the problem, so Braun went there with a group of engineers to look into it. They installed a new set of plugs in a car and in less than an hour's driving in the Loop and along Lake Shore Drive, they had fouled out and the engine was missing badly. No one was yet certain why.

Much to Turlay's and Braun's dismay, Compound Carburetion was awarded much of the blame. However, Braun knew that about fifteen percent of the 1941 Series 40 cars had been built with the single carburetion setup carried over from 1940 and without even a calibration change—and these cars were experiencing the same frequency of plug fouling as the dual carbureted jobs. Finally, he managed to convince Chayne that the failure was really AC's not CC's, and the result was a reversion to 14 mm plugs. Production was changed immediately, and dealers in the field bored and tapped cylinder heads by the thousands during the conversion program. Subsequently Chayne asked AC engineers to make up some 14 mm plugs using the new 10 mm insulators. It was his thought that the additional gas flow in the space between the insulator and the plug body would give Buick a wider operating range of conditions on the plug— and it did exactly that. This experiment led to further spark plug development work within General Motors, and Ford picked up the same idea about five years later.

The AC oil filter problem at Buick was simply a matter of faulty construction. The filter was a glued-together powdered-glass concoction which fell apart in service and sometimes caused extensive engine damage. It was a very large sore point within the corporation; the two divisions split the cost of necessary customer repairs until a quality filter could be built and installed in production.

Despite the peskiness of these problems, the 1941 Buick came on strong in the marketplace. It was a very positive-looking car, very modern. A "powerful" appearance was how chief engineer Chayne put it. "Buick's a hon' for '41!" was ad man Kudner's phrase on a Valentine-bedecked promotional flyer.

The Buicks for '41 were more "together" than ever before. The front license plate bracket was, for the first time, designed as an integral part of the bumper. The fender-mounted headlamps were slightly farther forward and farther apart than they had been on 1940 cars. Front fenders on all series extended back to the front doors and blended smoothly into the shape of the doors and rocker panels. Cars were lowered from 9/16ths to 2¾ inches below their 1940 counterparts. The spare tires on all sedan bodies were mounted vertically. On coupes and phaetons, they were carried flat on the floor, there was not the height sufficient to permit their standing upright. Rear directional signal indicators were now carried in a horizontal position just below the taillamps with an arrow indicating turn direction on all models except the Estate Wagon. (Estate Wagons continued with directionals in the tailgate ornament assembly.) Integral gravel shields were provided at the rear giving a clean-cut finished appearance. A new chrome-plated spear ornament was fitted to the rear fender or to the fender skirts.

All bodies had wide floors carrying integral running boards concealed by the doors. Exposed running boards and fender-mounted sidemounts were gone forever from all Buicks. Series 40 and 60 bodies were an all-new design, Series 50 and 70 were carried over. The Estate Wagon for 1941 was developed around the new 40-60 styling and was now a Special model. In addition it was provided new and better weather strip seals around the doors, a continuous hinge on the back window to prevent water leaks and neat, efficient windlaces around the doors. All in all, it was a much better car—and a real beauty.

A more colorful Bedford cord was given the Series 40, and a new Canada cloth was available in new patterns. For the first time, all series featured automatic switches on the front doors which operated the domelight when opened. The front seatback on the Series 40 had an attractive trim panel with an ashtray in the center.

In developing the colors for the 1941 cars Buick chose sixty-seven from the approximately sixteen hundred available. The colors were

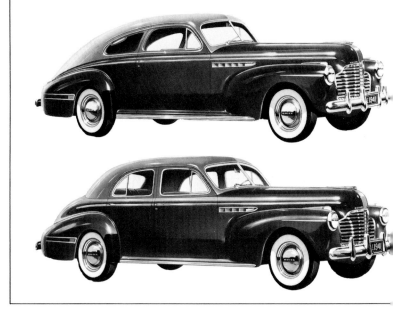

Buicks for 1941. From the top: Century 66S Sedanet, Super 51 Four-Door Touring Sedan, Roadmaster 71C Convertible Phaeton, Special 46S Sedanet. Right: Century 61 Four-Door Touring Sedan; Art Kudner advertises the '41.

You'll hardly believe your gas gauge!

Buick SPECIAL *4-door Sedan, model 47, $1021.* ★

IT takes only a moment to see how sleek and stylish this Buick really is—and not much longer to learn that its spacious room is just the thing you want in your new car for '41.

But it's not till you put the new Buick FIREBALL engine through its paces that you find out something new about *power*—and discover that Buick's in a class by itself when it comes to tight-fisted *thrift!*

The first '41 Buicks were hardly out on the road before happily-surprised owners found they were getting from 10% to 15% *more* miles per gallon.

They were saving money every mile because Buick gives you the thrift of the so-called "economy speeds" that others boast about.

It's thrift that's *constant*—for the extra power of the FIREBALL engine with Compound Carburetion*allows the use of a more economical gear ratio in our regular high gear.

And Compound Carburetion itself keeps gasoline costs low because only *one* smaller-than-average carburetor is working *all* the time—while another cuts in with more power when you

need it for a hill or sudden spurt.

The result is penny-pinching economy every mile you travel—good reason to travel *now* to your nearest Buick dealer's.

For if you want to see a money saving husky at work, just let a Buick take care of your pennies—and watch the dollars take care of themselves!

*Optional on the Buick Special at slight extra cost; standard on all other series.

BUICK PRICES BEGIN AT
★*delivered at Flint, Mich. State tax, optional equipment and accessories—extra. Prices subject to change without notice.* **$915** for the Business Coupe

"Best Buick Yet"

EXEMPLAR OF GENERAL MOTORS VALUE

---

then tested for fading, chalking and durability. From those successfully passing the test, Buick chose a line of seventeen colors and color combinations, with two-tones again offered. Models 41 and 46-S were available in Super-Equipped versions which upgraded the interior to Series 60 specs. Convertible coupes now had power-operated tops. Seat cushions and backs in the open cars were pleated when smooth grain leather trim in one of five colors was specified.

The radio grille casting, one large piece mounted with four large shouldered studs, carried all the switches, ash trays and air control knobs for the defroster. A major advantage of this new grille was that the driver no longer had to grope under the dash for these controls as he had been forced to in the 1940 cars.

Thanks to Curtice and electrical engineer Harry Doane, a unique optional radio was available: a dual short-wave/standard broadcast receiver called Super Sonomatic. Due to its price tag of $72.50, not many were installed, and they are extremely rare today. Buick used the radio this one model year only, although Chevrolet which had picked up on the idea offered it on both 1941 and 1942 cars.

Dashboards on the 1941 cars were finished in a grain harmonizing with the interior, save for the convertible which was finished in car color, and the 90-L which was black. Dash panels and glove compartment doors were a new damascene finish, and the instruments a new brushed copper and cream combination. For the first time, hoods were a one-piece stamping held in place with a new type of hood latch. To open the hood, the latch was pulled out and the safety button released. This design gave easier access to the engine compartment than the old-style center hinges or so-called "alligator hood." By simply releasing both latches at the same time, the entire hood assembly could be removed from the car without loosening a bolt.

And on February 3rd, 1941, there were four new Special models designated Series 40-A. They were on a shorter (by three inches) 118-inch wheelbase and used bodies that Curtice talked Chevrolet into providing him. His aggressive assault on the upper reaches of the marketing scale, he obviously thought, should be matched with an attack on the lower-priced end. Chevrolet apparently was much more amenable in this regard than Cadillac had been.

A record-smashing 370,229 new Buicks were retailed during the 1941 model year by 3038 Buick dealers. The company now had the capacity to build some seventy-six cars per hour and was operating the Flint assembly plant in two shifts totaling sixteen hours a day. Manufacturing departments were working three shifts totaling twenty-two-and-a-half hours; some departments with limited facilities were on seven-day operations.

Only a catastrophe, it seemed, could prevent Buick from even higher records with its 1942 cars.

229

Chapter Thirteen

BUICK TURNS TO WAR

"It is no secret that car designers and engineers have been up against an unusual situation this year," chief engineer Chayne wrote in the October 1941 edition of *The Buick Magazine*. A classic example of understatement.

By the final months of the 1941 production run, it had become obvious to everyone at Buick that the United States would eventually be drawn into World War II. Thus attention was being diverted from thoughts of autos to thoughts of arms, and there was less excitement than usual in Flint that fall about the introduction of the 1942 Buick line. Government quota restrictions had been implemented in August; public relations releases assured customers that these were not confined to Buick but instead to all manufacturers involved in operations using critical materials. During the new model announcement week, Harlow Curtice mentioned that Buick engineers and production men were already working with Army technicians to adapt the Buick engine to military use, but he hastened to add that any government work undertaken would co-exist with normal passenger car production. Somehow it had more the ring of hope than of expectation.

The new Buicks were introduced on October 3rd, 1941 "for the everyday use of the people of America." Where improvements could be made without sacrificing on defense needs, Buick made them. When materials had to be substituted, Buick used the best available. "In that they release needed materials, use machinery not immediately adaptable to defense purposes, and free men of usable skills for defense jobs," the company said, "these Buicks splendidly

measure up as 'defense cars.' "

The tone was subdued throughout. As Bill Hufstader noted, "In ordinary times, this might be the occasion of a little excusable boasting on our part, since the model year just closed saw Buick production reach a new, all time high. . . . However, we are less concerned now with our achievements of the past season than with the making clear to you our attitude toward the new models for 1942. Since these models will remain without essential change until annual models again become the rule, we realized that they would have to uphold the good name of Buick for quite some time."

Sales of the 1942 models were extremely strong right from the start. Buyers were aware this might easily be their last chance . . . for a long time. In total, Buick would produce 94,442 automobiles before the final shutdown to complete war production, and the beginning of a period which Harlow Curtice would recall as the most difficult in his life.

The 1942 Buicks were available in six series and twenty-three models, including five Sedanets, one in each line except the Limited. Prices had been increased from $131 to $202 depending upon model. The Special 40-A was built on a 118-inch wheelbase, the Extra Special 40-B on 121 inches. The Series 50 Super was 124 inches, the Series 60 Century 126, the Series 70 Roadmaster 129, the Series 90 Limited 139.

Most bodies were carryovers with new sheet metal. The Series 50 and 70, however, were new, both wider and lower than '41, with more room in front, and four inches added to the rear seat. Instruments were rearranged, and interior trim and twelve-inch defroster outlets were new.

On all series, a finger grip was added to the hood latch. Bumpers were larger and more massive, curving around the body at both front and rear. The Series 50 and 70 received a new taillamp and directional signal treatment, as well as a separate reflector button mounted on the rear fender and visible from the side of the car in addition to the rear.

The grille ornament was new, and the steering post now fully adjustable. On Super and Roadmaster two-door sedans and convertibles, fenders termed "Airfoil" gave a sweeping line which flowed across the door and ended at the rear fender. The result was an extremely streamlined look. Buick was the only General Motors car to have it. The other GM divisions were not happy about the fact.

On all Series 40, 60 and 90 cars and on the four-door body styles of the 50 and 70, the front fender contour extended just beyond the middle of the front door. The rear fender line on the other Series 50 and 70 cars was brought forward on the rear door. Use of these extended fenders permitted wider door openings both front and rear, and made

possible the use of concealed entrance steps without flaring of the rocker panels. Fender skirts were standard on all series, except the 40 and 60 where they were available at extra cost. Rear quarter windows were provided the Extra Special, Century and Limited sedans, one wide single window was given the Super and Roadmaster sedans. The Special also used an undivided rear window, all convertibles had rear quarter windows.

The familiar Buick cowl-type ventilator had been eliminated, replaced by screened fresh air intake vents near the grille and controlled by a cable and knob assembly at the bottom of the chrome center dash section. The Buick-designed Weather Warden Venti Heater was standard on the Limited, optional on all other series. A new radio grille on the Series 50 and 70 provided for tuning at the top of the dash instead of at the bottom. Locks which prevented the opening of the rear door from inside the car when the rear lock button was depressed were now available on all sedans optionally. Electric power replaced the former vacuum for all convertible tops. Super and Roadmaster convertibles now used the sedan-type windshield header radio antenna.

The thought that public reaction to the Buicks might be "nothing new in '42" had long worried Chayne and his engineers. About nine months before introduction, engineering specifications actually called for a fluid coupling and clutch for the 1942 line, as well as replaceable bearing inserts for connecting rods. But both ideas were dropped well before production plans were finalized. Engineering was proud, however, that its 1942 radiator grilles were stamped from cold rolled steel; due to restrictions, many manufacturers had been forced to die casting.

Aluminum pistons were continued on the large series 165 hp engines. A cast iron material called Domite, lighter than the cast iron used previously and with a Lubrite coating to retain oil and prevent scuffing during break-in, was substituted for the Special and Super. Horsepower of the smaller series engines without the optional Compound Carburetion dropped to 110 hp. (It was 118 with the dual carburetors.) Because of the heavier pistons in the smaller engines, a stronger connecting rod with a new heat treatment was used, along with longer life "Oil-Cushion Bearing Finish," to prevent early rod bearing failures.

Bearing longevity in the earlier engines utilizing cast iron had never particularly pleased Buick engineering, and Chayne had feared that it would be even worse now because of an increase in stroke on the small engines. Fortunately, a bearing development program undertaken on the aluminum piston engines was successfully concluded just about the time Buick found it necessary to return to cast iron, and it helped a good deal.

The "Oil-Cushion Finish" involved a process new to crankshaft and piston pin production. Instead of polishing and lapping the surfaces of crankpins and crankshaft journals to a smooth, highly polished degree, Buick lapped them in such a way that thousands of microscopic depressions per square inch were left on the surface. These depressions served as tiny reservoirs to trap the oil when the load was momentarily lightened during rotation, and held extra film in reserve to supplement the regular oil film when demands on the engine were increased through sudden acceleration or loading. The process was said to "help maintain a constant oil cushion between shaft and bearing surfaces."

Crankshafts at the GM Allison Aircraft engine plant used shot peening to seal minute surface cracks and strengthen the forging. Shot blasting, much like shot peening, was used to give further strength to the 1942 connecting rods. Chayne was quick to point out that the old-style connecting rods for the smaller engines could not be used with the new cast iron pistons. They were simply not strong

UNTIL TOTAL VICTORY, WE DEDICATE OURSELVES TO THE OBJECTIVE..."WHEN BETTER WAR GOODS ARE BUILT, BUICK WORKMEN WILL BUILD THEM."

Page preceding: Hellcat. Left: The 1942 Special Model 41. This page: Workers show their patriotism on February 3, 1942, with the last Buick built before World War II.

The Varnes H-3 Hydram Drilling Machine for automobile master rod production was set on its side and moved out of Factory No. 13 to make way for aircraft engine machinery.

enough to withstand the additional piston weight.

The longer wheelbases on the Series 50 and 70 made possible the mounting of the rear springs just ahead of the rear axle instead of over it, which reduced side rail deflection. The Buick ride was further improved through the use of twenty-percent softer rate rear springs, improved shock absorber valve calibrations and new wide rim wheels. The new rims pushed out the bead of the tire and made the sidewall almost vertical. Tire and wheel stability were greatly improved, heelover was prevented on turns, and the new design helped get maximum mileage from tire casings. The rear stabilizer bar could now be eliminated. Although pictured in 1942 sales literature, whitewall tires were no longer available in production due to material shortages.

Refinements to Compound Carburetion included a new accelerator pump in the front carburetor, a new block-out for the rear carburetor to make it more sensitive to cold operating conditions and to prevent stumble, and refinements in the idle system. Also improved was the location of the crankcase ventilator tube to eliminate the possibility of oil fumes in the carburetors, and fuel lines were routed away from the exhaust manifold, being carried first to the rear

carburetor to keep fuel cooler. For 1942 production Buick was using a quality check no other manufacturer could claim: Each combustion chamber was individually tested and held to exact blueprint dimensions.

Parking brakes were now applied by foot not hand. Ironically, a new directional signal switch dictated by material shortages turned out to be a better and longer lasting item than the original.

Things began happening quickly after Pearl Harbor. The first change came on December 11th, a price reduction to compensate for Buick's being unable to ship cars to dealers with a spare tire and tube. Then, on January 14th, 1942, came the first H models. Obviously Buick was aware its automobile production days were numbered, but serial records were retained on these final cars. With the H cars, the number of available models dropped from twenty-three to fifteen. Eliminated from the Series 40-A were the three-passenger special business coupe and the six-passenger four-door sedan. The series was now designated H-40-A, shared its taillamp and reflector assembly with all other series, and its chrome-plated die-cast radio grille was replaced by a painted metal stamping. Chrome plating on the cars was now confined to bumpers and outside door handles; everything else was now painted or, as Buick termed it, "defense finished." Escutcheons were made of plastic, and belt and rocker moldings were omitted on all closed cars. The Series 40-B, now H-40-B, lost its six-passenger four-door sedan with Super Equipment and its Super-equipped six-passenger Sedanet. Other changes were much the same as the H-40-A, although for these cars the belt and rocker moldings were retained.

The new H-60 Series was similarly changed, though losing no models from its original lineup. No models were deleted either from the H-50 and H-70. But all these cars now had plastic interior door handles in either grey or brown to harmonize with trim. Although it is not generally known, the Series 90 was completely dropped from the line; there were no H-90's built. The Limited nameplate would not see production again until the introduction of the 1958 cars.

Oil capacities were reduced in all Buick engines when the conversion to the H Series was made, this possibly through the elimination of oil filters as standard equipment. The compression ratio on the big engines was reduced from 6.7 to one to 6.3.

Though engineering specifications do not indicate H Series cars with anything but chromed bumpers, some of the last cars came through with their bumpers painted. Old-time Buick employees remember seeing them leaving the plant. The consensus: "They looked like the devil."

Gradually, all production shut down. Linden, New Jersey produced its final Buick two days before Christmas. Flint's last car came off the assembly line just before noon on February 4th, 1942. Southgate, California ended February 7th. Conversion and mounting of Estate Wagon bodies was completed May 13th. Just 16,601 Buicks were built in calendar 1942.

In the meantime, on January 1st, 1942, the government—except for vehicles deemed "essential"—banned the sale of all cars and light trucks. Government tire allotment for that month was announced at 357,000 new tires, 114,191 for car production, 242,783 for trucks and buses. The 500,000-600,000 various cars in the hands of dealers throughout the country would be rationed beginning February 2nd. General Motors announced that its five car divisions would buy back any new cars still on hand at a dealer's request, hoping this way they might be more equitably distributed around the country. Subsequently, the government liberalized new-car rationing procedures, but the threat of fuel rationing continued, and new-car sales remained low. America's thoughts moved out of the automobile showroom.

In 1940 William S. Knudsen had left the General Motors presidency to head the National Defense Advisory Committee. At New York Automobile Show time of 1941, he addressed manufacturers regarding the urgent need for a half billion dollars worth of air-

Loading Sundstrand Hydroscrew miller onto flatcar for storage elsewhere.

plane parts and components. Some of his listeners were caught by surprise. Not Harlow Curtice. A few months earlier, in fact, he had told Knudsen that Buick was ready any time. Shortly after, Knudsen asked Curtice to take on Pratt & Whitney aircraft engine production. "Sure," Curtice said. "How soon can we start?"

He caught the next plane to New York to receive approval of the GM board of directors, then flew to Washington with his production men to meet with the War Department. From there they traveled to Hartford, Connecticut to spend a day at the Pratt & Whitney plant. Within a week of the Knudsen request, Buick was already making plans for the construction of a completely new plant to do the job.

Red Curtice hated red tape. He never let it stop him. Advised there were matters of licensing to be worked out with Pratt & Whitney, as well as contracts to be signed with the government, he said "sure" and charged ahead, sending his men to Hartford to study production techniques and scouting for a place to put up his new plant. Initially, a site near Grand Blanc, a small town a few miles south of Flint, was optioned, but the government in the meantime raised its contract from 500 engines a month, first to 1000, then 3000, then 4400. Grand Blanc was now too small, and with so many GM divisions in the Flint

The M-18 Hellcat, shown above at the factory and below in test maneuvers at the Buick proving grounds. These Buick press release shots carried the notation, "This photograph has been approved by military censors."

area converting to wartime production, it no longer afforded the skilled labor necessary. Consequently, Curtice found 120 acres in Melrose Park, Illinois on the west side of Chicago, and on March 17th, 1942, ground was broken there. On September 17th, Curtice was handed the key to the new plant. There was shatter-proof glass in all its windows and, at the insistence of Army engineers, metal blinds were installed which could be closed automatically at night blacking out all light in the event of an air raid.

Interesting things resulted at Melrose Park, one of them regarding the testing of completed engines. When the test cells for the engines were designed, alternators with slip couplings were installed in every test area, the slip coupling allowing the alternators to run at 900 rpm no matter what the engine speed. The electrical power generated from engines on test was fed back into the electrical system for plant operation—and the surplus was sold to the city of Melrose Park. Buick saved some $80,000 a month. Each engine was run through a six-hour "green test," torn down and inspected, then subjected to another three-hour acceptance test before shipment. Throughout the nine hours, with every engine, Buick was generating electricity.

Initially, there were a few problems. Tested in a cold room at 50 degrees below zero, the engines would not start and run properly. The fuel systems were equipped with primer pumps but though their capacity was found to be sufficient, their end nozzles were too small to meter enough fuel. Engineers, in operating the pumps fast enough to keep a cold engine running, were actually working up a sweat—at 50 below! Subsequently, Buick's carburetion engineer Adolph Braun designed a larger fuel nozzle for the primer. Army Ordnance tested and accepted it. With the improved version, only two or three pump strokes were required to start a cold engine and keep it running—and test engineers cooled off considerably.

When automobile production ceased, Curtice put into motion at Buick a conversion operation which he said was more extensive than that undertaken by any other automobile manufacturer in America. Every factory building in the Flint operation would be devoted exclusively to war work. Fully sixty-five percent of Buick's automobile machine tools would be reworked or redesigned. War production and sales to the government in 1943 alone would amount to $391,000,-000, total sales would be more than a billion dollars. Buick wartime employment would peak at 44,600 workers, more than twice the number that would be necessary during the early postwar period when Buick returned to building cars again. Floor space would be increased from 5,600,000 square feet in 1941 to 8,200,000 in 1943.

Military production was not completely new to Buick. During the First World War, its D-4 trucks had been used as ambulances in France, and in addition the company had built tanks for Great

Below: Charlie Chayne showing Harlow Curtice the aviation test cell which generated electricity as it used it in the Melrose Park defense plant. Above and right: Curtice, Major E.H. Bowman and Buick-built aero engines.

Britain, the Liberty aircraft engine, mortar shells, and thousands of wheel rims, axles and forgings. But the World War II effort could only be described as Brobdingnagian.

At the time of Pearl Harbor, Buick's Plant 11 was one of the largest automobile engine producing facilities in the world. During calendar year 1941 it had been responsible for building 234,083 Buick engines. On February 3rd, 1942, the last one was assembled. Exactly six days later, the first peacetime equipment was moved out—and war machines moved in. It was not an easy thing for Buick men to watch. Patriotism mingled with a sort of emptiness, a knot in the

At the Buick War Training Headquarters, sales manager Bill Hufstader took charge of a school to teach mechanics the service of Pratt & Whitney aviation engines.

stomach as production lines and installations which had taken years to develop and perfect were ripped out. All sub-assemblies, inspection stations, temperature control testing room equipment, hoists, etc. were removed to storage. The long pits built into the floor through which the return conveyors ran were filled in and new block flooring laid. In a scant two weeks, the proud engine assembly line was a memory.

Most difficult to remove from Plant 11 had been two connecting rod presses. They weighed sixty tons apiece, rested in pits fourteen inches below the floor, and were so tall that the top of the building barely cleared them. A twelve-foot-square section of the roof had to be cut out above each press and special steel "A" frames fabricated which ran from the plant floor up through the hole in the roof. A network of chain falls in the hands of expert millwrights saw to the removal. The presses were then tipped on their sides, laid on steel skids, and caterpillars dragged them to railroad flatcars.

When rocker arm production for the Pratt & Whitney engines, initially built in Plant 13, had to be moved to Plant 11, the forty-seven machines involved—along with their stock and equipment—were quickly put on the road for the more than half-a-mile journey. At 7:00 on Sunday morning, April 19th, 1942, the men of the third shift in Plant 13 shut off the power to their machines. By 10:30 a.m. some of the milling equipment was already cutting into stock. By 4:30 p.m. finished rocker arms were being turned out.

Two days after Pearl Harbor, Curtice had informed his production group that Buick would be casting aluminum cylinder heads for the Pratt & Whitney engine. Another new building was necessary, the site chosen was the old Liberty engine plant in Flint, construction on the new facility—designed to be the largest aluminum foundry in the world—began on February 17th; five months later the first cylinder heads were coming off the assembly line.

Another Buick defense project begun in early 1942 was the T-70. As first conceived by the Army, it was to be a highly mobile tank destroyer, to weigh about eight tons, to travel at approximately 35 mph, and to be capable of carrying a five-man crew and a 37 mm cannon. The first prototype, mounted with a 57 mm cannon instead, was completed by Buick in early July. After tests in Flint, Detroit and Texas, the Tank Destroyer Command decided to think even bigger and asked that the second model be a sixteen tonner, with a 75 mm gun and a speed capability of just over 50 mph. This one was completed in October and when tested reached nearly 60 mph. Then the Army decided upon more changes, a 76 mm cannon, machine guns and even more weight.

Originally, plans called for diesel power, although the first pilot model was built using a Buick engine. As the weight of later prototypes increased, a radial-type aircraft engine—the Wright Whirlwind—was tried. It gave Buick engineers some trouble, operating properly up to about 85 degrees ambient temperature, but then it began to lose pistons. A very poor fuel pump and fuel delivery appeared to be the major stumbling block; engineer Braun corrected it by changing carburetor metering and got satisfactory results at 150 degrees. The Army was satisfied too, and placed an initial order for six T-70's with Buick. As these were being built, the order was increased to an even thousand at a price tag of more than fifty million dollars. Later the T-70 designation of the tank was changed to M-18. But everyone referred to it by its nickname. It was called the Hellcat.

Shortages of vital materials caused production problems for the country's military program throughout the war but perhaps none was more acute than the need for copper in the construction of brass car-

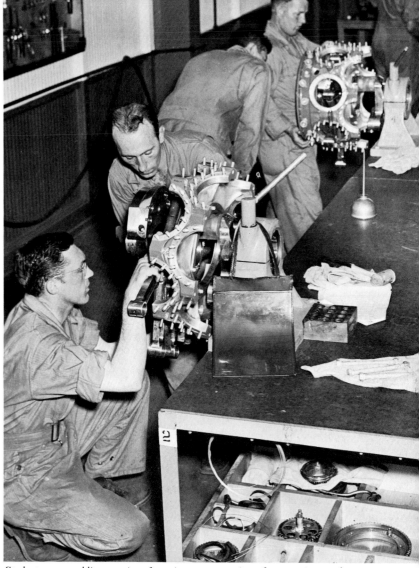

Students reassembling an aircraft engine power section after practice teardown.

tridge shell cases. In January of 1942 Curtice was approached by Army Ordnance and advised that a "desperate situation" existed due to ammunition shortages.

During World War I some success had been realized by both Germany and the United States in the use of steel cartridge jackets, but the technique had not been perfected nor had records been kept of the process used. The first attempts by Buick now used low carbon steel

WHEN BETTER AUTOMOBILES *war goods* ARE BUILT BUICK WILL BUILD THEM

Assembling and lapping gears for the 90 mm anti-aircraft gun mount.

... so nice to come home to!

No, the fighting isn't over. Nor is Buick's war work finished.

But victory in Europe is releasing many fighting men to come home — and permitting the country to turn, at least in part, to the making of things they will find nice to come home to.

To many a fighting man, this will mean such pleasures as an open road, a glorious day — and a bright and lively Buick.

The roads are here. The days come with each rising sun. And the bustle that now enlivens Buick's factories is the make-ready process for getting back into the production of cars.

We aim to make those Buicks all that returning warriors have dreamed about — cars that from go-treadle to stop light will fit the stirring pattern of the lively, exciting, forward-moving new world so many millions have fought for.

This is the 1942 Buick which sets the high standards to be surpassed in new models now being made ready.

WHEN BETTER AUTOMOBILES ARE BUILT
BUICK
WILL BUILD THEM

BUICK DIVISION OF **GENERAL MOTORS**
Every Sunday Afternoon — GENERAL MOTORS SYMPHONY OF THE AIR

The Army-Navy "E" proudly flies over all Buick plants

Victory in Europe signaled WWII was near an end, and this famous ad, featuring a yellow 1942 Buick convertible, was an indication Buick was preparing for the postwar boom.

with no alloys. The result was not promising. Later tests with the same grade of steel but with alloys proved successful but there was a snafu here too; the alloys necessary were more difficult to obtain than copper. So experiments followed using plain-carbon steel and a small amount of manganese. *Voila!* The end of passenger car production released the sheet metal stamping plant, and by the end of the month the facility was converted to work on 75 mm cartridge cases.

The metallurgy and ballistics involved in this operation was extensive and complicated. Not until May of 1943 was Buick ready to go to the Aberdeen military proving ground with two hundred rounds for testing. The results with both American and French guns were a triumph. Three days later Buick was asked to build half a million shell cases. Production commenced at four hundred an hour.

In total, Buick was assigned more than thirty separate war production operations. Among them, the following records were realized: 424,000 steel cartridge cases, 19,428 tank power trains, 9,719,000 20 mm shell bodies, 2507 Hellcat tank destroyers, 2952 mounts for anti-aircraft guns.

The pace had been a killing one for virtually everyone at Buick. The hours were long and exhausting, the pressure formidable and unrelenting. With no new cars to manage sales of, Bill Hufstader became head of a Buick school in Flint devoted to the training of men

to service the Pratt & Whitney engine. Some 2700 men selected by the Army would be put through the eleven-week course. Buick public relations diverted its efforts to press releases devoted to the progress being made in conserving war matériel and to company development of new methods to produce war goods at lower cost. Buick advertising took patriotic themes—or nostalgic ones, like the famous ad Art Kudner developed featuring a yellow 1942 Buick convertible and entitled, "So Nice To Come Home To." Sadly, Buick would lose its advertising director during the war. Art Kudner died in 1944.

The state of war could not endure forever. Early on, General Motors had announced to its dealers that those retaining their franchises for the duration would be given new car distribution priority for two years over newly appointed dealers when it was all over. Dealers who stayed existed meagerly on used cars, parts and service. At Buick, Curtice and Hufstader worked hard to keep their organization together. They were successful; in December 1941 there were 2947 Buick dealers in the United States, in December of 1943 the total stood at 2509—or a loss of a mere fifteen percent of the retail sales force. Late the year following, as the tide of battle turned in favor of the Allies, Harlow Curtice could begin thinking about the day coming soon when his plants could turn aside from cartridge shells and tanks, when Buick could begin again.

Chapter Fourteen

HARDTOPS, PORTHOLES AND CHROME

When World War II ended in 1945, Buick was in an enviable position. Like the other automakers, it had to serve warmed-up 1942 models for 1946 palates because war production did not permit new car tooling. But to Buick's advantage, the 1942 models had been among the most advanced in styling, and Buick's Fireball Eight engine was one of the industry's most respected powerplants.

From a production standpoint, Buick was in a good position to begin again quickly. Both Buick and Fisher Body, which supplied the division's bodies, had preserved their prewar tooling. Furthermore, near the end of the war, the federal government's War Production Board had permitted Buick to reactivate engine assembly to manufacture 500 replacement engines, using 1942 tooling.

Before the 500 engines had been completed, the war had ended—so Buick had its postwar engine production immediately ready to start.*

Yet another advantage for Buick was that it was part of General

---

*The replacement engine program was expanded to offer complete engine assemblies which would fit any 1937 through 1942 Buick. The 248- and 320-cubic-inch Buick straight-eights were available and Buick dealers advertised that a complete new engine could be installed in twelve working hours. As design changes and improvements were incorporated in production engines, such as aluminum pistons and precision bearings, the replacement engines included these parts. Every replacement engine had an "RE" stamped on the engine number pad and when the "RE" engine was installed in the car, the original car engine number was transferred to the pad just below the "RE" number. Nearly 100,000 replacement engines were built between 1945 and 1953 when the program ended. Some were used as power sources for irrigation pumps in the Southwest.

Motors, whose chief executive, Alfred P. Sloan, Jr., announced a $500 million program for reconversion from military to civilian production, plus modernization and expansion.

But Buick's real ace was that it was still headed by the dominant Harlow H. Curtice, destined to become GM's top executive in less than a decade, and a man who would be remembered decades later by many who worked closely with him as the strongest manager they had ever known.

Not long after Sloan announced the big postwar expansion program, Curtice put in his bid for a large share of it. Describing his needs in internal memos, Curtice was persuasive with facts and figures. He pointed out that an estimated 20.9 million cars would be on the road January 1st, 1946, compared with a normal or potentially existing 29.7 million. "On this basis, there will be an immediate backlog of demand for 8.7 million cars," he wrote. Curtice estimated the immediate postwar market would require U.S. production of six million cars a year for three years, compared with prewar capacity of four million cars. Since Buick's penetration of the market during the last four prewar years averaged 8.4 percent, he emphasized, Buick would have to produce 500,000 cars a year in the projected postwar market just to stay even.

Curtice apparently got most of what he wanted. On July 22nd, 1945, he announced that Buick's greatest peacetime expansion was about to begin, with new factories totaling 1.3 million square feet of floor space in fifteen buildings. This would give Buick, in Flint, working space for 22,000 employees and production of 550,000 cars a year. When the program was essentially completed in December 1947, Curtice called it one of the most significant developments in Buick history and said the Flint Buick complex was "the most advanced, modern manufacturing setup in the country." And the expansion had been completed largely before postwar inflation became rampant. This fact would be pointed to in later years as a major factor in Buick's high profitability for GM.

Further expansions followed, and Buick, which had begun in Flint in 1903 with a one-story building 80 by 200 feet, had by 1953 some ten million square feet of floor space.

Projecting production of more than half-a-million Buicks a year turned out, however, to be a lot easier than actually producing them. Buick's simplified 1946 lineup, announced October 7th, 1945, included the Series 50 Super on a 124-inch wheelbase, the Series 70 Roadmaster on a 129-inch wheelbase and the Series 40 Special on a 121-inch wheelbase. These were continuations of 1942 sizes and numbers. But though production got off to a fast start, events occurred beyond Curtice's control. The UAW struck General Motors on November 21st, 1945, shutting down operations for 119 days—until

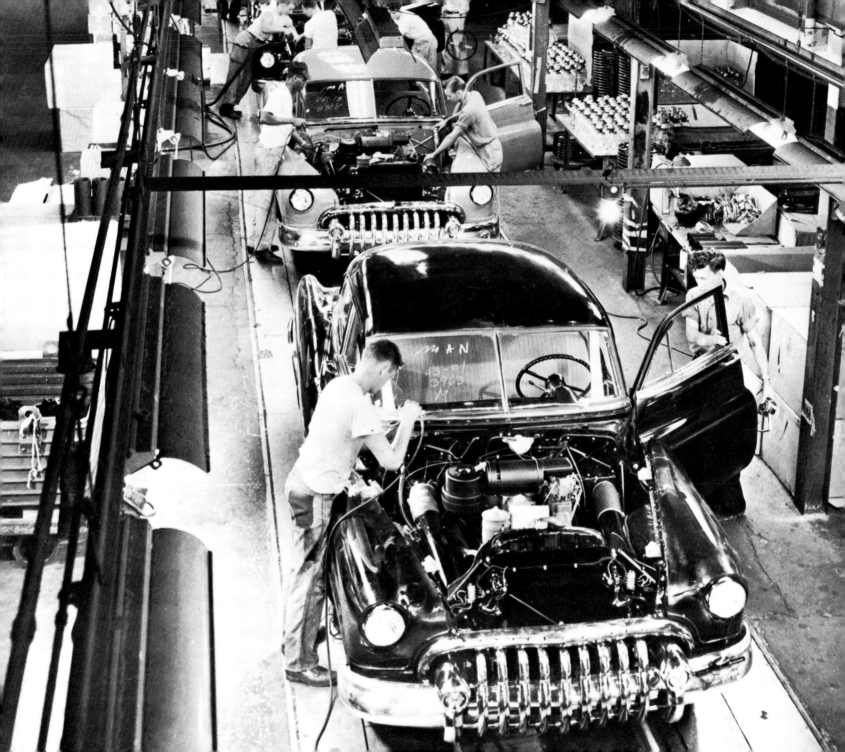

Page preceding: The Buick assembly line in Flint, 1950. Above and below: Harley Earl and his Y-Job as it was before the war—and after, in 1947.

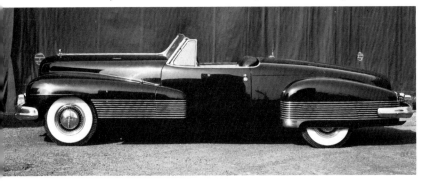

March 19th, 1946. Buick was struck about a month longer over local issues. In the meantime, steel companies sold the steel Buick had reserved to other manufacturers.

"We had to do a lot of talking and invest a lot of money with the steel companies to get them to increase capacity for us," recalled Anthony G. De Lorenzo, then one of Curtice's closest associates, later the GM vice-president of public relations.

Buick promoted the 1946 cars, despite the minimal changes, as "fresh, smart-as-tomorrow new models." They traced some of their styling influence to the Y-Job, the prototype dreamed up in 1938 by GM design chief Harley Earl, and built on a production Buick

chassis fixed up by Charlie Chayne and crew.

Among Harley Earl's guiding design principles for the whole of his career was lowering and lengthening the American automobile "at times in reality and always at least in appearance . . . because my sense of proportion tells me that oblongs are more attractive than squares." The Y-Job was certainly in keeping with Harley Earl's principles. In addition to being undeniably oblong, it featured disappearing headlights, flush-type door handles, a convertible top completely concealed automatically by a metal deck, electrically operated window regulators, and small wheels with airplane-type air-cooled brake drums.

The car was completed late in 1939 and Buick made known its existence with a press release and photographs in the spring of 1940. The press promptly voiced its opinion that here was a "Car of the Future." Because the immediate future was World War II, nothing much was heard of the Y-Job thereafter, though it was used as a rolling testbed for other innovations as time went on. And Harley Earl drove it as his personal transportation during the war years.

The Y-Job proved, however, to be almost as much production Buick as personal Earl. The vertical bar grille idea graced the few '42 model year Buicks built before Pearl Harbor put a stop to production. And other Y-Job features found their way into the postwar Buicks as well, notably the hood ornament which the 1940 press release had referred to as a "machine gun sight" and which postwar came to be known more familiarly as the Buick "bombsight." Kids loved it. There would be a lot of them stolen in the almost dozen years following in which the bombsight guided Buicks down the road.

Modifying the design of the hood ornament for the 1946 Buicks was the task of Ned Nickles. He was Harley Earl's protégé, hired by him just before the war on the strength of drawings Nickles submitted to GM. A Wisconsin native, the son of a papermaker and not formally educated beyond secondary school, Nickles had taught himself car design. He did it mostly during classes in general science at Kaukauna High School, which didn't please his teachers much, though the punishment dealt him wasn't harsh; he was made to stand in front of the room and, sometimes, show the class the drawings he had done. After graduation, he went to work for his father, until at age twenty-three he spotted a *Life* magazine article about Detroit and its cars, and sent some sketches and a request for a job to the man at General Motors whom a typographical error had rendered as "Earl Harley." A terse note followed several weeks later telling him to report to work the following Monday morning.

Nickles was the flamboyant sort, which appealed to Earl. After working in several GM design studios and doing camouflage work on GM tanks and trucks during World War II, he was named Buick's chief designer in 1945. There wasn't much he could do for the '46 cars, but he was already thinking ahead. And sketching. One day soon he would have to stand in front of a room again and show what he had done.

For 1946, the Super was to be produced in four body styles (sedan, sedanet, convertible, wagon), the Roadmaster in three (all the foregoing save the wagon) and the Special in two (sedan and sedanet). Buick built 2482 cars in late 1945 and 156,080 in calendar 1946, which was fifth best among U.S. automakers, 7.2 percent of the industry. (The '46 model year total was 158,728.) Without the strike, Buick would have been fourth. The production figures listed, incidentally, represent the United States only. Buick would recommence production in Canada in 1951, after a nine-year hiatus.

Besides the gunsight hood ornament, to survive until 1958, the few styling innovations for 1946 included a more massive grille and the elimination of a fender crease. The fenders were described as "sweeping airfoil," there were smoothly fitting rear wheel shields, and chrome trim was simplified, though some body hardware and knobs which had been made of plastic in 1942 returned to the chrome of prewar days. Mechanically, Buick returned to the aluminum pistons that had been unavailable on some models just before the war. The "several score major design changes" which Buick exaggerated had been incorporated in the 1946 line also included a new method of precision finishing of the cylinder walls, revised carburetion and rear axle gears, and a new system of operating the windshield wipers "for the first time in an absolutely noiseless fashion." *Business Week* noted that a "neat trick is the rear-wheel lock operated by a bolt inside [the fender skirt] to make rear tire thefts difficult when the door is locked." (This was a feature on four-door Series 50-70 only.)

One of the most interesting Buicks of the model year was the Super convertible, production of which was announced by Curtice on August 11th, 1946. It had push-button controls, hydraulically operated, not only for the top, but also for the windows and seat adjustments.

The Super moved down the Buick assembly line first, in October 1945. The low-priced Special did not become available until November 1946—more than a year later. The strike and shortages of raw materials delayed its introduction. And, significantly, an auto-starved public was willing to buy whatever came off the line—it was a great time to be a car salesman. Getting the lowest-priced Buick ($1522-$1580, compared to the Super's $1741-$2594 range) into production, therefore, was understandably not Buick's highest priority, especially when it would use up materials needed for bigger, and more profitable, cars.

During the 1946 and 1947 model years, Buick offered special driv-

From the left, around the seated Harley Earl: Bob Lauer, Steve McDaniel, Bill Mitchell, Ned Nickles. Below: Portholes and bombsight by Nickles.

ing controls—without charge—to disabled veterans of World War II. "These special controls are made available with the sincere hope that their use may in some measure help to overcome physical handicaps of many disabled veterans," Buick said in a brochure. The controls were designed so that veterans who had lost hands or legs could operate them.

The postwar period also saw the expansion of facilities to build Buicks in a number of plants around the country, along with Oldsmobiles and Pontiacs, under the direction of the B.O.P. Assembly Division. Before the war, Buick assembly began in South Gate, California (October 1936) and in Linden, New Jersey (April

1937). After the war, production began at Fairfax, Kansas in 1946; Doraville, Georgia in 1948; Framingham, Massachusetts and Wilmington, Delaware in 1949; Arlington, Texas in 1954.*

Buick made few changes for the 1947 model run, but moved up to fourth place with calendar-year production of 267,830 cars, 7.5 percent of the industry. (The total for the model year was 277,134.) The "bonnetful of Fireball power at your command," as Buick put it, was advertised as delivering 110 and 144 bhp in 248- and 320-cubic-inch powerplants respectively. The only major styling change was in the grille. Although it followed in motif the 1946 version, it was now more three-dimensional, more massive. This grille, which was continued in theme but with variations through the 1954 model year, is one of the most famous of all Buick identifications, perhaps surpassed only by VentiPorts, or portholes, which arrived in 1949. A familiar memory to those who lived through the early postwar years, the Buick grille has recently shown up in campy posters and movie advertisements, when artists desire a ready identification of the era. And there is the tinge of nostalgia, too, to one of Buick's advertising lines for its cars of '47: "Choose any one, as your tastes or the measurements of your garage may dictate, and you may be sure you've put your money in the smartest possible place."

In 1947, Buick put its money on an Estate Wagon addition to the Roadmaster series. And, more significantly, Buick led the industry in one body style, the convertible, with 37,743 sales, taking a hefty 22.9 percent of the softtop market.

Something else of importance happened during 1947, a severing of a link to the Buick past. On March 18th, eighty-five-year-old William Crapo "Billy" Durant, the man who had taken the marque from obscurity to ubiquity and who had then founded General Motors, died at his apartment overlooking Gramercy Park in New York City. In 1942 he had suffered a stroke at the Durant Hotel in Flint and had been confined to a wheelchair for the last several years of his life. His widow Catherine said he was penniless when he died, though it is known that such men as Chrysler, Sloan and Mott had provided him with some funds during his last years.

*There would be various adjustments through the years. Linden did not produce Buicks between 1963 and 1976. Doraville stopped in 1970, Wilmington in 1975. Framingham did not build Buicks between 1961 and 1970. In 1964 production switched from Arlington to Baltimore, and then Fremont,. California and Leeds, Missouri were added. In 1973, Norwood, Ohio and Van Nuys, California became Buick production points. In 1976, Tarrytown, New York was introduced; in 1977, Willow Run; in 1978, Lordstown, Ohio. Until 1967, Canadian production was largely for Canada. Beginning that year, and running through 1969, Canada shipped Buicks to the United States. Buicks were also sent to the United States from Canada between 1974 and 1978, including Skyhawks built at Ste. Therese, Quebec.

In 1948 Buick introduced Dynaflow, the first Buick automatic transmission since the trials of a decade earlier, and became the first American-built car to use a torque converter. Dynaflow was offered initially only on the Roadmaster, and only as a $206 option.

The prospect of a Buick automatic transmission for '48 had been rumored through much of 1947. In August, *American Machinist* declared that "signs are overwhelmingly in favor of Buick's definitely coming out with a new automatic development on its 1948 models." In its November issue, *Fortune* commented that "on the much-discussed subject of automatic transmissions, Buick now thinks it has the answer." Through much of this period, Curtice declined to confirm the rumor. Indeed, he had been putting out smokescreens stating there would have to be more refinements developed before Buick would consider abandoning the conventional transmission.

Before the year ended, however, Curtice announced that "Buick's answer to no-shift, clutchless driving" was just about ready, without mentioning its name. In mid-January 1948 he was ready with the name; Dynaflow was here. And a reporter, after test-driving a Dynaflow-equipped Roadmaster, wrote this impression: "The most pronounced sensation . . . is the total absence of the noises and interrupted car movement associated with gear shifting whether it is done manually or by automatic shift. The car just glides forward and the only sound is the purr of the motor."

In the sales brochure, Buick heralded Dynaflow as "a new triumph of motoring . . . It's driving magic . . . a new kind of drive . . . wonderfully smooth under every conceivable condition of acceleration and speed . . . and wonderfully simple and safe in operation. You never use a clutch pedal—there is none. You never sense any lags, any halts—there are none. And not only is there no shifting for you to do—no gears ever shift anywhere in the car."

But Dynaflow's torque converter drive, which had been used during World War II on Buick-built M-18 (Hellcat) tank destroyers, was not quite as good as the sales brochure boasted. Owners noticed that Dynaflow had sounds of its own, and there was a noticeable lag as the transmission worked to catch up to acceleration. "Come on, Dyna, flow," a driver would sometimes joke during these sluggish intervals. There was also some problem with leakage in the early production models and gas mileage suffered.

Still, Dynaflow was a success. By 1954 fully eighty-five percent of new Buicks were being sold with it.

Buick's Hellcat days had also contributed to another innovation for '48. A synthetic rubber formulation had been determined during military testing to have frictional characteristics providing unique damping properties. This rubber composition was used in the new system of "controlled frequency" engine mounting, which included

Above: The Super sedan for 1946 and the Super convertible for 1947.
Below: The Roadmaster convertible and sedan for the 1948 model year.

two front mounts and a rear mount composed of two pieces located at the torque tube ball joint. The system was so designed that the frequency of the engine on its mountings eliminated or damped all other vibrations whether induced by engine operation or by transmitting road vibrations from the chassis. The result of all this, Buick said, shielded passengers against tiring pulsations, alleviated road noise, and made engine sensation almost imperceptible. Buick engineers were proud of it, and had not Dynaflow stolen its thunder, probably the innovation would have received wider publicity.

Four engine power ratings were available in 1948 Buicks: the 40 Special, 110 hp; the 50 Super, 115 hp; the 70 Roadmaster with standard transmission, 144 hp; the 70 Roadmaster with Dynaflow, 150 hp. For Dynaflow, the engine was fitted with a new crankshaft and flywheel, its compression ratio increased from 6.6 to 6.9 to one, and new hydraulic lifters were part of the package.

To improve performance and oil economy, Buick adopted as standard equipment a new piston ring setup, claimed to be the first major application of the steel "Flex-Fit" oil control ring. There was also a new oil filter to keep engine oil cleaner, and a revised front suspension system on the Series 40 and 50 with higher springs to provide increased ride clearance. New, too, was the three-spoke flexible steering wheel, "leaving the upper half of the wheel entirely unobstructed," and carrying a redesigned monogram bearing the series designation as well as an altogether new semi-circular horn ring.

Calendar-year production for '48 reached 275,503 units, 7.0 percent of the industry total, still good for fourth place. (Model year production totaled 219,718.) But, more significantly, during 1948 Buick's leadership changed.

General manager Harlow Curtice and general sales manager William Hufstader, both of whom had led Buick during fifteen momentous years—from the depths of depression to recovery, through the military production of World War II, then into postwar production and finally Dynaflow—went on to bigger jobs at General Motors. Curtice, who was on his way to the GM presidency, was named executive vice-president of the corporation, and Hufstader vice-president in charge of distribution.

They were honored in Flint on November 4th, 1948, at a civic tribute dinner attended by 1300 at the IMA Auditorium. The community ovation was genuine. When Curtice took over at Buick, the marque was on the verge of oblivion, and Flint was being referred to as "a ghost town" by some writers. When he left, Buick had regained its position of prestige and prosperity.

Of all the men who have led Buick, none but Durant had as great an impact on its success as Harlow "Red" Curtice.

Curtice's climb up the corporate ladder of General Motors scarce-

247

ly lessened his interest in, or control of, Buick. His immediate successors as general manager in Flint—easy-going Ivan L. Wiles from 1948 to 1956, and rough-talking Edward T. Ragsdale from 1956 to 1959—were fine men in their own ways, but neither was a strong leader, at least compared to Curtice. Curtice may not have actually "run" Buick from the day he left his office in Flint in 1948 until his retirement from General Motors in Detroit in 1958—but if he didn't, he fooled a lot of top Buick executives.

A former general manager said, "Curtice used to go in on Saturdays and run Buick." A car designer agreed: "Even after Curtice became president of GM [in 1953], he ran things at Buick. Nobody wanted to stand up to him." An executive noted, "Curtice made the decisions."

There seem to be few disagreements on this, and even those are hedging. Said another executive: "Curtice didn't really run Buick in the '50's, but maybe Wiles and Ragsdale just went along with him." Wiles in fact went to Curtice privately after being appointed Buick's head man and asked Curtice to "turn him loose." Curtice laughed and agreed—insofar as he was psychologically able to.

Curtice maintained his home in Flint and commuted to Detroit almost daily in a twin-engine Lockheed. (The plane had Buick-built Pratt & Whitney engines installed in a hangar at Flint's Bishop Airport.) On many Saturday mornings while president of General Motors, he would meet with Buick top executives in the general manager's office. "Curtice loved Buick, and he never rode in any other kind of car, even when he was GM president," said one executive of the period. "In fact, when he was GM president, he secretly talked Fisher Body into selling bodies to Buick for $25 under the price to other divisions."

On Saturday afternoons, Curtice would hold court at the Flint City Club on the top floor of the Durant Hotel, a suite of rooms that had originally been planned as Billy Durant's apartment when the hotel was built in 1920. One day Flint's mayor, George M. Algoe, told Curtice that he had just bought a Cadillac "and, Red, it's the best car I ever had." Curtice stared icily at him for a moment, then said, "George, I think maybe that's too much car for you." Algoe replied, "Red, I got the message." The next day Algoe traded in his Cadillac for a Buick.

Tony De Lorenzo, who had joined Buick as representative for the Kudner advertising agency in 1946 and who became one of Curtice's closest confidants, recalls that "Curtice was, most of all, dynamic. He had a fast grasp of things, made decisions quickly after checking all sources, and he was a prodigious worker. If he had a fault it was that sometimes maybe he moved a little too fast."

Mary Gainey Turnbull, one of Curtice's secretaries for decades af-

ter 1935, said, "One thing was his drive. He never asked anyone to give more of themselves than he was willing to give. His memory was unbelievable. People liked Mr. Curtice. Some who didn't know him well thought he was very austere. 'Oh, no,' I would tell them, 'He's not that way at all. Underneath, he is a very kind, thoughtful man.' "

Joseph D. Turlay, who designed Buick straight-eight engines, the first Buick V-8 and the famous V-6 of a later period, said Curtice "was probably the best executive and most forceful man I have ever worked for. He was fire and energy." Turlay also remembers that Curtice was thorough in everything he did, including cutting costs. In one such economy drive, Curtice even ordered that all nuts be reduced by a few thousandths of an inch to save a fraction of a cent a car. "But then we found we had to change all of the sockets on the assembly lines to fit them, so I don't know if we saved much."

One man who might have known was Curtice's successor as general manager of Buick. Ivan L. Wiles had been Buick's comptroller since 1941.

Born in Goodland, Indiana, the son of a bank executive, Wiles was an aviation cadet in World War I (the war ended before he completed training) and worked his way through Wabash College in Crawfordsville, Indiana, by waiting tables and working as a teller in his father's bank. In his senior year he and a friend successfully operated a college store, selling food, cigarettes and second-hand books. Along the way he also earned a Phi Beta Kappa key.

His first job was as an accountant with the Marmon Automobile Company in 1922. But he was there only a few months, going on to similar positions with other accounting firms and becoming a certified public accountant in 1927. In 1928 he went to Oakland Motor Company, predecessor of Pontiac, and three years later, aged thirty-two, he was promoted to assistant comptroller at Buick. Nine years later the comptrollership was his and now, in 1948, he was Buick's general manager.

Wiles, interviewed at age eighty-one for this book, said he felt he had "a pretty good foundation" for the job, even though his background was as a "bean counter." As he explained, "When I was an assistant at Oakland, my boss made me go out into the plant when I wasn't busy to learn what was going on in every department. Once, I had to weigh every part of an automobile, every component, because we were getting in trouble on exports because of weights. By doing this, I got to know what every part was. Also, I had worked my way through college. Still, I realize that possibly some of the other guys, those who ran engineering and manufacturing, were unhappy that a comptroller got the job. They probably felt they should get it. But I had good communications with the top people. I told the leaders of the Buick departments that they knew more about their

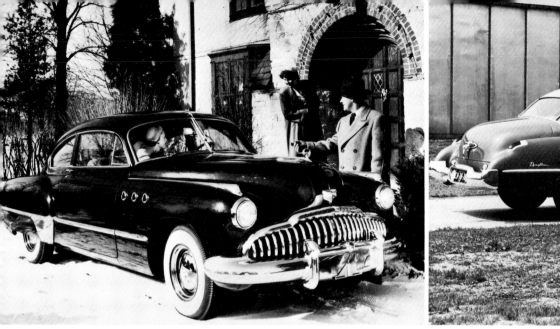

Dior's "New Look" was revolutionizing women's fashions. Buick's new look for 1949 included a Super Sedanet and, most significantly, a Roadmaster Riviera hardtop.

areas than I did, but that I was the liaison with the central office."

Wiles became Buick general manager at a fortunate time. New styling was in the works for 1949, and Buick still had a strong engineering staff headed by Charlie Chayne.

Both the Roadmaster and Super series received body-length fenders, panoramic curved windshield and rear window, and one-piece wraparound bumpers in '49. The Special would not be restyled until mid-year. But the real star of the '49 Buick show was the Roadmaster Riviera Hardtop Coupe.

According to some Buick sources, the hardtop convertible styling was an idea of Edward T. Ragsdale, who moved up from Buick assistant chief engineer to manufacturing manager in '49. Ragsdale noticed that his wife Sarah always bought convertibles but never put the top down—she just liked the sporty look. This gave him the idea for convertible styling in a hardtop car.

Other sources say this story is not true at all—that Ned Nickles, who was in charge of Buick styling, had built a scale model of a "hardtop" in 1945, that Curtice liked it and wondered if it could be produced, and that Ragsdale was called in to answer that question. Ragsdale decided it could, and then worked out a lot of the tooling that made it possible.

The best source for the truth today is Nickles. He says both versions are true.

"The hardtop convertible was done at 40 West Milwaukee in Detroit, at a GM Styling experimental studio," Nickles explains. "We had ⅜ths scale models there. It was about 1945. Ragsdale came into a meeting, and I think Curtice was also there. Ragsdale looked at my model of the hardtop and said that his wife always wanted convertibles because she liked the styling, but never put the top down because it made her hair blow around. So I had already designed the hardtop, but Ragsdale did show an interest. Everybody liked the car. Curtice had a lot to do with it from that point."

Curtice's powerful position within the corporation got the hardtop exclusively, at first, for Buick. The basic differing element in hardtop convertible styling was that the B-post, the center side pillar, was eliminated. Chrysler had made seven Town & Country cars with similar hardtop styling in 1947, but these were hardly more than prototypes. Buick built more than 4000 hardtop Rivieras in 1949, the first of hundreds of thousands it would produce over the next few years.

"A stunningly smart new body-type conceived and styled by Buick," the brochures declared proudly. " . . . the racy look of a convertible with the suave and solid comfort of a fine sedan. It has the swift, greyhound lines that give sportive zip and zest to the convertible—but with a permanent crown of solid, sturdy steel

overhead." One reporter put all this rather less elegantly: "It will please aging sports who want the zip of a convertible but not its wind-blast and rattles." If so, there were a lot of aging sports. Riviera styling was a smash hit.

A few of the Roadmaster Rivieras had another Nickles' styling device, the "sweepspear," a chrome side decoration that began in the front fender as a slim horizontal molding and became wider as it swept in a downward curve along the doors, dipping to the base of the leading edge of the rear fender, and then kicking up over the rear wheel openings. It would become another long-lived Buick identity feature, changing in detail though not in concept.

But Nickles himself says that yet another styling device he put on the 1949 Roadmaster and Super models became the most famous of all Buick identifications. Buick called them VentiPorts, with a "sleek and nautical sweep . . . chrome-ringed . . . gleaming and ultra-smart . . . their name [deriving] from the fact that they serve as heat outlets for the engine compartment." Other designations would follow for what in essence were merely holes, and one of the more clever styling recognition devices in automotive design history. One nickname they received—mouseholes—probably resulted from the famous cartoon by the inimitable Russell Brockbank, depicting a Buick motoring down a country lane with a little mouse jumping out of one of the VentiPorts.

However termed, they happened almost accidentally. Nickles had cut holes in the sides of the hood of his own 1948 Roadmaster convertible and behind them installed amber lights attached to the distributor. The lights, flashing on and off, suggested an unusually powerful engine with a flaming exhaust. If you look at the Buick Bug—that famous racer of 1910—you get the idea. When the Bug at Flint's Sloan Museum is started—the writer once drove it around the Indianapolis Speedway track—flames dance out of the four portholes in the hood while the big engine is idling.

However, Nickles says he got the inspiration essentially from World War II fighter planes. Ragsdale saw Nickles' custom work one day, was aghast and told Curtice how Nickles had "ruined" his convertible. Curtice was intrigued and had Nickles bring the car around from the garage. Unlike Ragsdale, he liked the portholes so much that, even though the 1949 Buicks were only seven months from production, he ordered them used on the new cars. But without the lights.*

This was an example of the Curtice flair for showmanship. Some

---

*The early '49 Roadmasters and Supers had hoses attached to the ports to vent the engines. The hoses were removed and the holes plugged in the middle of the '49 model year. Thereafter VentiPorts were decorative.

published assessments of the man contend he had wild taste in automobiles. Nickles does not agree. "Curtice was conservative in his dress and speech," he notes. "I don't think he was radical in his styling tastes, more middle of the road."

On styling in general during this period, Nickles adds: "I have heard criticism of the amount of chrome we used on those postwar Buicks, but I come from a different perspective than some of these writers. You have to judge things in the context of their times. We had just come through a war, and you couldn't get chrome during the war. So, in the postwar years, we were entertaining people with chrome on cars. I think the cars fit in well with the times."

There was also some entertainment in the designations Buick copywriters came up with for various features. The steering was called "Permi-Firm," coachwork was joined to frame with "Silent Zone" body mountings, the interior acoustic installation pad was a "Sound-Sorber" top lining, the suspension "Quadruflex Coil" springing. The ventilating and heating system was revised and renamed "WeatherWarden." The radio remained "Sonomatic," the instrument panel was "Pilot-Centered." The controlled-frequency engine support introduced the year previous became "Hi-Poised" mounting which prevented "vibration build-up" and provided "cruising as the clouds know it."

Such comfort was not universally admired, however. *Motor Trend* noted that "the combination of soft tires, soft springs and soft seats gives you the feeling of riding on a Beautyrest mattress on wheels . . . but it heels over in turns like a marshmallow . . . a tendency of nearly all cars with such a soft ride." *Consumer Reports*, on the other hand, found the Buick's roadholding ability commendable and noted that the car "inspires owner confidence by its bulk, its stability, and its roadability at high speed, and gratifies by its powerful and prompt response to the accelerator. What else could a buyer require at the price?" The magazine answered its own question with "Plenty." The best *Consumer Reports* could say about the Buick's maneuverability in traffic was that the "high fenders and low hood give the driver a much better than average indication of where the car is, vis-à-vis other cars or obstacles." Doubting that the Buick attributes could be had at a lower price, the magazine nonetheless offered the opinion that a potential purchaser could avoid in other cars such Buick penalties as "inordinate thirst" and "garage-bursting size." The Consumers Union people also didn't like the Buick's ash tray, "about the flimsiest CU has so far seen."

Despite mixed reviews, Buick produced a record number of cars in calendar 1949—398,482 (model year, 327,321). Of these, 4343 were the Roadmaster Rivieras, listing at $2985 and which included Dynaflow and pushbutton windows. This production figure was bet-

Buicks for 1950, from the top: Roadmaster Riviera sedan; Special sedan; Super Riviera hardtop; the factory-built custom Model 71 for King Ranch.

ter than a quick glance indicates, for although the Roadmaster Riviera hardtop had first been shown to the public at the General Motors exhibition in New York in January 1949, it did not become available to customers until July.

The '49 Special was even slower in arriving. Although some 1948-styled Specials were sold as 1949 cars, this Buick model was effectively out of production from December of 1948 until mid-summer of 1949, when the redesigned version began coming off the line. Base priced at $1819, with Dynaflow optional, and produced in two-door sedan, four-door sedan and three-passenger business coupe form, the new Special was introduced to the public on August 8th. It created something of a sensation, and proved an indicator of what would follow for the entire 1950 Buick line.

Copywriters called the new Special "traffic-handy size," in seeming answer to the Consumer Union criticism. Despite a half-inch increase in wheelbase, the Special's overall length was decreased three-and-a-half inches, this partly because of the innovation of a combination grille-bumper. It consisted of a one-piece bumper faceplate which wrapped around the lower part of the front fenders, two bomb-shaped bumper guards into which were mounted the parking lamps and directional signals, and nine vertical bumper grille bars that curved over the bumper. The Buick portholes went from round to oval and were positioned in the hood just forward of the windshield instead of in the fender. And the new front fender skirts, inside the front fender, Buick said, "actually perform three functions, besides being neater and more attractive than formerly." These were 1) to prevent mud and dirt thrown up by the front wheels from entering the engine compartment; 2) to aid in reducing engine compartment temperature; 3) to permit a separate straight-through air duct to the car interior as a part of the heating and ventilating system.

That the new Special caused a stir in the industry is reflected in an internal memo fired off to his dealers three weeks after its introduction by E.C. Quinn, general sales manager, Dodge Division, Chrysler Corporation. "Your first impression of the car was probably the same as mine," he wrote, "—it looked like a 'big package'—and a lot of car for the money. But I think you'll agree that the pictures become a lot different when you take a close look." He then proceeded with facts and figures, noting that Dodge's comparable models, the Meadowbrook and the Wayfarer, were lower priced, and if "some buyer . . . insists on comparing the Coronet with the Buick," Dodge still fared better because the Special's price advantage was within fifty cents of the cost of putting foam rubber cushions on the Special (they were standard on the Coronet), and moreover the Special was equipped with neither an oil filter ($5.30) nor the steering wheel with horn ring ($17.30) nor chrome moldings on the fenders

Buicks for 1951, from the top: Super DeLuxe sedan; Roadmaster Riviera; Super convertible; Super Estate Wagon. Roadmaster Estate Wagon at right.

and assorted other accoutrements which to the Dodge man indicated the Special was "stripped." "What do you suppose would happen if the next Coronet every dealer received came without a horn ring, without chrome moldings, without arm rests, etc? It doesn't take much imagination to answer that one," he exhorted. "We would be swamped with protests from all of you—that the car no longer lived up to its name. . . . Of course, Buick will sell Specials. But it is my conviction that what inroads Buick will make with the Special will be chiefly into its own G.M. family—Pontiac and Oldsmobile—rather than into Dodge." He didn't sound terribly convinced.

Apparently the people out there believed there was more to a Buick than a horn ring and chrome, and that the traditional Buick virtues were worth any inconvenience resulting from the lack of an armrest. Some 81,817 of the new Specials were built and sold before the end of 1949—and the introduction three days after Christmas of the Buick line for 1950.

The Special remained as it was, though it was now officially given a 1950 model year designation, which of course in styling it had been all along. With the Special as precursor, the redesign and relocation of the Buick VentiPorts was extended to all models for 1950, and so was the combination bumper-grille. After its novelty wore off, this last proved controversial. Some people decided the grille was just plain ugly. Others were concerned that a low-speed crash would lead to expensive repairs, since the vertical grille bars extended in front of, and over, the bumper. Buick claimed that because the bars were mounted separately and could be replaced singly, the cost would be reduced. Nonetheless the grille arrangement—expensive to manufacture (the bars varied in size and shape and thus led to a proliferation of part numbers and headaches for the people in Buick stockrooms) and unlikely to win any popularity contests—would be dropped at the end of the model year.

But there was more to the 1950 line than portholes and bumpers. For one thing, the Super had a new engine, designated F-263 (its cubic-inch displacement) and designed to take advantage of the higher octane fuels recently introduced by the petroleum industry. With a higher 7.2 to one compression ratio, a Dynaflow-equipped Buick now produced 128 hp instead of the former 120. More compact in design, there was no weight penalty—and Buick even claimed an enhanced operating economy.

In reporting the new engine, however, *Steel Magazine* indicated that it might be a stopgap: "While embodying many new features the F-263 makes no sharp break from tradition . . . such as was taken by Oldsmobile and Cadillac when they started manufacture of entirely new V-8 overhead-valve engines. Rather it is a further refinement of a basic design, suggesting that it may be a few years before Buick will

Pictured here is the ROADMASTER *Estate Wagon —also available in the* SUPER *Series*

It's named "Estate Wagon" for very good reasons

HERE is something vastly more than a car for transporting guests and their luggage from the station—or a week's supply of groceries from the store.

While it's true that the rear seat flips ingeniously over to form a carpeted platform, more than six feet from front to back and almost five feet wide—this smartly styled conveyance manages to look distinguished, even when playing truck at the wish of its master.

You might say it "doubles in class"—for it's equally at home before the stately porticos of a mansion or sweeping serenely through the night to a white-tie-and-tails affair.

It has, of course, every Buick feature—Fireball power—Dynaflow Drive—four coil-springed wheels and honest heft that level the miles with majestic smoothness.

In its ROADMASTER version, this is the costliest of Buicks. It is built for those who want something finer than fine—and of course, that makes possession ultraexclusive.

Have you ever examined the Estate Wagon? Better ask your Buick dealer to arrange a viewing of this "limited edition" soon.

BUICK Division of GENERAL MOTORS

No other car provides all this:

DYNAFLOW DRIVE • FIREBALL POWER
4-WHEEL COIL SPRINGING • DUAL VENTILATION
PUSH-BAR FOREFRONT • TORQUE-TUBE DRIVE
WHITE-GLOW INSTRUMENTS • DREAMLINE STYLING
BODY BY FISHER

WHEN BETTER AUTOMOBILES ARE BUILT BUICK WILL BUILD THEM

"Smart Buy's Buick"

venture to the V-8 field. From the looks of things, however, and on the basis of experimental work in progress, there is coming a wholesale shift to V-type overhead valve engines . . ."

For '50 Buick remained content to proliferate in models, nineteen of them now. "Visitors to the plant in Flint," Buick said, "never cease to be amazed by the variety of cars that come down . . . the fast moving line at ninety-second intervals." There were DeLuxe versions of the Special and the Roadmaster—and the Riviera hardtop styling was extended to the Super series—and the Riviera name, probably unwisely, to long wheelbase and center-pillared four-door sedans in both the Super and Roadmaster series. But borrowing the look and designation of the Riviera was the result of its popularity. In announcing these derivatives, Ivan Wiles simply said the public liked it, "so there it is." Added to the Special, previously available only in fastback (Jetback) configuration, was a bustle-back body Buick called Tourback. This style was also added to the Super and Roadmaster. Both the latter series featured a larger one-piece curved windshield and a back window in which "the blind spots are reduced to a minimum." Despite increased wheelbases, overall length decreased, lines were lower, and bodies wider.

Both *Consumers' Research Bulletin* and *Consumer Reports* complained of the scant knee and shoulder room in the new Buicks. But the consumers who bought cars apparently didn't read the magazines or just disregarded them, for Buick production for calendar 1950 totaled 552,827, which was 8.2 percent of the industry and kept Buick solidly in fourth place. (Model year total was 670,256, including the Specials built in 1949.) A couple of weeks before Christmas of 1950, a large delegation of GM executives and officials journeyed to Flint to congratulate the Buick organization on the best year in its history.

The year following, the United States was again at war, in Korea, and Buick again had a military job to do. The division which had built Liberty engines in World War I, and bomber engines and tanks in World War II, now had a contract to build J-65 Sapphire turbojet engines and an automatic transmission for tanks. The British-designed Sapphire was the powerplant for the American-designed Republic F-84-F Thunderjet fighter, and by war's end Buick had delivered 4300 of these engines to the U.S. Air Force.*

But the division was obviously happiest in this period building cars. Changes were minimal for '51, and mostly decorative—though the Special was now given the Super's engine, which provided that line more performance and allowed Buick to concentrate production on just two powerplants (the 263 and the 320). The Special series was also expanded with a two-door convertible and hardtop and four varieties of Tourback not previously offered. On all models, Buick drew in its teeth in 1951, putting the grille vertical bars back behind the bumper, a move that was generally greeted with satisfaction.

*Buick produced jet engines in Willow Springs, Illinois, near Chicago, using half of a 1.3-million-square-foot building for assembly and testing. Fisher Body used the other half to make auto body stampings and components. Some of the jet engine work was also done at Flint. Buick began construction of a plant just north of Flint to house part of the jet engine parts production and sub-assembly operations. However, a production cutback as the Korean conflict wound down made the plant unnecessary for Buick and it was transferred to GM's Ternstedt Division and is now the Fisher Body Coldwater Road plant.

Buicks for 1952, the Roadmaster Riviera four-door sedan (above) and Super Riviera two-door hardtop (below). Advertising the '52's (right).

There was a phaseout of some of the Jetback styles, and at model year's end all of the Buick fastbacks would be discontinued. The division had concluded that streamlined styling was less a virtue than usable stowage space; Consumer's Union had reported that when the Jetback's trunk lid had been opened before a panel of selected motorists, they all laughed or hooted. Perhaps taking a fresh look themselves, the people at Buick recognized why. The sales figures of Jetbacks helped too.

Overall styling, less the Jetback, remained pretty much the same for '52—and mechanical revisions were few. Interesting among the latter was the four-barrel carburetor, designed primarily by Adolph Braun, Buick's carburetor engineer. According to one source, GM's top management, upon visiting Buick's test lab to find out why the

This is the day You've dreamed of

Someday you've hoped to find it—a car that expresses your ideal of all that a supremely fine automobile should be.

It would be, of course, exquisitely appointed, expressing restrained luxury in every detail of its fabrics, finish and fitments.

It should have power so great that no demand you would ever make could find its limit. And it should travel with hushed and distinguished silence.

It should ride the highway with confident poise—steady, level, haughtily superior to road conditions that disturb the going of lesser cars.

It should be obedient—willing and effortless in its response to your hand on the wheel, your toe on its gas treadle or brake.

And with all its proud size and power, it should be thrifty to maintain—thrifty in its use of fuel—not so much because pennies are important to you, as because these are the tokens of modern and expert engineering.

Today is the day you can make those dreams come true. You can make them come true in a ROADMASTER.

As you may know, this year's ROADMASTER has the highest horsepower in Buick history, and an Airpower carburetor that needs less fuel at 40 than was formerly used at 30—lets loose a mighty reserve of power when needed.

To Dynaflow Drive's infinite flexibility, this year's ROADMASTER adds Power Steering.*

And a million dollars' worth of engineering, research and special components have gone into perfecting its ride.

But no technical terms can describe for you this great car's spirit—its eagerness and the friendly companionship that it somehow makes you feel.

You need to see it, drive it, know it. Just say the word, and your Buick dealer will arrange this for you.

BUICK *Division of* GENERAL MOTORS
*Equipment, accessories, trim and models are subject to change without notice.
Optional at extra cost on ROADMASTER only.

Custom Built
ROADMASTER
by BUICK

When better automobiles are built Buick will build them

6-passenger Super Convertible

How smooth is smooth? Drive a Buick and see

You can learn a lot about comfort—or the lack of it—by watching what happens in situations like these:

On uneven roads—you'll notice that some cars slow down to a crawl, where a Buick rolls along with scarcely a bobble.

On curves—you'll notice the bodies of some cars on an outward sway. But there's a road-hugging security to a Buick.

At stop lights—you'll notice that some cars have a "rocking chair" motion when brakes are applied. But Buicks dip gently to a smooth, poised stop.

We could name more than a dozen engineering features that make this difference in a Buick.

Each individual Buick wheel has its own

soft coil spring. Each Buick wheel has wide-base rims and ample-sized tires, to give the car a better stance.

There's a special transverse radius rod extending from the frame on one side to the rear axle on the other side—to control sidesway and "side shift" on curves. And Buick shock absorbers have two sets of cylinders and pistons to control upsurge and downthrust.

Every Buick has a solid X-braced frame and a V-braced torque-tube keel to keep its going firm and weave-proof.

Even the mighty Fireball 8 Engine of a Buick is specially Hi-Poise mounted to give a smoother transmission of power—and Dynaflow Drive* also plays an important part in the way a Buick rides.

But why go into technicalities—when you can sample this Million Dollar Ride any day in the week—for the asking?

Whatever it takes to make driving a pleasure, you'll find in this nimble performer.

How about trying one out today?

*Equipment, accessories, trim and models are subject to change without notice. *Standard on Roadmaster, optional at extra cost on other Series.*

Sure is true for '52

When better automobiles are built
BUICK
will build them

SEE YOUR NEAREST BUICK DEALER

---

engine was pulling so much horsepower in dynamometer testing, discovered the four-barrel for the first time and immediately wanted it for Oldsmobile too. "I screamed foul," recalled Braun. "We had developed the carburetor and I wanted it as a Buick exclusive." GM compromised, giving Olds the carburetor* but making that division use smaller secondary ports than on the Buick version, holding down horsepower for one year. Oldsmobile, however, brought its car out a few days ahead of the new Buick—and claimed the four-barrel carb as an Oldsmobile innovation. Which didn't seem exactly Marquis of Queensbury rules. But no matter.

Success has a tendency to ameliorate sleights of hand or slights of

attribution—and the Buick, despite carping by the automotive press, remained in good favor by the automotive customer. The car was solid and stylish—with its sweepspear, its portholes (four per side on Roadmaster, three on Super and Special), the varying but always identifiable grille, the cachet of hardtop styling. And power steering became a newly offered option during 1952 for the Roadmaster and Super.

Production for calendar 1951 had been 404,695 cars for 7.5 percent of the industry, for 1952 the figures were 321,048 and 7.4 percent. Reflected in these were the restrictions forced by the Korean War, in addition to a steel strike.

Buick was coasting along nicely.

But there were changes in the offing.

---

*Cadillac would also have it in '52.

Chapter Fifteen

THE RECORD AND THE CRASH

Buick's postwar momentum continued well into the 1950's, making the Ivan Wiles years prosperous—even though there were a number of major personnel changes early in the decade.

Some of Harlow Curtice's chief assistants from his Buick days eventually joined him at the corporate level. Tony De Lorenzo went to Detroit in 1949 and was soon vice-president in charge of GM public relations. In 1951, chief engineer Charles A. Chayne left Buick to become vice-president in charge of the GM engineering staff. Also, Otis L. Waller, who had succeeded Hufstader as general sales manager in 1948, retired because of ill health in 1950 and Albert H. Belfie succeeded him.

De Lorenzo had filled the function of Buick public relations director from his arrival at Buick at the tail end of the 1946 strike, though he was actually a public relations representative for the Kudner agency, which had Buick's account. "But I dealt directly with Curtice, and not with my ad bosses," De Lorenzo said. Steve Richards was briefly in charge of Buick PR as the Kudner man before Waldo McNaught became Buick's first official public relations director in 1950. McNaught retained Richards and also hired Gerald H. Rideout as an assistant. Rideout would succeed McNaught in 1959.

The Fifties was a free-wheeling time in public relations, and McNaught was a master promoter of lavish press parties, Motoramas and other events. Along the way, he also initiated and promoted the Buick Open Golf Tournament, which set PGA attendance records with one-dollar tickets in the late 1950's and through most of the 1960's. The tournament was held at Warwick Hills, a country club backed by McNaught in Grand Blanc, near Flint. (Dropped for some years, the tournament returned in the late 1970's.)

Chayne, who left an impressive legacy at Buick, was succeeded by Verner P. Mathews, who had started as a Buick chassis engineer in 1927. To Joe Turlay, Buick's top engine designer of the period, the choice of Mathews was a return to less audacious times. Turlay was in a good position to judge chief engineers. He had started under Ferdinand A. "Dutch" Bower, whom he once regarded as "a real conservative." Turlay thought Chayne a radical, at least compared with Bower. "Chayne pushed through new things Bower had held back, such as aluminum pistons," Turlay said. "Mathews, though a conservative, was a good manager. He didn't understand all of the technical aspects, but he made the right decisions, over and over."

As for Belfie, he had originally planned to enter the auto business at Buick, and headed from his home in Michigan's Upper Peninsula to a promised job as a Buick metallurgist. However, by the time he got to Lansing, fifty miles from Flint, he had only eight cents left in his pocket, so he took a job with Lansing-based Oldsmobile. Belfie had a sales job in the B.O.P. sales department when it disbanded in 1933 and he transferred to Buick as business manager.

Despite the fact Buick had a new public relations director and new general sales manager, some of the division's most showy promotions of the early 1950's came out of engineering and styling—no doubt with corporate blessings from Curtice, who hardly concealed his continued paternal interest in Buick.

Buick experimental cars began hitting the show circuit in the early Fifties, this program again part of the Charles Chayne legacy. Actually only one car was initially planned in 1951, a successor to the Y-Job. Chayne observed at the time that it was planned "to see if we could better our mark of 'good after ten years' by doing one that would be still fresh and new after fifteen years." The program was not far along before Buick realized there wasn't room enough in one car for everything the division wanted to try.

Consequently, approval was given for two cars, with Harley Earl to have command of one, called LeSabre, and another, the XP-300, to reflect the Chayne way of thinking. The mechanics for both would be Chayne's responsibility. Stylists and engineers traditionally think differently. As Chayne himself lamented, "The stylists always want to build cars very low and never seem to understand that underneath the body must be certain things that make the car go and stop." With this program, however, it was agreed that "we could go as far off the beaten path mechanically as we planned to go style-wise."

One of the results was a 215-cubic-inch V-8 engine with an ultra-high compression ratio, a supercharger, a thirsty demand for

methanol/gasoline fuel, and a 335 brake horsepower rating. Pains were taken to acknowledge the experimental nature of these exotic, super-streamlined dream cars, though veteran journalist Griff Borgeson enthused, "Take off the blower and the alcohol tank . . . then look again. This may be tomorrow's Buick engine." And this was great publicity for Buick.

Both the LeSabre and XP-300 bodies were aluminum, and even Charlie Chayne's XP-300—his lamentations to the contrary—was only 39.1 inches high at the cowl, 53.4 with convertible top up. "I told Mr. Earl we would let him put the people in the car just as low as he wanted and we would put the 'works' in the front and rear," Chayne explained. This pretty much dictated a two-passenger car because room for more would have meant an "excessively long wheelbase." The final products were spectacular.

Among the innovations in creature comfort were power seats operated by a pushbutton hydraulic mechanism, hydraulic jacks operated from the instrument panel which permitted lifting the car for tire changes before leaving the driver's seat, and a back window that could be lowered while the top was in position. Although the cars were designed for light weight with aluminum and magnesium used where possible, all of the accessories made the cars so heavy that, at first, the springs were flattened to the stops and the hydraulic jacks would not lift the car. Changes were made to fix these problems.

Ralph Watts of the *Detroit News* was among the journalists covering a "breakfast for the brass" at the GM proving ground in the latter part of 1951, where the main course was the XP-300 and the guests "ate it up. . . . At one point in the demonstrations, Chayne and

his boss, 'Gasoline Charley' Wilson [GM president Charles Wilson], hit more than 110 miles an hour around the track." Not to be outdone, Buick general manager Ivan Wiles then took the car out and reportedly put it up to 140.

Both the LeSabre and the XP-300 received appreciative nods from the show-going public in 1952.

Page preceding: James Murphy driving a 1954 Century 66R at Milwaukee. Below: Ivan Wiles (left), Chayne, a 1905 and 1951 Buick, and XP-300.

But it was the production Buick the following year that really made the big news.

Buick celebrated its Fiftieth Anniversary in 1953 in grand style. It introduced the first Buick production V-8 engine in the Roadmaster and Super, and it gave the automobile collecting field a modern classic—the Skylark. To mark the anniversary, Buick also used an

Above: XP-300 and experimental LeSabre. Below: Joe Turlay, early and late in his Buick career; the narrow-vee prototype engine he designed for Chayne.

emblem, in the center of the steering wheel, depicting an antique Buick and noting the 1903-1953 dates. The car pictured was actually the original Flint 1904 model. The mistake was not recognized by Buick—official histories have always identified the car as a 1903—and probably at the time quibbling over a year might have seemed insignificant anyway. The important fact was that the Buick Motor Company (later Buick Motor Division) was now fifty—a longevity rare in the American automobile industry.

On his usual upbeat note, general manager Wiles predicted on December 3rd, 1952 that by 1960 Buick would be selling 750,000 cars a year. As it happened, that figure would be surpassed in 1955, for a record that would stand for twenty-two years, indicating—unfortunately—that the achievement would also bring calamity in its wake. Buick production for the United States for 1953 would be a healthy 485,353 for the calendar year, 488,805 for the model.

The most famous Buick of '53 was, of course, the Skylark. It began rather haphazardly. According to Kenneth Amrhein of Bay City, Michigan, who has owned four Skylarks and has extensively researched their history, Ivan Wiles saw some drawings made by Ned Nickles for customizing his own 1951 Roadmaster convertible and ordered a prototype built to Nickles' specifications. The car was unveiled as a 1953 model in early July of 1952 as Buick's "answer to the European sports car," and Wiles indicated it would be produced "if there are enough inquiries." Obviously there were. Obviously, too, Flint was anxious to have a top-of-the-line, limited-production Buick to celebrate its anniversary.

And the Skylark was a celebration, at $4596 the most luxuriously

standard-equipped Buick produced to that time. It had power brakes, power steering, power windows, power seats, and a power aerial for the foot-controlled Selectronic radio. The owner's name was engraved on a gold-colored emblem plate placed on the hub of the steering wheel. Based on the Roadmaster chassis of 121½-inch wheelbase, Skylark styling showed a little XP-300 influence in its front-end design, a nicely notched beltline and sweepspear swooping over cutout rear wheel openings, and rear taillights of double-bubble motif. With its convertible top up, the Skylark stood less than five feet tall and was sumptuously fitted inside with soft-tanned cowhide available in four color combinations.

Wide whitewall tires called attention to one of the Skylark's loveliest features. The prototype used Carlo Borrani wire wheels imported from Italy, the production version chrome-plated spoke wheels designed and produced by Kelsey-Hayes in Michigan to Buick specifications. As Amrhein wrote, "Buick's wheels, with their forty spokes and skinny hubs, are among the most beautiful ever made in their own right; no one has to get right on top of them to see they are wire wheels."

At least two hardtop versions of the '53 Skylark are in existence, and these are a puzzlement. Amrhein, who has devoted a considerable amount of time to the subject, believed initially they were special models built at Fisher Body for GM officials, but has since learned they were built in Buick Engineering to test the Skylark hardtop idea. Nickles says no GM design work was done on these '53 cars, and Wiles and other Buick officials of the time claim no knowledge either, nor do the cars show up in GM records.

What is definitely known is that in the 1953 model year Buick sold 1690 Skylark convertibles. For 1954, only 798 were produced. Instead of being based on the Roadmaster chassis, as in '53, the '54 was pretty much a renovated Century convertible, built on that series' chassis with its 3.5-inch shorter wheelbase. In 1954 the look of Skylark styling was extended to the entire Buick line, and its racy silhouette was no longer unique. Skylark had been planned as a limited production model from the beginning. Amrhein has noted there were never any plans to go beyond 1954, that in fact the only reason the car was built beyond 1953 was because GM styling chief Harley Earl wanted it. Nickles says he designed the Skylark for both model years.

Two features were not unique to Skylark even in 1953: Twin-Turbine Dynaflow and the Buick V-8. The former, with twin turbines in the torque converter between pump and stator, was said to increase torque output by ten percent, providing faster and quieter acceleration at reduced engine speeds. It was an evolution of the Dynaflow design credited largely to Oliver K. Kelley's crew at GM Technical

Buicks for 1953. Above and below: Skylark, two-door Roadmaster and Super Rivieras. Right: Four-door Roadmaster Riviera, Special, Super Estate Wagon.

Center, with follow-up work by Buick engineer Rudolf J. Gorsky. The V-8 was something of a revolution for Buick.

Between 1948 and 1952, V-8 production in the United States practically doubled—from 18.9 percent to 33.5 of the industry. Buick had to notice. Buick had, in fact, anticipated it. Development of high compression V-shaped engines had been begun in 1944, was accelerated after the war, and really got to moving after the high compression Cadillac V-8 was introduced in 1949. Buick's V-8 was the division's first major engine innovation since the introduction of the straight-eight in 1931, and Flint engineers were careful to emphasize that they did not believe the V engine had any inherent advantages over an in-line. "The cylinders don't seem to care whether they stand up straight or lean over," one of them was quoted as saying.

But the V-8 configuration did have advantages: The engine's proportions lent themselves to contemporary styling trends, and ease of driving and better handling were evident with a lighter weight power unit. The increased rigidity of a V engine was certainly more suitable for the higher compression ratios made available with improved fuels. And in an SAE paper, Verner Mathews and Joe Turlay noted another reason: It was time for a change. The basic tooling of the large series engine had hardly been disturbed since the introduction of the Century in 1936. (The 263-cubic-inch engine of the Special had been retooled in 1950.)

Like every other manufacturer that had one, Buick proclaimed its engine as the most advanced V-8 ever placed in a standard-production American automobile. Units with varying angles of 22.5 and 35 degrees had been developed, and were seriously considered until balance problems and manufacturing difficulties—and, most

Below right: General manager Ivan Wiles and general manufacturing manager Ed Ragsdale (left) photographed with a milestone Buick in June of 1953.

important, a profile that was too high—ruled them out. Ultimately Buick reached the same 90-degree V-8 solution as did its sister divisions of Cadillac and Oldsmobile, and Ford and Chrysler. But Buick's version did boast some interesting features all its own. It was an unusually compact unit, this because of the use of very short connecting rods and the vertical positioning of the valves in the combustion chamber. "A simple way to visualize this combustion chamber," wrote John Bond in *Road & Track*, "is to think of it exactly like the four-valve Model J Duesenberg with one pair of valves removed."

The Buick used a bore and stroke of 4.0 by 3.2 inches, for a stroke/bore ratio that was the lowest in any American production engine at that time. A specially shaped piston crown resulted in a compression ratio of 8.5 to one which was, Buick proudly boasted, the highest in the industry (though the others caught up quickly enough), and Buick's V-8 was the first to have originated with a 12-volt electrical system. Displacement was 322 cubic inches, and horsepower developed in the Roadmaster with four-barrel carburetor was 188. In the Super with two-barrel it was 170. Ten thousand hours of dynamometer testing and more than a million miles of road testing in cars running at the GM proving grounds preceded Buick's V-8 introduction.

"I had a free hand on the 90-degree V-8, which was an awfully good engine," recalled Joe Turlay. "Chayne and I quarreled about the early narrow V-8 a lot. He had ideas I couldn't make work, big bearings and so forth. Finally, I told him this cannot be done. He said he was surprised I had stayed with it as long as I did. Finally it was decided the narrow V-8 would not fit well under the new low hoods, so Chayne turned me loose on the more conventional 90-degree V. Chayne had all kinds of ideas, but not always good judgment. He was a funny guy to work with. His thought processes were unlike mine. But after awhile, things changed, and nobody could have treated anyone better than he treated me."

Turlay recounts that Curtice's involvement was often welcome, for him particularly on the V-8. "Curtice had a habit of dropping over to engineering when Chayne and Ragsdale were out of town, asking how a project was coming. He would ask, 'Is this the way you would do it?' After I designed and developed the V-8, they put someone else in charge to take it into production. Some troubles did ensue. Curtice came to Buick, he must have heard something. Shortly after, they put me back on, to get it straightened out."

Helping Turlay was John F. Crouter, later in charge of basic engine design. Once everything was straightened out and the engine was in production and the new Buicks were introduced, it was time for the enthusiast press to take over. Auto buff magazines called the engine the "nailhead" because of its small valves. But Turlay con-

Buicks for 1954. Above: Special and Roadmaster two-door Rivieras. Below: Four-door Roadmaster Riviera with factory accessory wire wheels. Right: The Skylark convertible, Century Estate Wagon and Century convertible.

tends that the valves were not too small—that engines with large valves did not perform as well. "I doubt if any passenger car engine ever had a more thorough development of its breathing characteristics as affected by part shape and size, valve size and valve timing," he said. The new V-8—shorter by 13½ inches, lower by four inches, lighter by 180 pounds than the former straight-eight, and just 26.56 inches wide—was combined with the new Dynaflow design to make quite a difference in the Buick performance. In November 1952, *Motor Trend* had reported a zero-to-sixty time of 17.1 seconds with a '52 Roadmaster with straight-eight engine and single-turbine Dynaflow. In June 1953, *Popular Mechanics* needed only 14.5

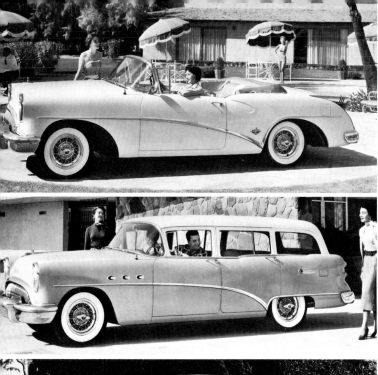

seconds to get to sixty with a '53 Buick with V-8 and Twin-Turbine Dynaflow.

Turlay contends that Buick's big V-8's (including the 322 and the later 364 and 401) were among the best, and often the best, American engines for power torque and fuel economy. GM's sound laboratories also rated it the quietest in several model reports and, said Turlay, "it was also one of the most durable engines made."

If the new Buicks' power was immediately apparent, a problem in its ability to stop was not. In a push from management to try to meet the competition, Buick moved too quickly to install power brakes on 1953 Roadmasters and Skylarks. After a few months, a major

problem became apparent—one of the seals, made of plasticized rubber, in the power-assisted cylinder would fail and the car would be left without brakes. The unit was provided by an outside supplier, but Buick had not done adequate long-term testing.

Charles D. Holton, who was Buick's chief brake engineer of the time, recalls the problem with horror. As complaints flooded Buick, the division had to supply so many replacement cylinders (with the problem solved) that for months it could not supply any of the advertised optional power brake units for 1954 models. Ralph Nader, in his book *Unsafe At Any Speed*, used the Buick power brake failure as an example of his contention that the industry was too willing to put inadequately tested equipment on cars. Nader also criticized Buick's handling of the problem: quietly telling dealers to make the fixes instead of announcing a public recall.

Buick was also having a problem in this period with its brake drums. For some years, its foundry had been turning out cast-iron brake drums that were good most of the time, but sometimes were not. Holton said no one really figured out why, though it was suspected that a soft constituent would sometimes appear in the casting, causing performance problems. He notes Buick was making some progress in trying to solve the problem, innovating a desulfurizing process and other techniques to develop more uniform castings. But Holton had also made some experimental aluminum brake drums, and GM's Fabricast Division in Bedford, Indiana was looking for aluminum castings work.

The result of the work by Holton, engineer Frank Daley and Fabricast was a front brake drum of finned aluminum that was used on one version of the 1957 Roadmaster and on all 1958 Buicks except Special—a development that turned Buick's brake reputation around. Instead of having one of the worst brake systems in the industry, it then had, by far, the best. Aluminum is lighter than cast iron and is a better conductor, and the fins helped even more to dissipate heat. Holton patented a method of attaching a cast-iron liner to the inside of the drum to provide a stronger rubbing surface for the brake linings. But in 1953, these improvements were a long way off.

Air conditioning was available on a Buick for the first time in '53, with the air unit housed on the shelf in the trunk and filtering cool air through ducts above the windows into the passenger compartment. Not available, though widely seen and publicized, was a show-circuit sport convertible called the Wildcat and built primarily to test the use of fiberglass in automobile body construction. It featured a concave grille and buffer bombs integrated into a massive wraparound front bumper which actually looked more fish-like than feline, twin hood scoops, fender-top vent ports and a slim sweepspear inset on a not particularly attractive line from bumper to bumper. Fortunately, all

263

this was not predictive of the production Buicks to come. The new Buicks would be more Skylark than Wildcat.

On July 10th, 1950 Buick had formally requested its styling studio to gather ideas for a completely new car for '54—a head start on the GM minimum lead time of twenty-one months for a new model. It was extra time well spent. The new cars were so good-looking that Buick designers would still be talking about them with admiration twenty-five years later.

With the show car XP-300 as instigator and the production Skylark as bellwether, all the '54 Buicks were crisp and clean and strikingly modern looking. The hood was lowered, the deck lid raised, and the body closer to the ground. Buicks were longer, the lines less rounded. Available wheelbases were trimmed to two and lengthened to 127 inches for Super and Roadmaster and 122 inches for the rest of the line. There were more bars in the Buick grille, but they were narrower and respaced for aesthetic effect. Two-door models had full rear-wheel cutouts, and there were wide panoramic windshields with reverse slanting pillars on some models and vertical pillars on others. Rear windows were from three to four-and-a-half inches wider.

The overall effect of the '54 line made previous Buicks look suddenly old-fashioned. Any Buick owner questioning before their introduction whether this was the year to trade in for a new car had no doubt after the '54's made their debut. Only rarely is it that advertisement can be accused of understatement. "The Beautiful Buy" was all many Buick ads said. It was a becoming modesty.

The engineering department had come up with a refined front suspension, new direct-acting shock absorbers attached directly to the frame and independent of the springs, thus replaceable without changing the front end alignment and contributing to what Buick advertising called the "Million-Dollar Ride." Steering linkage and geometry were improved for more stability, less strain and better steering control. One road test report enthused that "finger-tip steering is literally possible."

But more exciting was the return of the Century, which combined the light Special chassis and the powerful Roadmaster V-8 engine. This thrilled performance buffs. The new Century cruised easily at 100 mph. At the time, the redoubtable Floyd Clymer said it was "one of the three fastest American stock cars." More recently, historian and car designer Jeffrey I. Godshall called it the "classiest family hot rod since the original Ford V-8."

The big Roadmaster itself could scarcely be lambasted for toodling. Road testers for the English *Autocar* magazine did zero to sixty in 12.6 seconds in one, with top speed hitting a hundred on the button. And with little effort. "The Buick Roadmaster is a fine example of a

Buick show cars. Above: The 1953 Wildcat. Center: Wildcat II from 1954. Below: The Landau, also from 1954, with 127-inch wheelbase, V-8 engine.

At the Wisconsin State Fair Speedway in 1955, Les Snow (No. 45), Bill Kearney (No. 14), Pat Flaherty (No. 96) in their Buick Century 66R's.

quality American car," the magazine concluded, "which . . . fulfills admirably its function of taking a number of people and their belongings long distances without fuss."

New also for 1954 was the Special's engine. The tooling for the straight-eight which had been installed four years earlier was rendered obsolete. Buick had decided to go V-8 all the way. The Special's powerplant was an underbored 322, with bore and stroke of 3.65 by 3.2 inches, displacing 264 cubic inches, and developing 150 hp with Dynaflow, 143 without.

And still there was more.

In March of 1954, a convertible was added to the Century line, making five separate convertibles offered by Buick—one in each series plus Skylark. Apparently there was a lot of sunshine in Flint those days. Buick was among the most committed proponents in the industry of open-air motoring.

And in the dashboard of all '54's was the first real innovation in speedometer instrumentation since speed dials first were installed. Instead of a needle pointing to the miles-per-hour number, a red bar moved from left to right, like a horizontal thermometer. The idea and engineering for this device was credited to Ralph O. Helgeby, an AC Spark Plug Division engineer.* The name given it was a good one: Redliner. The device itself, however, brought mixed reactions.

Modern was the keynote throughout the new Buick line. With wood considered passé, the Estate Wagon was now all steel. In 1940 the Biehl company in West Reading, Pennsylvania had built Buick's all-wood station wagon body, with Hercules of Evansville, Indiana following for 1941 to 1948. From 1949 to 1953, the Ionia Body Company (Michigan) had produced a combination steel and wood body for Buick, and followed this with an all-steel body from 1954 through 1958.

It all worked, beautifully. In calendar 1954, Buick built 531,463 cars (9.65 percent of the total market), vaulted over Plymouth and marched smartly into third place in the industry. It was the first time Plymouth had been out of third since 1931. The higher-priced Buick had suddenly bested one of the "low-priced three."

Jerry Rideout recalls overhearing a conversation between then-GM president Curtice and Wiles that year. Said Curtice: "Ivan, do you like being in third place?" Wiles allowed that he did. "Then,"

*Helgeby, besides being an engineer, was a pioneer aviator. He had been in the first group of pilots ever issued licenses in Norway, during World War I, and was a military pilot in neutral Norway at the same time Germany's fabled "Red Baron," Manfred Von Richtoften, was the scourge of the skies a few hundred miles away. Helgeby, who flew an antique biplane around Flint until past age eighty, was the oldest pilot in Michigan licensed to fly without a copilot.

Above: The hardtop Super Riviera for 1955. Below: '55 ad from The Saturday Evening Post. Right: Flanking the first '55, from left, Verner Mathews, purchasing director Floyd Compson, comptroller Kenneth Hendershott, Ivan L. Wiles, Ed Ragsdale, general sales manager Albert H. Belfie. Opposite: The two-door Super Riviera as shown in the 1955 sales catalog.

replied Curtice, "you'd better start acting like a third-place manufacturer and build more cars."

Wiles did as he was told, responding in 1955 with a gigantic gain in production: 781,296 cars, an increase of nearly 250,000 units. That year Buick produced 9.84 percent of all the automobiles made in the United States. The 21,877 cars built in Canada also set a Buick record.

The 1955 model year, which like the calendar resulted in a record U.S. production (738,814 cars) plus another record in Canada (23,762), was notable for reasons other than numbers, however.

Buick joined the horsepower race with a vengeance.

Horsepower was raised from 200 to 236 in the Roadmaster and Century, increased from 150 to 188 in the Special and—most dramatically, with the addition of four-barrel carburetion for the first time—zoomed from 182 to 236 in the Super series. It should be noted that these figures were Buick's and, like everyone else's in the industry, tended toward hyperbole—more so as time went on. There was a lot of horseplay in the horsepower race.

But undeniably these were impressively more powerful Buick engines. Contributing to this were the increased size of valves, carburetors and intake manifolds. Compression ratios were boosted to 9.0:1 in the top series Buicks, and from 8.1:1 to 8.4:1 in the Special. A new camshaft provided longer valve opening and higher exhaust lift. Im-

proved pistons reduced friction loss. Aluminum alloy connecting rod bearings were a Buick first.

These engine changes invited some speed-enhancing revisions for the Dynaflow transmission. Variable Pitch was the new designation, and it was a device operating on the same principle as that of an airplane propeller. "When you press the gas pedal to the floor board," Buick explained, "twenty spinning stator blades change their pitch in Dynaflow oil to produce a liquid-smooth safety-surge of power for quick passes and instant getaway. . . . Hold the pedal at cruising speed and you get brand-new gasoline savings."

Acceleration times were cut by nearly a second. "This means just that much less time the driver is exposed to oncoming traffic when passing another car," said Buick coyly. What Buick was really saying was that Flint had produced one of the hottest cars in the country.

Magazine driving reports proved it. No other American car—not even the awesome Chrysler 300—matched the 0-60 time of 9.8 seconds scored with a Century by *Motor Trend* during its round of 1955 road tests.* *Science & Mechanics* reported the same results, and recommended the Century as "sort of a hotrod dressed in mink

---

*In fact, a privately sponsored 1955 Buick Century initially won the 1955 Daytona 500 with Fireball Roberts driving. This surprised race officials as the Chrysler 300 was the odds-on favorite. However, the Buick was later disqualified on an engine technicality and the Chrysler declared the winner.

[for anyone with] a big appetite for spectacular stock car acceleration." Top speed was 108 mph.

Later in the year *Motor Trend* tried out a Special and Roadmaster and, though the acceleration was not head-snapping, the former averaged a 104.1 mph top speed, the latter 109.2, over four quarter-mile runs. *MT* was also impressed with the diverse range of Buicks available and that "Buick brings to buyers something unique"—a kinship among all cars in the line in both engineering and styling, a definitive Buick identity.

A new body style was introduced, the four-door hardtop which, Buick said, "combines . . . for the first time . . . the airy grace of the Riviera . . . the added space of the Sedan." In truth, there was very little that was either airy or graceful about any of the Buicks for 1955. They appeared more heavy and massive, and it was no illusion; the frame side rails had to be extended seven inches with a new cross member added at the front simply to support the new design. The famous Buick vertical grille bars gave way to a network of mesh that was called Wide-Screen Grille, with two huge bullet-shaped protrusions and a formidable bumper that wrapped all the way around to the front wheel openings. At the back, tail- and back-up lights were encased in heavy chrome, which reminded showgoers of the similar treatment on the experimental Wildcat II (a cute 1954 show car with plastic body, V-8 engine, four carbs and 100-inch wheelbase) that had

Buicks for 1956. Above: The four-door Riviera in the Special line, the two-door Riviera in the Super line. Below: Roadmaster four-door sedan.

quickly followed the original. Still, aesthetics aside, the customers loved the '55's.

But 1955 was a mixed blessing for Buick. True, it set records that took decades to surpass. But some Buick veterans are convinced that the division also built far beyond its true production capacity, sacrificing Buick's reputation for quality for temporary sales success. As a result, they contend, the cars were not well finished, customers became angry, and Buick went into a tailspin from which it barely recovered.

That answer is probably too pat. A variety of factors contributed to Buick's problems in the late Fifties. One of them indeed was quality control. But there were engineering failures, and in 1957 the styling was disastrous. People began turning to smaller cars in the wake of a recession which began in 1956, and Buick had an image of a big gas guzzler, though Turlay says Buick was at least as good as the competition. There was an internal feud between engineering and manufacturing. There was poor management.

Of 1955 production, one Buick official of the time recalled: "We were building engines so fast we were building some of them off the assembly line, on hand trucks. We were running the foundry three shifts, running overtime beyond capacity. We got into a quality control problem. Then the quality problems became noised around. There was a problem with the rear axle. A number of them failed after 20,000 miles. Still, I don't know if you can blame anyone. Most anyone would have tried to build what they could sell."

Said another executive: "I knew one guy who had twelve rear axles put in his car. It needed a new design. There was a big feud between engineering and manufacturing—engineering wanted to design a new axle, manufacturing wouldn't do it." (Some question that number of axle failures on one car, and contend that the internal feud was no greater than usual, while not denying there was friction.)

Amid the bickering, the '56 line was introduced. There were some changes, though not the ones needed. All Buicks now shared the 322-cubic-inch engine, the two-barrel carburetor being used for the Special, four-barrel for the Century, Super and Roadmaster. Dynaflow was standard on those cars, optional on the Special. The Special now had one of the biggest and most powerful engines of any car in its class. But the brake drum problem had not been seen to, nor the rear axle matter.

There was all-new sheet metal at the front, a vee-profile hood and the revised grille and bumper appeared just as massive as before. But the taillight treatment, which eliminated the previous heavy chrome and large circular backup light in the center, was more subdued. Full wheel cutouts both front and rear were featured on all models. The Buick portholes were more oval in shape and "ringed by blisters," noted a Ford Motor Company internal memo summarizing the "confirmed information" obtained, nefariously no doubt, about the new Buicks before their introduction.

Apparently Ford concluded Buick was an easy target in '56. Throughout the model year, the company bombarded its Mercury dealers with comparative analyses of the two competing cars. "Buick Special and Century Mark Time Again . . . " was the headline of one, another denigrated the Super as continuing "down the typical Buick groove with its emphasis on sheer bulk, with advertised horsepower, like June, 'busting out all over.' " The rear suspension coil springing—"a device continued only by Buick and Nash after its trial and progressive abandonment by other manufacturers"—was attacked, and the larger brake linings of the Mercury, providing "twenty-eight percent more braking area for weight of car," pointedly mentioned. What Ford called Buick's "standstill styling" was given extensive examination. The revised portholes: "They have changed every year since 1949. But this can hardly be called a major styling change, much less an improvement." The new grille: "located immediately behind the front bumper where it would seem to be directly vulnerable to even slight bumps." The full-wheel cutouts: "give a feeling of 'nakedness' . . . a styling feature rapidly becoming outmoded." The rear end design: "Buick has made a pass at improving the appearance of the tail-light ensemble. The back-up light has traded places with the red-button reflector, and the over-all effect is not quite so 'chromy.' However, the boxy deck lid contour has been retained . . . "

Be aggressive, Mercury dealers were advised, don't be awed by Buick's "past prosperity." Take the car on. The "Big M" can do it.

Meanwhile, in Flint, complacency mixed with optimism. "Best Buick Yet," the promotion said. "Breath-taking beauty from every point of view."

Buick was gearing up its tooling to produce one million cars a year. The optimism was both misplaced and expensive.

Ivan Wiles said he hoped Buick would forge a sales record of 900,-000 in '56, but that was not to be. After the first quarter of the year, car sales declined. The anticipated spring upsurge failed to materialize. So Buick cut output.

As it turned out, it would not be necessary for Wiles to worry about making his prediction come true. On March 6th, 1956 he was elected to the new position of GM executive vice-president in charge of dealer relations. The idea, according to Curtice, was to give GM's 18,500 dealers a direct line of communication to the corporation's top management. Wiles held the job only a year before retiring because of health problems from which he fully recovered. He said he was the first and last man to have that job, since it happened that the dealers didn't make use of it.

Of the Wiles years at Buick, one executive noted, "You or I could have held the job at that time. Buick was moving up, and Wiles didn't work too hard. He once told me, 'This is the easiest job I ever had.' "

Wiles himself mentioned to the writer that the highlight of his years at Buick was "that I could fill the job."

On his relationship with Curtice, he said: "Curtice was a dominating man. I understood him. You had to have facts to support any decision. One time when Curtice was still head of Buick, Bill Hufstader came to me and said, 'I can't get raises for anyone out of Curtice. Do you have this problem?' I said, 'no, I just tell him how long the fellow's been there, how much other people in similar jobs are making, how long since he's had a raise, and say he should get ten percent. And I always get it.' Hufstader said, 'Hell, I don't do that, I just tell him I think the guy ought to have a raise.' Curtice didn't like that. He had to have facts."

Did Curtice run Buick when Wiles was in charge? Wiles replied to the question: "I remember once I went to Detroit when I was general manager. It must have been after some decision Curtice had made at Buick. I told him I now had the experience and if I were to have this job, I should be making the decisions. He laughed and said, 'You're on your own.' He loved it when you fought back."

Edward T. Ragsdale, who had been Buick's general manufacturing manager since 1949, succeeded Wiles. His timing was just the opposite of his predecessor's—it was all bad. Possibly no manager could have turned Buick around in this period. The new models for 1957 and 1958 had already been approved, a mild recession was setting in, and the public was turning away from mammoth cars.

Ragsdale was a native of Hopkinsville, Kentucky. He had shown early aptitude as an inventor and draftsman and, shortly after graduating from high school, he joined the Maxwell Motor Company as a tool designer. During World War I he was in the aviation branch of the Army Signal Corps and, while attached to the British flying service, he invented a machine-gun mount and a gauge for applying wires to planes, both of which were used by the British.

In 1920 Ragsdale joined the Pierce-Arrow Motor Company in Buffalo, New York, where he met and married Sarah Judd, whose personal car styling preferences helped boost the hardtop styling concept. Ragsdale has been credited with a number of improvements on windshield and body construction of the Pierce-Arrow.

In 1923 Ragsdale moved to Buick as a body draftsman. In 1935 he became body engineer, and in '39 assistant chief engineer, the position he held when he was named general manufacturing manager. He seemed a logical choice for Buick's top spot.

Buick retained third place in the industry in 1956, with U.S. calen-

When better automobiles are built Buick will build

Magnificent IS THE WORD FOR IT

WE SET OUT with one goal in mind in building this car —

To make it the most luxurious automobile our stylists and skilled craftsmen could create.

And we believe that when you see it, sit in it and drive it, you will —in all honesty—consider it the most magnificent fine car on the American scene today.

Naturally, the superb and spacious new interior of the ROADMASTER 75 is what you will judge first—and we invite that judgment.

For the seats are meticulously fashioned in glove-finish wool broadcloth or nylon, with backs topped in supple, hand-buffed leather. They are thickly layered with contoured foam rubber. They are wide, deep, superbly soft—and flanked by luxurious doors fully upholstered and cushioned from floor line to window.

The chromed and safety-padded instrument panel, the wide-sweeping armrests integral with the doors, the deep-pile carpeting underfoot—even these have been designed to a striking new excellence.

With equal pride, we invite your judgment of the magnificent performance to be enjoyed in ROADMASTER 75.

For only here—among all the world's fine cars—do you have the absolute smoothness and instant obedience of Variable Pitch Dynaflow—plus the swift and silent might of Buick's newest and most powerful V8 engine.

MOTORING'S NEWEST ADVANCE—AIR-COOLED ALUMINUM BRAKES

Add to this the extra luxury and surety and smoothness of air-cooled aluminum front brakes—*the newest and finest in the fine-car field* —and you have the heart of the story on ROADMASTER 75.

Your Buick dealer will be honored to have you meet this magnificent automobile. See him this week.

BUICK *Division of* GENERAL MOTORS

Roadmaster 75
CUSTOM BUILT BY BUICK

Buicks for 1957. Left: Century Riviera, advertisement for Roadmaster 75. From the top: The hardtop styling provided the Century station wagon and dubbed "Caballero"; Roadmaster convertible; Special sedan; Super hardtop.

dar year production of 535,364 and model year production of 572,-024. The totals were highly respectable, but not close to Wiles' 900,-000 prediction.

Buick would prefer to forget 1957. As one reporter noted matter-of-factly, the "driver is immediately aware of new styling." It was a total redesign though retaining, as one admiring reviewer put it, "Buick's traditionally substantial look." The cars were longer and lower, the sweepspear was rerouted and had a baked enamel center line in tangerine; on the Roadmaster Riviera coupe, chrome ribs were extended from the front windshield post, over the roof, down the rear windows, and across the trunk. The three-piece rear window treatment featured on the Special, Century and Roadmaster was strictly derriere-garde. A one-piece rear window was standard only on the Super, a no-cost option for Roadmaster. Hardtop styling was added to the station wagon, conventional four-door styling was reintroduced in the Century.

There were chassis refinements. An additional universal near the differential of what *Motor Trend* called Buick's "rather bulky but trouble-free torque tube drive" kept the tunnel hump size down despite the lower silhouette. A new ball-joint front suspension improved handling to some extent, though a pillow remained the widely-used metaphor for the Buick ride. "Stiffer shocks would make connoisseurs happier," commented *Motor Trend*, "and would perhaps please even soft-ride lovers; they would stay in their places better on curves. One attribute with which stiffer shocks would certainly please all hands would be elimination of bottoming on rugged dips."

Though performance wasn't affected appreciably, the Buick engine was bigger yet: 364 cubic inches and a 10.0 to one compression ratio for Century, Super and Roadmaster brought an increase of forty-five percent more horsepower, Buick said. The new figure was 300. For the Special with 9.5 to one compression ratio, horsepower was quoted as 250. A public relations official remembers shuddering when Ragsdale, asked at a news conference about poorer fuel economy of the new engines, replied, "Well, we have to keep the gas companies happy."

The superlatives sprouted like violets in April. Ragsdale called the 1957 line "the greatest value we have ever offered the motoring public." "New 'dream car' styling," the press releases ballyhooed. It was, instead, a nightmare.

Recalled one Buick executive: "The styling was awful in 1957, particularly those split rear windows. Plymouth looked at them, and said, 'Suddenly it's 1949.' A dealer came in from California to see the new cars, then went back to the coast and told the other dealers to buy all the used cars they could get, because that would be all they'd sell. But Curtice loved that '57. He showed me those new cars and said, 'My God, they're beautiful!' "

Said Buick chief designer Ned Nickles: "We did have some off years in styling. And there was the competition. They were doing some things right in that period."

At the beginning of the 1957 model year, Ragsdale predicted that Buick would build about 675,000 cars—twenty-five percent more than the 551,000 produced in the 1956 model year. He talked about hanging onto third place.

Instead, Buick built only 405,098 in the model year and 407,283 in the calendar. And tumbled back into fourth place. Plymouth had redesigned too—and came up with a winner.

Nothing much could be done immediately. Buick would pretty much have to go with the unpopular styling for 1958. The tooling was already committed, although the three-piece back window was gone. Instead the division decided to try to overwhelm the public with gingerbread, resulting in what became known as the "chromiest" Buick ever built: gaudy louvers and chrome on the rear fenders, twin gunsight ornaments on each front fender, and what Ragsdale called "the most dazzling grille design in the history of Buick." It consisted of small chrome squares, 160 of them, each with four triangular surfaces to reflect light. It was called a Fashion-Aire Dynastar Grille, and was topped by new Vista Vision dual headlamps. A garish ribbed aluminum, chrome-trimmed rear quarter panel rerouted the sweepspear again, but it was still there. The VentiPorts were not. With all the other geegaws on the car, there wasn't room for them anyway.

But another Buick tradition was revived, the Limited name, for a top-of-the-line Buick with rear fenders eight inches longer than the Roadmaster and "trimmed with three banks of chrome-capped louvers to make it more distinctive from the rest of the line." It was that. And it was huge. A joke making the rounds noted that the car was appropriately named because "limited" was what parking places would be if too many of them were sold.

A custom-built version was run up especially for Dale Robertson who was starring at the time in the Buick-sponsored television show, "Tales of Wells Fargo." Complete with a gun rack holding two Winchester rifles, a leather holster with Colt revolver on each door, upholstery in natural Danish calf, carpeting of natural Jersey hide, a golden steer's head superimposed on the Buick hood emblem and a solid walnut panel with "Wells Fargo" in raised chrome letters replacing the rear fender louvers, it was displayed at automobile shows throughout the country, and then grandly presented to Robertson.

Interestingly, Buick seemed to devote more effort to press agentry

Buicks for 1958. From the top: Special and Limited four-door Rivieras,
Century sedan. Page opposite, from the top: The Roadmaster 75 four-door
Riviera, Century convertible, actor Dale Robertson with the custom-built
"Wells Fargo" on a Limited chassis, the Super four-door Riviera sedan.

of this sort than to publicizing the one major improvement for the '58 line: the adoption of the air-cooled aluminum front brake drums with a radial fin design and cast iron linings for faster cooling of the rubbing surfaces. They had been in development for several years and had been introduced the year previous on the top-of-the-line Roadmaster 75 (and not publicized then, either). The new brakes were now fitted to all models save the Special. Credit for their development has been given to Charles D. Holton and Frank Daley in Buick's brake engineering section; Walter Boehm, who was responsible for metals development in the foundry; and Berlin B. Brambaugh, top engineer for brake lining composition at GM's Inland Division.

Though, as mentioned previously, the aluminum drums gave Buick the industry's best brakes, Ragsdale didn't talk about brakes much. Nor would he make a prediction on whether Buick would regain third place, noting that his forecast of the previous year "didn't exactly come true." He said only that he hoped "to capture a greater percentage of industry sales."

He said a lot more about the developments which were probably the reason advertising copywriters coined the dreadful slogan "Air Born B-58 Buicks" for the new cars. He shouldn't have. "With the all new air-poise suspension, which literally floats the car on four columns of air," he enthused, "and the new flight-pitch Dynaflow transmission which provides a spectacular increase in performance, Buick attains a new high in automotive engineering." This was not prediction, it was bald statement. And Ragsdale was wrong again.

He was not the only one. "We've taken the bounce out of rough roads and reduced the possibility of bottoming when the car hits a big bump," said Oliver K. Kelley.

Kelley, whose nickname was "O.K.," was Buick's new chief engineer, replacing Verner Mathews in 1957. As head of the transmission development group of General Motors, he had been credited with the development of Dynaflow. Kelley, a native of Finland, was regarded by some of the engineers at Buick as a radical. One thought that was an understatement. Some looked upon many of his ideas as difficult to translate from concept to blueprint. But others saw him as an excellent "hands-on" engineer. Whichever is the valid assessment, air-poise and triple turbine were not among Buick's better engineering ideas, though air suspension, it should be emphasized, was a corporate—not a Buick—development. Other GM cars tried it too.

To explain it simply, four rubber bellows filled with compressed air formed the air-poise suspension system. Buick claimed that regardless of the load, the car would be kept at a constant level at all times. A high-pressure tank, fed from a compressor run by the engine, was mounted on the car frame. The air in the bellows was to be kept at

100 p.s.i., counteracting roll and sway on curves or crowned roads. Each bellows was composed of a chamber consisting of a metal container, into which a rubber diaphragm was compressed by means of a plunger connected to the suspension. An added feature was a lift actuated by a lever under the instrument panel. It permitted the driver to raise the car body five-and-a-half inches and was designed primarily for use in tire changing, getting out of deep mud or snow, or when a high curb interfered with door opening.

It was one of those ideas that looked good on paper. In practice, it tended to leak, resulting in loss of pressure.* Nor, even when healthy, did it always do what it was supposed to. As Don Francisco wrote in *Motor Trend*: "Some types of dips at street intersections would cause the rear to bottom with a thud that shook the whole car. This happened only on dips that had the right angle and depth but it didn't matter whether there was a load in the car or not. Some dips that wouldn't make the rear end bottom would cause it to bounce unusually high. As it wasn't possible to tell from looking at a dip whether the car would bottom or bounce, I got to the point where I would just grit my teeth for all of them and take what came."

Not many people were persuaded to buy Buick's optional air suspension. For 1959 the self-leveling device would be used only at the rear, and by 1960 it would be gone.

Three turbines instead of two, ostensibly to increase torque output, was the other less-than-meritorious idea for 1958. It was termed Flight Pitch Dynaflow that year, and simply "triple turbine" in the few subsequent years it was offered. In some ways, it was a good transmission, according to Buick engineers who were around during its development period. Actually it was a corporate idea, with Buick trying to produce it. But problems there were aplenty. It was so complicated that it was difficult to manufacture. "Make it out of gold, but make it work," Ragsdale shouted in desperation to a Buick engineer one day as the problems continued and production time neared. Joe Turlay was assigned to head a team including Charles S. Chapman, who had come to Buick from Chrysler in the late 1950's to help further develop the triple turbine, Kenneth W. Gage, formerly with Hydra-Matic Division, and John Lindsay from GM Engineering to get the triple turbine perfected to the point it could be manufactured. Despite the major improvements they made, triple turbine had strange handling characteristics. "A stop watch told you it was doing fine, but your sensibilities told you (inaccurately) that it was slipping like a son of a bitch," said Turlay. Ultimately, it was too expensive. Buick invested $86 million in tooling for triple turbine, only to scrap it a few years later. "It practically broke us," said one

*This usually occurred overnight when the car was on its knees. On the road, the pressure would pump up again.

Buick executive.

Nothing seemed to be working right in Flint. To make matters worse, the Buicks were bigger, and the public was beginning to think smaller. As a palliative perhaps, GM offered Buick dealers a new car to sell—the Opel, built by the GM subsidiary in Rüsselsheim, Germany. It had a 99-inch wheelbase and a 90-cubic-inch four-cylinder engine, and looked like it might fit right inside of a Buick. But it wouldn't help Buick much right away.

In 1958 Buick production dropped to 241,908 for the model year and 257,124 for the calendar. Buick fell to fifth place in the industry.

Desperate to pull out of the slump, the division offered a lineup for 1959 that was a complete break from the past. Ragsdale said the new models provided "the most revolutionary change" in Buick history.

"It is given to a man once in a lifetime to introduce a completely new line of cars," he rhapsodized. "These things happen only once every two or three decades. We at Buick feel we are on the threshhold of an event that most of us will not witness again."

Gone were the portholes. Gone was the sweepspear. Gone even were the names. In their place were LeSabre (French for "the sword"), Invicta (Latin for "unconquerable"), Electra (Greek for "brilliant"). Ragsdale had selected the names himself, from more than a thousand choices. This may have been his only completely unfettered decision. Though these were the first cars designed under Ragsdale's leadership, designers claim that Curtice made the final choices. And the styling itself was very much Harley Earl. Stung by the public acceptance accorded the Flightsweep look of the 1957 Chrysler line, Earl decided to give the people what they wanted in maximum dosage. The fins flaring outward from the rear deck of the new Buicks were called "Delta wing." Those flaring outward from the rear decks of the other division cars were designated by other names. High style, they called it then. Low camp, it's considered today.

But one thing was certain, the cars from Flint were different. " 'They don't look like Buicks,' is the spontaneous comment heard most often"—and that is a direct quotation from a press release issued by Buick on September 15th, 1958. Such a sentence would have been heresy for the division only a few years before.

Mechanical refinements were less spectacular than the styling, though in retrospect perhaps more noteworthy. The horsepower race had to be attended to, and it was, with a new 401-cubic-inch engine for the Invicta and Electra series. LeSabre was powered by the predecessor 364-cubic-inch unit. The fine brake system was even further improved, with air cooling added to the rear drums. The power steering, which in recent years had become heavier as the cars themselves did, now required less than two-and-half pounds of effort

Buicks for 1959. Gone was the traditional sweepspear. Gone were the portholes.

to turn the wheel. Handling was improved all-around.

In *Mechanix Illustrated*, after taking one of the new Invictas out in the rain at the GM proving grounds, the inimitable Tom McCahill wrote: "This '59 Buick is one hell of a road car, with the traction of a leech. Many a lesser car on this wet road surface would have been off the shoulder like a French evening gown and sailing to parts unknown. You could no more have taken these bends at 60 mph with last year's Buick than you could sprout antlers on a rabbit. Oscar (sic) Kelley, the old fox, knew all this beforehand or he wouldn't have been sitting there in the front seat with me." Even so, Buick engineers say a mistake was made in '59 when, for some reason, front stabilizers were removed. They were back by 1960.

Press reports on the '59's generally were good, very good as a matter of fact. Buick took to snipping quotations from the reviews, as movie producers do, and published them widely. Indeed, there was an opening night aura to the whole of Buick promotion this year. When *Motor Trend* named the Invicta four-door hardtop the "best-looking car overall" in the industry (the Invicta also took "best-looking wagon" honors), Buick heralded the news virtually like a marquee.*

The September 16th debut of the new cars was the earliest for any manufacturer in the postwar period, this an attempt to get a jump on the competition. And it worked at first; for a time the public seemed to accept the new Buicks. But Murphy's law apparently continued to reign in Flint. A steel strike halted production for a few weeks in the

*Buick also had a new advertising agency. Kudner was dropped and in 1958 replaced by McCann-Erickson, an outgrowth of A.W. Erickson Company, founded in 1901, and H.K. McCann Company, founded in 1912. McCann-Erickson retains the Buick account to this day.

Electra 225, 1959 Indy pace car. Tony Hulman surrounded by Buick Dealers William R. Krafft, Robert Ogle, Robert Halcomb and R.P. Dellen.

late fall, and when it ended public enthusiasm for the cars faltered. Perhaps after thinking about it for a while, people decided a Buick that was more like a Buick was what they wanted after all. The revolution had gone too far. The production figures for calendar and model year respectively were 232,579 and 285,089—and Buick fell all the way to seventh place in the industry.

By then Ed Ragsdale was gone. In three years he had seen Buick production fall from nearly ten percent of the total industry and third place, to less than five percent and seventh. The new cars he had been so proud of for 1959 had not caught on. Buick had introduced such innovations as air suspension and triple turbine, and they had been disappointments. Buick's reputation for quality had declined.

In the factory, workers who were not on layoff worried that the division might be folded by the corporation, though this was apparently never seriously considered. Ragsdale had been a Curtice man, but Curtice had retired as GM chief executive in 1958.* In his place were Frederic G. Donner as chairman and chief executive, and John F. Gordon as president. Ragsdale and Gordon were not on friendly terms. In the spring of 1959, Ragsdale retired early.

Said one Buick executive: "I remember a conference of GM executives in 1958, when Curtice was still president. Gordon and Ragsdale were shouting at each other. It was embarrassing, I walked away. When Gordon became president, I had a feeling Ragsdale would not last too long."

Some Buick insiders were critical of Ragsdale, saying he appoint-

ed inferior managers to important positions. One man was named to a key manufacturing post because, Ragsdale reasoned, he had only a year to go before retirement and the job would help him out in his pension. A magnanimous gesture, but not a particularly astute one.

Still, some key Buick officials of the time have good things to say about Ragsdale.

"I knew him very well and liked and admired him," said Turlay. "He was straightforward and courageous. He and Curtice both favored styling that was too heavy and ornate . . . but Curtice accepted the blame for some of the 'Chrominess.' "

Ivan Wiles also has a kindly view: "Ragsdale was an excellent manufacturing engineer and manufacturing manager. He was innovative as hell. Hours meant nothing to him. He had only a high school education, and yet he became an engineer. Remarkable, really. But I think some of the people in the corporate office may have looked down on him because of his lack of education. So maybe after a few years he said to hell with it and left. I didn't have the feeling that he was retired before he wanted to be."

Others who were closer to Buick at that time are convinced, however, that Ragsdale was told to retire, that he had wanted to continue. Ragsdale stayed around Flint for a time, but complained to Wiles that he spent too much of his time running civic errands for people to whom he had once given orders. Wiles advised him: "Never retire where once you were famous." Ragsdale took the advice. He moved to Sarasota, Florida, and died there in 1971, aged seventy-four.

In 1959 the new leaders of General Motors looked around for someone who could bring Buick's luster back. They decided the man to do it was Edward D. Rollert.

---

*Curtice had been heard to remark that Buick, the one car division he could always count on, had finally let him down. Harlow Curtice's strong ties to Buick remained to his final days.

Chapter Sixteen

RISING UP FROM ADVERSITY

A former Buick general manager has said that "it's lucky Buick was attached to a big prosperous corporation" in 1959 and 1960. The implication was that the division might not otherwise have survived its nosedive.

There was even speculation among some employees that Ed Rollert was being brought in to close the place. But that was never a thought of GM top management, according to corporate insiders. Men such as Alfred P. Sloan, Jr., then still honorary GM chairman, could remember the days when Buick was the only GM car worth talking about. And Harlow H. Curtice, still a board member though retired as GM chief executive, remained Buick's Number One supporter. Buick was a great name. Only a few years earlier it had been highly profitable.

Basically, what the division needed was a strong manufacturing man to take a firm hand. GM chose Rollert, whose career to that point had been marked with versatility, independence (he left GM for two years in mid-career) and success. A native of Crete, Illinois and a graduate of Purdue University with a master's degree in chemical engineering, he had come to Flint in 1934 as a student engineer at AC Spark Plug Division. There he rose to successive positions of chief process engineer, chief tool and die designer, master mechanic and assistant works manager. From 1946 to 1948 he was manufacturing manager of the Elgin Watch Company, then returned to GM to become production manager of its New Departure Division.

After a short defense assignment with Fisher Body, Rollert was transferred to the Buick-Olds-Pontiac (later GM Assembly Division) plant at Kansas City, Kansas, where he became manager in 1951. The Kansas City plant was unusual—it was GM's first dual-purpose facility, with production split between automobiles and military jet planes. When output in one was down, the plant shifted to production of the other. Rollert handled the assignment well, and in 1955 was named general manager of GM's Harrison Radiator Division.

Buick's new general manager, therefore, had a wide variety of manufacturing experience when he succeeded Ed Ragsdale in the spring of 1959. He immediately set about to rebuild Buick's reputation as a producer of high-quality cars. Rollert also began to put together his own management team, including John Gretzinger, in charge of reliability and quality control; Lowell A. Kintigh as chief engineer; Roland S. Withers as general sales manager, and Robert L. Kessler as general manufacturing manager. Of these, Kessler was the last to arrive, in January 1961.

Gretzinger was forty-seven years old and had been chief engineer of GM's Allison Division, with extensive experience in guided missile work—a field necessarily emphasizing reliability. During World War II he was assigned as a major to the Hermes guided missile research and development program, was later an AC project engineer in Flint and in the 1950's was chief engineer at the Kansas City plant managed by Rollert, where he continued his work on jet engines.

Arriving at Buick in August 1959, he was given a broad mandate by Rollert to improve quality control. "Gretzinger was the first to have the power to shut the line down if he didn't like the quality," said Kessler. "He was hard-nosed, but he was good."

As for Rollert, Kessler found him to be "down to earth, had his feet on the ground. I argued with him. He didn't want a yes man. When I went to Ed with something, he listened. If there was one man who brought Buick back, it was Ed Rollert."

Gerald H. Rideout, named Buick public relations director in August 1959 when Waldo McNaught became manager of divisional relations for GM in Detroit, said: "Rollert was a workaholic. He had arthritis that was painful if he sat for long, so he was always pacing around. Buick needed a good, strong manufacturing man in 1959, and Rollert was that kind of man." Rollert roamed the plant, showing up in corners where no one could ever recall seeing a general manager before. Designers remember that he would sometimes walk into their departments and make his own marks on a blueprint. He rubbed some members of his staff the wrong way with his brusque demeanor, but no one could deny that he knew the business.

By the end of 1959 Rollert had found his chief engineer. Lowell Kintigh, who had been assistant chief engineer at Oldsmobile, succeeded Oliver K. Kelley, who moved on to become technical assistant

to the general manager of GM's new Defense Systems Division.

Kintigh was fifty-three, a native of Goshen, Indiana and—like Rollert and Kessler—a graduate of Purdue. He had been with Olds nearly thirty years, during World War II had held several important defense engineering assignments and was later an experimental engineer. According to Joe Turlay, Buick's chief engine designer, Kintigh was not considered a design man but was "the best judge of automobiles I ever met." This was high praise from Turlay, who never got along with Kintigh. Kintigh could drive a car, then sit down and tell each engineer what he had done right and what he had done wrong. He liked to test cars.

Said Turlay: "He'd take us to the mountains of Colorado, and we'd drive new Buicks like hell, 100 miles an hour on those mountain roads. I don't know what it proved, but we had a good time."

Roland Withers, formerly general manager of GM's United Motors Service, succeeded Edward C. Kennard, who had been general sales manager since 1957 and now became assistant general sales manager in charge of the eastern half of the United States, Kennard later was named general manager of Cadillac.

The new team created some friction. One executive remembers that there were "two armed camps. They apparently cooperated but some were fighting the new regime. The people Rollert put in were in no case better. There was no improvement." He also said that most of the quality control improvements were "window dressing." Another executive, acknowledging that this was true in some cases, added, "but some good things happened. Gretzinger did a good job because he had Rollert's backing."

Whatever the veterans at Buick thought of the new regime, they could not deny the lamentable sales figures of the late 1950's that proved something was very wrong. A shakeup of some sort obviously had been necessary.

Given the lead time required to get new models ready, as well as the complexities of manufacturing, promoting and selling automobiles, Rollert could not immediately turn Buick around. The division built only 253,999 cars in the 1960 model year. Calendar-year production of 307,804 units was better than the 232,579 of calendar '59 but, compared to the tremendous increases of other manufacturers, was nothing to boast about. Buick fell to ninth place in the industry, its lowest position since 1905.

For 1960 Buick had sculptured side sheet metal and more subdued tailfins which to some observers made it a more pleasing car than 1959. The public, unfortunately, was less than enthralled.

Rollert tried, though. From the beginning he pushed for quality and at new-car introduction in October 1959, he called the new Buicks the most reliable the division had ever built. Then he exaggerated some and added, "Quality in manufacture, plus our sculptured styling and fresh new features make these the most outstanding cars we have ever produced."

Reliability was his main goal. Privately, he asked Rideout to come up with a demonstration that would dramatically prove to the public that the Buick had it. Rideout met with the owner of the Daytona (Florida) Speedway, and together they came up with a plan. They

Page preceding: 1963 Riviera. Below: At a party at the Hotel Durant in 1959, from the left, Lowell Kintigh, Ed Rollert, Oliver K. Kelley. In portraits, Robert Kessler, Lee Mays. Page opposite, at the top: Dan Gurney in the Buick-powered, Mickey-Thompson-built car for Indy 1962; at the bottom, Buicks at Daytona for the 1963 Pure Oil Performance Trials.

would show that a Buick could be driven 10,000 miles in 5000 minutes—an average speed of 120 miles an hour. That would prove reliability—plus.

Planning was elaborate. Buick engineers developed a method for refueling two test cars—1960 Invictas—on the fly by having a fueling car come up behind them and shoot fuel into the tank from a long flexible pipe, similar to midair jet fueling. NASCAR race drivers were hired. Buick suppliers, including a tire company, wanted in on the publicity. The first car's engine had a mechanical problem but the second one completed the 10,000 miles in the prescribed 5000 minutes. Rideout prepared a publicity release. But GM president John Gordon found out, called Rollert and immediately demanded that it be shelved. The stunt smacked of racing, Gordon raged.

A Detroit newspaperman heard about the flap, called Rideout, and asked him what he would do if he had the information. "The same damn thing you're going to do," replied Rideout, slamming down the phone. The story ran. Eventually Rollert was given permission to show a film of the event to dealers, but the widespread publicity Buick had hoped to gain was never realized. In the mid-1970's, Rideout showed the film again at a Buick Club of America national meet in the Buick Administration Building.

Some of the "fresh new features" Rollert talked of for 1960 were an adjustable "Mirromagic" instrument panel that could be tilted to the easiest reading position, independent heating controls for the front and rear seats, and a revised exhaust system with the muffler mounted crosswise to the frame. A nod was given to Buick tradition

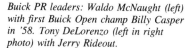

Buick PR leaders: Waldo McNaught (left) with first Buick Open champ Billy Casper in '58. Tony DeLorenzo (left in right photo) with Jerry Rideout.

Below: John Burnside (left) shakes hands with Ed Kennard at finish of '66 Mobil Economy Run.

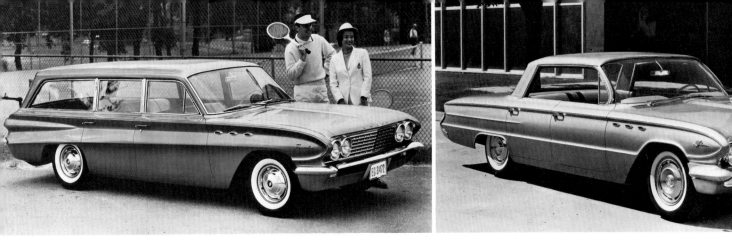

with the return of the VentiPort, LeSabre and Invicta each getting three per side, the Electra four. There was also an exclusive Buick option, Twilight Sentinel, that turned on the headlights automatically at dark, turned them off at daylight. This feature was to return as an option twenty years later, in 1980.

The 1960 front end treatment included dual headlights and a concave grille. LeSabre continued to use the 364-cubic-inch V-8, with one version a no-cost-option economy engine (9.0 to one compression ratio as opposed to the 10.25 to one of the standard) which could function efficiently, Buick said, on "lower-octane regular gasoline without sacrificing vital performance characteristics." The 401 was retained on the other models. With triple turbine dropped, only one automatic transmission was available on Buicks, the twin turbine which in recent years had ceased being called Dynaflow and instead was simply Turbine Drive. (Manual synchromesh was continued, though demand for it in '59 had been only about one percent of sales and it would be discontinued for the larger Buicks the following year.) Among chassis changes were a heavier stabilizer bar in front and improved shock absorbers.

In its road test of a 1960 Invicta, *Motor Trend* noted among the "Things We Like," good passenger comfort, reasonable gas mileage, smooth transmission and engine, quiet and comfortable cruising, easy handling, excellent brakes—and among the "Things We Don't Like," the short legroom for center rear seat and the lack of sun protection through the rear window. Buick seemed to be doing more things right already.

Meanwhile, at corporate headquarters, further plans were being made.

In May of 1960, General Motors announced that Buick, Oldsmobile and Pontiac would each introduce a new small car in the fall—the Special, the F-85 and the Tempest respectively. Buick's

Special nameplate, dropped only two years before, was back again. But some automobile feature writers preferred recalling the original introduction of the name twenty-six years earlier when the car carrying it was credited with saving Buick from disaster. "Will the Buick Special do it again?" was widely asked.

Building the small B.O.P. cars was a response to the marketplace, and the success enjoyed by such cars as the American Motors' Rambler and what seemed to be the ubiquitous Volkswagen from Germany. In the fall of 1959 the Big Three had responded with the Chevrolet Corvair, the Ford Falcon and Chrysler's Plymouth Valiant. Now, for 1961, Buick, Olds and Pontiac would get their somewhat larger compacts.

Planning for the new small cars had begun as early as 1957, and the cooperation among the three divisions—which had been willed by corporate headquarters—was closer on this project than ever before. It was not, however, always smooth. "At one point, Pontiac refused to go along on the engine," recalled Turlay. "Then Oldsmobile insisted on redoing the engines we provided."

A small aluminum V-8 of 215 cubic inches which had been developed by GM Engineering staff was redesigned for manufacturing by a Buick engineering team headed by Turlay. His recollection: "The corporation wanted to make the engine at Buick, the chassis at Olds, some parts at Pontiac. We had meetings at the GM Technical Center, trying to coordinate divisions. The idea was—and it wouldn't have worked—that the Tech Center would do the engineering and the divisions the manufacturing. On the aluminum V-8, they made the drawings. Our suppliers wouldn't bid on them because of tolerances, etc. The corporation, as planned, turned the engine over to us to manufacture. I made design changes. It had been designed under my recommendation, but I redrew every drawing."

An automobile engine of aluminum was nothing new, of course—

the XP-300 and LeSabre had an experimental high performance version, and aluminum had been used in some form in some production cars for many years. What the new Special represented was the first mass-produced aluminum V-8 in an American-built passenger car. It weighed only 318 pounds; it developed 155 bhp. This was news. *Road & Track* called it an "absolute jewel." In *Sports Cars Illustrated*, the respected technical journalist Karl Ludvigsen compared its introduction to the 1948 debut of the high compression V-8 by Cadillac and Olds, and predicted that Buick's new powerplant would be America's "most widely copied engine in the next ten years"—and also the most widely desired in one segment of the market. "Obviously this Special V-8 is going to be in furious demand among enthusiasts for all kinds of sporting uses," he wrote, "most especially for engine swaps in all popular imported sedans and sports cars. Why? A highly typical imported car engine, the 1.6-liter Volvo four, weighs almost exactly the same as this remarkable V-8, at less than half the displacement!" The title of the article was "Buick Built a Better Engine."

Coupled to this better engine was an optional automatic transmission which Buick called Dual Path Turbine Drive, a combination of the Buick torque converter and planetary gearing. Prototypes for it had been developed by GM Engineering Staff under the direction of G.K. Hause; the production unit was finalized by Buick. This compromise resulted in a transmission better in performance and economy than any earlier design.

In the fall of 1960, the new Buick Special was introduced. On a 112-inch wheelbase—eleven inches shorter than Invicta—it was available initially only in four-door sedan and wagon models. Initially, too, no one knew exactly what it was. No designation in vogue seemed to fit. Detroit quipsters decided it was either a jockey-sized big car or a giant-sized compact. *Road & Track* just parenthesized the Buick slogan to "when better (sized) cars are built . . ." *R&T* liked the new Special—"anyone used to the modern 'big' car will find the Special a delight to drive, and will find himself the owner of a car having ample, though not ostentatious, prestige." The Special did owe a debt to the Corvair—some of its inner body/chassis structure was the same but, as *Road & Track* noted, "the outside skin is so extensively revised that there is absolutely no visible clue as to this." Tom McCahill, with his formidably figurative way with words, said it "has more new angles than a broken plate glass window." He also called it "a well-calculated compromise . . . less compact than some cars on the market . . . more power than any of the new smaller cars I have tested up to this writing." *Motor Trend* called it "sensibly-sized."

The sensible Special cruised easily at around 80 mph, accelerated from rest to sixty in twelve seconds or under, and boasted gas mileage

Buicks for 1961. Page opposite: Special station wagon, LeSabre four-door hardtop. From the top: LeSabre Estate Wagon, Special DeLuxe, Electra 225.

in the 18-22 mpg range. The sensible Special also weighed (at 2700 pounds) 1600 pounds less than conventional Buicks—quite a departure from the slogan Buick had earlier bruited about, "more pounds per dollar than any other car on the road."

"A new concept from a most conservative firm" was one press reaction—and that meant more than size. Buick's portholes, three of them, were there for ready marque identification, but underneath was something brand-new for Buick. The traditional torque-tube drive had been replaced by an open driveshaft. The new drive line consisted of a front and rear propeller shaft with a standard universal

Buick announces the Skylark convertible!

Happily timed to capture the foot-loose, fancy-free feeling of Spring—the sparkling new Skylark *convertible*. Sports car adventure in a luxurious, new dimension. With lush vinyl interior. Deep pile carpeting. Front bucket seats. Electrically operated top. The take-off who-o-o-sh of the 190-h.p. *aluminum*

Skylark V-8 with 4-barrel carb. Choice of 3-speed transmission, optional Dual-Path Turbine Drive* or sporty 4-speed floor-mounted stick shift. Drive this mint-new companion for the hardtop Skylark at your Buick dealer's. (He's got Spring trading fever!)

BUICK MOTOR DIVISION — GENERAL MOTORS CORPORATION
*OPTIONAL AT EXTRA COST.

ONLY BUICK DEALERS HAVE THE NEWS FOR SPRING!
NEW SKYLARK CONVERTIBLE! NEW BUICK WILDCAT! BUICK SKYLARK

joint at each end, joined together with a constant-velocity universal joint in the center. Some observers assumed the change had been made specifically to reduce the size of the transmission hump, but much more significant was the improvement it rendered to the Buick's handling. And the constant-velocity joint, dividing the angles equally between the two driveshafts, effectively cancelled the ordinary vibrations produced by conventional driveshafts.

The new drive line necessitated a redesign of the Buick's rear suspension, which now comprised coil springs mounted on heavy trailing arms and operating forward of the axle. A second set of upper arms attached to the differential housing, running forward and outward for better lateral stability. Tubular shocks were mounted behind the rear axle. Though front suspension remained conventional, it was distinguished by its attachment as a subassembly—together with steering, hubs and brake drums—to the body/frame through three rubber-mounted isolation points.

Interestingly, in its overall review of what might be expected from Detroit for '61, *Motor Trend* hypothesized that since the Buick staff had been spending most of its time on the new Special, "there are no changes expected beneath the body" of the rest of the cars in the line. But when the rest of the line was introduced, with the Special, it too had the new drive line. The torque tube, a Buick tradition which in principle could be traced back to 1907, was abandoned completely.

For 1961, even the muted tail fins were, thankfully, finally gone. And the styling overall was considerably more pleasant. There was still a lot of chrome, but the sense of the convoluted was minimized in the sculpturing. There was also an attempt to stem the tide of model proliferation, though it would be short-lived. Invicta was limited to two- and four-door hardtops and a convertible, with four-door sedan and two wagons dropped. Electra models remained as before, but the top-of-the-line Electra 225 was confined to a Riviera four-door hardtop and convertible.

In looking for ways to improve Buick's image, Rollert and Withers wanted to blunt its reputation as a gas-guzzler. That reputation was no longer justified, they determined, and they needed a demonstration to prove it.

The well-known Mobilgas (later Mobil) Economy Run had been operating on the West Coast since 1936 and in 1950 it was expanded. Buick dealers had entered cars in the Mobil runs in the late 1950's, but with disappointing results.

Withers assigned John W. Burnside, an engineer in the Buick parts department, to manage Buick's effort in the 1961 Economy Run. Burnside worked closely with the engineering department in this effort and achieved good results in the Pure Oil Trials at Daytona Beach.

In the 1961 Mobil run, the Buick Special V-8 won first in its class with 24.7075 miles per gallon from Los Angeles to Chicago (2560 miles). The second place car was also a Special with V-8.

This was the beginning of a number of successes. The Special V-8 again won its class in 1963 when the run was from L.A. to Detroit. In '64, Buick was the big winner: first in three classes when forty-five cars competed in the first cross-country run from L.A. to New York, ending at the New York World's Fair. Firsts were taken by the Special V-6 (25.2986 mpg), Special V-8 (23.7441) and LeSabre V-8 (21.3670). LeSabre also won in 1966 and 1968, after which the runs were discontinued.

These victories were used extensively in sales promotion and advertising and went a long way toward reducing Buick's gas-guzzler image. Burnside, who started with Buick as a time-study man in 1943, later held such sales department jobs as exhibit and display manager, sales promotion manager and market research manager. In 1971 he was named manager of customer service. One of the most knowledgeable Buick employees about the company's history, he assisted the authors extensively in research for this book.

In March of 1961—mid-model year—there was another new

Buicks for 1962. Advertisements for the Skylark and the Wildcat. Above: Electra 225. Below: The Special convertible, a car for collectors today.

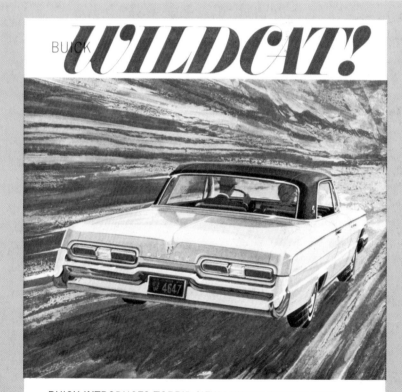

BUICK **WILDCAT!**

BUICK INTRODUCES TORRID NEW LUXURY SPORTS CAR! FIRST WITH THE SURE-FOOTED SOCK OF ADVANCED THRUST!

Here now—Buick's new, family-size package of sports car fun! WILDCAT! Only car of its kind with Advanced Thrust positioning of the engine over the front wheels. Result? Arrow-straight tracking even in stiff crosswinds. Pancake-flat cornering on curves. An exhilarating feel of sure-footed power behind the wheel. Plus the practical beauty of colorful vinyl interior. Front bucket seats divided by

a console with tachometer and Turbine Drive stick shift. The extra luxury of smart fabric overlay to highlight the Landau roof. See the WILDCAT! Your Buick dealer is eager to show it—and talk Spring trade! Buick Motor Division—General Motors Corporation.

BUICK WILDCAT!

Only Buick dealers have the news for Spring! New Buick Wildcat! New Skylark Convertible!

Buicks for 1963. From the left: Special, Electra 225, Wildcat, Invicta.

Find secret places . . . in the adventurous new Buick Skylark. Powerful aluminum V-8 engine, choice of 3 silk-smooth transmissions. Dashing bucket seat interior. Despite its modest price, a "limited edition" car, every inch a quality Buick.

a very personal car '63 Buick

Buick with a fondly-remembered old name: the Skylark, basically a trim option of the Special. With the same 112-inch wheelbase, the new Skylark used a version of the Special's 215-cubic-inch V-8 that was tweaked to 185 hp, primarily with the addition of four-barrel carburetion and a boost in compression ratio from 8.8 to 10.25 to one. Its top speed was an even one hundred.

In 1962 Buick introduced a V-6 engine for the Special. Because it was the first instance in which such an engine had been offered in a major American motorcar, it was a major news story. But nobody then could realize how important the little V-6 would become.

Even more fascinating, given its subsequent history, is the fact that the V-6 wasn't one of those ideas which resulted from years of planning. Most ideas in a mammoth corporation do. But not this one. Instead, it was based on the realization by Buick that the aluminum V-8 was too expensive for the low-priced Special, and something new was needed. But the development of an engine requires years, and Rollert wanted one in less than twelve months, in time for the '62.

Turlay relates: "Pontiac had taken half of a V-8 and made it a slant-4. Rollert said we'd better do it too. I said I can make a 90-degree V-6 that will beat the four all ways, by eliminating two cylinders of the V-8. 'How do you know?' Rollert asked. I'd done it on paper. 'Let's get to it,' said Rollert. We got it into full production in less than a year. It had a new crankcase, but the rods, pistons and valves were nearly the same as those of the V-8. I even made a patent application, but found some writer had mentioned in a publication the idea of a 90-degree V-6. Getting the V-6 was a selling job as well as engineering. We had to sell the V-6 to management, lend cars with V-6's in them to key vice-presidents. We had preliminary meetings to smooth the way. Generally, you go into a final meeting, and you find people want to think about it. We made sure the engine was sold before the final meeting."

The 198-cubic-inch V-6, basically the V-8 with two cylinders eliminated, had a cast iron block instead of aluminum. It was about fifty pounds heavier than the aluminum V-8 but about that much lighter than the new Chevrolet 194-cubic-inch in-line six. Working

under Turlay on experimental models of the V-6 was Cliff Studaker. Nelson W. Kunz, William B. Hoffman and, in production, Ed Holtzkemper have also been credited with helping turn the Turlay idea into reality.

Hurriedly designed in the months before 1962 model introduction, the V-6 would survive at Buick through 1967. The entire manufacturing line was later sold to Kaiser Jeep, where it showed up in the Jeep CJ-5 and the Jeepster. The engine was mothballed sometime after American Motors Corporation acquired Jeep in 1969. But it came back in 1974, and to Buick. In one of the more interesting adventures of any automobile engine, a refined V-6 would lead Buick into the fuel-economy era of the mid-1970's and, turbocharged, would power the sports version of the luxurious Riviera of 1979 and beyond. By 1980, Buick would be posting signs on its home plant and along the freeways near Flint proclaiming the factory as "Home of the Turbocharged V-6."

In 1962 the Special's new engine resulted in Buick's earning the "Car of the Year" award of *Motor Trend* magazine for "pure progress in design, originative engineering excellence and the power concept for the future expressed in America's only V-6 automobile engine." In an article carrying his byline, Lowell Kintigh quoted various glowing reviews of the V-6 appearing in the national press and concluded, "new ones keep coming . . . The men in engineering at Buick like this. After all, engineers have the same capacity as actors for that warm feeling of pride in their own professional accomplishments." There were a lot of curtain calls in Flint that year, and nobody complained when Buick erected two elaborate billboards on the freeway near Flint, calling the city "Buicktown."

For 1962 the Special was available in standard, Special DeLuxe and Skylark versions, with the V-8 standard in the Skylark. Convertibles were also now offered in Buick's compact. Indeed, the 1962 Special convertible with V-6 engine is one of the more intriguing and attractive cars in Buick history, and it could be a "sleeper" in the car collecting hobby. (The Special had been offered neither in a convertible nor with a V-6 in 1961, and in '63 seemed to lose its styling sport-

iness, which makes the '62 Special very special indeed.) One top Buick executive, who asked not to be named, noted that "if we had kept that little '62 Special and emphasized that small car, instead of letting it get big, Buick would be on top of the world today." The V-6 Special provided a top speed potential just a tad under 100 mph. "That engine doesn't know it's not an eight" was the very quotable conclusion of Buick sales manager Roland Withers. "Six for Savings—V for Voom" was the advertising tagline.

Hindsight aside, the people in Flint were beginning to feel just a little top-of-the-world themselves in 1962. Press reaction to the new Buicks was spectacular.

Dale Shaw in *Stag* called the Special with V-6 Detroit's best car in thirty years, and described its prowess in language appealing to readers of a men's magazine—and doubtless equally favorably received in Flint: "This terrific boost in power is due partly to the fact that the V-6—unlike the V-8—fires on one side and then the other alternately, left bank then right bank, causing a ram effect when a cylinder takes in gas and air. . . . Another reason . . . is the fact that the block design allows a big fat piston to be used, floating in an unusually husky 3.625-inch cylinder. Six of these bullish cylinders generate 135 horsepower. . . . Apparently possessing full knowledge of the 1962 Buick Special threat, both Ford and Chevrolet are out this year with completely compact-standard models half-heartedly designed to compete . . . the Fairlane series is powered by an in-line six that musters a mere 101 horsepower, forcing you to a V-8 to beat Special's 135-horsepower V-6 . . . Chevy II? Its little in-line six rates only 120 horsepower. And neither of these sixes has the performance or economy of V-6. Nor does overall construction compare with Buick's. . . . Actually, Buick Special is a fine automobile produced by a maker of deluxe automobiles with the specific aim of taking the malcontents away from 'Big Two' (Ford and Chevy) and with the added objective of supplying the cream of the so-called compact field, where buyers have found all too often they were not getting enough car for the open road."

Road & Track was equally enthusiastic about the Skylark with

Buick chief stylists, above and below, from the left: W.F. Lange, S.F. Parker, B.N. Smith, D.R. Holls, D.C. Lasky, E.F. Taylor, R.C. Hill, W.A. Kady.

aluminum V-8, now up to 190 hp with an increase in compression ratio to 11.0 to one. Said that magazine: "There was a time, not too long ago, when we would have laughed if anyone had told us that Buick would one day build a car we'd like to own. . . . But Buick's done it and, frankly, we're pleased to admit that our former conclusions may have been a bit hasty . . . it was the consensus of our staff that the Buick Skylark is one of the best all-around cars available today."

As an added fillip, Mickey Thompson chose the aluminum Buick V-8 (which he modified to pull 330 horsepower on dynamometer test) for his Harvey Aluminum Special for the '62 Indy 500. "Old hands,"

it was said, issued "dire warnings" that the engine wouldn't last. Dan Gurney qualified the car at 147.88 mph for eighth place on the grid, and raced it for ninety-two laps before a rear-end gear problem forced him to the side. The engine was just fine.

The big Buicks for '62 had most of their thunder stolen, of course, by the inherent specialness of their sister line. There hadn't been a great deal to talk about in any case. The 364-cubic-inch engine was dropped from LeSabre, and all the big cars now used the 401, in the LeSabre at 280 hp, in the Invicta and Electra at 325. All Electras were given the 225 designation. There was one very appealing new model, however. It was called Wildcat, and was marketed—as noted

by *Motor Trend*—as Buick's "performance image personification" (zero to sixty in 8.1 seconds, a 115 mph top). It was in essence an Invicta two-door hardtop to which were added numerous luxurious touches including a vinyl top, special side trim, a special vinyl interior and seating in what *MT* called a "bucket-seat palace."

In 1958 Ned Nickles had moved up to Advance Styling for the corporation. And a new generation of Buick chief stylists was ushered in: William Lange and Stanley Parker immediately following Nickles, Bernard Smith from mid-'61, David R. Holls for '63 through '67 models, Donald C. Lasky following him, and in turn being followed by Edward F. Taylor, Ronald C. Hill and Wayne A. Kady in the early Seventies. The look of the Buick was their charge during these important years when the division was climbing out of the abyss. Already there was the general consensus that Buicks were looking good. And already Buick was climbing.

During calendar 1962 the division produced 415,892 cars to move into sixth position in the industry. The model year figures were 245,-683 of the big cars and 154,467 Specials, including 20,600 wagons.

There would be another production increase in 1963, but that wouldn't be the best news from Buick that year. Not by a long shot. The best news was a model which brought attention back to the big Buick. The best news was called the Riviera. The name had been in use since 1949, but this Riveria was entirely different. It became a modern classic the day it was introduced. It was originally not intended to be a Buick.

Ned Nickles recalled: "All stories about the '63 Riviera are wrong. The original sketch was made by me in my apartment. It was not meant to be a Buick. It was to be LaSalle II, a Cadillac. We made a complete full-size model. Cadillac turned it down. It stayed around under cover. Mitchell [GM styling chief Bill Mitchell] showed it to Rollert, who became interested. The car went through very much as it was."

Chuck Jordan, now chief of GM design staff, remembers a strong involvement by Mitchell. His recollection: "It had been more like a fighter plane. Mitchell went to London, saw a Rolls-Royce in front of the Savoy Hotel, came back and said, 'You know what we got to do, make it a Ferrari-Rolls-Royce.' We needed that cross, that sporty elegance. The course was redirected. We got some drawings in that idiom." Supposedly, the sharp, elegant lines of the Rolls had been softened by fog, inspiring Mitchell's vision.

And following is Mitchell's version: "Ford had gone to our Motoramas, studied some of our show cars, and come up with the four-seat T-Bird. We didn't care much. Nickles had a room at GM Styling. I perceived that we needed a Cadillac LaSalle. Cadillac didn't have the facilities, didn't need the car much. Chevy was giving

Buick, Olds and Pontiac fits with its sales, so Gordon [GM president John Gordon] said, 'let them compete for it.' Olds wanted to put a blower on it—they weren't too good then—Pontiac wasn't much interested, but Rollert really went after it.

"I was stubborn. Nobody was going to change it. While it was being done, I went down to Gordon's office. He wanted very sheer lines, flat and angular. I saw a Rolls at the Claridge in London, not the Savoy. Gordon took a personal interest. The car was done in Nick's [Nickles'] room. The Riviera, and the Corvette, those were my two favorites."

One Buick engineer remembers Kintigh and Rollert trying out a "pre-test" Riviera at the GM proving ground at Mesa, Arizona. Kintigh took the car around a sharp turn and almost left the road. Enraged, he stepped out of the car and shouted to engineers in a trailing car: "Take this goddam thing back to the barn and start over from the ground up."

But by the time Buick engineers were through with the chassis, Riviera was a fine handling vehicle. Cliff Studaker gives much of the credit to Phillip C. Bowser, then in charge of Buick research and development. "He was a chassis expert, and he really made that car's ride," said Studaker.

The Riviera was produced in only one model, a hardtop coupe. Its wheelbase was 117 inches, length overall 208 inches. The standard engine was the 401, rated at 325 hp at 4400 rpm. A fifty-dollar option was a bored-out version of 425 cubic inches, rated at 340 hp, and available only with 10.25 to one compression ratio and four-barrel carburetion. Standard were leather bucket seats and a console. Weight was 3998 pounds. Price was $4333. But more significant than anything else was the styling, the sharply sculptured roofline, the sheer side panels, the low silhouette, and especially that unique frameless side window glass.

John R. Bond referred to it as a "GM T-Bird" in *Road & Track*, *Motor Trend* said it aroused GM dream car memories, *Car and Driver* saw Bentley S-2 Continental concept influences. The following year, having received some complaints from its sports car readership, *Car and Driver* noted: "Our opponents assert that the car is a big heavy Buick and therefore completely undesirable for people who have enjoyed Jaguars, 300 SLs, or even Corvettes. Actually the Riviera is different from the other big Buicks, and it stands alone among American cars in providing a combination of luxury, performance and general roadworthiness that approaches Bentley Continental standards at less than half the price." *Ward's Automotive Yearbook*, that factual appraiser of the industry not wont to tossing adjectives about, called it "a marvelously balanced prestige car."

Buick built 40,000 Rivieras in the 1963 model year, which was

precisely the number the division intended. Like the Skylark of a decade earlier, the Riviera was a prestige builder for the marque. Exclusivity was a prerequisite. Its low volume was by design.

Everything else seemed anticlimactic. But there were other Buicks in 1963. The Wildcat name was given to a series, the one formerly known as Invicta. (The Invicta name remained only on a station wagon.) This year styling identity among Buicks was replaced by a studied differentiation. The Wildcat had its own grille design with brushed stainless steel moldings extending down the sides from the headlight to the middle of the front door. The Electra 225 was distinguished by long straight rear fenders reaching back beyond the body panel, and concave taillights. LeSabre had its own look. The American tendency to make little cars ever bigger was at work. Specials, though remaining on the same wheelbase, were longer by four inches and restyled front and rear to appear more massive.

New options were a tilting seven-position steering wheel in the big cars, and Superlift shock absorbers (a sealed piston chamber utilized with the normal shock) for owners who loaded their trunks down with peat moss or other heavy commodities, this available with the Special as well. A cruise-control option for turnpike driving could be had with all Buicks save the Special.

In 1964 virtually all Buicks except the Riviera got bigger. The only noticeable change to the latter was underneath the hood: a 425-cubic-inch V-8 with a 10.25 to one compression ratio, four-barrel carburetion and 340 horsepower standard. A second four-barrel carb was optional. There were a couple of other revamped engines as well for the other Buicks: a V-6 of 225 cubic inches and 155 hp, and a 300-cubic-inch V-8 of 210 hp. Turbine Drive was revised into Super Turbine 300 and 400, both the torque converter plus two (in the 300) or three (in the 400) forward speed ratios. The Special and Skylark received a new 115-inch wheelbase, a three-inch increase over the predecessor, and Skylark wagons went to 120 inches. The increase in overall length in the Specials was nearly a foot. General press consensus was that, especially with the 425 engine option, the Wildcat name for a Buick was no misnomer.

More power, more length, more width, more room—"more" seemed to be the keynote for '64. Styling represented the most gentle of facelifts.

But the important thing for Buick was that it was coming back. Calendar-year production rose from 291,285 in 1961 to 415,892 in '62 to 482,731 in '64. There was a new pride in Flint, and much of it was reflected in the Riviera. The Riviera had been the perfect car for Buick to market, not only for its styling, but simply because it gave the division a car unlike anything else in the GM stable. Oldsmobile would introduce its front-wheel-drive Toronado for '66, but until it did Buick had the star of the GM show, a car in a class all its own. Uniqueness would become ever more rare as the years progressed.

In fact, tracing Buick through the 1960's and 1970's and into the '80's provides a picture of the industry in microcosm. There was, first, more models and more muscle—then, and increasingly, concern with safety, serviceability, emission controls, fuel economy. Every manufacturer had to contend with the growing effort by the Federal Government to regulate the automobile. At times the industry fought, at times it gave in, at times it cooperated with some enthusiasm, as would be the case with GM president Edward N. Cole and the catalytic converter. Though that didn't happen often.

At General Motors, the growing need to respond to government regulation, in addition to the internal emphasis placed on making more components interchangeable, would inevitably strengthen the corporate hold on the car divisions, and lessen their individual personalities. Former general managers will argue with each other about how much power the head of a division retained, but it seems fair to say that the Harlow Curtice-type of strong manager was going out of style.

For some time, it seemed, model proliferation and muscle cars were not. At Buick, the number of models grew from twenty-six in 1964, to thirty-nine in '65, to fifty-three in '66. In 1965, Buick offered two new performance cars, Gran Sport versions of Riviera and Skylark which, the engineers boasted, could do zero to sixty in seven seconds. Enthusiast magazine road testers were only a little slower

Buick '65 Buick

This is the year Buick conquered inner space.
This Buick Sportwagon is how.

It won't hold an elephant.
But for people (adults and kids), pets, bundles–it's great. This Buick Sportwagon boasts a cargo volume of 97.8 cubic feet. Useful space. Convenient. Ready to meet your specific needs. For instance: Need more people room? Order the model with the forward-facing third seat. Want extra luggage space? Just fold that third seat down and load up. Obviously, this 120-inch-wheelbased Sportwagon is a full-sized wagon. To say the least.
And see that Skyroof? Not only does it look pretty, it gives you more headroom. It also gives you a breezy, out-in-the-open ride without the breeze. And heat and glare are blocked by Buick's new kind of shaded glass.
You really will get more out of this Buick Sportwagon.
Naturally. We put more in. From the inside out. Your move. Wouldn't you really rather have a Buick?

Buick Motor Division · General Motors Corporation

Page opposite: The Special sedan and the Wildcat hardtop for 1964. Above: Wildcat convertible for 1965. Below: '65 Wildcat sport coupe; the '65 Skylark Gran Sport (with "portholes"). Right: '65 Riviera.

than the Buick engineers: *Car Life* needed 7.4 seconds, *Motor Trend* 7.8, each with the Skylark. With its 400-cubic-inch engine rated at 325 hp, the Skylark was a patent attempt by Rollert to attract the youth market which he saw headed in the direction of the new Ford Mustang and Pontiac GTO, among others.

The Riviera Gran Sport simply added another twenty horsepower (to 360) to the big 425-cubic-inch engine introduced the year previous, plus a specially calibrated transmission for higher shift speeds, a positive traction rear axle delivering power equally to both rear wheels, and a higher axle ratio for faster acceleration. The ride and handling option included heavy duty suspension, rear track bar bushings and faster steering. "Inside, it's luxurious Buick-bred silence," said *Car and Driver.* "Outside, it's Daddy Warbucks' high-powered runabout." Because of its tighter suspension, the Gran Sport stood about an inch lower than the standard Riviera. Both featured a new Riviera styling idea which was widely applauded: disappearing headlamps. Receiving commendation, too, was the placement of the taillamps in the bumper. Basically, the body lines were unchanged. The Riviera was crisper, cleaner and, some said, more elegant than ever.

It was inevitable that Riviera styling would eventually show its influence in the rest of the Buick line, and in '65 it did. Roof lines were more sloping, hoods were lower, rear decks shorter. The cleanliness of Riviera design found its way into the Skylark especially where, in a 180-degree departure from the norm, some of the previous year's trim was deleted, with nothing new added. Among the many models were three in Special and Special DeLuxe, four in Skylark, seven in LeSabre, ten Wildcats ("Wouldn't it be fun to drive one of these babies to Riverside?" asked one advertisement of the hottest "cat"), seven Electras and one Riviera, plus the Gran Sports of Riviera and Skylark. But for all the models more, there was one less, the LeSabre station wagon. Wagons were offered in Special and Skylark only.

The 1965 calendar year saw Buick produce 653,838 cars, for seven percent of, and fifth place in, the industry. Though not quite back to where it had been in the early Fifties, Buick clearly had turned the corner and was heading that way.

On June 24th, 1965, Ed Rollert was promoted to GM group vice-president in charge of the car and truck group. (He was still a vice-president, heading the Overseas Operations, Non-Automotive and Defense Group, when he died on a hunting trip in South Dakota in November 1969.)

His successor was Bob Kessler, his general manufacturing manager and a fellow Purdue alumnus. Kessler, in fact, had been an All-American basketball player for the Boilermakers. He joined GM in 1936 in the process department of Delco-Remy Division; by 1959,

290

Buicks for 1966. Above: Skylark four-door hardtop. Page opposite, from the top: Special sedan, Wildcat convertible, Riviera and Electra 225 hardtop

The tuned car. For young people of all ages.

What makes a car a car is styling, performance, ride and handling. Only when they're all tuned together is the car a Buick. Like this '66 Wildcat Gran Sport.

We have a secret formula for rejuvenating tired drivers. It's called "Buick tuning."

You know how well your car's engine runs after a tuneup? Buick tuning has the same effect on the whole car. Not just the engine. The whole Buick. Everything blends with everything else. Styling. Performance. Ride. Handling. All tuned to work together in harmony. That's what the tuned car is. A Buick.

Where the tuned car comes from. It comes from ideas, yes. But we don't really trust ideas until we see how they prove out. So we put our ideas in cars and take them out on the road for exhaustive testing.

Do we test on orthodox proving grounds? Sure—in Phoenix, Arizona, for example. But since we couldn't tune a car on a proving ground alone (and since you won't be driving on one, either), we don't ship our cars out there. We drive them—testing all the way.

Where else do we test and tune, test and tune? The answer is: everywhere. Anywhere a road can teach us something about the roads you drive.

Safety is everybody's business. Including ours. The tuned car is tuned for safety, too. Which is why every model comes with an outside rear view mirror. And a padded dash. And seat belts front and rear. And a shatter-resistant inside mirror. And padded sun visors. And automatic backup light. And dual-speed windshield wipers and washers.

What the tuned car can do for

you. Will a new 325-hp Wildcat make a new driver out of you? We think so. You may find yourself enjoying those little unexpected trips to the grocery store. With the 340-hp Wildcat Gran Sport version (it has the larger engine, a special ride and handling package, Positraction rear axle and—naturally—everything tuned to match), you may just find yourself arranging to forget things so you can go back again. Don't blame us. Just think how much fun it will be to feel like you've just gotten your driver's license. Ah, youth.

Wouldn't you really rather have a Buick?

1966 Buick. The tuned car.

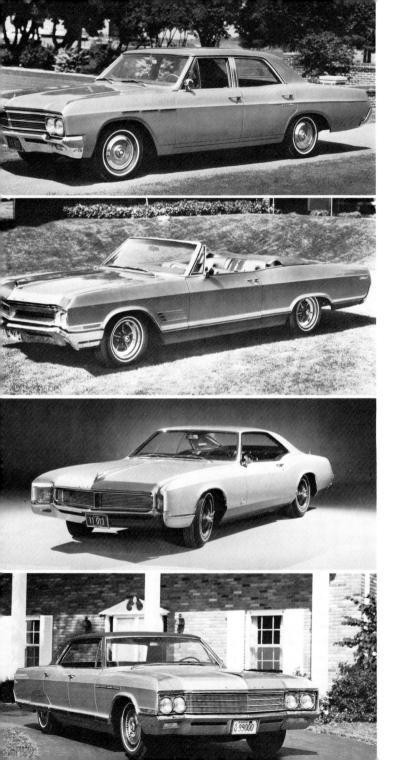

after a series of promotions, he was works manager there. At Buick he had succeeded an excellent manufacturing man, Donald F. Taylor, who went to the new post of production control and purchasing manager.

Robert J. Breeden was named general manufacturing manager to succeed Kessler. Breeden had once been plant manager at GM's Saginaw Steering Gear Division and had for a year shared Buick manufacturing manager duties, under Kessler, with George R. Elges, who was later to become Buick general manager.

About his nearly four years as Buick general manager, Kessler would later note that he was most proud of the team he had— Kintigh, Withers and Breeden in particular.

With the departure of Rollert, the era of long-term general managers in Flint seemed to be over. In the next thirteen years, from 1965 to 1978, Buick would have no fewer than five of them. Some were not around long enough to see the cars they approved get into production. But through it all, Buick was generally growing in strength with only an occasional backslide, in the '66 calendar year for example when production of 580,421 cars slipped the division back into sixth place in the industry.

Riviera received its first major restyling that year: a new grille, longer hood, a more sloping windshield, modified fastback roof and rear deck—and no window vents. "The Riviera is bound to change the driving habits of thousands of Americans," quipped *Motor Trend*. "They no longer will have a window-vent frame to cling to." And they would get used to it; the vent would soon be eliminated on most automobiles. David Holls was especially happy about this Riviera. It remains his personal favorite of the cars he styled during his four-year tenure: "There was just a flair about it I liked, I still do." Available for the first time was a front bench seat instead of buckets for less sporty Riviera owners. And both Riviera and Riviera Gran Sport now had the 425-cubic-inch V-8. What neither had was front wheel drive. Nor was it planned for the near future.

There had been considerable speculation that Riviera would go the way of Toronado, enough of it that the people in Flint became worried. "I'd like to take this means of telling you that it just isn't so . . . ," wrote sales manager Withers in a rather unusual letter to all media representatives on the Buick mailing list. Citing facts and figures—"As an example, the 1966 Riviera went to market October 14. In the first thirty days it has substantially outsold its predecessors"—Withers concluded that "all of this is my way of saying that the 1966 Riviera is doing just fine—even better than we expected—and we have no intentions of tampering with such a successful formula."

Extending a successful formula was something else. Now there was

Above: Special DeLuxe station wagon (left) and the Sportwagon for 1966. Below: Skylark four-door hardtop and Electra 225 convertible for 1967; the four-barrel 430 V-8.

a Gran Sport version of the Wildcat, in hardtop and convertible.

For the 1967 model year, Gran Sport was abbreviated officially to GS—enthusiast magazines had begun doing so the year previous—and Buick offered the GS 400, built on the Special wheelbase, in convertible, coupe or hardtop. The 400 represented the number of cubic inches in the Buick's entirely new V-8 engine.

The new engine was unexpected, in view of the GM trend toward ever-increasing standardization of components among divisions. But as engineer Cliff Studaker, who developed the engine, explained, "We here felt we needed a new big V-8. The old design dated basically from 1953 and we had developed it about as far as we could. It took some selling—but we finally got the front office okay."

There were two versions of the new big V-8, the 400-cubic inch rated at 340 bhp at 5000 rpm, and a 430-cubic-inch rated at 360 bhp at 5000 rpm for Wildcat, Electra and Riviera lines. Four-barrel carburetion was standard. The old 401/425 engines were gone. There were a couple of important reasons for the change. The first was breathing flexibility. The earlier engine featured vertical valves with a pent roof combusion chamber, necessitating a valve actuating mechanism in which the pushrods passed through bosses drilled in the cylinder heads crossing the valve guides with the rocker arms and doubling back to actuate the valves. Valve and port sizes were limited in this arrangement. In the new engine there was a domed chamber (Buick engineers called it a "slanted saucer") designed by Turlay before his retirement, with conventional rocker arms and pushrod placement, and a 15-degree angle between valve and cylinder axes. This was similar to the very efficient combustion chamber of the small aluminum V-8 Buick had introduced in 1960, and used in all the later small engines including the V-6.*

Since the industry trend seemed to be away from the classic wedge chamber, this was a surprise as well. But the domed chamber with small quench area had a significant feature and represented the second important reason for the change. It boasted considerably less surface area in relation to displacement volume than the conventional wedge. While this did not reduce octane requirement, it did result in higher efficiency (power and fuel economy) and less emission of hydrocarbons. Already the Federal Government was beginning to take a hard look at the smog problem.

Buick's brakes, still recognized as the best in the industry, were made even better for '67. Front power discs were optional on most models, aluminum brake drums were extended to GS 400 and

---

*When Buick stopped building that original aluminum V-8, Rover of England bought the rights to the engine with all engineering and factory drawings and hired Turlay to help get it into production. Rover is still building that engine.

Above: The Wildcat from Buick for 1967. Below: Advertising the new Riviera.

'67 proves again that it takes Buick to top Buick. A lot of people thought Riviera was perfect, with its trend-setting look and new ventilation system. But now Riviera is—yes—improved. And this is how:

With hazard flashers at all corners, and the GM-developed energy-absorbing steering column. The day-night, vinyl-coated mirror. The new braking system, with dual master cylinders. Standard.

And Riviera now connects a 430-cubic inch, 360-horsepower V-8 to Super Turbine automatic, and to the kind of ride and handling that live up to Riviera's looks: clean, smooth, married to the road.

And because bucket seats and a center console and such are available, you can make the '67 Riviera even more personal. Now the question is: How soon can you make it to your Buick dealer's?

BUICK '67
THE TUNED CAR

Sportwagon, and on the larger cars the system was improved through use of a larger power booster, better linings and a doubling of the number of fins in the brake drums.

The new Buicks were well received in the enthusiast magazines. Even the "big, solid, heavy, roadworthy" Buicks that "your dad used to drive" won plaudits—though most enthusiasm was reserved for the "semi-luxury car on a smaller scale" (the Skylark), and the GS 400 "that'll shut down the best of them over a quarter-mile, burn the rear tires like a drag strip 'rod,' and then drift quietly all the way home with never a trace of roughness." The GS 400, with its paint stripes, hood scoops and wide tires, was seen as the "Gran Sleeper" or "dark horse of the year"; *Car Life* found the Wildcat "more friendly than fierce . . . a super/tabby"; and *Car and Driver* editors admitted that they essentially went "clean out of our skulls" for the Riviera Gran Sport.

While the press emphasized muscle, Buick itself promoted modishness. "The Magazine for the In Crowd" was the subtitle of the house organ introducing the new cars, with the top models in the fashion industry—Suzy Parker, Wilhemina, Penny Ashton, Delores Wettach, Jean Shrimpton, Dolores Hawkins—draped languorously over them in photographs and saying very nice things about them in captions.

It was a good year.

In 1967 Buick regained fifth place in the industry from Olds. And for the first time, some of the Buicks built in Canada (6523 of the 15,-664 produced there) were for the U.S. market. The following year Canada would build 46,405 Buicks, and 32,282 of them would cross the border.

For 1968, Buick mixed things up. All intermediate models had new bodies and shorter wheelbases, and the base Special was dropped. So was the V-6, replaced by the in-line six of 250 cubic inches and 155 horsepower built by Chevrolet.* The front office had won that one.

The small 340-cubic-inch V-8 was revised into the 350, and more closely resembled the 400/430 units than it did its predecessor, mainly for exhaust emission reasons. What had previously been the GS 340 with the old engine became the GS 350 with the new.

New too was an emphasis on safety, that word even being mentioned before "styling" in press releases from Flint. Among the safety features touted were improved door latches, larger outside rear-view mirrors, side marker lights on front fenders and rear quar-

---

*GM did not hide the fact that divisions built engines for each other, although later the corporation would be successfully sued because, it was said, customers were not clearly informed of the practice. Buick press releases for '68 did not specify the in-line six as being Chevrolet-built, but virtually all enthusiast magazines reporting the new "Buick" engine did.

Buicks for 1968, from the top: Skylark, LeSabre, Wildcat and Electra 225. Page opposite: Skylark convertible and LeSabre four-door hardtop for '69.

ter panels, safety armrests.

This bewildering array of models, engines, stripes, scoops and cars which were invariably described as lower and wider and more lithe than the year previous, was keeping Buick competitive. Not a breaker of new ground, but a sure-footed contender in the marketplace. By 1968, Buick had left its lean years of nearly a decade behind. The division set a record for production in Flint of 350,826 cars, surpassing the 309,946 built in 1950. Nationally, production hit 673,655, the second best in Buick history, and the Canada-U.S. total was 698,454.

Chief engineer Lowell Kintigh was named GM's director of forward planning in April of 1968 and was succeeded by Phil Bowser. Bowser had joined the GM research staff in 1950 after graduation from Ohio State. After a few years in Chevrolet's research and development department, he was named director of research and development at Buick engineering in December 1957. Four years later he was named assistant chief engineer in charge of experimental testing, chassis development, acoustics and production engineering.

By 1969, Buick was back in what it once considered its natural sales position—fourth place. Buick production of 713,832 cars in the calendar year was second only to the record 781,296 of 1955 in the United States, and only the second time U.S. Buick production had topped 700,000. Flint production also set a record, 347,736—and Canada had its second-best Buick production year, 37,896. U.S. production for the model year was 665,422.

There were only minor styling changes for 1969. Mostly, there was emphasis on safety and performance features. Variable ratio power steering was introduced to Wildcat, Electra and Riviera models. And there was a Turbo Hydra Matic (THM) 350 transmission option which comprised a three-element torque converter and two planetary gearsets. But more attention was paid to a new suspension called Accu-Drive which Buick engineers boasted provided "the best directional stability ever experienced in an automobile." They accomplished this by utilizing the principle called "camber thrust," the side force generated when a rolling wheel is leaned or cambered. Buick

used it as a stabilizing force by lowering the lower control arm inner pivot and raising the upper control arm inner pivot. Because of this relocation, when the wheel moved over an undulation, it tipped outward at the top, instead of inward, producing a positive camber angle and providing an opposing force. The two forces would effectively cancel each other out, keeping the car on a more nearly straight path. The new safety features Buick emphasized included an anti-theft ignition lock on the redesigned collapsible steering column, headrests, larger rear-view mirrors again and impact bars within doors and quarter panels of some models.

But Buick may have said too much, at new-car introduction, about an automobile that wasn't even a Buick. It was the new Opel GT, built by GM's German subsidiary, which Buick dealers would offer later in the model year as part of their Opel inventories. Kessler told the auto writers that he couldn't talk about it yet, but "we just wanted you to get a look at it." That little bit of showing off resulted in automotive feature writers finding a lot more to say about the Opel GT, some describing it as a cross between a Corvette and an American Motors AMX, than they did the Buick line. "When better cars are built, Buick will import them," one reporter would note. But because both small cars and imports were coming into increasing favor in the U.S. marketplace, the Opel would prove a boon for Buick dealers, with sales in some years nearing 100,000.

In early April 1969, Buick had a new general manager: sixty-year-old Lee N. Mays. On the 7th of that month, Bob Kessler was named general manager of Fisher Body; only six months after leaving Buick, he would suffer a major illness but would recover and become vice-president in charge of the manufacturing staff before retirement in 1976.

His successor in Flint was a native of Findlay, Ohio and a 1931 graduate of Ohio State University. Lee Mays had spent most of his GM career in sales. He got there in an unusual way. At OSU, his fraternity adviser was vice-president of a big Ford dealership in Columbus and hired Mays as an odd-job employee. Less than three months later the general manager died, the owners put Mays in charge, and he quickly discovered the business had been losing money heavily for several years. Mays convinced the owners to switch car lines, and a change from Ford to Chevrolet was made in 1933. Two years later, Mays decided to quit, but was persuaded by Chevrolet to stay in the organization and was made a district sales manager.

Through the years he gained something of a reputation as an organizer who could pull things together and get the job done. In 1962 he was named general sales manager of Cadillac; in 1967 he took the similar job at Chevrolet.

Reportedly, Mays was anxious to retire (there were reports of a clash between Mays and Chevy's new general manager, John Z. DeLorean), but he was talked into staying on a few more years to run Buick. This was a period of great shifting at the top level of GM management. The senior managers of the corporation's car and truck divisions had fewer than three years in their jobs. Observers complained they needed a program to figure out who was doing what. Perhaps it didn't matter much. Mays has said that general managers didn't have much power anymore, anyway.

In the days of Ivan Wiles, it was customary for general managers of Buick to go to GM headquarters only twice a month, for one administration and one styling meeting. By the late 1960's, they were going two or three times a week. Mays, close to retirement and with much of his Buick time to be spent in Detroit in any case, didn't move to the Flint area, a fact which caused some grumbling among community leaders accustomed to Buick managers being involved in city affairs.

Though a salesman by background, Mays said, predictably, that quality was his most important goal at Buick. In 1970 he announced new Buick testing procedures, including air monitoring, in which partially assembled engines were run on compressed air to check for defects, and new processes for checking all electrical and vacuum systems before they were dropped on a chassis.

For the younger and older segments of the marketplace, general sales manager O. Franklin Frost said there would be two themes: "Automobiles to Light Your Fire" and "Wouldn't You Really Rather Have a Buick?" (Frost, assistant general sales manager since 1963, had received the top sales job in 1968 when Roland Withers became president of GM of Canada.) There is no need to indicate which slogan was for which group, nor which has endured the longest.

In 1970 the Special, which certainly had more rebirths than any other Buick in history, was dead again, replaced by the Skylark and Skylark 350. The restyled Skylark featured a longer hood, shorter rear deck and the side impact bars in doors and rear quarter panels

introduced the previous year on the larger cars.

Styling changes on the bigger Buicks, including Riviera, were confined primarily to new grilles, bumpers and ornamentation. Serviceability, a word being heard more frequently in these years, was used at Buick to describe snap-on speedometer cable connections, air conditioner outlet hoses that could be disconnected quickly, and a steering column designed to reduce the time required to replace

directional signal switches.

Muscle car remained very much in the automotive lexicon too, and this year at Buick it translated to a new 455-cubic-inch engine (replacing the 430) generating 370 bhp and 510 lb/ft of torque. The GS version, of course, was now the GS 455—and there was a Stage I package that provided high-lift cam, positive traction rear axle and dual exhaust system, among other speed sundries. The 370 horse-power rating would be Buick's highest in the muscle-car era that was rapidly coming to a close. *Car Life* tried one of the first GS 455's off the line, at the GM proving grounds in Mesa, Arizona, did zero to sixty in 6.5 seconds, with a 129.5 mph top, and concluded it was a nice car to "take home to mother, or to the dragstrip on grudge night."

Buick's model year production totaled a healthy 666,501 cars, but

Buicks for 1970, from the top: Electra 225, Riviera, the new Estate Wagon.

calendar-year production dropped to 459,931 because of a UAW strike against GM. Still, the division retained fourth place.

In 1971, Buick produced one of the most controversial cars it has offered in modern times—a restyled Riviera with a rear end that swept down to a point, or "nostril," as one designer put it. More often it was referred to more traditionally. Not since the Thirties had a major manufacturer offered a style that could be called a boattail. This one could. The design was selected while Kessler was general manager, but Lee Mays was in charge when it was introduced.

Mays publicly called it "a classic new design that is a triumph of automotive styling." Privately, however, he hated the boattail Riviera and spent much of the rest of his Buick career trying to get rid of it. "Sure, some people liked it, some people like anything," Mays told the writer. "I could never find anyone who admitted they designed it."

Jerry Hirshberg does. Hirshberg, later chief designer of Buick Studio 2 where the larger and intermediate Buicks are designed, acknowledges that he was responsible for the boattail Riviera, trying to interpret a concept of GM styling chief Bill Mitchell's.

"It is a peculiar car to look back on," says Hirshberg. "Bill Mitchell was the prime mover on the car; he wanted a classic. The boattail was my first big assignment as chief designer of advanced Buick, and I threw myself into the work.

"At first it was supposed to be on a smaller body, the A-body. But then it was built on the B-body, and that didn't help. On a smaller car it could have been kind of interesting. It was one of the more painful exercises I've ever been through. The car looked slightly eccentric. But so would a Corvette if it were the size of a Cadillac.

"I will say I have taken a gentle ribbing around the office about it, but the car did have aspects I like myself. Mitchell wanted a classic. And to Bill's credit, he liked a little controversy. Too often, we are intimidated by all the regulations. But I think the boattail was a mistake."

Ned Nickles, in retirement, agrees. From a styling viewpoint, the boattail Riviera, he said, "was a disaster and the ones the next few years after were no good." But there are people so fond of the cars that they carefully restore them. Kessler today says he thinks the boattail was a "nice, distinctive car" but that Buick didn't do a good job of marketing it.

The last word goes to Mitchell, who comments: "What hurt the boattail was to widen it. It got so wide, a speedboat became a tugboat."

There were more changes of names and models in '71. Wildcat was dropped, Centurion added—but the latter, said Buick officials, was not a name change for the same car. Wildcat had evolved from

Buicks for 1971, from the top: Skylark Custom, the controversial boattail Riviera, Centurion, Electra Limited. Page opposite, from the top, Buicks for 1972: the Skylark 350 Sun Coupe, the Electra Limited, and the Riviera.

Buick's small muscle car, the Century, and its role was now filled by Skylark GS. No, Centurion was to be a more formal, more luxurious regular-size car than LeSabre.

The big Buicks this year had new sheet metal, more "turn under," as the stylists say, for easier entrance and exit, though some customers complained that the inward curve at the bottom of the body required mud flaps to protect the finish. Roofs of the larger cars had a new Fisher Body lamination construction, an additional steel panel on the inside. The convertible was fading, dropped this year from Electra, but retained in LeSabre, Skylark and GS.

All Buick engines were revamped with lower compression ratios to operate on low or no-lead fuel for less exhaust emission. Exhaust valves in all engines were nickel-plated for greater durability using low-lead gasoline. Like other GM cars, Buick offered a new pressurized ventilation system on all models and a "glide-away" tailgate on Estate Wagon.

The 1971 model year had started slowly because of the sixty-seven-day UAW strike against GM. But the pent-up demand set up records after the first of the year. In the first quarter of 1971, Buick produced 229,470 cars, in March it built 85,526, both records.

Despite the introduction of Centurion, Mays said Buick was doing its part to roll back model proliferation. Nine models were eliminated—including two in GS and three in LeSabre 455. The 455 was merely available as an option. The low-volume Skylark thin-pillar coupe was dropped.

One innovation was MaxTrac, a device developed by AC Spark Plug Division which used a small computer and two sensors, one near the speedometer drive in the transmission and the other on the left front disc brake, to regulate wheelspin for greater traction. Automobile writers doubtless felt occasional need of a crash course in space age technology during these years. They did admirably however, throwing in exclamation points only when credulity was strained. Said *Road & Track* of MaxTrac, "Buick's system uses a black box to sense differences of speed between rear and front wheels: if the rear wheels get over 10% faster than the front the control system modulates engine power by interrupting the ignition! Interruption can take place up to fifty times per second." But a system that interrupted ignition was not compatible with the coming sophisticated emission systems. After two or three years, MaxTrac was gone.

In 1972, Buick built 688,557 cars in the calendar year (none in Canada for the first time since '51) and 679,921 in the model year.

In 1972, too, Buick offered sun roofs for the first time in decades, the Skylark Sun Coupe with a folding vinyl sun roof, gold-colored nameplate and special carpet colors of bright gold or bright red—and

Buicks for 1973, from the left: The Apollo, Riviera GS, Electra Limited, Centurion. Below: Advertising the car Lee Mays was most proud to introduce.

a power-operated steel sun roof on Riviera. Another styling option was a short vinyl top on the Skylark 350 coupe, a feature that would later carry the traditional coachbuilding term of landau.

But styling was given only a cursory nod in the Buick public relations releases this year.

A sign of the times, at the new-car introduction, was the curtain in Buick's auditorium opening to reveal two shiny Buicks, both with their front bumpers caved in. Previously, it would have been unthinkable to spotlight anything except a flawless showroom model. But on this day, auto writers surged forward to fondle a crinkled hood, run their hands over a dented bumper, examine a crunched grille. The damaged cars were displayed to back up Buick's claim that its bumpers met federal 1973 crash barrier standards a year early. The standards would require that cars be able to withstand a 5 mph barrier crash—equal to a 10 mph crash into a parked car—without damage to safety equipment. The standard did not require that the bumper itself withstand the impact without damage.

Emission control standards were also being tightened, and Buick introduced two new corporation-developed systems for emission control and combined them with modifications to the basic engine. The job of the engineering staff was not merely to meet the standards, but to meet them while retaining engine performance, no small feat. Buick's new controls were an integral air injection reactor system (AIR) on all 455 engines and, to meet California standards for oxides of nitrogen emissions, an exhaust gas recirculation system (EGR). Buick was the first GM division to use EGR. The function of AIR was to inject air into the exhaust ports to induce further burning of hydrocarbons and carbon monoxide. EGR was designed to dilute the incoming fuel-air mixture from the carburetor with exhaust gases to lower peak combustion temperatures, thus reducing the formation of oxides of nitrogen. Both AIR and EGR used internal passages in the intake manifolds and heads rather than external tubing to conduct air to the exhaust gas ports. EGR would be standard on all models the following year.

In July 1972, Buick completed its second biggest model run, 679,-

921, behind only the 738,814 of 1955.

The 1973 model year brought attractive new styling to Buick's intermediate line, and the name game was on again. Skylark was dropped. The intermediates were now called Century, reviving another famous name in Buick history. There was a luxury model named Regal. Another trim option was Century Luxus in formal coupe, sedan and wagon. With introduction of the new body style, the small convertible was dropped. Only one Buick softtop remained, Centurion.

The Regal, which Lee Mays would later claim as the model he was most proud to have introduced, was set apart with a more formal roofline, different rear quarter windows as well as a vertical pattern grille instead of the horizontal of the Century.

Buick had twenty-five models in LeSabre, Centurion, Century, Riviera, Electra and top-of-the-line Electra 225. On the big cars, styling revisions were in the front and rear, incorporating a new bumper system with hydraulic energy absorbers.

By '73 all Buicks had center pillars to meet federal requirements for occupant protection in rollovers, but Fisher Body still referred to some of the cars as "hardtops." Auto writers accused Fisher of changing the definition, for its officials were claiming that "hardtop" meant that the car did not have a frame going over the top of the door windows. But, the press observed, when the door was closed, the car looked a lot like a sedan.

In February 1973 new compacts for Buick, Olds and Pontiac were ready for announcement. Buick's, called the Apollo, went on display at the Chicago Automobile Show in February and in dealer showrooms in April. The car was assembled at GM Assembly Division plants in Norwood (Ohio) and Van Nuys (California), was 10.5 inches shorter than Century and, at 3277 pounds, 570 pounds lighter. It was offered in hatchback coupe, thin-pillar coupe and thin-pillar four-door. Apollo was on a 111-inch wheelbase, one inch less than the Century coupe, five less than the Century sedan. At $3200, it was priced to favorably fill the void in Buick showrooms between the Opel (about $2600) and the Century (about $3700). The standard

engine was the 250-cubic-inch Chevy six; optional was the Buick V-8. "Corporate gingerbread"—which was Chris Packard's phrase in *Motor Trend*—to the contrary, there was no denying the new Buick's parentage. Packard said the Apollo "may just be the best Nova yet" and suggested the Buick V-8 as the best engine choice. "When was the last time you saw a Buick V-8 torn down?" he quoted a friend as asking. "See, you can't remember because they just don't break."

Also in February, GM announced it would offer air bag passive restraints as an option on Buick Riviera and Electra, and Oldsmobile 98 and Toronado, in the 1974 model year. The year previous an experimental fleet of 1000 Chevrolets had been equipped with the devices. On December 6th, 1973, a blue Electra Limited rolled off the line at Factory 4 in Flint with the first Buick air bag. An Olds Toronado had been produced with the device the previous week. Air bags were expensive and controversial. After several years, little promotion and few sales, they were dropped, though in the early 1980's there would be renewed pressure for the feature.

Lee Mays retired at the end of 1972 and was succeeded as Buick general manager by George R. Elges, the forty-nine-year-old former general manager of Cadillac. A native of Erie, Pennsylvania, Elges had joined Cadillac in 1941 and graduated from General Motors Institute in Flint in 1950. Between 1964 and 1966 he had been assistant manufacturing manager and manufacturing manager at Buick. Then he went back to Cadillac as general manufacturing manager, becoming the head man of that division in July of 1969.

In contrast to the reserved Mays, Elges was an effervescent general manager. He was also, using his own words, an "incurable optimist." For a time it looked as though he would have plenty to be optimistic about. When the 1973 model year ended, production totaled 821,165 cars. The great model year record of 738,814 which Buick set under Ivan Wiles in 1955 had finally been surpassed.

Elges went to a Flint luncheon club and confidently predicted that Buick would break the 1955 calendar year record as well. Buick was booming. Onward and upward.

And then the Arabs turned off the oil.

Chapter Seventeen

MEETING THE NEW CHALLENGES

Under normal circumstances, Buick officials would have rejoiced over the statistics of 1973. The division set model year production and sales records and went on to break the calendar year production mark, building 826,206 cars—a handsome increase over the old record, set in 1955, of 781,296. (The U.S.-Canadian total was 803,-173 in '55; there was no Canadian Buick production in '73.)

But within a few weeks after the introduction of the 1974 models, an event in world politics sent sales tumbling. The sharp decline wiped out general manager George Elges' hopes—which had seemed certain of fulfillment—that the 1955 sales record of 744,861 would fall, too.

The price of gasoline had increased a dramatic thirty-nine percent in the first nine months of 1973. But that was just the beginning. On October 6th, war broke out in the Middle East. On October 16th, the Organization of Petroleum Exporting Countries (OPEC) announced a seventy percent increase in prices and the next day declared that its Arab members would cut production five percent each month until Israel withdrew from Arab territories taken in the 1967 war "and the legal rights of the Palestinian people are restored."

OPEC also declared that the United States and the Netherlands, because of their friendship with Israel, would be cut off completely. There is some doubt as to how effective the announced cutoff really was, but gas prices shot up and fuel was suddenly in short supply.

The impact on automobile sales, particularly big-car sales, was almost immediately devastating.

More than 20,300 people had been employed at Buick in Decem-ber of '73. But by early spring of 1974, more than half had been laid off for various periods as gasoline stations closed periodically around the country. Economic conditions were so uncertain that buying any car seemed risky.

In the midst of this period—a really frightening time for Buick—something interesting was going on behind the scenes. There are two stories, at least, about how it started. Jerry Rideout, Buick's public relations director, recalls that Elges, while touring dealerships across the country, was interviewed by a reporter in his hotel room in Pittsburgh. The reporter casually mentioned he was driving an old Buick with a V-6 engine and "I'll bet you wish you had it now." That set Elges to thinking about what had become of the V-6—and could it be the answer to Buick's problem?

The other version starts on a golf course in the Dominican Republic. Chief engineer Phillip C. Bowser, on vacation there in early December 1973, was playing a round with Richard E. Denzer of the GM Technical Center. The shock waves of the oil embargo were already being felt so it was inevitable that Bowser and Denzer would begin discussing ways Buick could do something about fuel economy.

Bowser wondered aloud what had happened to the tooling and dies for the old V-6. The pair continued playing golf. But the more Bowser thought about the V-6, the more excited he became. Finally he placed a call to Flint, to Clifford G. Studaker, assistant chief engineer for power trains. Could Studaker find out what happened to the V-6 machinery?

Studaker was more than a little interested. He had worked on the original development of the V-6, under Joe Turlay, and understood the economical little engine. Studaker turned to Donald F. Taylor, manager of production control, who found that the machinery Buick had sold was in a mothballed Kaiser Jeep plant in Toledo, Ohio.

Within a few weeks, Taylor was actively negotiating with American Motors—by then the new owner of Kaiser Jeep—to either buy engines from American Motors, lease the Toledo plant or buy the equipment back.

Meanwhile, Buick engineers were looking for a V-6 to tinker with. Kaiser Jeep wasn't building them anymore. Engineers called around to Flint junkyards and finally salvaged one of the old engines. There was no vacation for Buick engineers at Christmastime, 1973. By late December, word that Buick was interested in the engine was leaking internally, and on December 29th *The Flint Journal* published the first speculative article about the possibility of the V-6's return.

Edward N. Cole, GM's president, learned of Buick's idea. He called from Detroit: "I hear you're thinking of the V-6. Do you have one running in a car?" Buick engineers checked. Yes, they'd just gotten ten it installed.

Page preceding: 1976 Indianapolis 500 Pace Car. Buicks for 1974, from the top: Riviera, Regal Colonnade, Electra Limited Landau and LeSabre Luxus.

"Good," said Cole. "Bring it down here. I want to drive it—today."

About an hour later, Studaker showed up at the GM Building in Detroit with the car, and he and Cole drove it directly to Toledo to join in the continuing negotiations with American Motors. There were reports that Cole was particularly interested in the V-6 because it could fit into the newly planned Chevy Monza-Buick Skyhawk-Olds Starfire cars in place of the Wankel engine, if the rotary's development stalled—which it did, partially because of mediocre fuel economy.

The talks with American Motors took several turns. AMC considered building the engine and selling it to General Motors, but the firms couldn't come to terms on price. Finally, in March 1974, AMC agreed to sell the tooling back to GM and let GM build its own engine.

Buick was now faced with what seemed an impossible task—to bring the equipment back to Flint, reinstall it, re-engineer the engine for the latest pollution controls and for lead-free gasoline—a necessity first articulated by Ed Cole who was pushing the catalytic converter—and get it into production by late summer for the 1975 model-year start.

There were several helpful factors. American Motors had done a good job of mothballing the machinery in Toledo—it had been well-greased and was in good shape. And Buick engineers found they could set up the equipment quickly because the old anchors for it were still in the floor. The holes and depressions were covered merely by a thin layer of concrete which could be easily chipped away.

George R. Polen, who was placed in charge of the engineering redesign of the V-6, said he remembered that Buick set up a "war room" with charts indicating every step that had to be taken to get the engine launched. Robert J. Breeden, general manufacturing manager, took personal supervision of the overall project.

Since the V-6 was originally a sawed-off version of the Buick V-8, the pistons and much of the engine "dress" of the latest Buick V-8, including pollution controls, could be fit directly onto the redesigned V-6. The inherent imbalance of a 90-degree V-6 engine was largely overcome by tuning the motor mounts to isolate engine vibration from the body. (The building of an even-firing V-6 would not come until 1978.)

An American Motors top executive was later overheard to remark: "We thought the V-6 was rougher than a cob. But Buick has done a good job with it. They seem to have turned a sow's ear into a silk purse." A good quote, but hardly accurate. The V-6 had been a silk purse from its conception.

One of the built-in problems of getting a new engine ready for market is having it driven 50,000 miles so it can be certified by the Environmental Protection Agency. In the case of the Buick V-6, it was driven day and night at the GM proving grounds near Milford; when one driver took an hour off for lunch, another would take over.

By August 1st, 1974, Elges was able to announce that Buick was ready with its V-6 for 1975-model production, adding that "I have been in this business for more than thirty years and I have never heard of anyone setting up an engine line in that short space of time." It had been just 137 days. The norm was eighteen months.

Buick was making other moves to try to sell its cars in the dark days of the first fuel crunch. The writer, then *The Flint Journal's* automotive editor, was invited by the division to take a 1974 Electra on a trip to northern Michigan to see how far he could travel on one tankful of gas. Also on board were a young Buick test engineer (Gary A. White) and a public relations representative (David G. Gosler)— and a $2500 machine called a long-range fuel board which produced fuel economy readouts. The trip, mostly over freeways partially covered with snow in January 1974, was made at an average speed of about 55 miles per hour. The Electra, with 455-cubic-inch engine using regular gas, had fuel economy of about 15.5 miles per gallon (considered good at that time) and the tank of gas endured 386 miles—from Flint to Montreal River, Ontario (north of Sault Ste. Marie)—before the red warning light on the gas gauge flickered.

In the same month, Elges told a Flint luncheon club that he was looking for ways to convert to small car assembly in Flint (it didn't happen) and wanted to build more of Buick's intermediates there to get employees back to work. The Buick general manager also noted: "I wish I could tell you . . . that Buick is going to turn this thing around immediately and that the announced layoffs will not last very long—but I can't. But I can tell you I personally am spending ninety percent of my time trying to make it happen and some key Buick people are spending 100 percent of theirs trying for the same objective."

For the manager of a major manufacturing firm, Elges made a rare speech that day: "It's just possible that all of us have been playing the numbers game too long. Why should a nation such as ours, with six percent of the world's population, use one-third of the total world's energy? Much of what we have been doing can be summed up in one four-letter word—more. More electricity, more food, more cars, more of everything. In our business, if we sell 700,000 Buicks in one year, it's almost natural to think we've got to get 800,000 the next. Sure, it's great to set new goals and objectives—that's how we became a great industrial nation. But perhaps the time has come when we have to shift the emphasis from just more to moderation, with more moderate goals."

These were especially unusual words for a man from Buick. At 1974-model introduction the previous fall, Buick's general sales manager, O. Franklin Frost, pitching in for the ailing Elges, had pointedly mentioned "the large number of people" who were not ready to give up the benefits of larger cars, and emphasized that more than half of Buick's projected 1974 sales was expected to come from the standard and luxury Buicks. Frost suggested that if customers wanted both big cars and fuel economy, they could realize a twenty-three percent saving by driving an Electra at 50 mph instead of 70. Buick "challenges small car trend" was a headline in the *Detroit News*.*

From his hospital bed, Elges had indicated to a reporter his pleasure with the progress of the smaller Buick idea—"The Apollo is going great"—but at that point, like Frost, he spent more time talking big Buick, and the Riviera as "our bright hope for 1974."

"We've cleaned up the back end and made it more conventional," he said. Gone was the boattail effect that Lee Mays, and apparently a lot of potential customers, disliked. But now there was criticism that the Riviera, though no longer controversial, was entirely undistinguished. Gone too was the Centurion, never a popular model and one which had been confused in name with the Century. It was succeeded by LeSabre Luxus.

Both Riviera and LeSabre featured a pillared roof design with fixed rear side windows which had been introduced on GM intermediates the previous year. A four-door Regal was added. A new GM high-energy ignition system was standard with some engines, optional with others. It produced greater voltage than regular breaker or solid-state ignition systems, with more precise firing because the charge was distributed electronically, not mechanically, and added reliability because of its unitized construction.

There were new energy absorbing bumpers in the rear, steel-belted radial ply tires on all wheels, and a seatbelt interlock system that was soundly disliked. This last, required on all U.S. cars for the '74 model year, made it necessary for the driver and any right front passenger to buckle the combined lap-shoulder belt before the car would start. Critics complained that a heavy bag of groceries on the seat also required buckling up before a car would start, and backyard mechanics worked out ways to cheat the system.

But this had been an annoyance. The oil embargo had been a disaster, throughout the United States, and especially in Flint. Buick production plummeted from 826,206 in calendar 1973 to 400,262 in 1974. Model year production fell from 821,165 to 495,063.

"I've never seen a division make such a complete change in such a

---

*Frost retired at the end of 1973 and was succeeded by Robert D. Burger, who had been in the Olds sales department for twenty-four years. John D. Duffy, Jr. succeeded Burger in 1977.

short time," George Elges said during new-car introductions in September. For the 1975 model year, Elges had a lot to talk about—and it was, literally, small talk.

First, there was the introduction of the Skyhawk, shorter by twenty inches than any other model in the line. It had a ninety-seven-inch wheelbase and used the reconstituted V-6 engine. Like its cousins, the Oldsmobile Starfire (which also used the Buick V-6) and the Chevrolet Monza, the Skyhawk was derived from the basic H-body of the Chevy Vega and had some of the aerodynamic look of the

Chevrolet Camaro. All three cars were originally built only at Sainte Thérèse, Quebec, Canada. Perhaps the Skyhawk's greatest contribution to Buick was in the advertising use of a real hawk, which became identified with the entire line over the next few years—even, strangely, the Skylark.

Next, "for additional emphasis on smaller size cars," Elges said, "two familiar Buick names have been returned to the lineup." The division revived Skylark on a hatchback and regular coupe model of the compact Apollo, and reinstituted Special on a version of the Cen-

Buicks for 1975. This page: The Indianapolis 500 Pace Car and an ad for its replica; one of the forty convertibles provided for use by the Indy Festival Committee. Right, from the top: Skylark, Special and LeSabre.

tury coupe that was especially engineered for economy. The Apollo was available as a four-door sedan with Chevrolet-built straight-six standard, and in two coupe models with V-6 standard. The Century Special was a two-door with V-6 and weight reduction measures. The V-6 was also standard on other Century models including Regal, though Century wagons used the 350 V-8.

LeSabre, Electra and Riviera received some styling refinements and the Riviera was shortened three-and-a-half inches with redesign of the grille and bumpers. Most noticeable, and featured on all Elec-

tra and Riviera models and the Skyhawk coupe, were the new rectangular headlamps. Also new was a trim option on the Electra that was called Park Avenue: plush, pillowed velour with 60-40 split seats in front, a velour-covered console separating, and the same motif carried into the rear for the appearance of individual seats. Officials said the Park Avenue was the most prestigious car Buick had ever offered. Elges said it was his idea, and Rideout agrees. "Elges' strong forte was styling," noted Rideout. "The Park Avenue and the Landau top came from him."

But the biggest news from Buick for '75, of course, was the emphasis on its new smallness. And its economy. In the EPA's city-suburban driving cycle, Buick claimed fuel usage improvements ranging from thirteen percent on intermediates to twenty-nine percent on the compacts with V-6. In engineering tests, a Buick compact with V-6 averaged 20.4 miles per gallon; in proving ground tests, the V-6 was getting 15 mpg in city driving, 18.3 in city-suburban and 25 at a steady 55 miles per hour.

One reason was the catalytic converter.

Catalytic converters are exotic devices. A converter is basically a stainless steel can spliced into a car's exhaust system and filled with a catalyst, a substance that helps a chemical reaction take place without changing its own form in the process. Its initial job was to change hydrocarbons and carbon monoxide, which are pollutants, into water vapor and carbon dioxide, which aren't. The nice thing about the converter is that it takes the burden of cleaning the air from the engine, and therefore allows engineers to retune the engine for better performance and economy.

AC Spark Plug Division in Flint, a few miles from Buick, was chosen by GM president Ed Cole to develop the catalytic converter. AC's involvement began on December 9th, 1969, when the division's general manager, George W. Chestnut, was sitting with Cole on a GM prop-jet headed for Rochester, New York.

"I'd like you to find us an exhaust system," said Cole, who then launched into a discussion of the converters. Chestnut did not know what a catalytic converter was. He excused himself, walked to the rear of the plane where AC's chief engineer, Thomas E. Hustead, was seated, and said, softly: "I think you'd better join us."

Hustead blinked. "I can't even spell catalyst," he thought.

It was a top-level project all the way. Cole was intimately involved in it, visiting AC at least fifteen times in two years, and discussing the converter project on the phone with Hustead almost daily.

Cole began to have two identities at AC, one as GM president, another as GM's chief engineer. Therefore, he was referred to by two names. When the AC engineering staff talked about Cole as president, they called him Cole. When they talked about Cole as chief

Photographed for the Buick Motor Car Company, Flint, Michigan. U.S.A. Division of General Motors Corporation.

The day everything changed.

THE HORSE was more than sleek flanks, flaring nostrils and sinewy beauty. It represented a way of life. It was the status quo.

Ah, but the car. It was simply a machine trying to shoulder its way into a lifestyle that was still not completely at ease with machines.

There had to be a confrontation.
The machine had to be put in its place.
And so in some unremembered pasture, on some unremembered day, the people lined up to watch some unremembered horse defend their way of life.
What they saw was history.

It didn't matter that the car had won.
The mere fact that it was there was a victory.
The automobile had arrived. And the technology and tempo of an entire country—indeed, the entire world—had changed forever.

McCann-Erickson, Buick's advertising agency, created this ad exclusively for a special Bicentennial issue of Time magazine in 1976.
It struck a popular historic note with the public, won advertising's "Oscar," the national Cleo award, among other advertising honors.
It was later issued as a limited edition sepia print 13½'' x 19''. Photographer Reed Miles, Art Director John McCluney.

engineer, they referred to him as Eloc, Cole spelled backward. Conversationally, they could discuss Cole's mandates and Eloc's engineering opinions.

AC's staff tried to develop base metal (such as copper) catalysts, but finally acknowledged it would have to use platinum and palladium, which are "noble" metals available in quantity only from South Africa and the Soviet Union.

Flint was suddenly a city of major international business interest. The AC executive dining room looked and sounded like the United Nations, as representatives from Germany, France, Italy, England and Japan moved in and out. Hustead remembers meeting with a group of back-slapping Russians in the GM Building in Detroit one day. But GM decided not to buy from the Soviet Union. It wanted to sell all palladium, no platinum, and AC wanted mostly platinum, with little palladium.

The GM people were dealing with different kinds of people than they had ever talked to before. One was Sir Albert Robinson, a Churchillian figure from Johannesburg, South Africa. It turned out that he practically controlled the free world price of platinum and palladium. He went to Flint and stolidly refused to give GM any price break on these metals, no matter what the volume. He had his price, and GM could take it or leave it. GM would have to sign a ten-year contract for the metals whether it would need them for that long or not. And GM could not use the metals for anything except catalysts.

AC finally dealt with another man, Bing Jackson, who operated the Impala Mines in South Africa. But Bing and Sir Albert played tennis together in Johannesburg. GM finally agreed to pay $44 million a year for ten years, with an escalator clause, for its supply of platinum and palladium. It had nowhere else to go.

There was a great deal of concern within the industry about whether the cost of catalytic converters was worth the slightly cleaner air that would result. But Cole's enthusiasm for the converter prevailed, even though one catalyst expert at GM Research laboratories indicated the devices were still something of a mystery.

Dr. Richard Klimisch was quoted by Hugh Wells in "The Changing Challenge," a GM publication: "Catalysts have an aura of alchemy about them, black magic, even with chemists. The normal sequence of research and development is almost always turned around in catalyst technology. Somebody finds a catalyst maybe by a clumsy accident. Then we spend twenty years trying to find out why it works. I hesitate to say this, and I'll probably lose a lot of friends, but we really don't understand many catalysts."

Regardless, thanks to AC's ability to get the job done, GM was able to move from a situation of no converters on its 1974 cars to all converters on the 1975's.

As the industry changed, bringing the new technology of black magic to pollution controls, one of the standard options of the automobile from its earliest days was fading out.

In July 1975 a woman from Atlanta was almost in tears upon calling Buick headquarters in Flint and being told it was too late to order a 1975 Buick convertible. She was among about 200 people who made a late decision to buy a Buick softtop after learning it was about to be phased out. For most, it was too late. For the Atlanta woman, Buick officials scouted around dealerships and found one.

Since Buick had begun building cars with folding tops in 1909, it

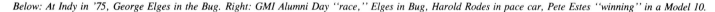

Below: At Indy in '75, George Elges in the Bug. Right: GMI Alumni Day "race," Elges in Bug, Harold Rodes in pace car, Pete Estes "winning" in a Model 10.

had produced 1,028,798 of them, about one out of every seventeen Buicks. The last two, LeSabres, were built July 18th, 1975, at the GM Assembly Division plant in Fairfax, Kansas. (To arrive at the total figure, Buick officials counted early cars listed as roadsters as the first convertibles, but actually there were removable tops available for Buicks going back to 1904, maybe 1901.)

With the end of the '75 model year, the convertible era was all but over at General Motors. Cadillac went one more year with its Eldorado softtop and Corvette continued to offer a detachable top, but Buick, Chevrolet, Oldsmobile and Pontiac would make no more.

At Buick, convertible production had reached its peak in 1967 when 46,528, about ten percent of Buick output, were built. From that time, demand fell steadily until it hit 3627 in 1974. Output in 1975 totaled 4559.

The death of the convertible was blamed on safety requirements and concerns, cost, air conditioning, vandalism, vinyl tops that made coupes look more like convertibles, and high-speed freeways. Advertising emphasis was also no longer heavy on top-down models. Whatever the reasons, the fact was indisputable—the true convertible was gone. There are a lot of people who still mourn its demise.

The convertible from Flint was given an impressive final salute, however. It played a significant role during the nostalgic period for Buick which began in the mid-1970's and carried through Buick's 75th anniversary year of 1978. Forty gleaming white LeSabre convertibles with special decals were shipped to Indianapolis Speedway in the spring of 1975 for use by the Indy 500 Festival Committee.

Buick had been chosen to pace the racing classic that year. The pace car itself, however, was a Century Custom coupe, with red, white and blue decals, a 455-cubic-inch engine of 325 horsepower and two removable roof panels installed by Hurst Performance, Inc., of Brighton, Michigan. (Buick built 1800 pace car replicas with the decals and Hurst hatches, but with 350 V-8's instead of the modified 455.)

Indianapolis saw another Buick that year, the famous racing Buick Bug. It was shipped from the Sloan Museum in Flint to the Speedway, where Greg Fauth, a Buick buff from Flint, and Donald Mates, a restorer from Chicago, tuned it up after Jim Johnson of the museum staff set it running. George Elges and the writer both took turns driving the car around the speedway track that had not yet been fully completed when Louis Chevrolet and Wild Bob Burman had shown up there with two Bugs in 1910. The surviving Bug is believed to be Louis Chevrolet's.

Elges had so much fun at Indianapolis that he was easily persuaded to take part in another event on June 22nd, 1975. In a "race" along streets surrounding General Motors Institute in Flint as part of GMI

Buicks for 1976. Above: Skyhawk. Below: Century. Below right: Special. Above right, from the left: Singer Marty Robbins, the Indy Speedway's Tony Hulman, and Buick general manufacturing manager Robert J. Breeden.

Alumni Day, Elges in the Buick Bug was beaten by General Motors president Elliott M. "Pete" Estes, who was behind the wheel of a 1910 Buick-owned Model 10 which Buick later donated to the Sloan Museum. Elges said the race was not fixed, but observed that "Mr. Estes is my boss." Pete Estes finished with his shirt soaked with antifreeze, the result of the radiator cap coming off mid-race. Finishing third was GMI president Harold P. Rodes—in the 1975 Buick pace car.

But the most interesting exercise in nostalgia for Buick during the decade was a project to tie in with the 1976 U.S. bicentennial. The Federal Government urged communities to develop their own historical projects to commemorate the country's 200th birthday, but nobody said you had to commemorate an event of 200 years earlier.

A group of Flint men, with no urging from Buick, decided to go back to 1904. The idea began with Charles E. Hulse who, ironically, is a collector of curved-dash Oldsmobiles, though a dabbler in Buick history. He thought an effort should be made to recreate the original Flint Buick, the famous car that Walter Marr and Thomas Buick had driven from Flint to Detroit and back in July of '04.

It was not a preposterous notion. Hulse knew, from two existing photographs, that the original Flint Buick was hardly more than an engine, chassis and buggy seat. He also knew that none of the thirty-seven Model B Buicks built in 1904 is known to exist, but that the Sloan Museum had one of the two known 1904 Buick engines. Fred Hoelzle, an early Buick employee, had found it in a shipping crate at Buick years earlier and persuaded company officials to keep it.

Furthermore, the museum owned a poorly restored 1905 Buick with a chassis scarcely different from the '04. It was a Model C originally owned by Fred A. Aldrich, Durant-Dort Carriage Company secretary, and rescued from a field by early Buick dealer Ed Lunt.

Hulse's proposal: Put the '04 engine together with the '05 chassis, add a buggy seat and some other components, using the two photos and some early descriptions as guides, and take the result on a commemorative Flint-Detroit roundtrip using the 1904 route of Marr and Tom Buick. Local antique car owners were interested in Hulse's idea. A committee was formed, with Hulse and Greg Fauth as co-chairmen. James L. Johnson, the museum's technician, and his father, Gerald Johnson, did much of the work.

The re-creation was a labor of love. Eventually the committee decided not to use the chassis from the Aldrich car, but did use both of its axles, transmission and gear levers. (The museum has another '05 Model C, so it was not dismantling a needed display model.) A new chassis was built. The car was barely completed in time to leave Flint on July 9th, 1976, exactly seventy-two years from the date Marr and Tom Buick had started out. The replica, with no windshield, no body and no fenders—just like the original—required four-and-a-half hours to travel the sixty miles to Detroit, mostly because everyone who had a hand in it, plus the writer, took a turn at the wheel.

The car was met by officials and the press at the Detroit Press Club on Howard—the street where, between 10th and 12th, Buick had been in '02-'03. The following morning, the Johnson father-son team started on the trip back to Flint, their mission being to beat the Marr-Buick time of 217 minutes for the same run on July 12th, 1904. The replica left at 10:00 a.m. from the GM Building in Detroit. "We ought to beat Marr because we've got paved roads and an engine that's rested for about seventy years," said Bob Burnham, a committee member who drove the press convertible.

But the replica began developing problems—carburetor adjustments were needed on the road to Lake Orion, a cotter pin sheared near Metamora, the car stalled in downtown Oxford and again in rural Lapeer County. Finally, it began running smoothly and the Johnsons put up one last burst of speed. A small crowd was waiting at East First and Saginaw streets in downtown Flint as the replica arrived—twelve minutes later than Marr and Buick in 1904. It didn't matter. The replica was lined up on First Street so it could be photographed in exactly the same spot as the Marr-Buick car had been in '04, and then it was retired to the Sloan Museum, where it can be seen today—perhaps a unique example of an antique car recreated for a museum.

The 1904 Buick was an example of a piece of Buick history

recreated in the 1970's. But another part of history was lost. Ironically, when the Buick (now UAW) Freeway was built on a north-south path through Flint, one of the homes in its path was that of James H. Whiting, the man who brought Buick to Flint in 1903. It was razed in 1973. But Flint, awakened to an interest in its heritage, worked to save another historic building: the original office of Billy Durant, the Durant-Dort Carriage company. It was named a national historic landmark and plans were made for the raising of

funds for its renovation.

For the 1976 model year, more contemporary news was made when Buick concluded, in a last-minute decision, to use the V-6 engine in one of its full-sized cars, the LeSabre.

Elges commented that when some of the division's bright young engineers first tried out the idea on chief engineer Phil Bowser, "he almost threw them out of his office." Describing the sequence of events at the press preview in September 1975, he added, "but they kept after him, and finally Phil agreed to try it and that was really all it took." The LeSabre, the only six-passenger car then on the market with a V-6, was perhaps the world's most fuel-efficient full-size car, claimed Elges. It was getting about 21 mpg on the highway and 16 in city driving tests.

At its re-introduction, the V-6 had been standard on ten Buicks; for the new model year, it was standard on fifteen of the twenty-eight models in the line. And the V-6 had improved performance, a newly calibrated carburetor with a metering system and fuel level control tailored specifically for it. "It still sounds funny though," wrote Bob Hall in *Motor Trend*. "The noise of one of these V-6's is rather hard to describe, but it was, well, strange enough to make some people ask us if the car was rotary powered."

The sound of sales being rung up in Buick dealerships was, well, kind of strange too. But welcome. Elges credited the V-6 with the division's ten percent increase in sales—a modest improvement but one indicating that Buick was headed in the right direction.*

For 1976 the rectangular headlamps introduced previously on some models were now awarded to LeSabre, Regal and Century as well. Century and Regal had lower body sheet metal with flared wheel openings front and rear, and new grilles. Styling changes on the Electra, Riviera and LeSabre were limited to new grilles and the new headlamps, plus interior modifications. With the convertible gone from the lineup, Buick offered four special roof treatments: electric sunroof on Electra, Riviera, Regal and Century; the "astro-roof," a heavily tinted glass sunroof with sliding shade on Electra and Riviera; a fixed-glass roof with wide brushed metal molding on Skyhawk; and Hurst hatches on Century Custom and Regal coupes.

Placing the V-6 in the LeSabre wasn't the only example of moving more fuel-efficient engines into bigger cars. The same young engineers who convinced Bowser to do that came back to him with the idea of using the 350 V-8 instead of the 455 V-8 in the Electra.

Hurrah for the red, white and Buick.

Old Glory's colors are in great abundance these days. Well gosh, why not? It's a big year for the good ol' U.S. of A. There's something else in great abundance these days. It's Buick's Century. Which would suggest that something interesting is happening to America's automotive set of values. Think of it. All that affection and popularity for a Buick.

Well, Century has changed a lot of thinking about what Buicks are all about.

See, this Buick is smaller. Sleek. With practical considerations like High-Energy Ignition, standard radial tires, and a super little V-6 engine that has caused quite a stir all by itself.

Just how practical these considerations are can be brought to light by the following. A Buick Century, equipped with standard V-6 engine and available automatic transmission, got an estimated 25 mpg in the EPA highway test and 17 mpg in the city test (for California ratings, see your Buick dealer).

Of course, these are only estimates. The mileage you get may vary according to your driving habits, the condition of your car, and its available equipment.

But in a year where belt-tightening is as prevalent as flag-waving...well, Century has proven itself to be something America needs.

But because it's a Buick, it can take care of wants as handily as it satisfies needs.

For all it's pragmatism, Century has smoothness, quietness, comfort, good looks, and plenty of little touches the kinds of things people want, whether the car they buy is intended to help them economize or not.

Anyway, it really isn't so surprising that the mid-sized Buick Century has been such a successful automobile. People who have to cope with 1976 economics have become fairly adept at spotting a good thing.

Join the parade.

BUICK *Dedicated to the Free Spirit in just about everyone.*

*Elges also pushed for a more youthful Buick image, which he felt was assisted by the emblem of the Skyhawk, which was now known as "The Free Spirit Hawk." A basswood carving of the hawk by Georg Keilhofer of Frankenmuth, Michigan was photographed for the cover of the 1976 national sales catalogue.

Left: Buick celebrates the Bicentennial in an advertisement in '76, and its 75th Anniversary with fireworks in 1978. Above and below: The 1904 Buick re-creation for the Bicentennial, with Gerald Johnson and his son Jim in dusters, on the road, and upon arrival in Flint on East First Street near Saginaw. In the photograph above, Brennan Smith is at left.

That idea worked too, though it was less of a surprise.

Bowser says it's a little strong to say he almost threw the young engineers out of his office on the V-6/LeSabre idea, though he acknowledges he was none too encouraging. One of his questions was whether the car would have enough performance, although a more important consideration was that Buick already had more demand for the V-6 than the capacity to build it. But he added: "I didn't tell them to forget about it. We've got a good performing young group, and I like to encourage them."

George Polen, originally in charge of the engineering redesign of the V-6 and by 1975 staff engineer of advanced design, said that "Bowser studied our analysis and the vehicle potential, and he also agreed we should build and test a car."

A few weeks later—it was now July of 1975—Bowser was test-driving a 1976 Buick compact on the Buick Freeway (not yet open to the public) when he noticed a '76 LeSabre coming up behind him.

"What's that doing here? I thought we were testing compacts today," Bowser remarked to his companion, Cliff Studaker. Replied Studaker: "It's a job with a V-6 that the boys cooked up for you to drive."

Bowser tried out the car and was impressed.

"He loved it," said Polen. "It had the performance of a Regal." Already another assistant chief engineer, Carlisle R. "Cardy" Davis, had discussed a V-6 LeSabre with Wes Brush of Buick's sales department and learned of the department's enthusiasm for the idea. LeSabre had been selling well, but in a shrinking market for full-size cars, and the idea clicked of giving it an image as a full-size car with gas economy. Before the month was over, Elges had driven the car and ordered it into production as soon as possible. Although a number of people were involved in the V-6/LeSabre package, two young engineers, David Fulks and Edward Stadler, were among the key men in producing that package.

The V-6 engine had several advantages over the straight six. Because of its compact size, it could be fit into smaller engine compartments, an advantage that would be more important on the smaller cars of a few years later. It was also of lighter weight, and Buick engineers said a V-6 got better fuel economy because of more even fuel distribution with the carburetor closer to all pistons than in the straight six. Said Joe Turlay: "The 90-degree V-6 had the best inherent fuel distribution of any engine I ever tested. With a dual carburetor, the short manifold branches and even firing on each bank, nearly ideal conditions resulted."

A more quotable analysis of the V-6's fuel economy came from Phil Bowser. "We give some of the credit to serendipity," he said. "It's like a kiss in the dark. You don't know where it came from, but you like it."

Only a few days after the new Buicks were placed on the market, Elges was promoted to group vice-president in charge of the GM car and truck group, and David C. Collier was named general manager of Buick.

Collier had been president and general manager of GM of Canada since 1973, and was a Canadian by birth, a native of Hardisty, Alberta. He had earned a teaching certificate from the University of Alberta in 1948 and graduated from the University of Montana in 1956. Later he received a master of business administration from the Harvard Graduate School of Business. Collier joined the GM Financial Staff in Detroit in 1957 as a summer trainee and became a member of the comptroller's staff in 1958. In 1965 he was named assistant

comptroller of GM of Canada, and in 1971 treasurer of General Motors.

Because he had risen from humble beginnings—in his youth he had worked in a cement plant and handled milk cans in addition to polishing marble in a monument factory—Collier was named a Horatio Alger award winner in 1979.

In the same group of personnel changes which brought Collier to Flint, Bowser was named general manager of Delco Moraine Division and Lloyd E. Reuss (pronounced Royce) succeeded him as Buick chief engineer.

Tall and reserved, Collier contrasted sharply with the shorter and more outgoing Elges. But Collier was also considered a strong general manager, and in his first interview in Flint said he would try to project a quality image at Buick. The division received a boost in that direction with the appointment of Reuss, who was thirty-nine when he arrived in Flint, and who has been called by Buick engineers a "fantastic" chief. Said one of his assistants: "Reuss had a good perspective. He could see the big picture. We had turbochargers when he came, but we wouldn't have had the turbo without him."

What he meant was that Reuss was open to suggestion. Reuss joined Buick just in time to be handed the problem of what to do for the 1976 Indianapolis 500. Buick was the first automaker since Packard in 1916-1917 to provide the pace car two years in a row.

Buick's engineers and the division's sales department were intrigued with the possibility of coming up with a V-6 that could meet the strict requirements for Indy—90 miles an hour by the middle of the third turn, 110 mph coming out of the fourth, and at least 120 by the time the pace car reached the pit entrance.

For this kind of performance, Buick engineers decided, a turbocharger would be necessary.

The idea of using the V-6 in the pace car, and boosting its power with a turbocharger, actually preceded Reuss. In fact, according to Cliff Studaker, the idea of turbocharging the V-6 began with a Boy Scout Explorer Post, sponsored by Buick Engineering, that was formed in 1974.

As a project, the post turbocharged a V-6 to try to get the performance of a V-8. Buick engineering had done some development work on a turbocharged 401-cubic-inch V-8 in the mid-1960's, so some background was available. The post's project was successful. "The engine's performance was impressive," Studaker said.

When Buick's advance design engineers, under Polen, looked around for a way to boost the pace car's V-6, they looked back on the Explorer Post's success and decided to give it a try. By now Reuss was chief engineer and supported the idea wholeheartedly. On October 29th, all Buick dealers were notified that the V-6 would power

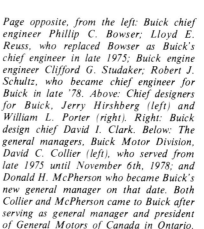

Page opposite, from the left: Buick chief engineer Phillip C. Bowser; Lloyd E. Reuss, who replaced Bowser as Buick's chief engineer in late 1975; Buick engine engineer Clifford G. Studaker; Robert J. Schultz, who became chief engineer for Buick in late '78. Above: Chief designers for Buick, Jerry Hirshberg (left) and William L. Porter (right). Right: Buick design chief David I. Clark. Below: The general managers, Buick Motor Division, David C. Collier (left), who served from late 1975 until November 6th, 1978; and Donald H. McPherson who became Buick's new general manager on that date. Both Collier and McPherson came to Buick after serving as general manager and president of General Motors of Canada in Ontario.

the 1976 Indy 500 pace car.

Kenneth R. Baker, assistant staff engineer of advanced design, heading a group which included Thomas F. Wallace and Jeff K. Lane, senior project engineers of advanced design, now had the job of putting together a package that would do the job. While they concentrated on the engine principally, they also looked for ways to lighten the car. They succeeded in reducing weight by 470 pounds, excluding the change from V-8 to V-6, by using aluminum hood, trunk lid, fenders and radiator supports, eliminating hydraulic bumper reinforcements, side guard beams, catalytic converter, spare tire and jack, and employing magnesium wheels and a lightweight bumper.

The 231-cubic-inch engine, the first V-6 ever used in any Indy pace car, had its horspower rating tripled. The turbocharger, supplied by Rajay Industries, accounted for the greatest horsepower boost. Other gains were made by using a specially-calibrated quadrajet carburetor, modified ignition, special spark plugs and modified camshaft and cylinder heads. The stock cast-aluminum pistons were replaced with pistons of forged aluminum of a lower compression ratio, the Turbo-Hydra-Matic transmission was the one usually used with Buick's big 455 V-8, and there was a higher ratio rear axle and a modified suspension system with higher rate springs, larger stabilizer bars, fast ratio power steering and heavy duty shock absorbers. Aerodynamic drag was reduced by using spoilers on the front bumper and trunk lid.

The car which resulted from all this was one that could get the Indy job done. Easily. In some tests it topped 130 mph by the time it reached the pit entrance.

No replicas of the pace car were built, but Buick did produce 1290 Centuries for the market with the pace car colors—orange, black and gray—and tape emblems, some with twin removable Hurst hatches, but none (except the one back-up car) with the special engine and weight-reduction features. Both the '75 and '76 pace cars are in the Sloan Museum.

The turbocharged V-6 was not yet ready for the marketplace for the 1977 model year, but Buick had other things to talk about. General Motors chairman Thomas A. Murphy had announced the previous fall that nearly three out of every four cars sold by GM by 1980 would be in the weight class with compacts, and Buick was the first of the GM family to introduce the first of these, because it was the first division to show off its '77 lineup.

Smaller, but not small, was the word for the new Electra, LeSabre and Riviera, all scaled down. LeSabre was ten inches shorter, 2.7 inches narrower and 665 pounds lighter than the previous year's model, and similar downsizing was performed on the other big Buicks.

On Skylark, Century and LeSabre, Buick offered a special economy package with a specially-calibrated V-6 with vacuum spark regulator, and a 2.56 rear axle ratio. Five engines were available for '77, the V-6 and four V-8's, including a new 301-cubic-inch unit built by Pontiac.

Styling changes included pillared roofs and doors with full frames around the glass on all Electra, LeSabre and Riviera models; new front-end design on Electra and LeSabre—and portholes—and new

Buicks for 1977. Left: Riviera. Above: LeSabre Custom. Below: Regal.

grilles on Century, Regal and Skyhawk. Also offered was a new factory option: citizens' band radio.*

Things began to look good in Flint. The year following they looked even better.

In August 1977, Buick introduced its 1978 Regal Sport Coupe with turbocharged V-6 engine. A turbocharged LeSabre coupe

---

*In 1941, incidentally, Buick had a short-wave option built in the AM radio.

quickly followed. The division wasn't the first in GM ever to offer a turbocharger. Oldsmobile had had one on its old F-85 and Chevrolet on the Corvair Spyder. But neither of those had lasted very long and, now, Buick was leading a vanguard on turbocharging in the fuel-economy era.

"Don't call it a turbo," one Buick engineer was quoted as saying to a reporter, "or people will get the idea it's a muscle car or our answer to the Porsche Turbo, and it's neither. With this car we're trying to be gymnasts, not muscle men."

Reuss was less cautious. The Regal Sport Coupe was "the performance car of the future," he said, because it was an economy car too since the turbocharger "works only when you want it to." In other words, at normal highway speeds, the device wasn't operative, but with the depression of the accelerator, the turbocharger pumped a heftier air-fuel mixture into the cylinders, boosting power from a normal 105 bhp to 150 with two-barrel carburetor, 165 with four-barrel. The key to the system was the "Turbo Control Center," a small electronic control that detected engine knock and advanced or retarded the spark as needed for top-efficiency running. Collier said it was a first in the auto industry. Automotive writers found it intriguing. And Buick's newest advertising slogan fit well—"A Little Science. A Little Magic."

The engine used was the 231 V-6—also called the 3.8-liter V-6 as metrification took hold in the industry—and the aim with turbocharging was to extract the same performance from it as the 350 V-8, while not diminishing the V-6's fuel economy. The general consensus was that this had been achieved. "This is the car that will lead Detroit down the road to turbocharger happiness," predicted *Car and Driver.* "Nice work," said *Road & Track.*

Buick was taking no chances. Cardy Davis, by now director of reliability and quality control, ordered each turbocharged V-6 Buick coming off the line to be road tested for two miles. Special arrangements were made with the city to do this on a street near the Flint Buick complex. It had probably been fifty years since any major American carmaker has instituted such a program. But, as Davis boasted a little, "Buick is pioneering a new era in the industry, the turbocharging of a family car, and we are going to make certain these cars are right before they go into the hands of the customers."

Besides the turbocharger, the V-6 for '78 was notable for another reason. It was now an even-firing engine, the result of Cliff Studaker's direction. There hadn't been time for its development when the decision for the engine's resuscitation had been made a few years earlier. In its earlier configuration, the 90-degree V-6 used a crankshaft with three crankpin throws spaced 120 degrees apart, with firing impulses coming at 90- and 150-degree intervals. This characteristic of uneven timing spacing resulted in idle smoothness problems. Now, by "splitting" each crankpin by an included angle of 30 degrees, the throw was advanced 15 degrees for the cylinders on the right bank and delayed 15 degrees for the cylinders on the left, and equal intervals of 120-degree timing between cylinders were produced. A clever idea. It made for a smoother engine.

There were now three V-6's in the Buick lineup: the 3.2-liter version standard on all intermediates except the wagon, the 3.8-liter and the turbocharged 3.8-liter.

Downsizing continued. The Regal Sport Coupe, with striking new styling, was almost a foot shorter and 560 pounds lighter than its predecessor. It was mounted on a 108.1-inch wheelbase, four inches shorter than previously, had an overall length of 199.6 inches compared with 209.8, and weighed 3142 pounds compared with 3701. And better design resulted in more interior room.

Like the Regal, the Century was also more than a foot shorter and about 600 pounds lighter than previous models, as were the intermediates of all GM cars that year. A sloping "aerodynamic" rear end design, which turned out to be unpopular, was a styling feature of all the intermediates except Regal. Century was offered in three lines—Special, Custom and Limited. Skyhawk got new trim, Skylark and LeSabre had new interior decor and a new grille, and the Electra and Riviera had a new grille and taillight design. The Electra Park Avenue was now available as a coupe.

In February 1978, at the Chicago Automobile Show, Buick unveiled a 75th anniversary edition of the Riviera, the LXXV Riviera. This car, of which 2899 were produced, had a lower body in silver and the upper in black, including a black hood and trunk lid and black vinyl top. The interior was finished in gray leather with instrument panel trim plates in dark brushed silver and a sport steering wheel with dark brushed silver accent.

Buick held its 75th anniversary bash that June, in Flint, of course, and to coincide with the national meet of the Buick Club of America at the Buick Administration Building. Some 36,000 people visited the Buick complex during an open house, more than 600 antique Buicks paraded through downtown, and Buick spent more than $25,-000 to put on the largest and most spectacular fireworks display ever seen in Flint. The finale was 648 aerial shells, fired three at a time, then six at a time, then nine, then twelve, with the last burst 150 aerial explosions.

Flint and Buick had a lot to celebrate. In the 1977 model year, Buick had set records for U.S. production (845,234), U.S. plus Canadian production (877,622) and Flint production (416,459). In the 1977 calendar year, the Flint plant set a record (393,045), though the calendar U.S. record (826,206) had been set in 1973 and the U.S.-

Buicks for 1978. The LeSabre Sport Coupe, with turbocharged V-6 engine.

Canadian record (845,335) was set in '76. But calendar 1977's U.S. total (801,202) was the fourth best in history, and the U.S.-Canadian total (824,616) was third best. And 1978 totals in various categories would rank between the second and fourth best. Just as in 1953, when it celebrated its 50th, Buick could enjoy its 75th anniversary from a perspective of prosperity.

Collier was promoted to executive in charge of General Motors' new finance group on November 6th, 1978, and was succeeded as Buick general manager by Donald H. McPherson, also a native of Alberta, Canada. It was the second time McPherson had succeeded Collier. When the latter had moved to head Buick in 1975, McPherson had followed him as president of GM of Canada. Fifty-five years old and with a background in design, McPherson had been chief engineer of Chevrolet from 1966 to 1972, when he was named director of engineering with responsibility for all design decisions concerning Chevrolet cars and trucks.

Two days after Collier's promotion, Lloyd Reuss was promoted to chief engineer at Chevrolet. His successor at Buick was Robert J. Schultz, forty-eight years old, who had been with Oldsmobile for twenty-two years before being sent to Flint in 1977 to head the emissions control system project center at AC Spark Plug Division.

In 1979 there was a new Riviera and immediately it was clear that Riviera was back at last as a styling leader, with engineering to match. Some Buick officials called it the best Buick ever, and magazine writers were inclined to agree.

The '79 Riviera came in two models, the standard version with 350 V-8 engine supplied by Oldsmobile, and the S Type with turbocharged Buick V-6 engine, along with stiffer springs and anti-sway bars, revised shock absorber valving, wider steel-belted radial tires and a more responsive power steering. There was independent

Regal Coupe had new styling.

suspension front and rear. And, optionally, four-wheel disc brakes. But most significant of all, the '79 Riviera was the first Buick to feature front wheel drive. An old rumor finally true.

The S Type was named "car of the year" by *Motor Trend* magazine, the first Buick to get that trophy since the original V-6 Special of 1962. Reported that magazine: "The Riviera S offers luxury with taste and performance with comfort. Though it is plush, it rides and handles extremely well for a car of its type. Its styling is crisp and modern, but not at the expense of utility . . . though the Riviera is certainly not a car for the masses, it offers excellent value, especially when compared to cars costing twice as much."

The manufacturer's list price for the standard Riviera was $10,-371. The base price for the S Type was $10,648. A full run down the option list could bring the sticker price to more than $14,000.

Car and Driver noted that although the new Riviera was derived from the same body as the totally new Oldsmobile Toronado and Cadillac Eldorado, "the Riviera somehow manages to make the others look like rather plain sisters. It is the first of the square-cut GM designs—the look originated on the Cadillac Seville—that really works. . . . The Riviera is somehow plumper, more substantial and far happier with itself. They even speak wistfully of it at Oldsmobile, which should tell you something of its appeal." Concluded the magazine: "The steering is quick and tight . . . and the ride tells you there is a road underneath. Traditional Buick buyers will hate it. We think it has a shot at being the neatest car of Detroit's new crop. After a long dry spell, it's safe to say the Riviera is back from the brink."

Road & Track quibbled a little, complaining about the use of warning lights instead of gauges on the instrument panel, and the fact that the car was a four-seater whereas, with a little better interior

design, it could have seated five. But generally the magazine was impressed and called the turbo V-6 "the car's one best feature."

George Elges, Buick's manager when the car was being planned, said he had asked the designers what they would do if they had a free hand on the new Riviera. "They told me they would hark back to the old original classic of 1963," he remarked.

According to Jerry Hirshberg, who took both credit and blame for the boattail Riviera, the advance work on the '79 E-body cars—Riviera, Eldorado, Toronado—was done in David North's advanced design studio, but Bill Mitchell was principally responsible for the design development. Hirshberg, who would be succeeded as chief designer for Buick in 1980 by William L. Porter, designed the front end himself. David I. Clark, who is credited with designing the high-styled 1978 Regal, said he tuned up the exterior after North did the basic body architecture.

"The first Riviera [1963] had a fantastic body," said Clark. "It inspired the '79 Riv."

Chuck Jordan, GM design chief, agrees: "You can see just a hint of the '63 Riviera in the 1979 version, notably in the rear fender."

Hirshberg calls the 1979 Riviera "a truly successful style, maybe the last of that kind of statement. It has a high personality. Of any of the E-bodies, it has the most identity."

Although the standard version of both Riviera and Riviera S sported warning lights instead of gauges, buyers who wanted to spend an extra $700 or so could get trip monitor digital instrumentation in mid-model year. Buick's answer to *Star Trek*, with this computerized system, a group of buttons could be pushed for digital readouts of such data as fuel range, trip odometer, engine temperature and rpm, speed, voltage and travel computations such as miles remaining on a trip and estimated time of arrival based on the average speed maintained to that point.

Less exotic and standard features included push-button windows, air conditioning, AM-FM stereo radio, automatic level control, six-way power seats, electric door locks, tinted glass, cornering lights, side-window defrosters and remote outside rearview mirrors.

For the first time since it was introduced, the Riviera was not built in Flint in 1979. All three of the E-body cars (including Toronado and Eldorado) were produced at the same GM assembly division plant in Linden, New Jersey. In the fifteen years the Riviera was built in Flint, production ranged from a high of 52,872 in the 1969 model year to a low of 17,300 in 1975.

Aside from the Riviera, changes on the 1979 lineup were mostly limited to styling and engineering refinements. One new model was the Century Turbo Coupe, bringing the turbo V-6 to the Century line for the first time. The model included front and rear spoilers, first 319 used by Buick on the 1976 Indianapolis 500 pace car, some special lettering and paint, and special handling and suspension equipment.

In the spring of 1979, the new General Motors X-body cars, downsized models with front wheel drive, were introduced. These corporate cars, the Buick Skylark, Pontiac Phoenix, Oldsmobile Omega and Chevrolet Citation, were initially produced at GM's assembly plant at Willow Run, Michigan. They were the result of the most expensive new-car development program in GM's history, $1.5 billion, not including $1 billion in new production facilities. In the new reality of high fuel prices, these cars, which would achieve about 27 mpg on the EPA city-highway driving cycle, would carry GM well into the 1980's.

The standard engine was a 2.5-liter four-cylinder made by Pontiac, the optional unit a 2.8-liter V-6 from Chevrolet. The X-body cars had a 104.9-inch wheelbase, about six inches shorter than their 1979 counterparts, and weighed about 2500 pounds, a reduction of about 800 pounds.

Planning for these models had begun in 1974, during the worst of the first energy crisis. Originally the X-body was intended only for Chevrolet and Pontiac, but by 1976 Buick and Oldsmobile were included in the thinking.

Buick's design work on the basic corporate body shell, led by David Clark, was successful. The Skylark, offered in two-door and four-door body styles and Limited and Sport Coupe trim options, as well as standard, was considered by many observers to be the most attractive of the new corporate cars.

Introduced just as a new gasoline shortage and higher gasoline prices were settling in, the X-cars proved so popular that, within a few months, orders were backed up a half year, even though dealers refused to discount from the list price and in some cases were adding hundreds of dollars to it. Although the Skylark initially listed at $4769, a customer could spend well over $8000, even by adding only the most popular options. And there were upward price adjustments during the model run.

Later there would be widely publicized controversies about the X-car brakes, but most of the early reaction to these cars was very positive. Writers and customers alike seemed pleased with the new models' interior room, performance and appearance.

In the fall of 1979, Buick had something else new: a diesel-powered car (5.7-liter V-8 engine made by Oldsmobile) as an option on Electra coupes and sedans and Electra and LeSabre Estate Wagons. A 4.1-liter V-6, a bigger displacement version of the 3.8-liter V-6, was standard on Electra. The new Electra was about 200 pounds lighter than its 1979 counterpart.

Also for 1980, the Century aeroback (fastback) design was

Buicks for 1979, from the top: Riviera S Type, Skyhawk, Century Turbo Coupe. Buicks for 1980, right, from the top: Electra Limited coupe, Century Limited sedan, LeSabre Limited coupe, Electra Park Avenue sedan.

replaced with a notchback in the four-door, though coupes retained the fastback styling. Riviera, Skylark and Skyhawk were minimally changed, and Skyhawk was dropped before the end of the calendar year. Buick traded Skyhawk for more Skylark production.

In the first few months of 1980, Buick was the only U.S. automaker to sell more cars than in the same period a year earlier. The division set all-time sales marks for January and February. By mid-summer 1980, while the entire U.S. auto industry was in a slump—causing huge losses at Ford, government assistance to Chrysler and red ink at GM—the Buick division was performing better than any other of the Big Three marques, comparing sales with year-earlier figures. General sales manager John D. Duffy, Jr. credited the V-6 engine and styling for the relative success in a recessionary period. The V-6 had turned around Buick's old image as a producer of gas-guzzling cars; the division was the only automaker to offer a V-6 in a car as large as Electra.

The success of styling was evident in Skylark, the GM X-body car that was in the greatest demand through much of the '80 model year, even though it was the highest-priced of the four GM X-bodies and even though it varied only in styling and trim levels from the others. The four-door Century styling was so popular—"Our Little Limousine," it was advertised—it boosted Century sales by 121 percent in January, even though the two-door aeroback version, an older style, had sold so poorly it was phased out in February.

Duffy, who became general sales manager in 1977 when Robert Burger was named GM vice-president of marketing, said, "We've got the strongest product line I've experienced since I first came here thirty-four years ago." Buick moved into the fourth sales position—behind Chevrolet, Ford and Oldsmobile but ahead of Pontiac and the financially ailing Chrysler nameplates—production totaled 854,011 in the '80 model year. In the short run, at least, there would be more diesels. In February 1980, LeSabre joined Electra and the big wagons as being available with a diesel option. And for 1981, the 5.7-liter diesel became an option on Riviera.

Among other engines for model year '81, the 4.1-liter V-6, not turbocharged, was standard on the Riviera, the 3.8 turbo V-6 remaining base for the sports version. A vertical grille was given the Skylark, and there were subtle appearance changes given other 1981 Buicks. The major styling change was on the Regal, which now had a forward-sloping hood and a redesigned rear deck with a small spoiler, or lip, in the sheet metal to reduce drag. New for '81, too, were self-sealing tires on all models, the torque converter and automatic overdrive for better fuel economy (the converter had been used on some '80 models sporadically), and onboard computer controls for the emission-control system.

From the top: Skylark Limited, Century Limited, Riviera and Electra for '81.

But while new-model cars were capturing the public spotlight, other events were taking place, far behind the scenes, which would have a major impact on Buick in the 1980's. Among them were significant efforts to solve the long-standing conflict between management and labor. Buick workers had not been officially involved in the 1936-37 Flint sitdown strikes which had led to GM's recognition of the UAW; the sitdowns were at Fisher Body and Chevrolet. UAW Local 599 at Buick was, however, the main impetus behind the "30 and Out" early retirement plan accepted by the Big Three automakers in 1973.

In the 1960's and early 1970's, labor-management relationships at Buick were among the worst in the corporation. That old pattern was severely jolted, however, by the oil embargo of late 1973 that nearly shut Buick's Flint complex. Late in the summer of 1975, Buick general manager George R. Elges attended a meeting in Detroit between GM leaders and top UAW executives which resulted in a new level of understanding between labor and management. That meeting led to another, at the Local 599 hall, initiated by Buick's personnel director, Wilbur J. (Bill) Rowland, with Albert Christner, Local 599's president. It was said to have been the first time a personnel director had ever been in the union hall.

Out of that meeting came still another, the later-famous "Halloween Party" on October 31, 1975. The date was a coincidence—the result of several delays—but Rowland capitalized on it by buying a pair of Halloween masks depicting the devil and suggesting he and Christner wear them to the meeting. They walked into the meeting wearing the masks, then removed them. The idea, Rowland told an interviewer, was that "we would take off the masks we had been wearing for forty years and begin to deal with each other in a straightforward, one-on-one manner." The sight of the personnel director and union chief wearing masks broke the ice at the tense meeting of managers and union leaders. And that meeting set the tone for big improvements in labor-management relationships.

On the occasion of Buick's 75th anniversary in 1978, general manager David Collier told an interviewer: "Over the years, management tended to forget employees were individuals and this created conflicts. I think current relationships are better. Management is trying to create an atmosphere of mutual respect and dignity for the individual." That those relationships had improved was observable in 1979, when Local 599 became the first UAW local in the United States to settle its local contract—in advance of the national GM-UAW contract. The improvement was also seen in successful efforts in the late 1970's to lure corporate work to the Flint complex. It would become more notable a few years later.

Change was coming to the auto industry—and to Buick—in ways that could hardly be predicted. Buick's 450-acre complex—filling an

Personnel Director Bill Rowland (top left) and Local 599 president Al Christner (above left) helped harmonize Buick's labor relations. Foundry (above right) was shut down in 1980.

area two miles long and a half mile wide on the North side of Flint, on what was once the Hamilton Farm—was GM's largest U.S. manufacturing center. It was second in size only to the Opel plant in West Germany among the corporation's worldwide operations. The division could boast of more than 10 million square feet of floor space, 75 miles of power conveyors, 22 miles of steam mains, 14 miles of rail track and 5.5 miles of roads. Besides assembling full-size and intermediate cars, it produced engines, brake and axle assemblies, springs, transmission components, plastic parts and sheet metal panels.

Change at the complex was constant. Assembly of Rivieras was moved to New Jersey in 1979. The foundry, a Buick fixture for most of its history, was phased out on August 15, 1980. Production of Type 350 automatic transmissions was being phased out, but the torque converter for a new automatic transmission for front-wheel-drive cars was being phased in. Buick's plastics operations were growing, and

in 1979 Buick won the GM contract for making trailing axles for all of the front-wheel-drive X-body cars.

On November 30, 1979, the Buick foundry poured its last V-8 engine block and by April of 1980 Buick was out of the business of building V-8 engines. But V-6 engine production was ever growing. And Buick engineers were developing experimental three-cylinder engines that for a time looked like one answer to the energy problem.

In 1980, McPherson said Buick was going through a major transition. "Old things are going out, and new production is coming in—I don't know if I'll be around to see the total transformation." As it turned out, he wasn't. On December 1, 1980, McPherson was named group executive of GM's Car and Truck Group. His successor? None other than Lloyd E. Reuss, Buick's former chief engineer. Reuss' return would place him at the center of one of the most remarkable periods in Buick's remarkable history. *323*

Chapter Eighteen

CHALLENGE AND CHANGE

Challenge and change reshaped Buick in the fiercely competitive Eighties. The division bucked a severe industry-wide slump early in the decade, then set consecutive sales records in the mid-Eighties. In 1984, for the first time in any year, Buick sales worldwide topped one million. Later in the decade, they would drop to nearly half that—and then the stage would be set for another resurgence.

Buick management and UAW Local 599 thawed a relationship that had been rancorous for years, then applied their new understanding to Buick's biggest manufacturing challenge in eight decades. This was the task of saving car assembly at Buick's "home" complex in Flint by promising to turn its aging facilities into the country's most innovative and efficient assembly operation. That promise became the $300-million-plus "Buick City" project, achieved after teams of Buick and Local 599 representatives traveled to sites away from the complex investigating a "clean sheet" approach to assembly. Before they were done, management and union representatives had journeyed across Europe and to Japan to study the state-of-the-art assembly methods of more than a dozen other automakers. Their work resulted in a plant that was ranked, by decade's end, as the No. 1 quality plant in North America and No. 2 in the world, in an independent measurement of cars built for sale in North America and their factories.

Buick City, that most dramatic of Buick's manufacturing projects (described in the next chapter), would also be its last. By mid-decade, General Motors had changed Buick and the other GM car divisions to marketing and marketing-engineering organizations. Exclaimed one veteran Buick executive in 1985: "We've seen more changes here in the last five years than in the previous fifty."

Three men led Buick through this period. The first, Lloyd E. Reuss, faced the dilemma of the complex's assembly future when he took over as general manager December 1, 1980. In the little more than three years he held that position, Buick met that challenge; became more involved in motor sports, electronics and high-tech engines; placed new emphasis on customer satisfaction; made giant strides in the quality of work life, employee training and labor relations in general; initiated the two-seater Reatta project; and set sales and production records.

Donald E. Hackworth, Reuss's immediate successor, would face a different kind of challenge—leading Buick into a new era, with a new mission resulting from the GM reorganization. Hackworth would assure that Buick would continue to define the Buick product; he placed renewed emphasis on customer satisfaction and support of motor sports activities; and he committed Buick to an active participation and leadership in community affairs.

Edward H. Mertz, who succeeded Hackworth in 1986, set the stage for Buick's resurgence by sharply focusing on the division's image and future direction and then leading the team that developed new models to meet that focus.

By 1980, when Reuss returned to Buick as general manager, he had accumulated 21 years of GM engineering and management experience. He was born in Belleville, Illinois, on September 22, 1936, graduated from the University of Missouri at Rolla in 1957 and served two years as a lieutenant in the U.S. Army Corps of Engineers.

He joined GM in 1959 as an experimental engineer. A few months later he moved to the Chevrolet engineering staff where he eventually became chief engineer for the Camaro and Nova. In 1973 he was promoted to manager of product planning at Chevrolet. From 1975 to 1978 he served as Buick chief engineer before returning to Chevy as director of engineering.

When he was chief engineer, Reuss aimed to give Buick a more youthful, dynamic image. On his return a few years later, he simply picked up where he had left off. In 1981, for the fifth time, a Buick was pace car for the Indianapolis 500. Buicks had enjoyed this honor before in 1939, 1959, 1975 and 1976. The 1981 pace car was a Regal with what Buick called a "very special" 4.1-liter V-6 engine.

The stock 4.1 was not then offered on Regal, but was standard on Electra and Riviera and optional on LeSabre. Developed by Buick engineers in cooperation with Baker Engineering of Grand Rapids, the pace car version was naturally aspirated—unlike its turbocharged predecessor in the '76 race. It produced 281 horsepower at 5100 rpm, compared to 125 hp at 4000 rpm for the stock 4.1 engine. Heavy duty and reworked production components were used. The car was metallic

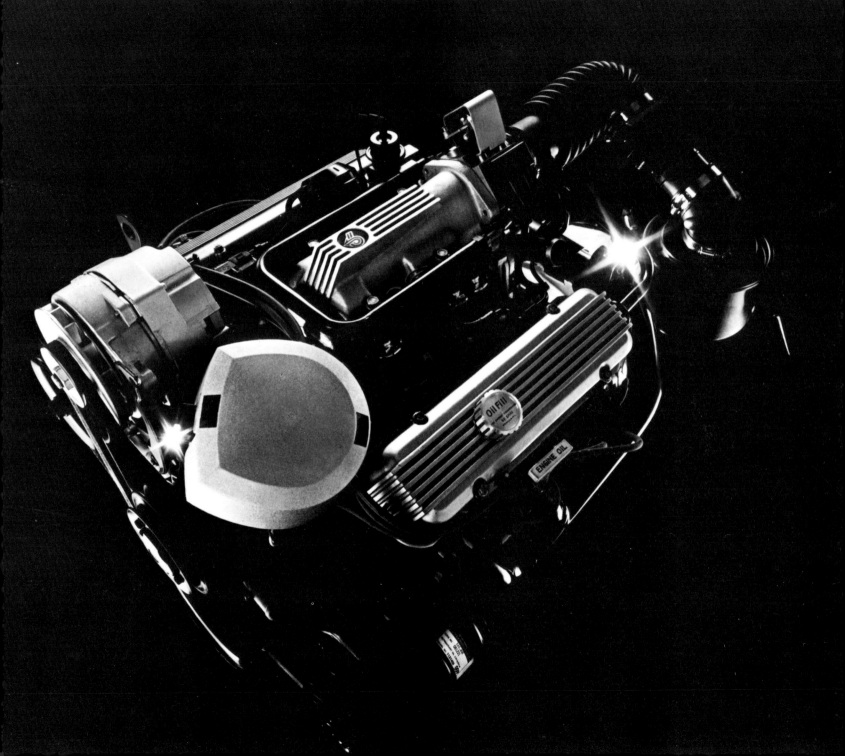

Previous page: This 3.8-liter V-6 shows the result of Buick's engine beautification effort. Left: 1981 Indy 500 pace car, a Regal. Above: Herbert A. Fishel (center) and Joseph M. Negri (right). Right: 1982 Buicks: From top, Century Limited Coupe, Grand National Regal, Skyhawk Coupe, Riviera Convertible.

silver with "maple" (dark maroon) on the center hood section, and wide stripes of orange, maple and dark brown along the sides. The same car also paced the July 4th "Race to the Clouds"—the 58th Pikes Peak Auto Hill Climb.

Cars such as this were the responsibility of Buick Special Products Engineering, which Reuss had created as chief engineer and placed under the direction of Herbert A. Fishel, whom he had brought in from Chevrolet. Fishel held the post until 1982, when he took a similar job at Chevy. Joseph M. Negri, who had worked for Fishel on the three-cylinder engine project, succeeded him at Buick. Special Products was an elite group of a dozen engineers, covering all the disciplines: engine design, electronics, body design, aerodynamics.

For 1982, Century went front-wheel drive and Buick introduced its smallest car, the Skyhawk, built on the J platform. But neither was ready by August 1981, so Reuss first introduced the carryover lineup. That included a new Regal sedan and Regal Estate Wagon, and improvements in the V-6 turbo. The 4.1-liter V-6 was now available in Regal, while Riviera, LeSabre and Electra were largely unchanged. Skylark received an optional high-output 2.8-liter V-6 engine and an improved standard 2.5-liter inline 4 with electronically controlled throttle body fuel injection.

To improve turbo response and maintenance, changes were made to increase air velocity through the turbine and compressor, heat the carburetor plenum with exhaust gas instead of engine coolant, increase the oil flow to the turbo and provide a new torque converter in transmissions used with turbo engines. A five-quart oil pan replaced the four-quart sump.

A 4.3-liter V-6 diesel was optional in Regal coupe, and the 5.7-liter diesel V-8 was available in Regal, LeSabre, Electra, Riviera and Estate Wagon. Overdrive transmissions, said to improve fuel economy ten to twenty percent, became standard in Electra and Riviera, and optional in LeSabre. Limited Edition models were offered later in the model year: Riviera T Type, with a 3.8-liter turbo V-6, custom grille, aluminum wheels and special suspension; Regal Somerset, with light sandstone and dark blue accent paint and wire wheels; and LeSabre F/E (Formal Edition), with blue/gray paint combinations, special steering wheel and wire wheels. The T Type concept had been a Reuss idea when he was chief engineer, though he had called it E Type, taking that name from Jaguar. "E could stand for anything you wanted it to; in my mind, it meant European type," Reuss explained. "The design studios came up with the image we wanted, and someone down there named it T Type."

On November 30, 1981, Buick introduced the front-drive Century, featuring a new 3.0-liter V-6 and a 4.3-liter V-6 diesel as options, in Custom and Limited coupe and sedan. A 2.5-liter four-cylinder engine with electronic fuel injection was standard. This wedge-shaped car became very popular, succeeding the Regal as Buick's volume leader within two years.

On February 10, 1982, at Daytona International Speedway, Buick introduced its Grand National Regal (called Regal Grand National in later years), a limited edition of the Regal coupe—the car which had brought Buick the Manufacturer's Trophy in the 1981 NASCAR Winston Cup series, the first of two straight trophies for Buick. Reuss considered those trophies important in Buick's drive for a new image. The Grand National, said Reuss, "will be used to help Buick dealers capitalize on the success of the Buick nameplate on the NASCAR circuit. Buick has undergone a subtle, but significant, change of image over the past few years, with more youthful, contemporary products

that feature increasing technical sophistication. Grand National will help to emphasize the idea that Buicks can be exciting, fun-to-drive cars." The new model included T-top roof, silver-gray and charcoal-gray paint with red accent stripes, blacked-out grille and trim, a front air dam and rear spoiler, and the 4.1-liter V-6 with four-barrel carburetor. Only 215 were produced, a few with 3.8-liter V-6 turbos.

And on February 25, 1982, Buick finally got its J car. "Bearing a distinct family resemblance to the new Buick Century, the front-wheel-drive Skyhawk carries the aerodynamic wedge shape of the fuel-efficient future," Buick announced. Engines included the standard 1.8-liter inline 4 with two-barrel carburetor, and two optional choices: a 1.8-liter inline 4 with fuel injection and overhead camshaft and a 2.0-liter inline 4 with two-barrel carburetion. Reuss introduced the Skyhawk at the Chicago Auto Show, and said that it and Century indicated how Buicks would look in the years ahead.

Another model unveiled at the show spoke more of nostalgia than of the future. It was a Riviera convertible; for the first time since the 1975 LeSabre, Buick was selling soft tops. American Sunroof Corporation executed the conversion to Buick specifications. The car was offered in white or red, with a white top and dark red leather seats, and was continued through the 1985 model year.

The 1982-85 Riviera convertibles, which helped lead the domestic industry back into soft tops after a six-year absence, received favorable press reviews and by 1986 were called "instant collectibles" by *Collectible Automobile* magazine. *Popular Mechanics* described Riviera as "the Rolls-Royce of American convertibles . . . a stunning $25,000 package." Ed Noble, in the *Oakland [Michigan] Press*, said Riviera is the "classiest of all convertibles slipping down the road." He called the car's headliner (included for 1984 and 1985) a "thoughtful touch . . . to cover all those arms and bows that make convertibles work." Explained Reuss: "We're working to provide some unique models with specific personalities." Most convertibles had 5-liter V-8 engines but some were equipped with a 4.1-liter V-6 or, in 1984 and 1985, a 3.8-liter turbo V-6. Of interest to collectors, these were the model-year totals: 1982—1,248 (898 white, 350 red, 107 V-6); 1983—1,750 (1,114 white, 636 red, 128 V-6); 1984—500 (280 white, 220 red, 11 V-6, 47 turbo V-6); 1985—400 (150 white, 250 red, 49 turbo V-6).

Through these slump years for the U.S. auto industry, Buick was performing very well. Model-year sales had been 700,083 in 1980; 756,186 in 1981 and 694,742 in 1982. But market penetration had increased significantly—from 7.6 percent in 1980, to 8.4 percent in 1981, to 9.0 percent in 1982. Buick was firmly in fourth place in the U.S. industry and its gains against the competition were impressive.

For 1983, Buick expanded on the T Type theme and added a Skyhawk wagon. T Type models of Skyhawk, Skylark, Century (two- and 324-3

four-door), Regal and Riviera featured specific engine-transmission-final drive combinations, "grand touring" suspensions and special trim. The optional 3.0-liter V-6 for Century offered improved driveability, thanks to computer control of exhaust gas recirculation into the intake manifold. The onboard computer still controlled air-fuel ratio, spark timing, idle speed and early fuel evaporation. A new automatic transmission with overdrive was available in mid-model year. Regal, Buick's volume leader, was offered in T Type form with the 3.8-liter turbo V-6, and the turbo was refined further with computer-regulated exhaust gas recirculation. There was no Regal Grand National in 1983.

Reuss continued his drive for customer satisfaction, stating Buick intended to become measurably better in that area than the rest of the industry. He announced a revised new-vehicle inspection and delivery process, a technical assistance hotline for dealer technicians and plans for a customer assistance hotline.

Darwin E. Clark, assistant general sales manager for service, said Buick's definition of customer satisfaction had evolved from mid-1981. A core group of high-level executives from planning, reliability, service and sales examined what was really important to a customer, such as fixing a car right the first time and having it ready when promised. Clark stressed that resulting projects were being implemented at a deliberate pace. "We are talking about a process here, not a program," he said. "Others have not been completely successful because they rushed in without adequate planning, preparation and training, and we are not going to repeat those mistakes."

In 1983 Reuss announced Questor, a concept car described as a test bed for innovative ideas in electronics. According to Reuss, the show car, developed by Buick and GM's Delco Electronics Division, was designed to demonstrate "the leadership of Buick and General Motors in electronics technology." Jon Bereisa, who became manager of electrical systems development, was brought into the Buick organization from Delco Electronics. He was largely responsible for conceiving the electronics portion of Questor, which certainly met Reuss' goal.

Questor had a laser key entry system, an automatic level, attitude and spoiler control system, a "systems sentinel" which monitored the status of key equipment, a map and navigation system, automatically aimed headlamps, theft deterrent system, television rear-view mirror system, voice-actuated radio-telephone, road surface traction monitoring system, and a touch-command center for entertainment, comfort and convenience functions. Questor, which used 14 micro-computers, became popular with automotive reporters who wanted to discuss cars of the future. Exterior design was largely attributed to Steven Pasteiner in David Clark's Buick Design Studio No. 2. In this period, Buick's big cars were designed in Buick Design Studio 1 under Bill Porter, its

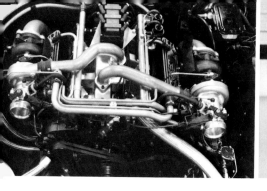

smaller cars in Studio 2 under Clark, and interior design for all Buicks was done in Buick Interior Design under Paul Tatseos.

In 1983, the Indianapolis 500 pace car was again a Buick. This time it was a Riviera convertible, powered by a twin-turbocharged 4.1-liter Buick V-6 engine. Said Reuss: ''Although the Riviera might not fit at some racing events, it is a natural for the Indianapolis 500. Both the Riviera and the race are classics—American traditions.'' Reuss said the engine, developing 450 horsepower, ''may well be the most technically sophisticated powerplant ever to appear at the Indianapolis Motor Speedway, in a pace car or in a race.''

A Delco digital onboard computer controlled all major engine functions, including sequential-port fuel injection. Twin mass air-flow sensors from AC Spark Plug were linked to the computer to control the air-fuel mixture, and AC high pressure in-tank pumps delivered the fuel. The computer also controlled the ignition system, idle speed and turbo waste gate. The engine used many standard Buick heavy duty components and the twin turbochargers were modified production units. The car's main color was cream, with light chocolate brown on the sides. Real wood was used for the trim and steering wheel. Dennis ''Duke'' Nalon, whose name was synonymous with the famous Novi race cars, drove both the 1981 and 1983 pace cars.

On top of everything else, Buick's U.S. domestic sales of 810,435 in the 1983 model year broke the old record of 799,321 set in 1973—just before the first oil embargo. Market penetration rose again, to 9.2 percent. For the calendar year, sales of 845,083 beat the old record of 800,586 set in 1978. Calendar-year production topped 900,000 for the first time, totaling 905,608.

GM Chairman Roger B. Smith spoke at a civic celebration in Flint's Hyatt Regency Hotel in September 1983, traveling to GM's birthplace to commemorate the corporation's 75th anniversary. Among those gathered for the celebration were the seven men still living who had been general managers of Buick. Ivan L. Wiles (manager from 1948-1956) at 85 was the elder statesman of the group. (Wiles died at age 88 on November 9, 1986, in Scottsdale, Arizona.) The others were Robert L. Kessler (1965-1969), Lee N. Mays (1969-1972), George R.

Opposite: 1983 Buicks: From top, Electra Sedan, Regal Sedan, Skyhawk Limited Wagon, Riviera T Type. Above: 1983 Indianapolis 500 pace car was the Buick Riviera Convertible with sophisticated twin-turbo V-6 (left). Below: Electronic instrument panel made news in Buick's exciting Questor, which debuted in 1983.

Left: Buick's six living former general managers meet current manager Lloyd Reuss in 1983: From left, Kessler, Mays, Wiles, Elges, Reuss, Collier and McPherson. Right: From top, Edward H. Mertz, Buick's chief engineer in the early 1980s, and Donald L. Runkle, assistant chief engineer for powertrain.

Elges (1973-1975), David C. Collier (1975-1978), Donald H. McPherson (1978-1980) and, of course, Lloyd Reuss.

They all reminisced. Joked Wiles: "I got along good with [Harlow] Curtice; that's probably why I succeeded him." And Kessler stated, "Buick has the most loyal group of employees I've ever seen. We took a survey and found eighty percent of the employees had relatives working there. They all wanted to do the job." Mays remembered pollution from the powerplant being a big issue. "They were talking about particulates and I didn't even know what particulates were—I didn't know a hydrocarbon from a carbohydrate . . . next thing, it was water pollution. Everything all of a sudden was polluted and it was all my fault." Elges recalled the oil embargo: "The gas shortage was my big crisis, and reactivation of the V-6 was my big accomplishment." Collier said he just "fell into" Buick's Quality of Work Life program begun by Elges, Bill Rowland and Local 599's Al Christner. The union invited him to the Reuther Education Center at Black Lake in northern Michigan. "I think it was the first time GM officials were in the place for a meeting like that." Said McPherson: "Buick must have more surviving general managers than any other division. Seeing so many surviving is kind of encouraging." And Collier volunteered: "Reuss

is the best damned thing that ever happened to Buick."

For 1984, Buick emphasized high-technology powerplants, advanced electronic systems and aerodynamic styling. Two 3.8-liter V-6s, one with sequential-port fuel injection (SFI) and the other with multi-port fuel injection (MFI), were introduced. The 3.8-liter SFI turbo was standard on T Type Riviera and Regal and optional on Riviera convertible; the 3.8-liter MFI was optional on Century.

With MFI, an onboard computer measured the air and fuel needs of all six cylinders collectively and activated the six injectors once each engine revolution. SFI took the process a step farther. Its electronics measured the fuel and air needs of the engine, and calibrated the intake charge to provide the correct mixture needed at the intake port of each individual cylinder, just before it fired in sequence. SFI was developed because of the need for even greater fuel metering precision over a wider operating range, from idle to cruising to full power boost. The SFI's precision made it the natural choice for the 3.8-liter turbo, the all-out performance engine developed for Riviera T Type, Regal T Type and Regal Grand National (which for '84 was back in the lineup).

The MFI and SFI development work had started under George M. Claypole, a staff project engineer in Buick Special Products Engineering. Claypole had worked with SFI during experiments with a three-cylinder back in 1979. He had developed experimental six-cylinder engines using SFI hardware from the Robert Bosch Corporation of Southfield, Michigan (a subsidiary of the Bosch firm in West Germany), a computer from Delco Electronics, and other equipment from AC. That work was turned over to a group headed by Ernest Thrapp, assistant staff engineer, and from that point, the job of developing production fuel-injected Buick engines moved forward on two fronts.

Gerry Pierce and Paul Young, senior project engineers, led development of the 3.8-liter MFI V-6, with Pierce spending months at the Desert Proving Grounds in Mesa, Arizona, and Young working in Flint. Three other project engineers, Ron Yuille, Jim Royer and Steve Ives, began to work on the SFI engine, under the direction of Ron Kociba, assistant staff engineer for turbo engines.

Many others contributed to the new engines. Senior project engineers Bob Gardner and Dennis Bogden developed a major innovation, an all-electronic ignition system called Computer Controlled Coil Ignition, which eliminated the distributor. The system consisted of three ignition coils, an electronics module and engine position sensors. Signals from the sensors and the on-board computer controlled the charging and discharging of the coils. Two spark plugs always fired at the same time, one on the combustion stroke of one cylinder and the other on the exhaust stroke of another.

Meanwhile, Dan Richardson and Larry Carrion, Buick senior project engineers, developed—with AC engineers—the mass air flow sensor. This device measured the mass, rather than the volume, of air entering the intake manifold, thereby eliminating the effect of temperature or altitude on fuel/air metering. The signal from the sensor fed into the onboard computer, which calculated the amount of fuel necessary to mix with the air to form the desired air-fuel ratio. Although fuel injection is more expensive to produce than carburetors, Claypole pointed out that both MFI and SFI offered great advantages. These included considerable weight reduction and more precise fuel, power and emission control—plus fewer parts and a much neater underhood engine package.

Edward H. Mertz, who had succeeded Robert J. Schultz as Buick chief engineer in November 1981, claimed the turbocharged SFI engines were among the most sophisticated production turbo engines in the world. Mertz, a Grosse Pointe, Michigan, native and 1959 graduate of Notre Dame, had been chief engineer for body engineering at Fisher Body and chief engineer of passenger cars for Chevrolet before arriving at Buick.

Reuss brought Mertz to Buick to develop advanced engines and other technology. Highly respected by Buick engineering personnel, he advocated high technology in the work place as well as in the product.

Buicks for 1984: All-black Regal Grand National (top) and Century Olympia, a model tied to Buick's status as official car of the 1984 Olympic games in L.A.

He brought Buick engineering into the forefront in office automation. More importantly, he brought in Donald L. Runkle to develop engine innovations and he also brought Kenneth R. Baker back from a GM electric car project to develop leading-edge electronics at Buick. The team Mertz created would, within a few years, place Buick in a leadership position in engine design and electronics applications.

Runkle, assistant chief engineer for powertrains from 1982 to 1984, had been staff engineer at Chevrolet and chief engineer for Impala, Caprice and Camaro before arriving at Buick. He was credited not only with giving Buick engines a beauty treatment that contrasted sharply with the jumbled and disorganized underhood appearance of the past, but also with starting a new engine program scheduled to emerge in the Nineties.

Through this period, the man in charge of Buick ride and handling was George W. Drew, assistant chief engineer in charge of chassis, production engineering and experimental test and development. Retaining the famous Buick "ride" was a challenge as cars became shorter and smaller and began using unibody construction, rather than a separate frame, to reduce weight in the push for fuel efficiency. "Despite all that," observed Drew, "our small cars still do not ride like small

cars. I think that's a mark on the wall.''

Mertz had reorganized Buick's product engineering department in 1982, establishing three vehicle chief engineer positions, each responsible for different car line programs. These positions were held by Kenneth R. Baker, David S. Sharpe and Thomas F. Wallace. Baker was also responsible for overall electrical and electronics coordination, including development of Buick's TV-like Graphic Control Center, at a time when Buick was GM's lead division for application of automotive electronics.

Also, as part of that reorganization, Anna S. Kretz was named manager of electrical, electronics and the micro-processor laboratory, and she assumed overall coordination responsibility for all Buick electrical and electronics applications. Kretz, a native of Poland and a graduate of Oakland (Michigan) University, had become the first woman to achieve bonus-eligible status at Buick Engineering when she was named staff engineer-electrical in 1981.

Women and minorities moved higher into Buick management in the late Seventies and early Eighties. On March 1, 1977, women first achieved bonus-eligible status in sales when June Lazar became manager of car distribution and later a zone manager, and G. Lynne Dower became a zone manager. Dower later owner a Buick dealership near Dallas, Texas. Perhaps the most widely known of Buick women em-

Above: Olympic torch exchange in front of the Buick Administration Building in Flint on May 22, 1984. Below: Paula McGee, Flint Mayor James A. Sharp and Pam McGee, an Olympic gold medalist in basketball from Flint, in an Olympic Torch Run Riviera.

ployees in the Eighties were Helen M. Turi, an employee of more than 40 years who was promoted from public relations director's secretary to administrator and then to senior staff assistant in public relations; Frances E. Baese, who was executive secretary for seven Buick general managers starting with Ed Rollert; and Lynn L. Salata, product planner in charge of the Buick Reatta. Additionally, Sharon J. McQuigg, Linda D. Hamilton, Jan A. Mills, Deborah A. Rau and Julie K. Welker became assistant superintendents; and Carol Perelli became an exterior designer of Buicks at GM Design.

Nelson B. Gonzalez, a Brazilian native of Spanish ancestry, was the first member of a minority group to become a plant manager at Buick, and was one of the first minority plant managers in the corporation. Claude A. Verbal, who began his Buick career in research and development in product engineering in 1964, became the first black to reach bonus-eligible status at Buick when he became superintendent of quality control for the sheet metal, axle and forge plants in 1977. Eddie L. Wright, also black, was later named superintendent in the Engine Plant. In the sales and service department, the first black zone manager was William E.L. Powell, in the Portland, Oregon, zone in the early Eighties. By the end of the decade, Powell was assistant general sales manager-administration. He became general manager of GM Motors Holding in 1992.

For 1984, Buick offered an industry first: cellular telephones. Cellular technology, developed by AT&T, provided higher-quality mobile communications and made the service available to millions of users nationwide, compared to the few hundred thousand users possible with conventional radio-telephone technology. At first, the cellular phone was a factory endorsed, dealer-installed option on Riviera in Chicago. As cellular technology became more available, the option was expanded to other cars and other parts of the country.

Buick also became more involved in motor sports, offering for 1984 a Stage II intake manifold and Stage I piston for the 4.1-liter V-6. These parts were available through Buick dealers for use on the track, joining the heavy duty blocks, heads, head gaskets, crankshafts, connecting rods, pistons and valves which dealers already offered.

When announcing such off-road goodies, Buick could point to race track successes like Ron Cosner, whose super stock Regal set a record over the quarter mile of 9.91 seconds with a speed of 131.38 mph; and Robert Overby, whose Stage II V-6 Regal developed 500 horsepower and ran off with Detroit and Pocono victories in the IMSA (International Motor Sports Association) Kelly Challenge series. This was the first non-Chevy-powered car ever to win in that series. At the Bonneville Salt Flats, a Buick V-6-powered 1977 Skyhawk entered by John Thawley in the Bonneville National Speed Trials set the E/Production record at 167.6 mph in 1984. Car show visitors around the country could tour the Buick exhibit and see the Buick Regal that took Bobby Allison to the driver's championship on the 1983 NASCAR circuit; and the PPG pace car, a Skyhawk modified by Buick, GM's design staff and PPG, Inc., to pace CART (Championship Auto Racing Teams) races around the country. In April 1985, Patty Moise, driving a 1985 Somerset, became the first woman to qualify on the front row of an American road race with the second best qualifying time in the Road Atlanta Kelly Challenge Series race. She finished second.

Buick also announced it had improved its Electronic Product Information Center (EPIC) system to provide even more information than the system just rolled out the previous year. EPIC offered a wide range of Buick product and feature information on a video display that could be operated by the customer. One version helped dealers check the status of ordered vehicles, locate desired vehicles anywhere in the country and access public data bases. Each dealership enrolled in the program received a microcomputer, display screen, keyboard and printer linked to a central computer at Buick headquarters in Flint.

From a design standpoint, 1984 was largely a facelift year. One newcomer was the front-drive Century Custom and Estate Wagon, replacing the rear-drive Regal wagon. The rear-drive Electra was also nearing an end. It would be succeeded by the front-drive version the following spring.

The 1984 Regal Grand National featured the 3.8-liter SFI turbo engine, sport steering wheel, tachometer and boost gauge, and came in any color you wanted, as long as it was black.

One special-edition Buick was the Century Olympia Limited sedan to commemorate Buick's participation as the official car and a sponsor of the twenty-third Olympic Games in Los Angeles in the summer of 1984—a sponsorship negotiated by comptroller LeRoy D. Bence, Jr. and Jack Faerber, administrative assistant general sales manager. The sedan carried U.S. Olympic identification on the front fender, deck lid and hood ornament. The car, accented with gold-colored body stripes and gold-colored aluminum wheels, also sported a decklid luggage rack and headrests embroidered with the U.S. Olympic logo.

The excitement of Olympic sponsorship was brought home to the Flint Buick complex on May 22, 1984, as the Olympic torch, carried across the country by runners, was relayed along Division Street in the middle of the complex, then past several thousand spectators on the Buick Administration Building lawn. Three Buick employees—Dennis R. Council, Ronnie Bartels and Daniel B. Donigan—and the daughters of two others—Shelaen Williams and Tina Mitchell—carried the torch.

Buick also provided a fleet of cars, including Riviera ''pace cars,'' to accompany the torch runners across the country, creating an interesting engineering problem for a team headed by Claypole. Claypole had been project manager for the 1983 Indy 500 pace car's dual turbocharged V-6. In one year, he would switch goals from building reliability at the Indy 500 race to building durability at a snail's pace. He had to modify a fleet of Buicks to survive 84 days of travel, 12-16 hours a day, in all climates and altitudes—moving at just 2 to 12 miles per hour.

Such slow speeds subjected the cars to the equivalent of seven years of average driving in one short summer, Claypole said. His team devised a computer-controlled electric cooling fan, a hand-held box with a rocker switch to regulate constant engine rpm at low speeds, a special radiator from Harrison Radiator, and experimental high-density light-weight batteries from Delco Remy. A team headed by B. E. "Butch" Beckman, foreman in the test-car build area, worked late nights to modify the Olympic Buicks, and Dan Nicholson, a GMI student at Buick, coordinated maintenance as the cars traveled across the country.

Buick didn't get the Indy pace car privileges in 1984, but Buick Special Products Engineering had a keen interest in that year's race. A team headed by Ron Kociba worked with McLaren Engines, which was modifying the Buick V-6 for the Indianapolis 500. While the torch cars were creeping across the country, two Buick-powered Indy cars sped around the track fast enough to qualify for the 500. Scott Brayton and Pat Bedard both used V-6 turbocharged Buick engines—Stage II stock block powerplants. They were the first stock blocks ever to break 200 mph in Indy qualifying. Bedard set a record of 201.915; Brayton quickly broke it at 203.637. Unfortunately, neither car completed the 500. Bedard miraculously survived a terrible crash; Brayton finished 18th among 33 entrants, completing 172 of the 200 laps before an oil tank problem sidelined his car.

Buick continued sports sponsorships such as the Buick Open golf tournament, which drew record crowds to Warwick Hills at Grand Blanc, near Flint, in the mid-Eighties. And in 1984 it began sponsorship of the World Championship Tennis Finals and the short-lived Cherry Bowl football game at the Pontiac Silverdome.

Within the Buick complex, internal communications were emphasized more than ever before. By the mid-Eighties, there were more than a dozen small in-plant newspapers, a magazine called *Inside Buick*, and an internal cable television network. Bill Lamb, who hosted the "Buick Factory Whistle" radio show for 23 years, began TV interviews with employees for the internal network.

In advertising, Buick's living logo celebrated its tenth anniversary in 1984. This was a red-tailed hawk named Happy, trained by J. David Siddon of Grant's Pass, Oregon. "I don't think there's a bird anywhere that's been photographed and filmed as much as Happy," said Siddon of the Hawk featured in Buick ads. Happiest of Happy's talents was

its ability to land—on command—on a Riviera hood ornament. Harold E. Savage, Buick's advertising director, said surveys indicated the bold bird had a positive influence on younger potential buyers. But the hawk trademark, like the Skyhawk itself, was about to go away. By decade's end, both Skyhawk the car and the hawk symbol were gone. Buick would place new emphasis on the tri-shield as its symbol.

More momentous developments in the first half of 1984 would result not only in a change in Buick's leadership, but in the biggest change in Buick's mission and structure in its history.

Rumors of a massive reorganization of General Motors surfaced late in 1983. On January 10, 1984, GM Chairman Roger B. Smith announced that GM's North American Automotive Operations would be split into two integrated car groups functioning as self-contained business units. Each would be totally responsible for its product, including engineering, manufacturing, assembly and marketing, and each would be accountable for its quality, performance and profitability. Buick's Reuss was named to head one of the two huge organizations—the Chevrolet-Pontiac-GM of Canada (C-P-C) Group. Robert C. Stempel, who had been general manager of Chevrolet, was named to head the other, the Buick-Oldsmobile-Cadillac (B-O-C) Group.

"Buick was a unique place to work," Reuss told the writer in 1985. "There was so much cohesiveness between the city and the organization. And Buick has a tremendous amount of tradition. I have fond memories of Buick and the Flint area—in fact, I think I never had a job that was as much fun."

Donald E. Hackworth, 46, a GM vice president and president of GM of Canada, was named to succeed Reuss as Buick general manager. Born in Circleville, Ohio, on February 19, 1937, he had been a submarine crewman in the U.S. Navy before graduating from Ohio State University in 1963. That year he joined GM's Delco Moraine Division in Dayton, Ohio. In 14 years he progressed from foreman to general foreman, superintendent, general superintendent, manufacturing manager and works manager at Delco Moraine. In 1977 he completed the senior executive training program at Stanford University.

The following year he was named director of manufacturing facility planning on the Worldwide Product Planning Group in Detroit, and in 1979 he moved to Oldsmobile as general manufacturing manager. In December 1981, he became president and general manager of GM of Canada and a GM vice president. Like Collier and McPherson, he moved directly from that position to general manager of Buick.

Hackworth moved to Flint knowing he would be at the forefront of a massive transition at Buick. For the first time, Buick, like the other GM car divisions, would not actually be making cars. Most of the giant Flint Buick complex would belong to manufacturing and engineering arms of the B-O-C Group. The number of people working

Cars powered by Buick V-6 turbo engines, driven by Pancho Carter (top photos) and Scott Brayton (bottom, in 1984 Indy car), drew much attention during qualifying for the 1985 Indianapolis 500. The only Buick-powered cars trying to qualify in a Cosworth-dominated field, both set records as Carter won the pole and Brayton qualified second. Carter's four-lap record average was 212.583 mph and Buick became the first American production-based engine on the Indy pole since 1931. Brayton won an award for his record 214.199 mph one-lap average, but lined up second because his transmission failed on the fourth lap. Joe Negri and Ron Kociba of Buick Special Products Engineering won the prestigious Louis Schwitzer Award from the SAE Indiana Section for innovation and engineering excellence in the 500. Sports Illustrated described the engine as "perhaps the racing powerplant of the future." Although both cars left the race early, Kociba lauded the qualifying success and vowed: "We'll be back."

directly for Buick would drop from more than 17,000 to less than 1,000. But Hackworth was not willing to define the new Buick organization as entirely a marketing arm of the group. As GM executives moved forward with studies on how to implement the new organization, Hackworth insisted that the B-O-C car divisions—or Buick, specifically—have their own engineering organizations. Buick should define its product, besides handling marketing, sales and after-sales customer satisfaction, he argued. He prevailed.

As for the former Flint Buick complex, much of it would come under the direction of an organization called the C/H Product Team, formed to carry out the functions of producing the C car (including the front-wheel-drive Electra introduced as a 1985 model), and the H car (including the new front-drive LeSabre introduced as a 1986 model) for the B-O-C Group.

Edward D. DuCharme, Buick's last general manufacturing manager and the C/H Product Team's first manufacturing manager, said one of the important advantages of the new organization would be simultaneous engineering of both the product and the process. ''The biggest change is that we're going to be a more product-oriented organization,'' DuCharme explained. ''Under the old system, the engineers would design something, then throw it over a wall, and the manufacturing guys would engineer a process to build what came over the wall. By taking the wall down and with both groups working together, you get a better product.''

Although the C/H Product Team had general control of the Flint complex site, four large plants in the Flint complex—the Engine Plant under William W. Tennant and two transmission machining plants and

the Torque Converter Plant under William F. Aikman—were placed under a different B-O-C Group organization, the Powertrain Team. That team would be responsible for engines and for the marriage of engines to transmissions for the Group. As time went on, the organizations and their names would be ever changing.

The formal change in structure took effect July 1, 1984. By then, Hackworth was moving quickly to define the new Buick organization. Even as this process continued, there were new cars to introduce. First was the front-drive Electra, introduced on March 27 as a 1985 model. It was offered in Electra, Electra T Type and Park Avenue versions. Depending on model, the 1985s had shed between 600 and 900 pounds in their new configuration. Compared to the 1984 rear-drive models, the new cars were two feet shorter overall, rode on a wheelbase shorter by eight inches, were four inches narrower, and about two inches lower. Inside, however, most dimensions were within an inch of their predecessors. Unique to Electra was a hood that opened from the rear, making the engine more accessible.

The new Electra received an enthusiastic welcome from the press, particularly the T Type with 3.8-liter MFI V-6, which Road & Track called ''a stunningly good American sedan.'' John R. Dabels, Buick's general director of marketing and sales planning, said of this car, ''When Lloyd Reuss first proposed the Electra T Type, many of us had trouble with this concept. The Electra had a long history of being a boulevard car and we thought there was no way we could make a T Type out of an Electra. Reuss proved us wrong. Not only is the T Type a superb automobile, but it is also generating sales for the regular Electra and Park Avenue.''

Opposite page: From left, Donald E. Hackworth, chief engineer David S. Sharpe, and 1985 Park Avenue. Counterclockwise from right: More '85 Buicks: Electra T Type, Regal Grand National, Century T Type, Somerset Regal.

In advertising, Buick highlighted an engineering test of the Electra T Type in the Australian Outback (picturing a car equipped with "roo bars"—sort of a cowcatcher for kangaroos) and in the twisting, winding roads of the Austrian Alps. Popularity of the new Electra was so high that production at GM's Wentzville, Missouri, Assembly Plant could not keep up with early demand.

This period of reorganization and new-model introductions also allowed a few moments to look to the past. On April 24, 1984, Celdine Schneder, a 41-year Buick employee, drove the last rear-drive Electra off the Flint assembly line. It was the 2,620,875th rear-drive Electra built. Beneath its floor carpeting and trunk coverings, it carried the names of more than 1,200 people who helped build it. Later in the year, a drawing was held for the car, sponsored by UAW locals 599 at Buick and 581 at the Fisher Body Flint Plant, which for 59 years built bodies for rear-drive Buicks. The proceeds of the drawing went to help restore Flint's Durant-Dort Carriage Company office building, a national historic building where GM founder Billy Durant had been headquartered in his carriage days.

In 1984, his first year at Buick's helm, Hackworth presided over the division's second straight record-breaking performance. Sales totaled 940,611 in the United States for the model year and 941,611 for the calendar year. Sales of Buicks in Canada and overseas pushed the totals over the million mark for the first time: 1,001,945 for the model year; 1,004,679 for the calendar year.

One model targeted for export was the LeSabre Golden Hawk, developed by Duane R. Tangue, Buick assistant staff engineer for export and advanced engineering. Conceived for sale in Saudi Arabia, Kuwait and Oman, the special 1985 LeSabre sported Arabic lettering on the sides, as well as a gold-plated luggage rack, hood ornament and other gold-plated accents. A gold-plated Buick hawk insignia was incorporated into the hood ornament, wheel hubs and steering wheel. A prototype displayed at the Kuwait Auto Show in 1983 drew a great deal of interest. Only two Golden Hawks were made—a black one sold in Kuwait and a white one. Buick's emphasis was clearly on the domestic—not overseas—market.

For 1985, the big news besides the Electra was the Somerset Regal, positioned between Skyhawk and Century, which Hackworth said was aimed at smaller, sporty-yet-luxurious imports. A new version of the 2.5-liter four-cylinder transverse-mounted engine with throttle body fuel injection was standard on this new front-drive N-body model. The optional engine was a new 3.0-liter V-6 with multi-port fuel injection.

Roy Nicholson, an assistant staff engineer, had been chosen to lead the design team for that engine. His team included Richard Barnum and Tom Halka, along with Gary Woodward of Rochester Products Division. The design team included Paul Hunkele, Mike Parise, Dan Kerr and Dan Richardson, all of Buick Engineering, and Jim Mottern, who served as Engine Plant coordinator.

The 1985 model year saw a lot of "lasts." Diesel engines were offered for the last time—changes in fuel prices and concerns about emissions caused GM to phase out the diesel for most passenger-car applications. To commemorate the rear-drive LeSabre's last year, the Limited Collector's Edition replaced the Limited. It included a special hood ornament and other identification. This was also the last year for Skylark on the X body and the last year for the Riviera styling that had won car-of-the year honors in 1979. A Limited Edition Riviera included real wood trim. One hundred 1984 and 1985 Rivieras were equipped with a Graphic Control Center (GCC), Buick's name for its computer system with the TV-like screen mounted in the instrument panel. These were test vehicles only, and were not for sale.

Most of the rest of the 1985 lineup was carryover. The black Regal Grand National, with its 3.8-liter SFI turbo, helped push Buick's youth image—particularly in a TV ad featuring the "Bad to the Bone" music of George Thorogood and the Destroyers.

(In 1985, the Classic Car Club of America reported that it had recently accepted all 1931-42 Series 90 Buicks as classics. In addition, the club had approved, on a "please apply" basis, a few custom-bodied models built between 1925 and 1948. The club's classification and technical services committee officials determine a car to be a classic on the basis of many factors, including coachwork, outstanding engineering, production volume and price.)

As soon as the 1985s were introduced, Hackworth completed his reorganization. Jim Perkins, Buick's general sales and service manager

since April 1982, had resigned in September of 1984 to become vice president of sales at Toyota. (He would later return to GM and become Chevrolet general manager.) His successor was William J. Atkinson, formerly assistant general sales manager-west at Pontiac. Most of Hackworth's other staff members were also new: David S. Sharpe, chief engineer; Jack W. (Jay) Qualman, director of strategic planning; Gilbert H. Cass, controller; and John C. Carlson, manager of personnel administration. Continuing as director of public relations was Thomas L. Pond. Phillip L. Ramsey's management information-systems operation was briefly associated with the new Buick organization; on January 1, 1985, it became part of GM's new wholly owned subsidiary, Electronic Data Systems.

Hackworth asked Sharpe to define Buick's engineering organization, a position close to the general manager's heart. Sharpe had joined Buick in 1968 in the test department of product engineering and had been senior staff engineer, program manager and vehicle chief engineer, among other positions. For the new Buick organization, Sharpe established a system of product-line managers, one to coordinate with each of the car platforms (such as C/H). The product-line managers reported to Timothy A. Logsdon, manager of product planning and advanced concepts and a member of Sharpe's staff. Other members of that staff were Joseph M. Negri, manager of special products (including motor sports), and James E. Queen, manager of customer satisfaction and engineering activities.

Hackworth took advantage of Buick's national wholesale seminar at the Opryland Hotel in Nashville in October 1984 to get his staff together to plan Buick's future. He called the meeting "a watershed," a time to make a historic shift in emphasis. Out of that meeting came short statements defining Buick's new role, including this one: " The mission of Buick is to provide high value transportation products and related services targeted at upscale buyers. These products and services will be of such value that they provide life cycle customer satisfaction . . . exceeding buyers' expectations throughout the consideration, purchase, ownership, service and re-purchase process."

As Hackworth prepared to reveal an important new lineup for the 1986 model year, the summer of 1985 was shaping up to be an eventful one. Buick invited all of its dealers to Flint for a 1986 new-model announcement program that Hackworth called "a hometown celebration to rival anything Buick has ever done." The elaborate event was staged by Harry W. Wagner, Buick's manager of shows, displays and exhibits for thirteen years. It featured a Broadway-style revue that spoofed the movie *Heaven Can Wait* while delivering sales messages, such as the importance of the women's market.

Later that summer, the UAW celebrated its 50th anniversary in Flint, with special recognition given the development of Buick City. The

This is the new Buick Electra.

Advertisement for the 1985 Electra T Type shows Buick's new marketing strategy for traditional luxury cars by emphasizing performance in Australian Outback.

first official production front-wheel-drive LeSabre rolled off the Buick City assembly line on schedule September 16, 1985. Shortly thereafter, Buick City's parent organization, the C/H Product Team (for the interim named Luxury Vehicles Product Team), got its first leader when 42-year-old J. T. Battenberg III, a Flint GMI graduate who had become general manager of England's Bedford Commercial Vehicle Division, was named product manager. Battenberg would soon become B-O-C group executive.

Perhaps the single most exciting feature of the 1986 Buicks was inside the Riviera—the Graphic Control Center, which replaced 91 buttons that would have been required to control as many functions using conventional systems. Backed by the computer expertise of Delco Electronics, the Riviera had seven to ten microprocessors, depending on options chosen. The driver could call up information on the "TV" screen in five areas: climate control, radio, trip monitor, gauges and diagnostic information. A summary appeared first, and by pressing the screen, the driver could call up more detailed information. Much of the Buick development work was done by Cary A. Wilson, assistant staff engineer-electrical, and Bob Kruse, project engineer-electrical.

The Riviera, with a normally aspirated 3.8-liter SFI V-6 engine standard, was downsized and restyled in what Buick called a "gentle wedge form" with improved aerodynamics. The Riviera T Type included a more sophisticated optional seat with power control of thigh, lumbar and seatback support and even headrest height.

The 1986 LeSabre—a totally new product of the Buick City assembly facility—now had a transverse-mounted engine, front-wheel drive and integral body-frame construction. Front suspension was by modified McPherson struts, rear suspension was fully independent, steering was rack and pinion, the standard engine was the 3.0-liter MFI V-6 and the optional engine was a 3.8-liter SFI V-6 with roller lifters to reduce internal friction. The four-door LeSabre had the traditional notchback styling of most front-drive Buicks, but the coupe was a fastback with a low drag coefficient.

There was other news for 1986 as well, such as a hatchback sport coupe Skyhawk, with blackout treatment and optional rear spoiler. Standard on the hatchback T Type and Limited coupes were hidden headlamps opened by electric motors.

Although the X body was no longer in production, Buick retained the Skylark name on a four-door version of the N-body Somerset (no longer called Somerset Regal). Skylark had been an important name for Buick since that first limited edition convertible in 1953, and Hackworth didn't want to lose the name when GM stopped making X bodies. A T Type Somerset was also offered, with an appearance and handling package including a front air dam, blacked-out moldings and special suspension and tires.

The Century received a new front-end panel and grille and an optional 3.8-liter SFI V-6, while Regal T Type and Grand National were equipped with a more powerful intercooled and turbocharged version of that engine. The intercooler, located in the air intake system between the turbocharger compressor and intake manifold, acted as a radiator to cool the air before it entered the engine, resulting in a denser charge and a 10 percent increase in horsepower and torque.

For the Electra, an electronic instrument cluster was optional, and a 3.8-liter SFI V-6 replaced the 3.8-liter MFI. An electronic braking system was standard on T Types and optional on other Electras. The rear-drive LeSabre and Electra Estate Wagons remained largely unchanged.

Some Buick dealerships could show off a new service system as well as new models. In 1985, Buick began a successful pilot of a computer-based diagnostic, service and communications tool called CAMS—Computerized Automotive maintenance System. CAMS, a joint development of Buick, Electronic Data Systems and IBM, gave dealerships the ability to diagnose and repair a car's electrical components more accurately and reliably than ever. By the end of 1986, more than 1,000 Buick dealers had CAMS units in operation.

Computer-based systems were now in wide use, notably in the Buick Customer Assistance and Technical Assistance Centers, which moved from pilot programs into full implementation.

The Customer Assistance Center handled complaints and questions called in to Buick headquarters by customers using a widely publicized toll-free number. The Technical Assistance Center allowed technicians at headquarters to solve specific service problems at dealerships by directly reading data from the engine via a computer link. The engine at the dealership could even be "revved" by computer from Flint.

Another example was OSCAR (On-Site Computer-Aided Research), a system of car-mounted sensors that provided data to a computer installed in a GMC van. Virtually instantaneously, engineers could determine how a test car was operating and what changes, if any, were required to meet performance specifications. Planned initially to assist racing teams using Buick V-6 engines, it also reduced engineering development time and costs on prototype passenger cars.

For the 1985-86 car show season, Buick displayed a concept car called Wildcat. The name had been used on three show cars in the Fifties and on later production models, but this was a car unlike any seen before. It incorporated four-wheel drive and a McLaren engine based on Buick's 3.8-liter V-6 block mounted just behind the seats. The top of the engine was visible through an opening in the rear deck. The original theme came from Center for Creative Studies students and Buick Design Studio 1; the final version, developed by GM Advanced Design Studio 2, was used to generate excitement about Buick engine technology (see box pg. 324-31).

Buick received worldwide attention for that technology when the only two competing Buick V-6-powered cars set records in qualifying 1-2 against a field of Cosworth-powered cars for the 1985 Indianapolis 500 (see pg. 324-11).

Some of the new models of 1986 were not successful. Riviera's instrument panel with its TV screen fascinated some customers but not many auto writers, and the down-sized styling was even more unpop-

This page: From top, 1983 NASCAR Grand National Champion Buick Regal, its driver Bobby Allison, 1984 Regals at IMSA Kelly American Challenge, driven by Robert Overby and Tommy Riggins. Opposite page: Women and minorities at Buick: From left, June Lazar and G. Lynne Dower, first bonus-eligible women at Buick, in 1977, as manager of sales distribution and as sales zone manager; Anna S. Kretz, first woman to achieve that status in engineering in 1981; Claude A. Verbal, first bonus-eligible black at the company in 1977; William E. Powell, first black sales zone manager.

ular. Sales began to plummet. The front-drive LeSabre was another slow starter. Buick City was just ramping up, and LeSabre production moved slowly as the plant struggled with the GM reorganization, combined work forces (as many transferred to Buick City from the closed former Fisher Body Flint Plant), new processes, balky robots and a new quest for quality. In a few years Buick City and LeSabre would become quality stars, all the more impressive because that required dramatic improvement following the rocky start of the mid-Eighties. For the moment, Buick had lost its momentum. Instead of heading for third place in industry sales, the division was headed for seventh.

But as Buick moved into the last half of the Eighties, one future product was already stirring considerable press interest. It was a two-passenger luxury car. Buick dealers had marketed the Opel GT in the early Seventies, but Buick hadn't had its own two-place car since before World War II. However, Buick product planners had been looking at two-seaters since the mid-Seventies. Among several pilot projects was a mid-engine sports car using X-body components and a high-performance L4 engine. Don Sullivan, manager of product planning, and Tom Patrick, strategic planner, were early sponsors of the car. Jay Qualman, who had joined Buick in 1977 as a senior car-line planner, pushed the idea of a short-stroke, high-output V-6. Chief Engineer Reuss liked the idea but objected to the mid-engine proposal, preferring the engine in the front.

Buick considered building such a car with two-plus-two seating in Japan, but McPherson thought the cost was too high and dropped the idea. "When I made that decision, the engineering department was in shambles, but the financial department was in ecstasy," he quipped. The two-seater sponsors suffered other disappointments along the way, but with Reuss' return as general manager, a new luxury two-seater approach emerged. By mid-1981, Qualman, by then strategic programs manager, had Reuss' backing to push the idea.

"We saw a good potential market for Buick in a car that had two seats, the styling of a sports car, and the comfort of a Riviera," said

Qualman. "If we could get the right combination of styling, comfort, handling, power and price, we could virtually create a new niche in the market."

When Qualman became manager of product planning in 1982, Lynn L. Salata was named strategic planning manager in Qualman's organization. She specifically concentrated on the two-place car program and helped carry the concept through final presentation to corporate leaders. Qualman, who was named Buick's general director of advertising in July 1987, was then in the unusual position of directing advertising for the car he helped conceive.

The assignment to develop a styling concept for the Buick two-place car reached GM Advanced Design Studio Number 2 in 1982. David S. McIntosh, the studio's assistant chief, won an internal competition with his concept drawing and completed a clay scale model in July. The car went through a series of detail changes, but the concept fiberglass model completed in early 1983 retained most of McIntosh's original flavor.

Developers wanted a name for the car to focus attention on the program and so they could make a nameplate to give a finished appearance to the full-size model. David R. North, then the studio's styling chief, suggested "Reata." North, who grew up on ranches in the west, said he remembered the word (pronounced Ree-OTT-ah) from his childhood. Also spelled "riata," it is defined in Webster's New World Dictionary as a Spanish-American term for lariat. But North had another reason for remembering the word. He had been "best boy," a member of the film crew, for the Fifties movie *Giant*, which takes place at a ranch called the Reata Ranch. Salata added another "t" for appearance and recommended "Reatta" to top management. The name was used by planners for several years before it was made official in the summer of 1986.

In March 1984, Buick received corporate approval to produce the two-seater. Hackworth, who by then had succeeded Reuss as general manager, said the key to approval was splitting the decision-making

The 1986 Buicks: This page: Riviera and its instrument panel with Graphic Control Center. Opposite page: From top, LeSabre Coupe, LeSabre Limited Sedan, Electra Park Avenue Sedan and Somerset T Type.

process on whether to build it and where to build it.

"We persuaded the corporation to first consider whether we could have the two-seater—we would come back later and recommend where to build it," Hackworth said. "That strategy worked. We won approval for the car."

Once the "go" decision was made, the small concept-car organization was expanded quickly to move the car—code-name GM33—to engineering design and production. Frank L. Colvin was the first vehicle program manager. When he was named manufacturing engineering manager for the Buick-Oldsmobile-Cadillac Group's Flint (former C/H) Product Team in late 1984, J. Robert Thompson, who had been manufacturing manager at Cadillac, succeeded him on December 1, 1984.

The program moved forward on a number of fronts. At GM Advanced Design 2, John K. "Kip" Wasenko, who had succeeded North, qualified the car for production by changing the hood slightly, adding 5-mph bumpers and making other detail modifications.

After decisions were made to use the assistance of British firms because U.S. suppliers were overworked at the time, Robert J. Merkle was sent to England in 1984 as project manager for manufacturing/process engineering for the car in the United Kingdom. Like most other members of the Reatta team, Merkle was motivated, he said, "by the uniqueness of the assignment."

The team was coming together. Randy A. Wightman, who had been a Buick staff engineer, was named the vehicle's chief engineer June 1, 1984. Donald R. Cantleberry, who had been with the program since

mid-1981 to oversee the initial packaging of the car at GM Design, became assistant chief engineer. Robert R. Haist later went to England as validations systems manager for Reatta. At Buick headquarters, Thomas C. Englin was named product line manager for the car.

British firms were placed under contract. Hawtal Whiting Design and Engineering Co., in Pitsea, was contracted for design and engineering, and prototype build. Abbey Panels, near Coventry, made the bodies in white and shipped them to GM's Bedford Truck, near Luton, for dipping in prime. Aston-Martin Tickford, also near Coventry, painted the bodies and assembled the rest of the vehicles. Lamb-Sceptre Ltd., of Bishop Stortford and Mildenhall, was contracted on assembly and sub-assembly process, tool design and manufacture, and to interface with product engineering on feasibility and prototype build. In Japan, Ogihara Iron Works of Ota City was contracted to build sheet-metal dies for the new car.

Off-site meetings had a definite international flavor with British and Japanese representatives discussing the program with representatives of GM and B-O-C design, engineering and manufacturing organizations and Buick product planners. Adding to the international flavor, one of the meetings was in Sarnia, Ontario, Canada. During one four-month period, engineers in the United States and England communicated weekly using satellite-beamed teleconferencing.

The development team went to a Bedford plant near Lisbon, Portugal, to study a special paint-dipping process that requires less space than usual, yet assures that the paint flows into every crevice of the car body. Most road testing of prototypes took place at the Bedford

Proving Ground at Millbrook, England. Lab testing and barrier testing in England was done at the Motor Industry Research Association facilities near Nuneaton. Mountain and desert testing that would normally have taken place near the GM Desert Proving Ground was done for several weeks in Spain because of its proximity to England.

Manufacturing tooling for the body that was designed and built in England was shipped to the United States for installation in the American plant, which was selected in late 1984. Reatta would be built in Lansing, Michigan, at a totally renovated plant that had once been part of the Oldsmobile complex.

Although rumors of a Buick two-seater had circulated in the press for several years, Buick executives did not publicly discuss the car until January 1985. On January 26, Buick announced that production of a new car would go to Lansing. Four days later, then-GM President F. James McDonald confirmed to reporters that the Lansing plant would build the two-seater for Buick. Bob Thompson, the program manager, would also be the plant manager.

While the Reatta project was entering its final stages, a change in Buick's leadership was announced. Edward H. Mertz, 49, chief engineer from 1981 to 1984, was appointed Buick general manager and a GM vice president on August 1, 1986. Mertz had been named chief engineer of B-O-C's Detroit Product Team in 1984 and manager of its Lansing Product Team in 1985. (As the GM reorganization evolved, the E/K/V Team was renamed Detroit Product Team and then absorbed by Cadillac; J/N evolved into Lansing Product Team and finally Lansing Automotive Division; C/H Product Team became Flint Product Team and then Flint Automotive Division). Mertz and Hackworth traded jobs, with Hackworth moving to head of Lansing Automotive Division.

As Mertz became personally involved in making final decisions on Reatta's wheels, upholstery and other details and trim—and on plans for a future convertible—Bob Thompson in Lansing moved Reatta closer to production.

Union and management worked closely together to develop innovative production methods. For example, employees developed a die-change system, using basically conventional equipment, that resulted in die changes in about 10 minutes. Die changes at one time required several hours. Employees even determined the plant's name: Reatta Craft Centre.

The Reatta was assembled under a "craft station" concept. Under this concept, the car is stopped in front of a group of workers, rather than passing by them on an assembly line.

"With the craft station process, the worker is able to pace the building of the vehicle, rather than the moving assembly line determining the pace," Thompson said.

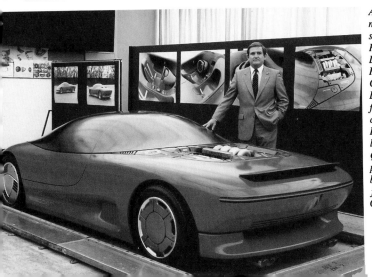

Above: Buick's senior staff under the new GM organization: From left, seated, William J. Atkinson, Gilbert H. Cass, Donald E. Hackworth, David S. Sharpe; from left, standing, R. J. Adams, Jack W. Qualman, John C. Carlson, Thomas L. Pond, and L. D. Robbins. Left: Hackworth with a full-size model of the 1985 Buick show car, the four-wheel-drive Wildcat. Right: Discussing the Reatta are (from left) Strategic Planning Director Jay Qualman; Lynn L. Salata, marketing planning manager; Donald R. Cantleberry, assistant vehicle chief engineer for the car; and David R. North, GM advanced design studio head.

As Buick began to develop its final marketing plans, Joseph J. Fitzsimmons at Buick headquarters in Flint was named marketing line manager for Reatta.

Meanwhile, Ed Mertz was carefully developing his plans for Buick's future. He worked with engineering and design people on new-product plans—and he ordered a thorough study of Buick's "image" and future direction. Buick wasn't the only GM division focusing on its future—they all were. In the highly competitive market of the late Eighties, GM recognized the need to muster its substantial resources to fight external competition and to limit direct competition between sister divisions. As a result, each car division was required to define its role.

Mertz said Buick's decisions on its future direction were about much more than "image"—they were about what he called "the essence of Buick." And he settled on one phrase to describe that essence: Premium American Motorcars.

"The words themselves do not convey the intensity of thought, planning and analysis that went into putting them together, nor the impact they will have on our future," he said. "When we say Premium, it's because our cars will be moving upscale, with added value and substance. American, in that we will—more than any other GM division—serve the needs of the domestic-oriented buyer. Motorcar, because the word conveys the prestige that capsulizes what makes a Buick a Buick."

His task force on future direction had distilled the texture of Buick's past to four other words that Mertz regarded as the elements that would chart the division's future: Substantial. Distinctive. Powerful. Mature.

Powerful was a word aptly describing one 1986-87 Buick that earned rave reviews in the automotive press. Writers discovered that the addition of an intercooler to the Regal Grand National's turbocharged 3.8-liter V-6 engine had created the quickest production car built in the United States. While Buick conservatively claimed the Grand National for those two years could reach 60 mph in 6.9 seconds, journalists found they could do even better: *Car and Driver* clocked its GN's 0-60 time as a stunning 4.9 seconds. Ron Yuille, later manager of engine development at Buick Special Products Engineering, headed the group in charge of developing the intercooled turbo. His key associates on the project included Ann Moss, Jeff Lane, Jim Royer, Steve Ives, Joe Vito, Bill Blackman and Herold Hadley.

Two other performance-oriented Buicks were produced in small numbers late in the 1986 model year. One was the Century Gran Sport, of which 1,029 were built. All were black and equipped with a rear spoiler and distinctive 15-inch aluminum wheels. Large "Buick" decals were placed in the trunk so the buyer could decide whether to use them. If they weren't used, the Buick name didn't appear on the car's exterior. The 3.8-liter SFI V-6 was standard, as were complete instrumentation, including tach, and a special suspension.

Even rarer was the 1986 LeSabre Grand National, of which only 117 were built to qualify the body style for NASCAR competition. These were among the first LeSabre coupes built at Buick City and were also all black (although white was also planned), with sport suspension, 3.8-liter SFI V-6, leather-wrapped steering wheel, 15-inch alloy wheels with Eagle GT tires and rear quarter-window close-outs.

Buick continued its practice of occasionally packaging special cars to be sold regionally when it offered the Somerset and Skylark Sport Edition only in California in 1986 and '87. These had specific packages of standard and optional equipment to appeal to Californians. Standard equipment included 14-inch Shelby aluminum wheels, Eagle GT blackwalls, Gran Touring suspension and wide body moldings.

While 1987 was largely a carryover year for Buick, there was a new LeSabre T Type coupe, designed to appeal to younger, nontraditional Buick buyers. Similar in concept to the LeSabre GN, its features included a front air dam, black exterior moldings and grille, Gran Touring suspension, quartz analog gauges and special aluminum wheels with Eagle GT tires. Later in the model year, the T Type received thermoplastic front fenders, a first for Buick. Like other LeSabres, the T Type had a 3.8-liter SFI V-6 with roller lifters and a four-speed automatic transmission. Development was credited to Jon Lauckner, product-line manager; Mike Doble, advanced concepts manager in Buick Engineering; and Chuck Jensen, project engineer.

Attracting a lot of attention in 1987 was a special "aftermarket" edition of the Regal Grand National that performed even better than the GN. ASC Incorporated (formerly American Sunroof) announced in February 1987 that it would offer 500 of the special models, called GNX, in cooperation with McLaren Engines. Even with a hefty suggested price tag of $29,290 (which dealers boosted substantially), demand for the GNX far exceeded supply.

Doble and Jensen were in charge of developing the prototype, with assistance from Jeff Lane at B-O-C Powertrain. Chief Engineer Dave Sharpe had started the GNX project when he asked Doble to see if he could develop a special car to mark the Grand National's farewell as rear-wheel-drive Regal production was phased out.

Starting with a heavily optioned 1987 Grand National, the GNX had such features as a ceramic turbine and dynamic oil seal in the turbocharger; a more efficient intercooler; recalibrated PROM (programmable read-only memory computer chip); an auxiliary transmission oil cooler; 16-inch aluminum alloy wheels with Eagle GT tires; a modified rear suspension with longitudinal torque bar and Panhard rod; modified wheel openings with fender flares; functional air exhausts (portholes!) in the front fenders; and full analog instrumentation. Unofficial horsepower numbers were over 300. *Car and Driver* wrung out a 0-60 clocking of 4.7 seconds in a prototype. The final production total for

Two limited-production Buicks for mid-1986: A total of just 117 LeSabre Grand Nationals (left) were assembled to qualify the body configuration for NASCAR competition. Nearly as rare was the Century Gran Sport (right), of which 1029 examples were built. Both were produced in black only.

GNX was 547.

As a result of all the publicity for GNX and for Regal Grand National performance, Grand National was suddenly hot in the marketplace. GN production, which had been 2,000 in 1984, 2,102 in 1985 and 5,512 in 1986, soared to 20,193 in 1987 (not including the 547 GNXs and 1,547 Regal T Types). In an unusual move, Buick went back into production of 1987 Grand Nationals after the end of normal 1987 production and built 10,634 between August and December 1987. Although they were built during the 1988 model year, the GNs produced during the extended run were 1987 models.

Robert A. Colvin, a Buick dealer in Springhill, Louisiana, bought the last GN off the line on December 11, 1987, although a B-O-C employee purchased the GN with the last vehicle identification number. The bodies were assembled at the B-O-C Flint Body Assembly Plant (formerly Fisher Body Flint Plant) and shipped to Pontiac Final Assembly. Colvin and his family followed his car through the assembly process and he wrote a dramatic account of the day for *Inside Buick*. After the body was dropped onto the chassis, he wrote, "one older lady walked over and gave me a big hug. She looked up with tears streaming down her cheeks and said, 'You take care of our car. You know it was really built by the best.'"

Although not a major year for new products, 1987 was a year of reorganization. Buick realigned its field sales and service operations, reducing field offices from 24 to 15 and creating a Dealer Assistance Center at Buick headquarters in Flint to work with smaller-volume dealers across the country. Robert E. Coletta, an assistant general sales manager, led the reorganization, called "Project Spearhead." The Dealer Assistance Center became operational in July 1987.

That same month, Coletta was appointed Buick general sales and service manager, succeeding Atkinson, who had moved to GM of Canada in a similar position. Coletta was a 30-year Buick veteran. A native of Memphis, Tennessee, he had joined Buick as a GMI co-op student in 1955. He served in various sales and service assignments in Jacksonville, Charlotte, Atlanta, Dallas, Chicago and St. Louis be-

California-only Somerset Sport Edition was offered in 1986-87.

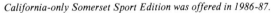

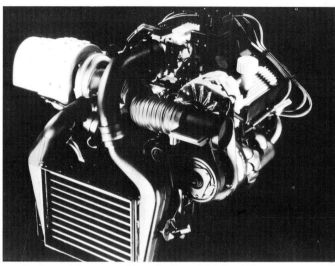

Above: The Regal Grand National became America's quickest production car in 1986, when a new intercooler boosted the output of its turbocharged 3.8-liter SFI V-6 (right) to 245 bhp. Below: The 1987 GNX, built in cooperation with ASC and McLaren Engines, was even faster. Production was limited to 547 units.

Below: LeSabre T Type coupe was new for 1987.

fore being appointed zone manager at Buffalo in 1978. He had similar jobs in New York and Detroit and became assistant general sales manager for the Midwest in 1983 and for the northeast in 1984.

Darwin Clark was promoted to the new position of general marketing manager, reporting directly to Mertz. Engineering and Strategic Planning were combined under Dave Sharpe, who became general engineering and planning manager. Another new member of Buick's senior staff was Comptroller Richard L. Payne, who succeeded 1985-86 Comptroller James R. Cooney. Tim Logsdon was named to the new position of general director of divisional planning under Sharpe. Jay Qualman was appointed general director of advertising, an assignment described by Mertz as representing an increased emphasis on advertising in Buick's overall marketing strategy.

The revamped organization would direct the introduction of what Mertz called "one of the most important new models Buick has ever introduced"—the front-wheel drive 1988 Regal. The Regal was to be the first of a major new line of GM mid-sized cars—developed under a multi-billion dollar program code-named GM10—to arrive in dealer showrooms. Regals would go on sale October 1, 1987, about six months in advance of GM10s from Oldsmobile and Pontiac that would use the same platform but entirely different sheet metal. "There are few times in a person's work life," said Mertz, "when he or she can be part of something very big, very important. This is one of those times. I can hardly overemphasize how we feel about this venture."

Regal was developed through a Product Development Team process, 324-21B

Buick's all-new 1988 front-wheel-drive Regal.

defined as a community of individuals representing various organizations within GM who work together to achieve common goals in a specified time frame.

David E. Fleming, product-line manager, who had been with the program since its early development in 1981, said, "we pushed the decision-making out to the people who were the most knowledgeable, and we involved key suppliers very early in the design process to get their ideas."

Another process, nicknamed "Mona Lisa" after the famous painting, was also an important part of Regal development. It was used by engineers to identify the best features on the best cars in the world. Regal's features and functions could be developed to compare with world-class standards. Regal was the first General Motors car to benefit from the Mona Lisa process.

Introducing Regal, Mertz said special emphasis was placed on ride and handling, durability and ease of maintenance and servicing. David Clark, chief of Buick Design Studio 2 during much of the design work, said the Regal was also the most aerodynamic Buick in history. Its drag coefficient, as measured in wind-tunnel tests, was .299 for a clay model and .305 for a prototype, about a 33 percent improvement over the former Regal. Two major design features, flush glass and "doors-into-roof" construction, were big factors. The design studio received the assignment to start work on Regal in 1982 and the design essentially jelled by May 1983. Steven D. Pasteiner, who helped design it, said he didn't try to build in a series of Buick design "cues" but instead developed what he called a stance of implied confidence.

Regal's engine was a 2.8-liter MFI V-6. Among what Mertz described as "small, thoughtful features" were lubricated-for-life suspension, easy access to fuses, electronics connectors and front suspension cartridges, and even remote jump-start terminals for emergency battery jumping.

In a March 1987 visit to the highly automated manufacturing complex, called "GM Autoplex," in Oshawa, Ontario, Canada, where Regal would be built, Mertz told an audience: "How our Regal is perceived by the public—in terms of quality, reliability and durability—is going to be critical to GM's future success . . . . Buick and the Oshawa plant will be telling the world that the new GM coupes are world class." He also noted that the connection between Buick headquarters in Flint and the plant in Oshawa renewed a historic partnership. The beginnings of GM of Canada could be traced to the 1905-08 period when Flint's Billy Durant and Oshawa's Sam McLaughlin reached agreement on the joint Buick-McLaughlin venture.

Also for 1988, Buick offered a new "3800" engine—a redesigned 3.8-liter SFI V-6—as standard on Riviera, Reatta, Electra and LeSabre T Type, and optional on other LeSabres. It had a redesigned cylinder block featuring a balance shaft gear-driven by the crankshaft for reduced vibration. Cylinder bores were relocated in the block, and intake manifold and cylinder heads were redesigned to increase fuel efficiency and reduce emissions. The engine was rated at 165 horsepower, compared with 150 on the regular 3.8-liter SFI V-6.

Another new engine, the Quad 4, a 16-valve, dual-overhead-cam four, made its Buick debut in the Skylark. (The Somerset name was dropped, and Skylark was used for the N-car coupe as well as sedan).

Skylark's base engine, a 2.5-liter four, received many improvements, including the addition of a balance shaft and lighter pistons to further enhance engine smoothness. The 3.0-liter V-6 was one optional powerplant but the Quad 4 received more attention. It was so efficient that it didn't need an EGR system in order to meet current emissions requirements. It had 150 hp and 160 ft. lbs. of torque and was engineered for a long service life.

Skylark coupes featured composite-headlamp front-end treatment. The most noticeable interior change was the new standard analog gauge cluster, which included a trip odometer. The electronic digital cluster was now an option.

Meanwhile, there was a Silver Anniversary Riviera sporting a special hood ornament and instrument-panel trim plate. The GCC, now called Electronic Control Center, had added capabilities, including a personal reminder calendar, speed alert and an optional compass.

Regal got off to a fast start, leading all American mid-size coupes in sales the first year. The 1988 Regal was named winner of *Home Mechanix* magazine's "Easy Maintenance Car of the Year" award. The magazine noted the engine compartment was well designed to encourage owner maintenance and cited a long list of features, from rust-resistant fasteners to lubricated-for-life suspension.

This was a busy time for Buick, especially for concept cars. Three

Above: The clay model of the Reatta approaches its final form in the GM design studio.
Right: Bob Thompson (left) Reatta program and plant manager, and Stan Pewoski, UAW Local 1618 shop committee chairman, inspect a Reatta's underside.

"one-off" models from Buick Engineering were based on production 1987 Riviera T Types. They were a convertible, turbo (with a 3.8-liter V-6 estimated at 250 hp and 300 lb. ft. of torque), and sport (featuring a de-chromed and de-badged body, matte-black grille, and rear spoiler). A concept convertible based on the front-drive 1988 Regal was displayed at major auto shows.

A silver-blue concept car, Lucerne, was introduced in New York City's Waldorf-Astoria Hotel at GM's "Teamwork and Technology—for Today and Tomorrow" exhibition in January 1988. Lucerne was described as a prestige/luxury front-drive coupe with exceptional comfort for four adults in a stylish environment.

It had flush glass and no door handles or other exterior trim. And it featured a Navicar computer navigation system, developed by GM's Delco Electronics Division from a system formerly known as ETAK. Navicar used advanced "dead reckoning"—through sensors on the wheels and steering—to track the car's location continually from a starting point entered by the driver.

Other features: interior surfaces trimmed in burled walnut and leather, hands-free cellular phone, optional computer terminal "for the mobile business person," four-wheel independent suspension and electronic ride control, electronically shifting four-speed automatic transmission, and 3.8-liter V-6 engine (a fuel-injected 32-valve V-8 was originally announced but never installed).

Perhaps most importantly, Lucerne advanced Mertz's vision of Buick's future direction. He said Lucerne had "grace and solidity" and was an example of "providing distinctive automobiles that are substantial and powerful . . . an example of how upscale cars built for mature buyers can be expressive and exciting."

It later became more exciting, transformed into a convertible to make an even more dramatic statement—and to give Lucerne several more years of life on the circuit.

Also in January 1988, the Reatta coupe and a concept Reatta convertible were unveiled at the Detroit Auto Show. The coupe would be introduced in dealer showrooms later that month as a 1988 model. Reatta was positioned as a luxury two-place car with a combination of sporty and aerodynamic styling, nimble handling and a comfortable and quiet "Buick ride." The 3800 V-6 with four-speed automatic transmission was the only powertrain offered.

"We believe Reatta has created virtually a new niche in the marketplace," said Mertz at the introduction. "Reatta has the elements of both a luxury car and a sports car, yet will be priced many thousands of dollars less than luxury and sports cars at the top end of the market." 324-21D

Mertz described Reatta as much more comfortable than most sports cars. Almost every conceivable feature was standard, including four-wheel power anti-lock disc brakes, Gran Touring suspension and Riviera's CRT instrument panel. All major exterior body panels except the roof and front fenders were double galvanized for added rust protection. The front fenders were constructed of a thermo-plastic material known as GTX, designed to protect against stone dings and low-impact damage. The slippery design had a drag coefficient of .34. The only extra-cost options were a power sunroof and 16-way adjustable driver's seat. Reatta was described by *Popular Science* in the "Best of What's New" as one of the outstanding products of 1988.

In the summer of 1988, more than 700 vintage Buicks were gathered in Flint as the Buick Club of America "came home" for its national meet to celebrate Buick's 85th anniversary. "There's a close relationship between your interest—the past—and our interest—Buick's future success," Mertz told BCA members at the awards banquet. He presented his General Manager's Trophy to the car he felt best exemplified Buick's heritage and future direction—a 1956 Roadmaster hardtop sedan owned by Peter Maguire of Baltimore. At least 28 states and three Canadian provinces were represented. Buick owners flew in from England, Sweden, the Netherlands, Australia, Colombia and South Africa. Before the year ended, there was another bow to heritage. A full-size statue of Billy Durant, Buick promoter and GM founder, was dedicated near two restored historical buildings—the Durant-Dort Carriage Co. headquarters and Flint Road Cart Co. factory—on December 8, 1988, the 127th anniversary of his birth. Among the attendees were two of Durant's granddaughters and several great-grandchildren.

For 1989, Buick offered extensively restyled Rivieras and Centurys, as well as a new luxury flagship—Park Avenue Ultra.

A suspension named DynaRide, introduced on some models in 1988, was standard on all 1989 Buicks except station wagons and those models equipped with Gran Touring suspension. DynaRide was described as a combination of deflected-disc shock absorber valving and other carefully tuned components that provided an unusually smooth and comfortable ride without sacrificing handling response.

Among new features, a compact disc player was available on Regal. Also new was a remote keyless entry system, which was optional on Reatta, Riviera, Electra/Park Avenue models (including the new Ultra) and Regal. An anti-lock brake system (ABS) was again standard on Reatta and Electra T Type and remained optional on other Electra/Park Avenue models and Riviera. Anti-lock brakes were available for the first time on Regal.

Riviera was 11 inches longer for 1989, mostly because of a new rear end design. The personal luxury coupe had a "stronger" vertical bar grille, new chrome bumper design, wider roof pillars and more curvaceous rear quarter panels.

Giving Riviera a new look was a major job. Under the leadership of Anthony H. Derhake, vehicle chief engineer for Riviera, the Riviera team compressed what would have taken three full years of development into one and one half years to meet market demands.

Century had a major facelift with more contemporary roofline, and rear-window treatment. Also new were the grille, front-end panel, fascia, body color bumpers, flush composite headlamps with wrap-around park and turn lamps, rear quarter panels, deck lid and full-width taillamps with center back-up lights. The new optional 3300 V-6, a 3.3-liter powerplant with multi-port fuel injection and roller lifters rated at 160 hp, replaced both previous optional engines, the 2.8-liter V-6 and 3.8-liter V-6.

Park Avenue Ultra was Buick's latest definition of a premium American motorcar. Its interior included leather on all surfaces of the seats, on the door panels and steering wheel, plus padded leather on the glove-box door. The 20-way power driver and passenger seats included the conventional six-way power adjustments, plus two-way power recliners, two-way power adjustable thigh and lumbar supports and four-way power adjustable headrests.

Reatta had minor changes. On the outside, there was a larger hood medallion. On the inside, detail changes included moving the electric trunk and fuel-door releases from the console to a more secure position inside the glove box and equipping the glove box with a new manual latch, replacing the previous electric release. Remote keyless entry was now standard.

Skylark received the 3300 V-6 replacing the 3-liter as an optional engine (the Quad 4 remained another option and the 2.5-liter Tech 4, now with balance shift and lighter pistons, remained standard). Buick marketed the Skylark Special Edition across the country and offered a Luxury Edition with formal vinyl top later in the model year.

In its last year, the subcompact Skyhawk was again offered in coupe, sedan and wagon models, as well as the sporty S/E coupe with concealed headlamps, Gran Touring suspension and gauge package. Back in the oil scare of the mid-Seventies, Buick had worked long hours to bring the economical Skyhawk to market. But now times were different. Full-size cars could get good fuel economy, too. GM was repositioning its divisions to attack separate segments of the market. For Buick and its upscale market, Skyhawk no longer fit. Its departure at the end of the 1989 model year was announced April 5, 1989.

In late February and early March 1989, Buick put on an unusual event for the press at Firebird Raceway in Phoenix. It took six experimental cars out of hiding and turned them over to the press for evaluation. There were two reasons for showing these cars. One was simply to get across the message that "powerful" is a key word if you're

Above: David Kimble cutaway of the 1988 Reatta coupe. Right: Fiberglass model of Reatta ultimately won GM corporate approval, minus the lift-off roof shown. With the model are David S. McIntosh (left), assistant chief of GM Advanced Design Studio No. 2, who drew original Reatta sketches, and Theodore T. Polak Jr., a designer. Below: The final design.

talking about Buicks. The other was to get the opinions of experienced writers on what a powerful Buick powertrain should be. Most of the concept cars had been developed by Advanced Concepts Manager Michael E. Doble and his organization at the request of Dave Sharpe, who wanted to test cars along several different lines.

They included three Reattas: a rear-drive coupe with a turbocharged and intercooled 3.8-liter V-6 (245 hp at 4400 rpm, 355 lb. ft. of torque at 2800, 0-60 in 7 seconds, top speed of 140 mph); a "high-boost" front-drive coupe developed by Larry Baker, Buick's manager of vehicle activities, with a hand-built 3.8-liter V-6 and many Grand National components and special Garrett high-response turbo (245 hp and 300 lb. ft. of torque, 0-60 in under 6 seconds, top speed estimated at 150 mph); and a "low-boost" front-drive coupe with turbo 3.8-liter V-6 (230 hp at 5100 rpm, 260 lb. ft. of torque at 2500 rpm, 0-60 in 8 seconds, top speed 140 mph).

There were two Regals—one a front-drive coupe with Eaton supercharged 3.8-liter V-6 with modified intake manifold and high-performance pistons (0-60 in 8 seconds, top speed of 130 mph). The other Regal was an extensively modified rear-drive coupe with turbocharged and intercooled 3.8-liter V-6 with many specifications of the former Grand National engine and raised hood with functional louvers (245 hp at 4400 rpm and 355 lb. ft. of torque at 2800 rpm, 0-60 in 6.5 seconds, top speed of 140). In contrast to these smaller cars was a rear-drive Electra Estate Wagon with a modified Grand National engine—and an unreal performance of 0-60 in 5.18 seconds.

There were a lot of differing opinions but a consensus favored supercharging over turbocharging. "The supercharged Regal is what a Buick should be—it should be in production now," was one view. Surprisingly, the writers in general applauded front drive over rear drive. "There may be a marketing need for a rear-drive Reatta but no engineering reason," said Dennis Simanaitis of *Road & Track*.

The concept car event had an important impact on Buick product plans. When Buick turned to extra-performance engines again late in the 1991 model year, it went with supercharging rather than the turbo, and the first supercharger application was in a Park Avenue Ultra—a front-drive model.

While Buick was testing new performance cars, it was also performing well on the race tracks in the late Eighties. Bobby Allison won the 1988 Daytona 500 in a LeSabre before a serious injury on June 19 at Pocono shelved his driving career. Ricky Rudd won the Watkins Glen International in a Regal. Bobby Hillin, Jr. and his Stavola Brothers teammates captured the Sears DieHard Racer of the Year award for completing the most racing miles during the Winston Cup series. Tommy Ellis won the NASCAR Busch Grand National title in a LeSabre and Buick V-6s won 22 of 30 races in that series.

Scott Brayton was the top Buick qualifier at the 1988 Indianapolis 500 (7th at 212.624 mph) but Jim Crawford all but stole the show. Despite severe foot and leg injuries from the previous year, Crawford led the Indy 500 by mid-race in a Buick V-6-powered car and was running second with less than 10 laps to go when a flat tire caused an unscheduled pit stop that dropped him to sixth in the final standings. It was the best finish ever for a Buick at the Indy 500. Tom Hessert in a Buick-powered car won the IMSA Camel Lights driver's crown. Kenny Bernstein, driving the world's only Buick Reatta-bodied funny car, brought Buick its second straight NHRA Winston drag-racing world championship.

In 1989, Buick's "low-deck" 3.3-liter V-6 debuted and set new stock-block qualifying records at Indianapolis. Crawford qualified fourth with a four-lap record pace of 221.450 mph. Tom Sneva upped the one-lap stock-block record to 223.178. On race day, Brayton matched Crawford's mark for the best Indy 500 Buick performance when he finished sixth. Ricky Rudd drove a Regal to a road-course victory at Sears Point in Sonoma, California, in NASCAR Winston Cup and Rudd and his King Racing teammates won the Sears Diehard award. Dick Trickle, at 47, became the oldest rookie of the year in Winston Cup, driving a Regal. Buick 4.5-liter V-6s dominated Busch Grand National stock car racing, winning 23 pole positions and 25 of 29 races. The top four positions in the final point standings went to Buick drivers Rob Moroso (champion), Tommy Houston, Tommy Ellis, and L.D. Ottinger.

In IMSA Camel Lights, Buick-powered racers established their dominance by winning both the manufacturers' and drivers' championships. At the season-opening 24 Hours of Daytona, Tom Hessert, Charles Morgan and John Morrison co-drove their Buick/Tiga to an incredible 55-lap margin of victory, a record for the class. Teammates Scott Schubot and Linda Ludemann made history in their Buick/Spice racer. Their S&L Racing entry produced eight of Buick's 11 wins. When the duo co-drove to victory at West Palm Beach, Ludemann became the first woman to win a GTP race in IMSA's 18-year history. Schubot beat fellow Buick driver Charles Morgan for the Camel Lights driver's crown. Wrapping up Buick's era of professional drag racing, Bernstein won three NHRA national events in his 1989 Reatta funny car and finished third in the final point standings. For the first time in recent history, a Buick won in the highly competitive stock car class at the 1988 Pikes Peak Auto Hill Climb as Colorado racing veteran Ralph Bruning sped to a six-second victory in a 1988 Skylark.

Mertz joined with Brock Yates, automotive journalist who created One Lap of America (and earlier the famous Cannonball Run), to announce that Buick would be the official car of the 1988 One Lap, an 8,500-mile auto rally that would circumnavigate the country, touch-

*bove: Lucerne concept car which starred in GM's "Teamwork and Technology" exhibit
id the later convertible version. Below: 1989 Riviera featured more curvaceous rear
anels. Bottom: Park Avenue Ultra became Buick's luxury flagship in 1989.*

ing both coasts, and starting and ending in Detroit. Buick's pace car was a red Reatta. Buick's official entry, a 1988 Riviera T Type driven by Karl Chevalier, with a crew of Phil Suomu and Daniel Lyons, won a trophy for finishing fourth and another for having the top American-built car in the final standings.

Near the end of the decade, there were two changes on Buick's senior staff. John E. (Jack) DeCou was named public relations director November 1, 1988. The position had been open since the retirement of Tom Pond nearly a year earlier.

DeCou, born in Flint, had been with Buick for most of his 31-year GM career and had held various engineering assignments, including senior staff engineer for body, engine and experimental activities. In 1984, he became manager of transmissions and drivetrains at B-O-C Powertrain and returned to Buick in 1987 as director of service engineering. DeCou had a bachelor's degree in physics and mathematics from Alma College and a master's degree in business administration from Michigan State University.

Tony Derhake became Buick's general engineering and planning manager November 1, 1989. He succeeded Dave Sharpe, who was named to a similar position at B-O-C headquarters. Derhake, who received a bachelor of science degree in electrical engineering from the University of Missouri-Rolla and attended the University of Illinois executive development program, joined GM in 1969 as a sales and systems engineer with Delco Electronics in Kokomo, Indiana.

Derhake moved to Cadillac in 1977 as a project engineer and through the years enjoyed a series of promotions, specializing in electrical and electronics systems. He was vehicle chief engineer for Riviera and later program manager for Eldorado and Seville before becoming Buick's chief engineer.

As the Eighties drew to an end, Ed Mertz had his team in place, Buick's future direction fully formed and his product plans for the early Nineties nearing reality. There was a feeling around the Buick Administration Building that tough times and hard work had led to solid progress. Buick had come through the GM reorganization, the launch of Buick City, the restructuring of image and several years of sales decline. (Model year sales totaled 601,289 in the 1987 model year, 566,261 in 1988 and 573,280 in 1989).

Now there were some signs of hope for a brighter future. For one thing, the quality was getting much better. For another, the public was beginning to understand that. A stunning accomplishment in a J.D. Power quality survey in June 1989 (described in Chapter 20) brought the message home. There would be no letup in competition from Japanese imports and there would be instability and economic recession in the years just ahead. But more than most domestic makes, Buick was ready for the Nineties.

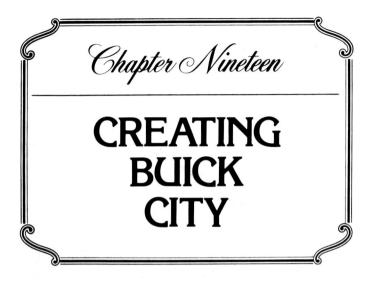

Chapter Nineteen

CREATING BUICK CITY

Buick's most famous manufacturing project was the result of an alarming situation.

"If you looked at corporate allocation charts, Flint Buick assembly was a surplus or 'down' plant," said Jim Hall, who would become production manager of trim, chassis and final assembly at Buick City, the facility he would help create. "It wasn't a game. The corporation was dead serious that we were not going to be in the assembly business. We knew we had to do something different."

In 1979, Hall was assistant superintendent of factory planning, on the staff of Ernest O. Vahala, then Buick's manager of manufacturing engineering. His assignment was spelled out by Edward D. DuCharme, who that year succeeded Bob Breeden as Buick general manufacturing manager. DuCharme had emphasized a program of giving managers of specific areas the responsibility of trying to attract corporate work to the huge Buick complex at Flint. Hall's job: Find work for the south half of the complex, which included the two assembly plants. It was a big job, because it looked like the old assembly plants would soon become vast empty spaces.

In the spring of 1980, GM announced it would spend $40 billion to build new plants, upgrade old ones and install equipment to reach a production capacity by 1984 of six million cars a year with unitized bodies, front-wheel drive and transverse-mounted engines. The corporation had determined that this configuration was best for combining fuel-efficiency with satisfactory interior space.

That scenario did not bode well for Buick assembly in Flint. Front-wheel drive production requires a different kind of assembly line,

meaning big expenses and months of "down" time to convert an existing plant with old rear-drive assembly lines. GM's Assembly Division was in the process of building a number of new $500-million plants around the country to produce the new cars much more efficiently than seemed possible in the old plants. And Buick faced an additional cost penalty because its bodies were trucked across town from the Fisher Body Flint Plant to the Buick complex for final assembly.

Don McPherson, then Buick general manager, had acknowledged when questioned at the 1980 Chicago Auto Show that Buick would be faced with two choices if it were to stay in the car assembly business in the front-wheel-drive era: building a new assembly plant or closing Buick for up to six months for conversion. There was, however, a third possibility—that the corporation might just close Buick assembly at Flint and allow plants elsewhere in the country to pick up the slack.

For a time, a big new assembly plant near Buick was considered. GM chose one site in Vienna Township, outside Flint but still in Genesee County. Flint Mayor James W. Rutherford offered an alternative: a site in Genesee Township which the City of Flint could then annex under an agreement with the township to share revenue. But the U.S. auto slump grew worse; the need for a new assembly plant faded.

Said DuCharme: "As time went on, as auto sales fell, as the financial situation changed, that plant was cancelled, and there was no assembly program for our facility. So we started looking—what can we do?" Under the timetable, the Flint complex would stop building big cars in August of 1983; intermediate-car production would end in August of 1984.

Buick executives sought alternatives. They had already looked at converting to build the front-drive Buick Riviera, Oldsmobile Toronado and Cadillac Eldorado, a job that was awarded to the Linden, NJ GM Assembly Plant starting in the 1979 model year. Undaunted, they looked on. "We looked at the J car, we looked at the N, we looked at the M van," said Hall. "We looked at what it would mean to be in here with military vehicles. We went very hard after the M van (a Chevrolet-GMC product). That program rattled around for quite some time. We were at the point where imminently we were facing going out of the assembly business."

Hall said Buick made twenty-six bids to the corporation for business. All were rejected, except for the van. And DuCharme ultimately decided he didn't want to assemble vans. "I thought it was the wrong business for us to be in. We said we had to take a worldwide look at what we have here to be leaders in the assembly business. What's going to sell us to everybody as being the ones to assemble a product?"

A broad base of Buick management was dedicated to the task. One leading proponent was Leland E. Furse, Jr., manager of Buick's as-

Above from left: Ed DuCharme; Jim Hall; Lee Furse; and Herb Stone. Preceding page: Bill Hutchinson poses with Furse, Stone and DuCharme as electricians Mike Maier and Mike Flynn adjust Buick City's robots.

sembly plants. "I went to management and said, 'Now, we really want to stay in business. I have a lot of good people here, and I don't want to see us lose the business. I am an old Buick guy, and I don't want to see Buick shut their doors forever on their assembly line."

Another was Bill Rowland, the personnel director who had earlier challenged tradition by developing a strong working relationship with the leadership of UAW Local 599. Rowland took a group of top Buick executives to a meeting of Japanese and American businessmen at the University of Nebraska in October 1981, and learned the meaning of words such as "kanban"—just-in-time delivery of components to the assembly line.

Following up that meeting, Rowland had challenged the executives to see how far they could cut costs by following the Japanese example. To emphasize the possibilities at Buick, Rowland opened a presentation for Buick managers in April 1982, with a slide that read: "Toyota City, Japan: Toyota City, U.S.A.—Flint."

Lloyd E. Reuss, who had succeeded McPherson as general manager late in 1980, recalled he was discussing Buick's future a short time later at a worldwide planning conference at the General Motors Technical Center. William B. Larson, then director of GM's Worldwide Planning Group, was listening. When Reuss used the term "Toyota City," Larson corrected him. "You mean 'Buick City,' " he said.

Reuss went public with the name in a speech before the Flint Area Chamber of Commerce at the Flint Hyatt Regency on June 2nd, 1982. Discussing Buick's strategic planning, he said that in one scenario "it was determined that eighty percent of the components for [one future] vehicle could be supplied within a 60-mile radius of Flint. In effect,

we could have our own 'Buick City,' shortening the supply line, reducing inventory, and at the same time improving quality by dealing with area suppliers who can be more responsive to our needs."

Later that month, Furse received approval from DuCharme to form a study team to advance the ideas, and the Buick City project began to take form.

It was somewhat ironic that Furse, in fighting to save Buick assembly, was again facing a Japanese challenge—this time in automobiles. He had been a hero in the Naval Air Corps in World War II, helping rescue a downed U.S. airman in the sea less than a mile from the Japanese shore. Furse, a Hellcat pilot, had been among fighter pilots making sweeps over Tokyo to destroy planes and hangars.

"They were very tough competitors in World War II and they're extremely tough competitors now," Furse said. "But I like to be a winner. And it's kind of like being a loser when you just close down the assembly operations and say we're not going to build any more Buicks forevermore. Buick was one of the cornerstones of General Motors; I just couldn't visualize Buick never assembling any more vehicles.

"And in looking at the studies that had been put together, it became evident to me that we weren't that far behind the Japanese in our assembly costs per se. It was just that we had put in a lot of extra things like inspection and repair that the Japanese don't do—and if I could get rid of the need for those kinds of operations, I could be competitive on a cost basis with the Japanese."

Buick managers also found some factors in their favor. Not only had they been successful in the quick re-introduction of V-6 engines after the 1973 oil embargo, but they also had developed a track record for success by converting the doomed foundry into the sole supplier of torque converters for the transverse-engine, front-wheel-drive automobiles—an effort that included help from the union local in developing innovative work arrangements. Management and the union had also worked together in bringing in additional engine business, engine cradles, components and plastics.

Furse named Frank Meer, superintendent of manufacturing engineering in assembly, as director of the study group. The other members and the areas they represented were: Don Smith, manufacturing engineering; Wayne Iben, financial; Clarence Root, materials management; Al Burdick, purchasing; Len Forbes, sheet metal fabricating; Bill Hutchinson, UAW Local 599 shop committee; Ray LaClair, labor relations; Len Ricard, corporate materials management; Bill Rehklau, industrial engineering; and Hall in manufacturing planning.

Furse said that at first, the study team was not trying for assembly of a specific car. "When we started the off-site meetings (the first was at Mr. Gibby's restaurant in Flint Township June 27th, 1982), we had no idea there was going to be an H car (front-drive 1986 LeSabre)," Furse said. "We just had a philosophy to assemble vehicles, and we didn't care what kind of vehicle it was. We wanted to get the next vehicle that came out. We had all these innovative ideas we were going to achieve to be competitive."

Hall remembered, however, that there had been some "pretty strong" talk about a front-wheel-drive program for the B car (rear-drive LeSabre) which reportedly was backed by Reuss, who was known as "a big-car man." That program had been curtailed because of the dollar crunch of the early 1980s. Hall's responsibilities included knowing GM's product plans for the next few years, and that information served him well.

While Buick managers looked for the key to landing the big job that would guarantee Flint's assembly future, they also sought to adopt the production of some rear-drive cars being displaced from other plants that were being converted to front-wheel drive. For the first time, the Flint Buick plant began assembling other cars as well as Buicks—first, big Chevrolets, then intermediate Oldsmobiles. That work kept the Flint assembly organization intact, buying time while Buick officials sought an overall solution to their problem.

The study team began its clean-sheet approach to assembly with a common goal—to go after the work and do it right. Participants recall there were strong-willed people in the meetings. Inevitably, there were arguments. One of the key questions was: Do you go after the work from a cost perspective—so many dollars a car; or from a purely qualitative perspective—what is the best way to build a car?

"It ended up that we decided to approach it from a quality perspec-

Helen Jacques drives the last Flint-built, rear-drive Regal off the assembly line on February 1, 1985. The plant was then closed for conversion to front-drive production.

tive first, and to let the costs fall where they wanted to be," Hall said. "This was the first time we had put together a plan before the corporation had asked for it. All the others were reactive planning. We said, 'Okay, we're going to put together this plan and when the corporation asks for it, we will be ready to respond with a very comprehensive program.' We started the selling early."

Bill Hutchinson, the union representative on the committee, had been a committeeman or shop comitteeman for twenty-eight of his thirty-four years as a Buick hourly employee. He had seen the change in labor relationships that had once been "miserable," but still wondered about his role: "The first time we put together some proposals and presented them to plant managers and the senior staff at Buick, my comments after the meeting were, 'What the hell am I doing here?' Because I thought my input would be minimal . . . but as the process went on, I saw why I was there. I think I had something to do with selling the project to the corporation."

The study group wanted to complete its plan by September 1982. But there was a continual progression of reviews through October and November. "These guys were off-site for nine months," said Furse. "I didn't think they were ever coming back. But they really did put together a hell of a package."

It was an audacious, high-risk plan. The study team's proposals, if properly implemented, would produce extremely high quality cars at a lower per-unit cost than any other plant in the United States. This would be achieved by a variety of innovations, such as requiring suppliers to provide only perfect parts (there would be minimal in-plant inspections and repairs), and by assuring that each assembler would do his job right the first time (intensive training and the personal motivation of employees were keys to this), thus markedly reducing inspection and repair costs.

The plan included an elaborate just-in-time system under which parts would be delivered at various points along the assembly line every few hours, eliminating the cost of large inventories. All supply containers would be returnable, cutting the cost of throw-away containers and the job of storing and disposing of tons of cardboard. One goal: The total elimination of waste. Sheet-metal parts such as fenders and hoods would be stamped and sent directly to the assembly line, greatly reducing handling (and thus the likelihood of damage) to those parts, and eliminating the need to place them in racks and store them.

Quick die changes—eight minutes instead of eight hours—would be implemented to produce the stampings needed immediately; the exact quantity of parts needed for a shift's production would be made for that shift, eliminating storage of extra parts. Suppliers would be allowed their share of input. For example, PPG Industries, which was named the coatings supplier for Buick City, was asked how it would paint a car if it were in charge; its officials said no one had ever asked them that question before. After recommending innovative ways to apply paint and other coatings, PPG was then given the job of teaching Buick employees how to do it. The assembly plant's success would depend a great deal on the motivation of employees.

Besides motivated employees, there would also be more than 225 robots along the assembly line. Defending the use of robots, DuCharme said, "If we're going to have job security, we're going to have to be competitive in the world market. If we're going to be competitive, we're going to have to be more productive. Of course, automation is part of that productivity."

Finally, in January 1983, it was decision time. GM's top management was to decide where the new H car would be built. For one brief period—24 hours—the study team was convinced it had lost the project to a GM plant in another state.

Hutchinson remembers being in a room, late at night, with Frank Meer and Jim Hall at the Flint Hyatt, awaiting news of the decision. They got word that the H-car assembly job had been given to the other plant. "I said, 'What the hell do I tell the union now?' Because there was nothing else on the horizon."

The next night, he was at a dinner meeting at Bosley's restaurant outside Flint with other members of the study team having, as Hutchinson put it, "an off-site among ourselves." Furse telephoned the group. He had just heard from DuCharme. The decision had changed. Buick would get the H car. "We were elated," said Hutchinson. "Quite a celebration." Said Furse: "I don't know what turned it around. We didn't have it and then the next day we had it. Reuss is the guy who got it turned around, but I don't know how he did it. I know the union-management relationship was a big factor."

Reuss has not commented on that for the record, but the important fact was that the decision was made. Thanks to the study group's effort, the enthusiastic backing by such men as DuCharme, Furse, Rowland, Buick comptroller LeRoy D. Bence Jr., Local 599's Christner and by Reuss' efforts at the top levels of GM, Buick City was a "go" project. Through a herculean effort by Buick management and Local 599, the job of assembling Buicks in the division's home town of Flint was saved. There would be a lot of work ahead, but it would be a lot different to develop an approved project than to win that approval.

Furse, named plant manager of Buick City, moved quickly to implement the plan. He created a "front-end load" team of forty people (it would grow to eighty after six months) to work solely on the project, and out of that group named a design team of ten management and five union representatives.

Various members of the design team visited the most modern auto plants they could find in Scandinavia, Germany, Italy, Spain, England and France. A materials management group went to Toyota City in Japan. With the benefit of this first-hand information, the team settled down to plan every detail of Buick City.

A program the size of this $300-million-plus project required a great many things to happen at once. It was important, for example, to inform Buick City suppliers of what the project required of them, particularly the development and continued production of perfect parts and the need for just-in-time delivery. Some suppliers would set up operations in the St. John Industrial Park adjacent to Buick and nearby.

To coordinate all these activities as well as the overall H-car program, Reuss named Herbert D. Stone program manager of Buick City

Opposite page: William Harchick, an assembly worker for 42 years, drives the last of 14 million rear-drive Buicks off the line on February 8th, 1985. Harchick retired the same day. From left are Ed DuCharme, manufacturing manager; Fred Myers, president of UAW Local 599; Jim Hall, production manager for trim, chassis and final assembly; Lee Furse, assembly plants manager; Flint Mayor James A. Sharp; Buick City "Mayor" Herb Stone; and Bill Hutchinson, Local 599's representative to the Buick City study team. This page, above, left to right, the study team: Frank Meer; Alan Burdick; Len Forbes. Left: Bill Hutchinson. Below, left to right: Wayne Iben; Ray LaClair; Bill Rehklau. Bottom, left to right: Leonard Ricard; Clarence Root; Don Smith.

on March 4th, 1983. Stone, a native of Sparta, Michigan and a graduate of General Motors Institute in Flint, had been Buick's director of reliability and quality control for five years. It wasn't long before he became known as the "mayor of Buick City."

The naming of Buick's quality-control director as program manager was a clear signal that quality was the No. 1 goal of Buick City. Stone had developed a strong quality program, begun under McPherson's direction, that included raising Buick's conformance-to-specifications goal from the reality of seventy-two percent in 1979 to an ideal ninety-nine percent.

The program, with strong input from Local 599, included the development of a quality task force, quality councils, quality coordinators, annual "best in class" meetings and quality-recognition awards. The program was not window dressing. Corporate indexes showed that Buick management and union members had made great strides. The only way to save jobs at the old complex, they had realized, was to be better than the competition. It was this kind of remarkable determination that kept work pouring into the Flint complex at a time when national employment in the auto industry was shrinking rapidly.

There were major organizational changes at Buick and throughout General Motors as the Buick City project moved forward. When the reorganization of GM was announced January 10th, 1984, Reuss was placed in charge of the Chevrolet-Pontiac-GM of Canada Group and was succeeded as Buick general manager by Donald E. Hackworth (see preceding chapter). Christner was defeated in his bid for re-election as president of UAW Local 599 by Fred Myers in June of that year. Rowland retired as Buick personnel director in December and, at his retirement party, was praised by Christner for the foresight which had helped save thousands of Flint jobs.

In fact, management of the Buick City project passed from Buick Motor Division to the Buick-Oldsmobile-Cadillac Group, and specifically to the C/H Product Team, July 1st, 1984, under the GM reorganization (the new GM organization is also explained in the preceding chapter). Many of the same people, however, were still overseeing development. Ed DuCharme was now the C/H Team's manufacturing manager; Lee Furse still headed Buick City assembly operations. Jim Hall, Frank Meer and Bill Hutchinson were still on the project.

Interest in the project continued to grow among the national and international news media, as well as among businesspeople in general. The interest was understandable: Buick City was being presented as a project that would result in the most efficient and innovative assembly plant in the country—and it was going to be built inside the walls of an old plant, in half the floor space of GM's bright new assembly facilities.

Stone went to New York in November 1984 to address the Confer-   *324-27*

After the last rear-drive car was completed, welders tore apart the old assembly equipment (above left) piling scrap outside the building (above right).

ence Board, an organization of senior executives of leading U.S. corporations, and said a starting point for the re-industrialization of America could well be found in the Buick City project. He said Buick City would "bring together more new ideas, more new equipment, more new processes, more new ways of working with our employees, suppliers and customers, than has ever before been accomplished in the automobile industry.

"Our plans entail sizable risks—for Buick and our suppliers. But our suppliers all understand the risks. They also understand the rewards. We're building Buick City without a safety net in a conscious attempt to force discipline into a manufacturing system that used to operate with convenient—but expensive—fallbacks." The risks, he said, had to be accepted. "The greater risk is, if you don't do what must be done, you will not be able to compete in a world market. Then it won't be risk that closes your operation—it will be economics."

News conferences hosted by Lee Furse, Jim Hall and Donald J. Charney, production manager of fabricating, body and paint, kept reporters abreast of what was happening in the assembly plants as change took place.

One popular exhibit was a room, called the Dimensional Certification Center, housing a 100-ton granite block which served as a vibration-free platform on which car bodies were placed for testing of crucial structural points with highly sensitive measuring devices.

Another was the Robogate, a device which held a car's underbody, side frames and roof panels in position while ten robot welders fastened them together to form the car's body. There were explanations of the project's paint system, featuring turbine-like spray nozzles whirring at 40,000 revolutions per minute, creating a mist of paint. A direct-current, high-voltage charge attracted the mist to the car body.

"We will match technology," said Furse, "with anybody in the world."

Officials emphasized that Buick City would produce seventy-five front-wheel-drive cars—Buick LeSabres and Oldsmobile Delta 88's—an hour in 1.5 million square feet of floor space, compared to three million square feet at GM's other "super" plants, such as Orion Township, Michigan, and Wentzville, Missouri.

Other plants within the Flint complex that were not part of car assembly were also tied to Buick City. The Engine Plant which was setting records with production of more than a million engines a year—making it the busiest V-6 plant in the world—would initially supply Buick City with all of its engines.

"Our people feel good about being part of Buick City and we intend to meet the challenge," said William W. Tennant, Engine Plant manager. "Like everyone else, we are working toward one hundred percent conformance to specs and to be the very best against world competition. We have to—it's the key to our survival."

As the project moved forward, Buick officials and the Flint complex assembly team took time out in February 1985 to mark the end of an era with two ceremonies.

On February 1st, a rear-wheel-drive Buick Regal rolled off the assembly line in Factory 40, ending assembly of mid-size cars at the Flint complex. Relief person Helen Jacques, a nine-year employee, drove the car off the line under the bright lights of television news crews. "The end of Factory 40's assembly is the beginning of the future," said Hall, who pointed out Factory 40 was producing GM's highest-quality G cars.

The second ceremony was held February 8th, when the last Flint-built rear-drive Buick LeSabre rolled off the line in Factory 04, the other final car assembly factory in the complex, with William Har-

The interior of the old Flint complex was almost completely gutted (above left). New equipment was lowered through the roof by helicopter (above right).

chick, who retired that day after 42-1/2 years in assembly, driving the car. It was, officially, the 14,039,956th rear-drive car assembled by Buick and the B-O-C Group in Flint. The count went back to those first thirty-seven Buicks built in the little plant on W. Kearsley in 1904 (but also included a few thousand that should properly be listed as Jackson-built Buicks in 1905 and for a few years thereafter).

The end of rear-drive assembly also marked the end of a 59-year period in which the Fisher Body Flint Plant, across town from Buick, had sent bodies to the Flint complex for final assembly. When the Buick City project had been announced, the plan was to close Fisher Flint. Since Buick City would build its own bodies, the Fisher plant would be unneeded. But because the Regal was such a strong seller, it was later decided to keep Fisher Flint open to continue to produce Regal bodies and send them to a reopened plant in Pontiac, Michigan, where final assembly would take place. About 1000 Fisher Flint employees would move to Buick City, but others who would have been laid off either continued to work at Fisher or were given transfer rights to Pontiac.

Lawrence A. Streng, who was manager of manufacturing engineering and facilities planning for Buick in this period, said this was the latest of several scenarios which had been considered by Buick to use Fisher Body facilities in the Flint area. Among others studied were having Buick City assembly located at the Fisher Body Coldwater Road Plant; using Fisher Flint as a second plant in which to build H cars (actually, the Willow Run GM assembly plant got that job); and a plan by Hackworth to use Fisher Flint to totally assemble Regals.

Hackworth had said he wanted more Regals; at his request a study was undertaken to see if the entire Regal, rather than just the body, could be built there. The plan received corporate approval; but at the last minute the other plan was instituted: to increase production of the G-car bodies at Fisher Flint and send them to the Pontiac plant, which was then unused, for final assembly. As a result Buick gained even more Regal production. The employment picture was about the same: thousands of jobs that would have been lost had Fisher closed were saved, at least for several years.

At the end of rear-drive production at the Flint complex, Hackworth said: "The real significance in the end of rear-drive assembly here lies in the beginning of an entirely new era for our industry. There have been more sweeping changes in our industry in the past few years than in most of the rest of our history and the inauguration of Buick City will bring the Flint complex to the leading edge of automotive manufacturing technology."

It was an occasion for such remarks. Flint Mayor James A. Sharp said the transition would place Flint "on the cutting edge of technology from here on." Buick City "mayor" Stone praised the cooperation of the union local and the Buick City design team for creating the project and said that "with hard work we can show that America can build the best quality products in the world."

Jim Hall told the workers—who would have several months off while the conversion took place—that the complex had also been building the best B cars in the corporation, "and how we go out [with top quality] is how we'll start up." Local 599 president Fred Myers singled out DuCharme for special praise: "I mean it sincerely—many people do not know what he's done for us." And DuCharme himself noted that "Flint will be a leader again in the production of automobiles."

On the day assembly ended, there was another ending. The Buick Railroad, which dated to 1936 when it had supplied the foundry with coke and pig iron, went out of business, its last few crew members transferred to other jobs. Trucks, not rail cars, would handle the hauling within the complex.

As such mementos of the past disappeared, innovations appeared. One was a new pilot line in which engines were placed on automatic guided vehicles, where the engines were "dressed" and then sent by the vehicles to the final assembly line.

Furse singled out the training of the Buick City work force as a historical event. "Both hourly and salaried employees are being assessed to determine the type of training or retraining programs they need to enhance their job skills at Buick City," he said. "This will be the first time in history that everybody has been trained in a totally participative style. In the past we concentrated on the hourly people, but forgot about the salaried people. The only way we can be successful is to train the total work force, starting with me and going right down the line. Certainly it will no longer be business as usual."

GM President F. James McDonald and other top GM officials toured Buick City on a regular basis. On one such tour, the group observed a quick die change that required only 9.5 minutes. Len Forbes, technical manager of fabricating operations, said, "nobody in the country can do it faster." Buick City officials claimed a North American record for a die change.

In late February 1985, the Wall Street Journal described the Buick City project as almost as important to the future of GM as the Saturn project announced a month earlier. The newspaper described Buick City as a test case for much of what GM wanted to accomplish with Saturn—cutting deeply into the Japanese manufacturing-cost advantage over U.S. automakers.

By then, crews had begun tearing out all the old tooling, rearranging the work space, installing new lines, capping old floors with new concrete, painting everything. The goals were to provide a clean, bright, attractive and high-tech work place, ready to start building pre-production front-drive cars by mid-summer, ready to begin production cars by Fall 1985.

On December 18th, 1984, the first pilot front-drive LeSabre body was completed at Buick City; by late February 1985, the first total car was completed on production tooling there. For the first time in fifty-nine years, the Flint complex was building its own bodies. "Match checks" of how all the parts had come together were said to be among the best ever in the corporation.

The proof of Buick City would be in how well all the promises, all of the planning, were delivered. As contractors moved their equipment into parking lots surrounding the old factories of the Flint complex, creating a staging area that looked like the preparation for the D-Day invasion, the mayor of Buick City sounded confident.

"We're convinced," said Herb Stone, "that when world-class cars come off an assembly line, one after another, day after day, that assembly line will be right here in Buick City."

BUICK LOOKS TO THE FUTURE—SINCE 1938

Wildcat (above), the concept car that joined the car-show circuit in 1985, added to the heritage of "one-offs" that have emphasized Buick's determination to remain on the leading edge of technology.

Following are some highlights of Buick's dream cars:

Y-Job, 1938: Designed by Harley Earl, the Y-Job was GM's first true dream car. Its aerodynamic styling incorporated disappearing headlamps and flush door handles. Additional advances included air-cooled brake drums and a soft top that automatically concealed itself beneath a hinged metal deck (see photograph, pg. 244).

XP-300 and LeSabre, 1951: These two dream cars shared aluminum bodies, supercharged V-8 engines fueled by a mixture of methanol and gasoline and power-operated seats, windows and lifting jacks (photos, pp. 258-259).

Wildcat I, 1953: This single-seater featured a V-8 with a twin-turbine automatic transmission. Its wheel discs were fixed: The wheels revolved around them (photo, pg. 264).

Wildcat II, 1954: This rakish convertible was Buick's first fiberglass-body dream car. Buick called it "a revolutionary front-end design with flying-wing fenders that flare straight out from the body, exposing the entire front wheel and part of the front-end suspension" (photo, pg. 264).

Wildcat III, 1954: This four-passenger convertible also used a fiberglass body. Its high-compression V-8 produced 280 bhp with four carburetors.

Centurion, 1956: A four-passenger coupe, the Centurion featured an all-glass top along with a "seeing-eye" television camera mounted in the rear jet-plane-like tailcone with a receiver on the dashboard to replace the rear-view mirror.

XP-75, 1958: The XP-75 premiered at the GM Golden Milestone parade in Flint. Its hand-built body was made by Pinin Farina.

Century Cruiser: A restyling of the Firebird IV of 1964.

Questor, 1983: This was a nonpowered test bed for innovative ideas in electronics (photos, pg. 324-5).

Wildcat, 1985: Buick's newest Wildcat was powered by a mid-mounted 3.8-liter 24-valve SFI V-6 producing 230 bhp at 6000 rpm. In addition to four-wheel drive, it offered an array of electronic controls, fiberglass/carbon-fiber body structure and clutchless manual-shift transmission.

This list does not include a number of "one-off" modified production cars such as special Rivieras (Silver Arrow I, II and III of the 1960s and an '87 convertible, Turbo and Sport) and the Flamingo convertible of 1961 nor Buick concept cars since 1985.

Opposite page, top to bottom: Workers install the front-drive assembly line; Area manager William A. Hildebrandt and production manager Donald J. Charney contemplate the new robots; Electricians Todd Turbin and Paul Muylle discuss the Robogate with area advisor Dave Nicholls and area manager Carl Kowalcyk.

Chapter Twenty

HEADING FOR THE 21ST CENTURY

As Buick began planning for the 21st Century, it could look back on the early Nineties as a period of resurgence in the face of economic hard times.

Ed Mertz's focus on "premium American motorcars" and a renewed sense of purpose throughout GM engineering and manufacturing had laid a strong foundation. Now a combination of new models that fit Buick's image, high quality rankings and positive press reviews began to build sales.

Buick led all automakers, domestic and import, in increased sales volume and increased market share in the 1991 model year. Sales rebounded from 518,275 in 1990 to 544,277 in 1991, which might have seemed a modest boost in a normal year. But 1991 was truly historic and disruptive—recession, the Persian Gulf War, coup and countercoup in the Soviet Union and then the collapse of the USSR, among other events.

At GM, events at the start of the decade were also historic. In December 1991, GM Chairman Robert C. Stempel announced there would be a massive downsizing of the corporation, with plant closings, staff cuts and an overall restructuring—B-O-C and C-P-C would be replaced by an integrated North American Operations (NAO) structure. In April 1992, Lloyd E. Reuss, the former Buick general manager who had been GM president since August 1990, was replaced as the corporation's president by John F. Smith Jr. GM said it would accelerate "the fundamental changes necessary to reduce costs, restore profitability to our core North American vehicle business and strenghthen GM's performance throughout the world."

Even in the period of change ahead, Buick would remember 1991 as a vintage year.

More impressive than Buick's increase of 26,000 units was the fact that Buick was up 5 percent in a down year—the total industry was down 9.5 percent and imports were down 6.4 percent. Buick was the only domestic automaker to show an increase. Buick had moved from seventh to fifth in industry sales in two years and its share of the domestic market was 6.5 percent, up almost a point or 16 percent in a year—even though volume leaders LeSabre and Skylark were in transition and out of production for months.

General Sales and Service Manager Robert E. Coletta attributed the surge to quality ratings, styling, great press reviews and excellent dealer support of new models. He said Buick had developed a clear vision of its future direction and built strong team work among engineers, designers, the manufacturing work force and dealers.

The automotive press could hardly have been more enthusiastic. Buick, said *Automobile* magazine, is "GM's most notable over-achiever." James V. Higgins, in the *Detroit News*, said Buick "is generally seen as GM's best focused division." *Fortune* and *Forbes* hit the news stands the same week in May 1991 with major Buick pieces teased on their covers. "There's nothing fancy about how Buick does it," wrote Alex Taylor III in *Fortune*. "In the past five years the division has rethought its marketing philosophy, overhauled its model line and straightened kinks in its relationship with other parts of GM." In *Forbes*, Jerry Flint posed the question, "What happened?" and then answered it: "Simple, a new general manager decided Buick should be Buick, not a hot rod nor a technological experiment. The division rediscovered its roots."

Taylor took his readers inside the Buick Administration Building:

> General Schwarzkopf (Gulf War hero) would feel right at home in Buick's War Room on the third floor of its Flint headquarters. Across the walls, interspersed with top-secret photos of future models, are charts, graphs and tables that track market share, model cycles, capital spending, service costs and dealer and customer satisfaction. The charts reflect a dramatic victory in the car wars. Everybody else's sales have been decimated, but Buick's are up—sharply.

Jerry Flint described Mertz:

> In an industry dominated by strong personalities with a flair for self promotion—from Lee Iacocca to John DeLorean—Mertz is a study in anticharisma. Slim and low key, he is endowed with a shy, self-deprecating manner. He avoids red meat, doesn't smoke and only occasionally sips wine. But he knows his Buick.

The *Chicago Tribune* devoted major space to a story, "The fall and rise of Buick," in which writer Jim Mateja said "Buick has returned

Darel Kimble

Buick senior management in 1991: Top (from left), General Sales and Service Manager Robert E. Coletta, General Manager Edward H. Mertz, Public Relations Director John E. (Jack) DeCou and General Marketing Manager Darwin E. Clark. Seated (from left), Chief Engineer Anthony H. Derhake, Assistant General Sales Manager-Administration William E.L. Powell, Administrator of Human Services John E. Carlson, Comptroller Richard L. Payne and Assistant General Sales Manager- Service L.D. (Jack) Robbins.

Left: Buick billboard thanks Buick City employees for top U.S. quality rating for 1989 LeSabre. Above: Tim Sprecher, plant manager at the time. Right: Herman Maass (left), production manager, and George Guernsey, Buick product satisfaction manager.

with adventurous new models, a visionary leader and a commitment to excellence.''

Buick's new quality reputation could be traced to June 1989. J.D. Power and Associates, a California-based market research firm, gave Buick a big boost. LeSabre was ranked No. 1 domestic and No. 2 among 154 domestic and import models sold in the United States in terms of fewest customer-reported problems in the first 90 days of ownership, in Power's Initial Quality Survey.

LeSabre sales had been rising anyway, but the widely reported Power results boosted them dramatically. Dealers reported customers carrying in news clippings (such as a *New York Times* article headlined "Quality survey makes Buick smile") and asking to see the car that was making the headlines.

The same survey ranked Buick overall as No. 1 domestic and No. 7 among all makes. Two more 1989 Power surveys, one on customer satisfaction after one year and one on sales satisfaction (treatment in the dealership), also ranked Buick in the top 10. In 1990, LeSabre repeated as No. 1 domestic in the Initial Quality Survey (though dropping to 6th overall) and again Buick was in the top 10 of all Power customer surveys. And then it happened again. In 1991 Buick could boast that only two automakers in the world had finished in the top 10 in all J.D. Power initial quality, customer satisfaction and sales satisfaction surveys over three straight years—Buick and Mercedes Benz.

Buick's success was shared with several plants. Buick City, the one-time Buick "home" plant in Flint, was ranked in 1989 by Power as No. 1 quality plant in North America and only a fraction of a point (less than one problem per 100 cars) behind a Japanese plant for No. 1 in the world. Lloyd Reuss's dream for Buick City had come true—with a lot of help from plant management and the work force. Buick City received a second Power quality award in 1990. In both years Buick opened Flint's AutoWorld amusement center for all Buick City employees and their families and posted congratulatory billboards on Interstate 75. In 1990 and 1991, GM plants at Ramos Arizpe, Mexico, and Oklahoma City—both of which built the Century—received Power quality awards (Oklahoma City was No. 1 in 1992).

Buick City's triumph was a stunning Cinderella story. After the struggle to save Buick production in Flint (see chapter 19) and create Buick City, the plant had faltered at the beginning. In the 1986 J.D. Power Initial Quality Survey, LeSabre was ranked a dismal 147th among 154 models. There were rumors the plant would be closed. But then things turned around. Credit goes to Plant Manager Tim Sprecher and his production manager, Herman Maass, as well as Flint Automotive Division Manager J.T. Battenberg III, Buick's customer satisfaction manager for LeSabre, George W. Guernsey, and managers and hourly workers from UAW Local 599. Sprecher said the material system led by George Johnson was unique and "competitive with anything in the world" and that plant Engineer Tony Otero "did a fantastic job to get the plant up and running."

Sprecher, however, said he would not attribute Buick City's success to any one person—but to the contributions of many. He noted, for example, that the plant's Shop Committee—Ray Davis, Dan Woods, Terry Burgess and Chairman Jim Yaklin—made a pledge to do everything possible to make Buick City succeed. "They said, 'We'll knock your socks off!' That was the missing ingredient—total organizational cooperation," Sprecher said.

Buick advertising, which had been using the slogan "The Great American Road Belongs to Buick" since 1988, could now confidently augment that campaign with a powerful message for the early Nineties: "Buick—the new symbol for quality in America."

(Buick City received an explosion of positive publicity in February 1992, when foreman Rich Richardson and line worker Michael Wilson called customer John Jacobs to apologize for a defect. Jacobs' brakes had gone out on his 1992 LeSabre in Maryland. Richardson tried to call the dealer for information but the number was the customer's. He missed Jacobs at home but called him at work the next day "because the defect was so important I thought we ought to tell him we are going to see it never happens again." Wilson also got on the phone and apologized—he said he had failed to bolt a bracket to a strut. Jacobs was so impressed at getting an apology call from a foreman and assembler that he called a newspaper and it was picked up nationally. Said Wilson: "Here is someone who has just turned in a Toyota (on a Buick) and we might've lost him. We're losing too many jobs to lose customers. The Buick LeSabre is one of the top quality cars in the world. I thought it was important for him to understand that this (brake problem) was very rare." Wrote *Flint Journal* columnist Andrew Heller: "Some people probably consider what they did a small thing. And they are right. But then reputations are both built and destroyed on small things. And if I were Buick, this is one small thing I'd shout from the rooftops. Or at least from the TV screens.")

In a speech at the National Press Club in May 1990, Mertz told the Washington Automotive Press Association that the quality of GM cars, on average, was more than competitive in "heart of the car" components such as engines and transmissions, and improving dramatically in all areas. Not only was Buick the highest quality domestic car in independent surveys, but the 3800 V-6 "is at the top in engine quality compared with engines from all other makers, foreign and domestic," he said.

Mertz was honored by *Design News* magazine in 1991 as quality engineer of the year for his work with LeSabre, an award that included a $10,000 donation to Mertz's alma mater, Notre Dame.

Buicks for 1990: Left (top to bottom), Regal Gran Sport Coupe, Riviera, Park Avenue Ultra, LeSabre Custom sedan. Above: tuned port 3800 V-6.

Buick was picking up more than quality rankings in 1991. The 1991 Park Avenue Ultra won four best-car awards ("Most Significant New Car—Domestic," *Dawn* magazine; "Car of the Year," Tom Keane, nationally syndicated writer; "Driver's Choice Luxury Car of the Year," *Motor Week*, national TV car-test program, which compared it with Lexus, Infiniti, Mercedes, Jaguar and domestics; "Best Domestic Car," Motor Press Association, a San Francisco-based organization of auto writers) as well as a "best buy" from *Consumers Digest*. Park Avenue Ultra also was second in domestic autos in *Financial World*'s "Best of Everything 1991 Quality Award Winners" behind the Lincoln Town Car.

Also in 1991, Regal and Skylark were rated among the best in class by *The Car Book*, Century was named "Safe Car of the Year—Domestic" by *Prevention* magazine (*Prevention* gave an award for 1992 to Century Estate Wagon), Roadmaster Estate Wagon won a design and engineering award from *Popular Mechanics* and Buick overall ranked second behind Ford in a *Design News* survey of engineers on the "car I would buy today," with LeSabre 4th and Regal 9th among individual models. Even *Consumer Reports*, often sharply critical of GM cars, gave the 1989 LeSabre a good recommendation. In a news release, it rated LeSabre "among a handful of American cars becoming more competitive with Japanese vehicles" and said it "shows a marked improvement" from the previous year.

All of this helped confirm Mertz's philosophy. When one interviewer in 1991 suggested to Mertz that "the bottom line is to make a profit," Mertz responded that Buick's bottom line "is to provide premium American motorcars that meet—and hopefully surpass—our customers' expectations. If we provide automobiles that fit our upscale image and that are of high quality and high value, then sales and profits will take care of themselves. But if you think of short-term profits

1990 Reatta convertible (above right) and new interior with analog gauges (top) replacing controversial "TV screen" instrument display.

first, you may make decisions that will hurt you in the long run."

Mertz saw Buick's quality rankings as proof of GM people doing a lot of things right. "A great deal of credit goes to the designers, engineers, managers and work forces in GM factories throughout North America," he said. "And our dealers deserve credit for outstanding execution of a host of customer satisfaction processes." He noted that another J.D. Power survey, this one measuring dealer attitudes, showed a big upswing in dealers' feelings about a Buick dealership as a financial investment and about Buick's product quality. And when asked to rate the future desirability of their franchises, 83 percent of the Buick dealers replied "excellent"—twice as high as the industry average.

Mertz traced Buick's success to the mid-Eighties when it developed its future direction by taking cues from what had been successful in

Dennis Holland and his daughter Julie in the 1909 Buick desert racer that won the 1990 Great American Race "Class Brass" award.

the past. Once the "premium American" focus was established, General Marketing Manager Darwin E. Clark worked with the Buick organization and GM Design Staff to develop an image conference to emphasize to division and corporate decision-makers just what Buick meant. The 1989 conference in the Design Staff dome, called "Essence of Buick," got the message across without spoken or written words but with symbols—an array of crystal, rich leather goods, fine china, futuristic concept cars, classic vintage Buicks and lifestyle exhibits to communicate the "premium American" image of Buick.

The most important step, though, was to translate image into product. Buick was restructuring its organization, creating business teams for each model, linking product, marketing, finance, public relations and other disciplines. The division began using more customer clinics, more marketing studies and more dealer involvement programs than ever before. It broke tradition by revealing once-secret concept cars to auto writers to get their opinions (see chapter 18). The mission, said Clark, "is to provide cars people really want—as opposed to cars we may think they want."

Buick's 1990 lineup featured a new convertible model of the luxury two-place Reatta and analog-gauge instrument panels in Reatta and Riviera to replace the CRT screen which had been strongly criticized by many auto writers.

Another important improvement was the 3.8-liter 3800 V-6 as an option in 1990 Regal coupes in the spring of 1991. Regal was finally getting the engine Buick had wanted from the beginning of the front-drive model. And this was an advanced 3800 with tuned port injection (TPI) and 170 horsepower (5 more than before)—an exclusive for the 1990 Regal. The 3800 TPI differed from the regular version most visibly in its new two-piece intake manifold with long tuned runners, substantially boosting mid-range torque.

The long-awaited Regal sedan was announced in September of 1989 as a 1990 model for mid-model year and was even nominated by *Motor Trend* as a Car-of-the-Year candidate. But quality concerns pushed

Essence concept car (above) previewed the 1991 Park Avenue (opposite).

back the start of production by several months, and Regal sedan was officially introduced June 7, 1990—as a 1991 model.

The most dramatic model of 1990 was the Reatta convertible—Buick's first soft-top since the 1985 Riviera and the first Buick convertible produced ''in house'' since the LeSabre in 1975. The manually operated top was said to be designed for easy operation. Some writers didn't think it worked all that easily but most gave the top operation high marks. It could be lowered quickly with a little practice and was concealed by a hard tonneau cover which was flush with the body.

Reatta's new instrument panel, shared with Riviera, featured vacuum-fluorescent analog gauges in addition to warning lights. Reatta was again powered by the 165-horsepower 3800 V-6 coupled to the four-speed automatic. A new auxiliary transmission cooler was situated in front of the radiator. Riviera and Reatta had driver-side air bags—the first air bags on Buicks since the early Seventies.

''The Reatta rates as one of America's best convertible buys,'' said veteran auto writer Tony Swan. ''It's a two-seater that avoids the stiff ride and cramped quarters of hard-edged sports cars but still delivers sporty handling and a sense of partnership between car and driver.''

Reatta was spotlighted at the 1990 North America International Auto Show in Detroit. The GM corporate exhibit featured members of UAW Local 1618 from the Reatta Craft Centre actually building a Reatta (the final two stages of a ten-stage operation) at Cobo Hall in front of showgoers and a live CNN worldwide TV audience. John McElroy, *Automotive Industries* editor interviewed by CNN, said ''no other auto show in the world brings down their hourly people. This sets the Detroit show apart . . . .''

The rest of the 1990 lineup had minor changes. LeSabre had a new front and rear design—notably a classic vertical-bar grille that instantly made the car look more luxurious—plus structural and engineering improvements for ride and handling. A standard Skylark coupe and sedan, entry level Skyhawk replacements, joined Skylark Custom coupe and sedan, Luxury Edition sedan and Gran Sport coupe. Park Avenue Ultra, the most luxurious sedan offered by Buick, entered its first full model year with structural and engineering improvements for ride and handling, as did Electra Limited, Electra T Type and Park Avenue. To add a customer satisfaction element, Buick began a Roadside Assistance Program in January 1990.

Park Avenue Essence, a concept car displayed at auto shows in 1989, foreshadowed one of Buick's most important new cars of the Nineties—the 1991 Park Avenue. Essence featured graceful exterior contours and instruments displayed in a wide, sweeping panel, and the Delco Navicar navigation system, similar to Lucerne's.

Buick introduced the 1991 Park Avenue and Park Avenue Ultra at a press luncheon in January 1990 at the North American International Auto Show—and launched the new models in dealer showrooms in July 1990. Mertz described Park Avenue and Ultra (the Electra name was dropped) as ''not only the most sophisticated six-passenger cars Buick has ever offered but, in terms of affordable luxury, among the most advanced automobiles available anywhere.''

While early customer reaction centered on the graceful and aerodynamic new exterior styling and wrap-around instrument panel, Mertz said the real pleasure was in the driving. The new models featured the 3800 TPI V-6 and the first electronically controlled four-speed automatic transmission ever offered in a GM luxury sedan. Mertz pointed out that the new powertrain ''provides effortless acceleration and precise and almost undetectable upshifts and downshifts in normal driving,'' an opinion widely shared by the press. The new 4T60-E transmission from Hydra-matic Division used the same computer that managed the engine to handle shift control electronically.

Donald L. Miles, chief engineer of V-6 engines for B-O-C Powertrain (later GM Powertrain), pointed out that electronic management of the engine, transmission and cruise control was integrated for the first time. He called the new powertrain ''significant for overall performance in areas drivers deem important—power on demand, instant starting, smooth idling, quiet running, pleasant shifting and excellent fuel economy (18 city/27 highway).''

Anthony H. Derhake, Buick's new chief engineer, described Park Avenue and Ultra to the press at Detroit. The new models offered ComforTemp dual climate controls for driver and front passenger, flush-mounted ''solar control'' glass to reduce wind noise and harmful sun rays, and an engine oil-life monitor and oil-level warning light.

Limited edition supercharged 1991 Park Avenue Ultra (above) and its powerplant (below) that became standard for Ultra in 1992.

The monitor, indicating when to change oil, used engine sensors to measure engine coolant temperature, rpm and vehicle speed and then calculated the oil life remaining based on actual driving conditions. Electronic "sun sensors" in the instrument panel compensated for the warming effect on interior temperature so selected temperatures could be maintained.

Park Avenue had a drag coefficient of 0.31, torque-axis engine mounts to isolate engine vibration further and an overall increase in length of eight inches for additional trunk space. Safety features included driver air bag, brake/transmission interlock and improved anti-lock brakes. An optional Gran Touring package included special suspension, 3.06:1 final-drive ratio, 15-inch aluminum wheels with Eagle GT + 4 blackwall tires and leather-wrapped steering wheel.

The new models were developed by teams of salaried and hourly employees from the B-O-C Flint Automotive Division. For the first time, suppliers approved the way their parts were processed by the plants. Adding to rigidity, precise fits and quality, the number of separate pieces needed to build the cars was reduced by 25 percent. For example, the whole side of the car was now made from one stamped piece, compared with 27 pieces previously.

To strengthen the quality process, hourly employees from the

Wentzville, Missouri, Assembly Center, where the cars were built, were assigned to engineering at Flint Automotive Division headquarters. They were part of a team that provided advice before the first prototypes were built to assure that the parts could be assembled easily and precisely in the plant.

William L. Porter, chief of Buick Design Studio No. 1, spoke of "a voluptuous quality to Park Avenue and Ultra that is really the essence of Buick." But that's not where Porter started. In the beginning, he acknowledged, he was trying to develop an evolution from the previous Park Avenue—a "Teutonic" approach, as he called it.

> We soon determined that this approach—somewhat stiff and rigid—was not really what we wanted. As a result, we finally shook off our Teutonic mind-set and experienced our first breakthrough toward our final theme.
>
> We finally hit on an approach of developing a shoulder through the upper part of the doors which projected forward. This shoulder idea—combined with a svelte side-view undulation in the belt line with a slight "hip" over the rear wheel—looked quite promising and had the potential of being much more expressive of the newly emerging definition of Buick's image.
>
> Adjectives like substantial, distinctive, powerful, mature and smooth described the new image. Our new shouldered look certainly conveyed that feeling and yet there was also a new graceful quality emerging—we had turned away from the Teutonic and were moving in the direction of a much more "romantic" theme.
>
> It then began to dawn on us that we were tapping into our own traditions. The greatest Buicks of the past had been unashamedly "romantic" cars.

The combination of all this advanced engineering and design creativity was obvious to everyone—Park Avenue and Park Avenue Ultra were smash hits in the news columns and with the public.

"Buick has created a galvanizing advancement, a new benchmark that breaks out of the previous Buick mold while redefining it at the same time," wrote Daniel Charles Ross in *Motor Trend*. "In the contest of front-drive American luxury sedans, the Ultra is the new King of the Hill," In the *Washington Post*, Warren Brown called Park Avenue's exterior "some of the best metal ever to come out of GM or anywhere else . . . . Even teen-agers like this one." Park Avenue Ultra, Brown said, is "a splendid comeback machine—proof that Americans can build fine automobiles and that many of those Americans work at General Motors."

Richard Truett, in the *Orlando Sentinel*, said Ultra "may be the finest all-around sedan that ever rolled out of General Motors. The car does everything well; it has great styling, a level of sophistication usually reserved for expensive imports and gets better than 25 mpg while hauling six passengers in luxurious comfort. Buick's 3800 V-6

Buicks for 1991: (Top to bottom) Century Limited, LeSabre Limited, Regal Gran Sport.

with tuned port injection establishes itself as one of the best V-6s being made today.''

And much more. *Car and Driver*'s Nicholas Bissoon-Dath said ''Park Avenue Ultra is such a turnaround vehicle that Buick, which is supposed to be GM's builder of traditional American luxury cars, is actually leading what we hope will be a corporate renaissance.''

Marshall Schuon, *New York Times*: ''Ultra is likely to put Buick back where it once was, as Middle America's aspiration.'' Gerry Kobe, *Automotive Industries*: ''Buick has the product and mind-set to wage war on any manufacturer that dares to stray into its path.'' And J. P. Vettraino, *AutoWeek*: ''Against the Lincoln Continental, Town Car and Acura Legend that Buick offered for comparison, the Park Avenue was the quietest . . . compared with the Legend, in which each shift comes like slap on the back of the neck, the Park Avenue seems a class apart.''

Automotive News placed four Buick executives on its ''all-star'' team—Mertz, Bill Porter for styling, Darwin Clark ''who implemented the marketing support and strategy that have catapulted Buick's market share more than a point over a year ago,'' and Jay Qualman, director of advertising, described as ''a solid executive (who) has been effective in developing and communicating the division's product image and quality message.''

The 1991 Park Avenue was introduced early but another 1991 model made its debut even earlier. Regal sedan, launched in June 1990, featured as optional the 3800 V-6 TPI, with the 3.1-liter V-6 standard. Like the coupes, the sedan was offered in Custom, Limited and Gran Sport versions and shared the same sophisticated chassis, with power four-wheel disc brakes and independent rear suspension. Yet the sedans had their own distinct design, with no exterior panels shared with the coupe.

''Regal sedan may be the best mid-size four-door yet offered by Detroit,'' wrote Paul Lienert in the *Detroit Free Press*. In the *Boston Globe*, John R. White called Regal ''a peach of an automobile.''

In August, Buick debuted the rest of its 1991 lineup, especially the return of a great name in its heritage—Roadmaster—on a new family of full-size vehicles featuring V-8 engines and rear-wheel drive. They were the extensively redesigned 1991 Estate Wagon, now called Roadmaster Estate Wagon, and the all-new 1992 Roadmaster and Roadmaster Limited sedans, which were to come in the spring of 1991.

The Roadmaster name was back for the first time since 1958. The full-size wagon received a major redesign for the first time since 1978 and was powered by a fuel-injected 5-liter V-8 with 170 horsepower—up 30 hp from the previous year.

The big news, however, was the announcement of Roadmaster and Roadmaster Limited sedans, featuring a 5.7-liter, fuel-injected V-8 as standard—180 hp at 4200 rpm and 290 lb.-ft. of torque at 2400 rpm. Limited had a new standard feature for Buick, variable-effort steering. Except for Estate Wagon, these were the first rear-drive Buicks since the 1987 Regal and the first Buicks with a standard V-8 engine since the 1985 Riviera. Roadmaster had 5,000-pound towing capacity—2,000 more than Park Avenue.

''Roadmaster was a great name for premium Buicks from 1936 until model names were changed for 1959—in fact, I don't know why we left that name on the shelf so long,'' Mertz said.

The return of Roadmaster was Mertz's idea. He felt Buick needed a larger ''flagship'' sedan and at one time considered a stretched Park Avenue. But the idea of a powerful rear-drive sedan based on the B body also had appeal. At Buick Exterior Design No. 2, studio chief Wayne Kady, using black tape on a large white board, created the outline of a concept Roadmaster late in 1987. Mertz ran the idea past his dealer council. ''I saw a sparkle in their eyes,'' he said. From the start he used the name Roadmaster. ''When I'd say Roadmaster, everybody knew what I meant. It saved a lot of time explaining the image I had in mind.'' A B-body Roadmaster with a big V-8 seemed like a good idea to almost everyone within GM. In retrospect, Buick officials wish they'd had more time and money to spend on interior refinements, but basically they were very pleased with Roadmaster's return.

The new Roadmaster had overall lengths of 217.7 (wagon) and 215.8 inches (sedan) and a wheelbase of 115.9 inches. This compared with Park Avenue's length of 205.2 inches and wheelbase of 110.8 inches. The new Roadmaster sedans were smaller than the last models in 1958 (219.1 inches length and 127.5 inches wheelbase), but their size, compared with other cars of the Nineties, inevitably led writers to the nickname ''Roadmonster.'' Even so, fuel economy was impressive for their size, 16 mpg city and 25 highway.

No portholes? Kady admitted he had considered them, but felt the front design of the new sedans did not offer an opportunity for their revival. He did make a nod to the past with a subtle design feature in the sail panel behind the rear window. It was a rectangular bar carrying the name Roadmaster—or an optional rectangular lamp in place of the bar—with four ''segments,'' as Kady described them, above and below the bar. He emphasized, however, that Roadmaster sedans featured contemporary technology.

Buick had considered a long list of names for its return to a rear-drive full-size car but Roadmaster kept surfacing.

''It's a very powerful name—and not just with people old enough to remember the Roadmasters of the Fifties,'' said Darwin Clark.

> It's interesting how that name affects people. We received suggestions from many sources. Our dealers wanted Roadmaster. Some of our own employees wrote memos urging us to bring

it back. Even some of the auto writers, when they asked us about rumors that we were considering Roadmaster, said they would like to see the name return. Ultimately, we selected this historic Buick name because we wanted to create a new classic in a traditional vein.

In his Detroit radio report, auto writer Al Fleming said "it's really terrific having the old monicker in showrooms again."

As an example of Buick business teams, Frank Porter was product line manager for Roadmaster, Pat Harrison marketing line manager and Greg Kretz product satisfaction manager. Analysts reporting to Ron Cieslak, director of business and product planning, were part of the team as were reps from sales promotion and public relations.

In the five months remaining in the model year after their debut—Roadmaster sedans were rolled out for southwestern dealers in April 1991 in Texas Stadium near the Arlington Assembly Plant where they were built—more than 20,000 were sold. Buick had found a niche in the market for a luxury car priced below Park Avenue, and a traditional customer group was ready to buy. Limousine Werks, based in Schaumburg, Illinois, quickly began marketing a Roadmaster limo through Buick dealers.

With the 1991 major model changes and 1992 Roadmaster sedans, Buick had a lot to talk about. Other models had minor changes. LeSabre received structural improvements, a new brake/transmission interlock, a new optional anti-lock brake system. The 2.5-liter Tech 4 and 3.3-liter V-6, the standard and optional engines for Skylark and Century, were improved. Regal coupe and sedan received new 15- and 16-inch aluminum wheels, a new full analog gauge cluster and other interior improvements.

Reatta for 1991 offered additional smoothness and performance with the Park Avenue powertrain—3800 TPI V-6 and electronically controlled automatic transmission. Other enhancements included a new steering gear for improved "on-center" feel and more acoustical insulation. There was a new 3.33 final-drive ratio for a quicker launch from 0 to 60 (writers figured about 9 seconds) and a revised engine mount system for less engine vibration and a smoother ride.

Reatta standard equipment now included Twilight Sentinel automatic headlights, a cupholder in the console armrest and a power "pulldown" to snug the rear of the convertible top. Convertible tops were available in black, white or tan. Exterior colors were Arctic White, Black, Sterling Silver Metallic, Gunmetal Gray, Maui Blue Metallic, Bright Red and Claret Red Metallic. Several hundred Reatta coupes were also painted a new Polo Green. A green convertible almost made it to production—but two days before the car was to be completed, Reatta production ended.

The announcement came March 5, 1991. GM President Lloyd E.

Reuss said Reatta would be discontinued at the end of the 1991 model year and the Reatta Craft Centre converted to building a future GM electric car. Mertz said Reatta's market segment did not grow to expected levels. But he credited the hand-crafted Reatta with helping Buick re-establish public awareness of the division's product direction.

"We introduced Reatta as a 'halo' car to attract customers who may not have considered Buick before," he said. "Partly through the overwhelming enthusiasm of the automotive press, we reached the market we were after—including many import owners." He noted Reatta met its sales goals in the 1988 and 1989 model years but sales declined in 1990. The production record was 4,708 coupes in the 1988 model year, 7,009 in 1989, 6,383 coupes and 2,132 convertibles in 1990 and 1,214 coupes and 305 convertibles (238 qualified for sale) in 1991. The production grand total was 21,751 Reattas, of which 19,314 were coupes and 2,437 were convertibles.

Executives and the press floated various theories for the demise. War and recession, perhaps, had taken their toll. Reatta was a discretionary car in non-discretionary times. The two-seater market was drying up. Buick was losing big money on Reatta and General Motors was losing much bigger money in its entire North American operations (but this was a Buick, not GM, decision). Some critics wanted lower prices or more power, or both. Although Reatta was not a financial success, Buick people did not consider it a failure. Reatta had drawn positive attention to Buick at a time the division needed the publicity. It helped reinforce Buick's "premium American" image. And, as almost any owner will tell you, Reattas are fine automobiles. Still, the cancellation was a disappointment to Buick people. It was one of the very few disappointments for the division in the early Nineties.

A Knight-Ridder newspaper article, pointing out that the last hand-built Reattas would be produced the week of May 10, 1991, reported that "knowledgeable sources said the car will attain collector status quickly and become a certified classic." Reatta certainly had many of the ingredients: good looking, sporty, luxurious, limited edition. Of the 305 convertibles for 1991, probably the most valuable Reattas, this is the exterior color breakdown: 110 white, 88 red, 44 black, 23 silver, 22 Maui blue, 13 garnet (maroon), and 5 gray.

Buick had a new concept car for auto shows in 1990 and 1991. It was the Bolero, a front-drive, aerodynamic mid-size sedan with future generation 3.3-liter 3300 V-6 generating 206 hp and 253 lb.-ft. of torque. Bolero's power was suggested by its aerodynamic shape, with a rear deck slightly higher than the hood, a steeply raked windshield, vertical bar grille and smooth lines throughout. One fiber optics light panel extended the width of the rear and others were used in the instrument panel and doors. The fiber optics created uniform lighting as well as easy maintenance.

Roadmaster returns. Above: 1992 Roadmaster sedan with 1991 Roadmaster Estate Wagon and 1949 Roadmaster.

Roberto Guerrero (above) drove a Buick/Lola to a qualifying record in the 1992 Indianapolis 500 to win the pole, but spun out on the parade lap and failed to start. Al Unser Sr. (below left) took his Buick-powered car to third place in 1992, best ever finish for a Buick in the 500. Jim Crawford (below center) was a top competitor for Buick at Indy. Buick driver Patty Moise (below right) set five international women's closed-course records in 1990 in a specially prepared Regal.

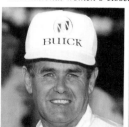

Above: 1991 Riviera with Gran Touring package. Below: 1991 Skylark Custom coupe.

Roadmaster body provided the basis for this Limousine Werks limo.

Designers had families in mind when they provided a built-in cooler in the rear package shelf, dual cupholders front and rear and portable radio headsets located in the rear of the front seats. Rear passengers could listen to their own music while in the car, and take the radios with them when they left.

Bolero was a teaser for 1992 Skylarks, dramatically redesigned compact coupes and sedans with the highest level of standard equipment—including anti-lock brakes—ever offered in compact Buicks.

"We wanted cars with real personality—with a look people haven't seen before," said Mertz. "These are provocative cars, inside and out."

Indeed they were. Auto writers argued about the styling. "It doesn't look like a Buick," said one. Another shot back, "I love it. It shows that somebody at General Motors isn't uptight."

When an *Automobile* writer suggested Skylark styling was controversial, Wayne Kady, who led the exterior design team, replied: "We were trying to be a little more flamboyant—bring a little romance, a little flair back into the car. Lately, cars have become so simple, they look boring. I'm tired of seeing these rounded-off designs; they look like a used bar of soap."

The unusual pointed nose was inspired, Kady said, by the 1939 Buick as a tribute to what he called "that famous styling trend-setter." But the rest of the car had free-flowing lines.

Skylark's interior rivaled the exterior in fresh design. The instrument panel swept across the cockpit and into the doors. On sedans the theme was carried into the rear door panels, an unusual design element. Paul Tatseos, Buick interior design chief, accurately observed that "this is probably the most dramatic instrument panel we've done in a long time."

Skylark Gran Sport coupe and sedan were sure to attract special attention. Instead of the new standard 2.3-liter "Quad OHC" engine (a single overhead cam four-cylinder), Gran Sports were equipped with the powerful 3300 V-6 which Buick would promote as an option on

all Skylarks, a new adjustable ride control system, Eagle GA 16-inch blackwall tires on cast aluminum wheels, body color grille, combination leather/cloth bucket seats and leather-wrapped steering wheel and shift lever.

Adjustable ride control allowed the driver to adjust the suspension feel for road conditions or personal preference—or leave it in automatic while a computer made the adjustments. The system, standard on Gran Sport and optional on other Skylarks, was operated by a computer that

1991 Reatta convertible. With only 238 produced for sale, this last Reatta soft top beca[me] an instant collectible. Below, 1990 Bolero concept car, a hint of the 1992 Skylark.

1992 Skylark Gran Sport sedan featured dramatic styling inside and out.

could change the shock absorber or damping rates at all four wheels, depending on the "g" forces acting on the chassis.

Skylark received "two thumbs up" from writer Tom Keane. "In an age when you can't tell one car from another because designers are going crazy with rounded, oval corners, this division of GM is going down a new path," he wrote. And Paul Dean, in the *Los Angeles Times*, wrote: "As a shape, all Skylarks are entertaining. As a performer, the peppier Gran Sport will impress everyone. As a value in a mechanical package, the line won't disappoint . . . Skylark GS becomes a maneuvering, handling fool that, frankly, is superior to any small American car ever."

Also for 1992, LeSabre Custom and Limited sedans had an all-new exterior and interior, new comfort and convenience features and new powertrain—the 3800 TPI V-6 and electronically controlled automatic transmission. While not quite as luxurious as Park Avenue, the new LeSabre had the same powertrain and many similar styling cues.

In *Motor Trend*, Don Sherman wrote one of the earliest 1992 LeSabre assessments, and it was a keeper: "Without hesitation, we can bestow an A grade on the exterior designers' craftsmanship. The LeSabre looks exactly how a Buick should look; muscular but not macho, flowing but not flamboyant . . . Mertz has every right to be proud of his division and the newest Buick. The LeSabre is a sweetheart of an automobile—nicely styled, thoughtfully engineered and conscientiously equipped." And Dan Jedlicka, in the *Chicago Sun-Times*, concluded after testing the 1992 LeSabre and Lexus ES300, that "Buick has an edge over Lexus under U.S. motoring conditions." Also, *Family Circle* named LeSabre 1992 Family Car of the Year.

For 1992, Park Avenue Ultra was clearly set apart with a standard supercharged 3800 V-6. The supercharged engine, which was introduced in 150 Ultras at the end of the 1991 model year, produced 205 hp at 4400 rpm and 260 lb.-ft. of torque at 2600 rpm and was clocked—conservatively as usual by GM—at 8.7 seconds for 0-60 mph compared 10.6 for the previous model. Others found it quicker. Kevin Smith of

Car and Driver timed it at 7.5 seconds and concluded: "With this kind of power, the handsome, capable Park Avenue moves another step closer to becoming what its tastily curvaceous lines promise: an American Jaguar with classic European touring-car refinements and equally classic Yankee stretch-out room."

Elsewhere, change was minor for 1992. Riviera now had solar control glass. Regal offered new seat designs and trims plus such new standard features as power door locks, dual covered visor vanity mirrors and two-speed windshield wiper. Century had minor additions to standard equipment.

By 1992, Buicks were well-equipped with safety and security features. Anti-lock brakes were now standard on Park Avenue, Riviera, Roadmaster, Estate Wagon, LeSabre Limited, Regal Limited, Regal Gran Sport and Skylark and optional on LeSabre Custom and Regal Custom. Air bags were standard for the driver on Park Avenue, Riviera, Roadmaster, Roadmaster Estate Wagon and LeSabre. Clearly these were destined to become standard equipment on all models within a few years.

While Buick in the early Nineties was churning out unprecedented numbers of new models, it was also moving forward with "non-product" strategies, such as golf sponsorships. Buick was the first major corporate sponsor in golf, starting with the inaugural Buick Open in 1958 at Warwick Hills in Grand Blanc, near Flint. The Buick Open soon became known for huge crowds drawn by major contestants (Palmer, Nicklaus, Player, Lema, et al), low prices and free parking. The first tournament was promoted by Waldo McNaught, Buick's public relations director, who was chairman in 1958 and 1959. Jerry Rideout, McNaught's assistant and then successor, promoted it from 1960 to 1969 and persuaded GM to reinstate the tournament in 1974. He turned it over to his successor as PR director, Thomas L. Pond, who chaired it from 1979 to 1987, after which Buick Sales Promotion took it over. In the early Nineties, Buick concluded that golf was the perfect fit for its image and customer base and broadened its participation in the PGA Tour with four tournaments—Buick Classic at Westchester Country Club in Harrison, New York; Buick Southern Open at Callaway Gardens at Pine Mountain, Georgia; and the Buick Invitational of California at Torrey Pines in La Jolla near San Diego, California, in addition to the Buick Open.

Buick also continued in motor sports, with Buick engines powering a third of the field in the 1990 Indianapolis 500. Kevin Cogan, ninth, was the highest finisher among the group. In NASCAR Winston Cup, Bobby Allison returned, but as an owner, not a driver, forming a team that fielded a Regal for driver Mike Alexander. Brett Bodine drove a Regal to victory in the First Union 400 at North Wilkesboro, North Carolina, Speedway. In Busch Grand National racing, Buick's 4.5 V-6 won 28 of 31 outings including victories by series champ Chuck Bown. In the ARCA Permatex Super Car Series, Bob Brevak won the title in a LeSabre. Patty Moise, driving a modified Regal with a V-8, set a women's closed-course record with a one-lap speed of 217.498 mph at the 2.66-mile Talladega Superspeedway in Alabama. She set four other women's records at the same time: one kilometer, 220.93 mph; 10K, 217.8; one mile, 215.9; and 10 miles, 216.

In 1991, Buick provided the engine for Willy T. Ribbs, the first black qualifier in the Indy 500. The first Japanese ever to qualify, Hiro Matsushita, also had a Buick-powered car. Nine Buick-powered cars qualified in the 33-car field, including five special Lola/Buick chassis specifically engineered for Buick's stock-block V-6. Gary Bettenhausen, a second-day qualifier who was, therefore, ineligible to win the pole, was fastest of all qualifiers with a four-lap average of 224.468 mph. That mark and a one-lap best of 224.635 gave Bettenhausen and Buick's Indy V-6 new stock-block qualifying records. But the best finish by Buick-powered cars in the race itself was an eighth by Stan Fox. In Busch Grand National, Buick's V-6 continued to dominate, winning 24 poles and 25 of 31 races. Bobby Labonte was series champ with Buick power and Harry Gant took five victories in a Regal. In IMSA Camel Lights, Charles Morgan and Jim Pace combined to win their class at the 12 Hours of Sebring in a Buick/Kudzu. In the Firestone Indy Lights (formerly American Racing Series), in which all cars are powered by Buick V-6s, Eric Bachelart was season champ in 1991 following Paul Tracy's 1990 championship.

When the new GM Motorsports Technology Group began managing the engineering resources of GM car-division motorsports programs on October 8, 1991—replacing Buick Special Products Engineering and similar operations at other divisions—Herb Fishel (Chevrolet and formerly Buick) was named director and Joe Negri (Buick) was appointed manager of engineering and technology for the group. Buick then decided to focus all of its efforts at the Indy 500 and CART events including Indy Lights. Jim Markwalder was named Buick's motors-

ports marketing manager, reporting to Darwin Clark.

Roberto Guerrero averaged 232.482 in his four-lap qualifying run for the 1992 Indianapolis 500, smashing the previous qualifying record by more than 7 mph and placing his Quaker State Buick/Lola on the pole. Overall, there were 12 Buick engines in the 33-car field. The stock-block Buick engine based on the production 3300 V-6 was the star of qualifying week.

The race itself was a bad-news, good-news event for Buick, and the bad news came first. Guerrero spun out on the parade lap and failed to start. In a "demolition derby" that saw only 12 cars finish, six of the Buicks crashed, three had engine failures, and one a transmission failure. John Paul Jr. finished 10th and the good news was that Al Unser Sr. finished third, the best ever for a Buick.

Buick had been official pace car since 1989 of the Interstate Batteries Great American Race, an annual cross-country tour/rally of antique cars. In 1990, Dennis Holland and his daughter, Julie, driving Holland's striking black 1909 Buick Model 17 desert racer (first Buick in Orange County, California, according to Holland), won the race's "Class Brass" award and was sixth overall after just missing a Class Brass victory the previous year. The race was routed through Flint in 1990 as a bow to Buick. Buick also participated in another unusual Flint event that year. A B-24 Liberator, a rare World War II bomber that had Buick-built Pratt & Whitney engines, stopped at Flint's Bishop Airport for press rides. The visit was a gesture from its owners, the Collings Foundation, to Buick for helping restore one of the engines.

One key non-product strategy moving forward was the "retail environment design program" headed by L. D. (Jack) Robbins, assistant general sales manager for service, who called it the most comprehensive facilities plan in the industry. Basically, Buick had developed architectural designs for future dealerships, but with flexibility for cost, size and other factors. Key features were a dome, canopy walkway, curved entry wall and landscaped plaza. Dealers were being encouraged to use the architectural plans drawn up by Buick. Jim Black, Buick's dealer facilities planning manager, said one element was moving service reception "from out back, where service was traditionally located, to the front of the building." It would take time, but Buick was building toward a future when premium American motorcars could be sold and serviced in dealerships that fit the image. The first new dealership built with the plans was Holiday Buick-Olds in Palmdale, California.

Buick could continue to promote quality ratings as it entered the 1993 model year. Park Avenue was rated "best overall American car value" in 1992 by IntelliChoice, an independent firm that ranked cars based on price, maintenance/fuel costs, insurance rates and other factors. And Park Avenue and Skylark generated the lowest rate of com-

1992 LeSabre Limited was an instant hit with customers and the press.

plaints among all full-size and compact cars in a 1989-91 study by the Florida attorney general's office, which also ranked Buick second among 36 brands. In May 1992, Buick was the only domestic automaker to place two cars in the top 10 in J.D. Power's annual Initial Quality Survey—Regal sedan 7th and Century tied for 9th.

For 1993, Buick would feature improved 3800 TPI V-6 engines and a restyled Regal sedan. The modified 3800 was lighter, had new low-friction roller rockers to reduce engine noise and vibration further, and a change in compression ratio from 8.5:1 to 9.0:1 to enhance performance and fuel economy. Torque was increased from 220 to 225 lb.-ft. and the torque and horsepower curves were reconfigured to provide better performance at all rpm levels. The result was a promised reduction in 0-60 times of about half a second and an improvement in fuel economy of one mile per gallon in the city.

A new base 2.2-liter four-cylinder engine in Century, although smaller in size, was more powerful, more fuel efficient and quieter than the engine it replaced. A new electronic monitoring system for Skylark protected the battery from going dead if interior lights were left on. All Regals now had electronically controlled automatic transmissions. Century offered a driver air bag.

While most models otherwise had minor improvements, Regal sedan received new front and rear styling including a new grille (that departed from Buick's traditional vertical bars), sculptured hood, new headlamps, revised quarter panels and larger wrap-around taillamps.

In its 90th anniversary year of 1993, Buick could take a brief breather to consider its heritage. It was displaying its own collection of historic Buicks in auto shows and in a permanent historical display in the lobby of the Buick Administration Building. Among them was a 1905 Model C believed to be the fourth or fifth oldest Buick in existence—apparently the first Buick sold in California (See Appendix 7). Buick Public Relations had produced a Buick video history with rare and never-before-collected motion pictures of such auto pioneers as Billy Durant, Ransom Olds, Louis Chevrolet, Henry Leland, Henry Ford, Charlie Nash, Boss Kettering, C.S. Mott, Sam McLaughlin, Walter Chrysler, Harlow Curtice, Dutch Bower and Charlie Chayne (but no film could be found of David Buick). The Buick Club of America planned major national and regional 90th birthday events.

Aristo Scrobogna, Billy Durant's last personal secretary, came to Flint from his home in New Jersey on May 14, 1991, to present Mertz with two historical artifacts for the lobby display—a letter Winston Churchill had written to Durant after World War I to thank GM for its war production, and a pewter statuette Durant had received during the Automobile Golden Jubilee in 1946 for being an important automotive pioneer. The trophy would be a permanent reminder that the founder of GM was originally a Buick man.

But not much time would be spent looking backward. The division was moving on with fresh concepts such as the "Essence of Buick People." Mertz personally created "people vision," working at home on ideas to empower employees to take leadership and develop self-confidence and team-building skills. He credited Coletta for inspiring new leadership methods when Coletta headed Project Spearhead, reorganizing the sales and service department.

Above: Holiday Buick-Olds in Palmdale, California, first dealership with Buick's new design. Below: Aristo Scrobogna (left), last personal secretary of GM founder and Buick promoter Billy Durant, presents the statuette Durant received in 1946 as an auto pioneer to Buick General Manager Ed Mertz.

Coletta had been part of sales and service for three decades and saw a lot of room for improvement.

"The organization was too autocratic," he said. "If you went to someone who wasn't your immediate superior, you'd get in trouble. We were losing good people, and losing the ideas of those who stayed. I knew, when I moved up to assistant general sales manager, I would be just like the others unless I made a move to change things."

Coletta studied new management techniques, created self-directed work teams in the field and began an educational process of empowering people to become leaders, to trust in their own abilities to get the job done.

Mertz, who saw the need to tap more fully into Buick's own talent if it was to move forward, was encouraged by Coletta's enthusiasm and confidence in his people. Mertz then spent long hours framing the foundation of the "Essence of Buick People.' When he announced it to employees in 1990, this was his vision of how Buick people should strive to act and interact with each other and their customers:

Team Focus—Working together for strength and support, succeeding together.

Confidence—Knowing where we're going and how we're going to get there, and feeling good about it.

Caring—Demonstrating genuine respect and trust for individuals, and concern for our customers.

Leadership—Displaying leadership no matter what our job responsibilities. Leadership is seeing something that needs to be done, and taking on the responsibility to make it happen.

Empowerment—Fostering and encouraging empowerment so that people feel free to speak up, to take risks, to make decisions on their own with all of our support.

Simplicity—Continuously identifying ways for our system to operate with less effort, allowing our energies to be focused on the important things.

"People vision" proved easier said than done, as Mertz acknowledged in *Inside Buick* in 1991.[1] "I was surprised when I learned recently that so few people comprehend what we're trying to achieve. I realize this vision is going to take patience and fortitude, perhaps even more than we had thought. People cultures aren't so easily molded by words. Even actions can be suspect if they aren't supported by continuity. We've yet to prove that this isn't just another program and that it will live long after the principal players have moved on."

This was frank acknowledgement that much needed to be done—and that a vision was something to aim for, that might never be fully achieved. Certainly Buick was moving forward. The same issue of *Inside Buick* that carried Mertz's remarks also included articles describing specific achievements by empowered teams. Training programs, structure of business teams and management attitude all began to show the influence of Mertz's vision. But early in the Nineties, no one was yet declaring victory.

Having its "people vision" as well as its future product direction defined, Buick looked at one more key business element, defining "customer vision." In 1992, a team of employees defined it as "Customer care that says 'you're family'" and added four descriptors: Welcome, trust, respect and appreciation. In the Mertz era, Buick was defining its future on all fronts. It was not surprising that when the incentives industry created a "national motivator of the year" award in 1991, Ed Mertz was the first winner.

While Buick continued to emphasize its American image, it was showing new interest in an international market it had largely ignored for half a century. Announcing the 1991 Park Avenue, Buick pointed out that it had better fuel economy than 37 similarly equipped mid-size, compact and subcompact models, including the Acura Legend,

every BMW and Porsche and even a 3-liter Hyundai. And when a Buick concept car named Sceptre debuted at the 1992 North American International Auto Show, it was described by Mertz as "a design statement that could attract those purchasers who have been drawn to the international brands."

Introducing Sceptre in Detroit, Mertz pointed out that Buick was "doing its bit for the balance of trade" by exporting 2,000 more cars (about 11,000 total) than Jaguar imported in 1991. And he observed that Buick was selling more cars to American "baby boomers" (people from ages 27-45) than BMW, Audi, Lexus and Infiniti combined. A week later, speaking before the *Automotive News* World Congress, he noted Buick's success in a domestic market that was increasingly global in makeup. He said there was no desire to disparage quality imports—but that customers needed to be reminded American cars were world competitive in quality, fuel economy, performance and price. Indeed, one week after that speech, the Japanese parliament, apparently trying to cool angry rhetoric on both sides of the Pacific, made a public gesture of conciliation to Americans by buying two Park Avenues. And a ship full of Roadmasters was among the first commercial shipments into Kuwait at the end of the Persian Gulf War in 1991.

As to where Buick was headed in product, Sceptre was a good indicator in mid-size sedan styling. Specific features included a 3.5-liter supercharged V-6, five-speed automatic transmission and air bags front and rear. Sceptre was rear drive, but Mertz said it might have front drive in production.

A concept car program in March 1992 offered more specific clues about the future. Seven cars with advanced engines—V-6s, supercharged V-6s and V-8s—were turned over to 50 auto writers for test drives at Phoenix International Raceway. The purpose was to show the writers where Buick was headed and also to get their opinions.

"Buick is considering both overhead valve and overhead cam engines for future powerplants," Derhake told the writers. "These concept cars represent advances in overhead valve engines that demonstrate the great potential of that technology."

It was an important point. While many auto writers had long favored dual overhead cam engines (used in many Japanese cars), Thomas G. Stephens, director of engineering for engines at GM Powertrain Division, delivered a strong message on the advantages of overhead valve engines used in most Buicks.

Stephens' organization was building both. Overhead valve engines have one intake and exhaust valve per cylinder, with each valve having pushrod linkages which pass through the engine. Dual overhead cam engines have two intake and two exhaust valves per cylinder, allowing more air to flow into the combustion chamber and more exhaust gas to flow out of it. OHV engines, described as "torquers," have better

---

[1] In 1991, *Inside Buick*, Buick's employee magazine, won its second international award. Its editor, Corby L. Casler, won the International Gold Mercury Award, called the Oscar of communications, for excellence in communications, from the International Academy of Communications Arts & Sciences. The magazine in 1985 had won an international "Moto" award for outstanding achievement in automotive journalism, presented to Lawrence R. Gustin, then the magazine's editor.

Sceptre, Buick concept car for 1992, was a hint of future "international" Buick design.

low-end performance and DOHC engines, described as "twisters," have better performance at high rpm. But Stephens saw technology converging so that an "extended range" 3800 V-6 (also called the ERV-6) could be described as "a torquer that'll do a decent twist."

Said Stephens: "With strong torque output, overhead valve engines can be matched with axle ratios that allow the engine to meet customers' needs for responsiveness and highway cruising capability while operating with low engine friction, thus providing very competitive fuel economy." He noted OHV engines are less complex than their DOHC counterparts, resulting in fewer parts, reduced cost and simplified manufacturing requirements. "These tightly packaged OHV designs also allow designers greater flexibility because they can be installed in less space in the engine compartment."

Looking toward the new century, he said GM would be working on overhead valve and overhead cam applications, new fuels such as reformulated gasoline, methanol and natural gas and, of course, electric vehicles. He said GM is "looking very seriously at two-stroke cycles" and other engines and fuels, although he declined to predict what percentage of each would be used at the start of the new century.

Engines in Buick's 1992 concept cars ranged from a supercharged 3.1-liter V-6 in a spirited Skylark Gran Sport to a 292-horsepower V-8 in a surprisingly quick Roadmaster. They included future generations of 3800 V-6 and supercharged versions of the advanced 3800s in Park Avenues and Park Avenue Ultras, as well as supercharged advanced 3800s in Regal Gran Sports.

Michael E. Doble, Buick's manager of advanced concepts, said he was particularly excited about the "customer's choice" Park Avenue Ultra. This car could be set up to meet a customer's wishes on ride

characteristics and aggressiveness of response and handling. Various levels of chassis/suspension "ride," throttle response and steering response and transmission shift frequency could be programmed into the car. In addition, there were adjustable memory settings for two drivers—allowing them to select their own radio and climate "presets," outside rear-view mirror positions and seat positions.

The writers confirmed Doble's opinion—the "customer choice" Park Avenue Ultra was, as several said, "a terrific idea." Nobody else has done anything like that, the writers said. Buick should move quickly to market its advantage, they advised. The powerful advanced engines in Roadmaster and Park Avenue also got plenty of good votes, as did the supercharged Skylark.

While engines dominated the discussions with the writers, Buick also showcased newly designed seats in most of the concept cars—as well as displays contrasting present and future seats. Buick was taking the first steps toward becoming a leader in seating designs.

Meanwhile, work was continuing on a sleek new generation of Riviera. And designs were being sketched for Buicks of the 21st century. The enthusiasm for motorcars that had germinated late in the 19th century was ever growing.

As Ed Mertz told *Design News* writer Charles J. Murray: "This is a car business. You have to have a passion for it. If we live it and breathe it and love it, we're sure to build better cars."

Innovation would continue at Buick. For the most part, that had been true for most of a century, since the days when David Buick, Eugene Richard and Walter Marr experimented with the valve-in-head engine, even before Billy Durant used Buick to build what became the largest industrial corporation in history.

Buicks for 1993: Park Avenue Ultra (above), Regal Limited sedan (below).

The Buick —

COLOR PORTFOLIO II

Page preceding: 1938 Special Model 46C with coachwork by Letourneur et Marchand | Above left: 1937 Century Model 61 Four-Door Trunk-Back Sedan
Above right: 1938 Special Model 46C Convertible Coupe | Below left: 1939 Special Model 46C Convertible Coupe
Below right: 1940 Limited Model 81 Four-Door Touring Sedan | Right: 1940 Century Model 66C Convertible Coupe

Above: 1940 Special Model 41C Convertible Phaeton \ Below: 1940 Limited Model 81C Convertible Phaeton

Above: 1941 Century Model 66S Sedanet | Below: 1942 Limited Model 91F Formal Sedan

Above left: 1947 Roadmaster Model 79 Estate Wagon by Hercules | Above right: 1947 Super Model 56C Convertible Coupe
Below left: 1948 Roadmaster Model 76C Convertible Coupe | Below right: 1949 Special Model 46S Sedanet | Right: 1949 Super Model 56C Convertible Coupe

Above left: 1950 Super Model 56R Two-Door Riviera | Above right: 1951 Special Model 48D Two-Door DeLuxe Sedan | Below left:
1951 Roadmaster Model 76C Convertible Coupe | Below right: 1952 Roadmaster Model 72R Four-Door Riviera | Right: 1953 Roadmaster Model 76X Two-Door Skylark

Above left: 1954 Super Model 56C Convertible Coupe | Above right: 1954 Skylark Model 100 Sports Convertible
Below left: 1955 Special Model 48 Two-Door Sedan | Below right: 1955 Roadmaster Model 76C Convertible Coupe

Above: 1956 Special Model 46R Two-Door Riviera
Below: 1957 Super Model 53 Four-Door Riviera

Left: 1957 Century Model 66C Convertible Coupe | Above left: 1958 Roadmaster Model 75 Four-Door Riviera
Above right: 1959 Electra 225 Model 4867 Convertible Coupe | Below: 1960 LeSabre Model 4467 Convertible Coupe

Above left: 1961 Invicta Model 4637 Two-Door Riviera | Above right: 1962 Special Model 4367 Skylark | Below: 1963 Riviera Model 4747 Two-Door Sport Coupe

Above left: 1964 Special Model 4027 Two-Door Coupe | Above right: 1965 Skylark Model 44467 Gran Sport | Below: 1965 Wildcat Model 46667 Custom Convertible Coupe

Above left: 1965 Electra 225 Model 48239 Four-Door Hardtop Sedan | Above right: 1966 Electra 225 Model 48467 Custom Convertible Coupe | Below left: 1967 Skylark Gran Sport Model 44617 Two-Door Sport Coupe | Below right: 1969 Wildcat Model 46667 Custom Convertible Coupe | Right: 1968 Wildcat Model 46487 Two-Door Sport Coupe

Left: 1971 Gran Sport Model 43437 Two-Door Sport Coupe, Stage I \ Above left: 1970 Electra 225 Model 48467 Custom Convertible Coupe
Above right. 1972 Riviera Model 49487 Two-Door Sport Coupe \ Below: 1974 Riviera Model 4EY87 Two-Door Hardtop Coupe

Above: 1975 Century Indianapolis 500 Pace Car \ Below: 1975 LeSabre Custom Model 4BP67 Convertible Coupe

Above: 1976 Century Indianapolis 500 Pace Car | Below: 1977 Electra Model 4CX37 Two-Door Limited Coupe

Left: 1978 Riviera LXXV, Model 48Z37, 75th Anniversary model | Above: 1979 LeSabre Model 4BP69 Four-Door Limited Sedan
Below: 1980 Riviera Model 4EZ57 Luxury Two-Door Hardtop

*Above: 1981 Regal Limited Coupe \ Below: 1983 Riviera Indianapolis 500 Pace Car \ Right: 1982 Century Four-Door Sedan *
Far right, top: 1984 Regal Grand National \ Far right, center: 1985 Somerset Regal \ Far right, bottom: 1985 Electra T Type

Above: 1986 Riviera T Type / Below: 1986 LeSabre Coupe / Opposite, top left: 1987 LeSabre T Type / Opposite, top right: 1987 Regal GNX / Opposite, bottom: 1988 Regal

Opposite: 1988 Reatta Coupe. Above: 1991 Reatta Convertible with 1938 Buick "Y-Job."

1991 Park Avenue.

Above left: 1992 Skylark Gran Sport Coupe. Above right: 1992 LeSabre Limited. Below: 1992 Roadmaster Limited.

Above: 1993 Regal Gran Sport Sedan. Below: 1993 Park Avenue Ultra.

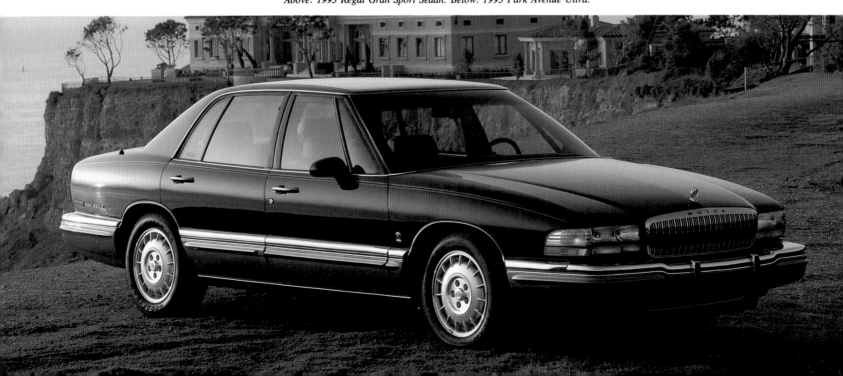

OWNER & PHOTOGRAPHER CREDITS

1938 Special by Letourneur et Marchand
Owner: Leonard J. Peterson   Photograph by Roy Query

1937 Century Model 61 Trunk-Back Sedan
Owner: David Crow   Photograph by Rick Lenz

1938 Special Model 46C Convertible Coupe
Owner: Wayne Yonce   Photograph by Rick Lenz

1939 Special Model 46C Convertible Coupe
Owners: Katie and Ron Kucharski
Photograph by William L. Bailey

1940 Limited Model 81 Four-Door Touring Sedan
Owner: Al Newman   Photograph by Rick Lenz

1940 Century Model 66C Convertible Coupe
Owner: Leonard J. Peterson   Photograph by Roy Query

1940 Special Model 41C Convertible Phaeton
Owner: Robert Coates   Photograph by Rick Lenz

1940 Limited Model 81C Convertible Phaeton
Owner: Harold B. Casey   Photograph by Roy Query

1941 Century Model 66S Sedanet
Owner: Oliver L. Ehresman   Photograph by Roy Query

1942 Limited Model 91F Formal Sedan
Owner: Guy B. Bennett, Jr.   Photograph by Roy Query

1947 Roadmaster Model 79 Estate Wagon by Hercules
Owner: Leonard J. Peterson   Photograph by Roy Query

1947 Super Model 56C Convertible Coupe
Owner: Leonard J. Immke, Jr.   Photograph by Roy Query

1948 Roadmaster Model 76C Convertible Coupe
Owner: John Bankhead   Photograph by Don Vorderman

1949 Special Model 46S Sedanet
Owner: Mario P. Romano   Photograph by Rick Lenz

1949 Super Model 56C Convertible Coupe
Owner: Anita Brooks Bennett   Photograph by Roy Query

1950 Super Model 56R Two-Door Riviera
Owner: Jim Hallameyer   Photograph by Rick Lenz

1951 Special Model 48D Two-Door DeLuxe Sedan
Owner: Frank Kozlevchar   Photograph by Roy Query

1951 Roadmaster Model 76C Convertible Coupe
Owner: Richard B. Boyer   Photograph by Rick Lenz

1952 Roadmaster Model 72F Four-Door Riviera
Owner: Dr. Marvin Speer   Photograph by Rick Lenz

1953 Roadmaster Model 76X Two-Door Skylark
Owner: Jack Tyrrell   Photograph by Rick Lenz

1954 Super Model 56C Convertible Coupe
Owner: Guy B. Bennett, Jr.   Photograph by Roy Query

1954 Skylark Model 100 Sports Convertible
Owner: Mr. Duran   Photograph by Rick Lenz

1955 Special Model 48 Two-Door Sedan
Owner: Robert Cushman
Photograph by William L. Bailey

1955 Roadmaster Model 76C Convertible Coupe
Owner: Burley Harding   Photograph by Rick Lenz

1956 Special Model 46R Two-Door Riviera
Owners: George and Melvia McKerle
Photograph by Rick Lenz

1957 Super Model 53 Four-Door Riviera
Owner: James G. Rossetti   Photograph by Rick Lenz

1957 Century Model 66C Convertible Coupe
Owner: Gary Offstein   Photograph by Rick Lenz

1958 Roadmaster Model 75 Four-Door Riviera
Owner: Burt Alleshouse   Photograph by Rick Lenz

1959 Electra 225 Model 4867 Convertible Coupe
Owner: Jack M. Lawson
Photograph by William L. Bailey

1960 LeSabre Model 4467 Convertible Coupe
Owner: Wayne Yonce   Photograph by Rick Lenz

1961 Invicta Model 4637 Two-Door Riviera
Owner: Jeff Frank   Photograph by Rick Lenz

1962 Special Model 4367 Skylark
Owner: Norman L. Milcherska   Photograph by Rick Lenz

1963 Riviera Model 4747 Two-Door Sport Coupe
Owners: Bill and Aida Colson   Photograph by Rick Lenz

1964 Special Model 4027 Two-Door Coupe
Owner: Guy B. Bennett, Jr.   Photograph by Roy Query

1965 Skylark Model 44467 Gran Sport
Owners: Alan and Mary Paulhamus
Photograph by Roy Query

1965 Wildcat Model 46667 Custom Convertible Coupe
Owner: Guy B. Bennett, Jr.   Photograph by Roy Query

1965 Electra 225 Model 48239 Four-Door Hardtop Sedan
Owner: Donald Naugle   Photograph by Rick Lenz

1966 Electra 225 Model 48467 Custom Convertible Coupe
Owner: Dick Osborne   Photograph by Rick Lenz

1967 Skylark Gran Sport Model 44617 Sport Coupe
Owners: Mr. and Mrs. Harry Scholman
Photograph by Rick Lenz

1969 Wildcat Model 46667 Custom Convertible Coupe
Owners: Mr. and Mrs. Donald Glaub
Photograph by Rick Lenz

1968 Wildcat Model 46487 Two-Door Sport Coupe
Owner: Howard Polland   Photograph by Rick Lenz

1971 Gran Sport Model 43437 Two-Door Sport Coupe
Owner: James A. Bennett   Photograph by Roy Query

1970 Electra 225 Model 48467 Custom Convertible Coupe
Owner: Dick Osborne   Photograph by Rick Lenz

1972 Riviera Model 49487 Two-Door Sport Coupe
Owner: Guy B. Bennett, Jr.   Photograph by Roy Query

1974 Riviera Model 4EY87 Two-Door Hardtop Coupe
Owner: Martin M. Schiff, M.D.
Photograph by Rick Lenz

1975 Century Indianapolis 500 Pace Car
1976 Century Indianapolis 500 Pace Car
Alfred P. Sloan Museum   Photographs by Roy Query

1975 LeSabre Custom Model 4BP67 Convertible Coupe
Owner: Leonard J. Peterson   Photograph by Roy Query

1977 Electra Model 4CX37 Two-Door Limited Coupe
Owners: Mr. and Mrs. Vernon Scrafield
Photograph by Rick Lenz

1978 Riviera LXXV, 75th Anniversary Model
Clark Brothers   Photograph by Rick Lenz

1979 LeSabre Model 4BP69 Four-Door Limited Sedan
1980 Riviera Model 4EZ57 Luxury Two-Door Hardtop
Buick Motor Division   Photographs by William L. Bailey

1981 Regal Limited Model 4AJ47 Two-Door Coupe
Buick Motor Division   Photograph by Roy Query

1987 Regal GNX and 1988 Regal photography by Roy Query; 1991 Reatta convertible (with 1938 "Y-Job") and 1991 Park Avenue photography by David Franklin;
1988 Reatta coupe, 1992 Skylark Gran Sport coupe, 1992 Le Sabre Limited, 1992 Roadmaster Limited, 1993 Regal Gran Sport sedan, and 1993 Park Avenue Ultra photography
by Gary D. Smith; all other photography courtesy of Buick Motor Division.

THUNDERING DOWN THE TRACK

In the first decade of this century, a colorful group of men and their Buick racing machines thundered out of the corners of the nation's race tracks and scorched across the pages of the record books. By the time the checkered flag had fallen for the last time, Buick had established its reputation as a dependable, reliable car—and had achieved a racing record that was the envy of many another automobile manufacturer.

Buick's sporting life began virtually with the beginning of the Buick. AAA historical records show that as early as August 27, 1904, a Buick driven by Walter Marr finished third in a 5-mile race at Grosse Pointe, Michigan.

In November of 1904, on Thanksgiving Day, Buick's New York and New Jersey agent H.J. Koehler drove a two-cylinder stripped chassis Buick up Eagle Rock near Newark, and not only won its class (for cars selling between $850-$1250) in the hill climb at 2 minutes 18-2/5 seconds, but slashed the best previous record in half as well. Buick claimed the car developed 22 bhp at 924 rpm, and the win was the "first conspicuous event that impressed the general public with the marvelous efficiency of the Buick car." Walter Marr, who was there and who was asked how this smallish engine could beat its larger competitors, replied: "It's a valve-in-head motor." No one was exactly sure what that meant at the time, but by December Koehler had sold two new Buicks with its surprising new engine.

In 1905, in July, the annual Glidden Tour was a thousand-mile run through four states, plus a climb to the top of Mount Washington. A Koehler Buick won the two-cylinder class in the latter with a time of 36 minutes 25-4/5 seconds. Driven by A.H. Weisser, the 1740-pound $1200 Buick had bested cars selling for three times its price. A Pope-Toledo, for example, was more than ten minutes slower up Mount Washington. During the 1905 season, Koehler upped his sales to seventy-five Buicks.

On October 27th, 1906 at Empire Track in Yonkers, New York, this same agent entered a 100-mile race for stripped touring cars. There were seven competitors: Cooper driving a Matheson, Keeler with an Oldsmobile, Bernin with a Mercedes, Wridgway with a Packard, two Cadillacs driven by Burne and Roberts—and Koehler with his Buick.

With the exception of one lap when the Oldsmobile took over, Cooper led the race with his Matheson for the first seventeen miles. Down the straightaway on mile eighteen, however, the Matheson lost a rear wheel, which ended the race for it, and for the Matheson's mechanic as well, who was thrown from the car and broke his collarbone. The Oldsmobile was in the lead once more, until lap fifty-eight when a tire change was necessary and Keeler was forced to the pits. This gave Koehler his chance, and his Buick—until then lying in second place—surged into the lead. With new rubber on his car, Keeler was again back on the track, overtook the Buick, and at mile ninety had tire trouble again. With fortune smiling, Buick led again—and to the finish, taking the checkered flag just 15-2/5 seconds ahead of Keeler. In another race that same day the Buick was victorious once more over the Oldsmobile—and had a much easier time of it—in a three-mile run for stock cars selling for $1500 or less.

From Thanksgiving Day of 1904 through Christmas of 1906, Koehler accumulated no fewer than thirty-six racing cups and medals. Racing success meant sales success. On October 1st, 1906 the agent placed an order with Buick for 500 vehicles, 350 two-cylinder cars and 150 fours. There must have been joy in Flint that day. The order represented about $700,000 and one-tenth of the factory output.

In the meantime, other distributors around the country—Charles S. Howard in San Francisco particularly—were experiencing much the same success as Koehler on the tracks. Buick had begun to pile victory on top of victory.

Meantime, too, Billy Durant noticed what was going on—and realized what a great idea all this was for publicity. He had had a trial run at Empire City, sent a Buick from New York to San Francisco in twenty-four days for a new coast-to-coast record, and in Los Angeles yet another Buick won its class in an endurance contest. This was in 1906, and was just the beginning.

Eventually Durant would bring together a racing team that would

Page preceding: The Buick team at Savannah, 1908. Above left: H.J. Koehler at Newark meet in 1905. Above right: A Koehler Buick, A.H. Weisser the driver, at Mt. Washington, 1905.

make the Buick name famous—and prosperous. Over the coming years such noted drivers of the period as Bob Burman, the Chevrolet brothers (Arthur, Louis and Gaston), Lewis Strang (a veteran with wins at Savannah, Briarcliff and Lowell already behind him), Hugh Easter, George DeWitt and Louis Nikrent, among others, would run with the Buick banner.

The real backbone of the team, however, consisted of "Wild" Bob Burman and Louis Chevrolet.

Born on a farm in Imlay City, Michigan in 1884, Burman was one of Buick's first employees and is given credit for testing the first Buick made in Jackson, Michigan. Thereafter he was chief tester for the Jackson Automobile Company, but soon found that racing automobiles was more to his liking than testing them and he quickly made a reputation for himself in motor sport. Durant persuaded Burman to return to Buick and immediately put him on the Buick team in 1907.

Burman's racing strategy was simple: "It either holds together and I win running wide open, or it breaks and I lose." He was a fearless competitor. His greatest exploit probably was in 1911, when he drove the Blitzen Benz over a mile course at an average speed of 142 mph. He was killed April 8th, 1916 driving a Peugeot in the Corona, California road race, an event he had helped to organize. Running down the backstretch on the ninety-seventh lap, a tire blew and flipped his car into the crowd. Burman, his mechanic and a track guard were killed. Five spectators were injured, several seriously. Burman was only thirty-two years old.

Louis Chevrolet was born in Switzerland on December 25th, 1878,

was educated in France and had his first experiences in racing and automobile engineering there. Emigrating to America in 1900, he was racing for Fiat in New York five years later. On March 6th, 1909, he transferred his allegiance to Buick and, in Flint, was instrumental in the design, construction and competition of Buick racing vehicles. While not the "wild" driver Burman was, he was extremely competent. In a head-to-head battle, Burman usually came out the winner—if his car held together. Chevrolet, on the other hand, lived to a ripe old age, dying of natural causes in 1941. His motto: "Never give up."

Louis Chevrolet was very strong and powerfully built. On one occasion, when cranking a large-engined race car, the engine backfired. A broken arm was the usual result in such cases. But Chevrolet held on—and actually bent the crank in his hands!

"That group of hellions" is how Peter Helck has described the early team drivers at Buick, and it is apt. Racing was usually a matter of each man running as hard as he could and as long as he could—until something broke or the race ended. A Buick race car was not a machine to be babied.

Loren Hodge, a mechanic on and the last surviving member of the Buick racing group, describes the team as "close to each other like members of a large family. It was long work and hard hours, but in the end success came. It was the team's job to make the Buick a better vehicle through trial and error." Early team managers were Eugene Richard, Walter Marr, Enos DeWaters and Dr. Wadsworth Warren. Bill Pickens followed. Mechanics in addition to Hodge were Otto Snyder, Charles Miller, Henry Parish, Tony Janette and David Carroll.

352

Above: Hugh Easter and his 1908 Model 10 racer at the Savannah International Light Car race that year, during one of the first twelve laps, and after crashing on the thirteenth.

The Buick team moved from race to race by rail car. Equipment included the race machines and a tow car for transportation to the track. A baggage car was leased from the railroad and outfitted with a complete machine shop, blacksmith's forge and room to carry eight race vehicles. Buick traveled in style.

By 1908 everything seemed to be slipping into place nicely. Durant staged a mock race with Burman driving a stripped-down Buick racer against an airplane for publicity purposes.

Even temporary reversals were turned to advantage, as witness the incident during the 250-mile road race in Lowell, Massachusetts, on September 7, 1908. Burman's 40hp Model 5 stock chassis was running a poor second to Strang, then driving an Isotta, when Burman suddenly pulled off the track and into his camp area. When he came back on the track, officials spotted a new radiator and front axle. Burman was promptly disqualified. Durant, who was there, promptly wired Buick's sales manager H.E. Shiland: "Model five and Burman behaved beautifully yesterday. No fault of either that we did not get second place. Three laps ahead of nearest competitor for that position on twenty-first round. Our disqualification perfectly just, due to our repair force not understanding the rules." Noblesse oblige—and probably mash for the publicity mill, since this would not be the last time Burman or Buick was to be disqualified for pushing the rules a bit too far.

September 26 and 27 saw three Buicks, Burman and a driver named Burke (apparently not a member of the team) in Montreal, Canada, for two days of racing. Of the fourteen events, Buick took eleven firsts, tied once and lost only twice. Most of the eleven victories belonged to Burman. "Burman is a dandy," the newspapers said. "His sensa-

tional driving electrified the crowds here." The fact he was driving a Buick was mentioned, too.

In mid-November 1908, Buick headed south to Savannah for the light car races on November 25, and the Grand Prize race on November 26. It was to be a memorable event.

Four Buicks were entered in the light car races, Burman in car number 8, Jeffers in number 16, Easter in number 14 and Hearne in number 11. All had four-cylinder "square" engines with 3-3/4-inch bore and stroke rated at 18 hp. Legend surrounds cars 8 and 16.

In most earlier racing cars, Buick had retained standard state-of-the-art suspensions. However, during a race preceding the Savannah event, an underslung Benz had been fortuitously wrecked just outside the Buick camp. In the dead of night, lanterns in hand, members of the Buick team quietly and carefully inspected the Benz's springing until they were convinced they understood its design and principles. Back in Flint the group built the necessary parts quickly and secretly, loaded them into the boxcar in separate crates and, once the doors were closed and the train on the way to Savannah, converted two of the team cars to underslungs!

It worked. Burman's fastest lap was 10 minutes 30 seconds, an average of 55.98 mph. He finished second in the 196-mile race with an average of 51.44 mph. Jeffers, in the other underslung, was out at 29.4 miles with a bent steering knuckle. Hearne came in fourth with an average of 49.6 mph.

Easter and his mechanic Thompson had quite a ride. At 127 miles, as the car was entering a corner, the rear axle cracked allowing the right rear wheel bearing and wheel to separate from the assembly. The

353

resulting wreck was spectacular. The car somersaulted in the air, passed over a corner worker while airborne, and landed in a ditch. Easter managed to stay with the car and was badly bruised. Thompson was thrown some 50 feet through the air, and although first reported to have been killed, was badly injured.

Burman had entered a 50hp 5-inch bore and stroke machine in the Grand Prize race. However, he suffered mechanical problems and retired after the third lap.

But 1909 brought spectacular victories. On February 21st Burman drove a Model 17 in the Mardi Gras Speed Contest in New Orleans and finished the 100-miler in 102 minutes 39-3/5 seconds—a full nine miles ahead of the second-place car. On February 22nd, another Model 17 won the Pasadena-Altadena Hill Climb for cars selling up to $2000. Daytona, Florida, on March 23rd, saw Strang win a 100-mile event for $1000-$1700 cars in 1 hour 34 minutes 1-1/5 seconds. In the same event, DeWitt driving a Model 10 won his class in 1 hour 44 minutes 34 seconds. At the Atlanta Hill Climb on March 27th, Model 10's won both first and second places in Class One; a Model 16 stock car took Class Four in 58 seconds, setting a course record; Lewis Strang won Class Six with the same car in 59 seconds; Burman captured Class Five with a Model 17 in 1 minute 4-4/5 seconds.

Buick continued its winning ways through the rest of March, April and May. On April 22nd, with Chevrolet, Strang and DeWitt the drivers, Buick won five of six events at the Lookout Mountain Hill Climb in Chattanooga, Tennessee. On to Nashville on the 29th, and Chevrolet won the one- and ten-mile free-for-all contests.

On June 8th the team was in Crown Point for the 232-mile Indiana Trophy Race, a ten-lap event limited to engines of 300 cubic inches maximum. Sixteen cars started, with Burman, Chevrolet and Strang in Buicks—and Buick heavily favored to win. Bad luck. Strang's car lost a gear at twenty-five miles, Chevrolet's Buick failed at thirty. Burman was leading the race when he broke a valve. Just barely able to keep running, he limped around the track until he found Strang's car off the edge of the course and helped himself to some available "spare parts" from it. Alert officials caught him in the act. Burman was disqualified.

No matter. Much more prestigious was the Cobe Trophy at Crown Point the following day, a 395.6-mile race with a 525-cubic-inch engine limit. Only twelve cars were entered in the event. Among them were Burman and Chevrolet, driving Marquette-Buicks.

The Marquette-Buicks were an interesting addition to the Buick stable. It is not known just when the team began using them, but several things are certain. They weren't "stock" Buicks, in reality little save for the engine was actually built by Buick at all. The factory felt it might be in some trouble if word of what the vehicles really were was passed around too quickly, so they were called "Buick 30's" for thirty horsepower. It was not until the following year that the appropriate addition of the word "Marquette" was made.

Among the myriad firms Durant acquired in putting together General Motors was a little-known car producer in Saginaw, Michigan called the Marquette Motor Company, builders at the time of the Rainier production car and high-quality race cars that were being campaigned around the country successfully. It was at Durant's suggestion that Louis Chevrolet went to Saginaw to see what might be done to come up with a faster machine for the Buick team. What Chevrolet wanted was virtually a hand-built race car, something not readily available from the Buick production line, and he got it. Another one was made for Burman—and they were both ready for the Cobe Trophy.

The race began at 8:00 a.m., the cars being dispatched at one-minute intervals. In typical fashion Burman charged into the lead on the first lap, but on lap three he lost control and went off the course, and by lap five was out of competition. A Knox then led briefly until it threw a rod, and subsequently Chevrolet in the other "Model 30" ran to the front of the pack. But he ran too hard—and developed engine trouble. His crew managed to get him going again, but only on three cylinders for the last three laps of the race.

Meanwhile a telegraph station which had been set up at the track was sending race progress reports back to Flint. The factory had located a telegraph key, and an operator in a small machine shop at Buick, and men were clustered around him. Among them was one of the forgotten men of the company, David Dunbar Buick. He was nervous, paced the floor constantly, chewed his cigar as news clattered in over the wire. When the word came that Chevrolet was back in the race but on one less cylinder, the entire group groaned.

Chevrolet and his Buick were now running twenty-two minutes behind Robertson's Locomobile. A Knox driven by Bourque had slipped into second. Suddenly the Locomobile was forced into the pits with ignition problems and remained there for thirty-three minutes. Drawing every ounce of available power from his three remaining cylinders, Chevrolet's Buick moved into second place as the Locomobile re-entered the race. Later acknowledging that he wasn't sure how he did it, Chevrolet then took his stammering machine past Bourque's Knox in the standings to win by 65 seconds.

The telegraph at Flint, quiet for awhile, burst to life with news of the three-cylinder victory and the room went wild. A failure in the Fairmount Park race of 1909 followed, but Buick was still savoring the Cobe Trophy triumph and didn't pay much attention.

Mechanical failures were frequent with the Buick team, and many people since have wondered why. The answer is simple. Little thought was given to preservation of the machinery. Indeed there seems to have been no master plan to the team at all. It was instead a diverse grouping of diverse individuals who decided themselves how the cars were to be driven. It was not unusual for two members of the Buick team to be locked in an intramural competition for the lead—with the closest competitor on a car not built in Flint (or Saginaw) miles or minutes behind. This was the sort of inner team rivalry

Opposite: Burman at Lowell in 1908. From the top: Hugh Easter leading the Motor Parkway Sweepstakes (preceding the 1908 Vanderbilt). He won his class; Burman at Indianapolis in 1909; Louis Chevrolet at Atlanta in 1909, before driving to victory in the Coca-Cola Trophy race.

Above left: The Buick racing team: Walter Marr (with beard and homburg) is seated on the car. In passenger seat respectively are Bob Burman and Louis Chevrolet. Above right and below: The Buick of Bob Burman and George DeWitt in the Brighton Beach Twenty-Four Hour Marathon of May 1910. A Simplex won, the No. 4 Buick placed fourth.

which two decades later would bedevil Enzo Ferrari and his scuderia of racing Alfa Romeos. As competition policies go, it was certainly not the wisest. But certain too is one other fact. The Buick team was always spectacular.*

The Indianapolis Motor Speedway opened in August of 1909. Thousands of people came to see the racing. Buick showed up with fifteen cars. In the event for machines with engines of from 231-300 cubic inches, Buick finished one-two-three, with Gaston Chevrolet, Lewis Strang and Bob Burman driving.

For the Prest-O-Lite Trophy, Louis Chevrolet, Burman and Strang all entered cars. Chevrolet and Burman ran first and second until the thirty-second lap when the former had problems with blowing dust and allowed four cars to pass him. Strang's car was out on lap thirty-six; he had had trouble with a fire in his engine early in the race, had managed to get back on the track, but only for awhile.

At 100 miles it was Burman with a five-minute lead and Chevrolet running fourth. Ten miles later Chevrolet had run himself back into the second position and held there until the fifty-third lap when he again fell back to fourth. On the next lap Bourque in a Knox made a strong move and got into second position. On lap fifty-eight, as the Knox came into the stretch, it swerved sharply off the track, hit an open ditch and overturned. Both driver and mechanic were killed.

On the sixty-seventh lap, Kincaid's second-place National was passed by Ellis in a Jackson. The Jackson continued to close on Burman for several laps and then passed the Buick at 202 miles. Eighteen miles later Ellis had opened up a lead of better than sixteen minutes on the Buick. With just thirty miles to go, the Jackson seemed a sure winner, but then just as the car drove by the judge's stand, its engine quit dead. The car coasted to the south end of the pit area, and by the time a bad magneto had been discovered, Burman had closed the gap, regained the front position—and went on to win by twelve minutes over Clements in a Stoddard-Dayton.

---

*Perhaps it was the lack of any coherent pit strategy which was one of the reasons for the lack of Buick success in the major sporting events of the day— the Vanderbilts, the Grand Prizes, the early Indy 500's. Certainly any objective perspective on the Buick achievement record must take into account the marque's inability to win the "Big One." And, in fact, Buick eschewed even entering some of these events. Likewise, Buick participation in twenty-four-hour marathons was spotty. Conceivably the rationale behind this could have been that a twice-around-the-clock or an event in which Buick would be pitted against the best Europe had to offer would require a rigid discipline within the team if a respectable showing was to be expected—and Buick managers had long since thrown up their hands regarding that. Major events were thus either not entered or, if entered, added little to the Buick racing success story. Where Buick shone was where its devil-may-care attitude toward team play hurt the least: class events, sprint racing and the like. And there the Buick record was quite incredible.

A more leisurely triumph was Lewis Strang's in the 100-mile G&J Trophy race, his Buick going the distance in 1 hour, 32 minutes, 48.5 seconds. The last event on the last day of racing at Indy was devoted to a 300-mile race with some of the fastest cars in the country. Unfortunately, after a National crashed through a fence causing three deaths, and a Marmon was subsequently involved in a serious accident, the race was stopped at 235 miles.

In mid-September of 1909 the press announced that Lewis Strang had a new car to drive for the Buick team. Called "The Earthquake," it had a long pointed nose and, reportedly, a Buick-built V-8 engine! Strang was personally responsible for the design and construction of the vehicle; newspaper articles noted that it was "too fast and too light to be run at full throttle" on most tracks. What this doubtless meant was that the car had terrible handling characteristics. Though Strang is known to have run practice laps with the machine and did plan to enter it in the Vanderbilt later that year, no record can be found to indicate that the vehicle ever made it to a starting line.

Meantime, other Buicks did. On October 30th, 1909, Louis Chevrolet and Buick entered the fifth Vanderbilt Cup Race on Long Island. The event was limited to engines of 301- to 600-cubic-inch displacement, and Chevrolet was there with 316 cubic inches. Wishart in a Mercedes led at the end of the first lap, with Chevrolet right on his tail. Chevrolet took the lead on round two, and kept it through the fourth lap. On the next one, however, a cracked cylinder put Chevrolet's Buick out of the race.

But Buick had a good fall season with wins at Lowell, Dallas, Long Island, Winnipeg, Amarillo, Atlanta, Phoenix, San Antonio and Los Angeles. Of particular note was the Atlanta run where Chevrolet, driving a Model 16 (Marquette-Buick), won the Coca-Cola Trophy— and the Los Angeles event at Ascot Park where a new record was set.

By December 18th and 19th, the dirt of the Indianapolis Speedway had been replaced by bricks, and a series of time trials held. Buick elected not to participate but to await instead the races scheduled for the following May. During 1909, Buick had won 166 first places, more than ninety percent of the events it had entered. By the beginning of 1910 Buick's racing record was unsurpassed.

On May 27th, 1910, Buick sent its cars to Indy for the races and received an unwelcome surprise. The "Model 30's," with engines from Flint and everything else from Saginaw, would not be allowed to compete. The reason: The required thirty-five units had not been built. The decision was announced by the AAA contest board, at 10:00 a.m. on the morning of the first races. The backbone of the team had been broken.

Buick was able to run in a few of the minor events with the production cars which had been brought along almost as an afterthought.

Two victories in eight races resulted on Friday, the first day. The best Buick could do on Saturday was a fourth by Arthur Chevrolet in a Model 16 in the 200-mile Wheeler & Schebler Trophy. The following Monday saw Buick win five- and ten-mile races for its piston displacement category in the "National Stock Car Championships"— along with Marmon, Knox and National. But this was not the bonanza that Flint had counted on.

The lesson was well learned. To preclude any problems arising in the forthcoming July races at Indy, forms were filled out listing the cars as entrants from the Marquette Motor Company and calling them Marquette-Buicks. These cars would be allowed to run. July 1st, 2nd and 4th would be the days for Buick's revenge.

Back in Flint, Louis Chevrolet, Bob Burman, Enos DeWaters and Buick chief engineer Walter Marr put their heads together. They wanted something to startle the competition when they returned to Indy. What they came up with was a pair of specially designed race cars so radically different from the racing norm that a double-take would be the usual spectator reaction.

The vehicles were designed and built in just three weeks. Officially they were called the Buick 60 Specials. Burman took one look at the car assigned to him and said it was the "Space Eater." Chevrolet decided to reserve judgment until he got his machine on the track. Ultimately the cars would come to be known as the "Buick Bugs" because of their rotund, insectean shape.

From their rounded fronts to their pointed rears, the Buick Bugs were streamlined, in an era when that term was not in vogue. The bodies were made of aluminum, and even the spoked wheels were covered with aluminum discs to cut down wind resistance. They were mid-ship single-seaters utilizing dead-center steering, the first race cars in this country so built. The specifications were hefty: 622-cubic-inch four-cylinder engines, a weight of 2600 pounds, a wheelbase of 102.5 inches. The cars were painted red with a big ram's head insignia on the hood. "That was to show 'em we were butting back into racing," Walter Marr said.

On June 28th, the team left for the Brickyard under the direction of Dr. Wadsworth Warren. With the two Bugs were two stock Model 10's, and two Model 16 Marquette-Buick roadsters. Two days later the team was at the track practicing. On the first day, Chevrolet blew a tire and rolled his Bug over; fortunately neither was injured. Both Bugs ran impressively in the time trials, each breaking 105 mph, Burman the better at 105.87. The Bugs were the fastest qualifiers at the meet, but neither of them would place in an event that weekend.

The team did well, however. On the first day of racing, five firsts, three seconds and a third were accumulated. Burman's only real disappointment was that he did not win the Speedway Helmet while driving his Bug, an award worth a handsome fifty-dollars-a-week to the winner for as long as he could defend his crown. The final two days of the meet saw the team breaking records and winning further

Below: The first outing of the Buick Bug, Burman with his at Indianapolis in 1910. Left: One of the last outings of the Bug, Ray Howard at Brighton Beach in 1912.

races, Burman for example in the Remy Grand Brassard Trophy.

The only real disappointments at Indianapolis were the Buick Bugs. Although extremely fast, the cars were also found to be extremely difficult to handle on the track. Interestingly, and perhaps because the cars simply looked awesome, it has long been held that they were consistent winners. But it can be documented that not only were they not that, but they did not race often either. Only a few more times, as a matter of fact. At a meet in Fort Erie on July 22nd and 23rd, 1910, Chevrolet won the five-mile free-for-all in his Bug. On Tuesday, March 28th, 1911, Burman in his set a record for fifty miles in the Straightaway Free-For-All at Jacksonville Beach, Florida. Two days later he set another record for a twenty-mile distance. In 1912 a Bug was raced at Brighton Beach in New York by Ray Howard. He led for the first six miles of a twenty-five-mile free-for-all but was then forced out with an overheated engine. After 1911 one of the Bugs was lost forever to history. Burman's machine eventually found its way into the hands of San Francisco distributor Charles Howard. Howard, many years later, gave the car to Charlie Chayne who in turn presented it to the Sloan Museum in Flint where it is on display today.

Three Marquette-Buicks—and Bob Burman, Louis and Arthur Chevrolet—were on hand for the Vanderbilt Cup Race held October 1st, 1910. And the "Buick Boys" were up to their usual tricks and traditional frantic pace. Louis ran his first lap at over 70 mph, with the other two Buicks tied for third, only seconds behind Belcher's Knox. Arthur was the first to go out with a broken chain drive. Louis and Burman then proceeded to lead the race, turning in lap averages of 74 and 75 mph, some four minutes ahead of the nearest competition. Chevrolet's car suddenly began to misfire and lose power, dropping him from first. Burman charged into the lead and turned another lap at 75 mph. But coming up through the field—and taking a leaf from the Buick team racing book—was Dawson on a Marmon. Burman was now only seventy-four seconds in the lead—not a wide enough margin by Buick standards—and was advised from his pit to pour it on. He did. He lost a chain and ruined his engine.

Only Chevrolet's Buick was left, holding on to third position behind Dawson's Marmon and the Disbrow National. All three cars were running within a five-minute span. Chevrolet moved up, and had the lead when Dawson pitted, then lost it when the Marquette-Buick needed a fuel stop. Back on the track, Chevrolet's car blew a tire on the backstretch. Still running at about 85 mph, he was pulled toward a ditch. He tried to straighten the car but the force on his steering broke the pitman arm and his vehicle went wildly out of control. His riding mechanic was caught under the car as it somersaulted and was killed instantly. The Buick careened, turned sharply to the

360

Above: Louis Chevrolet's Marquette-Buick didn't make it to the finish of the 1910 Vanderbilt. Below: At the Grand Prize in Savannah that year, Burman fared better, finishing third in his Marquette-Buick. Right: Louis Chevrolet in a racer in 1911, and his brother Arthur driving his Marquette-Buick in the inaugural running of the Indianapolis 500 in 1911.

right, knocked over a four-inch tree and crashed into a spectator's E.M.F. touring car. Its occupants were injured. Miraculously, Chevrolet suffered only a dislocated shoulder. Partly because of his injuries and partly because Durant wanted him elsewhere, Louis Chevrolet would not race again for nearly five years.

But in the Grand Prize race which followed on November 12th at Savannah, his brother Arthur and Bob Burman did. Their Marquette-Buicks, at 593.7 cubic inches, had previously been regarded as formidable, but they were dwarfed here by the Benz team of two cars: one of 736, the other 920 cubic inches. Still, in the time trials, Burman and Chevrolet were spotted as the ones to watch.

It was not one of their better days. Chevrolet was in second place on the first lap, went to third on the second, and then descended to tenth, ninth and eleventh positions until he broke a crankshaft and was out on the ninth lap. Burman drove what must have been one of the most conservative races of his career. For the first ten laps he was no better than eighth position. On laps twelve through nineteen, he moved steadily up until he sat in fourth. The last three laps he worked himself up to third, and there he finished with an average speed for the race of 67.07 mph, some 3.48 miles behind the two Benzes.

There were Buicks entered in that historic race which was the first Indianapolis 500. The year was 1911, and the great team drivers had begun to drift away. Durant was gone, and without him so was much of the support for the team. A letter written on Buick stationery dated February 9, 1911, signed by Wadsworth Warren, "Manager Racing Team," makes the comment that "our racing team has been disbanded." Charles Basle qualified for the 1912 Indy with a Marquette-

Buick but only drove 46 laps before retiring with a cracked crankcase. Arthur Chevrolet was also there with another Marquette-Buick but completed only 30 laps before going out with a broken crankshaft. Burman and Strang were there, too—driving a Benz and a Case.

For the third Grand Prize in Savannah on November 30th, there were two Marquette-Buick 100's. With bore and stroke unrestricted in the event, they were given larger four-cylinder engines (six-inch bore by five-and-a-quarter-inch stroke), improved carburetion and a high tension dual magneto. Basle and Cobe entered the cars. Burman showed up this time with a Marmon.

Cobe completed just over two laps in thirteenth and fourteenth positions respectively—and then crashed on lap three. Basle finished the first lap in twelfth place, made his way up to eighth, but was forced out of the race on the tenth round with engine trouble.

At the fourth Santa Monica race in California in May of 1912, there was one Buick, driven by a man named Devore. He swapped the lead with Ralph De Palma in a Mercer for the first six laps, but lost his engine on the seventh. In the 1912 Indianapolis 500, Billy Liesaw drove a Marquette-Buick but was out after seventy-two laps.

In 1913 a Buick won the 102-mile Corona Race on the West Coast—and set a new record in the process. It would be Buick's last. But as late as 1924, there would still be thirty speed marks remaining to Buick in the pages of the American Automobile Association record books—records set two decades before, during 1909, 1910 and 1911, when Buicks and the men who drove them combined to write one of the more thundering sagas of early American motor sport history.

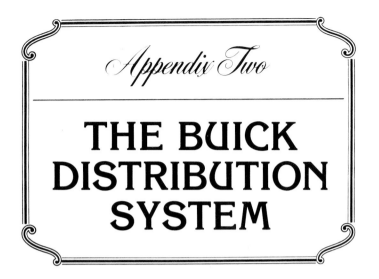

THE BUICK DISTRIBUTION SYSTEM

One advertisement and one newspaper story perhaps introduce the subject best.

First, the advertisement, from 1912. "The Car That Sells By the Train Load" was its headline, and a matter-of-fact listing followed: "30 car loads to Lincoln, Nebraska January 17th; 50 car loads to San Francisco January 25th; 36 car loads to Minneapolis January 25th; 59 car loads to Minneapolis January 30th; 20 car loads to Dayton, Ohio January 31st"—et cetera.

Next, the news story, from a San Francisco paper, a few years before: "Mr. Howard was in the east last week and before his return made arrangements to handle the 'Buick' automobile manufactured in Jackson, Mich., of which he has already sold 60 since the earthquake. He has contracted for 250 cars for the coming year."

The gentlemen to whom the carloads of Buicks were delivered, and one gentleman in particular who for nearly a half century received more of these shipments than anyone else, will be examined here. These men combined to form an organization that was the envy of the industry. These men combined to write what *MoToR* magazine in March 1938 called "a fascinating chapter in the history of American business." These men comprised the Buick distributorship network.

From the beginning the Buick network was strong. Durant laid the foundation, and when given the job of rebuilding Buick in the early Thirties, Curtice and Hufstader were quick to capitalize on it. As one dealer would later put it, "In the early days a Chevrolet was a Chevrolet, a Ford was a Ford, and a Plymouth was a Plymouth. But

if you were lucky enough to own a Buick or could become a Buick dealer, you really had something."

The stability and longevity of the Buick organization was frequently pointed to, and marveled at, in automobile trade publications. "Not all the men in it are greybeards, of course," noted *MoToR* in 1938, "but an extraordinarily large proportion of them have handled the line so long they have become institutions in the territories they serve." In that year no fewer than 116 dealers had been selling Buicks for more than a quarter century.

The Buick system, which served as the model for all of General Motors, was one of Billy Durant's first blueprints for success when he decided to take on the formidable challenge of saving the good car but ailing company founded by David Dunbar Buick. Durant was a master at working with margins and other people's capital, and his risk-taking was legendary, but he was astute enough, and fair enough, to do his utmost to assure that those trusting in his plans and investing in his schemes were well rewarded. That fact, plus the immediate sales success of the Buick, virtually guaranteed early dealers, and especially early Buick distributors, a sound financial investment and an unbelievable return on their money. Their aggregate earnings can never be documented but, as *MoToR* noted in '38, "the figure would be large enough to make an impression even in Washington." With words by Ben Black and music by Art Hickman, "Take Me on a Buick Honeymoon" was the title given a ditty published during the Twenties by the Howard Automobile Company. It was not one of the more stellar contributions to the lore of Tin Pan Alley, but the song remains an appropriate one in the Buick dealer network context. It was a honeymoon—and a long one.

For the first twenty years of its history, Buick built its retail organization around factory branches and a small but powerful group of wholesalers or distributors who were given the responsibility for bettering the sales and the market penetration in areas surrounding their primary locations. The area provided each distributor became his territory.

In 1904 Durant-Dort carriage sales agencies around the country had been the first showplaces for the Buick car. Within a year, however, Billy Durant was ready to put his larger plan into operation. He knew that to expand the sales and production capabilities of the fledgling Buick company he would need to find men who, while not necessarily strongly grounded in the automobile itself (and few were in those days), would nonetheless have sufficient business ability, capital and mechanical awareness to set up and run their own automobile businesses. It was also part of the Durant plan that, once established and profitable, these men would then assist others in their territory to set up their own agencies.

Page preceding: Buick distributors in 1929. On top step: C.C. Coddington, C.L. Whiting, G.G.G. Peckham, H.E. Sidles, A.S. Eldridge. On center step: Guy Garber. On bottom step: H.S. Leyman, H.K. Noyes, F.L. MacFarland, F.W.A. Vesper. In foreground: H.E. Pence. Above: The dealership in Chicago, photographed in 1909.

The thirteen distributors—Durant scarcely was the sort to be superstitious—were carefully selected and appointed in 1905: Charles S. Howard, Howard Automobile Company, San Francisco and Los Angeles; Harry K. Noyes, Noyes Buick, Boston; G.G.G. Peckham, Ohio Buick, Cleveland; Guy S. Garber, Garber Buick, Saginaw, Michigan; F.W.A. Vesper, Vesper Buick, St. Louis; Harry S. Leyman, Leyman Buick, Cincinnati; Harry E. Pence, Pence Automobile Company, Minneapolis; H.E. Sidles, Nebraska Buick, Lincoln; A.S. Eldridge, Eldridge Buick, Seattle; C.L. Whiting, Rochester, New York; A.G. Randall, Randall-Dodd Automobile Company, Salt Lake City; F.L. MacFarland, MacFarland Automobile Company, Denver; C.C. Coddington, Charlotte, North Carolina.

Each of these men would create a virtual empire with the Buick automobile. Most of them would become millionaires, some several times over. They were the Twentieth Century equivalent, in a sense, of the medieval feudal lord. Their territory was their fief. They held full and complete responsibility for any contacts made with the dealers they personally recruited and appointed within their respective territorial areas. Expansion and development of additional dealer locations, replacement of existing dealers and product promotions were all in their charge. Wholesale men from the Buick factory were authorized to contact the distributor and his managers only,

and they in turn carried the word to the dealers under them.

The plan worked nicely from the start. With this system, Durant was able to build a dealer organization quickly and at a minimum of expense to his company. And this, coupled with the display given the car by the Durant-Dort carriage people, made Buick one of the most widely exposed automobiles of the time.

The distributors were loyal and competent men. Durant had chosen well—and this, as history was to record, would serve him well too. In the years which followed, stories abounded in Flint of distributors rushing into town from far off territories with suitcases full of money to bail Durant and Buick out of a capital shortage or to help him meet a weekly payroll. In other instances, distributors would order large quantities of cars for their dealers, paying for them in advance so Buick would have capital upon which to operate or so Durant could tap the revenue for his plans elsewhere. In a very real sense, the success of Buick was tied to the success of these men.

As their wealth increased so did the number of dealers they appointed and controlled, and it was not long before these thirteen distributors became an extremely important and powerful force within both Buick and General Motors. The Buick company and the Buick car, of course, had during this same period become both a power in the marketplace and a success of awesome proportion. A conflict was perhaps inevitable. Or at the very least second thoughts on the part of

GM corporate management as to the desirability of having such a large part of the Buick fortunes vested in the hands of people outside the control of the company. It had been one matter to appoint these men when the industry was in its infancy and the Buick was but a baby, but as the industry—and Buick—matured and expanded, as the distributors grew increasingly more independent of the firm which had appointed them and began asserting their influence and power more aggressively, and as Buick found itself year upon year with more and more dealers which it could not contact directly, the whole situation became another matter indeed.

It was simply sound good business sense for General Motors to acquire the distributorships and thus gain the advantage of being able to work directly with the dealers in the various territories. MacFarland in Denver was the first distributor to sell out in 1925, then Randall-Dodd and Coddington in 1929, Sidles, Pence, Leyman and Vesper in 1930. Peckham followed in 1935, Eldridge in 1936, Whiting in 1937. By the mid-Thirties, of the original thirteen distributors, Noyes, Pence, Sidles and Coddington had died, and by 1938 only three of the original thirteen remained as distributors: Noyes Buick with most of New England, Howard with all of California, and Garber with the upper half of Michigan. Gradually they were brought into the GM fold as well. Garber was the last. After the other distributor agreements had been, or were in the process of being, terminated, Guy Garber personally asked Bill Hufstader to allow his company to continue. Hufstader agreed. The firm had always represented Buick well, and would continue to do so until the death of its owner in the early 1960's.

The role played by the Buick Thirteen—as they might be called— in the history of the company was incalculably significant. And their pioneering in the automobile industry itself carried with it the stuff of frontier romance. It was the strategy of Harry Pence, for example, to obtain new cars from Flint, round up the same number of drivers and then head west out of Minneapolis looking for buyers. The caravan would travel as far as necessary for Pence to sell all his cars, each driver returning home when the Buick he was piloting was sold.

In New England, on the other hand, Harry K. Noyes would get one new Buick from the factory, take it himself into the mountainous outskirts of his territory, sell the car, set up a local man as a dealer to handle the line, and then return home, sometimes by railroad, sometimes by oxcart. Ultimately, Noyes was responsible for the founding of 126 dealerships, and one of the finest and most efficient distributor operations in the world.

But of the thirteen, it was the career of Charles S. Howard which tends to stand out from the rest and which will be profiled here as representative of the trailblazing efforts of the Buick distributorship

"Rough Rider Charley," as Charles S. Howard was known during his racing days, with his mechanic Frank Murray (on the right), ready to do battle for Buick.

organization.

"The Howard Automobile Company. . .Largest Distributor of Automobiles in the World" was his slogan. In 1941, his biggest year, Howard was responsible for the sale of 30,000 Buicks. And certainly his territory was the largest of all.

Charles S. Howard was born February 28th, 1880 in Marietta, Georgia and was educated in both the United States and Canada. During the Spanish-American War, he served with Teddy Roosevelt and rode with the Rough Riders in the charge up San Juan Hill in 1898. After the war he migrated west, arrived in San Francisco with twenty-one cents in his pocket, liked the city and decided to settle there. The turn of the century found him engaged in a bicycle repair business on Van Ness Avenue, a likely enough enterprise for him since he had raced bicycles in New Jersey prior to his Rough Rider days. Early in 1903, however, he began spotting his first automobiles on the streets of San Francisco, and became interested. There were more of these machines in the East than in the West, he realized, so he left his bicycle business and returned to New York City where his father operated a piano manufacturing business. Next door to the Howard Piano Company was an agency for the Pope-Toledo automobile; a Pope-Toledo was Howard's first automotive purchase. The agency had been founded by A.G. (Glidden) Southworth, with partners Arthur Newton and Joseph Bell, and young Howard was soon a common sight in the Glidden Service Department. He had decided to become a racing driver, was continually tinkering with the Pope-Toledo to improve its speed potential, and proved himself quite successful in local racing events, earning nearly $5,000 in prize money.

The empire of Colonel Albert A. Pope, of which Pope-Toledo was part, was in the meantime foundering, and on one of his trips east Billy Durant arranged with the three partners in the Glidden firm to become the managers of the Buick factory branch in New York.* It was Southworth who introduced the go-getter Howard to Durant. Soon thereafter Durant hired him as a field man for Buick, and Howard began traveling the country to set up dealerships. Late 1904 found him back in San Francisco to arrange for the Pioneer Motor Company, a firm then handling Thomas Flyer, to take on Buick. He concluded those negotiations, brought in San Francisco reporters to tell them Buick would soon be building a commercial vehicle and would be involved in bidding for passenger vehicles to be used by the already famed Fairmont Hotel—and then hit the road again.

Returning in 1905 he discovered the main sales efforts of the Pioneer company had remained with the Thomas Flyer, a distressing situation which he presented to Durant. Realizing the potential in California, he suggested he be given the Buick franchise for San Francisco, promising to see to it that the car would be properly represented. In mid-1905, when he returned again to San Francisco, it was as the Buick dealer for that city.

Howard's first task was to find a building from which to operate. He decided on a modest location at the corner of Golden Gate and Larkin streets, and he hired a modest staff of two—a bookkeeper, and a mechanic named Frank Murray. During his first year, Howard sold eighty-five cars and discovered that horse sense, literally, was a valuable asset in the car business. A good many of the "trade-ins" he

---

*Eventually they went back into retailing, continuing at the same time, however, to direct the wholesale operations of the branch location. Though never a distributor, Glidden Buick in New York played an important part in the history of the marque and affected directly the lives of some of the men who were eventually to become distributors and leaders in Buick retailing. Among them was Charles Howard, as related above. And it was through the influence of the Glidden firm that Harry S. Leyman also became interested in Buick. Leyman had become acquainted with the three partners as a traveling factory representative for Pope-Toledo. After that firm folded, and after the proper introduction, he persuaded Durant to give him the Cincinnati territory. By the mid-1930's Leyman had become one of the wealthiest men in Ohio, with interests in numerous banks and finance companies. As for the three partners, by 1937 Glidden's sales volume had risen to 2887 new automobiles a year, and its service volume alone was totaling over two million dollars annually.

took when a purchaser moved up to a Buick had four hooves!

Things were moving along very nicely for Howard until the earthquake of '06. His building was destroyed, as was every other dealer's in the city, but he managed to save several of the cars he had on display and pressed them into service as ambulances and taxis to carry the injured and homeless. Fortunately his losses were covered by insurance and when the dust and smoke cleared he rebuilt his business and continued at another location on Golden Gate Avenue.

And he started something else. It was a natural for him, and an idea that was a favorite of Durant's as well. "Automobile racing has and will continue to have an important bearing on the automobile trade throughout the country. The benefits derived from the competition of motor cars, whether in track, road or hill climbing events, are hard to realize by dealers and agents," Howard said in 1908. "Often an agent or representative of a motor car figures he has only wasted money and time if his car fails to win the race in which it is entered. He does not give the circumstances of the reliability his car has gained the proper credit. I am strongly in favor of motor racing, and especially for stock cars. In fact, the competition for stock cars in speed and endurance is of the greatest interest to every man who is in the market for an automobile, and the result of a race on roads only demonstrates the value of the modern vehicle under ordinary touring conditions. I will always be ready to enter a Buick car in a road race for stock cars. . ."

True to his word, Howard and mechanic Frank Murray proceeded to enter every event they could find, and even organized of few of their own. They garnered trophies, awards, ribbons, accolades—and headlines, like "Buick Climbs to Top of Grizzley Peak," "Buick Speed Marvel a Sensation at Tanforan," "Buick Sets Mark for Diablo Hill Climb," "Buick Wins Perfect Score in 24 Hour Endurance Contest." His record, especially with the famous Buick White Streaks, became a legend in the California papers. In later years Howard credited racing competition, and the promotion of it, as one of the key factors which insured both his and the Buick's success.

There was another notion shared by Howard and Durant. From the very beginning of his association with the automobile, Howard proved to be expansionist-minded too. He appointed his first subdealer in 1906, Waterman Brothers in Fresno, and followed this with two more in Vallejo and Richmond. Then, after a quick visit to Durant, he returned home with the Buick distribution rights for eight western states—California, Oregon, Washington, Idaho, Nevada, Utah, Arizona, New Mexico—plus the territory of Hawaii. These rights allowed him to charge a commission or over-ride on every Buick automobile (two percent) and part (three percent) he sold to

A typical dealer driveaway scene from the Twenties, the new Buicks for 1926 set for travel to points throughout the United States, led by the Model 26-51 Brougham Sedan.

his dealers in these markets. Howard stockpiled the cars and components at a warehouse in San Francisco, distributed them as orders came in, and reaped a nifty profit.

In addition to his sub-dealers, Howard was busy acquiring additional dealerships of his own. The first, in 1909, was a southern headquarters in Los Angeles, placed under the direction of his brother Frank. Later to come were stores in Oakland, Alameda, Berkeley and East Oakland. By 1934 the main company in San Francisco had additional branches in Pasadena, Hollywood, Beverly Hills, Huntington Park, a second outlet in San Francisco, and four more branches in Los Angeles. The floor space in his buildings totaled a quarter of a million square feet.

In 1911 he found the time to tot up the sales figures for the entire Howard territory and discovered he was handling more automobiles than any other distributor in the world. His advertising and company stationery were immediately changed to note this fact. It was impressive then and it remains so today. By the early 1930's, his empire had grown too vast for him to control, and he sold off much of it. Yet, with only two states remaining in his territory—California and Nevada—and a country in the throes of the Great Depression, Howard could still make the "world's largest" claim in 1934.

Charles Howard was a colorful character. "Rough Rider Charley" they called him during his racing days, a reference to both his driving style and his earlier service with Teddy Roosevelt. In January of 1912 he earned another nickname which was to remain with him the rest of his life: "Train Load Charley." Howard had suffered supply problems during his early years and so when Buick expanded its production capability and could finally meet his demand, he was ready for his share. And his share was big by any standard, Buicks by the entire trainload. Again the press had a field day. Carloads of cars had been promoted by manufacturers before, but here was a man located thousands of miles away from the large eastern markets, selling Buicks in the wilds of the West, and ordering them in shipments complete from locomotive to caboose. Howard, being the promoter

he was, made the most of it. Entire page advertisements were placed displaying the wires he sent Buick's national sales manager asking for one, two or even three trainloads of Buicks at a time. When Buick wired back shipment confirmation, Howard saw to it that those telegrams got into the papers too. And, in Flint, Buick public relations made sure newspapers in the East knew all about Buick's super-salesman in the West.

Charles Howard was a big man in the Buick organization, and he was his own man at the same time. It was his responsibility, and authority, to distribute cars, keep dealers financially sound, locate dealers for new points, teach them how to promote and sell the product, hold technical repair schools, and in general administrate the business of every dealer in the territory. Howard patterned his zone and district managers after GM's own system.

Buick, though the major reason for Howard's success, was not the only car he sold over the years. When he first started in business, he also handled Apperson, and added National and Oldsmobile around 1909 when Durant purchased those firms and brought them into General Motors. By 1913, however, Howard was Buick all the way—and remained so until the Depression hit, when he was made a Pontiac dealer in 1932 and a Pontiac distributor in June of 1933. He retained that line until the B.O.P. was dissolved.

Durant and General Motors had obviously been good to Howard. And vice versa. Howard was a handy man for Durant to have as a friend.* Just before World War I, Durant found himself desperately short of cash. He approached Howard, who lent him the money he

---

*Their friendship survived until Durant's death in March 1947 and, after Howard died in 1950, the widows of the two men remained friends for years. During the early 1930's, having seen her husband make and lose several fortunes, Catherine Durant asked Howard's advice concerning possible investments with personal funds she had available. Howard recommended she invest in something that Durant could not touch should he again begin searching for money to promote a new venture. It was good advice, but it was not heeded. Durant later used her money—and lost it.

In Flint, in 1935, Buick dealers and salesmen from Ohio pose for a photograph before driving the new Buicks from the factory to showrooms throughout the Buckeye State.

needed, rumored to be about three million dollars. In exchange Howard received some GM stock. This was not a bad deal. That stock later became a substantial part of the Howard fortune.

The Howard business remained at the Golden Gate address until 1913 when a new and much larger building was especially designed and constructed on Van Ness Avenue in the heart of automobile row. The facility was well laid out, its showroom lavishly furnished. Employees were well treated, and the firm enjoyed a good reputation; turnover was extremely low, productivity concomitantly high. Howard's great success was his congeniality and his canny ability to choose good managers.

Around 1930, with his business in capable hands, Howard began to indulge in hobbies. First he bought a yacht and, with a group of scien-

tists aboard, sailed to the Galápagos islands to explore. In 1935 he organized a five-month safari into Africa. That year he also became involved in thoroughbred racing, bought a horse named Sea Biscuit, and when the animal was retired in 1940 it was as the top money horse ($437,730) of its era. Two other noted horses in the Howard stable were Noor and Kyak II.

During the years Howard was turning his attention to his personal hobbies, Buick was struggling for its survival. Peak sales had come in California in 1927. In 1928 they were down 5000 cars from the year before, in 1929 down another 1300—and thereafter down further still, until 1932 when total Buick sales in the state slid to an unglamorous 3497 units. This decline was matched in Buick distributorships across the country. The problem was not on the West

Coast. It was in Flint.

Buick was desperately trying to restyle, retool and recapture past glory and profitability with a new look and a new straight-eight engine. But the downhill rush was on, and the Depression was adding to the cascade of troubles. This was a new and most unpleasant situation for Buick and its sales organization. Even Howard who had twice been wiped out by fire—in the earthquake of '06, and then two years later when a cigarette-smoking employee carelessly refueled a car in the company garage—had never had to cope with anything like it. By 1932 Buick sales in California were only seventeen percent of what they had been in 1927.

As 1933 approached, and sensing impending disaster, Howard called a meeting of his top managers. Revenue from new car sales could no longer be relied upon to keep dealers solvent. New markets would have to be developed and dealer internal expenses trimmed at every possible corner. Three avenues were open: 1. increasing used car sales; 2. emphasizing service department sales through promotional advertising and facilities expansion; 3. augmenting the sale of parts and supplies necessary for good service. The Howard management team lost no time.

Used cars were reconditioned with a vengeance, axles straightened, engines rebuilt, bodies repainted, brakes adjusted, new tires installed; direct mail, radio and newspaper advertising was focused upon the prospective used car buyer. Then the Howard Automobile Company turned its attention to service departments. Where facilities had once been devoted almost entirely to the get-ready of new cars, they were now either modernized with updated service equipment or they stood vacant. And a chain of Authorized Buick Service Stations was inaugurated. Actually this wasn't a new idea; previously distributors had often found that a local dealer had capital enough for a Buick sales building and showroom but not a complete service department. By farming this branch of the business out, the distributor was still able to add a new dealer. In the early days of the business, money and experienced automotive people were in short supply and it was an arrangement that worked well under the circumstances. It worked well again in the Great Depression. About the only stipulation for these service stations was that the men be well trained in Buick repairs and that genuine Buick parts purchased from the distributor be used. Thus Howard was able to handily increase the market for his parts business.

Direct mail lists of Buick owners eventually requiring service were prepared and in one ambitious project a staff of six telephone operators was hired by Howard to contact 17,000 customers in the Los Angeles area advising them of the new and expanded service facility available. A device called a "Lubrometer" was installed by Howard in the dash of every new and used car sold. It acted as a reminder to the driver telling him when his maintenance services were due.

With all this attention, Buick service boomed. And the lean years slid by for the Howard organization with comparative ease. Howard emerged from the Depression with his usual confidence.

Meantime things were happening in Flint. Harlow Curtice had come to the helm of Buick in 1934. Shortly after his appointment, he journeyed to California to meet his largest distributor. The two men got along well. Curtice was anxious to accelerate the phase-out of Buick distributors, but knew this was not the time to move on Howard. He needed Howard's strength.

By the time war clouds gathered, however, Curtice had brought Buick back to a solid position—indeed it was the glamour car of the industry—and now the power wielded by those remaining in the old Durant-style distributor system really nettled him. And some of Howard's managers did not make things any easier. When the government war freeze on new cars was instituted by the rationing board, word went out from the main Howard office in San Francisco to all dealers in the territory: "If you have new Buicks in stock, advise us. We want them back in the San Francisco warehouse." Technically, these cars were the property of the dealers who held them but most responded to the demand and cars were driven and towed by the dozens back to San Francisco for redistribution or sale by the parent company. News of this move reached the ears of both Curtice and sales manager Hufstader in Flint and there was a considerable gnashing of teeth—but again nothing could be done. The war years would be at least as rough on dealers as the Depression had been and Curtice needed all the muscle he could get.

War's end, however, found him in the strongest position possible, staring happily at what appeared to be an almost bottomless new-car void. In October 1947 the Howard organization was taken over by Buick and all dealers formerly controlled by it were brought directly under Buick aegis. This left Howard with only the locations he personally owned. Charles Howard did not fight the change nor was he bitter toward Buick and Curtice for having requested it. He was sixty-seven years old now and in failing health. In 1905 he had begun as the Buick dealer for San Francisco. In 1950, when he died, he was that still.

Like his colleagues of the Buick Thirteen, the distributors who decades before had listened to Billy Durant and believed in him and wanted to be part of the adventure he said the Buick motorcar would be, Charles S. Howard had played his important role in Buick history. "When Better Automobiles Were Built," he was there to sell and promote them.

Appendix Three

HERALDRY & MASCOTS OF THE MARQUE

The name of the person responsible for stylizing the Buick trademark in cursive script, which was to endure for decades, is not known for sure—though it has been said to have originated with Billy Durant. The year the script was first used was 1908, and five years later the oblong background was added to form the official Buick emblem. Though the Buick "signature" would be slimmed as years went by, its basic character would remain.

The familiar blue-and-white Buick emblem appeared on the faceplate of the standard Boyce motometer (Senior size) which was fitted to various Buicks prior to 1927. But then Buick began to look for other identity features. For model year 1927, Buick chose to adorn some of its cars with a hood ornament.

The Ternstedt company of Detroit, prolific producer of such ornaments, or mascots, for the industry in this period, was commissioned by Buick to design its mascot series. To collectors and students of mascot history today, the Buick hood ornaments were among the finest to be produced by Ternstedt, and the very first was the most splendid of all.

This was the figure used for 1927 long-wheelbase and open cars, the head of a lovely young girl with rippling curls and flowing headdress and very much in the art nouveau mode. The year following, her countenance became more stern and she wore a Grecian-type winged helmet. Then, in 1929, the Buick goddess was gone, replaced by a god.

Interestingly, the god was Mercury, and resembled the mascot used by Florist Telegraph Delivery. Ternstedt designers may have been influenced by the design used on F.T.D. delivery vehicles, many of which—coincidentally—were Buicks. Buick's Mercury mascot of 1929 was, however, shown in company advertising that one year only—and for 1930 no Buick hood ornament was offered either as a standard cap or deluxe accessory.

But for 1931 there were two mascots available. A winged figure-eight to signify Buick's adoption of a straight-eight engine was used as the standard radiator cap. Offered at additional cost as a deluxe accessory was a revised design of the Mercury. This figure, devoid of the traditional cadeuces and winged heels, carried an orb surmounted by a single wing very similar to that on the standard cap. Although this Mercury was a more popular seller, neither it nor the 1929 predecessor found wide use on Buick motorcars. There was a reason. So fragile was the mascot at the ankle that one good twist by a heavy-handed filling station attendant separated Mercury from his pedestal.

In 1932 the standard cap was continued, but a new deluxe accessory mascot was introduced. A figure of exquisite grace, it was a young running nude girl with her scarf flowing behind her. This design may have been inspired by the famous modern dancer Isadora Duncan whose death in 1927, when her long scarf became wrapped in the wire wheels of an Amilcar, had been widely reported.

The year 1933 brought a modified design to the standard cap, with the "8" more angular and the diameter of the cap enlarged. The nude continued unchanged. In 1934 the relocation of the radiator cap under the hood of a motorcar signalled the end of the era of the radiator mascot. At Buick, however, the lovely nude was to remain available as an accessory through the 1935 model year. Although she put on a few pounds as she grew older, she remained otherwise the same—and during the last years was attached to a chrome strip which bolted to the radiator shell. Thereafter Buick hood ornamentation followed the industry trend to the nondescript, amorphous shapes concomitant to the age of streamlining.

In 1937, however, something new was added: a Buick crest. Unlike the spurious crests used by many manufacturers, this one was genuine, the ancestral arms used by the ancient Scottish family of Buick as a heraldic device on its armor. After years of being the forgotten man in Buick history, David Dunbar Buick was remembered again.

Because no representation of the original shield was available, the design was executed from a description in the Burke book of heraldry published in 1851: "Gu. A bend chequy, ar. and az. detw. A Buck's head erazed in chief, and a cross couped and pierced, or, in base." This translates to "gu" for gule (red), the color of the field; "a bend" the diagonal from upper left corner to lower right; "ar." for argent

VALVE-IN-HEAD

Buick

MOTOR CARS

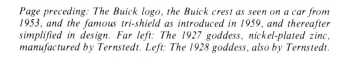

Page preceding: The Buick logo, the Buick crest as seen on a car from 1953, and the famous tri-shield as introduced in 1959, and thereafter simplified in design. Far left: The 1927 goddess, nickel-plated zinc, manufactured by Ternstedt. Left: The 1928 goddess, also by Ternstedt.

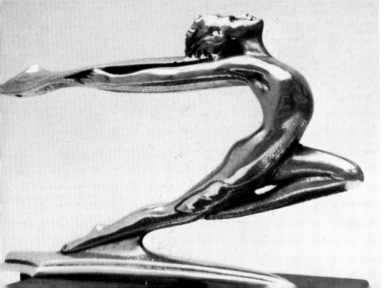

Page opposite: Buick's Mercury from 1929 (left above) and 1931 (left below) and the Mercury used by Florist Telegraph Delivery which may have influenced Buick versions. Above left: The 1931-1932 standard winged eight cap (top) and the version for 1933 (center). Above: The 1932-1933 Buick goddess. Left: Buick's goddess for 1934-1935. All of these Buick mascots were zinc diecast, chrome plated, and were manufactured by Ternstedt. Photographs of, and research for, the Buick mascots by W.C. Williams.

(silver) and "az." for azure, the color of checks on the bend. The "Buck's head" phrase indicated the deer design in the upper right-hand corner of the shield ("chief") and the cross in "or" (gold) in the lower left corner. "Erazed" signified the jagged broken edge of the buck's neck, "couped" the smoothed edges of the cross, "pierced" the round perforation of it, through which the red color of the field was visible.

The familiar Buick tri-shield emblem, incorporating all the elements and colors of its predecessors, was adopted in 1959.

THE BUICK STARS IN HOLLYWOOD

Hollywood. The name has magic. Practically every company that ever built a car wanted to be successful there. Hollywood was style, Hollywood was publicity. A motorcar pictured with a movie star was always worth a few good columns of newsprint. And a motorcar featured in a motion picture, a motorcar which figuratively would be driven into thousands of theatres across the country, a motorcar which literally would become a moving picture show? Now that was the sort of promotion that was beyond the purchasing power of even the most inflated advertising budget.

Beginning in 1934, and continuing through the 1940's, the Buick was far and away the most prominent motorcar in Hollywood films. In *Flamingo Road*, Joan Crawford played a carnival hootchy-kootchy dancer who married well and drove a 1941 Roadmaster convertible sedan. In *In This Our Life*, Bette Davis was a spoiled rich girl with a 1941 Roadmaster convertible coupe. And Humphrey Bogart drove a 1940 Limited convertible sedan to his saloon in *Casablanca*. More recently, Paul Newman was hauled back to jail in a 1941 Special Estate Wagon as *Cool Hand Luke*.

The Buick story in Hollywood is really the story of the Howard Motor Company and two general managers responsible for that store, C.B. Dixon and Phil Hall. The Buick franchise in Hollywood had been a part of the Howard Automobile Company empire since it first opened around 1910 as one of three locations owned by Charles S. Howard's brother Frank. (To differentiate ownership between northern and southern California, Howard stores in the south were designated Howard Motor Company rather than Automobile Com-

pany, the name given the main location in the north.)

In 1912, during the waning days of the nickelodeon era, C.B. Dixon became manager of the Hollywood Buick business. He recognized, probably earlier than most, that well-made silent films would mean a whole new industry, would carry motion pictures out of the "grub-houses" and into theatres, and would make nationwide celebrities of the people appearing in them. An acquaintanceship with movie actors would thus provide a readymade tool for the best publicity to be had for his store—and it would be practically free.

Dixon enlisted the assistance of several Hollywood photographers, and thereafter no one who ever appeared on celluloid, and who entered his Buick agency, left without having his picture taken. The photographs were used in newspaper advertisements and press releases, and were blown up into gigantic prints for showroom display: Cecil B. DeMille, John and Douglas Fairbanks, Babe Hardy, Clara Bow, Clair Adams, Constance Talmadge, Jean Hersholt, William Desmond, Ruth Renich, the Our Gang group, among many, many others—and with each of them was one of Dixon's Buicks. Still, he did not discriminate; screen credits were not an absolute prerequisite for his attention. Both Jack Dempsey and Will Rogers purchased Buicks from Dixon and were photographed with them. And Dixon proved himself a pretty good set designer too. In one instance, he had a large box constructed with one side open and the famous Buick script cleverly mounted inside. It became an effective, and widely talked about, promotion piece when it appeared on different vacant lots around Hollywood. When the franchise changed locations in July of 1919, the Los Angeles *Evening Press* reported: "The thousands of visitors who thronged the new Buick headquarters in Hollywood during the formal housewarming held by C.B. Dixon . . . went away in the belief that Dixon had succeeded in producing a combination of utility, comfort, and charm that had been thought here-to-fore impossible in the merchandising of motor cars."

The photographic record Dixon left behind—many of the pictures personally autographed to him—remains today as a tribute to his foresight and skill as a salesman and promoter. He inaugurated the alliance between Buick and the Hollywood community. He, in effect, set the stage.

Then Phil Hall took over. And it was under his direction that the bond between car and screen became permanent—and the envy of every other car maker in the country. During the great Buick years which followed, Hall would count among his customers and personal friends such stars as Bob Hope, Bing Crosby, Cary Grant, Eddie Cantor, Jerry Colona, Marie Wilson, Olivia De Havilland, Bette Davis, Ronald Colman, Alexis Smith, Fanny Brice, Al Jolson, Ruby Keeler, Jack Benny, Lucille Ball, Desi Arnaz, Gordon MacRae,

Phil - its marvellous
- it works!
might even get another
one next year - K.
Cary.

Page preceding: Cary Grant and his 1941 Century. Above: Original Hollywood Buick branch; Phil Hall's showroom. Below: On a movie set at Warner's in 1934, amid film people and regional Buick personnel, are Phil Hall, Bill Hufstader and Dutch Bower (second, sixth and seventh from left, standing); Harlow Curtice and C.S. Howard (third and sixth from left, seated). The pretty actresses are Patricia Ellis and Kay Francis. Page opposite: Press clipping of a famous sale; advertising the "Gold Diggers" and Buick of '35.

Alan Ladd, the Who's Who of Hollywood.

Born in Greeley, Colorado in 1899, Hall had arrived in California in 1921 with visions of becoming a movie actor. He landed a few bit parts in the next two years, *Honor First* starring Jack Gilbert and *Black Orchid* with Ramone Navarro and Barbara Lamar among the more notable—but most of the time he was, as he tells it, "between tests," a euphemism which, then and now, translates to "unemployed."

In mid-1923 Hall met New York stage personality Edna Wallace Hoper and they became friends. She was touring the Southwest at the time promoting her line of cosmetics and she needed an advance man. Hall took the job and soon found himself learning as much about black and white facial clays as he knew about stage makeup. He also learned his employer was something of a character.

His first assignment was in Texas. The show traveled in a touring car equipped with dual mounted rear spares. There were two different canvas spare tire covers, one lettered "Edna Wallace Hoper & Buick," the other "Edna Wallace Hoper & Cadillac." She didn't care which one was used: "It all depended on which dealer was the biggest chump!"—which one was willing to pay a few dollars for the advertising.

Arriving in Oklahoma City a few weeks later, Hall's assignment was to secure a typewriter, at no charge naturally. He could think of no way to convince a local merchant that the lending of such a machine to Edna Wallace Hoper would benefit the store owner's business, so he decided to part company with the show, return to Hollywood and resume his movie career. Within a few months he was selling cars.

He began in the spring with the Star, Billy Durant's newest motorcar—but by the summer decided prospects for selling Durant's first motorcar might be better. He applied for a job as a salesman with the Howard Motor Company, and C.B. Dixon hired him on a thirty-day trial basis. It was not until the final hours on the final day that Hall finally sold a Buick, to Harry Kerr, a casting director for whom he had worked, and the Model T Ford traded in on it to Kerr's brother. (In those early days of retail car selling, a salesman would not receive his commission on the new unit sale until any used car trade had also been sold.) Later during 1923 Hall sold actor Brandy Hurst his first car. Hurst got behind the wheel, not knowing how to drive, and promptly steered the Buick into a fire plug. It was not an auspicious beginning.

But Hall stuck with it, until early 1925 when he left for New York to visit an ailing relative and work a while selling Buicks for the Brown Buick Company in White Plains. In early 1926 Dixon wired him with the offer of the sales manager position and travel expenses

HORTON UP IN AIR, BUT SIGNS BUICK ORDER

In Warner Bros.' "GOLD DIGGERS OF 1935," Buick is featured with Dick Powell and the Berkeley Girls. Warner Bros. consistently choose Buick for shots of lavish musical revue display, and for those depicting people in the modern manner. Today's Buick is exquisitely styled. It harmonizes perfectly with the advanced and newly created styles which Warner Bros. productions display.

Hollywood—*Creator of Style*— *Chooses* BUICK *for Its Own*

In brilliant Hollywood—where picture directors and stars create the styles for a nation—Buick plays the star style part. A world once ruled by Paris now looks to Hollywood; and there Buick is the featured car. In production after production, for the hit pictures of the year, Buick is chosen . . . just as it is favored by those who value the prestige of modish, modern design. ¶ All you have ever known or heard of Buick size and roominess . . . of Buick quality and dependability . . . luxury, performance and economy . . . is now surpassed. To see Buick today is to feast your eyes upon aristocratic, sparkling style. To drive it is to gratify your enthusiasm for unsurpassed performance and to enjoy the unprecedented ease and simplicity of the newest automatic operating features. To ride is to know the finest of all fine motoring. ¶ Twenty-five beautiful models, in four series. Four popular price groups, $795 to $2175, list prices at Flint, Mich. Prices subject to change without notice. Special equipment extra. Favorable G.M.A.C. terms.

$795 *and up, list prices at Flint.*

BODY BY FISHER . . . A GENERAL MOTORS PRODUCT

WHEN BETTER AUTOMOBILES ARE BUILT—BUICK WILL BUILD THEM

---

to the West Coast. It was obvious why Dixon wanted him back. After a faltering start, Hall had become one of Dixon's top salesmen. He had even sold Ronald Colman his first car and, having learned his lesson, taught him how to drive it.

Hall was soon back in California. In 1926 Buick delivered over 1000 new cars in Hollywood. In September that year the 1927 model was introduced and 143 were despatched to Hollywood customers in that one month. "The picture people just loved Buick"—and Hall's Buick career was off and running. He held his sales manager job until January of 1933 when Frank Howard died and his three franchise locations—Hollywood, Pasadena and Beverly Hills—again became part of the parent Howard Automobile Company in San Francisco.

With that transition, Dixon was transferred to another of the stores, and Hall was made general manager of the Hollywood agency.

It was not the best of times in America, and this was a particularly bad period for Buick. But Hall eagerly accepted the challenge. Already he had proved he was a born salesman, and the actor in him had brought out a deft, if somewhat zany, facility for engendering publicity. He would find a way to promote and sell cars despite the Great Depression. He had always had lots of ideas.

In 1928, for example, he had assisted one of his salesmen in putting Edward Everett Horton into a Buick. Horton, a popular comedian and at that time the star of *Mary's Other Husband*, had been continually brushing off the salesman, saying he was too busy to leave

377

On movie lots in Hollywood: Cinematographer Darrel Foss with a 1920 K-44 roadster; Will Rogers, a 1928 Master Six 28-58 coupe; Our Gang, a 1925 Master Six 25-51 brougham.

the Plaza Hotel where he lived to come in and sign the order. Nineteen twenty-eight happened to be the year Buick introduced its Silver Anniversary car, so Hall decided to combine a solution to the Horton problem with some publicity for the new anniversary models.

Horton's room was located nine stories up in the hotel. Hall hired a safe mover and asked him to build a special platform reinforced with four-by-four spreaders to support a new Buick phaeton. He then contacted Lloyds of London and told them what he planned to do. "No difficulty with coverage," he was told and the policy was issued. After the platform had been built and its hoists installed on the Plaza's roof, Hall had his salesman get into the Buick with his order pad. Pathé News had been alerted and set up a camera on the sidewalk to record "the first airborne sale in history."

The signal was given and the hoists began to turn. Up went the car, salesman and order pad. At the fourth story, one of the supporting ropes caught on a building cornice and nearly dumped the whole stunt back onto the street below, but it was freed and the Buick scaled the remaining five stories without further incident. Horton had known nothing about what was going on until after it had begun. Surprised and delighted, he waited until the platform reached his window, then climbed out into the car and signed the order. His Buick was delivered the next day—downstairs.

The publicity was smashing. The following morning, Thursday, August 2nd, Los Angeles papers carried headlines like "Horton Up In Air But Signs Buick Order" and gave Ralph Johnson, the daring salesman, high marks for his perseverance. And Pathé News sent the cinematic account of this "New Method to Get Prospect's Name on Dotted Line" into movie theatres all over the world. An ironic footnote occurred a few days later when Hall talked to Lloyds of London representatives. Because of a technicality, the insurance had not actually been in force.

Thereafter Hall confined sales techniques to less risky ventures. But usually with the same successful results. Another occasion found another of his salesmen unable to complete a deal with a lady in town. Hall took the salesman with him in his car, parking a couple of blocks from the prospect's home. They jogged the rest of the way and arrived, in a sweat and panting, at her door. When she opened it, Hall gasped out—in dying breath fashion—that they had run all the way to let her know they had finally found a buyer for the old Packard in her garage. She produced its keys and title immediately. The Packard became the trade-in, and the new Buick was the sale.

In 1934, with the advent of knee action suspension, Hall parked a new Buick at the corner of Hollywood and Vine, its front wheel just touching the famous nose of Jimmy Durante. This was supposed to be the only bump the car would not take.

From the top: Laurel and Hardy in a 1930 Series 40 Model 30-45 phaeton; Jack Holt with a dashing sport roadster, the '30 Series 40 Model 30-44; Loretta Young with the Series 60 Model 67 sedan she purchased in 1932.

Above: Emil Jannings and his 1928 Master Six Model 54C Country Club Coupe; Humphrey Bogart, Barton McLane and a 1936 Limited Model 90L ready to film a scene for Bullets or Ballots. *Below: Gloria Swanson and her Roadmaster Model 80C from 1936; Ida Lupino with her Roadmaster Model 71C from 1941. Page opposite: Bob Hope and Jerry Colona with a 1946 Super Estate Wagon; Chuck Connors, Virginia Mayo and assorted stars with a 1955 Special 46C.*

And that was the year, too, that the Buick became a movie star. Earlier Sol Dolgen of Warner Brothers' promotion department had telephoned Hall asking to borrow a car for a film the studio was in the process of shooting. Hall was gladly willing. From that one phone call came a formidable triumvirate: Howard Automobile Company, Warner Brothers—and Buick. Another heady trio would follow: Howard Automobile Company, Paramount—and Buick. Hall would work with other studios as well, but it was to Warner's and Paramount that most of his Buicks were delivered, and their films in which most of his Buicks appeared. Hall sold virtual fleets of the cars to those studios for use by executives, actors, production staff and especially, of course, for use in motion pictures. Any vintage film buff who is also a car enthusiast has to wonder at times during late-show TV viewing if Buick might not have been the only car in town. It became as ubiquitous in films as popcorn in theatres. One Humphrey Bogart picture titled *Bullets or Ballots* used so many of the motorcars from Flint that the production crew was soon calling it *Bullets or Buicks*.

In the summer of 1934, soon after he took the helm of Buick in Flint, Harlow Curtice—with sales manager Bill Hufstader and chief engineer Dutch Bower—headed west to inspect the Howard territory. Phil Hall was the group's host and guide in Hollywood—and the visit provided him the opportunity to suggest to Hufstader that Buick's preeminence in films might be capitalized upon in advertising. Hufstader took the idea back to Flint, and there followed a splendid series of advertisements in *The Saturday Evening Post*, then the largest weekly circulation magazine in America, showing off the Buick as a movie star.

Thereafter Hall became a frequent giver-of-advice to Flint on a variety of Buick topics. Since he was located in what was considered the most style-conscious spot in the country, Buick management of-

ten asked his reaction to a new idea or a new model under consideration. For obvious reasons, Hall was always interested in styling. Cars designed for the conservative Midwest or the more cosmopolitan East might not necessarily find favor on the more flamboyant Pacific Coast. His personal favorite among Buicks, for example, was the 1940 Super, because the folks out west had long been disenchanted with running boards. When Buick took them off, Hall's sales took off too. He never could get enough of that particular model to sell.

Hall was incessantly badgering Curtice and GM Styling to produce cars amenable to the high fashion taste of his Hollywood clientele. There is a story that it was largely due to his persistence that GM Styling worked up the prototype which became the 1963 Riviera. Subsequently, when corporate management people could not decide whether Cadillac or Buick should market the car, they interviewed dealers associated with both lines on the issue. Hall carried the ball for Buick. History has recorded the result.

In June 1950, following the death of Charles S. Howard, Phil Hall bought the dealership he had been managing for so long. The Howard Automobile Company sign came down; Phil Hall Buick went up. The one-time actor had come full circle. And he was still brimming with ideas. In 1954, over lunch with Curtice and Hufstader, both of whom had by this time moved on to executive positions with GM in Detroit, Hall mentioned one of them: to put Buick back into third place in sales—where Plymouth, it seemed, was firmly entrenched—by using General Motors Acceptance Corporation, GM's financing arm, "as the bridge from the assembly line to someone's garage."

Curtice was interested but skeptical. As a result of litigation some years earlier, GM had been asked by the government to closely regulate the activities of GMAC and its divisional car lines, and he didn't want any legal snarls. But Hall's idea was intriguing. At that time the standard length for an automobile retail finance contract was thirty months. With an extension to thirty-six, Hall said, the buyer could pay the same monthly rate for either a Plymouth or a Buick and, given the option, he was sure there were a lot of people who would make the decision for Buick, because at the end of the three years, the Buick buyer would have a more valuable car. Curtice was convinced; GMAC inaugurated the thirty-six-month plan within a week. And in 1954, with a good-looking, well engineered car and a new financing scheme, Buick moved into third place in the industry, remaining there through 1956. In 1955 Hall delivered 1655 new Buicks to Hollywood customers, 243 of them in September, his best month ever.

Buicks delivered in Hollywood, of course, weren't always exactly like Buicks delivered in Dubuque. The sunshine factor made convertibles a popular body style, and what might be called the snazziness factor made side-mounted spares a very desirable option. The Hollywood agency frequently found itself in the custom styling business. Long before running boards left Buick on some 1940 models, Hollywood customers were bringing in their cars to have them removed, with front and rear springs then heated to lower the car for a racier appearance. Both Jack Benny and George Raft had their Buicks so modified. Cary Grant asked for one-way glass—so he could see but not be seen—in his Century. For the popular film *Topper*, Hal Roach Studios wanted a special car—and got a 1937 Series 80 with special sports roadster coachwork by Bohman & Schwartz.

In modern times, Buicks would again have presence in motion pictures. The most noticeable example was in the Academy Award-winning *Rain Man* of 1988 when a 1949 Roadmaster convertible was in the center of action throughout, sharing a starring role with Tom Cruise and Dustin Hoffman as they drove across the country.

Appendix Five

THE BUICK SHIFTS FOR ITSELF

Automatic transmissions, or at least crude attempts at them, have been around the American automobile scene almost as long as there has been an American automobile to put them on. The 1904 Sturtevant built in Massachusetts used a transmission with three speeds, all of them engaging automatically as engine revolutions increased, automatic downshift a feature, and governor controlled, with a "foot button" to engage the unit. A two-speed planetary was, of course, standard on all the cars Henry Ford built from 1903 through 1927. By 1910 the sliding gear transmission had come into general use, the one notable exception being the Model T Ford.

In the middle Teens, the Owen Magnetic featured an electric transmission. "No mechanical clutch to manipulate," its makers claimed; ratio changes were effected without shifting gears, though a selector lever was involved. The car weighed at least 600 pounds more and was priced some $750 higher than its competition. The Premier used the Cutler-Hammer, an electric shift using solenoids chosen and energized by the operator with the depression of the clutch pedal. The energized solenoid moved a plunger connected to the shift fork and accomplished the shift to the preselected gear. Logically, "preselective" was the term given to the Cutler-Hammer transmission and other devices operating on the same principle.

Further attempts were the de Lavaud automatic transmission, which proved a disaster for Citroën, and the Spontan transmission developed by Swedish engineer Fredrik Ljungstrom who brought it to the United States and managed to get it installed in three demonstrators, a Nash and two Essexes in early 1930. Further varia-

tions included the Tyler Automatic, the Vickers-Coats Hydraulic Torque Converter and the Salerni Fluid Flywheel. Noble sounding ventures all.

By 1933 Reo offered automatic gear changing in a rather compact unit. At a speed of about 16 mph, a governor took over and a clutch was activated placing the transmission in direct drive. On deceleration the governor weights were overcome by spring tension in the clutch assembly and the unit shifted itself into low gear. The unit was developed by Reo engineers and pretested for more than two years. It was eventually made available as standard equipment on the Royale and optionally on the Flying Cloud series. The transmission was a two-speed for normal driving—but its automatic feature, mounted behind conventionally selective gearing, in effect produced a four-speed transmission. When additional torque was required for hilly terrain or difficult driving conditions, the driver manually placed the unit into low gear, in which the car would travel about thirty miles an hour. A standard clutch was used for disengagement, and the selection to low and reverse options was completed through a control handle on the instrument panel. Pushed in, with the clutch pedal disengaged, the control handle selected normal running speeds or third and fourth gear; pulled out, it engaged the low gear or first and second automatic speeds; an eighth of a turn, with clutch disengaged, brought in reverse. Though this was obviously the most sophisticated attempt at a semi-automatic production car transmission in the United States thus far, field failures were rife. It was not a success.

The idea of an automatic or semi-automatic transmission remained a compelling one to automobile manufacturers, however. Many men were poor drivers, most women hated the gearshift lever, for years the cacophonous clashing of gears had been a song of the American road. A car which would "shift for itself," and do so practically and flexibly, held an undeniable appeal.

The General Motors Research Center had been established in 1920 to study and develop new products and innovations for the GM family of cars. From the very first, transmissions had been a focus of attention. Electrical units were tried and found to be successful in buses and other large commercial vehicles, but their use in passenger cars was concluded to be impractical by the mid-Twenties.

About the same time, a transmission using hydraulic principles and turbines was being studied. But the greatest promise seemed to come from a concept called the "infinitely variable," or simply the IV, transmission—so designated because it could operate with a large number of ratios and speeds in an uninterrupted sequence rather than the definite number of fixed steps or gear changes in the standard transmission.

Automatic development work was begun at General Motors at the

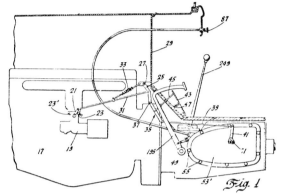

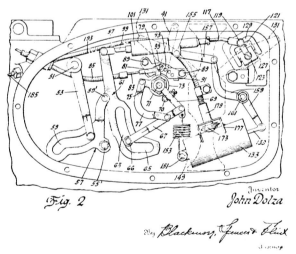

Dec. 11, 1934.   J DOLZA   1,983,745

ROLLER TYPE TRANSMISSION CONTROL

Filed Feb. 10, 1933   5 Sheets-Sheet 1

Fig. 1

Fig. 2

Inventor

John Dolza

By Blackmore, Spencer & Flint

Attorney

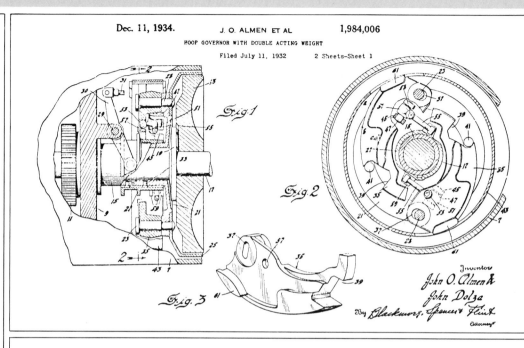

Dec. 11, 1934.   J. O. ALMEN ET AL   1,984,006

HOOP GOVERNOR WITH DOUBLE ACTING WEIGHT

Filed July 11, 1932   2 Sheets-Sheet 1

Fig. 1

Fig. 2

Fig. 3

Inventor

John O. Almen &

John Dolza

By Blackmore, Spencer & Flint

Attorney

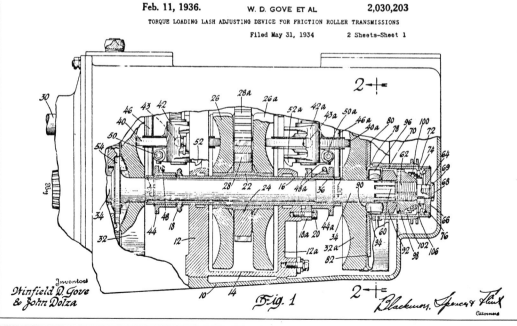

Feb. 11, 1936.   W. D. GOVE ET AL   2,030,203

TORQUE LOADING LASH ADJUSTING DEVICE FOR FRICTION ROLLER TRANSMISSIONS

Filed May 31, 1934   2 Sheets-Sheet 1

Fig. 1

Inventors

Winfield D. Gove

& John Dolza

By Blackmore, Spencer & Flint

Attorney

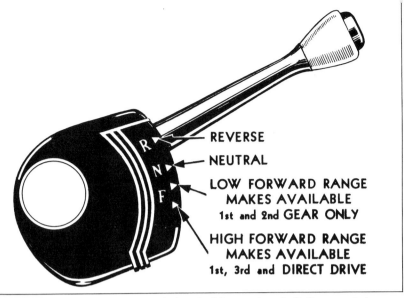

REVERSE

NEUTRAL

LOW FORWARD RANGE
MAKES AVAILABLE
1st and 2nd GEAR ONLY

HIGH FORWARD RANGE
MAKES AVAILABLE
1st, 3rd and DIRECT DRIVE

Page preceding: Patents which evolved from work on the Roller transmission. These pages: Buick's Self Shifting Transmission for 1938, the illustrations from the manual which announced that "It's Simpler, Safer, Easier, Thriftier and more Efficient." It was also short-lived, produced only that model year.

Starting—Lever in Low Range Position

Low Range gives the maximum power for climbing steep hills

The lever may be moved to High Range Position without disengaging the Clutch

instigation of Alfred P. Sloan, Jr. Like several of GM's top management people in the mid-1920's, Sloan was not a good driver. It would require an automatic transmission, he said, to "make the automobile for everyone. Women, poor drivers like myself, etc." He was chauffeured almost everywhere.

With Sloan's directive, Charles Kettering checked around and found a Citroën with a friction transmission on display at the Paris Automobile Salon. General Motors Research acquired the patent rights to the device and started work on a GM unit in a department called Dynamics, under the direction of John Otto Almen. By the late 1920's development had reached the point where eventual production of an IV transmission seemed a likely possibility and further work was assigned to Buick Engineering to determine if the project could be successfully completed. Cadillac would soon join in, but the major thrust and effort would be Buick's. Work at both divisions was to center around the larger series cars, although Buick would devise at least two different sizes of the transmission, one for the Series 50 and 60, one for the 80 and 90. (Engineering would later okay only the Series 90 for production.)

Assistant chief engineer Owen Nacker handled the project for Cadillac. Dutch Bower selected John Dolza as Buick's director. With the relocation of the project to Flint, several of the research engineers from Detroit moved with it. John Almen was to contribute a good deal, especially in the critical area of metal fatigue. And there was Jacob Ehrlich, chief analyst at GM Research; Winfield Gove, project engineer responsible for rollers and races; Andrew Lazlow, project engineer for development of the centrifugal clutch, and Earl Pierce, responsible for governor development. From Buick, in addition to Dolza, were engineers Robert Schilling and Joe Turlay, among many others. "It was the biggest staff I ever worked with," remembered Turlay.

The IV transmission or the Roller, as it came to be known, had been installed in cars at GM Research in Detroit. But the work there had been preliminary. When it moved to Buick, one thing didn't change. Development remained highly secret, conducted in locked rooms and kept hidden from the regular engineering people.

Millions of dollars were spent on the Roller transmission at Flint. Part of this was because of Dutch Bower. Dolza would have been content to build one or two working models but Bower preferred twenty. Even at this experimental stage, Bower thought in big numbers. Whenever anything was ordered for the Roller, it was ordered in volume. Engineers today recall large storage bins filled to the brim with handmade experimental parts. A component subsequently found to be incorrectly designed, or later changed, meant that all the additional pieces had to be scrapped.

The Roller transmission ran in a parafin-based, very light weight oil and was friction drive, utilizing three torus races nine inches in diameter, one at each end and one in the center. The races were made by New Departure of the highest quality ball bearing steel using three different heat treats for strength. The unit's governor was called a "hoop," because of the ring shape of its main spring. As engine power was applied to the input drum, it turned the inner toric race and transmitted torque to the outer races, through the rollers, which were compressed between the races in proportion to the output torque—and increased the friction between races and rollers. To obtain the proper friction load with the highest efficiency, a torque-loading device was devised by Gove and Dolza at the back of the transmission. Reverse gear was located at the front and was shifted in and out manually. Using the variable and adjustable properties of the transmission, it was possible for the unit to operate over a range from a 3.1x1 reduction to a 1.8x1 overdrive.

When the transmission arrived at Buick, it had a four-bar-type linkage which proved ineffective. Joe Turlay set up a cut-and-try program, testing various combinations until he came up with a geneva linkage movement which solved early development problems. Not without some difficulty. "I got so mad at the thing, it became an obsession," Turlay remembered. "I worked day and night, often didn't stop to eat when mealtimes rolled 'round. It was the only way I could handle the frustration, not stop to think about it but just keep working—that was my m.o."

Apparently it was the *modus operandi* of many of the other engineers on the project as well. Turlay also remembered being down in the dynamometer room with Dolza and some other engineers, working out some problem, and hearing the whistles blowing in the New Year. "We had no time off," he said, "maybe Christmas morning, but that was about it."

Several fluid couplings were tested on the Roller units at Buick but engineers feared they would absorb too much power. Instead, a completely mechanical automatic clutch was designed which would engage at just above idle speed. Cadillac apparently utilized the clutch pedal and friction clutch throughout, indicating there were development differences between the two groups, though they did cooperate extensively.

Performance of the unit as installed in a Buick passenger car is difficult to visualize today. Controls for the test cars were set so the engine would operate at peak output and power under full throttle. Performance was simply astounding. It was possible to burn rubber right up to 50 mph and then run on out strongly to the vehicle's maximum speed. With everything set correctly, you just stepped on the gas, the engine proceeded to peak revs, and stayed there while the car accelerated.

Many who drove test cars with Roller transmissions for the first time insisted the car had no power because the engine could not be heard at maximum rpm. Doubters were always invited to take the wheel of an identical car with a standard transmission and race a Roller-equipped job—and the Roller would win every time. John Dolza: "It was not always the noisiest fellow, the one that does the most work."

The transmissions for the Series 50 and 60 cars weighed 304.25 pounds, for the 80 and 90, 362.0 pounds. Corresponding weights for standard transmission 1932 Buicks were 113.43 pounds for the Series 50, 137.6 pounds for the 60 and 152.0 pounds for the 80 and 90. To compensate for the additional weight, the experimental vehicles in which the Roller transmissions were installed had larger displacement engines, achieved through a quarter inch added to the stroke. This made for 244 cubic inches for the Series 50 (vis-à-vis 230 cubic inches for the stock Series 50), 287.3 for the 60 (272.6 stock) and 362.0 for the 90 (344.8 stock).

The results under proving grounds test conditions were good. In the Series 90, for example, a stock 1932 version accelerated from 10 to 30 mph in second gear in 5.7 seconds. The Roller-equipped car could do it in 4.6. Acceleration from 10 to 60 mph with the production 90 was 26.4 seconds using high gear, 20.6 for the Roller. The Roller won the top speed contest 77.0 mph to 74.5.

On a country run from Flint to Toledo, Ohio and then from Flint to Saginaw, a 1932 stock Model 57 averaged 41 mph and 11.5 mpg. With the Roller, it averaged the same speed and 11.6 mpg. In city driving the stock car ultimately did win one, bettering the Roller vehicle by 1.6 mpg over a 170-mile test.

To back up, follow same procedure as with a conventional synchro-mesh transmission

Finally, Buick engineers said they were all set, the Roller was ready to go to market in the Series 90. They were in for a big disappointment. Cost projections had shown the retail price for the option, based on a first-year expected sales volume of 10,000 units (which was probably high), would have to be set at $500. In Depression dollars that was a lot of money. And there was another factor. Durability of the transmissions during testing had been troublesome. Initially the units were failing after 5000 miles, Turlay remembered, and though the last versions were capable of 50,000, "all those initial failures still lingered in the memory of many."

Harlow Curtice made his decision. After careful consideration, he recommended to Sloan that the project be dropped. Sloan went along. Dolza nearly quit. Dutch Bower had quite a time convincing him otherwise, but he succeeded and Dolza continued his career with GM for another twenty-four years.

The Roller was a great device arriving in the depths of the Great Depression. During development Dolza had been told that successful completion of the transmission project might be the single factor needed to pull the automobile industry out of its sales slump. About the only practical application to come out of the research was at New Departure. There were no three-phase variable speed electric motors in use at the time, and New Departure built a device similar to the basic operation of the Roller to get variable speed electric motor applications for use in machine tool drives.

Meantime, Oldsmobile—and especially its chief engineer Charles L. McCuen—had been keeping a watchful eye on the progress at Flint. And, at Cadillac, the man responsible for development of the synchronizer introduced in 1928 had begun another program even before the final decision was made regarding the Roller. Assistant chief engineer for Cadillac since 1929, Earl A. Thompson had also followed the Roller closely. By 1932 it was his feeling that an automatic transmission using step ratios and hydraulic servo mechanisms would be more practical. Development ensued, and some things still didn't change. The sign on the door at Cadillac read, "Military Transmission—Keep Out—This Means You." The government had nothing to do with what was going on.

Among the men working in the Thompson group were Ralph F. Beck, Walter B. Herndon, William L. Carnegie and Maurice S. Rosenberger. Thompson had made a free-hand sketch of a two-speed gearbox (no controls were shown) which was to be a full torque shifting unit. It was meant to prove the feasibility of a fully automatic, step-ratio transmission. Eventually it did prove exactly that. The sketch was signed by Thompson and witnessed by Cadillac chief engineer Ernest Seaholm on March 11th, 1932. Typical of Thompson's thoroughness, it was accurate in every detail.

The success of the first prototype was phenomenal. The automatic unit shifted smoothly and the car speed-throttle opening shift pattern functioned as planned. The basic principle of automatic shifting without relaxation of torque, in a step-ratio unit, was proven. Carnegie and Rosenberger were later brought into the project.

Routine development took the unit from a simple two-speed to a four-speed. By 1935 progress had been made, but the design was still far from being marketable. In January that year, due to the expense being absorbed by Cadillac, General Motors decided to move development work back into the corporation and place it in a Product Study Group under GM engineering vice-president Ormond E. Hunt. Early in 1936, with the enthusiastic support of McCuen (now the general manager of Oldsmobile) and under the direction of chief engineer Harold T. Youngren, Oldsmobile began to take over the Thompson designs in an effort to prepare them for production.

At this stage, the unit still utilized the normal friction clutch and pedal, and was a semi-automatic four-speed planetary design. The clutch pedal had to be used when starting out in low, the transmission then shifting automatically into second; with the steering-column selector lever moved to the high range position, it went into third, shifting thereafter into fourth automatically. When starting off with the selector in the high position, the transmission automatically shifted from first to third, skipping second, and then into fourth. The clutch pedal had to be depressed, and a button on the control lever pushed, for reverse.

In first gear, the two planetary units were utilized, the front one using a 1.418 reduction, the one at the rear a 2.228. Clutches and bands were applied and released as the unit went through its gear changes. In low gear, both planetaries were in reduction for a ratio of 3.159x1. In second gear the front planetary went into direct drive without reduction and drove the rear planetary which was now operating at its 2.228x1. In third gear the front planetary proceeded into its 1.418x1 reduction and the rear unit was in direct drive. In fourth, both planetaries were operating without reduction and there was a direct coupling through the transmission.

Both planetaries functioned in reduction for reverse which was brought into mesh between the friction clutch and the drive on the front planetary unit. Two pumps provided oil under pressure for operating the planetary clutches and servos.

Suddenly, Flint was again on the automatic transmission scene. In 1936 Buick was asked to build the unit for Oldsmobile. Buick did not want the transmission for its own cars and Buick's production manager wanted nothing to do with the project, period. The main concern was with tolerances and potential manufacturing problems. But Buick had the largest transmission production facility of all the

GM car divisions, was building its own high quality standard transmissions (in addition to those for Oldsmobile), and was the logical source to which GM might turn. All this must have smarted a bit, given the Roller development work and Buick engineers' faith in that design. But, with many grumbles about the potential problems ahead, work proceeded in Flint.

Buick set up an entire empty factory building and purchased the necessary tooling. Nearly five million dollars was spent before the first units came off the line in early 1937. In May that year Oldsmobile began advertising the "Automatic Safety Transmission." It was initially available as an eighty-dollar option on the 1937 eight-cylinder cars. Buick was charging Oldsmobile $180 for each unit built.

Corporate offices in Detroit wanted Buick to have the same advantage as Oldsmobile in available transmission options and "suggested" Buick offer the unit in its 1938 car. The Oldsmobile, with universal joints at both ends of its Hotchkiss drive to absorb the shock of gear change, was much more forgiving on the jar or "bump ratio" than the Buick with its solid torque tube. Buick engineers knew this and did not embrace the option with open arms.

Entering production in October of 1937 as the "Self Shifting Transmission," the unit was available only on the 1938 Series 40. Cars equipped with the option had a 3.651 rear axle ratio compared to a 4.40 ratio for the conventional transmission cars. Buick claimed a better fuel economy figure and less oil consumption due to the difference in ratios. In addition, the Self Shifter option received a shorter driveshaft and torque tube, a new steering column, speedometer drive gear and minor frame changes.

Enthusiasm at Flint remained lukewarm. Men at the proving grounds responsible for driving both the earlier Roller transmissions and the later Self Shifters claimed the Roller units superior in both driveability and durability. However, the step-ratio unit had been designed with available materials and contemporary know-how—had been, in other words, a reasonable compromise. Buick engineers still didn't like it. And they did not keep that fact to themselves.

Oldsmobile expanded the option for installation on its six-cylinder line in 1938 and continued offering the unit on 1939 cars. Buick installed about 3000 Self Shifters on 1938 models and was delighted to forget about the whole thing the following year. The transmission was not really a success for either division. Its principal triumph was as a bellwether.

Meantime, at Buick, the engineers were not idle. They didn't like fluid couplings as used in the first Hydra-Matics. Some had been hooked experimentally to standard clutches, but the results were dismal, there was little control. During World War II, the Development

Smooth as a Bird's Flight
Dynaflow Drive

Dynaflow, as seen in longitudinal cross section, as advertised to the world.

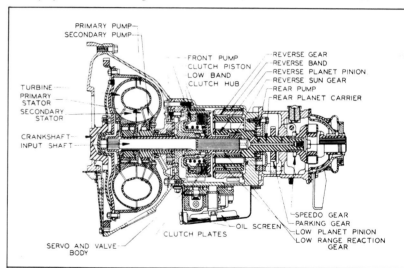

group in Central Office worked out a torque converter transmission first used on the Buick Hellcat tank destroyers, and work continued to ready a lighter version for passenger car use. Buick people were virtually alone in encouraging the development; they knew a torque converter was essential with their torque tube drive.

In the summer of 1945, Oliver K. Kelley, then head of the Central Office Engineering group, brought a test car to Flint to show Charlie Chayne what a transmission equipped with a torque converter could do. Chayne asked Kelley to stay overnight and the next day persuaded Harlow Curtice to take car and Kelley back to Detroit so Buick's president could personally drive it. Curtice was impressed.

Taking their cue from the Kelley test car, Buick engineers began a program on their own automatic which resulted in the Dynaflow.* Completed and tested by the time the 1947 line entered production, Buick was raring to go. Again, however, there was disappointment ... but not for long. The project this time was not stopped, just delayed, GM Central Office wanted more testing before introduction. Buick had worked long and hard. Finally, in 1948, it had Dynaflow, available as an option on the Roadmasters. For the first time since the 1938 cars, Buick had an automatic.

Buick copywriters got to work: "Imagine driving a car that glides swiftly from standstill to and through all speed ranges with the utter and uninterrupted smoothness of a skier swooping down a ski-slope. Imagine the sheer comfort and ease of motoring all day through city and turnpike traffic with nothing to do but steer and step on the gas treadle or brake pedal. . . . Imagine zooming up hills as though they were level . . . surging past speeding cars with effortless ease . . . stopping completely at traffic signals . . . starting off again fleet as a hare and reaching 45 in a handful of seconds. . . ."

Probably because they thought long technical descriptions would confound the public, or perhaps because they were confounded themselves, the copywriters didn't attempt to explain Dynaflow except cursorily, devoting one page of a fifteen-page brochure to its mysteries, the rest to "what the results are." But the motoring press was intrigued and immediately set its technical writers to work.

Defined as rudimentarily as possible, Dynaflow was the hydraulic torque converter in conjunction with an epicyclic two-speed gear mounted directly behind it. It comprised five elements: primary pump, turbine, secondary stator, primary stator, secondary pump. Turning with the flywheel, the primary pump imparted velocity to the oil. The turbine, carried on the end of the shaft, transmitted power to the gearbox. The secondary stator, primary stator and secondary pump were mounted on over-running clutches in order that they could rotate freely or remain fixed according to conditions. On a level road, the converter worked like a simple fluid coupling, with the primary and secondary pumps and the turbine all revolving at practically the same speed, and the stators freewheeling on the stationary reaction shaft. In accelerating or hill climbing, the primary pump worked harder, issuing oil from the turbine with such high velocity that the freewheeling stators on the fixed shaft were

stopped in their motion. As the oil flowed through them, the shape of their blades changed the direction of the oil and it impinged on the back of the vanes of the secondary pump causing it to run at a higher speed than the primary pump. When the fluid flow balance was reestablished, the pressure on the back of the secondary pump vanes was eliminated, the secondary pump ceased to run faster than the primary pump and became locked to it via the freewheel clutch, while—with this reduced reaction—the stators began freewheeling once again. More simply put, when the speed of the driving member was greater than that of the driven member, the torque output to the rear wheels was greater than that of the torque input from the engine, the multiplication of torque being of a ratio of 2.25 to one. The epicyclic gear, of course, was to allow a still lower ratio for extreme road conditions and to provide for a reverse gear.

Probably Buick copywriters, however, said it best: "You just start the engine . . . set a lever . . . step on the gas . . . and go!"

Dynaflow was a sufficiently new and sufficiently mysterious concept to have its share of problems once put into production. But customers liked it. Within six years fully eighty-five percent of Buick motorcars were Dynaflow equipped.

And by that time Dyna had gone double. Twin Turbine Dynaflow was introduced on 1953 Buicks. It utilized the torque multiplying characteristics of a planetary gear set in conjunction with the torque multiplying ability of a hydro-kinetic torque converter to augment engine output whenever driving conditions demanded greater torque than the engine could supply. Within the turbine casing were two turbines and a converter pump, driven by the engine, which energized the converter oil. Oil projected through the turbines returned to the pump with almost as much energy as when projected, and was further energized by the rotating pump, and sent back again. This build-up of energy force resulted in considerably greater torque and a smooth uninterrupted power flow. A unique aspect of the design was that all the power transferred was through the gear set and first turbine at low speeds; gradually the torque diminished as the second turbine torque increased until it did all the work at higher speeds. "There is a feeling of great controllable power," *The Autocar* editors said in their test of a Model 72R Buick Roadmaster lent to them by Lendrum & Hartman in London, "and getting away from a standstill can be made to resemble being in a high-speed lift!"

By 1955 there was another new wrinkle: variable pitch. Commercially used for some time in airplane and motorboat applications, the variable pitch stator blade replaced the former fixed stator blade in Dynaflow and provided a flexibility which could be profitably used in controlling the optimum angle under cruising and performance conditions. The year following, to increase low end car performance,

---

*If one man should be credited with the invention of Dynaflow, however, that man would be O.K. Kelley.

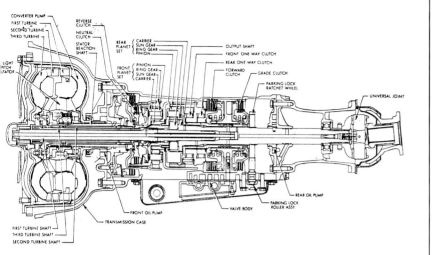

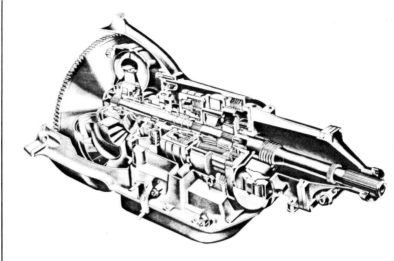

Dynaflow descendants, the Flight Pitch of 1957 and the Super Turbine of 1964, the illustrations from papers presented to the Society of Automotive Engineers.

there was the addition of a fixed blade stator between the first and second turbine. From Twin Turbine to Variable Pitch to added Fixed Blade Stator, each brought an enhanced efficiency to Dynaflow.

In 1957 Buick introduced a transmission called the triple-turbine "Flight Pitch" Dynaflow which allowed a continuous variation of the stator blade pitch. It utilized three turbines, each geared at its own speed ratio to the driven shafts, and still employed no shifts in the design. Its most important feature was a five-element torque converter in combination with two planetary gearsets. This consisted of an engine driven pump member, three turbines and the stator. Some development problems were encountered in keeping the transmission cool enough on hard operation in hilly terrain but by increasing torque converter and cooling oil flow from two gallons per minute to four-and-one-half in high stator angle, the problem was overcome. But triple turbine was enormously expensive: $86 million in tooling.

When the new Buick Specials were introduced in 1961, Buick Engineering came up with a new "downsized" unit called the "Dual Path Turbine Drive" to fit into the smaller vehicle. A number of trans-axle configurations were considered but it was finally decided that the benefits in terms of increased passenger room did not offset development costs and other problems inherent in this type of design. Engineering prototypes of the "Dual Path" transmission were first designed and built under the direction of G.K. Hause of the General Motors Engineering Staff and were then tested by Buick.

As completed for production, the unit weighed only eighty-four pounds without oil, ninety-five with. This weight factor made vehicles equipped with the transmission ten pounds lighter than a similar

car equipped with a manual transmission! The transmission was a step ratio and shifted very smoothly. Even though it was lighter in weight than other comparable units, it had a basic capacity considerably greater than for just the engine it was mounted behind.

For 1964 the Special was completely redesigned with a new chassis, a new body, and was available with two new engines: a 225-cubic-inch V-6 and a 300-cubic-inch V-8. The V-8 was also to be used in the LeSabre. To fill its requirements for these new vehicle and engine applications, Buick engineers developed a transmission called the "Buick Super Turbine 300." It utilized a three-element variable pitch torque converter with a two-speed Ravigneaux gearset. The unit was water-cooled with a cooler by-pass valve to provide lubrication in case of a restriction in the cooler line caused by foreign material or very cold oil. A lubrication pressure blow-off valve was incorporated to maintain a maximum lubrication pressure of 22 p.s.i.

Following this project Buick transmission engineers cooperated in a joint design and development program with Chevrolet which resulted in the 1969 model introduction of the Turbo Hydra Matic (THM) 350, still a mainstay at Buick and in many other General Motors car lines.

There have been ups and downs since Buick's first tentative experiments in this field. Still, on historical balance, the Buick achievement has been impressive. Today's Buick transmissions evolved from Dynaflow and Dyna—forgive us—flowed in a continuum from the pioneering work on the Roller. In the over half a century of perfecting a car that would shift for itself, Buick's role should not be lightly regarded.

Appendix Six

AROUND THE WORLD WITH BUICK

Around 1904, Buick illustrated a catalogue with a drawing of Uncle Sam pulling a Buick stationary engine across a globe. The catalogue's title was "Known All Over The World." Twenty years later, Buick set out to prove that not only was it known around the planet, but that it could travel around it as well.

The idea was not so much to prove that Buick was mechanically able to make the trip. That, the company sniffed, could be taken for granted. The idea of Buick and General Motors Export Company, which planned the trip jointly, was that Buick and GM had a strong service organization—so strong it could support sending a Buick around the world without a regular driver or mechanic.

A 1925 Standard Six Touring export model was selected. The fun began on December 20th, 1924. The "Around the World Buick" was shipped that day on the S.S. *Aurania*, bound for Liverpool, England. It arrived there December 30th and was driven by various distributors under General Motors Ltd., London, through such cities as Manchester, Birmingham and Stratford-on-Avon to London, getting appropriate publicity along the way. After being photographed at Buckingham Palace, it was shipped January 6th, 1925, to Amsterdam. There Buick distributor G.F. Bakels took over the car, touring Haarlem, The Hague and Rotterdam before delivering it to Paul Cousin, Buick distributor in Brussels, Belgium on January 11th.

A Cousin's representative drove the Buick to Paris, where French distributor Christian Lie took over. Large amounts of newspaper publicity appeared along the route through Avignon to Marseilles. The only mechanical fixes on the European continent were a check of valve clearances and a slight brake adjustment. On January 26th, it was shipped to Port Said, Egypt, in a crate.

Egyptian Buick distributor S. Gregorakie & Company drove the car through Cairo, had it photographed at the Pyramids and Sphinx, then headed back across the Suez Canal and into Palestine. Several blowouts were the only problems. On February 4th, at Gaza, the car was delivered to S. Audi & Preres, Buick distributor of Beirut, Lebanon. The Buick passed through Jerusalem, Nazareth and Haifa on its way to Beirut, where it arrived February 5th. There it was driven to various public places to the usual publicity.

The next day it left for Baghdad, accompanying one of the Nairn Transport Company's regular trans-desert convoys. "From Damascus to Baghdad, a distance of 540 miles," wrote the distributor, "no water was put in the radiator, nor was it required, the engine remaining quite cool on the journey." From Baghdad, the Buick was taken by a representative of Hills Brothers Company to Basra, a port on the Persian Gulf. It was a rough trip. Once, some bridging boards across a culvert gave out under the weight of the car, but there was no damage. The four-wheel brakes were used to advantage in slowing for the ditches. The car was shipped from Basra to Bombay, and started across India on February 23rd.

The Calcutta dealer found the car to be in good shape, except for a bent rear mudguard, and by March 1st, it was in Delhi. On April 15th it was shipped to Colombo, Ceylon and the Buick dealer there, C.A. Hutcon and Company. It rained much of the time in Ceylon.

On April 1st, the "Around the World Buick" arrived in Perth, Australia. Delivery was taken by Dalgety & Company. The 1825-mile trip from Perth to Adelaide was rugged and required seven days. The Buick traveled through bogs and mud, then followed a water course, from which some boulders were removed, from a cliff down to a lower level. "We filled in huge holes, said our prayers, engaged low gear and cautiously slithered down the pass," wrote the distributor. "We landed safely at the bottom, thankful that it was a Buick we were driving."

From Adelaide to Melbourne required four more days, and on April 15th the car was turned over to Lanes Motors Pty. Ltd., and that distributor toured Victoria "where it created a large amount of interest." Shipped back to San Francisco, then driven across the United States, the "Around the World Buick" arrived back in New York on June 25th, having traveled 16,499 miles through fourteen countries.

Buick's global experience has not, of course, been confined to one spectacular journey of one specific Buick motorcar. Buick has through the years been well represented on this planet, and in two places especially—Canada and England, where the adventures were

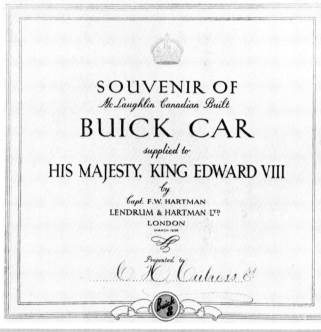

SOUVENIR OF
McLaughlin Canadian Built
BUICK CAR
supplied to
HIS MAJESTY, KING EDWARD VIII
by
Capt. F.W. HARTMAN
LENDRUM & HARTMAN LTD
LONDON
MARCH 1936

Presented to
C. H. Culross Esq.

perhaps less death-defying than the cliffs near Adelaide, but were equally as dramatic for other reasons. In England, where the prestigious house of Lendrum & Hartman of London was sole concessionaire for the marque, a Royal romance led to a memorable Buick episode. It might never have happened except that Canada was a Dominion and from Ontario, McLaughlin-Buick could ship cars to the United Kingdom with tax and tariff benefits.

In synopsis, the McLaughlin Carriage Company, as it was called in the Nineteenth Century, became the McLaughlin Motor Car Company in 1907 and, under the direction of R.S. "Sam" McLaughlin, the largest and most successful automobile producer in Canada. The Buick played a very important role in this.

Sam McLaughlin's grandparents had emigrated to Canada from Northern Ireland in 1832. His father Robert, born the first son of John McLaughlin in 1836 near Tyrone, Ontario, spent his first thirty-four years working the family farm and helping to clear the land. However he soon found he had a talent for wood carving and made axe handles in the family barn, selling them at a local market. In 1866 he married Mary Smith. One of their wedding presents was fifty acres of timbered land. After building their log home, Robert had plenty of raw material left to make axe handles, and to branch out too into the production of whiffle trees and wagon parts. A business was born. And soon thereafter, two sons, George and his younger brother who would be nicknamed Sam.

In 1867 Robert McLaughlin had put the finishing touches on a cutter he had designed and built, and from that point forward the building of wagons and sleighs became the main focus of his interests. As the enterprise grew, so too did the need for more room. From the barn in Tyrone the operation was moved to the larger community of Enniskillen. There one of his first major steps was the construction of a blacksmith shop. His previous dependence on the talents of traveling "smithies" who were not always around when he needed them had made keeping production on an even schedule difficult. His own shop meant iron work when he wanted it, and his business mushroomed.

In just two years it was necessary for him to find even larger quarters in Enniskillen, and it was now that he built the first McLaughlin carriage. He entered it in a county fair, and he won a first prize. He immediately turned his entire production to carriages and sleighs, formed the McLaughlin Carriage Company and came up with the slogan, "One Grade Only, And That The Best"—which was a good one and the precise truth. In 1876, when his business had expanded so that convenient banking facilities and rail transportation were needed, he moved his firm to Oshawa. There were already two other carriage works in town when he arrived, but they were no match for

the McLaughlin line. They were out of business within months.

Robert McLaughlin's son George had already entered the family business, but young Sam was initially enthused with bicycling as a sport and in bicycle racing—and trying his hand at several other professions. Finally in 1887, tiring of all these false starts, he became an apprentice in the McLaughlin upholstery shop. Three years later, as a journeyman, and wanting to broaden his experience in carriage building, he left Canada for Watertown, New York where he joined the H.H. Babcock Company.* Further learning experience with two other Eastern carriage makers followed, and he returned to the family firm in Oshawa in 1892 as foreman of the upholstery shop.

A catastrophe showed the strength of the company. Two weeks before Christmas in 1899, the McLaughlin plant was destroyed by fire. By July 1900, with the help of a loan of $50,000 from the city of Oshawa, the company was back in business. Sales for the year topped 25,000 units, despite the fire. Soon thereafter the firm was reorganized as the McLaughlin Carriage Company Ltd., with Robert and his two sons as shareholders. By now McLaughlin was listing 143 different designs of sleighs and carriages in its catalogue.

An Oshawa schoolteacher, who moonlighted keeping the McLaughlin books and who eventually was hired by the company full time, introduced the family to the horseless carriage. Oliver Hezzlewood purchased an automobile for himself, and young Sam found the contraption fascinating. Foreseeing the potential competition such a machine might give the carriage industry, Sam wondered aloud if perhaps they should not be doing some investigating. His brother agreed, but his father was a completely committed carriage man, and consequently no investigation was made formally. But Sam was spending his vacations in the United States visiting such successful factories as Peerless, Reo and Thomas. By 1905 he decided to do more than investigate; with Hezzlewood he contacted automobile maker Charles Lewis of Jackson, Michigan regarding the purchase of springs, axles, bodies and other components. Before any agreement would be signed, however, Sam made it a condition that two cars built by Lewis be shipped to Oshawa for testing, to insure McLaughlin was purchasing quality components. It was one of the best decisions he ever made. The two cars arrived, and they were just awful. When they both broke down continually on a test run, Sam and Hezzlewood cancelled the deal.

Meantime, Billy Durant learned of all this and, aware from his carriage days of the lofty reputation of the McLaughlin firm, stepped

---

*Coincidentally, it was at H.H. Babcock where a member of the Brunn family would learn his trade too. And the name Brunn, of course, was later to become associated with Buick's entry into the custom car luxury market.

in with an invitation for Sam to meet with him. Burned once, Sam took no chances this time, purchased a Buick beforehand in Toronto and found the car to be acceptable. But the negotiations with Durant hit a couple of snags, and Sam returned to Oshawa without a contract from Durant or a deal with Buick.

By now the McLaughlin family was united in the decision to move the firm into the horseless age. And the McLaughlins decided to do it on their own. They equipped a factory building with assembly machinery, hired Arthur Milbraith as their engineer, and ordered machine parts and castings from Cleveland. The plan was to build their own bodies and machine their own engines in the Oshawa shop.

The prototype McLaughlin was called the Model A and was a beautiful creation. Its two-cylinder engine was larger than the contemporary Buick's, and its coachwork featured flared fenders and a streamlined hood. Arrangements to purchase enough material for the first one hundred cars were made, and then engineer Milbraith suddenly became very ill.

The McLaughlins were desperate. They asked Durant if he might send them an engineer. Instead, Durant himself went to Oshawa and in short order negotiated a fifteen-year contract to supply the McLaughlins with Buick engines and other items they needed on a cost-plus basis. The McLaughlins would engineer and build their own bodies, which would be along similar lines to the Buick's. The earlier car was abandoned completely, and the machinery to build it disposed of.

A recently discovered journal, now in the National Automotive History Collection of the Detroit Public Library, records the disposition of the first few hundred cars built by Buick at Jackson. On January 18th, 1908 Buick shipped four cars to the McLaughlin Carriage Company in Oshawa, none of them painted. These vehicles, numbers 760, 764, 767 and 769 in the journal, were probably sent for inspection and test purposes. All were Model D's.

Further shipments to Oshawa would be to the McLaughlin Motor Car Company Ltd. which was quickly formed, with Sam as president, Hezzlewood as vice-president, and George McLaughlin as treasurer. Robert McLaughlin, now seventy, was made a director and remained the head of the carriage company.

As Durant had done so effectively with the Buick, the McLaughlins also used their carriage organization as a distributorship for the new line of cars. During these early years, the carriages were built right alongside the motorcars in the factory. The patriarch of the family had acceded to the automobile but he was not yet convinced. During 1905 and 1906, Robert McLaughlin approved the printing of calendars for the carriage company with scenes depicting overturned motorcars and injured motorists as a

Opening Page: The King's Buick, the front cover of Captain Hartman's souvenir album. Above and below: The "Around the World" Buick of 1925 pictured with the Sphinx in Egypt and at Buckingham Palace in London.

McLaughlin carriage sailed safely by.

The first Buick-powered McLaughlin, a Model F, was completed in December of 1907 and was offered as a 1908 model. Models 5, 10, D, E and S were offered as well, and 154 cars in all were built in 1908.

Although the engines were Buick and the look was Buick, the McLaughlin offerings were more than just Canadian-built versions of the car from Michigan. Differences in color and interior design were the norm, and on a few occasions the McLaughlins even tried a motor that was not a Buick. The McLaughlin Model 7 in 1909 featured a four-cylinder T-head engine originally destined for the Welch car. And in 1916 McLaughlin used a Northway engine similar to the flathead powerplant in the Oakland, which probably made Buick shudder.

Things happened quickly. In 1915 McLaughlin arranged with Durant—who by now had been long ousted from General Motors and, with it, Buick—to build his new car, the Chevrolet Four-Ninety, in Canada. This decision necessitated another, the disposal of the carriage business; the space was needed for a Chevy assembly line. By now the original Durant/Buick agreement with the McLaughlins was nearing an end. Meantime Durant was effectively using Chevrolet to regain control of General Motors. The McLaughlins, wanting neither to sever their ties with GM nor go it alone with an exclusively Canadian-built car, decided to sell their company. On November 8th, 1918, the McLaughlin and the Chevrolet operation were absorbed into General Motors of Canada Ltd. In 1914, before the Durant takeover, GM had acquired half the Oshawa operation; on December 19th, 1918, after the Durant takeover, the balance was purchased. Sam and George McLaughlin were asked to stay on to run the GM of Canada operation as president and vice-president. Before Christmas of 1920, Durant was ousted for the second time—and irrevocably—from General Motors. Before Christmas of 1921, Robert McLaughlin died.

For the fifteen years of the McLaughlin-Durant contract, varying names were given to the machines. Some were called McLaughlins,

Robert Samuel "Sam" McLaughlin, as a young bicycle enthusiast, and as chairman of General Motors of Canada, entertaining Queen Mother Elizabeth during a Canadian visit in 1965.

some McLaughlin-Buicks. As pointed out in the Durnford and Baecher book, *Cars of Canada*, other models read "McLaughlin on the radiator, and McLaughlin-Buick on the hubcaps." Sales catalogues from 1908 to 1915 indicated McLaughlin-Buick on their covers, the catalogue for 1916 just McLaughlin. In 1918, the last year of McLaughlin independence, the production rate was 125 cars a week.

The McLaughlin name continued to appear alone sporadically on automobiles until 1923 when they all became McLaughlin-Buicks. Their individual distinction remained for a time, but eventually the car grew into a near copy of the Flint Buick. Nineteen forty-two was last year McLaughlin was part of the car's name. Because of the war, very few of the cars were built, and sales catalogues for this last of all McLaughlin-Buicks are extremely rare.

The cars were never called Buick-McLaughlins. During the Twenties, with the McLaughlin name prominent, sales catalogues touted the vehicle as a "Canadian Car Built By Canadians, For Service on

Sam McLaughlin on the occasion of his 100th birthday, September 8th, 1971.

Canadian Highways." Similarly, in England, because the cars were imported from Canada, the Buick would be heralded as a "Dominion Built Car" and an "Empire Product."

In 1927, two special cars were built on McLaughlin-Buick chassis for a visit to Canada that year by the Prince of Wales. These were the first of a number of cars to be produced for members of the British Royal family.* The others were destined to be sent to England.

Buick was not an unknown quantity in England. In fact, the name Buick was introduced there only a few years after it had become known in the United States. Beginning in the summer of 1907, Buicks were sold in England, and from 1911 and continuing to 1932 they were distributed by General Motors Export Company.

And there was the Bedford connection as well. In 1909 Bedford Motors began building motorcars using Buick chassis fitted with its own coachwork. Apparently the Buick part of the resulting vehicle was underplayed, although the association was a strong one. In 1911, in fact, one of the Marquette-Buick race cars was shipped across the Atlantic to Bedford for advertising purposes. Bedford took it to the famous Brooklands track and photographed it, but not before affixing a large Bedford nameplate to the radiator.

The sub rosa nature of the partnership was short-lived, however. In February 1912 Bedford chairman Lambie announced his company was about to merge with General Motors Export Company and that his firm would soon be selling Buick cars. By the end of the year he was doing exactly that, the cars were called Bedford-Buicks, and became part of the Buick line offered in England. Their coachwork, somewhat different from the standard Buicks, was of good quality. This arrangement continued, interrupted only by World War I, until 1920, at which time the Bedford name was dropped by General Motors, although it would surface again ten years later, this time as the nameplate for an English-built Chevrolet truck; a few months later it would be applied to an all-British two-ton vehicle built along Chevrolet lines.

The really fascinating story of Buick in England was not, however, with the Bedford people. It was with the Messrs. Lendrum and Hartman. This enterprise had its origins in 1919 in southwest London as Lendrum Motors, but the Dutch-born Lendrum was not long in business alone, teaming up quickly with Captain F.W. Hartman, formerly of the Royal Naval Air Service. The partnership was titled Lendrum & Hartman, and Lendrum decided to become a silent financial partner in the enterprise and leave the selling and management to Hartman. It was a good move, for Hartman was an excellent

*One of these vehicles is currently owned by Aubrey and Bernice Marshall of Toronto.

THE McLaughlin for 1908

BODY	Side entrance tonneau.	CARBURETOR . .	Special design.
SEATS	Five persons.	LUBRICATION . .	Constant stream of oil on all bearings, gear pump.
WHEEL BASE .	108 inches.		
GAUGE	56 inches.	MOTOR CONTROL .	On top of steering wheel.
TIRES	34 x 4 inches.	CLUTCH . . .	Cone, leather faced.
BRAKES	Hub, internal expanding also external contracting on driving shaft.	CHANGE GEAR . .	Sliding gear; selective type; speeds, three forward, one reverse.
SPRINGS . . .	Semi-elliptic.	TRANSMISSION CONTROL . .	Side lever.
FRAME	Pressed steel.		
HORSE POWER . .	Forty.	DRIVE	Shaft.
CYLINDERS . . .	Four, 4⅝ x 5 inches.	PRICE	$2750 f.o.b. factory. This price includes oil lamps, tail lamp, generator, gas headlights, horn, repair outfit,
MOTOR SUSPENSION .	Sub-frame.		
COOLING . . .	Water.		
IGNITION	Jump Spark.		
CURRENT SUPPLY .	Magneto and storage battery.	EXTRAS	Top. Autogas tank, Glass front.

McLAUGHLIN MOTOR CAR COMPANY, LIMITED
OSHAWA   ONTARIO

Above: Catalogue page from 1908. Below: 1932 Series 50 McLaughlin-Buick. Right: Advertising the Buick product—for French Canadians in 1932; by Lendrum & Hartman for N.A. Series of '35; in a 1938 Canadian magazine.

salesman and businessman and, moreover, he was a familiar figure in London's high society, which was a decided advantage for any new enterprise of the sort the partners were planning.

The motorcar business in general and special coachwork in particular was the focus of the partners' interest. Initially not franchised as a dealership, they sold used cars and custom-bodied vehicles, purchasing the chassis wherever they could. The turning point came in the early 1920's when it became known that General Motors was about to appoint another agent in London; to be considered for the franchise, any interested parties were required to travel to New York and deal with General Motors there. Captain Hartman set sail immediately. In a race across the Atlantic with at least one other prospect, Hartman won and he returned to England with franchises to sell Buick and Cadillac in London. By 1928 Lendrum & Hartman was one of three firms handling Buick in London, one of the 148 Buick outlets throughout England, Northern Ireland and the Irish Free State. The company was now doing business in central London at 26b and 26c Albemarle Street as Lendrum & Hartman Ltd.

Because of the taxation structure favorable to a car built in the Dominion of Canada, the McLaughlin-Buick became the mainstay of the Lendrum & Hartman enterprise. But, in 1924, when Hartman made a return trip to America, it was from Noyes Buick in Boston that he recruited one of his managers, Merle G. Armstrong, who would work in various of the L&H departments until the outbreak of World War II, when he returned to the States.

Unlike the stereotypical English businessman, Hartman was not at all stuffy. In the rigid upstairs-downstairs society of England in that era, he was something of a rarity. He was always very approachable by his employees, invariably paid more than the prevailing wage and delighted in visiting the service shop and playing at the blacksmith forge. Equally at home with members of the gentry on either side of the Atlantic, Hartman befriended Alfred P. Sloan, Jr., who was a guest at his home during visits to London.

The services of numerous coachbuilders were used from the beginning, among them Carlton and Maltby in England, Vanden Plas in Belgium. Custom installations on Buicks sold in England, even the smaller series, included division windows and sun roofs. And there was one firm contracted to install automatic hydraulic jacks at all four wheels so that no matter where a flat occurred, the car could be instantly and automatically jacked for tire replacement. That firm, Carlton, may have been associated with or a part of L&H, incidentally, since its address was next door on Albemarle Street.

Because McLaughlin did not build convertibles in all years and all series, whenever a client ordered a Buick convertible that would have to come from the States, Lendrum & Hartman was forced to pay the

import tax (a full 33-1/3 percent) required. For obvious reasons, L&H discouraged open air motoring, or suggested that it be done via coachwork from an English or Continental builder.

As business prospered, the company rented berths, installed along a canal near its service facility, from which crates with chassis units inside were shipped via barge from the London docks, unloaded with a crane and assembled in the production department.

In 1932 Lendrum & Hartman became even busier. Previously the title of "Sole Concessionaire" for Buick in the United Kingdom belonged to General Motors itself. But in November 1925 General Motors Ltd. took over the English company of Vauxhall and eventually most of the Buick agents became Vauxhall dealers. With major corporate interest now tending toward its new acquisition, GM looked about for someone else to take care of Buick. The decision was made for Lendrum & Hartman in 1932.

Suddenly as Sole Concessionaire, L&H found itself with a much larger stake in Buick, continuing with its retailing and service operations, and now adding to it the distribution of Buick cars and the appointing of dealers to sell them. The company was equal to the task.

There were some changes made. As Sole Concessionaire, Len-

OTHER COUNTRIES, OTHER COACHBUILDERS

The venture in England in 1909, in which Buick chassis were shipped to Bedford Motors, Ltd., of London, and fitted with British coachwork, was the first of such arrangements in foreign countries involving Buick. The Abadal Company of Barcelona, Spain, reportedly produced a small series of customized bodies on Buick chassis for European consumption between 1913 and 1922.

According to GM Overseas—and the records, officials admit, are meager—during the 1930's chassis were shipped to Antwerp, Belgium; Copenhagen, Denmark and Batavia, Java (now Indonesia) where assembly was completed. In 1930, Marquette-Buick chassis were delivered to Australia where the Holden Body Works (now General Motors-Holden's Ltd.) added its own four-door sedan coachwork. Late in the Thirties, Holden built sedan bodies on unassembled Buick chassis. In 1947, Holden built the last bodies for Buick chassis, turning thereafter to all-Australian cars, although apparently the first Holden in 1948 used a body designed by Buick in 1938 for projected use in the mid-Forties, a plan scrapped because of the war.

Also in the Forties, after the war, according to GM Overseas, Buicks were assembled in Egypt, South Africa and Venezuela. During the late Fifties, they were assembled as well at a small plant operated by GM in Bienne, Switzerland, and also in Mexico. In 1970 plans were made for assembly in Peru. In 1977, GM acquired forty-five percent ownership in a company named General Motors Iran Ltd. and took over a former Jeep assembly plant. The plant continued to build Jeeps and added an unusual assembly mix of Cadillac Sevilles, Chevrolet pickup trucks and Buick Skylarks from components shipped from the United States. Production there was interrupted sometime after the Iranian revolution began in 1979.

Although Buicks were never assembled in China, a Buick sales office was opened in Shanghai in 1929. And in the U.S.S.R., the ZIS which began production in 1936 used a straight-eight engine which bore an unmistakable resemblance to the Buick powerplant.

In small numbers, Buick chassis through the years were used as the base for special bodies by coachbuilders in England, France, Germany and other countries as well as U.S. firms. In addition, a number of companies have converted Buicks to hearses, buses, ambulances and other special-purpose vehicles in some volume. Prominent among these firms in America—which used numerous motorcars other than Buicks for their conversions—were the Flxible Company (Loudonville, Ohio), Eureka Company (Rock Falls, Illinois), Sayres & Scoville (Cincinnati, Ohio), Knightstown Body Company (Knightstown, Indiana), A.J. Miller Company (Bellefontaine, Ohio) and August Schubert Wagon Company (Oneida, New York). In 1980, Buick owned a V.I.P. limousine built by Armbruster/Stageway, Inc. (Ft. Smith, Arkansas) complete with six doors, push-button window between driver and rear compartment, color television set and wet bar in a custom console, among various other amenities. After 3,000 miles, the car—built on a 1980 Electra chassis—was sold for $20,528 to a Buick dealer on Long Island, New York. A limousine built off the Roadmaster sedan by Limousine Werks of Schaumburg, Illinois, and marketed through Buick dealers, was featured at Buick displays in auto shows in the early Nineties.

drum & Hartman began assigning letter designations to the English Buicks of different model years. The 1933 cars were CA, the 1934 and 1935's NA, and 1936's DA. Given what these letters in congregate spelled, obviously they were not randomly chosen. Possibly there was a meaning behind the designations for the three following years but unfortunately what CO for 1937, MO for 1938 and RO for 1939 deciphered to has been lost to history.

What all the Buicks of this period, regardless of designation, had was a special brass plate. Upon arrival in London, the body plates of all McLaughlin-Buicks were removed and replaced with one for Lendrum & Hartman which was restamped with all the appropriate vehicle information and affixed to the firewall. It was a nice touch.

A few of the Buicks with Lendrum & Hartman plates were now finding their way into Royal garages. In 1935 a 90 Series car was sold to Lady Patricia Ramsey, a grand-daughter of Queen Victoria. And in 1936 a delivery was made which is remembered by the company to this day.

One morning in late summer of 1935 the Prince of Wales arrived at the Albemarle Street showroom and asked to see Captain Hartman. At the time Hartman was two doors up the street getting a shave, but he was quickly summoned back and discovered the Prince wanted to purchase a Buick. Arrangements were made for Merle Armstrong to go to St. James Palace, a short distance away, to take the order. It was during this meeting that the Prince confided to Armstrong that he was certain no one in England would build him a car as he wanted it built, but only as they *thought* he wanted it built.

Lendrum & Hartman was determined to prove the Prince wrong. After receiving detailed instructions on the Buick as royally desired, and alternate Armstrong suggestions when a Royal prerogative was simply not translatable to coachwork, the Buick as the Prince really wanted it was reality—on paper. Armstrong personally took the order to Oshawa, and was instructed by Hartman to remain there until the car was completed.

The Prince's Buick began life as a standard 1936 Limited limousine. In the archives of the McLaughlin company is this description of what happened to it then:

> The rear quarter windows and the backlight were cut out and filled in with sheet steel hammered and planished to follow the curves of the roof and belt. A new, much smaller backlight opening was then cut in, flanged and welded. The drip moulding line which ordinarily appeared over the rear quarter was then carefully effaced, so that a smooth unbroken surface was presented.
>
> The wooden framework was then built up to carry the rear quarter companions, which would occupy the spaces formerly

taken up by the rear quarter windows and ventilators. As much
work as possible was carried out at the benches, so as to permit
as many workers as practical to be employed to the best advantage. With this in mind, the rear quarter companions were built
up as separate units. Each one contained a mirror, held in place
by a chrome plated casting completely surrounding it, with a
flush lamp, reflector and switch. In a semi-cylindrical section
immediately adjoining the mirror section, was installed a vertical reading lamp, engine-turned from solid brass, and heavily
chrome plated. This lamp had a universal movement, so that it
could be pointed in any direction desired. When the reading
lamps were not in use, a solid panel covered to match the interior trim was arranged to slide forward in felt-lined channels
and close off the compartment.

Additional framing was built up at the rear window, and a

silk blind, actuated by a small electric motor which could be
operated at will from either the passenger's compartment or
the driver's seat was installed so that all mechanism and cords
were completely concealed.

Due to the long rear quarters, the surface of which was no
longer broken by a flat window, and due to the low, narrow
backlight, additional strainers and formers had to be built in to
carry the lines of trimming around in smooth curves in order to
preclude any flat spots, either in the quarters or in the headlin-
ing.

During this framing process, the series of compartments
which would eventually house the canteen equipment, smoker's
set and the hot water heating system, were being assembled into
one unit ready for trimming and completing for installation
into the main centre partition. The compartment containing

The Buick of King Edward VIII. Page opposite: Inside the King's car, and outside the factory in Canada, with Sam McLaughlin, his executives and workmen. Above: Unloading at Southampton. Below: Captain Hartman with the King's car; Mrs. Simpson's Roadmaster is behind it, and in the photograph below. Left: The Royal car as featured in an English magazine advertisement.

the heater system was carefully blocked off by baffles and insulating material to avoid the transferring of heat to the adjoining sections of the cabinet.

Meanwhile, the No-draft ventilators, specially fabricated for the rear doors instead of those ordinarily fitted into the rear quarters, were now in place, glass was being installed, the garnish mouldings screwed into location.

Then came the fitting into position of the partition cabinet unit. The upper lids were arranged to fold down and form luncheon trays, and consisted of black glass surrounded by a one-piece casting of chrome plated brass, supported by heavy chrome quadrants on each side. As no standard or suitable hardware was available which would be tasteful enough for a special job of this nature, the necessary parts were designed and specially made.

A point worthy of note is that particular attention was paid that all fastening screws or clips should be entirely concealed. A sandwich box of nickel silver was hand fabricated to match the canteen equipment, which was completed in every detail, and included a silver cocktail shaker, vacuum ice jar, large and small silver cups, silver topped cordial bottles, silver cigarette and tobacco boxes, which were all neatly tucked away in holders and recesses, to be readily accessible upon opening the cabinet lids. Two sliding drawers fitted into the bottom of the cabinet, of special size to accommodate London Telephone Directories. A partition in one drawer permitted carrying a washable linen holdall, in which [there was] a long spoon, a silver lemon knife, a combination measure, corkscrew and crown top opener, and a pair of ice cube tongs.

With the filling in of the rear quarter windows and the downsizing of the rear window, the car was a very private vehicle.

In January 1936 King George V died and the Prince who had ordered a Buick was now King Edward VIII, waiting for its delivery.

In late February the Royal car, together with a 1936 Roadmaster which the then-Prince had also ordered at the same time as his own car, arrived at the London docks from Canada. The Roadmaster was for a "friend" of his. Her name was Mrs. Wallace Warfield Simpson.

Both cars had been carefully crated to prevent shipping damage, and they were met at the docks by a specially selected team from the Hartman organization. Taken to the service facility, they were prepared for delivery, no detail too small, no expense spared. The Simpson vehicle had sustained some trunk damage en route, and it was quickly repaired. Captain Hartman cabled the McLaughlin firm congratulating them on an outstanding job. The McLaughlin people responded, saying that their work was "undertaken with intense pride and the result represents our utmost skill and care."

Though mention was not made in the description from the

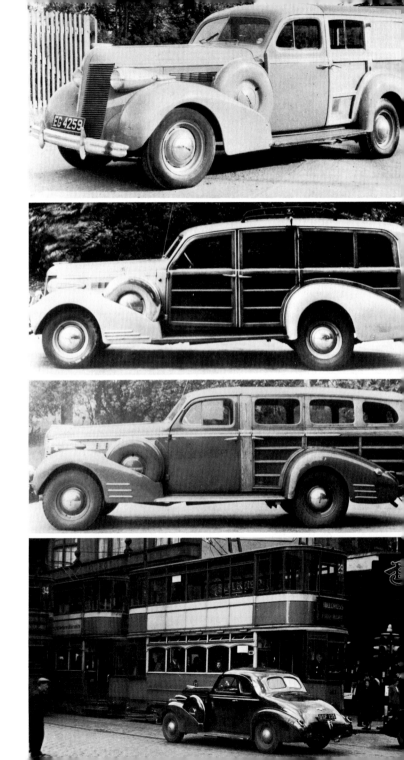

Buicks in England. Page opposite, from the top: 1937 McLaughlin Special with body by Arlington; 1937 shooting brake by Hales; 1938 variation, body builder unknown; '38 Lendrum & Hartman Series MO coupe in Scotland. This page, from the top: 1937 Century drophead coupe; '37 Century fixed head coupe; 1937 drophead with coachwork by Carlton; Lendrum & Hartman publicity photograph for the Series RO Special drophead coupe of 1939.

McLaughlin archives, the King's car had been built with two batteries and a throw-over switch so that a continually fresh battery would be available for service. This precaution was found to be advisable due to the heavy electrical demands of the vehicle. There were hydraulic lifting jacks all around, of course.

No mention was made either of the fact that two identical Royal vehicles were built. The second car was ordered by Captain Hartman himself and was stored at the Lendrum & Hartman facility in the event any difficulty was experienced with the King's vehicle. It was simply a back-up car and it is doubtful that the King even knew it existed. License plates, assigned for the life of the car in England, were registered as follows: The car delivered to the King carried CUL 421, the substitution vehicle CLN 6. Mrs. Simpson's Roadmaster was CUL 547. It is rumored that a replacement for the Simpson vehicle may have been shipped as well but no license number for this vehicle is known and the details surrounding its existence are cloudy.

In early March the vehicles were delivered to the King and Mrs. Simpson. As an appropriate touch for a Royal occasion, Captain Hartman had large red leather-bound albums made up as souvenirs of the presentation of the Royal car. Following a title page announcing that the vehicle was a "McLaughlin Canadian Built Buick Car Supplied to His Majesty, King Edward VIII" were a series of ten high quality 8-by-10 photographs of the car's appointments and pictures of the vehicle posed in front of the Oshawa factory and at Hyde Park. How many of these albums were made is not known, certainly very few. One is in the possession of Nicola Bulgari, the owner of the Royal car, CUL 421, today.

While all of England was being persuaded to believe that the King had purchased an "Empire Made Automobile," across the ocean in Flint, Buick was having a merry fling with advertisements proclaiming that for the first time in the history of the British Empire, an English King had purchased a car "other than of British make."

Following the delivery of the Royal car, trusted and long-time Lendrum & Hartman employee Russell Johns was given the task of maintaining and servicing the vehicle. Upon Captain Hartman's personal orders, the car was to want for nothing—and he was instructed to visit the Royal Mews* once a month to assure that it did not. Any expense to service the vehicle was absorbed by Hartman.

One evening Merle Armstrong visited the Royal Mews while Johns was working on the car and casually asked the head chauffeur how Buick's service compared with that of such other suppliers of

---

*Derived from the days when it meant a horse stable, the term "mews" initially also defined a "garage," although the latter term generally became more prominent. Buckingham Palace preferred to continue calling its garage a mews.

Above: The 1939 Roadmaster for the Duke of Windsor. Above right and below: The 90L of 1938 built for the Duke of Windsor. Page opposite, left: The 1938 90L for the Duchess of Kent. Page opposite, right: Sam McLaughlin, his wife, and one of two McLaughlin-Buicks built for the Royal Tour of '39.

vehicles to the Royal family as Daimler. He was told that the Buick attention ranked far above the others and that thought was being given to hiring Johns away from Captain Hartman. Armstrong carried this message back to his employer and in short order Johns found himself hired full-time for the Royal Mews. His official salary there was less than he had been making at L&H. Captain Hartman made up the difference out of his own pocket. (Daimler took the Royal Buick as well as the Johns appointment as a personal affront.)

There was good reason for all this special attention. The Royal Buick helped business. Sales really boomed at Lendrum & Hartman, and although Buicks of that period were attracting attention all by themselves, undoubtedly the increased favor the marque began enjoying was in good measure due to the Royal patronage. Consider the sales estimates through the years: 150 cars, 1932; 200 cars, 1933; 800 cars, 1934; 850 cars, 1935; 1000 cars, 1936; 2000 cars, 1937; 2000 cars, 1938. Documented figures for these years are not available, regrettably, nor even an estimate for 1939, the last year for many to come that new Buicks would be sold on a regular basis in England.

Before everything changed, there were more Royal Buicks built. When all the figures were totted up from McLaughlin and Lendrum & Hartman, the total number of Buicks produced for Royal service was an impressive one. There had been the two cars McLaughlin supplied for the 1927 Royal Tour of Canada, and the 1935 90-L delivered to Lady Patricia Ramsey. There was the 1936 90-L car, and its (never needed) replacement, for King Edward VIII. There was the 1936 Roadmaster for Mrs. Simpson and in which, incidentally, she made her legendary escape to Cannes in the midst of the abdication crisis. After giving up his throne, the former King, now the Duke of Windsor, purchased a 1938 90-L as a replacement for the '36. A 1937 90-L went to the Duke of Kent, a 1938 90-L to his Duchess. Then a 1939 90-L was bought by the Duke of Kent, and two more 1939 90-L's were built for the Royal tour of Canada by King George VI and Queen Elizabeth. (One of these 1939 tour vehicles is now owned by

Vern Bethel of Vancouver, British Columbia, the other by Larry Norton of Oshawa, Ontario.) A 1939 Roadmaster sedan went to the Duke of Windsor.

Added to these deliveries should be all the titled, though not Royal, customers of Lendrum & Hartman. Their business was considerable. The Buick that was born in America had found wide favor among the British upper classes.

With the onset of World War II, automobiles could no longer be shipped into the United Kingdom. The American Red Cross purchased some thirty vehicles from the company in 1939 for war service. Thereafter Lendrum & Hartman's facilities were taken over by the government for the testing and rebuilding of Packard and Sterling marine engines. A small corner of the shop only was allowed for the service of L&H motorcars.

The war years were particularly harsh ones for the company. Both its founders died, Lendrum in the early months of the conflict, Captain Hartman on September 5th, 1942. Hartman's widow immediately took over the business, but there wasn't much of it, even after peace came. From 1946 to 1954, Lendrum & Hartman was prohibited from importing automobiles because of the English war debt and balance of trade problems. The country was bankrupt. Lendrum & Hartman's situation was a virtual mirror image. With the death of Mrs. Hartman in 1958, the business was purchased by the Lex Group. There seemed to be hope for survival.

Incorporated in 1928, Lex Garages had become associated with General Motors in November 1957 through its acquisition of B&C Concessions Ltd. and its associate company, British and Colonial Motors Ltd. Among the B&C interests was the concession for Chevrolet and Oldsmobile in England. Since Lendrum & Hartman held the concessions for both Buick and Cadillac, Lex merged the two firms in the 1960's, later adding Pontiac to the line. After this merger, all automotive business of the firm was operated out of the buildings of Lendrum & Hartman at Albemarle Street.

In 1969 Lex made the decision to concentrate its motorcar interests on a limited number of franchises, domestically British Leyland and Rolls-Royce, with import attention devoted exclusively to the Lex Brooklands Volvo franchise. During the disposal of its other franchises, the Lendrum & Hartman business was sold to several of that company's managers. No longer, however, was the grand Albemarle address theirs. L&H was initially moved out of there to Kings Road, Chelsea, during the Lex period. Today the company is at 122-124 King Street, in Hammersmith, a suburb of West London. Volvo has the magnificent buildings in Albemarle.

Although Lendrum & Hartman still distributes cars and appoints dealers, it is on a much diminished scale. In 1963 sales were more than 2000 units. They are now about a quarter of that annually. There are a mere eight dealers under the concessionaire. Business is more difficult too. A growing number of restrictive regulations imposed by the British Government make it very expensive to import and sell American cars in England. Lights, brake master cylinders, window glass and many other components must be revised to meet the code. If a right-hand-drive conversion is desired by a customer, he must be prepared to pay for the 400 manhours the conversion will now take. Things have changed a lot since the days of the Royal Buicks.

David Norton, England's leading historian on Lendrum & Hartman and Buick in England, often walks past the former L&H service facilities on Old Oak Lane, and even more wistfully along Albemarle Street. He likes to talk of "hallowed ground." Rarely are the British given to overstatement. Among the synonyms for hallowed is revered—the connotation of reverence is "an intrinsic merit and inviolability in the one honored and a corresponding depth of feeling in the one honoring." As an enthusiast and a scholar, that very well defines Dave Norton's recollection of the great days of Lendrum & Hartman. And it does well by the company too. It was an era to be revered.

405

OLDEST BUICKS AND OTHER LORE

THE OLDEST SURVIVING BUICKS

As Buick approached its 90th anniversary (officially 1993), research intensified on two questions that had long puzzled Buick historians and collectors: One, do any of the 37 Buicks built in 1904—the first production Buicks—survive? And, two, whether they do or not, which is the oldest surviving Buick?

A quick review: One experimental Buick was built in Detroit about 1900 by David Dunbar Buick's Buick Auto-Vim and Power Co., and another in 1902-03 by its successor, Buick Manufacturing Co. The company was reorganized as Buick Motor Co. in 1903 and moved to Flint, Michigan, late that year. In 1904, after another reorganization, it began production in Flint with 37 cars—most or all of which were probably the Model B (a few students of Buick history believe some 1904 Buicks were Model Cs). In 1905, production was moved to Jackson, Michigan, and, according to new information, 729 Model C Buicks were built that year (the Model C run ended with 58 produced in 1906).

The earliest 1904 Model B Buicks had two-cylinder engines with pushrods on the bottom, 83-inch wheelbases and a narrow (rather than wide) molding along the front of the hood. The Model C had similar engines but with pushrods on the top, 85- to 87-inch wheelbases (all measured to date have 87) and the wider molding. There are other differences but these are the easiest to see. Some experts claim there were "late" 1904 Model B Buicks with Model C characteristics, and advertisements late that year seem to support this theory. Also, Model Bs were advertised toward the end of 1904 as 1905 models. (Actually,

the Model B was never advertised as a 1904 model.)

The oldest known surviving Buick is a Model C owned by Harold Warp Pioneer Village, a "living" museum in Minden, Nebraska. The car was probably built in April 1905, the second month of production of this model.

While no Model B Buicks are known to exist, the Alfred P. Sloan Museum in Flint, Michigan, has a replica of the first 1904 Flint Buick, a Model B. It was created by using one of two known surviving Model B (pushrods-on-bottom) engines, as well as axles and transmission from a 1905 Model C (one of two Model Cs in the museum's possession) and replica parts. The replica, with no body or fenders, looks exactly like the car in the photos of the July 1904 Flint-Detroit-Flint test run (photos, page 313).

Model C Buicks can be ranked by engine number, frame number and Selden patent number, when available. The earliest models apparently had no frame number (which should be on the rear rail near extreme right) and some other frame numbers are missing—apparently rusted or sandblasted away or painted over. Engine numbers are on the flywheel. The ranking system is uncertain—engines and Selden patent plates can be switched—but you have to start somewhere.

The oldest known surviving Buicks, ranked by engine and Selden number when available:

Rank	Selden	Engine	Frame	Owner
1904 MODEL B				
X-1		(1904)	New	Alfred P. Sloan Museum, Flint, Mich. (replica)
1905 MODEL C				
1.	22935	2873		Harold Warp Pioneer Village, Minden, Neb.
2.		2938		Grant Burns, Costa Mesa, Calif.
3.	26201	3006		Charles Schalebaum, Ridgewood, N.J.
4.		3044		Buick Motor Division, Flint, Mich. (*)
5.			348	Richard I. Braund, Elroy, Wis.
6.		3050	537	Robert Coombes Jr., La Canada, Calif.
7.		3076	562	Alfred P. Sloan Museum (1904 replica parts car)
8.	26253	3081		Nat'l Museum Sci. & Tech., Ottawa, Canada
9.	30667	3359		Imperial Palace Casino, Las Vegas, Nev.
10.		3399	604	Lowell Anderson, Glenham, S.D.
11.	32969	3459	701	J.B. Nethercutt, Sylmar, Calif.
12.		3476	713	Sloan Museum
13.	33105	3555	745	Warwick Eastwood, Pasadena, Calif. (**)
14.	No engine or nos.			Duane Dreesen, Hartington, Neb.

(*)—Flywheel number now 8014 but original number of 3044 recorded.
(**)—Although considered a 1905 Model C, No. 13 was likely built in 1906, at the end of the Model C run.

Oldest known surviving Buick, now in Minden, Nebraska, with former owners Alton Walker and his wife Elizabeth.

Former Imperial Wheel factory in Jackson, Michigan, was the assembly plant for 1905 Model C Buicks. Components were shipped there from Flint.

Note: Production months of the surviving 1905 Model Cs can be estimated based on the following information. In 1951, William G. Gregor of Flint recorded in a letter (to Warwick Eastwood, owner of No. 13) these Model C production totals by month based on factory records available at the time: *1905*: March—38, April—109, May—141, June—78, July—78, August—174, September—31, October—37, November—26, December—17. *1906*: January—17, February—35, March—2, April—3, May—1. Totals: 1905—729. 1906—58. Grand total—787.

Gregor once owned No. 9 and said it was built August 31, 1905. Gregor said his examination of now-missing factory records showed frame numbers were not necessarily used in sequence: "They may have built car number 537 one day, and two or three weeks later, brought in the frame and assembled car number 490." But, in the absence of comment by Gregor, it is believed engines were installed at least roughly in numerical order.

Based on this information and suppositions, these are the likely production months of the surviving Model C Buicks: No. 1—4/1905. Nos. 2 and 3—5/05. Nos. 4-8—6/05. No. 9—8/31/05. No. 10—11-/05. Nos. 11 and 12—12/05. No. 13—2-5/06. *Note*: Among those who believe Model Cs were built in 1904 is Greg Fauth, a student of Buick history who, among other evidence, cites a brief history of Buick written in the 1920s by Harley J. McKinney, a Buick advertising man in that era. McKinney wrote: "The first Buick type cars manufactured were the models 'B' and 'C.' A few of the 'B' models were constructed for test and experiment purposes, and the model 'C' was this company's first product offered for sale to the public. The first year's production of the model 'C' totaled 37 cars." Yet McKinney was not always accurate and there is evidence to contradict those statements. The Model B shows up for 1904 in the first Buick catalog and on all official lists. Also, the first Buick ads, late in 1904, are for a "1905 Model B," indicating the Model B was being sold late in 1904 and possibly into the new year.

NOTES ON OWNERSHIP:

No. 1—Probably built in April 1905, the second month of production. Collector Alton H. Walker of Pebble Beach, California, bought it from a Mr. Riley of Los Altos, California in about 1946. Warwick Eastwood, owner of No. 13, said Walker used parts of No. 6 to improve No. 1. Walker once wrote that he owned five Model Cs over the years. One seems to have disappeared, its parts probably used to restore others. The red No. 1, with bright brass and cape cart top, was bought by the Harold Warp Pioneer Village museum in Minden,

Nebraska, from Walker for $3,500 on October 3, 1957. It is on permanent display at the museum. The car is said to have no frame number (a reported chassis number is probably only a part number).

No. 2—Probably built in May 1905. It was said to have been the first Buick sold by the Buick agency in Denver, Colorado, and then bought back and owned by the agency for many years until it went out of business. Richard Williams of Garden Grove, California, bought it from Harold Cohan of Denver Buick in April 1971 and Grant Burns of Costa Mesa, California, bought it from Williams in May 1976.

No. 3—Probably built in May 1905. This is an unusual two-seater with a downward sloping rear deck that may have been added later. It once had a painted inscription on the hood: "Oldest car, oldest driver in Concord, N.H." William Pollock of Pottstown, Pennsylvania, bought it and restored it around 1957. The blue car was sold twice in 1991.

No. 4—Probably built in June 1905. Through the decades, this car has likely had more publicity than any other Model C. A photo of it, painted a light color, appeared in *The Buick Bulletin* in 1919, with an article describing it as the first Buick sold on the Pacific Coast. Charles S. Howard, early Buick distributor in California, sold it in 1905 to a Dr. A.J. Villain and later bought it back, displaying it as an antique at car shows even before 1919, according to the article. A photo exists of the car in a parade in the Twenties or Thirties. Howard's Model C was entered in antique car races in the Thirties. Buick Motor Division owns trophies it won July 4, 1935 (the Shell Oil Co. Trophy), in an "antiquated car race" as part of a San Francisco citizens celebration, and on July 10, 1936, where it went 25 laps, or 5 miles, in 10 minutes and 8/10ths seconds, at San Francisco Speedway, both years entered by the Howard Motor Company, and driven by George H. Hoadley. In those years it was painted a dark color and had a brass (and incorrect) "1904" brass inscription which remained on its radiator cover until recently. Alton Walker bought it in 1970 from Charles S. Howard III and sold it to Ernest and Ted Faggart, owners of the Faggart Buick dealership in Porterville, California, in 1978. There's a metal license plate on the dashboard, issued by Oakland, California, with a number of 98 and date of January 1, 1905 (but the 5 appears to be a strikeover of 6). The Faggarts concentrated on a major mechanical restoration and painted the car maroon with black fenders. As a result of this research on the earliest Buicks, and after the car was carefully inspected by Warwick Eastwood, Greg Fauth and the writer (Gustin), Buick Motor Division bought it from the Faggart family in November 1991 and displays it in the lobby of Buick headquarters in

Above: Grant Burns (behind car) with the second oldest known Buick. Below: Two-place Model C, No. 3 on list, before Pollock restoration. Bottom: No. 6 on list, before and after (bottom right) restoration and conversion to two-seater by Warwick Eastwood.

Above: No. 4 on list, now owned by Buick, shown here in 1991 in Porterville, California, with (from left) then-owners Ted Faggart and his father Ernest, and expert inspectors Warwick Eastwood and Greg Fauth.

1905 Buick,

Flint. It is the Model C pictured in this book's color section.

No. 5—Probably built in June 1905, was previously owned by Clifford Beauchamp of Waukegon, Illinois, whose name showed up in old lists. Richard I. Braund, retired Army National Guard brigadier general, has owned the car for several decades. It is in restoration. Braund confirms it has no engine number (the engine was extensively restored) but there is no recent confirmation of the frame number. This car has the original cape cart top. Braund has made sketches of the original stripes—"quite elaborate," he says—on both the body and chassis to help other restorers.

No. 6—Probably built in June 1905, was in a deteriorated condition when Warwick and Douglas Eastwood bought it from Alton Walker. The Eastwoods changed it to a two-seater during a major restoration and painted it red before selling it to the Coombes family. The 1905 transmission is now on a 1908 Model F owned by Coombes and the 1908 transmission is on the 1905. The Eastwoods were not sure how the rear of a two-seater should look so they used the 1906 Model G rear end as a guide.

No. 7—Probably built in June 1905, was originally owned by Fred A. Aldrich, an early executive with the Durant-Dort Carriage Co. of Flint and close associate of Billy Durant, founder of General Motors. It was later owned by early Flint Buick dealer Ed Lunt. Before Lunt got it, the car had weathered outside for a number of years and it was restored with many "wrong" pieces, some collectors say. Its transmission and axles are now on the Sloan Museum's Model B replica and the engine is displayed separately.

No. 8—Probably built in June 1905, is now owned by the National Museum of Science and Technology in Ottawa, Ontario, Canada. It was previously owned by E. Murray Billings, an Ontario car dealer whose family had it many years, and Ron Fawcett, a car restorer near Oshawa, Ontario, who restored it for him. Billings, who went to some lengths to try to prove the car was a 1904 or even a 1903, once reported that the Ontario license plate (No. 332), that was with the car when his family bought it, was issued in 1904. But, despite his claims, it looks like a 1905 car.

No. 9—The complete ownership record of this car is recorded. It was said to have been built August 31, 1905 (onetime owner William Gregor had access to now-missing factory records). Buick Chief Engineer Walter Marr (who built the first Buicks) personally drove it to Detroit. It was delivered to Ohio Auto Sales in Cleveland and sold to a Mr. Dickerman, principal of the Cleveland high school. Three years later it was traded back to Ohio Auto Sales and sold to W.J. Mack of Butler, Indiana, for $450. Mack is said to have become the third person in Butler to own a "gas buggy" and drove it in the summers of 1908 and 1909. Then he rolled it into his bicycle repair shop, jacked up the wheels, covered it with a tarpaulin and let it sit for 40 years. Bill Gregor of Flint heard of the car and eventually persuaded Mack to part with it and Gregor's wife wrote a check for it.

It was then said to be in great shape. It was later sold to Dr. C.L. Bowers of the Detroit area and then to Jack Skaff of Flint. Now restored (to the chagrin of some collectors who saw it as the best original-condition Model C), it is displayed at the Imperial Palace Casino's Automotive Collection in Las Vegas, billed as the "world's oldest known Buick" (which it now apparently isn't).

No. 10—Probably built in October 1905, was the first car owned by Lowell Anderson's grandfather, Gerhard Anderson, before 1920, and for a time its engine was used to power a mill. Reportedly the cowl served as the roof of a chicken coop. Lowell Anderson's father, Palmer, put the car back together again in the early Fifties. The body had been stored but not all the parts could be found. Other collectors say it now has some 1906 or 1907 parts. Anderson, who also has about 60 tractors, said he keeps the car in a barn as a sentimental family heirloom.

No. 11—Probably built in December 1905, is another car once owned by Alton Walker. He bought it from Lena Lentz, widow of John Lentz. In a 1980 letter, Walker said: "I bought one supposed to be a 1904 but when it arrived it was a 1905 and I sold it to Jack Nethercutt and he is restoring it at Sylmar, California." It is part of a large Nethercutt collection of antique cars and is now well restored in the original royal blue.

No. 12—Probably built in December 1905, but possibly a 1906 car, was once owned by Charlie Chayne, former Buick chief engineer. Bill Gregor's 1951 letter quoted previously said Chayne "recently acquired it from a Buick dealer down East." It was donated to the Sloan Museum in the Sixties.

No. 13—Certainly built in 1906 and one of the last Model Cs produced, was bought in 1942 by Warwick Eastwood from Addie C. Johnson of Santa Monica, California, said to be a member of the family that originally owned it. It is beautifully restored and its photo was on the cover of the January 1991 *Buick Bugle*, magazine of the Buick Club of America.

No. 14—which has no identifying numbers or engine, was bought years ago from an Anderson family (no relation to the South Dakota Andersons) in Bristow, Nebraska, which bought it used in 1909. Current owner Duane Dreesen said the engine had blown and the flywheel (with the engine number) could not be found. It also has no transmission. Dreesen plans to restore it, using the original frame, axles, rear seat and miscellaneous original parts. He bought some 1906 parts from Palmer Anderson. Dreesen said he believes the remains of the engine he saw indicate the pushrods were on the top, as are all known Model C engines.

Publication of information similar to the above in the *Buick Bugle* in December 1991 did not result in discovery of any Model B or any more Model C Buicks. Two other Model Cs show up on some lists but a knowledgeable collector said one is a "replica" and, in the other case, the original rear seat of No. 6 is on a 1909 parts chassis owned by another collector. An early Buick, on some lists called a Model B, showed up in old lists as owned by Frankie Watts in Hendersonville, North Carolina, but has not surfaced recently. A Model C is rumored to be in Sweden but an antique Buick in a Stockholm museum has a flywheel number of 10684 and is probably a Model 10. A rumored Model C in Pennsylvania turned out not to be a Model C.

Note on Selden patent license numbers: Thomas Reese, considered an expert on Selden numbers, says numbers starting in the 22000 period "are consistent with 1905" although at least one 1905 Olds has a number of around 20000. Buick joined the Association of Licensed Automobile Manufacturers in November or December 1904, and probably began purchasing Selden licenses for its cars around them.

Information on the above is based on personal research (Gustin) and conversations and correspondence with owners as well as information from Greg Fauth, Jack Skaff, Terry Dunham, Ron Fawcett, Charles Hulse, Jim Johnson, Richard Scharchburg, Joe Kulcsar and Tom Reese, among others.

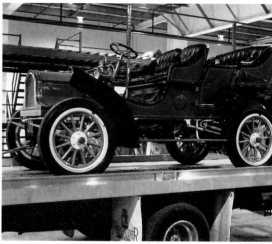

All other known surviving 1905 Model Cs: From left (top row) No. 5 before restoration started (now owned by Richard Braund), No. 7 before parts were used for the Sloan Museum replica, No. 8 in Canada, (middle row) No. 9 with onetime owner Bill Gregor (standing) and Buick Assistant General Sales Manager Robert Rudd, No. 10 on parade with Palmer Anderson in the front seat, beautifully restored No. 11 owned by Nethercutt, (bottom row) No. 12 at Sloan, No. 13 owned by Eastwood, No. 14 many years ago.

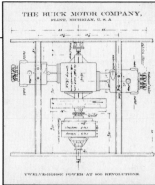

WILLIAM BEACRAFT, ENGINE BUILDER FOR BUICK

The photo above, showing production of Buick engines in the West Kearsley Street plant, dated 1904, has special historical interest. William Beacraft, Buick's first engine plant manager, is in the right foreground with the big mustache. He is working on a pushrods-on-top engine while the engine directly behind him has pushrods on the bottom.

The first Model Bs of 1904 had pushrods on the bottom and, sometime during 1904, the engine configuration changed. This photo apparently documents engine production in transition.

The 1922 *Buick Bulletin* published a feature article on Beacraft, described as "the dean of Valve-in-Head motor builders." It noted that when he took charge of Buick motor assembly, there were only 25 men in the shop. His first step on joining Buick was to acquaint himself with every detail of the motor, so he tore down one of the engines, inspected it carefully, and then reassembled it. He added that while he came to Flint to take charge of the department, he really assembled every engine himself, working alone because it was almost impossible to find skilled men.

Early pushrods-on-bottom Buick engine (top right).
Early Model B in 1904 photo (above).

BUICK'S RICH ADVERTISING HISTORY

For the record, Buick handled its own advertising from the beginning until 1915. Since then, there have been five agencies: Taylor-Critchfield (1915-18), Carl M. Greene (1919), Campbell-Ewald (1920-35), Kudner Advertising (1935-57) and McCann-Erickson (starting 1958).

Buick's most famous early advertising slogan can be traced to a paragraph in the 1911 Buick catalog: "We build nothing but high-grade automobiles, and when better automobiles are made, Buick will build them." A letter exists, dated September 5, 1912, from F.W.A. Vesper, then Buick assistant general sales manager, to Buick's law firm, Carton & Bray, advising that "we desire to have our slogan, 'When better automobiles are built, Buick will build them,' copyrighted if at all possible." Vesper is usually credited for the slogan.

In light of more recent events, an interesting ad surfaced from the Twenties, headlined "Buick carries the desert mail." It starts: "Oil discovered in Irak! Overnight sleepy Bagdad became a feverish center of commerce . . . a new way, and a shorter one, had to be found to carry passengers and mail to Bagdad." It explains how the British

Navy and Nairn Transport Co. used a fleet of Buicks on an abandoned 500-mile camel trail from Beirut and quotes an army officer praising Buick's high speed "for hours on end" and "power to carry excessive weight over two ranges of mountains and the desert, without overheating. Our cars go to Bagdad and back again, 1000 miles, without adding a drop of water to the radiator."

In the Twenties, Harley J. McKinney, Buick advertising man and archivist, discussed Buick advertising philosophy in his brief history of the company: "The policy behind all Buick advertising is to tell the simple truth about Buick cars . . . if we can get the truth about Buick cars properly before (people) our manufacturing facilities will never be great enough to supply the demand. Buick advertising is never sensational [he didn't anticipate Art Kudner!] and exaggeration is frowned upon as a matter of good business policy . . . ."

And any discussion of Buick advertising would include mention of some great theme music, including "The Great American Road Belongs to Buick." But for those whose memories go back to television of the Fifties, the advertising song, "My Buick, My Love and I," written by Frank Skinner and Jack Brooks, is recalled: *How I love to drive my Buick/ with my love sitting by my side./ Pretty girl and shiny Buick,/ fills a fella with so much pride./ Driving down the road on Sunday/ with my car and my heart riding high,/ for I know very soon/ we'll take a honeymoon/ my Buick, my love and I.*

MOSCOW MOTORSPORTS

Researchers in Buick's archives were puzzled to find unidentified photos dated 1925 that showed Buicks in Russia, including one being cheered in Moscow's Red Square (page 126). Lawrence R. Gustin, then editor of *Inside Buick* magazine, sent the photos to a Moscow address suggested by the Soviet Union's embassy in Washington. Months later, a thick packet arrived from S. Ushakov, secretary of the Federation of Automobile Sports of the Soviet Union. It contained detailed information on the 1925 National Test Motor Run, a government-run endurance test of 78 cars from around the world, including 42 from the United States. The Russian run was 3,090 miles, 48 percent on earth roads, 44 percent on macadam, eight percent on mountain roads, on a route from Leningrad to Moscow.

Five Buicks, probably Model 55s with "touring type" bodies, were entered. One, driven by an American driver named Levstrem, "left the run for some reason and there is no information about it." Another was a judge's car. But the others did extremely well. One, No. 37 driven by a Russian, Solomatin, won first prize of the State Trade Committee, a silver bowl with cups covered with enamel, "for the totality of abilities," which would appear to be the top overall award. Another, No. 40 driven by an American named Fatter, received the Organizing Committee's prize, a notebook with silver board, "for endurance and strong construction." And No. 38, the car photographed in Red Square, won the prize of the Ministry of Communication Means, a silver tea set, "for dynamic." The car, driven by a Russian, Kuznetsov, on a one-kilometer (0.62 mile) course on the Vladimirskoe motor road near Moscow, was clocked in 71.85 km/h (44.5 mph) from a standing start and 99.8 km/h (61.8 mph) from a running start.

After an article was published about all this, former Buick executive John Burnside found a letter dated January 27, 1926, from J.D. Mooney, president of GM Export, to Buick President Harry H. Bassett. Mooney noted that Buick won four of the five prizes it was possible for a car of its rating to obtain, including the government prize for general excellence, first prize in its class for economy, first prize in the speed trial from a flying start and first prize in the speed trial from a dead start. "Conditions in Russia up to a year or less ago have been, as you know, hardly of a nature to encourage the development of the automobile business, particularly on the part of foreign countries," Mooney wrote. He told Bassett the "remarkable showing" might pres-

Ad boasts of Russian triumphs; sheet music boasts of Buick Speed.

ent "an opening." While that turned out to be overly optimistic, the victories in Russia should have been remembered as a notable moment in Buick history. Instead they would have been forgotten had not some unidentified photos been found in an obscure file.

BUICK IN POPULAR CULTURE

As Buick Advertising Director Jay Qualman points out, Buick is mentioned an uncommon amount of the time in books, articles, movies and cartoons instead of "car" or "big car." Just a few examples: Woody Allen, in *Annie Hall*: " There's a spider in the bathroom the size of a Buick." Gary Shandling on television: "My father would hide in the woods and hit deer with his Buick. He'd use the gun sight on his hood to line 'em up." A Gary Larson cartoon: "Hey! Ernie Wagner! I haven't seen you in, what's it been—20 years? And hey—you've still got that thing growing outta your head that looks like a Buick!" Comedian Jay Leno has used whole skits about his vintage Roadmaster, with lines about cleaning Toyotas out of the wheel wells. Back around 1910, there was a song, "I Love My Horse and Wagon, But Oh! You Buick Car," with music by Bernie Adler and words by Victor H. Smalley, and with photos of race drivers Louis Chevrolet, Lewis Strang and Wild Bob Burman on the sheet music cover. Recently, Buicks have been featured in rock videos, in song titles ("Aliens Ate My Buick") and even in the names of bands (acknowledged Buick "nut" Arlen Roth named his band "the Roadmasters"). The list goes on.

SUNKEN TREASURE

During World War I, Buick built 1,320 of the 20,478 V-12 Liberty engines produced for aircraft (the others were built by Hall-Scott and Packard). But several other Liberty configurations were produced: two with 4 cylinders, 52 with 6 cylinders and 15 with 8 cylinders. All 15 V-8s were built by Buick in Flint. One somehow was obtained by a Harry N. Snavely and mounted in a mahogany speedboat named Liberty the Second. Reportedly, it once set a world record of more than 70 mph and was once clocked unofficially at 78 mph.

In racing trails on Conneaut Lake in Pennsylvania on September 2, 1922, Liberty the Second was running at 58 mph when it suddenly rolled over and sank, with Snavely and his mechanic escaping without injury. Despite attempts to recover it, Liberty the Second remained on the bottom for nearly 63 years—until its recovery in 1985 by divers William Houghton, a funeral director, and Brian Simpson, a Pennsylvania state trooper. The recovery of the 20-foot boat and its Buick Liberty engine was a local sensation. Both were in good condition. One expert said the engine "looks as if it could run right now." The engine was reassembled and brought back to life by Gary Worthington, engineer and ex-aircraft mechanic, working with Roy Palmer, a retired aircraft maintenance supervisor, and the hull was restored by Runabout Restorations near Lake Fenton, a few miles from Flint. Plans were made by a foundation to display the boat and its Buick engine at a museum at Conneaut Lake.

Liberty the Second brought to the surface after 63 years at the bottom of Conneaut Lake in Pennsylvania, and its Buick engine after restoration.

COLLECTING

The hobby requires separate volumes. There are many references, including *Seventy Years of Buick*, George H. Dammann, Crestline Publishing; *Buick Buyer's Guide*, (Cars from 1946), Richard M. Langworth, Motorbooks International; *Guide to Buick Gran Sports* and *Guide to Buick Grand National, T-Type and GNX*, both by Steven L. Dove, 1928 Sherwood Forest, Houston, Texas, 77043. Microfilm of old Buick shop manuals may be obtained from GM Photographic, Micrographics Department, P.O. Box 1449, Warren, Michigan 48090, for a fee. Other addresses: Buick Club of America, P.O. Box 898, Garden Grove, California 92642. Alfred P. Sloan Museum, 1221 E. Kearsley Street, Flint, Michigan 48503. Richard Scharchburg, GMI Alumni Historical Collection, 1700 W. Third Avenue, Flint, Michigan 48502. Ray Knott, Riviera Owners Association, P.O. Box 26344, Lakewood, Colorado 80226. Lawrence R. Gustin, Buick Public Relations, 902 E. Hamilton Avenue, Flint, Michigan 48550 (co-author of this book and author of *Billy Durant: Creator of General Motors*.)

COLLECTING GRAN SPORTS

Some Buicks have attracted unusual collector interest over the years, notably 1953 and 1954 Skylarks, many Rivieras including 1983-'85 Riviera convertibles, all Regal Grand Nationals and GNXs and now Reattas, particularly convertibles. Of particular interest are Gran Sports of the Sixties and Seventies.

From 1965 to 1975, Buick produced more than 140,000 Gran Sport models. They were part of the Skylark and Special series from 1965 to 1967 and on the GM B-body from 1968 to 1972. From 1973 to 1975, the Gran Sport models became an option package on Century.

In 1967, '68 and '69, Buick offered the California GS, a high-styled coupe designed exclusively for the California market. It was patterned after the GS400, which had a 400 cubic inch V-8. The California GS had a 340 V-8. More than 9,000 of the California models were produced in those three years.

A Stage 1 package was offered in 1969 through 1972 that provided a modified 400 cubic inch V-8 with 350 horsepower, high-lift cam, positive traction rear axle and dual exhaust system.

In addition to Buick Gran Sport models, 44,523 Gran Sport versions of the Riviera were produced from 1965 to 1975. By year, 3,355 Riviera Gran Sports were produced in 1965; 5,718 in 1966; 4,837 in 1967; 5,337 in 1968; 5,272 in 1969; 3,505 in 1970; 3,175 in 1971; 2,171 in 1972; 3,933 in 1973, 4,119 in 1974; and 3,101 in 1975.

Interested in Gran Sports? Talk to Richard Lasseter, founder and president of the 4,800-member Buick GS Club of America, 1213 Gornto Rd., Valdosta, GA 31602.

Former Buick and GM executives reunited in 1926: Walter Chrysler (at left), Charles Nash (fourth), Alfred Sloan (sixth), William Durant and Ransom Olds (at right).

BUICK EXECUTIVES

PRESIDENTS AND GENERAL MANAGERS

1899 - 9/10/03	David Dunbar Buick (Ben Briscoe financial backer May-September 1903. David Buick stayed with the company in other positions until 1908).
9/10/03 - 11/26/04	James H. Whiting (formally president 1/19/04; William C. Durant actually in charge from 11/1/04 until late 1910).
11/26/04 - 11/3/08	Charles M. Begole (ending date questionable. One GM list places William M. Eaton as Buick president starting 11/3/05. Eaton was placed by Durant in GM presidency in October, 1908).
11/3/08 - 12/13/10	William M. Eaton (see note above)
12/13/10 - 2/16/11	Charles W. Nash (acting president)
2/16/11 - 12/10/12	Thomas Neal (as president, GM. Nash still headed Buick)
12/10/12 - 6/1/16	Charles W. Nash (as president, GM. Walter P. Chrysler headed Buick)
6/7/16 - 1/13/20	Walter P. Chrysler, president (During a reorganization in 1917, William C. Durant, who returned to GM as president 6/1/16, was formally elected president of Buick, serving one hour and resigning. Chrysler was again elected president)
1/13/20 - 10/16/26	Harry H. Bassett, president (died in office)
11/20/26 - 4/1/32	Edward T. Strong, president
4/1/32 - 10/23/33	Irving J. Reuter, president (under temporary Buick-Olds-Pontiac)

Those below had title of general manager:

10/23/33 - 11/1/48	Harlow H. Curtice
11/1/48 - 3/5/56	Ivan L. Wiles
3/5/56 - 4/30/59	Edward T. Ragsdale
5/1/59 - 6/30/65	Edward D. Rollert
7/1/65 - 3/31/69	Robert L. Kessler
4/1/69 - 12/31/72	Lee N. Mays
1/1/73 - 9/30/75	George R. Elges
10/1/75 - 11/3/78	David C. Collier
11/6/78 - 11/30/80	Donald H. McPherson
12/1/80 - 1/9/84	Lloyd E. Reuss
1/10/84 - 7/31/86	Donald E. Hackworth
8/1/86 -	Edward H. Mertz

CHIEF ENGINEERS

1904 - 1914	Walter L. Marr (Also several times 1900- 1903; departure year is approximate).
1914 - 1929	Enos A. DeWaters
1929 - 1936	Ferdinand A. Bower
1936 - 1951	Charles A. Chayne
1951 - 1957	Verner P. Mathews
1957 - 1959	Oliver K. Kelley
1959 - 1968	Lowell A. Kintigh
1968 - 1975	Phillip C. Bowser
1975 - 1978	Lloyd E. Reuss
1978 - 1981	Robert J. Schultz
1981 - 1984	Edward H. Mertz
1984 - 1989	David S. Sharpe
1989 -	Anthony H. Derhake

GENERAL SALES MANAGERS

1904 - 1906	Charles Van Horne
1906 - 1910	Harry E. Shiland
1910 - 1916	Richard H. Collins

(Above based on published articles. William C. Durant later wrote that he set up the Buick sales organization in Boston, delegating Bill Meade as his chief of staff. While not carrying the title, Durant was effectively heading Buick sales from 1904 to 1910).

6/1/16 - 5/1/21	Edward T. Strong
5/1/21 - 4/1/32	C. W. Churchill (In the Depression, sales operations were directed by William Bless, Buick-Olds-Pontiac sales manager).
11/1/33 - 10/31/48	William F. Hufstader
11/1/48 - 6/1/50	Otis L. Waller
6/1/50 - 8/30/57	Albert H. Belfie
8/30/57 - 1/1/61	Edward C. Kennard
2/1/61 - 10/31/68	Roland S. Withers
11/1/68 - 12/31/73	O. Franklin Frost
1/1/74 - 4/30/77	Robert D. Burger
5/1/77 - 3/31/82	John D. Duffy Jr.
4/1/82 - 9/18/84	Jim Perkins
10/1/84 - 8/1/87	William J. Atkinson
7/24/87 -	Robert E. Coletta

Appendix Eight

THE BUICK PRODUCTION RECORD

	UNITED STATES CALENDAR YEAR	U.S. MODEL YEAR EXPORTED UNITS	PRODUCTION IN CANADA MODEL YEAR	CALENDAR YEAR
1904	37	—	—	—
1905	750	—	—	—
1906	1,400	—	—	—
1907	4,641	—	—	—
1908	8,820	—	154	—
1909	14,606	—	423	—
1910	30,525	—	847	—
1911	13,389	—	962	—
1912	19,812	—	967	—
1913	26,666	—	881	—
1914	32,889	1,783	1,098	—
1915	43,946	1,865	1,012	—
1916	124,834	7,736	2,859	—
1917	115,267	2,806	3,418	—
1918	77,691	4,672	6,317	—
1919	119,310	2,771	6,654	—
1920	115,176	8,700	6,499	—
1921	82,930	1,614	4,100	—
1922	123,152	563	15,690	—
1923	201,572	148	17,255	—
1924	160,411	7,607	10,684	—
1925	192,100	9,575	11,464	—
1926	266,753	8,050	12,344	—
1927	255,160	8,714	14,042	—
1928	221,758	5,780	10,986	—
1929	196,104	8,932	7,131	—
1930	119,265	8,651	4,603	—
1931	88,417	2,366	3,582	—
1932	41,522	636	2,026	—
1933	40,620	412	2,382	—
1934	78,757	7,328	4,091	—
1935	107,611	4,825	3,272	—
1936	179,533	10,720	4,722	—
1937	227,038	13,954	6,880	—
1938	173,905	12,156	5,081	—
1939	231,219	10,478	4,673	—
1940	310,995	7,934	4,477	—
1941	316,251	7,199	3,098	—
1942	16,601	2,274	211	—
1945	2,482	—	—	—
1946	156,080	9,070	—	—
1947	267,830	16,491	—	—
1948	275,503	14,456	—	—
1949	398,482	10,211	—	—
1950	552,827	—	—	—
1951	404,695	—	11,148	—
1952	321,048	—	6,940	—
1953	485,353	—	9,303	9,470
1954	531,463	—	13,846	15,564
1955	781,296	—	23,762	21,877
1956	535,364	—	14,738	19,799
1957	407,283	—	15,884	14,870
1958	257,124	—	12,465	14,163
1959	232,579	—	11,742	9,187
1960	307,804	—	9,279	9,336
1961	291,285	—	7,096	7,480
1962	415,892	—	8,648	9,252
1963	479,399	—	11,373	14,383
1964	482,731	—	19,629	15,782
1965	653,838	—	19,095	23,437
1966	580,421	—	23,014	17,819
1967	573,866	—	7,462	15,664[1]
1968	652,049	—	32,784[2]	46,405[3]
1969	713,832	—	61,846	37,896
1970	459,931	—	792	480
1971	751,885	—	480	936
1972	688,557	—	552	—
1973	826,206	—	—	—
1974	400,262	—	—	11,083
1975	535,820	—	35,171	29,449
1976	817,669	—	24,053	27,666
1977	801,202	—	32,388	23,414
1978	810,350	—	7,970	12,002
1979	787,123	—	7,200	3,168

	U.S. CALENDAR YEAR	U.S. MODEL YEAR
1980	783,575	854,011
1981	839,966	856,996
1982	751,332	739,984
1983	905,608	808,416
1984	987,833	987,980

	NORTH AMERICAN CALENDAR YEAR	NORTH AMERICAN MODEL YEAR
1985	1,001,461	1,002,906
1986	775,966	850,103
1987	538,863	648,687
1988	583,526	578,128
1989	556,186	598,234
1990	516,607	527,671
1991	601,383	560,244

[1] with 6,523 units to United States

[2] with 21,830 units to United States

[3] with 32,282 units to United States

The model year figures which follow were compiled from official Buick records. Model designations and terminology are as used by Buick in its data sheets for each year. An "X" in a model designation through 1949 indicates that the car or chassis was exported.

YEAR/MODEL/DESCRIPTION	MODEL
Passenger capacity in parentheses	UNITS

1904 *
Model B - Touring (5)	37

1905 *
Model C - Touring (5)	750

1906 *
Model F - Touring (5)	1,207
Model G - Runabout (2)	193
	1,400

1907
Model D - Touring (5)	523
Model F - Touring (5)	3,465
Model G - Runabout (2)	535
Model H - Touring (5)	36
Model K - Runabout (2)	13
Model S - Runabout (2)	69
	4,641

1908
Model D - Touring (5)	543
Model F - Touring (5)	3,281
Model G - Runabout (2)	219
Model S - Runabout (2)	373
Model 5 - Touring (5)	402
Model 10 - Runabout (3)	4,002
	8,820

1909
Model F - Touring (5)	3,856
Model G - Runabout (2)	144
Model 6A - Roadster (2)	6
Model 10 - Runabout (3)	8,100
Model 16 - Roadster (2)	497
Model 17 - Touring (5)	2,003
	14,606

1910
Model F - Touring (5)	4,000
Model 2A - Truck	1,098
Model 7A - Touring (7)	85
Model 10 - Runabout (3), Surrey (4), Toy Tonneau (4)	11,000
Model 14 - Roadster (2)	2,048
Model 16 - Roadster (2), Surrey (4), Toy Tonneau (4)	2,252
Model 17 - Touring (5)	6,002
Model 19 - Touring (5)	4,000
Model 41 - Limousine (5)	40
	30,525

1911
Model 2A - Truck	902
Model 14 - Roadster (2)	1,252
Model 21 - Touring (5)	3,000
Model 26 - Runabout (2)	1,000
Model 27 - Touring (5)	3,000
Model 32 - Roadster (2)	1,150
Model 33 - Touring (5)	2,000
Model 38 - Roadster (2)	153
Model 39 - Touring (5)	905
Model 41 - Limousine (5)	27
	13,389

1912
Model 2A - Truck	761
Model 28 - Roadster (2), Roadster (4)	2,500
Model 29 - Touring (5)	6,000
Model 34 - Roadster (2)	1,400
Model 35 - Touring (5)	6,050
Model 36 - Roadster (2)	1,600
Model 43 - Touring (5)	1,501
	19,812

1913
Model 3 - Truck	199
Model 4 - Truck	461
Model 24 - Roadster (2)	2,850
Model 25 - Touring (5)	8,150
Model 30 - Roadster (2)	3,500
Model 31 - Touring (5)	10,000
Model 40 - Touring (5)	1,506
	26,666

1914
Model 3 - Truck	101
Model 4 - Truck	738
Model B-24 - Roadster (2)	3,126
Model BX-24 - Roadster (2)	239
Model B-25 - Touring (5)	13,446
Model BX-25 - Touring (5)	1,544
Model B-36 - Roadster (2)	2,550
Model B-37 - Touring (5)	9,050
Model B-38 - Roadster (2)	50
Model B-55 - Touring (7)	2,045
	32,889

1915
Model C-4 - Truck	645
Model CX-4 - Truck	748
Model C-24 - Roadster (2)	3,256
Model CX-24 - Roadster (2)	186
Model C-25 - Touring (5)	19,080
Model CX-25 - Touring (5)	931
Model C-36 - Roadster (2)	2,849
Model C-37 - Touring (5)	12,450
Model C-54 - Roadster (2)	352
Model C-55 - Touring (7)	3,449
	43,946

1916
Model D-4 - Truck	1,152
Model DX-4 - Truck	1,347
Model D-34 - Roadster (2)	1,768
Model DX-34 - Roadster (2)	163
Model D-35 - Touring (5)	13,969
Model DX-35 - Touring (5)	944
Model D-44 - Roadster (2)	12,978
Model DX-44 - Roadster (2)	541
Model D-45 - Touring (5)	73,827
Model DX-45 - Touring (5)	4,741
Model D-46 - Coupe (3)	1,443
Model D-47 - Sedan (5)	881
Model D-54 - Roadster (2)	1,194
Model D-55 - Touring (7)	9,886
	124,834

1917
Model D-34 - Roadster (2)	2,292
Model DX-34 - Roadster (2)	238
Model D-35 - Touring (5)	20,126
Model DX-35 - Touring (5)	1,097
Model D-44 - Roadster (2)	4,366
Model DX-44 - Roadster (2)	100
Model D-45 - Touring (5)	25,371
Model DX-45 - Touring (5)	1,371
Model D-46 - Coupe (3)	485
Model D-47 - Sedan (5)	132
	55,578

1918
Model E-4 - Light Delivery Truck	2,410
Model E-34 - Roadster (2)	3,800
Model EX-34 - Roadster (2)	172
Model E-35 - Touring (5)	27,125
Model EX-35 - Touring (5)	1,190
Model E-37 - Sedan (5)	700
Model E-44 - Roadster (3)	10,391
Model EX-44 - Roadster (3)	275
Model E-45 - Touring (5)	58,971
Model EX-45 - Touring (5)	3,035
Model E-46 - Coupe (4)	2,965
Model E-47 - Sedan (5)	463
Model E-49 - Touring (7)	16,148
Model E-50 - Sedan (7)	987
	128,632

1919
Model H-44 - Roadster (2)	7,839
Model HX-44 - Roadster (2)	176
Model H-45 - Touring (5)	44,589
Model HX-45 - Touring (5)	2,595
Model H-46 - Coupe (4)	2,971
Model H-47 - Sedan (5)	501
Model H-49 - Touring (7)	6,795
Model H-50 - Sedan (7)	531
	65,997

1920
Model K-44 - Roadster (3)	19,000
Model KX-44 - Roadster (3)	200
Model K-45 - Touring (5)	85,245
Model KX-45 - Touring (5)	7,400
Model K-46 - Coupe (4)	6,503
Model K-47 - Sedan (5)	2,252
Model K-49 - Touring (7)	16,801
Model KX-49 - Touring (7)	1,100
Model K-50 - Sedan (7)	1,499
	140,000

1921
Model 21-44 - Roadster (3)	7,236
Model 21-X44 - Roadster (3)	56
Model 21-45 - Touring (5)	31,877
Model 21-X45 - Touring (5)	1,192
Model 21-46 - Coupe (4)	4,063
Model 21-47 - Sedan (5)	3,621

417

* - See bottom right corner of page 431 for a more detailed explanation of early Buick production.

Model 21-48 - Coupe (4)	2,606
Model 21-49 - Touring (7)	6,429
Model 21-X49 - Touring (7)	366
Model 21-50 - Sedan (7)	1,460
	58,906

1922

Model 22-4SD - Light Delivery Truck	403
Model 22-34 - Roadster (2)	5,583
Model 22-X34 - Roadster (2)	5
Model 22-35 - Touring (5)	22,521
Model 22-X35 - Touring (5)	29
Model 22-36 - Coupe (3)	2,225
Model 22-37 - Sedan (5)	3,118
Model 22-44 - Roadster (3)	7,666
Model 22-X44 - Roadster (3)	9
Model 22-45 - Touring (5)	34,433
Model 22-X45 - Touring (5)	449
Model 22-46 - Coupe (4)	2,293
Model 22-47 - Sedan (5)	4,878
Model 22-48 - Coupe (4)	8,903
Model 22-49 - Touring (7)	6,714
Model 22-X49 - Touring (7)	71
Model 22-50 - Sedan (7)	4,201
Model 22-50L - Limousine (7)	178
Model 22-54 - Sport Roadster (3)	2,562
Model 22-55 - Sport Touring (4)	900
	107,141

1923

Model 23-4SD - Special Delivery Truck	2,740
Model 23-34 - Roadster (2)	5,768
Model 23X-34 - Roadster (2)	8
Model 23-35 - Touring (5)	36,935
Model 23-X35 - Touring (5)	63
Model 23-36 - Coupe (3)	7,004
Model 23-37 - Sedan (5)	8,885
Model 23-X37 - Sedan (5)	1
Model 23-38 - Touring Sedan (5)	6,025
Model 23-39 - Sport Roadster (2)	1,971
Model 23-41 - Touring Sedan (5)	8,719
Model 23-44 - Roadster (2)	6,488
Model 23-X44 - Roadster (2)	3
Model 23-45 - Touring (5)	45,227
Model 23-X45 - Touring (5)	47
Model 23-47 - Sedan (5)	7,358
Model 23-48 - Coupe (4)	10,846
Model 23-49 - Touring (7)	5,906
Model 23-X49 - Touring (7)	25
Model 23-50 - Sedan (7)	10,279
Model 23-X50 - Sedan (7)	1
Model 23-54 - Sport Roadster (3)	4,501
Model 23-55 - Sport Touring (4)	12,857
	181,657

Note: One millionth Buick produced March 1923

1924

Model 24-33 - Coupe (4)	5,479
Model 24-X33 - Coupe (4)	30
Model 24-34 - Roadster (2)	4,296
Model 24-X34 - Roadster (2)	113
Model 24-35 - Touring (5)	21,854
Model 24-X35 - Touring (5)	4,294
Model 24-37 - Sedan (5)	6,563
Model 24-X37 - Sedan (5)	103
Model 24-41 - Double Service Sedan (5)	14,094
Model 24-X41 - Double Service Sedan (5)	25
Model 24-44 - Roadster (2)	9,700
Model 24-X44 - Roadster (2)	68
Model 24-45 - Touring (5)	48,912
Model 24-X45 - Touring (5)	1,561
Model 24-47 - Sedan (5)	10,377
Model 24-X47 - Sedan (5)	20
Model 24-48 - Coupe (4)	13,009
Model 24-X48 - Coupe (4)	4
Model 24-49 - Touring (7)	7,224
Model 24-X49 - Touring (7)	885
Model 24-50 - Sedan (7)	9,561
Model 24-X50 - Sedan (7)	71
Model 24-50L - Limousine Sedan (7)	713
Model 24-X50L - Limousine Sedan (7)	33
Model 24-51 - Brougham Touring Sedan (5)	4,991
Model 24-X51 - Brougham Touring Sedan (5)	24
Model 24-54 - Sport Roadster (3)	1,938
Model 24-X54 - Sport Roadster (3)	52
Model 24-54C - Country Club Special Coupe (3)	1,107
Model 24-55 - Sport Touring (4)	4,111
Model 24-X55 - Sport Touring (4)	324
Model 24-57 - Town Car (4)	25
	171,561

1925

STANDARD SIX SERIES

Model 25-20 - Coach (5)	21,900
Model 25-X20 - Coach (5)	65
Model 25-21 - Double Service Sedan (5)	9,252
Model 25-X21 - Double Service Sedan (5)	56
Model 25-24 - Roadster (2)	3,315
Model 25-X24 - Roadster (2)	108
Model 25-24A - Enclosed Roadster (2)	1,725
Model 25-24S - Sport Roadster (4)	501
Model 25-25 - Touring (5)	16,040
Model 25-X25 - Touring (5)	5,452
Model 25-25A - Enclosed Touring (5)	4,450
Model 25-25S - Sport Touring (5)	651
Model 25-26 - Double Service Coupe (2)	4,398
Model 25-26S - Sport Coupe (4)	550
Model 25-27 - Sedan (5)	10,772
Model 25-X27 - Sedan (5)	1,448
Model 25-28 - Coupe (4)	7,743
Model 25-X28 - Coupe (4)	119

MASTER SIX SERIES

Model 25-40 - Coach (5)	30,600
Model 25-X40 - Coach (5)	25
Model 25-44 - Roadster (2)	2,975
Model 25-44A - Enclosed Roadster (2)	850
Model 25-45 - Touring (5)	5,203
Model 25-X45 - Touring (5)	701
Model 25-45A - Enclosed Touring (5)	1,900
Model 25-47 - Sedan (5)	4,200
Model 25-48 - Coupe (4)	6,799
Model 25-X48 - Coupe (4)	4
Model 25-49 - Touring (7)	2,826
Model 25-X49 - Touring (7)	756
Model 25-49A - Enclosed Touring (7)	500
Model 25-50 - Sedan (7)	4,606
Model 25-X50 - Sedan (7)	164
Model 25-50L - Limousine Sedan (7)	768
Model 25-X50L - Limousine Sedan (7)	189
Model 25-51 - Brougham Sedan (5)	6,850
Model 25-X51 - Brougham Sedan (5)	2
Model 25-54 - Sport Roadster (3)	1,917
Model 25-X54 - Sport Roadster (2)	103
Model 25-54C - Country Club Coupe (3)	2,751
Model 25-55 - Sport Touring (4)	2,774
Model 25-X55 - Sport Touring (4)	382
Model 25-57 - Town Car (4)	92
Model 25-X57 - Town Car (4)	1
	166,483

1926

STANDARD SIX SERIES

Model 26-20 - Two-Door Sedan (5)	40,113
Model 26-X20 - Two-Door Sedan (5)	807
Model 26-24 - Roadster (2)	1,891
Model 26-X24 - Roadster (2)	84
Model 26-25 - Touring (5)	4,859
Model 26-X25 - Touring (5)	4,674
Model 26-26 - Coupe (2)	10,531
Model 26-26S - Experimental	1
Model 26-27 - Four-Door Sedan (5)	43,375
Model 26-X27 - Four-Door Sedan (5)	636
Model 26-28 - Coupe (4)	8,271
Model 26-X28 - Coupe (4)	66

MASTER SIX SERIES

Model 26-40 - Two-Door Sedan (5)	21,867
Model 26-X40 - Two-Door Sedan (5)	154
Model 26-44 - Roadster (2)	2,654
Model 26-45 - Touring (5)	2,630
Model 26-X45 - Touring (5)	839
Model 26-47 - Four-Door Sedan (5)	53,490
Model 26-X47 - Four-Door Sedan (5)	117
Model 26-48 - Coupe (4)	10,028
Model 26-49 - Sedan (7)	1
Model 26-X49 - Chassis	115
Model 26-50 - Sedan (7)	12,690
Model 26-X50 - Sedan (7)	62
Model 26-50T - Taxicab (7)	220
Model 26-51 - Brougham Touring Sedan (5)	10,873
Model 26-54 - Sport Roadster (3)	2,501
Model 26-X54 - Roadster (2)	67
Model 26-54C - Country Club Sport Coupe (3)	4,436
Model 26-55 - Sport Touring (4)	2,051
Model 26-X55 - Sport Touring (4)	429
Model 26-58 - Coupe (4)	1
	240,533

1927

STANDARD SIX SERIES

Model 27-20 - Two-Door Sedan (5)	33,190
Model 27-X20 - Two-Door Sedan (5)	870
Model 27-24 - Sport Roadster (4)	4,985
Model 27-X24 - DeLuxe Sport Roadster (4)	271
Model 27-25 - DeLuxe Sport Touring (5)	3,272
Model 27-X25 - DeLuxe Sport Touring (5)	4,222
Model 27-26 - Coupe (2)	10,512
Model 27-26S - Country Club Coupe (4)	11,688
Model 27-26CC - Collapsible Top Coupe (4)	1
Model 27-27 - Four-Door Sedan (5)	40,272
Model 27-X27 - Four-Door Sedan (5)	1,448
Model 27-28 - Coupe (4)	7,178
Model 27-X28 - Coupe (4)	94
Model 27-29 - Town Brougham Sedan (5)	11,032

MASTER SIX SERIES

Model 27-40 - Two-Door Sedan (5)	12,130
Model 27-X40 - Two-Door Sedan (5)	441

Model 27-47 - Four-Door Sedan (5)	49,105
Model 27-X47 - Four-Door Sedan (5)	322
Model 27-48 - Coupe (4)	9,350
Model 27-50 - Sedan (7)	11,259
Model 27-X50 - Sedan (7)	233
Model 27-50T - Taxicab (7)	60
Model 27-51 - Brougham Sedan (5)	13,862
Model 27-54 - DeLuxe Sport Roadster (4)	4,310
Model 27-X54 - DeLuxe Sport Roadster (4)	189
Model 27-54C - Country Club Coupe (4)	7,095
Model 27-54CC - Convertible Coupe (4)	2,354
Model 27-X54CC - Convertible Coupe (4)	19
Model 27-55 - DeLuxe Sport Touring (4)	2,092
Model 27-X55 - DeLuxe Sport Touring (4)	605
Model 27-58 - Coupe (5)	7,655
	250,116

Note: Two millionth Buick produced November 1927

1928
STANDARD SIX SERIES
Model 28-20 - Two-Door Sedan (5)	32,481
Model 28-X20 - Two-Door Sedan (5)	61
Model 28-24 - Sport Roadster (4)	4,513
Model 28-X24 - Sport Roadster (4)	251
Model 28-25 - Sport Touring (5)	3,134
Model 28-X25 - Sport Touring (5)	2,741
Model 28-26 - Coupe (2)	12,417
Model 28-26S - Country Club Coupe (4)	13,211
Model 28-27 - Four-Door Sedan (5)	50,224
Model 28-X27 - Four-Door Sedan (5)	1,863
Model 28-29 - Town Brougham Sedan (5)	10,840

MASTER SIX SERIES
Model 28-47 - Four-Door Sedan (5)	34,197
Model 28-X47 - Four-Door Sedan (5)	378
Model 28-47S - DeLuxe Sedan (5)	16,398
Model 28-X47S - DeLuxe Sedan (5)	7
Model 28-48 - Coupe (4)	9,002
Model 28-49 - Touring (7)	2
Model 28-50 - Sedan (7)	10,827
Model 28-X50 - Sedan (7)	206
Model 28-51 - Brougham Sedan (5)	10,258
Model 28-X51 - Brougham Sedan (5)	45
Model 28-54 - Sport Roadster (4)	3,853
Model 28-X54 - Sport Roadster (4)	85
Model 28-54C - Country Club Coupe (4)	6,555
Model 28-55 - Sport Touring (5)	1,333
Model 28-X55 - Sport Touring (5)	132
Model 28-58 - Coupe (5)	9,904
Model 28-X58 - Coupe (5)	11
	235,009

1929
SERIES 116
Model 29-20 - Two-Door Sedan (5)	17,733
Model 29-X20 - Two-Door Sedan (5)	90
Model 29-25 - Touring (5)	2,938
Model 29-X25 - Touring (5)	3,204
Model 29-26 - Business Coupe (2)	8,745
Model 29-X26 - Business Coupe (2)	1
Model 29-26S - Sport Coupe with Dickey Seat (4)	10,308
Model 29-27 - Four-Door Sedan (5)	44,345
Model 29-X27 - Four-Door Sedan (5)	3,262

SERIES 121
Model 29-41 - Four-Door Sedan, Close-Coupled (5)	10,110
Model 29-44 - Sport Roadster (4)	6,195

Model 29-X44 - Sport Roadster (4)	184
Model 29-46 - Business Coupe (2)	4,339
Model 29-46S - Sport Coupe with Dickey Seat (4)	6,638
Model 29-47 - Four-Door Sedan (5)	30,356
Model 29-X47 - Four-Door Sedan (5)	335
Model 29-X471 - Four-Door Sedan chassis	228
Model 29-48 - Coupe (4)	4,255

SERIES 129
Model 29-49 - Touring (7)	1,530
Model 29-X49 - Touring (7)	633
Model 29-50 - Four-Door Sedan (7)	8,058
Model 29-X50 - Four-Door Sedan (7)	319
Model 29-50L - Imperial Sedan Limousine (7)	736
Model 29-X50L - Imperial Sedan Limousine (7)	169
Model 29-51 - Four-Door Sport Sedan (5)	7,014
Model 29-X51 - Four-Door Sport Sedan (5)	105
Model 29-54CC - DeLuxe Convertible Coupe (4)	2,021
Model 29-X54CC - DeLuxe Convertible Coupe (4)	91
Model 29-55 - Sport Touring (5)	1,122
Model 29-X55 - Sport Touring (5)	311
Model 29-57 - Four-Door Sedan (5)	5,175
Model 29-58 - Coupe (5)	7,311
	187,861

1930
MARQUETTE SERIES
Model 30-30 - Two-Door Sedan (5)	4,630
Model 30-X30 - Two-Door Sedan (5)	92
Model 30-34 - Sport Roadster (4)	2,397
Model 30-X34 - Sport Roadster (4)	239
Model 30-35 - Phaeton (5)	889
Model 30-X35 - Phaeton (5)	1,281
Model 30-36 - Business Coupe (2)	2,475
Model 30-36S - Special Coupe (4)	4,384
Model 30-X36S - Special Coupe (4)	121
Model 30-37 - Four-Door Sedan (5)	15,795
Model 30-X37 - Four-Door Sedan (5)	328
Model 30-371 - Stripped Chassis	972
Model 30-X371 - Stripped Chassis	1,008
Model 30-X372 - Stripped Chassis	396

SERIES 40
Model 30-40 - Two-Door Sedan (5)	6,101
Model 30-X40 - Two-Door Sedan (5)	43
Model 30-44 - Sport Roadster (4)	3,476
Model 30-X44 - Sport Roadster (4)	163
Model 30-45 - Phaeton (5)	972
Model 30-X45 - Phaeton (5)	128
Model 30-451 - Stripped Chassis	72
Model 30-X451 - Stripped Chassis	840
Model 30-X452 - Stripped Chassis	320
Model 30-46 - Business Coupe (2)	5,695
Model 30-X46 - Business Coupe (2)	21
Model 30-46S - Special Coupe (4)	10,719
Model 30-X46S - Special Coupe (4)	29
Model 30-47 - Four-Door Sedan (5)	47,294
Model 30-X47 - Four-Door Sedan (5)	202
Model 30-X471 - Stripped Chassis	2,056

SERIES 50
Model 30-57 - Four-Door Sedan (5)	22,926
Model 30-X57 - Four-Door Sedan (5)	213
Model 30-58 - Coupe (4)	5,275

SERIES 60
Model 30-60 - Four-Door Sedan (7)	6,583
Model 30-X60 - Four-Door Sedan (7)	67
Model 30-60L - Limousine (7)	690
Model 30-X60L - Limousine (7)	146
Model 30-601 - Stripped Chassis	840

Model 30-X601 - Stripped Chassis	84
Model 30-61 - Four-Door Special Sedan (5)	12,508
Model 30-X61 - Four-Door Special Sedan (5)	49
Model 30-64 - Sport Roadster (4)	2,006
Model 30-X64 - Sport Roadster (4)	3
Model 30-64C - DeLuxe Coupe (4)	5,370
Model 30-X64C - DeLuxe Coupe (4)	11
Model 30-68 - Coupe (5)	10,216
Model 30-69 - Phaeton (7)	807
Model 30-X69 - Phaeton (7)	811
	181,743

1931
SERIES 50
Model 50 - Two-Door Sedan (5)	3,616
Model 50X - Two-Door Sedan (5)	11
Model 54 - Sport Roadster (4)	907
Model 54X - Sport Roadster (4)	70
Model 55 - Phaeton (5)	358
Model 55X - Phaeton (5)	30
Model 551X - Phaeton Chassis	232
Model 552X - Phaeton Chassis	60
Model 56 - Business Coupe (2)	2,782
Model 56C - Convertible Coupe (4)	1,531
Model X56C - Convertible Coupe (4)	9
Model 56S - Special Coupe (4)	5,733
Model X56S - Special Coupe (4)	24
Model X57 - Four-Door Sedan (5)	33,184
Model X57 - Four-Door Sedan (5)	174
Model 571 - Stripped Chassis	1,248
Model X571 - Stripped Chassis	360
Model X572 - Stripped Chassis	108

SERIES 60
Model 64 - Sport Roadster (4)	1,050
Model 64X - Sport Roadster (4)	28
Model 65 - Phaeton (5)	463
Model 65X - Phaeton (5)	32
Model 651X - Phaeton Chassis	160
Model 652X - Phaeton Chassis	24
Model 66 - Business Coupe (2)	2,732
Model 66S - Special Coupe (4)	6,489
Model 66SX - Special Coupe (4)	12
Model 67 - Four-Door Sedan (5)	30,665
Model 67X - Four-Door Sedan (5)	110
Model 671 - Stripped Chassis	1,392
Model 671X - Stripped Chassis	252
Model 672X - Stripped Chassis	48

SERIES 80
Model 86 - Coupe (4)	3,579
Model 87 - Four-Door Sedan (5)	14,731
Model 87X - Four-Door Sedan (5)	38

SERIES 90
Model 90 - Four-Door Sedan (7)	4,159
Model 90X - Four-Door Sedan (7)	43
Model 90L - Limousine (7)	514
Model 90LX - Limousine (7)	106
Model 901 - Stripped Chassis	636
Model 901X - Stripped Chassis	36
Model 91 - Four-Door Special Sedan (5)	7,853
Model 91X - Four-Door Special Sedan (5)	5
Model 94 - Sport Roadster (4)	824
Model 94X - Sport Roadster (4)	19
Model 95 - Phaeton (7)	392
Model 95X - Phaeton (7)	68
Model 951X - Stripped Chassis	290
Model 96 - Coupe (5)	7,705
Model 96X - Coupe (5)	10

Model 96C - Convertible Coupe (4)	1,066
Model 96CX - Convertible Coupe (4)	4
Model 96S - Country Club Coupe (4)	2,990
Model 96SX - Country Club Coupe (4)	3
	138,965

1932
SERIES 50
Model 55 - Sport Phaeton (5)	69
Model 55X - Sport Phaeton (5)	37
Model 552X - Stripped Chassis	20
Model 56 - Business Coupe (2)	1,726
Model 56C - Convertible Coupe (4)	630
Model 56CX - Convertible Coupe (4)	13
Model 56S - Special Coupe (4)	1,905
Model 56SX - Special Coupe (4)	9
Model 57 - Sedan (5)	10,803
Model 57S - Special Sedan (5)	9,766
Model 57SX - Special Sedan (5)	175
Model 571S - Stripped Chassis	504
Model 571SX - Stripped Chassis	48
Model 572SX - Stripped Chassis	92
Model 58 - Victoria Coupe (5)	2,194
Model 58X - Victoria Coupe (5)	2
Model 58C - Convertible Phaeton (5)	380
Model 58CX - Convertible Phaeton (5)	20

SERIES 60
Model 65 - Sport Phaeton (5)	79
Model 65X - Sport Phaeton (5)	24
Model 66 - Business Coupe (2)	636
Model 66C - Convertible Coupe (4)	450
Model 66CX - Convertible Coupe (4)	2
Model 66S - Special Coupe (4)	1,678
Model 66SX - Special Coupe (4)	6
Model 67 - Sedan (5)	9,013
Model 67X - Sedan (5)	47
Model 671 - Stripped Chassis	372
Model 671X - Stripped Chassis	36
Model 68 - Victoria Coupe (5)	1,514
Model 68C - Convertible Phaeton (5)	366
Model 68CX - Convertible Phaeton (5)	16

SERIES 80
Model 86 - Victoria Traveler Coupe (5)	1,800
Model 87 - Sedan (5)	4,089
Model 87X - Sedan (5)	3

SERIES 90
Model 90 - Sedan (7)	1,368
Model 90X - Sedan (7)	19
Model 90L - Limousine (7)	164
Model 90LX - Limousine (7)	26
Model 901 - Stripped Chassis	192
Model 901X - Stripped Chassis	24
Model 91 - Club Sedan (5)	2,237
Model 91X - Club Sedan (5)	1
Model 95 - Sport Phaeton (7)	131
Model 95X - Sport Phaeton (7)	15
Model 96 - Victoria Coupe (5)	1,460
Model 96C - Convertible Coupe (4)	289
Model 96S - Country Club Coupe (4)	586
Model 97 - Sedan (5)	1,485
Model 98 - Convertible Phaeton (5)	268
Model 98X - Convertible Phaeton (5)	1
	56,790

1933
SERIES 50
Model 56 - Business Coupe (2)	1,321
Model 56C - Convertible Coupe (2)	346
Model 56CX - Convertible Coupe (2)	4
Model 56S - Sport Coupe (2)	1,643
Model 56SX - Sport Coupe (2)	10
Model 57 - Four-Door Sedan (5)	19,109
Model 57X - Four-Door Sedan (5)	150
Model 570 - Stripped Chassis	21
Model 570X - Stripped Chassis	1
Model 571 - Stripped Chassis	660
Model 571X - Stripped Chassis	108
Model 572X - Stripped Chassis	80
Model 58 - Victoria Coupe (5)	4,118
Model 58X - Victoria Coupe (5)	5

SERIES 60
Model 66C - Convertible Coupe (2)	152
Model 66S - Sport Coupe (2)	1,000
Model 67 - Four-Door Sedan (5)	7,450
Model 670 - Stripped Chassis	71
Model 671 - Stripped Chassis	328
Model 68 - Victoria Coupe (5)	2,887
Model 68C - Convertible Phaeton (5)	183

SERIES 80
Model 86 - Victoria Coupe (5)	758
Model 86C - Convertible Coupe (2)	90
Model 86S - Sport Coupe (2)	401
Model 87 - Four-Door Sedan (5)	1,545
Model 870 - Stripped Chassis	90
Model 88C - Convertible Phaeton (5)	124

SERIES 90
Model 90 - Four Door Sedan (7)	890
Model 90X - Four-Door Sedan (7)	12
Model 90L - Limousine (7)	299
Model 90LX - Limousine (7)	39
Model 900 - Stripped Chassis	24
Model 901 - Stripped Chassis	168
Model 91 - Club Sedan (5)	1,637
Model 91X - Club Sedan (5)	2
Model 96 - Victoria Coupe (5)	556
Model 96X - Victoria Coupe (5)	1
Model 97 - Four-Door Sedan (5)	641
	46,924

1934
SERIES 40
Model 41 - Four-Door Sedan, Built-In Trunk (5)	10,953
Model 41X - Four-Door Sedan, Built-In Trunk (5)	542
Model 411X - Stripped Chassis	432
Model 46 - Business Coupe (2)	1,806
Model 46X - Business Coupe (2)	2
Model 46S - Sport Coupe, Rumble Seat (4)	1,232
Model 46SX - Sport Coupe, Rumble Seat (4)	47
Model 47 - Four-Door Sedan (5)	7,425
Model 47X - Four-Door Sedan (5)	380
Model 470 - Stripped Chassis	37
Model 470X - Stripped Chassis	14
Model 471X - Stripped Chassis	744
Model 472X - Stripped Chassis	500
Model 48 - Touring Sedan, Built-In Trunk (5)	4,688
Model 48 - Touring Sedan, Built-In Trunk (5)	91

SERIES 50
Model 56 - Business Coupe (2)	1,078
Model 56X - Business Coupe (2)	4
Model 56C - Convertible Coupe (2)	506
Model 56CX - Convertible Coupe (2)	83
Model 56S - Special Coupe, Rumble Seat (4)	1,150
Model 56SX - Special Coupe, Rumble Seat (4)	42
Model 561CX - Stripped Chassis	12
Model 57 - Four-Door Sedan (5)	12,094
Model 57X - Four-Door Sedan (5)	711
Model 570 - Stripped Chassis	19
Model 570X - Stripped Chassis	66
Model 571X - Stripped Chassis	1,332
Model 572X - Stripped Chassis	276
Model 58 - Victoria Coupe, Built-In Trunk (5)	4,316
Model 58 - Victoria Coupe, Built-In Trunk (5)	89
Model 581X - Stripped Chassis	72

SERIES 60
Model 61 - Club Sedan, Built-In Trunk (5)	5,395
Model 61X - Club Sedan, Built-In Trunk (5)	234
Model 66C - Convertible Coupe, Rumble Seat (4)	253
Model 66CX - Convertible Coupe, Rumble Seat (4)	10
Model 66S - Special Coupe (2)	816
Model 66SX - Special Coupe (2)	9
Model 67 - Four-Door Sedan (5)	5,171
Model 67X - Four-Door Sedan (5)	194
Model 670 - Stripped Chassis	97
Model 670X - Stripped Chassis	32
Model 671X - Stripped Chassis	588
Model 68 - Victoria Coupe, Built-In Trunk (5)	1,935
Model 68X - Victoria Coupe, Built-In Trunk (5)	31
Model 68C - Convertible Phaeton, Built-In Trunk (5)	444
Model 68CX - Convertible Phaeton, Built-In Trunk (5)	143

SERIES 90
Model 90 - Four-Door Sedan (7)	1,151
Model 90X - Four-Door Sedan (7)	83
Model 90L - Limousine (7)	262
Model 90LX - Limousine (7)	166
Model 900 - Stripped Chassis	70
Model 900X, 901X - Stripped Chassis	325
Model 91 - Club Sedan, Built-In Trunk (5)	1,477
Model 91X - Club Sedan, Built-In Trunk (5)	30
Model 96C - Convertible Coupe, Rumble Seat (4)	68
Model 96CX - Convertible Coupe, Rumble Seat (4)	5
Model 96S - Sport Coupe, Rumble Seat (4)	137
Model 97 - Four-Door Sedan (5)	635
Model 97X - Four-Door Sedan (5)	19
Model 98 - Coupe (5)	347
Model 98X - Coupe (5)	1
Model 98C - Convertible Phaeton, Built-In Trunk (5)	119
Model 98CX - Convertible Phaeton, Built-In Trunk (5)	19
	71,009

1935
SERIES 40
Model 41 - Four-Door Sedan (5)	18,638
Model 41X - Four-Door Sedan (5)	535
Model 411X - Stripped Chassis	636
Model 46 - Business Coupe (2)	2,850
Model 46X - Business Coupe (2)	8
Model 46C - Convertible Coupe (4)	933
Model 46CX - Convertible Coupe (4)	67
Model 46S - Sport Coupe (4)	1,136
Model 46SX - Sport Coupe (4)	64
Model 47 - Four-Door Sedan (5)	6,250
Model 47X - Four-Door Sedan (5)	391
Model 470 - Stripped Chassis	173
Model 470X - Stripped Chassis	60
Model 471X - Stripped Chassis	468

Model 472X - Stripped Chassis — 1,284
Model 48 - Two-Door Touring Sedan (5) — 4,957
Model 48X - Two-Door Touring Sedan (5) — 70
SERIES 50
Model 56 - Business Coupe (2) — 257
Model 56C - Convertible Coupe (2) — 170
Model 56CX - Convertible Coupe (2) — 17
Model 56S - Special Coupe (4) — 268
Model 56SX - Special Coupe (4) — 11
Model 561CX - Stripped Chassis — 12
Model 57 - Four-Door Sedan (5) — 3,778
Model 57X - Four-Door Sedan (5) — 220
Model 570X - Stripped Chassis — 5
Model 571X - Stripped Chassis — 156
Model 572X - Stripped Chassis — 24
Model 58 - Victoria Coupe (5) — 1,589
Model 58X - Victoria Coupe (5) — 29
SERIES 60
Model 61 - Club Sedan (5) — 2,762
Model 61X - Club Sedan (5) — 92
Model 66C - Convertible Coupe (4) — 111
Model 66S - Special Coupe (4) — 257
Model 66SX - Special Coupe (4) — 4
Model 67 - Four-Door Sedan (5) — 1,716
Model 67X - Four-Door Sedan (5) — 76
Model 670 - Stripped Chassis — 94
Model 670X - Stripped Chassis — 11
Model 671X - Stripped Chassis — 204
Model 68 - Victoria Coupe (5) — 597
Model 68X - Victoria Coupe (5) — 6
Model 68C - Convertible Phaeton (5) — 256
Model 68CX - Convertible Phaeton (5) — 52
SERIES 90
Model 90 - Four-Door Sedan (7) — 609
Model 90X - Four-Door Sedan (7) — 42
Model 90L - Limousine (7) — 191
Model 90LX - Limousine (7) — 105
Model 900 - Stripped Chassis — 21
Model 900X - Stripped Chassis — 4
Model 901X - Stripped Chassis — 156
Model 91 - Club Sedan (5) — 573
Model 91X - Club Sedan (5) — 7
Model 96C - Convertible Coupe (4) — 10
Model 96CX - Convertible Coupe (4) — 1
Model 96S - Sport Coupe (4) — 41
Model 96SX - Sport Coupe (4) — 1
Model 97 - Four-Door Sedan (5) — 117
Model 97X - Four-Door Sedan (5) — 2
Model 98 - Victoria Coupe (5) — 32
Model 98C - Convertible Phaeton (5) — 38
Model 98CX - Convertible Phaeton (5) — 5
53,249

1936
SPECIAL SERIES
Model 41 - Four-Door Sedan (5) — 77,007
Model 41X - Four-Door Sedan (5) — 1,796
Model 410 - Stripped Chassis — 150
Model 410X - Stripped Chassis — 14
Model 411X - Stripped Chassis — 5,057
Model 46 - Business Coupe (2) — 10,912
Model 46X - Business Coupe (2) — 16
Model 46C - Convertible Coupe (4) — 1,488
Model 46CX - Convertible Coupe (4) — 162
Model 46So - Sport Coupe (4) — 1,086
Model 46SoX - Sport Coupe (4) — 17

Model 46Sr - Sport Coupe (4) — 1,390
Model 46SrX - Sport Coupe (4) — 104
Model 48 - Victoria Coupe (5) — 21,241
Model 48X - Victoria Coupe (5) — 82
Model 481X - Stripped Chassis — 192
CENTURY SERIES
Model 61 - Four-Door Sedan (5) — 17,806
Model 61X - Four-Door Sedan (5) — 397
Model 610 - Stripped Chassis — 66
Model 610X - Stripped Chassis — 5
Model 611X - Stripped Chassis — 1,044
Model 66C - Convertible Coupe (4) — 717
Model 66CX - Convertible Coupe (4) — 49
Model 66So - Sport Coupe (4) — 1,078
Model 66SoX - Sport Coupe (4) — 1
Model 66Sr - Sport Coupe (4) — 1,001
Model 66SrX - Sport Coupe (4) — 17
Model 68 - Victoria Coupe (5) — 3,762
Model 68X - Victoria Coupe (5) — 37
ROADMASTER SERIES
Model 80C - Convertible Phaeton (6) — 1,064
Model 80CX - Convertible Phaeton (6) — 165
Model 81 - Four-Door Sedan (6) — 14,985
Model 81X - Four-Door Sedan (6) — 343
Model 810 - Stripped Chassis — 12
Model 810X - Stripped Chassis — 6
Model 811X - Stripped Chassis — 516
LIMITED SERIES
Model 90 - Four-Door Sedan (8) — 1,590
Model 90X - Four-Door Sedan (8) — 119
Model 90L - Limousine (8) — 709
Model 90LX - Limousine (8) — 238
Model 900 - Stripped Chassis — 25
Model 900X - Stripped Chassis — 29
Model 901X - Stripped Chassis — 300
Model 91 - Four-Door Sedan (6) — 1,713
Model 91X - Four-Door Sedan (6) — 13
Model 91F - Formal Sedan (6) — 74
Model 91FX - Formal Sedan (6) — 1
168,596

Note: Three millionth Buick produced May 1936

1937
SPECIAL SERIES
Model 40X - Crated Knocked-Down Chassis — 6,493
Model 40C - Convertible Phaeton (5) — 1,689
Model 40CX - Convertible Phaeton (5) — 256
Model 41 - Four-Door Trunk-Back Sedan (5) — 82,440
Model 41X - Four-Door Trunk-Back Sedan (5) — 2,755
Model 410 - Stripped Chassis — 257
Model 410X - Stripped Chassis — 110
Model 44 - Two-Door Touring Sedan (5) — 9,330
Model 44X - Two-Door Touring Sedan (5) — 12
Model 46 - Business Coupe (2) — 13,742
Model 46X - Business Coupe (2) — 31
Model 46C - Convertible Coupe (4) — 2,265
Model 46CX - Convertible Coupe (4) — 134
Model 46S - Sport Coupe (4) — 5,059
Model 46SX - Sport Coupe (4) — 225
Model 47 - Four-Door Touring Sedan (5) — 22,312
Model 47X - Four-Door Touring Sedan (5) — 205
Model 48 - Two-Door Trunk-Back Sedan (5) — 15,936
Model 48X - Two-Door Trunk-Back Sedan (5) — 98
CENTURY SERIES
Model 60X - Crated Knocked-Down Chassis — 949
Model 60C - Convertible Phaeton (5) — 410

Model 60CX - Convertible Phaeton (5) — 15
Model 61 - Four-Door Trunk-Back Sedan (5) — 20,679
Model 61X - Four-Door Trunk-Back Sedan (5) — 461
Model 610 - Stripped Chassis — 69
Model 610X - Stripped Chassis — 8
Model 64 - Two-Door Touring Sedan (5) — 1,117
Model 64X - Two-Door Touring Sedan (5) — 1
Model 66C - Convertible Coupe (4) — 787
Model 66CX - Convertible Coupe (4) — 56
Model 66S - Sport Coupe (4) — 2,840
Model 66SX - Sport Coupe (4) — 33
Model 67 - Four-Door Touring Sedan (5) — 4,750
Model 67X - Four-Door Touring Sedan (5) — 21
Model 68 - Two-Door Trunk-Back Sedan (5) — 2,874
Model 68X - Two-Door Trunk-Back Sedan (5) — 23
ROADMASTER SERIES
Model 80C - Four-Door Phaeton (6) — 1,040
Model 80CX - Four-Door Phaeton (6) — 115
Model 80X - Crated Knocked-Down Chassis — 588
Model 81 - Four-Door Trunk-Back Sedan (6) — 14,637
Model 81X - Four-Door Trunk-Back Sedan (6) — 344
Model 81F - Formal Sedan (6) — 452
Model 81FX - Formal Sedan (6) — 37
Model 810 - Stripped Chassis — 8
Model 810X - Stripped Chassis — 10
LIMITED SERIES
Model 90 - Four-Door Trunk-Back Sedan (8) — 1,592
Model 90X - Four-Door Trunk-Back Sedan (8) — 118
Model 90L - Limousine (8) — 720
Model 90LX - Limousine (8) — 245
Model 900 - Stripped Chassis — 2
Model 900X - Stripped Chassis — 8
Model 90X - Crated Knocked-Down Chassis — 588
Model 91 - Four-Door Trunk-Back Sedan (6) — 1,229
Model 91X - Four-Door Trunk-Back Sedan (6) — 13
Model 91F - Formal Sedan (6) — 156
Model 91FX - Formal Sedan (6) — 2
220,346

1938
SPECIAL SERIES
Model 40C - Convertible Sport Phaeton (5) — 776
Model 40CX - Convertible Sport Phaeton (5) — 170
Model 40X - Crated Knocked-Down Chassis — 6,528
Model 41 - Touring Sedan (5) — 79,510
Model 41X - Touring Sedan (5) — 2,681
Model 410 - Stripped Chassis — 455
Model 410X - Stripped Chassis — 109
Model 44 - Two-Door Sport Sedan (5) — 5,943
Model 44X - Two-Door Sport Sedan (5) — 8
Model 46 - Business Coupe (2) — 11,337
Model 46X - Business Coupe (2) — 31
Model 46C - Convertible Coupe (4) — 2,473
Model 46CX - Convertible Coupe (4) — 152
Model 46S - Sport Coupe (4) — 5,381
Model 46SX - Sport Coupe (4) — 193
Model 47 - Four-Door Sport Sedan (5) — 11,265
Model 47X - Four-Door Sport Sedan (5) — 76
Model 48 - Two-Door Touring Sedan (5) — 14,153
Model 48X - Two-Door Touring Sedan (5) — 60
CENTURY SERIES
Model 60C - Convertible Phaeton (5) — 208
Model 60CX - Convertible Phaeton (5) — 11
Model 60X - Crated Knocked-Down Chassis — 684
Model 61 - Four-Door Touring Sedan (5) — 12,364
Model 61X - Four-Door Touring Sedan (5) — 309
Model 610 - Stripped Chassis — 73

Model 610X - Stripped Chassis	5
Model 66C - Convertible Coupe (4)	642
Model 66CX - Convertible Coupe (4)	52
Model 66S - Sport Coupe (4)	1,991
Model 66SX - Sport Coupe (4)	39
Model 67 - Four-Door Sport Sedan (5)	1,515
Model 67X - Four-Door Sport Sedan (5)	1
Model 68 - Two-Door Touring Sedan (5)	1,380
Model 68X - Two-Door Touring Sedan (5)	13

ROADMASTER SERIES

Model 80C - Four-Door Sport Phaeton (6)	350
Model 80CX - Four-Door Sport Phaeton (6)	61
Model 80X - Crated Knocked-Down Chassis	204
Model 81 - Four-Door Touring Sedan (6)	4,505
Model 81X - Four-Door Touring Sedan (6)	199
Model 81F - Formal Sedan (6)	247
Model 81FX - Formal Sedan (6)	49
Model 810 - Stripped Chassis	4
Model 810X - Stripped Chassis	15
Model 87 - Four-Door Sport Sedan (6)	466

LIMITED SERIES

Model 90 - Four-Door Touring Sedan (8)	644
Model 90X - Four-Door Touring Sedan (8)	62
Model 90L - Limousine (8)	410
Model 90LX - Limousine (8)	167
Model 90X - Crated Knocked-Down Chassis	264
Model 900 - Stripped Chassis	4
Model 900X - Stripped Chassis	9
Model 91 - Four-Door Touring Sedan (6)	437
Model 91X - Four-Door Touring Sedan (6)	4
	168,689

1939
SPECIAL SERIES

Model 40X - Crated Knocked-Down Chassis	5,820
Model 41 - Four-Door Touring Sedan (5)	109,213
Model 41X - Four-Door Touring Sedan (5)	2,260
Model 41C - Sport Phaeton (5)	724
Model 41CX - Sport Phaeton (5)	106
Model 410 - Stripped Chassis	395
Model 410X - Stripped Chassis	66
Model 46 - Business Coupe (2)	14,582
Model 46X - Business Coupe (2)	27
Model 46C - Convertible Coupe (4)	4,569
Model 46CX - Convertible Coupe (4)	240
Model 46S - Sport Coupe (4)	10,043
Model 46SX - Sport Coupe (4)	233
Model 48 - Two-Door Touring Sedan (5)	27,218
Model 48X - Two-Door Touring Sedan (5)	72

CENTURY SERIES

Model 60X - Crated Knocked-Down Chassis	456
Model 61 - Four-Door Touring Sedan (5)	18,462
Model 61X - Four-Door Touring Sedan (5)	321
Model 61C - Sport Phaeton (5)	249
Model 61CX - Sport Phaeton (5)	20
Model 610 - Stripped Chassis	55
Model 610X - Stripped Chassis	7
Model 66C - Convertible Coupe (4)	790
Model 66CX - Convertible Coupe (4)	60
Model 66S - Sport Coupe (4)	3,408
Model 66SX - Sport Coupe (4)	62
Model 68 - Two-Door Touring Sedan (5)	521
Model 68X - Two-Door Touring Sedan (5)	4

ROADMASTER SERIES

Model 80C - Sport Phaeton (6)	3
Model 80X - Crated Knocked-Down Chassis	132
Model 81 - Four-Door Touring Sedan (6)	5,460
Model 81X - Four-Door Touring Sedan (6)	159
Model 81C - Phaeton (6)	311
Model 81CX - Phaeton (6)	53
Model 81F - Formal Sedan (6)	303
Model 81FX - Formal Sedan (6)	37
Model 810 - Stripped Chassis	2
Model 810X - Stripped Chassis	9
Model 87 - Four-Door Sport Sedan (6)	20

LIMITED SERIES

Model 90 - Four-Door Touring Sedan (8)	650
Model 90X - Four-Door Touring Sedan (8)	36
Model 90L - Limousine (8)	423
Model 90LX - Limousine (8)	120
Model 90X - Crated Knocked-Down Chassis	168
Model 900 - Stripped Chassis	2
Model 900X - Stripped Chassis	6
Model 91 - Four-Door Touring Sedan (6)	378
Model 91X - Four-Door Touring Sedan (6)	4
	208,259

1940
SPECIAL SERIES

Model 41 - Four-Door Touring Sedan (5)	67,308
Model 41X - Four-Door Touring Sedan (5)	1,508
Model 41C - Convertible Phaeton (5)	552
Model 41CX - Convertible Phaeton (5)	45
Model 41T - Taxicab (5)	48
Model 410 - Stripped Chassis	320
Model 410X - Stripped Chassis	2,260
Model 46 - Business Coupe (2)	12,372
Model 46X - Business Coupe (2)	10
Model 46C - Convertible Coupe (4)	3,664
Model 46CX - Convertible Coupe (4)	99
Model 46S - Sport Coupe (4)	8,291
Model 46SX - Sport Coupe (4)	110
Model 48 - Two-Door Touring Sedan (5)	20,739
Model 48X - Two-Door Touring Sedan (5)	29

SUPER SERIES

Model 51 - Four-Door Touring Sedan (6)	95,875
Model 51X - Four-Door Touring Sedan (6)	1.351
Model 51C - Convertible Phaeton (6)	529
Model 51CX - Convertible Phaeton (6)	5
Model 510 - Stripped Chassis	3
Model 510X - Stripped Chassis	1,321
Model 56C - Convertible Coupe (6)	4,764
Model 56CX - Convertible Coupe (6)	40
Model 56S - Sport Coupe (5)	26,251
Model 56SX - Sport Coupe (5)	211
Model 59 - Estate Wagon (6)	495
Model 59X - Estate Wagon (6)	6

CENTURY SERIES

Model 61 - Four-Door Touring Sedan (5)	8,597
Model 61X - Four-Door Touring Sedan (5)	111
Model 61C - Convertible Phaeton (5)	194
Model 61CX - Convertible Phaeton (5)	9
Model 610 - Stripped Chassis	179
Model 610X - Stripped Chassis	98
Model 66 - Business Coupe (2)	44
Model 66C - Convertible Coupe (4)	542
Model 66CX - Convertible Coupe (4)	8
Model 66S - Sport Coupe (5)	96

ROADMASTER SERIES

Model 71 Four-Door Touring Sedan (6)	13,583
Model 71X - Four-Door Touring Sedan (6)	150
Model 71C - Convertible Phaeton (6)	235
Model 71CX - Convertible Phaeton (6)	3
Model 710 - Stripped Chassis	4
Model 710X - Stripped Chassis	216
Model 76C - Convertible Coupe (6)	606
Model 76CX - Convertible Coupe (6)	6
Model 76S - Sport Coupe (5)	3,921
Model 76SX - Sport Coupe (5)	51

LIMITED 80 SERIES

Model 80C - Convertible Phaeton (6)	7
Model 81 - Four-Door Touring Sedan (6)	3,810
Model 81X - Four-Door Touring Sedan (6)	88
Model 81C - Convertible Phaeton (6)	230
Model 81CX - Convertible Phaeton (6)	20
Model 81F - Formal Sedan (6)	248
Model 81FX - Formal Sedan (6)	22
Model 810 - Stripped Chassis	2
Model 810X - Stripped Chassis	3
Model 87 - Four-Door Sport Sedan (6)	14
Model 87F - Formal Sport Sedan (6)	7

LIMITED 90 SERIES

Model 90 - Four-Door Touring Sedan (8)	796
Model 90X - Four-Door Touring Sedan (8)	32
Model 90L - Limousine (8)	526
Model 90LX - Limousine (8)	108
Model 900 - Stripped Chassis	1
Model 900X - Stripped Chassis	1
Model 901X - Crated Knocked-Down Chassis	12
Model 91 - Four-Door Touring Sedan (6)	417
Model 91X - Four-Door Touring Sedan (6)	1
	283,204

Note: Four millionth Buick produced November 1940

1941
SPECIAL A-SERIES

Model 44 - Business Coupe (3)	3,258
Model 44X - Business Coupe (3)	3
Model 44C - Convertible Coupe (6)	4,282
Model 44CX - Convertible Coupe (6)	27
Model 44S - Sport Coupe (6)	5,269
Model 44SX - Sport Coupe (6)	21
Model 47 - Four-Door Touring Sedan (6)	13,992
Model 47X - Four-Door Touring Sedan (6)	147

SPECIAL SERIES

Model 41 - Four-Door Touring Sedan (6)	91,138
Model 41X - Four-Door Touring Sedan (6)	1,390
Model 41SE - Sedan, Super Equipment (6)	13,378
Model 41SEX - Sedan, Super Equipment (6)	24
Model 410 - Stripped Chassis	3
Model 410X - Stripped Chassis	1,344
Model 46 - Business Coupe (3)	9,185
Model 46X - Business Coupe (3)	16
Model 46S - Sedanet (6)	87,687
Model 46SX - Sedanet (6)	461
Model 46SSE - Sedanet, Super Equipment (6)	9,591
Model 46SSEX - Sedanet, Super Equipment (6)	23
Model 49 - Estate Wagon (6)	838
Model 49X - Estate Wagon (6)	12

SUPER SERIES

Model 51 - Four-Door Touring Sedan (6)	57,367
Model 51X - Four-Door Touring Sedan (6)	1,271
Model 51C - Convertible Phaeton (6)	467
Model 51CX - Convertible Phaeton (6)	41
Model 510 - Stripped Chassis	220

Model 510X - Stripped Chassis — 1,380
Model 56 - Business Coupe (3) — 2,449
Model 56X - Business Coupe (3) — 3
Model 56C - Convertible Coupe (6) — 12,181
Model 56CX - Convertible Coupe (6) — 210
Model 56S - Sport Coupe (6) — 19,603
Model 56SX - Sport Coupe (6) — 273

CENTURY SERIES
Model 61 - Four-Door Touring Sedan (6) — 15,027
Model 61X - Four-Door Touring Sedan (6) — 109
Model 610 - Stripped Chassis — 2
Model 66 - Business Coupe (3) — 220
Model 66X - Business Coupe (3) — 2
Model 66S - Sedanet (6) — 5,521
Model 66SX - Sedanet (6) — 26

ROADMASTER SERIES
Model 71 - Four-Door Touring Sedan (6) — 10,431
Model 71X - Four-Door Touring Sedan (6) — 122
Model 71C - Convertible Phaeton (6) — 312
Model 71CX - Convertible Phaeton (6) — 14
Model 710 - Stripped Chassis — 170
Model 710X - Stripped Chassis — 109
Model 76C - Convertible Coupe (6) — 1,845
Model 76CX - Convertible Coupe (6) — 24
Model 76S - Sport Coupe (6) — 2,784
Model 76SX - Sport Coupe (6) — 50

LIMITED SERIES
Model 90 - Four-Door Touring Sedan (8) — 885
Model 90X - Four-Door Touring Sedan (8) — 21
Model 90L - Limousine (8) — 605
Model 90LX - Limousine (8) — 64
Model 900 - Stripped Chassis — 3
Model 900X - Stripped Chassis — 1
Model 91 - Four-Door Touring Sedan (6) — 1,223
Model 91X - Four-Door Touring Sedan (6) — 8
Model 91F - Formal Sedan (6) — 293
Model 91FX - Formal Sedan (6) — 3
377,428

1942

SPECIAL A-SERIES
Model 44 - Utility Coupe (3) — 461
Model 44C - Convertible Coupe (6) — 1,776
Model 44CX - Convertible Coupe (6) — 12
Model 47 - Four-Door Touring Sedan (6) — 1,611
Model 47X - Four-Door Touring Sedan (6) — 41
Model 48 - Business Sedanet (3) — 559
Model 48S - Family Sedanet (6) — 5,981
Model 48SX - Family Sedanet (6) — 9

SPECIAL B-SERIES
Model 41 - Four-Door Touring Sedan (6) — 17,187
Model 41X - Four-Door Touring Sedan (6) — 310
Model 41SE - Sedan, Super Equipment (6) — 2,286
Model 41SEX - Sedan, Super Equipment (6) — 2
Model 410 - Stripped Chassis — 175
Model 410X - Stripped Chassis — 828
Model 46 - Business Sedanet (3) — 1,406
Model 46X - Business Sedanet (3) — 2
Model 46S - Family Sedanet (6) — 11,856
Model 46SX - Family Sedanet (6) — 77
Model 46SSE - Sedanet, Super Equipment (6) — 1,809
Model 49 - Estate Wagon (6) — 326
Model 49X - Estate Wagon (6) — 1

SUPER SERIES
Model 51 - Four-Door Touring Sedan (6) — 16,001
Model 51X - Four-Door Touring Sedan (6) — 264
Model 510 - Stripped Chassis — 30

Model 510X - Stripped Chassis — 504
Model 56C - Convertible Coupe (6) — 2,454
Model 56CX - Convertible Coupe (6) — 35
Model 56S - Sedanet (6) — 14,579
Model 56SX - Sedanet (6) — 50

ROADMASTER SERIES
Model 71 - Four-Door Touring Sedan (6) — 5,418
Model 71X - Four-Door Touring Sedan (6) — 21
Model 710 - Stripped Chassis — 86
Model 710X - Stripped Chassis — 48
Model 76C - Convertible Coupe (6) — 509
Model 76CX - Convertible Coupe (6) — 2
Model 76S - Sedanet (6) — 2,471
Model 76SX - Sedanet (6) — 4

LIMITED SERIES
Model 90 - Four-Door Touring Sedan (8) — 144
Model 90X - Four-Door Touring Sedan (8) — 6
Model 90L - Limousine (8) — 192
Model 90LX - Limousine (8) — 58
Model 91 - Four-Door Touring Sedan (6) — 215
Model 91F - Formal Sedan (6) — 85
94,442

1945

Total Production — 2,482

1946

SPECIAL SERIES
Model 41 - Four-Door Sedan — 1,649
Model 41X - Four-Door Sedan — 1
Model 46S - Sedanet — 1,350
Model 410 - Stripped Chassis — 2
Model 412X - Stripped Chassis — 1,500

SUPER SERIES
Model 51 - Four-Door Sedan — 74,045
Model 51X - Four-Door Sedan — 3,679
Model 56C - Convertible Coupe — 5,931
Model 56CX - Convertible Coupe — 56
Model 56S - Sedanet — 34,235
Model 56SX - Sedanet — 190
Model 59 - Estate Wagon — 786
Model 59X - Estate Wagon — 12
Model 510 - Stripped Chassis — 1
Model 511X - Stripped Chassis — 3,120
Model 514 - Stripped Chassis — 80

ROADMASTER SERIES
Model 71 - Four-Door Sedan — 20,597
Model 71X - Four-Door Sedan — 267
Model 76C - Convertible Coupe — 2,576
Model 76CX - Convertible Coupe — 11
Model 76S - Sedanet — 8,226
Model 76SX - Sedanet — 66
Model 711X - Stripped Chassis — 168
Model 713 - Stripped Chassis — 180
158,728

1947

SPECIAL SERIES
Model 41 - Four-Door Sedan — 17,136
Model 41X - Four-Door Sedan — 1,295
Model 46S - Sedanet — 14,278
Model 46SX - Sedanet — 325
Model 411X - Stripped Chassis — 624
Model 412X - Stripped Chassis — 504
Model 461 - Stripped Chassis — 108

SUPER SERIES
Model 51 - Four-Door Sedan — 76,866
Model 51X - Four-Door Sedan — 6,710
Model 56C - Convertible Coupe — 25,796
Model 56CX - Convertible Coupe — 501
Model 56S - Sedanet — 46,311
Model 56SX - Sedanet — 606
Model 59 - Estate Wagon — 2,031
Model 59X - Estate Wagon — 5
Model 511X - Stripped Chassis — 4,584

ROADMASTER SERIES
Model 71 - Four-Door Sedan — 46,531
Model 71X - Four-Door Sedan — 621
Model 76C - Convertible Coupe — 11,947
Model 76CX - Convertible Coupe — 127
Model 76S - Sedanet — 18,983
Model 76SX - Sedanet — 229
Model 710 - Stripped Chassis — 4
Model 711X - Stripped Chassis — 360
Model 713 - Stripped Chassis — 352
Model 79 - Estate Wagon — 300
277,134

1948

SPECIAL SERIES
Model 41 - Four-Door Sedan — 13,236
Model 41X - Four-Door Sedan — 815
Model 46S - Sedanet — 10,775
Model 46SX - Sedanet — 401
Model 411X - Stripped Chassis — 768
Model 461 - Stripped Chassis — 192

SUPER SERIES
Model 51 - Four-Door Sedan — 47,991
Model 51X - Four-Door Sedan — 5,456
Model 56C - Convertible Coupe — 18,311
Model 56CX - Convertible Coupe — 706
Model 56S - Sedanet — 32,860
Model 56SX - Sedanet — 959
Model 59 - Estate Wagon — 1,955
Model 59X - Estate Wagon — 63
Model 511X - Stripped Chassis — 4,140

ROADMASTER SERIES
Model 71 - Four-Door Sedan — 47,042
Model 71X - Four-Door Sedan — 527
Model 76C - Convertible Coupe — 11,367
Model 76CX - Convertible Coupe — 136
Model 76S - Sedanet — 20,542
Model 76SX - Sedanet — 107
Model 710 - Stripped Chassis — 1
Model 711X - Stripped Chassis — 372
Model 713 - Stripped Chassis — 646
Model 79 - Estate Wagon — 344
Model 79X - Estate Wagon — 6
219,718

Note: Five millionth Buick produced September 1948

1949

SPECIAL SERIES
Model 41 - Four-Door Sedan — 5,777
Model 41X - Four-Door Sedan — 163
Model 46S - Sedanet — 4,631
Model 46SX - Sedanet — 56

SUPER SERIES
Model 51 - Four-Door Sedan — 131,514
Model 51X - Four-Door Sedan — 4,909
Model 56C - Convertible Coupe — 21,426
Model 56CX - Convertible Coupe — 684

Model 56S - Sedanet	65,395
Model 56SX - Sedanet	865
Model 59 - Estate Wagon	1,830
Model 59X - Estate Wagon	17
Model 510 - Stripped Chassis	4
Model 511X - Stripped Chassis	2,388

ROADMASTER SERIES

Model 71 - Four-Door Sedan	54,674
Model 71X - Four-Door Sedan	568
Model 76C - Convertible Coupe	8,095
Model 76CX - Convertible Coupe	149
Model 76R - Riviera Coupe	4,314
Model 76RX - Riviera Coupe	29
Model 76S - Sedanet	18,415
Model 76SX - Sedanet	122
Model 710 - Stripped Chassis	3
Model 711X - Stripped Chassis	240
Model 713 - Stripped Chassis	400
Model 79 - Estate Wagon	632
Model 79X - Estate Wagon	21
	327,321

1950

SPECIAL SERIES

Model 41 - Four-Door Touring Sedan	1,141
Model 41D - Four-Door Touring Sedan DeLuxe	141,396
Model 43 - Four-Door Sedan	58,700
Model 43D - Four-Door Sedan DeLuxe	14,355
Model 46 - Business Coupe (3)	2,500
Model 46S - Sedanet	42,935
Model 46D - Sedanet DeLuxe	76,902
Model 410 - Stripped Chassis	1
Model 411D - Stripped Chassis	420
Model 430 - Stripped Chassis	1

SUPER SERIES

Model 51 - Four-Door Touring Sedan	55,672
Model 52 - Four-Door Riviera	114,745
Model 56C - Convertible Coupe	12,259
Model 56R - Two-Door Riviera	56,030
Model 56S - Sedanet	10,697
Model 59 - Estate Wagon	2,480
Model 510 - Stripped Chassis	7
Model 511 - Stripped Chassis	1,296
Model 513 - Stripped Chassis	165
Model 520 - Stripped Chassis	1

ROADMASTER SERIES

Model 71 - Four-Door Touring Sedan	6,738
Model 72 - Four-Door DeLuxe Riviera	54,212
Model 75R - Two-Door Riviera	2,300
Model 76C - Convertible Coupe	2,964
Model 76R - Two-Door DeLuxe Riviera	8,432
Model 76S - Sedanet	2,968
Model 79 - Estate Wagon	420
Model 710 - Stripped Chassis	1
Model 711 - Stripped Chassis	300
Model 713 - Stripped Chassis	237
Model 720 - Stripped Chassis	1
	670,256

Note: Six millionth Buick produced December 1950

1951

SPECIAL SERIES

Model 41 - Four-Door Sedan	999
Model 41D - Four-Door DeLuxe Sedan	87,848
Model 45R - Two-Door Riviera	16,491
Model 46C - Convertible Coupe	2,099
Model 46S - Two-Door Sport Coupe	2,700
Model 48D - Two-Door DeLuxe Sedan	54,311
Model 410 - Stripped Chassis	2
Model 411D - Stripped Chassis	1,104

SUPER SERIES

Model 51 - Four-Door DeLuxe Sedan	10,000
Model 52 - Four-Door Riviera	92,886
Model 56C - Convertible Coupe	8,116
Model 56R - Two-Door Riviera	54,512
Model 56S - DeLuxe Sedanet	1,500
Model 59 - Estate Wagon	2,212
Model 513 - Stripped Chassis	201
Model 521 - Stripped Chassis	2,808

ROADMASTER SERIES

Model 72R - Four-Door Riviera	48,758
Model 76C - Convertible Coupe	2,911
Model 76R - Two-Door Riviera	12,901
Model 76MR - Two-Door Riviera (Alt.)	809
Model 79 - Estate Wagon	679
Model 710 - Stripped Chassis	1
Model 713 - Stripped Chassis	209
Model 721 - Stripped Chassis	600
	404,657

1952

SPECIAL SERIES

Model 41 - Four-Door Sedan	137
Model 41D - Four-Door DeLuxe Sedan	63,346
Model 45R - Two-Door Riviera	21,180
Model 46C - Convertible Coupe	600
Model 46S - Two-Door Sport Coupe	2,206
Model 48D - Two-Door DeLuxe Sedan	32,684
Model 410 - Stripped Chassis	1
Model 411D - Stripped Chassis	744

SUPER SERIES

Model 52 - Four-Door Riviera	71,387
Model 56C - Convertible Coupe	6,904
Model 56R - Two-Door Riviera	55,400
Model 59 - Estate Wagon	1,641
Model 510 - Stripped Chassis	1
Model 513 - Stripped Chassis	51
Model 521 - Stripped Chassis	900
Model 561 - Stripped Chassis	72
Model 564 - Stripped Chassis	48

ROADMASTER SERIES

Model 72R - Four-Door Riviera	32,069
Model 76C - Convertible Coupe	2,402
Model 76R - Two-Door Riviera	11,387
Model 79R - Estate Wagon	359
Model 710 - Stripped Chassis	1
Model 713 - Stripped Chassis	81
Model 721 - Stripped Chassis	144
	303,745

1953

SPECIAL SERIES

Model 41D - Four-Door DeLuxe Sedan	100,312
Model 45R - Two-Door Riviera	58,780
Model 46C - Convertible Coupe	4,282
Model 48D - Two-Door DeLuxe Sedan	53,796
Model 411D - Stripped Chassis	504

SUPER SERIES

Model 52 - Four-Door Riviera	90,685
Model 56C - Convertible Coupe	6,701

Model 56R - Two-Door Riviera	91,298
Model 59 - Estate Wagon	1,830
Model 521 - Stripped Chassis	1,332
Model 561 - Stripped Chassis	48

ROADMASTER SERIES

Model 72R - Four-Door Riviera	50,523
Model 76C - Convertible Coupe	3,318
Model 76R - Two-Door Riviera	22,927
Model 76X - Two-Door Skylark	1,690
Model 79R - DeLuxe Estate Wagon	670
Model 720 - Stripped Chassis	1
Model 721 - Stripped Chassis	108
	488,805

Note: Seven millionth Buick produced June 1953

1954

SPECIAL SERIES

Model 41D - Four-Door DeLuxe Sedan	70,356
Model 46C - Convertible Coupe	6,135
Model 46R - Two-Door Riviera	71,186
Model 48D - Two-Door DeLuxe Sedan	41,557
Model 49 - Estate Wagon	1,650
Model 411D - Stripped Chassis	600

SUPER SERIES

Model 52 - Four-Door Riviera	41,756
Model 56C - Convertible Coupe	3,343
Model 56R - Two-Door Riviera	73,531
Model 520 - Stripped Chassis	1
Model 521 - Stripped Chassis	744

CENTURY SERIES

Model 61 - Four-Door DeLuxe Sedan	31,919
Model 66C - Convertible Coupe	2,790
Model 66R - Two-Door Riviera	45,710
Model 69 - Estate Wagon	1,563
Model 610 - Stripped Chassis	1

ROADMASTER SERIES

Model 72R - Four-Door Riviera	26,862
Model 76C - Convertible Coupe	3,305
Model 76R - Two-Door Riviera	20,404
Model 721 - Stripped Chassis	360
SKYLARK: Model 100 - Convertible	836
	444,609

1955

SPECIAL SERIES

Model 41 - Four-Door Tourback Sedan	84,182
Model 43 - Four-Door Riviera	66,409
Model 46C - Convertible Coupe	10,009
Model 46R - Two-Door Riviera	155,818
Model 48 - Two-Door Tourback Sedan	61,879
Model 49 - Estate Wagon	2,952
Model 410 - Stripped Chassis	1
Model 411 - Stripped Chassis	696

SUPER SERIES

Model 52 - Four-Door Sedan	43,280
Model 56C - Convertible Coupe	3,527
Model 56R - Two-Door Riviera	85,656
Model 520 - Stripped Chassis	1
Model 521 - Stripped Chassis	744

CENTURY SERIES

Model 61 - Four-Door Tourback Sedan	13,269
Model 63 - Four-Door Riviera	55,088
Model 66C - Convertible Coupe	5,588
Model 66R - Two-Door Riviera	80,338
Model 68 - Two-Door Tourback Sedan	270
Model 69 - Estate Wagon	4,243

ROADMASTER SERIES

Model 72 - Four-Door Sedan	31,717
Model 76C - Convertible Coupe	4,739
Model 76R - Two-Door Riviera	28,071
Model 720 - Stripped Chassis	1
Model 721 - Stripped Chassis	336
	738,814

Note: Eight millionth Buick produced April 1955

1956
SPECIAL SERIES

Model 41 - Four-Door Sedan	66,977
Model 43 - Four-Door Riviera	91,025
Model 46C - Convertible Coupe	9,712
Model 46R - Two-Door Riviera	113,861
Model 48 - Two-Door Sedan	38,672
Model 49 - Estate Wagon	13,770
Model 411 - Stripped Chassis	96
Model 413 - Stripped Chassis	576

SUPER SERIES

Model 52 - Four-Door Sedan	14,940
Model 53 - Four-Door Riviera	34,029
Model 56C - Convertible Coupe	2,489
Model 56R - Two-Door Riviera	29,540
Model 520 - Stripped Chassis	1
Model 521 - Stripped Chassis	336
Model 531 - Stripped Chassis	144

CENTURY SERIES

Model 61 - Four-Door Tourback Sedan	1
Model 63 - Four-Door Riviera	20,891
Model 63D - Four-Door DeLuxe Riviera	35,082
Model 66C - Convertible Coupe	4,721
Model 66R - Two-Door Riviera	33,334
Model 69 - Estate Wagon	8,160

ROADMASTER SERIES

Model 72 - Four-Door Sedan	11,804
Model 73 - Four-Door Riviera	24,779
Model 76C - Convertible Coupe	4,354
Model 76R - Two-Door Riviera	12,490
Model 721 - Stripped Chassis	144
Model 731 - Stripped Chassis	96
	572,024

Note: Nine millionth Buick produced November 1956

1957
SPECIAL SERIES

Model 41 - Four-Door Sedan	59,739
Model 43 - Four-Door Riviera	50,563
Model 46C - Convertible Coupe	8,505
Model 46R - Two-Door Riviera	64,425
Model 48 - Two-Door Sedan	23,180
Model 49 - Estate Wagon	7,013
Model 49D - Four-Door Riviera Estate Wagon	6,817
Model 411 - Stripped Chassis	144
Model 431 - Stripped Chassis	360

SUPER SERIES

Model 53 - Four-Door Riviera	41,665
Model 56C - Convertible Coupe	2,056
Model 56R - Two-Door Riviera	26,529
Model 530 - Stripped Chassis	1
Model 531 - Strippcd Chassis	384

CENTURY SERIES

Model 61 - Four-Door Sedan	8,075
Model 63 - Four-Door Riviera	26,589
Model 66C - Convertible Coupe	4,085
Model 66R - Two-Door Riviera	17,029

Model 68 - Two-Door Sedan	2
Model 69 - Four-Door Riviera Estate Wagon	10,186

ROADMASTER SERIES

Model 73 - Four-Door Riviera	11,401
Model 73A - Four-Door Riviera	10,526
Model 75 - Four-Door Riviera	12,250
Model 75R - Two-Door Riviera	2,404
Model 76C - Convertible Coupe	4,363
Model 76R - Two-Door Riviera	3,826
Model 76A - Two-Door Riviera	2,812
Model 731 - Stripped Chassis	96
Model 750 - Stripped Chassis	1
Model 751 - Stripped Chassis	72
	405,098

Note: Rivieras 75 and 75R had sweepspear, 73 and 76R had straight-side moldings; 73A and 76A had chrome moldings on rear deck only

1958
SPECIAL SERIES

Model 41 - Four-Door Sedan	48,238
Model 43 - Four-Door Riviera	31,921
Model 46C - Convertible Coupe	5,502
Model 46R - Two-Door Riviera	34,903
Model 48 - Two-Door Sedan	11,566
Model 49 - Estate Wagon	3,663
Model 49D - Four-Door Riviera Estate Wagon	3,420
Model 411 - Stripped Chassis	648
Model 431 - Stripped Chassis	360

SUPER SERIES

Model 53 - Four-Door Riviera	28,460
Model 56R - Two-Door Riviera	13,928
Model 530 - Stripped Chassis	1
Model 531 - Stripped Chassis	168

CENTURY SERIES

Model 61 - Four-Door Sedan	7,241
Model 63 - Four-Door Riviera	15,171
Model 66C - Convertible Coupe	2,588
Model 66R - Two-Door Riviera	8,110
Model 68 - Two-Door Sedan	2
Model 69 - Four-Door Riviera Estate Wagon	4,456

ROADMASTER SERIES

Model 75 - Four-Door Riviera	10,505
Model 75C - Convertible Coupe	1,181
Model 75R - Two-Door Riviera	2,368

LIMITED SERIES

Model 701 - Stripped Chassis	72
Model 750 - Four-Door Riviera	5,571
Model 756 - Convertible Coupe	839
Model 755 - Two-Door Riviera	1,026
	241,908

1959
LESABRE SERIES

Model 4411 - Two-Door Sedan	13,492
Model 4419 - Four-Door Sedan	51,379
Model 4435 - Estate Wagon	8,286
Model 4437 - Two-Door Hardtop Coupe	35,189
Model 4439 - Four-Door Hardtop Sedan	46,069
Model 4467 - Convertible Coupe	10,489
Model 4410 - Stripped Chassis	192
Model 4430 - Stripped Chassis	480
Model 4490 - Stripped Chassis	1

INVICTA SERIES

Model 4619 - Four-Door Sedan	10,566
Model 4635 - Estate Wagon	5,231
Model 4637 - Two-Door Hardtop Coupe	11,451

Model 4639 - Four-Door Hardtop Sedan	20,156
Model 4667 - Convertible Coupe	5,447

ELECTRA SERIES

Model 4719 - Four-Door Sedan	12,357
Model 4737 - Two-Door Hardtop Coupe	11,216
Model 4739 - Four-Door Hardtop Sedan	20,612
Model 4730 - Stripped Chassis	48

ELECTRA 225 SERIES

Model 4829 - Four-Door Riviera	6,324
Model 4839 - Four-Door Hardtop Sedan	10,491
Model 4867 - Convertible Coupe	5,493
Model 4830 - Stripped Chassis	120
	285,089

1960
LESABRE SERIES

Model 4411 - Two-Door Sedan	14,388
Model 4419 - Four-Door Sedan	54,033
Model 4435 - Estate Wagon (two seats)	5,331
Model 4437 - Two-Door Hardtop Coupe	26,521
Model 4439 - Four-Door Hardtop Coupe	35,999
Model 4445 - Estate Wagon (three seats)	2,222
Model 4467 - Convertible Coupe	13,588
Model 4430 - Stripped Chassis	144

INVICTA SERIES

Model 4619 - Four-Door Sedan	10,839
Model 4635 - Estate Wagon (two seats)	3,471
Model 4637 - Two-Door Hardtop Coupe	8,960
Model 4639 - Four-Door Hardtop Sedan	15,300
Model 4645 - Estate Wagon (three seats)	1,605
Model 4667 - Convertible Coupe	5,236

ELECTRA SERIES

Model 4719 - Four-Door Sedan	13,794
Model 4737 - Two-Door Hardtop Coupe	7,416
Model 4739 - Four-Door Hardtop Sedan	14,488
Model 4730 - Stripped Chassis	24

ELECTRA 225 SERIES

Model 4829 - Four-Door Riviera	8,029
Model 4839 - Four-Door Hardtop Sedan	5,841
Model 4867 - Convertible Coupe	6,746
Model 4830 - Stripped Chassis	24
	253,999

Note: Ten millionth Buick produced January 1960

1961
SPECIAL SERIES

Model 4019 - Four-Door Sedan	18,339
Model 4027 - Two-Door Coupe	4,232
Model 4035 - Station Wagon (two seats)	6,101
Model 4045 - Station Wagon (three seats)	798
Model 4119 - Four-Door DeLuxe Sedan	32,986
Model 4135 - DeLuxe Wagon (two seats)	11,729
Model 4110 - Stripped Chassis	576
SKYLARK: Model 4317 - Two-Door Coupe	12,683

LESABRE SERIES

Model 4411 - Two-Door Sedan	5,959
Model 4435 - Estate Wagon (two seats)	5,628
Model 4437 - Two-Door Hardtop	14,474
Model 4439 - Four-Door Hardtop	37,790
Model 4445 - Estate Wagon (three seats)	2,423
Model 4467 - Convertible Coupe	11,951
Model 4469 - Four-Door Sedan	35,005
Model 4430 - Stripped Chassis	96

INVICTA SERIES

Model 4637 - Two-Door Hardtop	6,382
Model 4639 - Four-Door Hardtop	18,398

425

Model 4667 - Convertible Coupe | 3,953

ELECTRA SERIES
Model 4719 - Four-Door Sedan | 13,818
Model 4737 - Two-Door Hardtop | 4,250
Model 4739 - Four-Door Hardtop | 8,978

ELECTRA 225 SERIES
Model 4829 - Four-Door Riviera | 13,719
Model 4867 - Convertible Coupe | 7,158
277,426

1962

SPECIAL SERIES
Model 4019 - Four-Door Sedan | 23,249
Model 4027 - Two-Door Coupe | 19,135
Model 4035 - Station Wagon (two seats) | 7,382
Model 4045 - Station Wagon (three seats) | 2,814
Model 4067 - Convertible Coupe | 7,918
Model 4119 - Four-Door DeLuxe Sedan | 31,660
Model 4135 - DeLuxe Wagon (two seats) | 10,380
Model 4167 - DeLuxe Convertible Coupe | 8,332
Model 4110 - Stripped Chassis | 624
Model 4347 - Skylark Two-Door Coupe | 34,060
Model 4367 - Skylark Two-Door Convertible | 8,913

LESABRE SERIES
Model 4411 - Two-Door Sedan | 7,418
Model 4439 - Four-Door Hardtop | 37,518
Model 4447 - Two-Door Sport Coupe | 25,479
Model 4469 - Four-Door Sedan | 56,783

INVICTA SERIES
Model 4635 - Estate Wagon (two seats) | 9,131
Model 4639 - Four-Door Hardtop | 16,443
Model 4645 - Estate Wagon (three seats) | 4,617
Model 4647 - Two-Door Sport Coupe | 12,355
Model 4667 - Convertible Coupe | 13,471

ELECTRA 225 SERIES
Model 4819 - Four-Door Sedan | 13,523
Model 4829 - Four-Door Riviera | 15,395
Model 4839 - Four-Door Hardtop | 16,734
Model 4847 - Two-Door Sport Coupe | 8,922
Model 4867 - Convertible Coupe | 7,894
400,150

Note: Eleven millionth Buick produced December 1962

1963

SPECIAL SERIES
Model 4019 - Four-Door Sedan | 21,733
Model 4027 - Two-Door Coupe | 21,886
Model 4035 - Station Wagon (two seats) | 5,867
Model 4045 - Station Wagon (three seats) | 2,415
Model 4067 - Convertible Coupe | 8,082
Model 4119 - Four-Door DeLuxe Sedan | 37,695
Model 4135 - DeLuxe Wagon (two seats) | 8,771
Model 4110 - Stripped Chassis | 768
Model 4347 - Skylark Two-Door Coupe | 32,109
Model 4367 - Skylark Two-Door Convertible | 10,212

LESABRE SERIES
Model 4411 - Two-Door Sedan | 8,328
Model 4435 - Estate Wagon (two seats) | 5,566
Model 4439 - Four-Door Hardtop | 50,420
Model 4445 - Estate Wagon (three seats) | 3,922
Model 4447 - Two-Door Sport Coupe | 27,977
Model 4467 - Convertible Coupe | 9,975
Model 4469 - Four-Door Sedan | 64,995

INVICTA/WILDCAT SERIES
Model 4635 - Estate Wagon (two seats) | 3,495
Model 4639 - Four-Door Wildcat Hardtop | 17,519
Model 4647 - Two-Door Wildcat Sport Coupe | 12,185
Model 4667 - Two-Door Wildcat Convertible | 6,021
RIVIERA: Model 4747 - Two-Door Coupe | 40,000

ELECTRA 225 SERIES
Model 4819 - Four-Door Sedan | 14,268
Model 4829 - Four-Door Pillarless Sedan | 11,468
Model 4839 - Four-Door Hardtop | 19,714
Model 4847 - Two-Door Sport Coupe | 6,848
Model 4867 - Two-Door Convertible | 6,367
458,606

1964

SPECIAL SERIES
Model 4027 - Two-Door Coupe | 15,030
Model 4035 - Station Wagon (two seats) | 6,270
Model 4067 - Convertible Coupe | 6,308
Model 4069 - Four-Door Sedan | 17,983
Model 4127 - Two-Door DeLuxe Coupe | 11,962
Model 4135 - DeLuxe Station Wagon (two seats) | 9,467
Model 4169 - Four-Door DeLuxe Sedan | 31,742
Model 4160 - Crated Knocked-Down Chassis | 768
Model 4255 - Skylark Sport Wagon (two seats) | 2,709
Model 4265 - Skylark Sport Wagon (three seats) | 2,586
Model 4337 - Skylark Sport Coupe | 42,356
Model 4355 - Skylark Custom Sport Wagon (two seats) | 3,913
Model 4365 - Skylark Custom Sport Wagon (three seats) | 4,446
Model 4367 - Skylark Two-Door Convertible | 10,225
Model 4369 - Skylark Four-Door Sedan | 19,635
Model 4330 - Crated Knocked-Down Chassis | 288

LESABRE SERIES
Model 4439 - Four-Door Hardtop | 37,052
Model 4447 - Two-Door Sport Coupe | 24,177
Model 4467 - Convertible Coupe | 6,685
Model 4469 - Four-Door Sedan | 56,729
Model 4635 - Estate Wagon (two seats) | 6,517
Model 4645 - Estate Wagon (three seats) | 4,003

WILDCAT SERIES
Model 4639 - Four-Door Hardtop | 33,358
Model 4647 - Two-Door Sport Coupe | 22,893
Model 4667 - Convertible Coupe | 7,850
Model 4669 - Four-Door Sedan | 20,144
RIVIERA: Model 4747 - Two-Door Coupe | 37,658

ELECTRA 225 SERIES
Model 4819 - Four-Door Sedan | 15,968
Model 4829 - Four-Door Pillarless Sedan | 11,663
Model 4839 - Four-Door Hardtop | 24,935
Model 4847 - Two-Door Sport Coupe | 9,045
Model 4867 - Convertible Coupe | 7,181
Model 4810 - Crated Knocked Down Chassis | 120
511,666

1965

SPECIAL SERIES
Model 43327 - Two-Door Coupe (V-6) | 12,945
Model 43427 - Two-Door Coupe (V-8) | 5,309
Model 43335 - Station Wagon (V-6 two seats) | 2,868
Model 43435 - Station Wagon (V-8 two seats) | 3,676
Model 43367 - Convertible Coupe (V-6) | 3,357
Model 43467 - Convertible Coupe (V-8) | 3,365
Model 43369 - Four-Door Sedan (V-6) | 13,828
Model 43469 - Four-Door Sedan (V-8) | 8,121

SPECIAL DELUXE SERIES
Model 43535 - Station Wagon (V-6 two seats) | 1,677

Model 43635 - Station Wagon (V-8 two seats) | 9,123
Model 43569 - Four-Door Sedan (V-6) | 10,961
Model 43569 - Crated Knocked Down Chassis | 72
Model 43669 - Four-Door Sedan (V-8) | 25,675
Model 43669 - Crated Knocked Down Chassis | 624

SKYLARK SERIES
Model 44327 - Two-Door Coupe (V-6) | 4,195
Model 44427 - Two-Door Coupe (V-8) | 11,877
Model 44337 - Two-Door Sport Coupe (V-6) | 4,501
Model 44337 - Crated Knocked Down Chassis | 48
Model 44437 - Two-Door Sport Coupe (V-8) | 46,698
Model 44437 - Crated Knocked Down Chassis | 336
Model 44367 - Convertible Coupe (V-6) | 1,181
Model 44467 - Convertible Coupe (V-8) | 10,456
Model 44369 - Four-Door Sedan (V-6) | 3,385
Model 44469 - Four-Door Sedan (V-8) | 22,239
Model 44469 - Crated Knocked Down Chassis | 96

SPORTWAGON SERIES
Model 44255 - Wagon (two seats) | 4,226
Model 44265 - Wagon (three seats) | 4,664
Model 44455 - Custom Wagon (two seats) | 8,300
Model 44465 - Custom Wagon (three seats) | 11,166

LESABRE SERIES
Model 45237 - Two-Door Sport Coupe | 15,786
Model 45239 - Four-Door Hardtop Sedan | 18,384
Model 45269 - Four-Door Sedan | 37,788
Model 45437 - Custom Two-Door Sport Coupe | 21,049
Model 45439 - Custom Four-Door Hardtop Sedan | 23,394
Model 45467 - Custom Convertible Coupe | 6,543
Model 45469 - Custom Four-Door Sedan | 22,052

WILDCAT SERIES
Model 46237 - Two-Door Sport Coupe | 6,031
Model 46239 - Four-Door Hardtop Sedan | 7,499
Model 46269 - Four-Door Sedan | 10,184
Model 46437 - DeLuxe Two-Door Sport Coupe | 11,617
Model 46439 - DeLuxe Four-Door Hardtop Sedan | 13,903
Model 46467 - DeLuxe Convertible Coupe | 4,616
Model 46469 - DeLuxe Four-Door Sedan | 9,765
Model 46637 - Custom Two-Door Sport Coupe | 15,896
Model 46639 - Custom Four-Door Hardtop Sedan | 14,878
Model 46667 - Custom Convertible Coupe | 4,398

ELECTRA 225 SERIES
Model 48237 - Two-Door Sport Coupe | 6,302
Model 48239 - Four-Door Hardtop Sedan | 12,842
Model 48269 - Four-Door Sedan | 12,459
Model 48437 - Custom Two-Door Sport Coupe | 9,570
Model 48439 - Custom Four-Door Hardtop Sedan | 29,932
Model 48467 - Custom Convertible Coupe | 8,508
Model 48469 - Custom Four-Door Sedan | 7,197
RIVIERA: Model 49447 - Two-Door Coupe | 34,586
600,148

Note: Twelve millionth Buick produced January 1965

1966

SPECIAL SERIES
Model 43307 - Two-Door Coupe (V-6) | 9,322
Model 43407 - Two-Door Coupe (V-8) | 5,719
Model 43335 - Station Wagon (V-6 two seats) | 1,451
Model 43435 - Station Wagon (V-8 two seats) | 3,038
Model 43367 - Convertible Coupe (V-6) | 1,357
Model 43467 - Convertible Coupe (V-8) | 2,036
Model 43369 - Four-Door Sedan (V-6) | 8,797
Model 43469 - Four-Door Sedan (V-8) | 9,355

SPECIAL DELUXE SERIES
Model 43507 - Two-Door Coupe (V-6) | 2,359
Model 43607 - Two-Door Coupe (V-8) | 4,908

Model 43517 - Two-Door Sport Coupe (V-6) — 2,507
Model 43617 - Two-Door Sport Coupe (V-8) — 10,350
Model 43535 - Station Wagon (V-6 two seats) — 824
Model 43635 - Station Wagon (V-8 two seats) — 7,592
Model 43569 - Four-Door Sedan (V-6) — 5,501
Model 43569 - Crated Knocked Down Chassis — 72
Model 43669 - Four-Door Sedan (V-8) — 26,773
Model 43669 - Crated Knocked Down Chassis — 1,176

SKYLARK SERIES
Model 44307 - Two-Door Coupe (V-6) — 1,454
Model 44407 - Two-Door Coupe (V-8) — 6,427
Model 44317 - Two-Door Sport Coupe (V-6) — 2,456
Model 44317 - Crated Knocked-Down Chassis — 96
Model 44417 - Two-Door Sport Coupe (V-8) — 33,086
Model 44417 - Crated Knocked -Down Chassis — 240
Model 44339 - Four-Door Hardtop (V-6) — 1,422
Model 44439 - Four-Door Hardtop (V-8) — 18,729
Model 44439 - Crated Knocked Down Chassis — 144
Model 44367 - Convertible Coupe (V-6) — 608
Model 44467 - Convertible Coupe (V-8) — 6,129

SKYLARK GRAN SPORT SERIES
Model 44607 - Two-Door Coupe — 1,835
Model 44617 - Two-Door Sport Coupe — 9,934
Model 44667 - Convertible Coupe — 2,047

SPORTWAGON SERIES
Model 44255 - Wagon (two seats) — 2,469
Model 44265 - Wagon (three seats) — 2,667
Model 44455 - Custom Wagon (two seats) — 6,964
Model 44465 - Custom Wagon (three seats) — 9,510

LESABRE SERIES
Model 45237 - Two-Door Sport Coupe — 13,843
Model 45239 - Four-Door Hardtop Sedan — 17,740
Model 45269 - Four-Door Sedan — 39,146
Model 45437 - Custom Two-Door Sport Coupe — 18,830
Model 45439 - Custom Four-Door Hardtop Sedan — 26,914
Model 45467 - Custom Convertible Coupe — 4,994
Model 45469 - Custom Four-Door Sedan — 25,932

WILDCAT SERIES
Model 46437 - Two-Door Sport Coupe — 9,774
Model 46439 - Four-Door Hardtop Sedan — 15,081
Model 46467 - Convertible Coupe — 2,690
Model 46469 - Four-Door Sedan — 14,389
Model 46637 - Custom Two-Door Sport Coupe — 10,800
Model 46639 - Custom Four-Door Hardtop Sedan — 13,060
Model 46667 - Custom Convertible Coupe — 2,790

ELECTRA SERIES
Model 48237 - Two-Door Sport Coupe — 4,882
Model 48239 - Four-Door Hardtop — 10,792
Model 48269 - Four-Door Sedan — 11,692
Model 48269 - Crated Knocked Down Chassis — 48
Model 48437 - Custom Two-Door Sport Coupe — 10,119
Model 48439 - Custom Four-Door Hardtop — 34,149
Model 48467 - Custom Convertible Coupe — 7,175
Model 48469 - Custom Four-Door Sedan — 9,368
RIVIERA: Model 49487 - Two-Door Coupe — 45,348
558,870

Note: Thirteen millionth Buick produced September 1966

1967
SPECIAL SERIES
Model 43307 - Two-Door Coupe (V-6) — 6,989
Model 43407 - Two-Door Coupe (V-8) — 8,937
Model 43417 - Two-Door Sport Coupe (V-8) — 3,692
Model 43335 - Station Wagon (V-6 two seats) — 908
Model 43435 - Station Wagon (V-8 two seats) — 1,688

Model 43369 - Four-Door Sedan (V-6) — 4,711
Model 43469 - Four-Door Sedan (V-8) — 5,793

SPECIAL DELUXE SERIES
Model 43517 - Two-Door Sport Coupe (V-6) — 2,333
Model 43517 - Crated Knocked Down Chassis — 24
Model 43617 - Two-Door Sport Coupe (V-8) — 14,408
Model 43635 - Station Wagon (V-8 two seats) — 6,851
Model 43569 - Four-Door Sedan (V-6) — 3,602
Model 43569 - Crated Knocked Down Chassis — 48
Model 43669 - Four-Door Sedan (V-8) — 25,361
Model 43669 - Crated Knocked Down Chassis — 696

SKYLARK SERIES
Model 44307 - Two-Door Coupe (V-6) — 894
Model 44407 - Two-Door Coupe (V-8) — 3,165
Model 44417 - Two-Door Sport Coupe (V-8) — 40,940
Model 44417 - Crated Knocked Down Chassis — 144
Model 44439 - Four-Door Hardtop (V-8) — 13,673
Model 44439 - Crated Knocked Down Chassis — 48
Model 44467 - Convertible Coupe (V-8) — 6,319
Model 44469 - Four-Door Sedan (V-8) — 9,213

SKYLARK GRAN SPORT SERIES
Model 44607 - Two-Door Coupe — 1,014
Model 44617 - Two-Door Sport Coupe — 10,659
Model 44667 - Convertible Coupe — 2,140

SPORT WAGON SERIES
Model 44455 - Wagon (two seats) — 5,440
Model 44465 - Wagon (three seats) — 5,970
Model 44855 - Custom Wagon (two seats) — 3,114
Model 44865 - Custom Wagon (three seats) — 4,559

LESABRE SERIES
Model 45239 - Four-Door Hardtop — 17,464
Model 45269 - Four-Door Sedan — 36,220
Model 45287 - Two-Door Sport Coupe — 13,760
Model 45439 - Custom Four-Door Hardtop — 32,526
Model 45467 - Custom Convertible Coupe — 4,624
Model 45469 - Custom Four-Door Sedan — 27,930
Model 45487 - Two-Door Sport Coupe — 22,666

WILDCAT SERIES
Model 46439 - Four-Door Hardtop — 15,110
Model 46467 - Convertible Coupe — 2,276
Model 46469 - Four-Door Sedan — 14,579
Model 46487 - Two-Door Sport Coupe — 10,585
Model 46639 - Custom Four-Door Hardtop — 13,547
Model 46667 - Custom Convertible Coupe — 2,913
Model 46687 - Custom Two-Door Sport Coupe — 11,871

ELECTRA 225 SERIES
Model 48239 - Four-Door Hardtop — 12,491
Model 48257 - Two-Door Sport Coupe — 6,845
Model 48269 - Four-Door Sedan — 10,787
Model 48439 - Custom Four-Door Hardtop — 40,978
Model 48457 - Custom Two-Door Sport Coupe — 12,156
Model 48467 - Custom Convertible Coupe — 6,941
Model 48469 - Custom Four-Door Sedan — 10,106
RIVIERA: Model 49487 - Two-Door Coupe — 42,799
562,507

1968
SPECIAL DELUXE SERIES
Model 43327 - Two-Door Coupe — 21,988
Model 43369 - Four-Door Sedan — 16,571
Model 43435 - Station Wagon (two seats) — 10,916

SKYLARK SERIES
Model 53537 - Two-Door Sport Coupe — 32,795
Model 43569 - Four-Door Sedan — 27,387

SKYLARK CUSTOM SERIES
Model 44437 - Two-Door Sport Coupe — 44,143
Model 44439 - Four-Door Hardtop — 12,984

Model 44467 - Convertible Coupe — 8,188
Model 44469 - Four-Door Sedan — 8,066

GRAN SPORT SERIES
Model 43437 - Two-Door Sport Coupe (GS 350) — 8,317
Model 44637 - Two-Door Sport Coupe (GS 400) — 10,743
Model 44667 - Convertible Coupe (GS 400) — 2,454

SPORTWAGON SERIES
Model 44455 - Wagon (two seats) — 5,916
Model 44465 - Wagon (three seats) — 6,083
Model 44855 - Wagon (two seats, wood grain) — 4,614
Model 44865 - Wagon (three seats, wood grain) — 6,295

LESABRE SERIES
Model 45239 - Four-Door Hardtop — 18,058
Model 45269 - Four-Door Sedan — 37,433
Model 45287 - Two-Door Sport Coupe — 14,922
Model 45439 - Custom Four-Door Hardtop — 40,370
Model 45467 - Custom Convertible Coupe — 5,257
Model 45469 - Custom Four-Door Sedan — 34,112
Model 45487 - Custom Two-Door Sport Coupe — 29,596

WILDCAT SERIES
Model 46439 - Four-Door Hardtop — 15,153
Model 46469 - Four-Door Sedan — 15,201
Model 46487 - Two-Door Sport Coupe — 10,708
Model 46639 - Custom Four-Door Hardtop — 14,059
Model 46667 - Custom Convertible Coupe — 3,572
Model 46687 - Custom Two-Door Sport Coupe — 11,276

ELECTRA 225 SERIES
Model 48239 - Four-Door Hardtop — 15,376
Model 48257 - Two-Door Sport Coupe — 10,705
Model 48269 - Four-Door Sedan — 12,723
Model 48439 - Custom Four-Door Hardtop — 50,846
Model 48457 - Custom Two-Door Sport Coupe — 16,826
Model 48467 - Custom Convertible Coupe — 7,976
Model 48469 - Custom Four-Door Sedan — 10,910
RIVIERA: Model 49487 Two-Door Sport Coupe — 49,284
651,823

Note: Fourteen millionth Buick produced April 1968

1969
SPECIAL DELUXE SERIES
Model 43327 - Two-Door Coupe — 15,268
Model 43369 - Four-Door Sedan — 11,113
Model 43435 - Station Wagon — 2,590
Model 43436 - Station Wagon (dual tailgate) — 6,677

SKYLARK SERIES
Model 43537 - Two-Door Sport Coupe — 38,658
Model 43569 - Four-Door Sedan — 22,349

SKYLARK CUSTOM SERIES
Model 44437 - Two-Door Sport Coupe — 35,639
Model 44439 - Four-Door Hardtop — 9,609
Model 44467 - Convertible Coupe — 6,552
Model 44469 - Four-Door Sedan — 6,423

GRAN SPORT SERIES
Model 43437 - Two-Door Sport Coupe (GS 350) — 6,305
Model 44637 - Two-Door Sport Coupe (GS 400) — 7,602
Model 44667 - Convertible Coupe (GS 400) — 1,776

SPORTWAGON SERIES
Model 44456 - Wagon (two seats) — 9,157
Model 44466 - Wagon (three seats) — 11,513

LESABRE SERIES
Model 45237 - Two-Door Sport Coupe — 16,201
Model 45239 - Four-Door Hardtop — 17,235
Model 45269 - Four-Door Sedan — 36,664
Model 45437 - Custom Two-Door Sport Coupe — 38,887
Model 45439 - Custom Four-Door Hardtop — 48,123
Model 45467 - Custom Convertible Coupe — 3,620

YEAR/MODEL/DESCRIPTION	MODEL UNITS
Model 45469 - Custom Four-Door Sedan	37,136

WILDCAT SERIES

Model 46437 - Two-Door Sport Coupe	12,416
Model 46439 - Four-Door Hardtop	13,805
Model 46469 - Four-Door Sedan	13,126
Model 46637 - Custom Two-Door Sport Coupe	12,136
Model 46639 - Custom Four-Door Hardtop	13,596
Model 46667 - Custom Convertible Coupe	2,374

ELECTRA 225 SERIES

Model 48239 - Four-Door Hardtop	15,983
Model 48257 - Two-Door Sport Coupe	13,128
Model 48269 - Four-Door Sedan	14,521
Model 48439 - Custom Four-Door Hardtop	65,240
Model 48457 - Custom Two-Door Sport Coupe	27,018
Model 48467 - Custom Convertible Coupe	8,294
Model 48469 - Custom Four-Door Sedan	14,434
RIVIERA: Model 49487 - Two-Door Sport Coupe	52,872
	668,040

Note: Fifteen millionth Buick produced October 1969

1970

SKYLARK SERIES

Model 43327 - Two-Door Coupe	18,620
Model 43369 - Four-Door Sedan	13,420

SPORTWAGON SERIES

Model 43435 - Wagon	2,239
Model 43436 - Wagon (dual tailgate)	10,002

SKYLARK 350 SERIES

Model 43537 - Two-Door Sport Coupe	70,918
Model 43569 - Four-Door Sedan	30,281

SKYLARK CUSTOM SERIES

Model 44437 - Two-Door Sport Coupe	36,367
Model 44439 - Four-Door Hardtop	12,411
Model 44467 - Convertible Coupe	4,954
Model 44469 - Four-Door Sedan	7,113

GRAN SPORT SERIES

Model 43437 - Two-Door Sport Coupe	9,948
Model 44637 - Two-Door Sport Coupe (GS 455)	8,732
Model 44667 - Convertible Coupe (GS 455)	1,416

LESABRE SERIES

Model 45237 - Two-Door Sport Coupe	14,163
Model 45239 - Four-Door Hardtop	14,817
Model 45269 - Four-Door Sedan	35,404
Model 45437 - Custom Two-Door Sport Coupe	35,641
Model 45439 - Custom Four-Door Hardtop	43,863
Model 45467 - Custom Convertible Coupe	2,487
Model 45469 - Custom Four-Door Sedan	36,682
Model 46437 - Custom 455 Sport Coupe	5,469
Model 46439 - Custom 455 Four-Door Hardtop	6,541
Model 46469 - Custom 455 Four-Door Sedan	5,555

ESTATE WAGON SERIES

Model 46036 - Station Wagon (two seats)	11,427
Model 46046 - Station Wagon (three seats)	16,879

WILDCAT CUSTOM SERIES

Model 46637 - Two-Door Sport Coupe	9,447
Model 46639 - Four-Door Hardtop	12,924
Model 46667 - Convertible Coupe	1,244

ELECTRA 225 SERIES

Model 48239 - Four-Door Hardtop	14,338
Model 48257 - Two-Door Sport Coupe	12,013
Model 48269 - Four-Door Sedan	12,580
Model 48439 - Custom Four-Door Hardtop	65,114
Model 48457 - Custom Two-Door Sport Coupe	26,002
Model 48467 - Custom Convertible Coupe	6,045
Model 48469 - Custom Four-Door Sedan	14,109
RIVIERA: Model 49487 - Two-Door Sport Coupe	37,336
	666,501

1971

SKYLARK SERIES

Model 43327 - Two-Door Coupe	14,500
Model 43337 - Two-Door Sport Coupe	61,201
Model 43369 - Four-Door Sedan	34,037
SPORT WAGON: Model 43436	12,525

GRAN SPORT SERIES

Model 43437 - Two-Door Sport Coupe	8,268
Model 43467 - Convertible Coupe	902

SKYLARK CUSTOM SERIES

Model 44437 - Two-Door Sport Coupe	29,536
Model 44439 - Four-Door Hardtop	10,814
Model 44467 - Convertible Coupe	3,993
Model 44469 - Four-Door Sedan	8,299

LESABRE SERIES

Model 45239 - Four-Door Hardtop	14,234
Model 45257 - Two-Door Sport Coupe	13,385
Model 45269 - Four-Door Sedan	26,348
Model 45439 - Custom Four-Door Hardtop	41,098
Model 45457 - Custom Two-Door Sport Coupe	29,944
Model 45467 - Custom Convertible Coupe	1,856
Model 45469 - Custom Four-Door Sedan	26,970

ESTATE WAGON SERIES

Model 46035 - Wagon (two seats)	8,699
Model 46045 - Wagon (three seats)	15,335

CENTURION SERIES

Model 46639 - Four-Door Hardtop	15,345
Model 46647 - Two-Door Sport Coupe	11,892
Model 46667 - Convertible Coupe	2,161

ELECTRA 225 SERIES

Model 48237 - Two-Door Sport Coupe	8,662
Model 48239 - Four-Door Hardtop	17,589
Model 48437 - Custom Two-Door Sport Coupe	26,831
Model 48439 - Custom Four-Door Hardtop	72,954
RIVIERA: Model 49487 - Two-Door Coupe	33,810
	551,188

Note: Sixteen millionth Buick produced June 1971

1972

SKYLARK SERIES

Model 43327 - Two-Door Coupe	14,552
Model 43337 - Two-Door Sport Coupe	84,868
Model 43369 - Four-Door Sedan	42,206
SPORTWAGON: Model 43436	14,417

GRAN SPORT SERIES

Model 43437 - Two-Door Sport Coupe	7,723
Model 43467 - Convertible Coupe	852

SKYLARK CUSTOM SERIES

Model 44437 - Two-Door Sport Coupe	34,271
Model 44439 - Four-Door Hardtop	12,925
Model 44467 - Convertible Coupe	3,608
Model 44469 - Four-Door Sedan	9,924

LESABRE SERIES

Model 45239 - Four-Door Hardtop	15,160
Model 45257 - Two-Door Sport Coupe	14,011
Model 45269 - Four-Door Sedan	29,505
Model 45439 - Custom Four-Door Hardtop	50,804
Model 45457 - Custom Two-Door Coupe	36,510
Model 45467 - Custom Convertible Coupe	2,037
Model 45469 - Custom Four-Door Sedan	35,295

ESTATE WAGON SERIES

Model 46035 - Wagon (two seats)	10,175
Model 46045 - Wagon (three seats)	18,793

CENTURION SERIES

Model 46639 - Four-Door Hardtop	19,852
Model 46647 - Two-Door Sport Coupe	14,187
Model 46667 - Convertible Coupe	2,396

ELECTRA 225 SERIES

Model 48237 - Two-Door Sport Coupe	9,961

Model 48239 - Four-Door Hardtop	19,433
Model 48437 - Custom Two-Door Sport Coupe	37,974
Model 48439 - Custom Four-Door Hardtop	104,754
RIVIERA: Model 49487 - Two-Door Coupe	33,728
	679,921

Note: Seventeen millionth Buick produced December 1972

1973

CENTURY SERIES

Model 4AD29 - Four-Dollar Pillar Sedan	38,202
Model 4AD37 - Two-Door Pillar Coupe	56,154
Model 4AF35 - Station Wagon (two seats)	7,760

CENTURY LUXUS SERIES

Model 4AH29 - Four-Door Pillar Sedan	22,438
Model 4AH57 - Two-Door Pillar Coupe	71,712
Model 4AK35 - Station Wagon (two seats)	10,645
REGAL: Model 4AJ57 - Two-Door Sport Coupe	91,557

APOLLO SERIES

Model 4XB17 - Two-Door Hatchback Coupe	9,868
Model 4XB27 - Two-Door Coupe	14,475
Model 4XB69 - Four-Door Sedan	8,450

LESABRE SERIES

Model 4BL39 - Four-Door Hardtop	13,413
Model 4BL57 - Two-Door Hardtop	14,061
Model 4BL69 - Four-Door Sedan	29,649
Model 4BN39 - Four-Door Custom Hardtop	55,879
Model 4BN57 - Two-Door Custom Hardtop	41,425
Model 4BN69 - Four-Door Custom Sedan	42,854

ESTATE WAGON SERIES

Model 4BR35 - Wagon (two seats)	12,282
Model 4BR45 - Wagon (three seats)	23,513

CENTURION SERIES

Model 4BP39 - Four-Door Hardtop	22,354
Model 4BP57 - Two-Door Hardtop	16,883
Model 4BP67 - Convertible Coupe	5,739

ELECTRA 225 SERIES

Model 4CT37 - Two-Door Hardtop	9,224
Model 4CT39 - Four-Door Hardtop	17,189
Model 4CV37 - Two-Door Custom Hardtop	44,328
Model 4CV39 - Four-Door Custom Hardtop	107,031
RIVIERA: Model 4EY87 - Two-Door Coupe	34,080
	821,165

1974

CENTURY 350 SERIES

Model 4AD29 - Four-Door Sedan	22,856
Model 4AD37 - Two-Door Coupe	33,166
Model 4AF35 - Station Wagon	4,860

CENTURY LUXUS SERIES

Model 4AH29 - Four-Door Sedan	11,159
Model 4AH57 - Two-Door Coupe	44,930
Model 4AK35 - Station Wagon	6,791

REGAL SERIES

Model 4AJ29 - Four-Door Sedan	9,333
Model 4AJ57 - Two-Door Coupe	57,512

APOLLO SERIES

Model 4XB17 - Two-Door Hatchback Coupe	11,644
Model 4XB27 - Two-Door Coupe	28,286
Model 4XB69 - Four-Door Sedan	16,779

LESABRE SERIES

Model 4BN39 - Four-Door Hardtop Sedan	11,879
Model 4BN57 - Two-Door Hardtop Coupe	12,522
Model 4BN69 - Four-Door Sedan	18,572
Model 4BP39 - Luxus Four-Door Hardtop Sedan	23,910
Model 4BP57 - Luxus Two-Door Hardtop Coupe	27,243
Model 4BP67 - Luxus Convertible Coupe	3,627
Model 4BP69 - Luxus Four-Door Sedan	16,039

ESTATE WAGON SERIES

Model 4BR35 - Wagon (two seats)	4,581
Model 4BR45 - Wagon (three seats)	9,831

428

ELECTRA 225 SERIES
Model 4CT37 - Two-Door Hardtop Coupe	3,339
Model 4CT39 - Four-Door Hardtop Coupe	5,750
Model 4CV37 - Custom Two-Door Hardtop Coupe	15,099
Model 4CV39 - Custom Four-Door Hardtop Sedan	29,089
Model 4CX37 - Limited Two-Door Hardtop Coupe	16,086
Model 4CX39 - Limited Four-Door Hardtop Sedan	30,051
RIVIERA: Model 4EY87 - Two-Door Hardtop	20,129
	495,063

Note: Eighteen millionth Buick produced May 1974.

1975
CENTURY SERIES
Model 4AD29 - Four-Door Colonnade Sedan	22,075
Model 4AD37 - Two-Door Colonnade Sedan	39,556
Model 4AF35 - Station Wagon	4,416

CENTURY CUSTOM SERIES
Model 4AH29 - Four-Door Colonnade Sedan	9,995
Model 4AH57 - Two-Door Colonnade Sedan	32,966
Model 4AK35 - Station Wagon	7,078

REGAL SERIES
Model 4AJ29 - Four-Door Colonnade Sedan	10,726
Model 4AJ57 - Two-Door Colonnade Sedan	56,646

APOLLO/SKYLARK SERIES
Model 4XB17 - Two-Door Hatchback Skylark	6,814
Model 4XB27 - Two-Door Coupe Skylark	27,689
Model 4XB69 - Four-Door Sedan Apollo	21,138
Model 4XC17 - Two-Door Hatchback Skylark S.R.	1,505
Model 4XC27 - Two-Door Coupe Skylark S.R.	3,746
Model 4XC69 - Four-Door Sedan Apollo S.R.	2,241

LESABRE SERIES
Model 4BN39 - Four-Door Hardtop	9,119
Model 4BN57 - Two-Door Hardtop Coupe	8,647
Model 4BN69 - Four-Door Sedan	14,088
Model 4BP39 - Custom Four-Door Hardtop	30,005
Model 4BP57 - Custom Two-Door Hardtop Coupe	25,016
Model 4BP67 - Custom Convertible Coupe	5,300
Model 4BP69 - Custom Four-Door Sedan	17,026

ESTATE WAGON SERIES
Model 4BR35 - Wagon (two seats)	4,128
Model 4BR45 - Wagon (three seats)	9,612

ELECTRA 225 SERIES
Model 4CV37 - Two-Door Custom Hardtop	16,145
Model 4CV39 - Four-Door Custom Hardtop	27,357
Model 4CX37 - Two-Door Limited Hardtop	17,650
Model 4CX39 - Four-Door Limited Hardtop	33,778
RIVIERA: Model 4EZ87 - Two-Door Hardtop	17,306
	481,768

1976
CENTURY SERIES
Model 4AD29 - Four-Door Colonnade Sedan	33,632
Model 4AD37 - Two-Door Colonnade Sedan	59,448

CENTURY CUSTOM SERIES
Model 4AH29 - Four-Door Colonnade Sedan	19,728
Model 4AH57 - Two-Door Colonnade Sedan	34,036
Model 4AK35 - Station Wagon	16,625

REGAL SERIES
Model 4AJ29 - Four-Door Colonnade Sedan	17,118
Model 4AJ57 - Two-Door Colonnade Coupe	124,498
SKYHAWK: Model 4HS07 - Two-Door Hatchback	15,768

SKYLARK SERIES
Model 4XB17 - Two-Door Hatchback	6,703
Model 4XB27 - Two-Door Coupe	51,260
Model 4XB69 - Four-Door Sedan	48,157
Model 4XC17 - Two-Door Hatchback S.R.	1,248
Model 4XC27 - Two-Door Coupe S.R.	3,880
Model 4XC69 - Four-Door Sedan S.R.	3,243

LESABRE SERIES
Model 4BN39 - Four-Door Hardtop	2,312

Model 4BN57 - Two-Door Hardtop	3,861
Model 4BN69 - Four-Door Hardtop	4,315

LESABRE CUSTOM SERIES
Model 4BP39 - Four-Door Hardtop	46,109
Model 4BP57 - Two-Door Hardtop	45,669
Model 4BP69 - Four-Door Sedan	34,841

ESTATE WAGON SERIES
Model 4BR35 - Wagon (two seats)	5,990
Model 4BR45 - Wagon (three seats)	14,384

ELECTRA 225 SERIES
Model 4CV37 - Two-Door Hardtop	18,442
Model 4CV39 - Four-Door Hardtop	26,655
Model 4CX37 - Two-Door Limited Hardtop	28,395
Model 4CX39 - Four-Door Limited Hardtop	51,067
RIVIERA: Model 4EZ87 - Two-Door Hardtop	20,082
	737,466

Note: Nineteen millionth Buick produced March 1976

1977
CENTURY SERIES
Model 4AD29 - Four-Door Sedan	29,065
Model 4AD37 - Two-Door Coupe	52,864

CENTURY CUSTOM SERIES
Model 4AH29 - Four-Door Sedan	13,645
Model 4AH57 - Two-Door Coupe	20,834
Model 4AK35 - Station Wagon	19,282

REGAL SERIES
Model 4AJ29 - Four-Door Colonnade Sedan	17,946
Model 4AJ57 - Two-Door Colonnade Sedan	174,560

SKYLARK SERIES
Model 4XB17 - Two-Door Hatchback	5,316
Model 4XB27 - Two-Door Coupe	49,858
Model 4XB69 - Four-Door Sedan	48,121
Model 4XC17 - Two-Door Hatchback S.R.	1,154
Model 4XC27 - Two-Door Coupe S.R.	5,023
Model 4XC69 - Four-Door Sedan S.R.	4,000

LESABRE SERIES
Model 4BN37 - Two-Door Sport Coupe	8,455
Model 4BN69 - Four-Door Sedan	19,827
Model 4BP37 - Two-Door Custom Coupe	58,589
Model 4BP69 - Four-Door Custom Sedan	103,855
ESTATE WAGON: Model 4BR35	25,075

ELECTRA SERIES
Model 4CV37 - Two-Door Coupe	15,762
Model 4CV69 - Four-Door Sedan	25,633
Model 4CX37 - Two-Door Limited Coupe	37,871
Model 4CX69 - Four-Door Limited Sedan	82,361
RIVIERA: Model 4EZ37 - Two-Door Coupe	26,138
	845,234

Note: Twenty millionth Buick produced May 1977

1978
CENTURY SPECIAL SERIES
Model 4AE09 - Four-Door Sedan	12,533
Model 4AE35 - Station Wagon	9,586
Model 4AE87 - Two-Door Coupe	10,818

CENTURY CUSTOM SERIES
Model 4AH09 - Four-Door Sedan	18,361
Model 4AH35 - Station Wagon	24,014
Model 4AH87 - Two-Door Coupe	12,434
REGAL: Model 4AJ47 - Two-Door Coupe	236,652
SKYHAWK: Model 4HS07 - Two-Door Hatchback	24,589

SKYLARK SERIES
Model 4XB17 - Two-Door Hatchback	2,642
Model 4XB27 - Two-Door Coupe	42,087
Model 4XB69 - Four-Door Sedan	40,951
Model 4XC17 - Two-Door Custom Hatchback	1,277
Model 4XC27 - Two-Door Custom Coupe	12,740
Model 4XC69 - Four-Door Custom Sedan	14,523

LESABRE SERIES
Model 4BN37 - Two-Door Coupe	8,265
Model 4BN69 - Four-Door Sedan	23,354
Model 4BP37 - Two-Door Custom Coupe	53,675
Model 4BP69 - Four-Door Custom Sedan	86,638
ESTATE WAGON: Model 4BR35	25,964

ELECTRA SERIES
Model 4CV37 - Two-Door Coupe	8,259
Model 4CV69 - Four-Door Sedan	14,590
Model 4CX37 - Two-Door Limited Coupe	33,365
Model 4CX69 - Four-Door Limited Sedan	65,335
RIVIERA: Model 4EZ37 - Two-Door Coupe	20,535
	803,187

Note: Twenty-one millionth Buick produced September 1978

1979
CENTURY SERIES
Model 4AE09 - Four-Door Special Sedan	7,364
Model 4AE35 - Special Station Wagon	10,413
Model 4AE87 - Two-Door Special Coupe	4,805
Model 4AH09 - Four-Door Custom Sedan	9,681
Model 4AH35 - Custom Station Wagon	21,100
Model 4AH87 - Two-Door Custom Coupe	2,474
REGAL: Model 4AJ47 - Two-Door Coupe	273,365
SKYHAWK: Model 4HS07 - Two-Door Hatchback	23,139

SKYLARK SERIES
Model 4XB17 - Two-Door Hatchback	608
Model 4XB27 - Two-Door Coupe	10,201
Model 4XB69 - Four-Door Sedan	10,849
Model 4XC27 - Two-Door Custom Coupe	3,546
Model 4XC69 - Four-Door Custom Sedan	3,822

LESABRE SERIES
Model 4BN37 - Two-Door Coupe	7,542
Model 4BN69 - Four-Door Sedan	25,431
Model 4BP37 - Two-Door Limited Coupe	41,872
Model 4BP69 - Four-Door Limited Sedan	75,939
ESTATE WAGON: Model 4BR35	21,312

ELECTRA SERIES
Model 4CV37 - Two-Door Coupe	5,358
Model 4CV69 - Four-Door Sedan	11,055
Model 4CX37 - Two-Door Limited Coupe	28,878
Model 4CX69 - Four-Door Limited Sedan	76,340
RIVIERA: Model 4EZ57 - Two-Door Coupe	52,181
	727,275

Note: Twenty-two millionth Buick produced December 1979

1980
CENTURY SERIES
Model 4AE35 - Wagon	6,493
Model 4AH35 - Estate Wagon	11,122
Model 4AH69 - Four-Door Sedan	129,740
Model 4AH87 - Two-Door Aero Coupe	1,074
REGAL: Model 4AJ47 - Two-Door Coupe	214,735
SKYHAWK: Model 4HT07 - Two-Door Hatch Back	8,322

SKYLARK SERIES
Model 4XB37 - Two-Door Coupe	55,114
Model 4XB69 - Four-Door Sedan	80,940
Model 4XC37 - Two-Door Limited Coupe	42,652
Model 4XC69 - Four-Door Limited Sedan	86,948

LESABRE SERIES
Model 4BN37 - Two-Door Coupe	8,342
Model 4BN69 - Four-Door Sedan	23,873
Model 4BP37 - Two-Door Limited Coupe	20,561
Model 4BP69 - Four-Door Limited Sedan	37,676
ESTATE WAGON: Model 4BR35 - Wagon	9,318

ELECTRIA SERIES
Model 4CX37 - Two-Door Limited Coupe	14,058
Model 4CX69 - Four-Door Limited Sedan	54,422
RIVIERA: Model 4EZ57 - Two-Door Coupe	48,621
	854,011

1981
CENTURY SERIES
Model 4AE35-Wagon	5,489
Model 4AH35-Estate Wagon	11,659
Model 4AH69-Four-Door Sedan	127,119
REGAL SERIES: Model 4AJ47-Two-Door Coupe	240,200

SKYLARK SERIES
Model 4XB37-Two-Door Coupe	46,515
Model 4XB69-Four-Door Sedan	104,091
Model 4XC37-Two-Door Limited Coupe	30,080
Model 4XC69-Four-Door Limited Sedan	81,642

LESABRE SERIES
Model 4BN37-Two-Door Coupe	4,909
Model 4BN69-Four-Door Sedan	19,166
Model 4BP37-Two-Door Limited Coupe	14,862
Model 4BP69-Four-Door Limited Sedan	39,006
ESTATE WAGON: Model 4BR35-Wagon	11,268

ELECTRA SERIES
Model 4CX37-Two-Door Limited Coupe	10,151
Model 4CX69-Four-Door Limited Sedan	58,832
RIVIERA: Model 4EZ57-Two-Door Coupe	52,007
	856,996

Note: Twenty-three millionth Buick produced March 1981

1982
CENTURY SERIES
Model 4AH19-Four-Door Sedan	83,250
Model 4AH27-Two-Door Coupe	19,715

REGAL SERIES
Model 4GJ35-Wagon	14,732
Model 4GJ47-Two-Door Coupe	136,258
Model 4GJ69-Four-Door Sedan	74,428

SKYHAWK SERIES
Model 4JS27-Two-Door Coupe	25,378
Model 4JS69-Four-Door Sedan	22,540

SKYLARK SERIES
Model 4XB37-Two-Door Coupe	21,017
Model 4XB69-Four-Door Sedan	65,541
Model 4XC37-Two-Door Limited Coupe	13,712
Model 4XC69-Four-Door Limited Sedan	44,290

LESABRE SERIES
Model 4BN37-Two-Door Coupe	5,165
Model 4BN69-Four-Door Sedan	23,220
Model 4BP37-Two-Door Limited Coupe	16,062
Model 4BP69-Four-Door Limited Sedan	47,224
ESTATE WAGON: Model 4BR35-Wagon	15,331

ELECTRA SERIES
Model 4CX37-Two-Door Limited Coupe	8,449
Model 4CX69-Four-Door Limited Sedan	59,601

RIVIERA SERIES
Model 4EZ57-Two-Door Coupe	42,823
Model 4EZ67-Convertible Coupe	1,248
	739,984

Note: Twenty-four millionth Buick produced June 1982

1983
CENTURY SERIES
Model 4AH19-Four-Door Sedan	114,443
Model 4AH27-Two-Door Coupe	13,483

REGAL SERIES
Model 4GJ35-Wagon	15,287
Model 4GJ47-Two-Door Coupe	151,667
Model 4GJ69-Four-Door Sedan	61,285

SKYHAWK SERIES
Model 4JS27-Two-Door Coupe	32,652
Model 4JS35-Wagon	10,653
Model 4JS69-Four-Door Sedan	19,847

SKYLARK SERIES
Model 4XB37-Two-Door Coupe	14,160

Model 4XB69-Four-Door Sedan	51,950
Model 4XC37-Two-Door Limited Coupe	7,863
Model 4XC69-Four-Door Limited Sedan	30,674

LESABRE SERIES
Model 4BN37-Two-Door Coupe	6,974
Model 4BN69-Four-Door Sedan	31,196
Model 4BP37-Two-Door Limited Coupe	22,029
Model 4BP69-Four-Door Limited Sedan	66,547
ESTATE WAGON: Model 4BR35-Wagon	18,887

ELECTRA SERIES
Model 4CX37-Two-Door Limited Coupe	8,885
Model 4CX69-Four-Door Limited Sedan	79,700

RIVIERA SERIES
Model 4EZ57-Two-Door Coupe	48,484
Model 4EZ67-Convertible Coupe	1,750
	808,416

Note: Twenty-five millionth Buick produced September 1983

1984
CENTURY SERIES
Model 4AH19-Four-Door Sedan	178,454
Model 4AH27-Two-Door Coupe	15,429
Model 4AH35-Estate Wagon (Custom)	25,975

REGAL SERIES
Model 4GJ47-Two-Door Coupe	166,039
Model 4GJ69-Four-Door Sedan	58,715

SKYHAWK SERIES
Model 4JS27-Two-Door Coupe	86,077
Model 4JS35-Wagon	13,668
Model 4JS69-Four-Door Sedan	45,648

SKYLARK SERIES
Model 4XB37-Two-Door Coupe	13,300
Model 4XB69-Four-Door Sedan	56,495
Model 4XC37-Two-Door Limited Coupe	7,621
Model 4XC69-Four-Door Limited Sedan	33,795

LESABRE SERIES
Model 4BN37-Two-Door Coupe	3,890
Model 4BN69-Four-Door Sedan	36,072
Model 4BP37-Two-Door Limited Coupe	28,332
Model 4BP69-Four-Door Limited Sedan	86,418
ESTATE WAGON: Model 4BV35-Wagon	17,563

ELECTRA SERIES
Model 4DR37-Two-Door Limited Coupe	4,075
Model 4DR69-Four-Door Limited Sedan	52,551

RIVIERA SERIES
Model 4EZ57-Two-Door Coupe	57,363
Model 4EZ67-Convertible Coupe	500
	987,980

Note: Twenty-six millionth Buick produced September 1984

1985
CENTURY SERIES
Model 4AH19 - Four-Door Sedan	215,928
Model 4AH27 - Two-Door Coupe	13,043
Model 4AH35 - Four-Door Wagon	28,221

REGAL SERIES
Model 4GJ47 - Two-Door Coupe	124,546

SKYHAWK SERIES
Model 4JS27 - Two-Door Coupe	49,325
Model 4JS35 - Four-Door Wagon	5,285
Model 4JS69 - Four-Door Sedan	27,906

SKYLARK SERIES
Model 4XB69 - Four-Door Sedan	65,667
Model 4XC69 - Four-Door Limited Sedan	27,490

SOMERSET SERIES
Model 4NJ27 - Two-Door Coupe	86,071

LESABRE SERIES
Model 4BN37 - Two-Door Coupe	5,156
Model 4BN69 - Four-Door Sedan	32,091
Model 4BP37 - Two-Door Limited Coupe	22,211

Model 4BP69 - Four-Door Limited Sedan	84,432

ESTATE WAGON
Model 4BR35 - Four-Door Wagon	13,366

ELECTRA SERIES
Model 4CX11 - Two-Door Sedan	5,852
Model 4CX69 - Four-Door Sedan	131,011

RIVIERA SERIES
Model 4EZ57 - Two-Door Coupe	64,905
Model 4EZ67 - Convertible	400
	1,002,906

Note: Twenty-seven millionth Buick produced September 1985

1986
CENTURY SERIES
Model 4AH19 - Four-Door Sedan	234,352
Model 4AH27 - Two-Door Coupe	14,781
Model 4AH35 - Four-Door Wagon	25,374

REGAL SERIES
Model 4GJ47 - Two-Door Coupe	91,230

SKYHAWK SERIES
Model 4JS27 - Two-Door Coupe	45,884
Model 4JS35 - Four-Door Wagon	6,079
Model 4JS69 - Four-Door Sedan	29,959
Model 4JS77 - Three-Door Hatch Back	9,499

SOMERSET SERIES
Model 4NJ27 - Two-Door Coupe	75,620

SKYLARK SERIES
Model 4NJ69 - Four-Door Sedan	62,235

LESABRE SERIES
Model 4HP37 - Two-Door Coupe	7,191
Model 4HP69 - Four-Door Sedan	30,235
Model 4HR37 - Two-Door Limited Coupe	14,331
Model 4HR69 - Four-Door Limited Sedan	43,215

ESTATE WAGON
Model 4BR35 - Wagon	18,126

ELECTRA SERIES
Model 4CX11 - Two-Door Sedan	4,996
Model 4CX69 - Four-Door Sedan	114,858

RIVIERA SERIES
Model 4EZ57 - Two-Door Coupe	22,138
	850,103

Note: Twenty-eight millionth Buick produced November 1986

1987
CENTURY SERIES
Model 4AH19—Custom Four-Door Sedan	88,445
Model 4AH27—Custom Two-Door Coupe	2,878
Model 4AL19—Limited Four-Door Sedan	71,340
Model 4AL27—Limited Two-Door Coupe	4,384
Model 4AH35—Custom Wagon	10,141
Model 4AL35—Estate Wagon	6,990

REGAL SERIES
Model 4GJ47—Two-Door Coupe	44,844
Model 4GM47—Limited Two-Door Coupe	20,441

Note: From 1982 to 1987, 30,022 Regal Grand Nationals were produced (1982—215, 1984—2,000, 1985—2,102, 1986—5,512, 1987—20,193). From 1980 to 1986, 22,806 Regal T Types were produced (1980—6,276, 1981—2,891, 1982—2,022, 1983—3,732, 1984—3,401, 1985—2,100, 1986—2,384). In 1987, 547 GNXs were produced.

SKYHAWK SERIES
Model 4JS27—Custom Two-Door Coupe	19,814
Model 4JS69—Custom Four-Door Sedan	15,778
Model 4JS35—Custom Wagon	3,061
Model 4JS77—Sport Hatchback	3,757
Model 4JT27—Limited Two-Door Coupe	1,556
Model 4JT69—Limited Four-Door Sedan	2,200
Model 4JT35—Limited Wagon	498

SOMERSET SERIES

Model 4NJ27—Custom Two-Door Coupe	34,916
Model 4NM27—Limited Four-Door Sedan	11,585

SKYLARK SERIES

Model 4NC69—Custom Four-Door Sedan	26,173
Model 4ND69—Limited Four-Door Sedan	7,532

LESABRE SERIES

Model 4HH69—Four-Door Sedan	6,243
Model 4HP37—Custom Two-Door Coupe	9,158
Model 4HP69—Custom Four-Door Sedan	60,392
(Includes T Type 4,123)	
Model 4HR37—Limited Two-Door Coupe	7,741
Model 4HR69—Limited Four-Door Sedan	70,797

ESTATE WAGON

Model 4BR35—LeSabre Wagon	5,251
Model 4BV35—Electra Wagon	7,508

ELECTRA SERIES

Model 4CX69—Limited Four-Door Sedan	7,787
Model 4CW11—Park Avenue Two-Door Coupe	4,084
Model 4CW69—Park Avenue Four-Door Sedan	75,600
Model 4CF69—T Type Four-Door Sedan	2,570

RIVIERA SERIES

Model 4EZ57—Two-Door Coupe	15,223
(Includes T Type 2,587)	
	648,687

1988
CENTURY SERIES

Model 4AH19—Custom Four-Door Sedan	62,214
Model 4AH27—Custom Two-Door Coupe	1,322
Model 4AL19—Limited Four-Door Sedan	39,137
Model 4AL27—Limited Two-Door Coupe	1,127
Model 4AH35—Custom Wagon	5,312
Model 4AL35—Estate Wagon	4,146

REGAL SERIES

Model 4WB57—Custom Two-Door Coupe	64,773
Model 4WD57—Limited Two-Door Coupe	65,224

SKYHAWK SERIES

Model 4JS27—Two-Door Coupe	13,156
Model 4JS69—Four-Door Sedan	14,271
Model 4JS35—Four-Door Wagon	1,707

SKYLARK SERIES

Model 4NC69—Custom Four-Door Sedan	24,940
Model 4NJ27—Custom Two-Door Coupe	19,590
Model 4ND69—Limited Four-Door Sedan	5,316
Model 4NM27—Limited Two-Door Coupe	4,946

LESABRE SERIES

Model 4HP37—Two-Door Coupe	8,829
(Includes T Type 6,426)	
Model 4HP69—Custom Four-Door Sedan	67,213
Model 4HR37—Limited Two-Door Coupe	2,474
Model 4HR69—Limited Four-Door Sedan	57,524

ESTATE WAGON

Model 4BR35—LeSabre Wagon	3,723
Model 4BV35—Electra Wagon	5,901
Model 4BB90—Stripped Chassis	37

ELECTRA SERIES

Model 4CX69—Limited Four-Door Sedan	5,191
Model 4CW69—Park Avenue Four-Door Sedan	84,853
Model 4CF69—T Type Four-Door Sedan	1,869

RIVIERA SERIES

Model 4EZ57—Two-Door Coupe	8,625
(Includes T Type 2,065)	

REATTA SERIES

Model 4EC97—Two-Door Coupe	4,708
	578,128

1989
CENTURY SERIES

Model 4AH69—Custom Four-Door Sedan	89,281
Model 4AH37—Custom Two-Door Coupe	6,953
Model 4AL19—Limited Four-Door Sedan	49,839
Model 4AH35—Custom Wagon	5,479
Model 4AL35—Estate Wagon	3,940

REGAL SERIES

Model 4WB57—Custom Two-Door Coupe	56,057
Model 4WD57—Limited Two-Door Coupe	32,700

SKYHAWK SERIES

Model 4JS27—Two-Door Coupe	7,837
Model 4JS69—Four-Door Sedan	13,841
Model 4JS35—Four-Door Wagon	1,688

SKYLARK SERIES

Model 4NC69—Custom Four-Door Sedan	42,636
Model 4NJ27—Custom Two-Door Coupe	12,714
Model 4ND69—Limited Four-Door Sedan	4,774
Model 4NM27—Limited Two-Door Coupe	1,416

LESABRE SERIES

Model 4HP37—Two-Door Coupe	7,219
(Includes T Type 5,389)	
Model 4HP69—Custom Four-Door Sedan	78,738
Model 4HR37—Limited Two-Door Coupe	2,287
Model 4HR69—Limited Four-Door Sedan	61,328

ESTATE WAGON

Model 4BR35—LeSabre Wagon	2,971
Model 4BV35—Electra Wagon	4,560
Model 4BB90—Stripped Chassis	212

ELECTRA SERIES

Model 4CX69—Limited Four-Door Sedan	5,814
Model 4CW69—Park Avenue Four-Door Sedan	71,786
Model 4CF69—T Type Four-Door Sedan	1,151
Model 4CU69—Park Avenue Ultra Four-Door Sedan	4,815

RIVIERA SERIES

Model 4EZ57—Two-Door Coupe	21,189

REATTA SERIES

Model 4EC97—Two-Door Coupe	7,009
	598,234

1990
CENTURY SERIES

Model 4AH69—Custom Four-Door Sedan	88,309
Model 4AH37—Custom Two-Door Coupe	1,944
Model 4AL69—Limited Four-Door Sedan	35,248
Model 4AH35—Custom Wagon	4,383
Model 4AL35—Limited Wagon	2,837

REGAL SERIES

Model 4WB57—Custom Two-Door Coupe	39,036
(Z13—Gran Sport 12,965)	
Model 4WD57—Limited Two-Door Coupe	18,787
(Sedans counted in 1991 figures)	

SKYLARK SERIES

Model 4NV69—Four-Door Sedan	46,705
Model 4NV27—Two-Door Coupe	4,248
Model 4NC69—Custom Four-Door Sedan	24,469
Model 4NJ27—Custom Two-Door Coupe	5,490
Model 4NM27—Gran Sport Two-Door Coupe	1,637
Model 4ND69—Luxury Edition Four-Door Sedan	3,019

LESABRE SERIES

Model 4HP37—Two-Door Coupe	2,406
Model 4HP69—Custom Four-Door Sedan	96,616
Model 4HR37—Limited Two-Door Coupe	1,855
Model 4HR69—Limited Four-Door Sedan	62,504

ESTATE WAGON

Model 4BR35—LeSabre Wagon	7,838
Model 4BB90—Stripped Chassis	161

ELECTRA SERIES

Model 4CX69—Limited Four-Door Sedan	2,621
Model 4CW69—Park Avenue Four-Door Sedan	44,072
Model 4CF69—T Type Four-Door Sedan	478
Model 4CU69—Park Avenue Ultra Four-Door Sedan	1,967

RIVIERA SERIES

Model 4EZ57—Two-Door Coupe	22,526

REATTA SERIES

Model 4EC97—Two-Door Coupe	6,383
Model 4EC67—Two-Door Convertible	2,132
	527,671

1991
CENTURY SERIES

Model 4AG69—Sedan (Special)	13,045
Model 4AH69—Custom Four-Door Sedan	81,424
Model 4AH37—Custom Two-Door Coupe	1,951
Model 4AL69—Limited Four-Door Sedan	15,273
Model 4AH35—Custom Wagon	3,102
Model 4AL35—Limited Wagon	1,729

REGAL SERIES

Model 4WB19—Custom Four-Door Sedan	59,496
Model 4WD19—Limited Four-Door Sedan	60,155
Model 4WB57—Custom Two-Door Coupe	17,428
Model 4WD57—Limited Two-Door Coupe	6,901

SKYLARK SERIES

Model 4NV69—Four-Door Sedan	57,323
Model 4NV27—Two-Door Coupe	5,108
Model 4NC69—Custom Four-Door Sedan	11,582
Model 4NJ27—Custom Two-Door Coupe	1,706
Model 4NM27—Gran Sport Two-Door Coupe	693
Model 4ND69—Luxury Edition Four-Door Sedan	928

LESABRE SERIES

Model 4HP37—Two-Door Coupe	695
Model 4HP69—Custom Four-Door Sedan	56,231
Model 4HR37—Limited Two-Door Coupe	486
Model 4HR69—Limited Four-Door Sedan	33,344

ESTATE WAGON

Model 4BR35—LeSabre Wagon	7,291
Model 4BB90—Stripped Chassis	175

PARK AVENUE SERIES

Model 4CW69—Park Avenue Four-Door Sedan	87,461
Model 4CU69—Park Avenue Ultra Four-Door Sedan	22,030

RIVIERA SERIES

Model 4EZ57—Two-Door Coupe	13,168

REATTA SERIES

Model 4EC97—Two-Door Coupe	1,214
Model 4EC67—Two-Door Convertible	305
	560,244

BUICK GRAN SPORTS—
1965-1975 PRODUCTION FIGURES

From 1965 to 1975, 145,507 Buick Gran Sports were produced. The breakdown: Skylark and Special series: 1965—15,780; 1966—13,816; 1967—19,626. GM B-body: 1968—26,345; 1969—19,257; 1970—20,096; 1971—9,170; 1972—8,575. Option on Century: 1973—6,637; 1974—3,355; 1975—1,288. Option on Apollo (GSX): 1974—1,562.

(While these numbers for 1904-1906 are officially recorded, an original factory production book, now lost, has been quoted with slightly different numbers. It reportedly recorded 729 Model C's built in 1905 and 58 in 1906. There are theories that a few Model C's may have been among the 37 cars built in 1904 but this has not been confirmed).

Appendix Nine

SELECTED SPECS FOR THE BUICK

The selected specifications which follow were taken from official Buick records. They are presented as a ready reference for the Buick enthusiast in order that he may trace the varying changes in models and series through the years. It should be noted that the first reference to a new model or series provides the specification information; subsequent references to that model or series indicate the changes made to those original specifications. For further descriptive data, the reader is referred to the index, which notes the sections of the text which relate to each production car.

MODEL YEAR: 1904

MODEL B. Two-cylinder, 4.5 by 5, 159 cubic inches, rated 15-21 hp. Wheelbase 83 inches. Tires 28x3 1/2. Price $950 side-entrance tonneau. Chain drive; cone clutch; two-speed planetary transmission; jump spark ignition; float feed carburetor; radiator continuous coil with water circulation by gear-driven pump; lubrication by gear-driven pump with automatic sight feed; angle iron frame; suspension by three-quarter elliptics front, half elliptics rear; right hand drive; tilting steering wheel; dark blue wooden body.

MODEL YEAR: 1905

MODEL C. Continuation of Model B with detail changes. Price $1,200 side-entrance tonneau. Wheelbase increased to 87 inches; foot-operated service brake added; cape cart top with side curtains available optionally; body royal blue with ivory wheels.

MODEL YEAR: 1906

MODEL F. Continuation of Model C with detail changes. Price $1250 with acetylene headlamps, oil side- and tail-lights included. Recirculating radiator eliminated water storage tank.

MODEL G. Two-seater runabout companion to Model F. Price $1150.

MODEL YEAR: 1907

MODEL D. Four-cylinder, 4.25 by 4.5, 235 cubic inches, rated 30 hp. Wheelbase 102 inches. Tires 32x4. Price for five-passenger touring car $2500 with top, storm front, gas and oil lamps, horn, set of tools. Crankshaft, multiple disc clutch and three-speed sliding gear transmission built in unit; shaft drive; suspension by semi-elliptics front and rear. Introduced in May 1906 as 1907 model.

MODEL H. Two-speed planetary transmission variation of Model D.

MODEL S. Two-seater runabout companion to Model D.

MODEL K. Two-seater runabout companion to Model H.

Notes: Original price range for new four-cylinder Buicks was $1750 to $2000. Pencilled-in corrections on a brochure issued by dealer H.J. Koehler indicate mid-year price revisions to $1875 for the Model D, $1775 for the Model H, $2525 for the Models S and K. Latter two cars on extended wheelbase of 106.5 inches.

MODELS F AND G. Wheelbase increased to 89 inches; belly pan added.

MODEL YEAR: 1908

MODEL 10. Four-cylinder, 3.75 by 3.75, 165 cubic inches, rated 22.5 hp. Wheelbase 88 inches. Tires 30x3. Price for three-passenger runabout $900 including acetylene headlights, oil side- and tail-lights. Jump spark ignition; gear-driven force-feed lubrication; cone clutch; two-speed planetary transmission; shaft drive; suspension by semi-elliptics front, full elliptics rear; body off-white color.

MODELS F AND G. Wheelbase increase to 92 inches.

MODELS D AND S. Price $1750 for both models.

MODEL 5. Four-cylinder, 4.625 by 5, 336 cubic inches, rated 34.2 hp. Wheelbase 108 inches. Tires 34x4. Price for five-passenger touring car $2500. Three-speed sliding gear transmission; suspension by semi-elliptics all around.

MODEL YEAR: 1909

MODEL 10. Wheelbase increased to 92 inches, toy tonneau added.

MODELS F AND G. Prices now $1000 for F, $1000 for G. Delivery truck added.

MODEL 6A. Successor to Model 5, using its engine, but for a 113-inch wheelbase two-seat runabout. Rated 50 hp claimed. Price $2750.

MODEL 17. Successor to Model D. Engine bore increased to 4.5 inches, for 318 cubic inches. Wheelbase increase to 112 inches.

MODEL 16. Successor to Model S. Same revisions as Model 17.

MODEL YEAR: 1910

MODEL 10. Substitution of gear-driven water pump by centrifugal type; available body styles a three-passenger runabout, four-passenger surrey and toy tonneau, two-passenger roadster. Base price increased to $1000.

MODEL F, MODELS 16 AND 17. Vertical tube radiator adopted. Surrey and toy tonneau available in Model 16.

MODEL 7. Four-cylinder, 5 by 5, 392.6 cubic inches, rated 40 hp. Wheelbase 122 inches. Tires 36x4. Price for seven-passenger touring car $2750. This model also sometimes referred to as the 7-A.

MODEL 19. Same specifications as original Model D, but with wheelbase increase to 105 inches and a price of $1400 for five-passenger touring car.

MODEL 41. Four-cylinder, 4.5 by 5, 318 cubic inches, rated 32 hp. Wheelbase 116 inches. Tires 36x4½. Price $2750. This was Buick's first closed car, a limousine with closed rear compartment, open chauffeur's compartment.

MODEL 2-A TRUCK. Two-cylinder, 4.5 by 5, 159 cubic inches, rated 16.2 hp. Wheelbase 110 inches. Tires 32x4. Price $950.

Notes: Centrifugal water pump introduced on Model 10 now extended to larger model Buicks; multiple disc clutch replaced cone; dual ignition adopted.

MODEL YEAR: 1911

MODEL 32. Successor to Model 10, with wheelbase decrease to 90 inches. Price for two-passenger runabout $800.

MODEL 33. Five-passenger touring car companion to Model 32. Wheelbase 100 inches. Price $950.

MODEL 14. Two-cylinder, 4.5 by 4, 127 cubic inches, rated 14.2 hp. Wheelbase 79 inches. Tires 30x3. Price $550. This was Buggyabout introduced late in 1910 as 1911 model, with a 14B variant featuring rear-mounted fuel tank instead of the 14's under-the-seat location.

MODEL 26. Four-cylinder, 4 by 4, 201 cubic inches, rated 25.6 hp. Wheelbase 106 inches. Tires 32x3½. Price $1050 for two-passenger roadster.

MODEL 27. Five-passenger touring car companion to Model 26. Price $1150.

MODEL 21. Successor to Model 19, with tire increase to 34x4, wheelbase increase to 110 inches, price increase to $1500.

MODELS 38 AND 39. Successors to Models 16 and 17. Wheelbase increase to 116 inches. Both roadster (38) and touring car (39) priced at $1850.

MODEL 41. Some references indicate 338-cubic-inch displacement.

MODEL YEAR: 1912

MODELS 34 AND 35. Successors to Models 32 and 33; with wheelbase increase to 91 inches and price increase to $900 for the two-passenger runabout Model 34; wheelbase increase to 102 inches and price increase to $1000 for the four-passenger touring Model 35. Three-speed sliding gear transmission adopted; foot accelerator added; motor, clutch and transmission built in unit; reversion to cone clutch.

MODEL 36. Apparently a variation of the two-passenger runabout Model 34, selling for same $900 price.

MODELS 28 AND 29. Successors to Models 26 and 27. Wheelbase increase to 108 inches. Prices $1025 for two-passenger Model 28, $1180 for five-passenger Model 29.

MODEL 43. Successor to Model 41, now a five-passenger touring car priced at $1725.

MODEL 2-A TRUCK. Base price raised to $980.

MODEL YEAR: 1913

MODELS 24 AND 25. Successors to Models 34, 35 and 36. Wheelbase 105 inches. Price for two-passenger Model 24 $950; for five-passenger Model 25 $1050.

MODELS 30 AND 31. Successors to Models 28 and 29. Prices now $1125 and $1285 respectively. Electric side and taillamps introduced.

MODEL 40. Four cylinders, 4.5 by 4.5, 255.3 cubic inches, rated 28.9 hp. Wheelbase 115 inches. Price for five-passenger touring car $1650.

MODELS 3 AND 4 TRUCKS. Four-cylinder, 3 by 5, 141.4 cubic inches, rated 14.4 hp. Wheelbases 100 and 122 inches, tires 33x4½ and 33x5, prices $1075 and $1225 respectively.

MODEL YEAR: 1914

MODEL B-55. Six cylinders, 3.75 by 5, 331.4 cubic inches, rated 33.7 hp.

Wheelbase 130 inches. Tires 36x4½. Price $1985 for five-passenger touring car.

MODELS B-36, B-37 AND B-38. Four-cylinder, 3.75 by 5, 220.9 cubic inches, rated 35 hp. Wheelbase 112 inches. Tires 34x4. Prices $1235 for two-passenger B-36, $1335 for five-passenger B-37, both open cars; and $1800 for two-passenger B-38 closed coupe.

MODELS B-24 AND B-25. Continuation of former Models 24 and 25.

Notes: Left-hand drive adopted; lubrication revised to splash system with gear-driven pump; fuel tank removed to rear of chassis on all cars except B-24 and B-25.

MODEL YEAR: 1915

MODELS C-24 AND C-25. Successors to B-24 and B-25. Wheelbases increased to 106 inches, prices lowered to $900 and $950 respectively.

MODELS C-36 AND C-37. Successors to B-36 and B-37, with prices lowered to $1185 and $1235 respectively.

MODELS C-54 AND C-55. Refinement of six-cylinder Buick, C-54 a two-passenger roadster at $1635, C-55 a touring car for seven passengers at $1650. The Buick six was said to develop 55 hp by brake test this year.

MODEL C-4 TRUCK. Continuation of former Model 4.

MODEL YEAR: 1916

MODELS D-44, D-45, D-46 AND D-47. Six-cylinder, 3.25 by 4.5, 224.9 cubic inches, rated 25.3 hp. Wheelbase 115 inches. Tires 32x4, 33x4½ for sedan. Prices $985 for D-44 two-passenger runabout, $1020 for D-45 five-passenger touring, $1350 for D-46 three-passenger coupe, $1875 for D-47 seven-passenger sedan.

MODELS D-54 AND D-55. Continuation of large six, now on 130-inch wheelbase, priced at $1450 for two-passenger D-54 roadster and $1485 for seven-passenger D-55 touring.

MODEL D-4 TRUCK. Continuation of former C-4 truck.

MODEL YEAR: 1917

MODELS D-34 AND D-35. Four-cylinder, 3.375 by 4.75, 170 cubic inches, rated 18.2 hp. Wheelbase 106 inches. Tires 31x4. Prices $660 for two-passenger D-34, $675 for five-passenger D-35 touring.

MODELS D-44, D-45, D-46 AND D-47. Tire sizes revised to 34x4 (35x4½ for sedan); prices now $1040, $1070, $1440 and $1835 respectively.

MODEL YEAR: 1918

MODELS E-34, E-35 AND E-37. Both open cars now priced at $795; E-37 five-passenger sedan, with 32x3½ tires, and priced at $1185, added.

MODELS E-44, E-45, E-46 AND E-47. These sixes now on 118-inch wheelbase, with passenger capacities revised to three for the E-44 roadster ($1265), four for the E-46 coupe ($1695) and five for the E-47 sedan ($1845). The E-45 touring car was now priced at $1265.

MODELS E-49 AND E-50. Six-cylinder, 3.375 by 4.5, 241.5 cubic inches, rated 27.3 hp. Wheelbase 124 inches. Tires 34x4½. Prices $1495 for E-49 touring, $2175 for E-50 sedan, both seven-passenger cars.

MODEL E-4 TRUCK. Delivery version now available at $790.

MODEL YEAR: 1919

MODELS H-44, H-45, H-46 AND H-47. Price revisions to $1595, $1595, $2085 and $2195 respectively.

MODELS H-49 AND H-50. Prices of seven-passenger sixes revised to $1885 and $2585.

MODEL YEAR: 1920

MODELS K-44, K-45, K-46 AND K-47. Prices now $1495, $1495, $2085 and $2255 respectively.
MODELS K-49 AND K-50. Prices now $1785 and $2695.

MODEL YEAR: 1921

MODELS 21-44, 21-45, 21-46 AND 21-47. Prices now $1795, $1795, $2585 and $2895 respectively.
MODELS 21-48, 21-49 AND 21-50. Seven-passenger sixes now at $2060 and $3295; four-passenger coupe (21-48) at $2985 added.

MODEL YEAR: 1922

MODELS 22-34, 22-35, 22-36 AND 22-37. Four-cylinder. 3.376 by 4.75, 170 cubic inches, rated 18.23 hp. Wheelbase 109 inches. Tires 31x4. Prices $935 for two-passenger roadster (22-34), $975 for five-passenger touring (22-35), $1475 for three-passenger coupe (22-36), $1650 for five-passenger sedan (22-37).
SIX-CYLINDER LINE. Prices reduced to $1495 for 22-44, $1525 for 22-45, $2135 for 22-46, $2435 for 22-47, $2325 for 22-48, $1735 for 22-49, $2635 for 22-50.
MODELS 22-54 AND 22-55. Three-passenger sport roadster and four-passenger sport touring body styles added to six-cylinder line, each priced at $1785. These cars introduced late during model year and more actively promoted as 1923 models the year following, the roadster also designated as the "Special 6-54."
TRUCKS. Designated variously as 22-SD-4 and 22-4SD; body styles available included open express, canopy top express and steel panel.

MODEL YEAR: 1923

FOUR-CYLINDER LINE. Continued at $865 for 23-34, $885 for 23-35, $1175 for 23-36, $1395 for 23-37. Model 23-38 five-passenger touring sedan at $1325 and Model 23-39 two-passenger sport roadster at $1025 added.
SIX-CYLINDER LINE. Continued at $1175 for 23-44, $1195 for 23-45, $1985 for 23-47, $1895 for 23-48, $1435 for 23-49, $2195 for 23-50, $1625 for 23-54 and $1675 for 23-55. Previous coupe (22-46) replaced by new 23-41 five-passenger touring sedan at $1935.
TRUCKS. Designation changed to 23-SD-4, with more body styles added, and a price range from $840 to $960.

MODEL YEAR: 1924

FOUR-CYLINDER LINE. Continued at $1395 for 24-33; $935 for 24-34; $965 for 24-35; $1495 for 24-37.
SIX-CYLINDER LINE. Engine upgraded, 3.375 by 4.75, 255 cubic inches, rated 27.34 hp. On a 120-inch wheelbase (tires 32x4): 24-41 Double-Service Sedan at $1695; 24-44 Roadster at $1275; 24-45 Five-Passenger Touring at $1295; 24-47 Five-Passenger Sedan at $2095. On a 128-inch wheelbase (tires 32x4½): 24-48 Four-Passenger Coupe at $1995; 24-49 Seven-Passenger Touring at $1565; 24-50 Seven-Passenger Sedan at $2235; 24-50L Seven-Passenger Limousine at $2385; 24-51 Five-Passenger Brougham Sedan at $2235; 24-54 Three-Passenger Sport Roadster at $1675; 24-54C Three-Passenger Cabriolet at $1945; 24-55 Four-Passenger Sport Touring at $1725; 24-57 Four-Passenger Town Car at $2795.

Note: Four wheel brakes introduced throughout Buick line. Starting serial number for 24-41, 1064365; for 24-44 1080924; for 24-45, 1082590; for 24-47, 1066220; for 24-48, 1092945; for 24-49, 1094945; for 24-50, 1096358; for 24-51, 1098017; for 24-54, 1098871; for 24-55, 1099384; for 24-33, 1060178; for 24-34, 1067827; for 24-35, 1069858; for 24-37, 1062144.

MODEL YEAR: 1925

STANDARD SERIES. Six cylinders, 3 by 4.5 inches, 191 cubic inches, rated 21.6 hp. Wheelbase 114⅜ inches. Tires 31x4.95. Body styles: 25-20 Five-Passenger Coach at $1295; 25-21 Five-Passenger Service Sedan at $1475; 25-24 Roadster at $1150; 25-24S Special Roadster at $1250; 25-24A Enclosed Roadster at $1190; 25-25 Five-Passenger Touring at $1175; 25-25S Special Touring at $1275; 25-25A Enclosed Touring at $1275; 25-26 Two-Passenger Coupe at $1375; 25-26S Special Coupe at $1475; 25-27 Five-Passenger Sedan at $1665; 25-28 Four-Passenger Coupe at $1565.
MASTER SERIES. Continuation of previous six-cylinder line. Double Service Sedan dropped. New body styles added: 25-40 Five-Passenger Coach at $1495, 25-44A Two-Passenger Enclosed Roadster at $1400; 25-45A Five-Passenger Enclosed Touring at $1475—on the 120-inch wheelbase. Added on the 128-inch wheelbase, 25-49A Seven-Passenger Touring Car at $1700. Prices on other models raised approximately $100 to $200.
Notes: Four-cylinder line dropped, not to return for nearly a half century. Starting serial number for 25-20, 1270600; for 25-21, 1253555; for 25-24, 1255155; for 25-24A, 1256855; for 25-25, 1257055; for 25-25A, 1266505; for 25-26, 1267755; for 25-27, 1239262; for 25-40, 1231217; for 25-44, 1268055; for 25-44A, 1269255; for 25-45, 1211720; for 25-45A, 1274355; for 25-47, 1246009; for 25-48, 1247809; for 25-49, 1275355; for 25-49A, 1293797; for 25-50, 1249865; for 25-50L 1251265; for 25-51, 1251305; for 25-54, 1276917; for 25-54C, 1252905; for 25-55, 1277417; for 25-57, 1298267.

MODEL YEAR: 1926

STANDARD SERIES. Six cylinders, 3.125 by 4.5, 207 cubic inches, rated 23.4 hp, boring out of engine resulting in sixteen percent increase in developed horsepower, to 60 hp. Paring of body styles to 26-20 at $1195; 26-24 at $1125; 26-25 to $1150; 26-26 to $1195; 26-27 to $1295; 26-28 to $1275. All other body styles dropped.
MASTER SERIES. Six cylinders, 3.5 by 4.75, 274 cubic inches, rated 27.34 hp, boring out of engine resulting in sixteen percent increase in developed horsepower, to 75 hp. Tires now 33x6. Paring of body styles on 120-inch wheelbase to 26-40 at $1395; 26-44 at $1250; 26-45 at $1295 and 26-47 at $1495. Paring of body styles on 128-inch wheelbase to 26-50 at $1995; 26-51 at $1925; 26-54 at $1495; 26-54C at $1765; 26-55 at $1525. The former Four-Passenger Coupe offered on the 128-inch wheelbase was now put on the 120-inch wheelbase and offered as 26-48 at $1795. All other body styles dropped.
Notes: Starting serial number for 26-20, 1398244; for 26-24, 1402767; for 26-25, 1403132; for 26-26, 1405970; for 26-27, 1406970; for 26-28, 1410986; for 26-40, 1412093; for 26-44, 1416599; for 26-45, 1417049; for 26-47, 1417931; for 26-48, 1423331; for 26-50, 1424431; for 26-51, 1425541; for 26-54, 1426441; for 26-54C 1426702; for 26-55, 1427302.

MODEL YEAR: 1927

STANDARD SERIES. Wheelbase now noted as 114½ inches. Two body styles added: 27-26S Four-Passenger Special Coupe at $1275 and 27-29 Five-Passenger Brougham at $1375. Models continued: 27-20 at $1195; 27-24 at $1195; 27-25 at $1225; 27-26 at $1195; 27-27 at $1295; 27-28 at $1275.

MASTER SERIES. Open cars dropped from 120-inch wheelbase line. Three-Passenger Convertible Coupe 27-54CC at $1925 and Five-Passenger Coupe 27-58 at $1850 added to 128-inch wheelbase line. Models continued: 27-40 at $1395; 27-47 at $1495; 27-48 at $1465; 27-50 at $1995; 27-51 at $1925; 27-54 at $1495; 27-54C at $1765; 27-55 at $1525.
Notes: Striking new color range available. Starting serial number for 27-20, 1638800; for 27-24, 1645990; for 27-25, 1646560; for 27-26, 1648850; for 27-26S, 1650550; for 27-27, 1651350; for 27-28, 1659714; for 27-29, 1744069; for 27-40, 1661435; for 27-47, 1665501; for 27-48, 1674874; for 27-50, 1677210; for 27-51, 1679040; for 27-54, 1681440; for 27-54C, 1682370; for 27-54CC, 1713361; for 27-55, 1684170; for 27-58, 1685110.

MODEL YEAR: 1928
STANDARD SERIES. Four-Passenger Coupe dropped. Models continued: 28-20 at $1195; 28-34 at $1195; 28-25 at $1225; 28-26 at $1195; 28-26S at $1275; 28-27 at $1295; 28-29 at $1375.
MASTER SERIES. On the 120-inch wheelbase, the former Two-Door Sedan (or Coach) dropped, and a 28-47S "DeLuxe" Four-Door Sedan added at $1575. On the 128-inch wheelbase, the Convertible Coupe introduced the year previous now dropped. Models continued: 28-47 at $1495; 28-47S at $1575; 28-48 at $1465; 28-50 at $1995; 28-51 at $1925; 28-54 at $1495; 28-54C at $1765; 28-55 at $1525; 28-58 at $1850.
Notes: Standard SAE gearshift pattern adopted. Radiator emblem now standard. Starting serial number for 28-20, 1888911; for 28-34, 1895218; for 28-25, 1896218; for 28-26, 1897326; for 28-26S, 1899576; for 28-27, 1901476; for 28-29, 1909376; for 28-47, 1911026; for 28-47S, 1917026; for 28-48, 1919026; for 28-50, 1921026; for 28-51, 1923126; for 28-54, 1925476; for 28-54C, 1926476; for 28-55, 1926976; for 28-58, 1927476. The starting motor number was 1960500 for the Standard Series, 1990500 for the Master Series.

MODEL YEAR: 1929
SERIES 116. Six cylinders, 3.312 by 4.625, 239.1 cubic inches, rated 26.33 hp. Wheelbase 115¾ inches. Tires 30x5.50. Former Sport Roadster and Town Brougham dropped. Prices varied to $1220 for 29-20; $1225 for 29-25; $1195 for 29-26; $1250 for 29-26S; $1320 for 29-27.
SERIES 121. Six cylinders, 3.626 by 5, 309.6 cubic inches, rated 31.4 hp. Wheelbase 120¾ inches. Body styles available: 29-41 Four-Door Country Club Sedan at $1450; 29-44 Four-Passenger Roadster at $1325; 29-46 Two-Passenger Coupe at $1395; 29-46S Four-Passenger Coupe at $1450; 29-47 Four-Door Sedan at $1520; 29-48 Four-Passenger Coupe at $1445. The "DeLuxe" Four-Door Sedan of the year previous was dropped.
SERIES 129. Engine as above. Wheelbase 128¾ inches. Added body styles: 29-29 Seven-Passenger Touring Car at $1550; 29-50L Imperial Sedan at $2145; 29-54CC Convertible Coupe at $1875; 29-57 Four-Door Sedan at $1935. The new Convertible Coupe replaced the former 28-54C Country Club Coupe, increased in price by $110. Models continued: 29-50 at $2045; 29-51 at $1875; 29-55 at $1525; 29-58 at $1850.
Notes: The new series designations referred to wheelbase length. These cars were also referred to promotionally as the "Silver Anniversary" Buicks. For the first time color options were available throughout the line. Starting serial number for 29-20, 2123926; for 29-25, 2131476; for 29-26, 2133798; for 29-26S, 2135823; for 29-27, 2137873; for 29-41, 2151760; for 29-44, 2155485; for 29-46, 2157107; for 29-46S, 2158507; for 29-47, 2159907; for 29-48, 2256956; for 29-49, 2166412; for 29-50, 2167092; for 29-50L, 2169424; for 29-51,

2169651; for 29-54CC, 2171618; for 29-55, 2172432; for 29-57, 2173190; for 29-57, 2175065. The starting motor number was 22225361 for the Standard Series, 2340300 for the Master Series.

NOTE: Hereafter, because of their increasing and varying number, model designations only will be given; for the specific body style to which they refer, the reader is directed to the production chart.

MODEL YEAR: 1930
SERIES 40. Six cylinders, 3.437 by 4.625, 257.5 cubic inches, rated 28.4 hp. Wheelbase 118 inches. Tires 19x5.50. Available body styles: 30-40 at $1270; 30-44 at $1310; 30-45 at $1310; 30-46 at $1260; 30-46S at $1300; 30-47 at $1330.
SERIES 50. Six cylinders, 3.75 by 5, 331.4 cubic inches, rated 33.75 hp. Wheelbase 124 inches. Tires 19x6.50. Two body styles, 30-57 at $1540 and 30-58 at $1510.
SERIES 60. Six cylinders, 3.75 by 5, 331.4 cubic inches, rated 33.75 hp. Wheelbase 132 inches. Tires 19x6.50. Available body styles: 30-60 at $1910; 30-60L at $2070; 30-61 at $1760; 30-64 at $1585; 30-64C at $1695; 30-68 at $1740; 30-69 at $1595.
MARQUETTE SERIES. Six cylinders, 3.125 by 4.625, 212.8 cubic inches, rated 23.44 hp. Wheelbase 114 inches. Tires 28x5.25. Available body styles: 30-30 at $1000; 30-34 at $1020; 30-35 at $1020; 30-36 at $990; 30-36S at $1020; 30-37 at $1060.
Note: The prices noted were effective December 8th, 1929—following the stock market crash—and represented increases of $35 in the Series 40; $45 in the Series 50; $65 in the Series 60; $25 in the Marquette Series. Starting serial number for 30-40, 2313806; for 30-44, 2317238; for 30-45, 2318640; for 30-46, 2319613; for 30-46S, 2321363; for 30-47, 2323633; for 30-57, 2334956; for 30-58, 2340326; for 30-60, 2341626; for 30-60L, 2343657; for 30-61, 2343927; for 30-64, 2436357; for 30-64C, 2346118; for 30-68, 2346908; for 30-69, 2348508; for 30-30, 10000; for 30-34, 11996; for 30-35, 12569; for 30-36, 13139; for 30-36S, 13991; for 30-37, 15012. The starting motor number was 2439253 for the Standard Series, 2489593 for the Master Series, 10000 for the Marquette Series.

MODEL YEAR: 1931
SERIES 50. Eight cylinders, 2.875 by 4.25, 220.7 cubic inches, rated 26.45 hp. Wheelbase 114 inches. Tires 18x5.25. Available body styles: 8-50 at $1035; 8-54 at $1055; 8-55 at $1055; 8-56 at $1025; 8-56C at $1055; 8-57 at $1095.
SERIES 60. Eight cylinders, 3.0625 by 4.625, 272.6 cubic inches, rated 30.02 hp. Wheelbase 118 inches. Tires 19x5.50. Available body styles: 8-64 at $1335; 8-65 at $1335; 8-66 at $1285; 8-66S at $1325; 8-67 at $1355.
SERIES 80. Eight cylinders, 3.333 by 5, 344.8 cubic inches, rated 35.12 hp. Wheelbase 124 inches. Tires 19x6.50. Two body styles available, 8-86 at $1535 and 8-87 at $1565.
SERIES 90. Same engine as Series 80. Wheelbase 132 inches. Tires 19x6.50. Available body styles: 8-90 at $1935; 8-90L at $2035; 8-91 at $1785; 8-94 at $1610; 8-95 at $1620; 8-96 at $1765; 8-96C at $1785; 8-96S at $1720.
Notes: All six-cylinder cars dropped. Synchromesh adopted. Starting serial number for 8-50, 2460544; for 8-54, 2461202; for 8-55, 2461629; for 8-56, 2461809; for 8-56C, 254723; for 8-56S, 2462161; for 8-57, 2462969; for 8-64, 2467004; for 8-65, 2467537; for 8-66, 2467729; for 8-66S, 2468534; for 8-67, 2470095; for 8-86, 2477656; for 8-87, 2478581; for 8-90, 2482849; for 8-90L, 2483903; for 8-91, 2483971; for 8-94, 2485873; for 8-95, 2486273; for 8-96, 2486463; for 8-96C, 2551043; for 8-96S, 2488013.

MODEL YEAR: 1932

SERIES 50. Eight cylinders, 2.9375 by 4.25, 230.4 cubic inches, rated 27.61 hp. Tires 18x5.50. Body styles available: 32-55 at $1155; 32-56 at $935; 32-56S at $1040; 32-56C at $1080; 32-57 at $995; 32-57S at $1080; 32-58 at $1060; 32-58C at $1080.
SERIES 60. Tires 18x6.00. Body styles available: 32-65 at $1390; 32-66 at $1250; 32-66S at $1270; 32-66C at $1270; 32-67 at $1310; 32-68 at $1290; 32-68C at $1310.
SERIES 80. Wheelbase 126 inches. Tires 18x7.00. Available body styles: 32-86 at $1540; 32-87 at $1570.
SERIES 90. Wheelbase 134 inches. Tires 18x7.00. Body styles available: 32-90 at $1955; 32-90L at $2055; 32-91 at $1820; 32-95 at $1675; 32-96 at $1785; 32-96S at $1740; 32-97 at $1805; 32-96C at $1805; 32-98 at $1830.
Notes: Two-Door Sedan and Sport Roadster dropped in Series 50; Sport Roadster and Four-Passenger Special Coupe dropped in Series 60; Sport Roadster dropped in Series 90. Five-Passenger Convertible Phaeton added in both Series 50 and Series 90; Four-Passenger Convertible Coupe Roadster added in Series 60. Wizard Control introduced. Starting serial number 2602732; starting motor number 2751922.

MODEL YEAR: 1933

SERIES 50. Wheelbase 119 inches. Tires 17x6. Body styles available: 33-56 at $995; 33-56C at $1115; 33-56S at $1030; 33-57 at $1045; 33-58 at $1065.
SERIES 60. Wheelbase 127 inches. Tires 17x6.50. Body styles available: 33-66C at $1365; 33-66S at $1270; 33-67 at $1310; 33-68 at $1310; 33-68C at $1585.
SERIES 80. Wheelbase 130 inches. Tires 17x7. Body styles available: 33-86 at $1540; 33-86C at $1575; 33-86S at $1495; 33-87 at $1570; 33-88C at $1845.
SERIES 90. Wheelbase 138 inches. Tires 17x7. Body styles available: 33-90 at $1955; 33-90L at $2055; 33-91 at $1820; 33-96 at $1785; 33-97 at $1805.
Notes: Sport Phaeton, Special Sedan and Convertible Phaeton dropped from Series 50; Sport Phaeton and Business Coupe dropped from Series 60; Sport Phaeton, Country Club Coupe, Five-Passenger Sedan, Convertible Coupe Roadster and Convertible Phaeton dropped from Series 90. Convertible Coupe, Sport Coupe and Convertible Phaeton added to Series 80. Fisher "no-draft" ventilation introduced. Starting serial number 2,659,523; starting motor number 2,811,457.

MODEL YEAR: 1934

SERIES 40. Eight cylinders, 3.094 by 3.875, 233 cubic inches, rated 30.63 hp. Wheelbase 117 inches. Tires 16x6.25. Body styles available: 34-41 at $925; 34-46 at $795; 34-46S at $855; 34-47 at $895; 34-48 at $865.
SERIES 50. Eight cylinders, 2.969 by 4.25, 235.3 cubic inches, rated 28.2 hp. Wheelbase 119 inches. Tires 16x7.00. Body styles available: 34-56 at $1110; 34-56C at $1230; 34-56S at $1145; 34-57 at $1190; 34-58 at $1160.
SERIES 60. Eight cylinders, 3.094 by 4.625, 278.1 cubic inches, rated 30.63 hp. Body styles available: 34-61 at $1465; 34-66C at $1495; 34-66S at $1375; 34-67 at $1425; 34-68 at $1395; 34-68C at $1675.
SERIES 90. Eight cylinders, 3.3125 by 5.00, 344.8 cubic inches, rated 35.12 hp. Wheelbase 136 inches. Tires 16x7.50. Body styles available: 34-90 at $2055; 34-90L at $2175; 34-91 at $1965; 34-96C at $1945; 34-96S at $1875; 34-97 at $1945; 34-98 at $1895; 34-98C at $2145.
Notes: Series 80 dropped. Club Sedan added to Series 60; Convertible Coupe, Sport Coupe and Convertible Phaeton added to Series 90. Independent Suspension (Knee-Action) introduced. Prices indicated for cars equipped with five wire wheels in Series 50, 60 and 90; five steel wheels in Series 40. Models

68C and 98C (Convertible Phaetons) available with six wheels only. For Series 50, 60 and 90, starting serial number 2,706,453, starting motor number 2,861,223. For Series 40, starting serial number 2,735,509; starting motor number 2,894,800.

MODEL YEAR: 1935

SERIES 40. Convertible Coupe (35-46C) at $925 added to the line. All other body styles continued at same prices as year previous.
SERIES 50, 60 AND 90. All body styles continued at same prices.
Notes: All base cars equipped with five steel wheels, except the Series 60 and Series 90 Convertible Phaetons which were available with six wheels only. Starting serial number for all series 277650. Starting motor number 4-2937408 for Series 40; 2922072 for Series 50, 60 and 90.

MODEL YEAR: 1936

SPECIAL SERIES 40. Wheelbase 118 inches. Tires 16x6.50. Body styles available: 36-41 at $885; 36-46 at $765; 36-46C at $905; 36-46S at $820; 36-48 at $835.
CENTURY SERIES 60. Eight cylinders, 3.4375 by 4.3125, 320.2 cubic inches, rated 37.81 hp. Wheelbase 122 inches. Tires 15x7.00. Body styles available: 36-61 at $1090; 36-66C at $1135; 36-66S at $1035; 36-68 at $1055.
ROADMASTER SERIES 80. Same engine as Series 60. Wheelbase 131 inches. Tires 16x7.00. Body styles available: 36-80C at $1565; 36-81 at $1255.
LIMITED SERIES 90. Same engine as Series 60. Wheelbase 138 inches. Tires 16x7.50. Body styles available: 36-90 at $1845; 36-90L at $1945; 36-91 at $1695; 36-91F at $1795.
Notes: The Sport Coupe in both Special and Century Series was available with either an opera or rumble seat. The only Convertible Phaeton was in the Roadmaster Series; a Formal Sedan was a new top-of-the-line body style in the Limited Series. The new eight-cylinder engine replaced the three first-generation Buick straight-eights introduced in 1931. Hydraulic brakes and "suicide doors" introduced. Starting serial number for all series 2830899. Starting motor number 42995239 for Series 40; 63001000 for Series 60; 83001000 for Series 80; 93001000 for Series 90.

MODEL YEAR: 1937

SPECIAL SERIES 40. Wheelbase 122 inches. Body styles available: 37-40C at $1145; 37-41 at $870; 37-44 at $810; 37-46 at $765; 37-46C at $905; 37-46S at $825; 37-47 at $845; 37-48 at $835.
CENTURY SERIES 60. Wheelbase 126 inches. Body styles available: 37-60C at $1345; 37-61 at $1060; 37-64 at $1000; 37-66C at $1095; 37-66S at $1015; 37-67 at $1025; 37-68 at $765.
ROADMASTER SERIES 80. Body styles available: 37-80C at $1565; 37-81 at $1275; 37-81F at $1395.
LIMITED SERIES 90. Body styles available: 37-90 at $1895; 37-90L at $1995; 37-91 at $1725; 37-91F at $1895.
Notes: Two- and Four-Door Touring Sedans, and Convertible Phaetons, added to both Series 40 and 60. The Sport Coupe in Series 40 and 60 available only with opera seats; the Convertible Coupe now the only body style with rumble seat. Formal Sedan added to Series 80. All-steel body construction adopted on Series 40 and 60 cars. Base cars equipped with five painted steel wheels; models 80C, 90, 90L, 91 and 91F available with six wheels only. Starting serial number for all series 2999497. Starting motor number 4-3166225 for Series 40; 6-3166225 for Series 60; 8-3166225 for Series 80; 9-3176225 for Series 90.

MODEL YEAR: 1938

SPECIAL SERIES 40. Body styles available: 38-40C at $1406; 38-41 at $1047; 38-44 at $981; 38-46 at $945; 38-46C at $1103, 38-46S at $1001; 38-47 at $1022; 38-48 at $1006.
CENTURY SERIES 60. Body styles available: 38-60C at $1713; 38-61 at $1297; 38-66C at $1359; 38-66S at $1226; 38-67 at $1272; 39-68 at $1256.
ROADMASTER SERIES 80. Wheelbase 133 inches. Body styles available: 38-80C at $1983; 38-81 at $1645; 38-81F at $1758; 38-87 at $1645.
LIMITED SERIES 90. Wheelbase 140 inches. Body styles available: 38-90 at $2350; 38-90L at $2453; 38-91 at $2176.
Notes: The Two-Door Touring Sedan dropped from Series 60, the Formal Sedan from Series 90. A Four-Door Sport Sedan added to Series 80. "Torque Free Springing," "Dynaflash Engine" and "Self Shifter" introduced. Starting serial numbers for all series 13219848 (Flint); 23238767 (South Gate); 33245765 (Linden). Starting motor numbers, all plants, 43396937 for Series 40; 63396937 for Series 60; 83396937 for Series 80; 93396937 for Series 90.

MODEL YEAR: 1939

SPECIAL SERIES 40. Wheelbase 120 inches. Body styles available: 39-41 at $996; 39-41C at $1406; 39-46 at $894; 39-46C at $1077; 39-46S at $950; 39-48 at $955.
CENTURY SERIES 60. Body styles available: 39-61 at $1246; 39-61C at $1713; 39-66C at $1343; 39-66S at $1175; 39-68 at $1205.
ROADMASTER SERIES 80. Body styles available: 39-80C at $1983; 39-81 at $1543; 39-81C at $1983; 39-81F at $1758; 39-87 at $1543.
LIMITED SERIES 90. Body styles available: 39-90 at $2350; 39-90L at $2453; 39-91 at $2074.
Notes: The Convertible Coupe in Series 40 and 60 now with opera seat; the rumble seat now gone from all Buicks. The former Convertible Phaeton with luggage compartment in Series 40 and 60 replaced by Convertible Sport Phaeton with trunk back. The Sport Sedan dropped from Series 40 and 60. The Sport Phaeton in Series 80 now available in trunk or plain back. Sunshine Turret Top introduced on models 39-41, 39-48 and 39-61. Turn-signals adopted as standard equipment. Pushbutton radio introduced. Starting serial numbers for all series 13388547 (Flint); 23395088 (South Gate); 33405088 (Linden). Starting motor numbers, all plants, 4-3572652 for Series 40; 6-3576652 for Series 60; 8-3576652 for Series 80; 9-3576652 for Series 90.

MODEL YEAR: 1940

SPECIAL SERIES 40. Wheelbase 121 inches. Convertible Phaeton (40-41C) now priced at $1355. Taxicab introduced.
SUPER SERIES 50. Engine, wheelbase and tires same as Series 40. Body styles available: 40-51 at $1109; 40-51C at $1549; 40-56C at $1211; 40-56S at $1058; 40-59 at $1242.
CENTURY SERIES 60. Body styles available: 40-61 at $1211; 40-61C at $1620; 40-66 at $1128; 40-66C at $1343; 40-66S at $1175.
ROADMASTER SERIES 70. Wheelbase 126 inches. Tires 15x7.00. Body styles: 40-71 at $1359; 40-71C at $1768; 40-76C at $1431; 40-76S at $1277.
LIMITED SERIES 80. Wheelbase 133 inches. Body styles available: 40-80C at $1952; 40-81 at $1553; 40-81C at $1952; 40-81F at $1727; 40-87 at $1553; 40-87F at $1727.
LIMITED SERIES 90. Wheelbase 140 inches. Body styles available: 40-90 at $2096; 40-90L at $2199; 40-91 at $1942.
Notes: A Taxicab was new to Series 40, the Estate Wagon to the new Series 50. All Convertible and Sport Coupes now had full rear seats. Starting serial

numbers for all series 13596807 (Flint); 23601856 (South Gate); 33611856 (Linden). Starting motor numbers 4-3786214 for Series 40; 5-3786214 for Series 50; 6-3812000 for Series 60; 7-3812000 for Series 70; 8-3812000 for Series 80; 9-3812000 for Series 90.

MODEL YEAR: 1941

SPECIAL SERIES 40-A. Same engine as Series 40. Wheelbase 118 inches. Tires 15x6.50. Body styles available: 41-44 at $915; 41-44C at $1138; 41-44S at $980; 41-47 at $1021.
SPECIAL SERIES 40. Body styles available: 41-41 at $1052; 41-41SE at $1134; 41-46 at $935; 41-46S at $1006; 41-46SSE at $1063; 41-49 at $1463.
SUPER SERIES 50. Body styles available: 41-51 at $1185; 41-51C at $1555; 41-56 at $1031; 41-56C at $1267; 41-56S at $1113.
CENTURY SERIES 60. Body styles available: 41-61 at $1288; 41-66 at $1195; 41-66S for $1241.
ROADMASTER SERIES 70. Body styles available: 41-71 at $1364; 41-71C at $1775; 41-76C at $1457; 41-76S at $1282.
LIMITED SERIES 90. Wheelbase 139 inches. Body styles available: 41-90 at $2360; 41-90L at $2465; 41-91 at $2155; 41-91F at $2310.
Notes: Limited Series 80 dropped. Letters "SE" in Series 40 models indicated Super Series equipment. The Sedanet a new body style in Series 40 and 60. Compound Carburetion introduced. Starting serial numbers 14034052 (Flint); 23994170 (South Gate), 34007924 (Linden) for Series 40-A; for all other series 13880012 (Flint); 23892008 (South Gate); 33897008 (Linden). Starting motor numbers 44074859 for Series 40; A4074859 for Series 40-A; 54074859 for Series 50; 64085000 for Series 60; 74085000 for Series 70; 94085000 for Series 90.

MODEL YEAR: 1942

SPECIAL SERIES 40-A. Body styles available: 42-44 at $1067; 42-44C at $1352; 42-47 at $1162; 42-48 at $1088; 42-48S at $1125.
SPECIAL SERIES 40-B. Body styles available: 42-41 at $1203; 42-41SE at $1287; 42-46 at $1098; 42-46S at $1156; 42-46SSE at $1214; 42-49 at $1551.
SUPER SERIES 50. Wheelbase 124 inches. Body styles available: 42-51 at $1381; 42-56C at $1560; 42-56S at $1329.
CENTURY SERIES 60. Body styles available: 42-61 at $1454; 42-66S at $1402.
ROADMASTER SERIES 70. Body styles available: 42-71 at $1590; 42-76C at $1811; 42-76S at $1517.
LIMITED SERIES 90. Body styles available: 42-90 at $2610.50; 42-90L at $2400.50; 42-91F at $2558.50.
Notes: Starting serial numbers for all series 14257442 (Flint); 24273684; (South Gate); 3426384 (Linden). Starting motor numbers 4457941A for Series 40-A; 4457971-4 for Series 40-B; 4457941-5 for Series 50; 4457941-6 for Series 60; 4457941-7 for Series 70; 4457941-9 for Series 90.

MODEL YEAR: 1946

SPECIAL SERIES 40. Model 41 Four-Door Sedan at $1580; 46S Sedanet at $1522.
SUPER SERIES 50. Model 51 Four-Door Sedan at $1822; 56C Convertible Coupe at $2046; 56S Sedanet at $1741; 59 Estate Wagon at $2594.
ROADMASTER SERIES 70. Model 71 Four-Door Sedan at $2110; 76C Convertible Coupe at $2347; 76S Sedanet at $2014.
Notes: Starting serial numbers for all series 14364445 (Flint); 24380001 (South Gate); 34390001 (Linden); 44415001 (Kansas City). Starting motor numbers 4558037-4 for Series 40; 4558037-5, Series 50; 4558297, Series 70. *437*

MODEL YEAR: 1947

SPECIAL SERIES 40. Model 41 at $1673 and 46S at $1611.
SUPER SERIES 50. Models 51 at $1929; 56C at $2333; 56S at $1843; 59 at $2940.
ROADMASTER SERIES 70. Models 71 at $2232; 76C at $2651; 76S at $2131. Model 79 Estate Wagon added at $3249.
Notes: Starting serial numbers for all series 14524131 (Flint); 24530001 (South Gate); 34542001 (Linden); 44536001 (Kansas City). "Identification of 1947 Model Buicks will be made by Serial Number as the Motor numbering series for the 1946 Models will continue through the 1947 Models."

MODEL YEAR: 1948

SPECIAL SERIES 40. Models 41 at $1809 and 46S at $1735.
SUPER SERIES 50. Models 51 at $2087; 56C at $2518; 56S at $1987; 59 at $3124.
ROADMASTER SERIES 70. Model 71 at $2418; 76C at $2837; 76S at $2297; 79 at $3433.
Notes: Dynaflow introduced. Starting serial numbers for all series 14801266 (Flint); 2482001 (South Gate); 34824001 (Linden); 44830001 (Kansas City); 64834001 (Atlanta). Starting motor numbers 4999881-4 for Series 40; 4999881-5 for Series 50; 4999881-7 for Series 70.

MODEL YEAR: 1949

SUPER SERIES 50. Wheelbase 121 inches. Tires 15x7.60. Body styles available: Models 51 at $2157; 56C at $2583; 56S at $2059; 59 at $3178.
ROADMASTER SERIES 70. Wheelbase 126 inches. Tires 15x8.20. Body styles available: Models 71 at $2735; 76C at $3150; 76S at $2618; 70 at $3734. Model 76R Riviera Hardtop Coupe added at $3023.
SPECIAL SERIES 40. Wheelbase 121.5 inches. Tires 15x7.60. Body styles available: Models 43 Four-Door Sedan at $1925; 46 Business Coupe at $1819; 46S Sedanet at $1872.
Notes: The "sweepspear" introduced on a few Rivieras; VentiPorts introduced on Roadmaster and Super models. The Special Series did not begin coming off the production line until mid-summer of 1949, in some Buick data sheets is indicated as a 1950 model. Starting serial numbers for the 50 and 70 Series 15020984 (Flint); 25030001 (South Gate); 35036001 (Linden); 45043001 (Kansas City); 5505001 (Wilmington); 65054001 (Atlanta); 75057001 (Framingham). Starting serial numbers for the 40 Series 15360001 (Flint); 25370001 (South Gate); 35374001 (Linden); 4530001 (Kansas City); 55388001 (Wilmington); 75397001 (Framingham). Starting motor numbers 5568000-4 for Series 40; 5220972-5 for Series 50; 5220972-7 for Series 70.

MODEL YEAR: 1950

SPECIAL SERIES 40. Models 43, 46 and 46S continued at $1909, $1803 and $1856 respectively. Body styles added: Model 41 Four-Door Touring Sedan at $1941, 41D DeLuxe version at $1983; 43D Four-Door DeLuxe Jetback Sedan at $1952; 46D Two-Door DeLuxe Jetback Sedan at $1899.
SUPER SERIES 50. Eight cylinders, 3.1875 by 4.125, 263.3 cubic inches, rated 32.51 hp. Models 51, 56C and 56S continued at $2139, $2476 and $2041 respectively. Model 59 Estate Wagon at $2844 and 56R Two-Door Riviera at $2139 added. A Four-Door Riviera Sedan (Model 52) on a special 126-inch wheelbase at $2212 also added.
ROADMASTER SERIES 70. Wheelbase 126¼ inches. Tires 15x8.00, Models 71, 76C, 76R, 76S and 79 continued at $2633, $2981, $2854, $2528 and $3407 respectively. Added were another Two-Door Riviera (72R) at

$2633 and a DeLuxe Estate Wagon (79R) at $3433. Two further new models, on a special 130¼-inch wheelbase, were a Four-Door Riviera (Model 72) at $2738, and its DeLuxe version (72R) at $2764. Estate Wagons carried 15x-8.20 tires.
Notes: Starting serial numbers for all series 15360001 (Flint); 25370001 (South Gate); 35374001 (Linden); 45380001 (Kansas City); 5538801—except 55417001-55417948 included on 1949 Series 50 and 70—(Wilmington); 65393001 (Atlanta); 75397001 (Framingham). Starting motor numbers 5568000-4 for Series 40; 5628758-5 for Series 50 Synchromesh, 5624734-5 Dynaflow; 5635021-7 for Series 70.

MODEL YEAR: 1951

SPECIAL SERIES 40. Eight cylinders, 3.1875 by 4.125, 263.3 cubic inches, rated 32.51 hp. Models 41, 41D, 45R, 46, 46C and 46S continued at $2138.92, $2185.13, $2224.93, $1986.51, $2561.14 and $2045.51 respectively. A new Two-Door Sedan (48) and its DeLuxe version (48D) added at $2079.92 and $2127.13.
SUPER SERIES 50. Models 51, 52, 56C, 56R, 56S and 59 continued at $2536.26, $2436.78, $2727.80, $2356.19, $2247.81 and $3132.82 respectively.
ROADMASTER SERIES 70. Models 72R, 76C, 76R and 79R continued at $3043.62, $3283.03, $3143.42 and $3780.46 respectively. A new Two-Door Riviera Coupe (76MR) added at $3050.65.
Notes: Starting serial numbers for all series 16031301 (Flint); 26050001 (South Gate); 36055001 (Linden); 46061001 (Kansas City); 56070001 (Wilmington); 66075001 (Atlanta); 76080001 (Framingham). Starting motor numbers 6240128-4 for 40 Series Synchromesh, 6240100-4 Dynaflow; 6240564-5 for Series 50 Synchromesh, 6240100-5 Dynaflow; 6240161-7 for Series 70.

MODEL YEAR: 1952

SPECIAL SERIES 40. Models 41, 41D, 45R, 46C, 46S and 48D continued at $2208.76, $2255.32, $2295.43, $2634.17, $2114.65 and $2196.88 respectively.
SUPER SERIES 50. Models 52, 56C, 56R and 59 continued at $2563.17, $2868.59, $2477.56 and $3295.73 respectively.
ROADMASTER SERIES 70. Models 72R, 76C, 76R and 79R continued at $3200.36, $3452.56, $3306.05 and $3976.73 respectively.
Notes: Starting serial numbers for all series 16436001 (Flint); 26456001 (South Gate); 36464001 (Linden); 46471001 (Kansas City); 56483001 (Wilmington); 66490001 (Atlanta); 76496001 (Framingham). Starting motor numbers 6646232-4 for Series 40 Synchromesh, 6646230-4 Dynaflow; 6647024-5 for Series 50 Synchromesh, 6646230-5 Dynaflow; 6652000-7 for Series 70.

MODEL YEAR: 1953

SPECIAL SERIES 40. The 46C Convertible Coupe now $2553.17.
SUPER SERIES 50. Eight cylinders, V-8, 4 by 3.2 inches, 322 cubic inches, rated 51.2 hp. Models 52, 56C, 56R and 59 continued at $2696.17, $3001.59, $2610.56 and $3429.73.
ROADMASTER SERIES. Eight cylinders, V-8, 4 by 3.2 inches, 322 cubic inches, rated 51.2 hp. Wheelbase 121.5 inches (125.5 for 72R). Models 72R. 76C, 76R and 79R continued at $3254.36, $3505.56, $3358.05 and $4030.73. Model 76X Skylark, on the 121.5-inch wheelbase, added at $5000.
Notes: Twin-Turbine Dynaflow introduced. Starting serial numbers for all series 16740001 (Flint); 2675001 (South Gate); 36774001 (Linden); 46783001 (Kansas City); 56799001 (Wilmington); 66808001 (Atlanta); 76815001

(Framingham). Starting motor numbers 6950620-4 for Series 40; V2001-5 for Series 50; V2001-7 for Series 70.

MODEL YEAR: 1954

SPECIAL SERIES 40. Eight cylinders, V-8, 3.625 by 3.2 inches, 264 cubic inches, rated 42.05 hp. Wheelbase 122 inches. Models 41D, 46C, 46R and 48D continued at $2265.32, $2563.17, $2305.43 and $2206.88 respectively. Model 49 Estate Wagon added at $3163.
CENTURY SERIES 60. Eight cylinders, V-8, 4 by 3.2 inches, 322 cubic inches, rated 51.2 hp. Wheelbase 122 inches. Body styles available: 61 Four-Door DeLuxe Sedan at $2520.17; 66C Convertible Coupe at $2963; 66R Riviera Coupe at $2533.56; 69 Estate Wagon at $3470.
SUPER SERIES 50. Wheelbase 127 inches. Models 52, 56C and 56R continued at $2711.17, $2963.59 and $2625.56 respectively.
ROADMASTER SERIES 70. Wheelbase 127 inches. Models 72R, 76C and 76R continued at $3269.36, $3520.56 and $3373.05 respectively.
SKYLARK. Designated "100"—on 122-inch wheelbase of Special and Century, with engine of Super and Roadmaster, and priced at $4483.
Notes: Estate Wagon models now all steel. Starting vehicle identification numbers A1001001 (Flint); A2001001 (South Gate); A3001001 (Linden); A4001001 (Kansas City); A5001001 (Wilmington); A6001001 (Atlanta); A7001001 (Framingham); A8001001 (Arlington). Starting motor numbers V273956-4 for Series 40; V273956-6 for Series 60; V273956-5 for Series 50; V273956-7 for Series 70 and Skylark.

MODEL YEAR: 1955

SPECIAL SERIES 40. Body styles available: Model 41 Four-Door Tourback Sedan at $2291.32; 43 Four-Door Riviera Sedan at $2409; 46C Convertible Coupe at $2590.17; 46R Two-Door Riviera Sedan at $2332.43; 48 Two-Door Tourback Sedan at $2232.88; 49 Estate Wagon at $2974.
CENTURY SERIES 60. Models 61, 66C, 66R and 69 continued at $2548.17, $2991, $2600.56 and $3175 respectively. New Model 63 Four-Door Riviera Sedan at $2733.
SUPER SERIES 50. Models 56C and 56R continued at $3224.59 and $2830.56. New Model 52 Four-Door Hardtop Sedan at $2876.17.
ROADMASTER SERIES 70. Models 76C and 76R continued at $3551.56 and $3453.05. New Model 72 Four-Door Hardtop Sedan at $3349.36.
Notes: Horsepower raised from 200 to 236 in Roadmaster and Century, 150 to 188 in Special, and 182 to 236 in Super. Variable Pitch Dynaflow introduced. Starting vehicle identification numbers 5B1001001 (Flint), 5B2 (South Gate), 4B3 (Linden), 4B4 (Kansas City), 4B5 (Wilmington), 5B6 (Atlanta), 5B7 (Framingham), 4B8 (Arlington). Starting motor numbers V720080-4 for Series 40; that same number with last digit of "6" or "5" or "7" designating Series 60, 50 and 70.

MODEL YEAR: 1956

SPECIAL SERIES 40. Eight cylinders, V-8, 4.0 by 3.2, 322 cubic inches, rated 51.20 hp. Models 41, 43, 46C, 46R, 48 and 49 continued at $2412, $2524, $2736, $2453, $2353 and $2771 respectively.
CENTURY SERIES 60. Models 63, 66C, 66R and 69 continued at $3020, $3301, $2958 and $3251 respectively. Model 61 Tourback Sedan dropped; Model 63D Four-Door DeLuxe Riviera Sedan added at $3036.
SUPER SERIES 50. Models 52, 56C and 56R continued at $3245, $3539 and $3199 respectively. Model 53 Four-Door Riviera Sedan added at $3335.
ROADMASTER SERIES 70. Models 72, 76C and 76R continued at $3498,

$3699 and $3586 respectively. Model 73 Four-Door Riviera Sedan added at $3687.
Notes: All Buicks now shared the 322-cubic-inch engine, with two-barrel carburetor for the Special, four-barrel for the Century, Super and Roadmaster. Dynaflow optional on Special, standard on the others. Starting vehicle identification numbers 4C1001001 (Flint), 4C2 (South Gate), 4C3 (Linden), 4C4 (Kansas City), 4C5 (Wilmington), 4C6 (Atlanta), 4C7 (Framingham), 4C8 (Arlington). Starting motor numbers 1460023-4 for Series 40; that same number with last digit of "6" or "5" or "7" designating Series 60, 50 and 70.

MODEL YEAR: 1957

SPECIAL SERIES 40. Models 41, 43, 46C, 46R, 48 and 49 continued at $2659.83, $2779.83, $2986.83, $2703.83, $2595.83 and $3046.83 respectively, Model 49D Riviera Estate Wagon added at $3166.83.
CENTURY SERIES 60. Models 63, 66C, 66R and 69 continued at $3354, $3598, $3270 and $3706 respectively. Model 61 Four-Door Sedan added at $3234.
SUPER SERIES 50. Wheelbase 127.5 inches. Models 53, 56C and 56R continued at $3681, $3981 and $3536.
ROADMASTER SERIES 70. Wheelbase 127.5 inches. Models 73, 76C and 76R continued at $4053.33, $4066.33 and $4394.33 respectively. New Riviera body styles introduced: four-door 73A and 75 at $4053.33 and $4483.33; two-door 75R and 76A at $4373.33 and $3944.33.
Notes: Engine specifications now V-8, 4.125 by 3.4, 364 cubic inches, rated 54.45 hp. Beginning this model year the vehicle identification numbers and the motor numbers were the same. The code was as follows, using 4 D1001001 as an example, the first digit identified the series (4 for 40, 6 for 60, etc.), the letter identified the year ("D" for 1957), the digit following identified the plant (1 for Flint, 2 for South Gate, 3 for Linden, 4 for Kansas City, 5 for Wilmington, 6 for Atlanta, 7 for Framingham, 8 for Arlington). The last six digits represented the basic number in sequence.

MODEL YEAR: 1958

SPECIAL SERIES 40. Models 41, 43, 46C, 46R, 48, 49 and 49D continued at $2448, $2560, $2766, $2489, $2388, $2862 and $2974 respectively.
CENTURY SERIES 60. Models 61, 63, 66C, 66R and 69 continued at $3007, $3119, $3346, $3056 and $3487.
SUPER SERIES 50. Models 53 and 56R continued at $3443 and $3308.
ROADMASTER SERIES 75. Models 75, 75C and 75R continued at $4251, $4263 and $4149. Series designation changed to 75 this model year.
LIMITED SERIES 700. Wheelbase 127.5 inches. Three body styles available: Model 750 Four-Door Riviera Sedan at $4651, 756 Convertible Coupe at $4663, 755 Two-Door Riviera Coupe at $4549.
Notes: Air-cooled aluminum front brake drums, introduced on Roadmaster 75 the year previous, now standard on all models except Special. Air-Poise Suspension and Flight Pitch Dynaflow (triple turbine) introduced. The letter "E" indicated 1958 in vehicle identification number.

MODEL YEAR: 1959

LESABRE SERIES. Retained 364-cubic-inch engine. Wheelbase 123 inches. Body styles available: Model 4411 Two-Door Sedan at $2485; 4419 Four-Door Sedan at $2545; 4435 Estate Wagon at $3025; 4437 Hardtop Coupe at $2586; 4439 Four-Door Hardtop Sedan at $2657; 4467 Convertible Coupe at $2847.
INVICTA SERIES. Eight cylinders, V-8, 4.875 by 3.64, 401 cubic inches, rated 56.11 hp. Wheelbase 123 inches. Body styles available: Model 4619 *439*

Four-Door Sedan at $3045; 4635 Estate Wagon at $3495; 4637 Hardtop Coupe at $3129; 4639 Four-Door Hardtop Sedan at $3192; 4667 Convertible Coupe at $3290.

ELECTRA SERIES. Same engine as Invicta. Wheelbase 126.3 inches. Body styles available: Model 4719 Four-Door Sedan at $3495; 4737 Hardtop Coupe at $3460; 4739 Four-Door Hardtop Sedan at $3595.

ELECTRA 225 SERIES. Same engine as Invicta. Wheelbase 126.3 inches. Body styles available: Model 4829 Four-Door Riviera Sedan at $3895; 4839 Four-Door Hardtop Sedan at $3895; 4867 Convertible Coupe at $3795.

Notes: Traditional Buick sweepspear and VentiPorts were dropped. The letter "F" indicated 1959 in vehicle identification number. The first digit in the number identified the series: 4 for LeSabre, 6 for Invicta, 7 for Electra, 8 for Electra 225.

MODEL YEAR: 1960

LESABRE SERIES. Models 4411, 4419, 4435, 4437, 4439 and 4467 continued at $2500, $2606, $3086, $2647, $2718 and $2862 respectively. Model 4445 Estate Wagon, with three seats, added at $3186.

INVICTA SERIES. All models continued at same prices. Model 4645 Estate Wagon, with three seats, added at $3595.

ELECTRA SERIES. All models continued at same prices.

ELECTRA 225 SERIES. All models continued at same prices.

Notes: The letter "G" indicated 1960 in vehicle identification number.

MODEL YEAR: 1961

SPECIAL SERIES. Eight cylinders, V-8, 3.50 by 2.80, 215 cubic inches, rated 39.20 hp. Wheelbase 112 inches. Tires 13x6.50. Body styles available: Model 4019 Four-Door Sedan at $2175; 4027 Coupe at $2125; 4035 Station Wagon (two-seat) at $2450; 4045 Station Wagon (three-seat) at $2525; 4119 Four-Door DeLuxe Sedan at $2300; 4135 DeLuxe Station Wagon (two-seat) at $2575; 4317 Skylark Coupe at $2395.

LESABRE SERIES. Models 4411, 4435, 4437, 4439, 4445 and 4467 continued at $2720, $3306, $2867, $2938, $3406 and $3082 respectively. The Four-Door Sedan became Model 4469 at $2826.

INVICTA SERIES. Models 4637, 4639 and 4667 continued at previous prices. All other body styles dropped.

ELECTRA SERIES. Wheelbase 126 inches. Models 4719, 4737 and 4739 continued at $3466, $3460 and $3566.

ELECTRA 225 SERIES. Wheelbase 126 inches. Models 4829 and 4867 continued at $3942 and $3795.

Notes: The letter "H" indicated 1961 in vehicle identification number. The first digit in the number identified the series: 0 for 4000 model Specials, 1 for 4100 model Specials, 3 for Skylark, 4 for LeSabre, 6 for Invicta, 7 for Electra, 8 for Electra 225.

MODEL YEAR: 1962

SPECIAL SERIES. Six cylinders, V-6, 3.625 by 3.20, 198 cubic inches, rated 31.54 hp. Wheelbase 112 inches. Tires 13x6.50. Body styles available: Model 4019 Four-Door Sedan at $2151; 4027 Coupe at $2101; 4035 Station Wagon (two-seat) at $2426; 4045 Station Wagon (three-seat) at $2501; 4067 Convertible Coupe at $2363; 4119 DeLuxe Four-Door Sedan at $2298; 4135 DeLuxe Station Wagon (two-seat) at $2573.

SPECIAL SERIES. With V-8 engine. Models 4119 and 4135 continued at $2368 and $2643. Model 4167 DeLuxe Convertible Coupe added at $2633. The Skylark now available as Model 4347 Coupe at $2548 and 4367 Convertible Coupe at $2756.

440 **LESABRE SERIES.** Models 4639 and 4667 continued at $3333 and $3286.

Body styles added: 4635 Estate Wagon (two-seat) at $3490; 4645 Estate Wagon (three-seat) at $3565; 4647 Sport Coupe at $3394; 4647 Wildcat Sport Coupe at $3574.

ELECTRA 225 SERIES. All Electras now designated 225. Body styles available: Model 4819 Four-Door Sedan at $3664; 4829 Four-Door Riviera Sedan at $4033; 4839 Four-Door Hardtop at $3789; 4847 Sport Coupe at $3674; 4867 Convertible Coupe at $3957.

Notes: The letter "I" indicated 1962 in vehicle identification number. The same code prevailed regarding first digit, with the addition that O or A indicated eight- or six-cylinder engines in the 4000 model cars, 1 or B the eight- or six-cylinder engines in the 4100 model cars.

MODEL YEAR: 1963

SPECIAL SERIES. With V-6 engine. Models 4019, 4027, 4035, 4045, 4067, 4119 and 4135 continued at $2363, $2309, $2659, $2740, $2591, $2521 and $2818.

SPECIAL SERIES. With V-8 engine. Models 4119, 4135, 4347 and 4367 continued at $2592, $2889, $2857 and $3011.

LESABRE SERIES. Models 4411, 4439, 4447 and 4469 continued at $2869, $3146, $3070 and $3004. Model 4435 Estate Wagon (two-seat) at $3526, Model 4445 Estate Wagon (three-seat) at $3606, and 4467 Convertible Coupe at $3339 added.

INVICTA AND WILDCAT SERIES. Models 4635, 4639, 4647 and 4667 continued at $3969, $3871, $3849 and $3961. All models except 4635 Estate Wagon carried Wildcat name.

RIVIERA. Eight cylinders, V-8, 4.1875 by 4.63, 401 cubic inches, rated 56.11 hp. Wheelbase 117 inches. Tires 15x7.10. Model 4747 Sport Coupe at $4333.

ELECTRA 225 SERIES. Models 4819, 4829, 4839, 4847 and 4867 continued at $4051, $4254, $4186, $4062 and $4365. Because the Riviera became its own "series," the 4829 Four-Door Sedan formerly referred to as Riviera became known as "Pillarless."

Notes: The letter "J" indicated 1963 in vehicle identification number. The first digit in the number identified the series as before, with the addition of 7 for the Riviera.

NOTE: Because of the proliferation of models in coming years, specific models will not be indicated here. The reader is referred to the production chart where there is a complete listing.

MODEL YEAR: 1964

SPECIAL SERIES AND SKYLARK SERIES. Six cylinders, V-6, 3.750 by 3.40, 225 cubic inches, rated 33.748 hp. Wheelbase 115 inches. Tires 14x6.50. Price range $2343-$2834.

SPECIAL SERIES AND SKYLARK SERIES. Eight cylinders, V-8, 3.750 by 3.40, 300 cubic inches, rated 45.0 hp. Wheelbase 115 inches, except for Skylark Sport Wagons on a 120-inch wheelbase. Tires 14x6.50 except for Skylark Sport Wagons at 14x7.50. Price range $2414-$3286.

LESABRE SERIES. Eight cylinders, V-8, 3.750 by 3.40, 300 cubic inches, rated 45.0 hp. Wheelbase 123 inches. Tires 15x7.10. Price range $2980-$3314. The two Estate Wagons used the 401-cubic-inch engine, 15x7.60 tires and were priced at $3554 (Model 4635) and $3635 (Model 4645).

WILDCAT SERIES. Continued with the 401 engine and 123-inch wheelbase. Price range $3164-$3455.

ELECTRA 225 SERIES. Continued with the 401 engine and 126-inch wheelbase. Price range $4059-$4374.

RIVIERA. Eight cylinders, V-8, 4.3125 by 3.64, 425 cubic inches, rated 59.51

hp. Wheelbase 117 inches. Tires 15x7.10. Price $4385.

Notes: The letter "K" indicated 1964 in vehicle identification number. First digit identified series: A for six-cylinder 4000 models, O for eight-cylinder 4000 models, B for six-cylinder 4100 models, 1 for eight-cylinder 4100 models, C for six-cylinder 4300 models, 3 for eight-cylinder 4300 models, 4 for LeSabre, 6 for Wildcat, 7 for Riviera, 8 for Electra 225.

MODEL YEAR: 1965

SPECIAL SERIES. Available as previous model year in V-6 and V-8, both on 115-inch wheelbase. Price range $2292-$2630, V-6; $2362-$2691, V-8.

SPECIAL DELUXE SERIES. Available likewise in V-6 and V-8, both on 115-inch wheelbase. Station wagon and sedan respectively $2727 and $2436 for V-6, $2796 and $2506 for V-8.

SKYLARK SERIES. Available likewise in V-6 and V-8, both on 115-inch wheelbase. Price range $2482-$2842. Former Skylark Sportwagon dropped to become Sportwagon Series.

SPORTWAGON SERIES. Eight cylinders, V-8, 3.750 by 3.40, 300 cubic inches, rated 45.0 hp. Wheelbase 120 inches. Tires 14.7.75. Price range $2925-$3214.

LESABRE SERIES. Specifications as previous year. Estate Wagon dropped. Price range $2888-$3027.

LESABRE CUSTOM SERIES. Price range $2962-$3257.

WILDCAT SERIES. Wheelbase 126 inches. Price range $3117-$3278.

WILDCAT DELUXE SERIES. Price range $3218-$3431.

WILDCAT CUSTOM SERIES. Price range $3493-$3651.

ELECTRA 225. Specifications as previous year. Price range $3989-$4121.

ELECTRA 225 CUSTOM. Price range $4168-$4350.

RIVIERA. Standard engine now the 401-cubic-inch unit. Price $4318.

Notes: Gran Sport versions of the Riviera (425-cubic-inch engine) and Skylark (400-cubic-inch engine) were claimed to do zero to sixty in seven seconds. Vehicle identification number coding changed as follows: 1st digit identified Buick Division, 2nd and 3rd digits identified the series (33 for Special six, 34 for Special eight, 35 for Special DeLuxe six, 36 for Special DeLuxe eight, 42 for Sportwagon, 43 for Skylark six, 44 for Skylark eight or Sportwagon Custom, 52 for LeSabre, 54 for LeSabre Custom, 62 for Wildcat, 64 for Wildcat DeLuxe, 66 for Wildcat Custom, 82 for Electra 225, 84 for Electra 225 Custom, 94 for Riviera). The 4th and 5th digits identified body style; the 6th digit the model year (5 for 1965), the 7th digit the plant location.

MODEL YEAR: 1966

SPECIAL, SPECIAL DELUXE SERIES. Price range $2348-$2853.

SKYLARK SERIES. Price range $2624-$2916.

SKYLARK GRAN SPORT SERIES. Eight cylinders, V-8, 4.1875 by 3.640, 400 cubic inches, rated 56.11 hp. Wheelbase 115 inches. Tires 14x7.75. Price range $2956-$3167.

SPORTWAGON AND SPORTWAGON CUSTOM SERIES. Continued in price range $3025-$3293.

LESABRE, LESABRE CUSTOM SERIES. Price range $2942-$3326.

WILDCAT AND WILDCAT CUSTOM SERIES. Price range $3233-$3701. Wildcat DeLuxe Series dropped.

ELECTRA 225 AND 225 CUSTOM SERIES. Price range $4022-$4378.

RIVIERA. Engine again the 425-cubic inch unit. Wheelbase 119 inches. Price $4424.

MODEL YEAR: 1967

SPECIAL AND SPECIAL DELUXE SERIES. Continued in price range

$2411-$2742, with V-8 for station wagon only at $2901.

SKYLARK SERIES. Continued in price range $2665-$2950.

GRAN SPORT SERIES. "Skylark" nomenclature dropped, and series more popularly known as GS 400, for 400-cubic-inch engine. Price range $2956-$3167. GS 340 coupe at $2845.

SPORTWAGON SERIES. Custom Series dropped. Price range $3202-$3340.

LESABRE AND LESABRE CUSTOM SERIES. Price range $3002-$3388.

WILDCAT AND WILDCAT CUSTOM SERIES. Eight cylinders, V-8, 4.1875 by 3.90, 430 cubic inches, rated 56.11 hp. Wheelbase 126 inches. Tires 15x8.45. Price range $3277-$3757.

ELECTRA 225 AND 225 CUSTOM SERIES. Same engine as Wildcat. Price range $4054-$4421.

RIVIERA. Same engine as Wildcat. Price $4469.

Notes: Vehicle identification coding of second and third digits revised to: 33 for Special, 35 or 36 for Special DeLuxe, 43 for Skylark, 44 for Skylark V-8 or Sportwagon, 46 for Gran Sport, 52 for LeSabre, 54 for LeSabre Custom, 64 for Wildcat, 66 for Wildcat Custom, 82 for Electra 225, 84 for Electra 225 Custom, 94 for Riviera.

MODEL YEAR: 1968

SPECIAL DELUXE SERIES. Six cylinders, 3.875 by 3.530, 250 cubic inches, rated 36.0 hp. Wheelbase 112 inches for coupe, 116 inches for sedan, prices $2513 and $2664 respectively.

SPECIAL DELUXE SERIES. Eight cylinders, V-8, 3.800 by 3.850, 350 cubic inches, rated 46.20 hp. Wheelbase 116 inches. Available as station wagon, for $3001.

SKYLARK SERIES. Six-cylinder engine and wheelbases same as Special DeLuxe Series. Price range $2638-$2666.

SKYLARK CUSTOM SERIES. Eight-cylinder engine same as Special DeLuxe. Wheelbases 112 inches for Sport Coupe and Convertible, 116 inches for Four-Door Hardtop and Sedan. Prices $2936, $3098, $3108 and $2924 respectively.

GRAN SPORT SERIES. Wheelbase 112 inches. GS 400 continued; GS 350 added with new 350-cubic-inch V-8. Price range $2926-$3271.

SPORTWAGON SERIES. Used new 350-cubic-inch V-8. Wheelbase 121 inches. Price range $3341-$3499.

LESABRE AND LESABRE CUSTOM SERIES. Used new 350-cubic-inch V-8. Price range $3141-$3504.

WILDCAT AND WILDCAT CUSTOM SERIES. Price range $3416-$3873.

ELECTRA 225 AND 225 CUSTOM SERIES. Price range $4200-$4541.

RIVIERA. Continued at $4615.

Notes: In vehicle identification code the number "34" now represented the GS 350 as well as Special DeLuxe; the GS 400 carried "46."

MODEL YEAR: 1969

SPECIAL DELUXE SERIES. Price range $2562-$3124.

SKYLARK AND SKYLARK CUSTOM SERIES. Price range $2715-$3152.

GS SERIES. Price range $2980-$3325.

SPORTWAGON SERIES. Price range $3465-$3621.

LESABRE AND LESABRE CUSTOM SERIES. Wheelbase 123.2 inches. Price range $3216-$3579.

WILDCAT AND WILDCAT CUSTOM SERIES. Wheelbase 123.2 inches. Price range $3491-$3948.

ELECTRA 225 AND 225 CUSTOM SERIES. Wheelbase 126.2 inches. Price range $4302-$4643.

RIVIERA. Continued at $4701.

Notes: Variable ratio power steering introduced to Wildcat, Electra and Riviera models. Turbo-Hydramatic 350 transmission available optionally.

MODEL YEAR: 1970

SKYLARK AND SKYLARK 350 SERIES. Replaced former Special DeLuxe series, with six-cylinder engine standard, V-8 available optionally. Price range of V-6 $2685-$2859.

SPORTWAGON SERIES. Wheelbase 116 inches. Price range $3210-$3242.

SKYLARK CUSTOM SERIES. Price range $3101-$3275.

GS AND GS 455 SERIES. Eight cylinders, V-8, 4.3125 by 3,900, 455 cubic inches, rated 59.5 hp. Replaced former GS 400 in sport coupe and convertible models. Price range $3283-$3469. The GS Sport Coupe continued at $3098.

LESABRE AND LESABRE CUSTOM SERIES. Wheelbase 124 inches. Price range $3453-$3816.

LESABRE CUSTOM 455 SERIES. Used the new 455-cubic-inch engine. Wheelbase 124 inches. Price range $3757-$3897.

ESTATE WAGON. Eight cylinders, V-8, 4.3125 by 3.900, 455 cubic inches, rated 59.5 hp. Wheelbase 124 inches. Price range $4081-$4226.

WILDCAT CUSTOM SERIES. Used the new 455-cubic-inch engine. Wheelbase 124 inches. Price range $4107-$4237.

ELECTRA 225 AND 225 CUSTOM SERIES. Used the new 455-cubic-inch engine. Wheelbase 127 inches. Price range $4461-$4802.

RIVIERA. Used the new 455-cubic-inch engine. Price $4854.

Notes: The Stage I package for the GS 455 developed 370 horsepower, Buick's highest in the muscle-car era. Vehicle identification coding of second and third digits revised to: 33 for Skylark, 34 for Sportwagon or GS with 350 engine, 35 for Skylark 350, 44 for Skylark Custom, 46 for GS 455, 52 for LeSabre, 54 for LeSabre Custom, 60 for Estate Wagon, 64 for LeSabre Custom 455, 66 for Wildcat Custom, 82 for Electra 225, 84 for Electra 225 Custom, 94 for Riviera.

MODEL YEAR: 1971

SKYLARK SERIES. Price range $2968-$3039.

SPORTWAGON. Continued only in tailgate model at $3515.

SKYLARK CUSTOM SERIES. Price range $3288-$3462.

GS SERIES. Continued in GS Sport Coupe and Convertible with 350-cubic-inch engine. Prices $3285 and $3476 respectively. The 455-cubic-inch engine available only optionally.

LESABRE AND LESABRE CUSTOM SERIES. Price range $3992-$4342. The 455-cubic-inch engine available only optionally.

ESTATE WAGON SERIES. Price range $4640-$4786.

CENTURION SERIES. Eight cylinders, V-8, 4.3125 by 3.900, 455 cubic inches, rated 59.5 hp. Wheelbase 124 inches. Price range $4564-$4678.

ELECTRA 225 AND 225 CUSTOM SERIES. Price range $4801-$4915.

RIVIERA. Wheelbase 122 inches. Continued at $5253.

Notes: MaxTrac introduced. Wildcat series dropped; Centurion took its vehicle identification code number of 66.

MODEL YEAR: 1972

SKYLARK SERIES. Price range $2925-$2993.

SPORTWAGON. Continued at $3443.

GS SERIES. Price range $3225-$3406.

SKYLARK CUSTOM SERIES. Price range $3228-$3393.

LESABRE AND LESABRE CUSTOM SERIES. Price range $3958-$4168.

ESTATE WAGON SERIES. Price range $4589-$4728.

CENTURION SERIES. Price range $4508-$4616.

ELECTRA 225 AND 225 CUSTOM SERIES. Price range $4781-$5059.

RIVIERA. Continued at $5149.

MODEL YEAR: 1973

CENTURY AND CENTURY WAGON SERIES. Eight cylinders, V-8, 3.800 by 3.850, 350 cubic inches, rated 46.2 hp. Wheelbases 116 and 112 inches. Price range $3400-$3943.

CENTURY LUXUS AND LUXUS WAGON SERIES. Engine and wheelbases as above. Price range $3669-$4109.

REGAL. Eight cylinders, V-8, 3.800 by 3.850, 350 cubic inches, rated 46.2 hp. Wheelbase 112 inches. Price $3813.

LESABRE AND LESABRE CUSTOM SERIES. Continued with 350 engine in price range $4021-$4240.

ESTATE WAGON SERIES. Continued with 455 engine at $4668-$4813.

CENTURION SERIES. Continued with 350 engine at $4359-$4557.

ELECTRA 225 AND 225 CUSTOM SERIES. Continued with 455 engine at $4837-$5127.

RIVIERA. Continued with 455 engine at $5244.

APOLLO. Six cylinders, 250 cubic inches, the L-6 built by Chevrolet. Wheelbase 111 inches. Introduced at $3200 February 1973.

Notes: All Buicks had center pillars to meet government regulations. In vehicle identification code a letter replaced the number to identify the series: B for Apollo, D for Century, F for Century Wagon, H for Century Luxus, J for Regal, K for Century Luxus Wagon, L for LeSabre, N for LeSabre Custom, R for Estate Wagon, P for Centurion, T for Electra 225, V for Electra 225 Custom, Y for Riviera.

MODEL YEAR: 1974

APOLLO SERIES. Price range $2904-$3053.

CENTURY 350 AND 350 WAGON. New designation. Price range $3628-$4144.

CENTURY LUXUS AND LUXUS WAGON. Price range $3927-$4310.

REGAL SERIES. Sedan on a 116-inch wheelbase added. Price range $4039-$4059.

LESABRE AND LESABRE LUXUS SERIES. New designation for top-of-the-line LeSabre. Price range $4191-$4532.

ESTATE WAGON SERIES. Price range $4894-$5057.

ELECTRA 225 SERIES. Price range $5146-$5259. Custom series continued at $5324-$5436. Limited series added at $5772-$5807.

RIVIERA. Continued at $5565.

Notes: Air bag passive restraints offered as option on Riviera and Electra. In vehicle identification code, P now identified LeSabre Luxus and X the Electra 225 Limited.

MODEL YEAR: 1975

SKYHAWK SERIES. Six cylinders, V-6, 3.800 by 3.400, 251 cubic inches. Wheelbase 97 inches. Price range $3859-$4172.

APOLLO/SKYLARK SERIES. Used Chevrolet-built L-6 as standard in Apollo four-door sedans. New Buick V-6 standard in all other models. Price range $3233-$4252.

CENTURY SERIES. Used new V-6. Name "Special" revived for new two-door coupe. Price range $3814-$3944.

CENTURY WAGON SERIES. Continued with the 350 V-8 at $4636-$4751.

CENTURY CUSTOM SERIES. Replaced former Luxus. Used new V-6. Price range $4154-$4211.

CENTURY CUSTOM WAGON. Replaced former Luxus. Continued with

350 V-8 in price range $4802-$4917.

REGAL SERIES. Used new V-6 in price range $4257-$4311.

ESTATE WAGON SERIES. Continued with 455 V-8 $5447-$5591.

LESABRE SERIES. Continued with 350 V-8 $4771-$5133. The "Custom" name revived for top-of-the-line LeSabre models.

ELECTRA 225 SERIES. Continued with 455 V-8 at $6041-$6516. Available now only as "Custom" or "Limited."

RIVIERA. Continued with 455 V-8 at $6420.

Notes: This was the last year for a Buick convertible model. New letter designations in the vehicle identification number were S for Skyhawk, B or C for Apollo/Skylark and E for Century "Special."

MODEL YEAR: 1976

SKYHAWK SERIES. Price range $3902-$4215.

SKYLARK SERIES. Price range $3434-$4397. Apollo name dropped.

CENTURY SERIES. Price range $3934-$4104.

CENTURY CUSTOM SERIES. Price range $4345-$5098.

REGAL SERIES. Coupe continued with V-6. The 350 V-8 standard in the sedan. Price range $4464-$4824.

LESABRE SERIES. The V-6 used in standard line (4BN39, 57 and 69). Price range $4746-$4870. The 350 V-8 retained in Custom line at price range $5045-$5165.

ESTATE WAGON SERIES. Price range $5590-$5730.

ELECTRA 225 SERIES. Price range $6366-$6851.

RIVIERA. Continued at $6797.

Notes: New letter designations in the vehicle identification number were T for Skyhawk, S, B for Skylark, C for Skylark S/R, W for Skylark S.

MODEL YEAR: 1977

SKYHAWK SERIES. Price range $3980-$4293.

SKYLARK SERIES. Price range $3642-$4695.

CENTURY SERIES. Price range $4170-$4363.

CENTURY CUSTOM SERIES. Price range $4627-$5218.

REGAL SERIES. Price range $4712-$5243.

LESABRE SERIES. Wheelbase 115.9 inches. Continued in price range $5032-$5092 for V-6 models, $5321-$5381 for 350 V-8 Custom models. LeSabre Sport Coupe at $5818.

ESTATE WAGON. Used the 350 V-8. Wheelbase 115.9 inches. Price $5902.

ELECTRA SERIES. Used the 350 V-8. Wheelbase 118.9 inches. Price range $6865-$7032.

RIVIERA. Used the 350 V-8. Wheelbase 115.9 inches. Price $7357.

MODEL YEAR: 1978

SKYHAWK SERIES. Price range $4145-$4413.

SKYLARK SERIES. Price range $3911-$4463. "Custom" line introduced.

CENTURY SERIES. Wheelbase 108.1 inches throughout line. Models now designated "Special" in $4413-$5020 price range, "Custom" in $4658-$5322 price range; "Limited" in $5017-$5127 price range.

REGAL SERIES. Wheelbase 108.1 inches. Used V-6 in all models. Turbocharged V-6 introduced on Sport Coupe. "Limited" version of two-door coupe. Price range $4884-$5957.

LESABRE SERIES. Used V-6 in all models including Custom. Turbocharged V-6 introduced on Sport Coupe. Price range $5450-$5836, Sport Coupe at $6346.

ESTATE WAGON. Continued at $6393.

ELECTRA SERIES. Price range $7251-$7816. New "Park Avenue" coupe and sedan introduced at $7951 and $8207 respectively.

RIVIERA. Continued at $9223.

Notes: New letter designations in the vehicle identification number were C for Skylark Custom, G for Century Sport Coupe, L for Century Limited, K for Regal Sport Coupe, M for Regal Limited, U for Electra Park Avenue.

MODEL YEAR: 1979

SKYHAWK SERIES. Price range $4380-$4598.

SKYLARK SERIES. Price range $4081-$4561.

CENTURY SERIES. Continued in Special, Custom, Sport and Limited models in price range $4698-$5561.

REGAL SERIES. Price range $5079-$6226.

LESABRE SERIES. Price range $5680-$6621. "Limited" designation replaced "Custom."

ESTATE WAGON. Continued at $6714.

ELECTRA SERIES. Price range $7756-$8598.

RIVIERA SERIES. Wheelbase 114 inches. The S Type with turbocharged V-6 and front wheel drive introduced. The 350 V-8 retained for standard version. Price $10,111; for S Type $10,388.

Notes: Letter designation in vehicle identification number for new S Type Riviera was Y.

MODEL YEAR: 1980

SKYHAWK SERIES. Price range $4985-$5202.

SKYLARK SERIES. Introduced in spring of 1979 among new General Motors X-body cars. Standard engine 2.5-liter four built by Pontiac, optional 2.8-liter V-6 from Chevrolet. Wheelbase 104.9 inches. Front wheel drive. Coupe and sedan in standard, Limited and Sport models. Price range $5151-$5910.

CENTURY SERIES. Continued in standard, Limited and Sport models. "Special" and "Custom" designations dropped. Former Custom Wagon now Estate Wagon. Price range $5537-$6210.

REGAL SERIES. Price range $6294-$6941.

LESABRE SERIES. Price range $6662-$7769.

LESABRE ESTATE WAGON. Used 301-cubic-inch V-8 built by Pontiac. Wheelbase 115.9 inches. Price $7660.

ELECTRA ESTATE WAGON. Used 301-cubic-inch V-8 built by Pontiac. Wheelbase 115.9 inches. Price $10,500.

ELECTRA SERIES. Six cylinders, V-6, 3.965 by 3.400, 252 cubic inches, rated 37.7 hp. Models designated "Limited" and "Park Avenue." Price range $9119-$10,370.

RIVIERA SERIES. Price range $11,480-$11,810.

Notes: Diesel engine (5.7-liter V-8 built by Oldsmobile) available optionally on Electra coupes and sedans, Electra and LeSabre Estate Wagons. Letter designation in vehicle identification code for new Skylark Sport was D.

MODEL YEAR: 1981

SKYLARK SERIES. Price range $6275-$7054.

CENTURY SERIES. Sedans and wagons only. Price range $6863-$7737.

REGAL SERIES. Price range $7310-$8242.

LESABRE SERIES. Price range $7462-$7839.

LESABRE ESTATE WAGON. Standard engine 5.0 liter V8 produced by Olds. Price $8439.

ELECTRA ESTATE WAGON. Standard engine 5.0 liter V8 produced by Olds. Price $10,942.

ELECTRA SERIES. Price range $9917-$11,046.

RIVIERA SERIES. S Type Renamed T Type. Price range $11,777-$12,961. *443*

MODEL YEAR: 1982

SKYHAWK SERIES. Reintroduced February 1982, as a front wheel drive series with 101.2'' wheelbase. Coupes and sedans in custom and limited models with 1.8-liter L4 engine as standard. Price range $7289-$7923.
SKYLARK SERIES. Price range $7469-$8209.
CENTURY SERIES. Continued as a front wheel drive model with 104.9'' wheelbase. Coupes and sedans in custom and limited models. 2.5-liter L4 engine produced by Pontiac as standard with 3.0 liter Buick V-6 optional. Price range $8972-$9573.
REGAL SERIES. Added sedans in standard and limited models and a four door, 2 seat wagon as the Regal Estate Wagon. Price range $8702-$9728.
LESABRE SERIES. Price range $8763-$9320.
LESABRE ESTATE WAGON. Price $10,656.
ELECTRA ESTATE WAGON. Price $12,898.
ELECTRA SERIES. Price range $11,701-$13,547.
RIVIERA SERIES. Added Convertible model at $23,983. Price range $14,261-$23,983.

MODEL YEAR: 1983

SKYHAWK SERIES. Added four door, 2 seat wagons in custom and limited models. 2.0-liter EFI L4 engine produced by Chevrolet became standard on all custom and limited models. A T Type coupe with a 1.8-liter overhead cam (OHC) and Electronic Fuel Injection (EFI) engine produced by Pontiac as standard. Also standard on the T type was a 5 speed manual transmission. Price range $6951-$7952.
SKYLARK SERIES. Sport model designation replaced by T Type (coupe only). Price range $7540-$9326.
CENTURY SERIES. Added T Type coupe and sedan with a 3.0-liter Buick produced V-6 as standard. Price range $8832-$10,168.
REGAL SERIES. Sport coupe renamed T Type. Price range $9175-$10,441.
LESABRE SERIES. Continued as custom and limited models. Price range $9446-$10,144.
LESABRE ESTATE WAGON. Price $11,339.
ELECTRA ESTATE WAGON. Price $13,867.
ELECTRA SERIES. Price range $12,645-$14,475.
RIVIERA SERIES. Price range $15,468-$25,190.

MODEL YEAR: 1984

SKYHAWK SERIES. Price range $7133-$8152.
SKYLARK SERIES. Price range $7545-$9557.
CENTURY SERIES. Wagons in custom and limited models added. July 1983, the T Type standard powertrain revised to a Buick 3.8-liter MFI (Multi-Port Fuel Injection) V-6 engine and 4 speed automatic transmission. Price range $9110-$10,674.
REGAL SERIES. Wagons discontinued. T Type standard engine 3.8-liter SFI (Sequential-Port Fuel Injection) Turbocharged V-6 produced by Buick. Price range $9487-$12,118.
LESABRE SERIES. Price range $9984-$10,940.
LESABRE ESTATE WAGON. Discontinued.
ELECTRA ESTATE WAGON. Price $14,483.
ELECTRA SERIES. Price range $13,155-$15,044.
RIVIERA SERIES. T Type standard turbocharged 3.8-liter V-6 engine from carburetor to Sequential-Port Fuel Injection. Price range $15,967-$25,832.

MODEL YEAR: 1985

SKYHAWK SERIES. Price range $7365-$8437.

SKYLARK SERIES. Sedans only continued in custom and limited models. Price range $7707-$8283.
SOMERSET REGAL. New front wheel drive coupes in standard and limited models with a 103.4'' wheelbase. 2.5-liter EFI L4 engine produced by Pontiac and 5 speed manual transmission standard with a 3.0-liter MFI Buick V-6 as optional equipment. Price range $8857-$9466.
CENTURY SERIES. Price range $9377-$11,418.
REGAL SERIES. Price range $9928-$12,640.
LESABRE SERIES. Limited model renamed LeSabre Limited Collectors' Edition, recognizing 1985 as the last year of rear wheel drive LeSabre production. Price range $10,453-$11,916.
LESABRE ESTATE WAGON. Reintroduced after 1 year absence. Price $12,704.
ELECTRA ESTATE WAGON. Price $15,323.
ELECTRA SERIES. Introduced April 1984, as a front wheel drive model with 110.8'' wheelbase. The Electra coupe and sedan standard engine was a 3.0-liter V-6 produced by Buick. Park Avenue and T Type coupes and sedans standard equipment engine was the 3.8-liter MFI Buick V-6. All models have a 4 speed automatic transmission. Price range $13,850-$15,752.
RIVIERA SERIES. The 5.0-liter V-8 produced by Oldsmobile is made standard in the Riviera coupe and convertible models. (T Type retains 3.8-liter SFI turbocharged V-6.) Price range $16,710-$26,797.

MODEL YEAR: 1986

SKYHAWK SERIES. Price range $7844-$9414.
SKYLARK SERIES. Sedans only continued in custom and limited models. Price range $9620-$10,290.
SOMERSET SERIES. T Type coupe added. (Regal dropped from Series name.) Price range $9425-$11,390.
CENTURY SERIES. Price range $10,228-$11,109.
REGAL SERIES. Price range $10,654-$13,714.
LESABRE SERIES. Continued as front wheel drive models on 110.8'' wheelbase. 3.0-liter V-6 engine with MFI, automatic with overdrive and air conditioner are standard on all models. Custom and limited coupes and sedans available. Price range $12,511-$13,633.
LESABRE ESTATE WAGON SERIES. Price $13,622.
ELECTRA ESTATE WAGON. Price $16,402.
ELECTRA SERIES. T Type coupe dropped. Price range $15,396-$17,338.
RIVIERA SERIES. Continued as completely restyled 108'' wheelbase coupes with transverse mounted 3.8-liter V-6 engine with SFI as standard. Luxury and T Type coupes available. Price range $19,831-$21,577.

MODEL YEAR: 1987

SKYHAWK SERIES. T Type models eliminated. Price range $8,522-$9,841.
SKYLARK SERIES. Price range $9,915-$11,003.
SOMERSET SERIES. T Type eliminated. Price range $9,957-$11,003.
CENTURY SERIES. T Type eliminated. Price range $10,844-$11,998.
REGAL SERIES. T Type eliminated. Price range $11,562-$12,303.
LESABRE SERIES. 3.8-liter V-6 engine with SFI becomes standard. Price range $13,438-$14,918.
LESABRE ESTATE WAGON SERIES. Price $14,724.
ELECTRA ESTATE WAGON SERIES. Price $17,697.
ELECTRA SERIES. Limited coupe dropped. Park Avenue coupe only two-door Electra model. Price range $16,902-$18,769.
RIVIERA SERIES. T Type Model dropped as a separate V.I.N. (T Type Option Package available @ $1,844.) Price $20,337.

MODEL YEAR: 1988

SKYHAWK SERIES. Price $9,284

SKYLARK SERIES. 3.0-liter V-6 engine and 2.3-liter Quad 4 engine optional. Price range $10,684-$11,791

CENTURY SERIES. Price range $11,643-$13,077

REGAL SERIES. Redesigned front-wheel-drive Custom and Limited coupes. 2.8-liter V-6 with 4-speed automatic transmission. Price range $12,449-$12,782.

LESABRE SERIES. 3800 V-6 engine standard in T Type and optional on all other LeSabres. Price range $14,560-$16,350

LESABRE ESTATE WAGON SERIES. Price $16,040

ELECTRA ESTATE WAGON SERIES. Price $18,954

ELECTRA SERIES. 3800 V-6 engine with 4-speed automatic transmission. Anti-lock brakes standard on T Type. Price range $17,479-$20,229.

RIVIERA SERIES. Special hood ornament and instrument panel trim plate commemorate silver anniversary. 3800 V-6 engine standard. Price $21,615

REATTA SERIES. Two-passenger luxury coupe introduced. 3800 V-6 engine, anti-lock brakes, Gran Touring suspension, theft deterrent system, hidden headlamps, fog lamps are among the numerous standard equipment. Price $25,000.

MODEL YEAR: 1989

SKYHAWK SERIES. Price range $9,285-$10,230

SKYLARK SERIES. 3.3-liter MFI 3300 V-6 engine replaces 3.0-liter V-6 as optional. 2.3-liter Quad 4 engine optional. Price range $11,115-$12,345.

CENTURY SERIES. New exterior styling. 3.3-liter MFI 3300 V-6 engine optional. Price range $12,199-$13,956.

REGAL SERIES. Gran Sport package added. 3.1-liter V-6 engine replaces 2.8-liter V-6 mid-year. Price range $14,214-$14,739.

LESABRE SERIES. Price range $15,425-$16,730.

LESABRE ESTATE WAGON SERIES. Price $16,770.

ELECTRA ESTATE WAGON SERIES. Price $19,860.

ELECTRA SERIES. Park Avenue Ultra four-door sedan introduced mid-year. Anti-lock brakes standard on Electra T Type. Price range $18,525-$21,325.

RIVIERA SERIES. New exterior styling. T Type model eliminated. Price $22,540.

REATTA SERIES. Price $26,700.

MODEL YEAR: 1990

SKYLARK SERIES. Two new models: standard coupe and sedan. Price range $10,465-$13,145.

CENTURY SERIES. Price range $13,150-$15,455.

REGAL SERIES. 3800 V-6 engine optional mid-year. Price range $15,200-$15,860.

LESABRE SERIES. T Type discontinued. New front and rear design. Price range $16,050-$17,400.

ESTATE WAGON. Offered previously as the LeSabre and Electra wagon. Price $17,940.

ELECTRA SERIES. Price range $20,225-$27,825.

RIVIERA SERIES. Air bag standard. Price $23,040.

REATTA SERIES. Convertible added. Air bag standard. Price range $28,235-$34,995.

MODEL YEAR: 1991

SKYLARK SERIES. Price range $10,725-$13,865.

CENTURY SERIES. Price range $13,685-$16,230.

REGAL SERIES. Custom, Limited and Gran Sport sedans added. 3.1-liter V-6 engine standard. 3800 V-6 engine with tuned port injection optional but standard on Gran Sport Coupe and Sedan. Price range $15,690-$17,917.

LESABRE SERIES. Price range $17,080-$18,430.

ROADMASTER ESTATE WAGON. Roadmaster name returns after 33 years on the rear-wheel drive Estate Wagon. New styling inside and out. Eight passengers and three seats. 5.0-liter V-8 engine and four-speed automatic transmission with overdrive. Air bag and anti-lock brakes standard. Price $21,445.

PARK AVENUE SERIES. Redesigned model available as Park Avenue sedan and Park Avenue Ultra sedan. 3800 V-6 engine with tuned port injection and electronically controlled 4-speed automatic transmission with overdrive. Air bag and anti-lock brakes standard. Price range $24,385-$27,420.

RIVIERA SERIES. 3800 V-6 engine with tuned port injection and electronically controlled 4-speed automatic transmission with overdrive standard. Anti-lock brakes standard. Price $24,560.

REATTA SERIES. 3800 V-6 engine with tuned port injection and electronically controlled 4-speed automatic transmission with overdrive standard. Price range $29,300-$35,965.

MODEL YEAR: 1992

SKYLARK SERIES. Custom coupe and sedan and Luxury Edition sedan discontinued. Completely redesigned coupe and sedan and Gran Sport coupe and sedan. 2.3-liter Quad OHC engine standard. Anti-lock brakes standard. Price range $13,560-$15,555.

CENTURY SERIES. Sedan (Special) added. Price range $13,795-$16,395.

REGAL SERIES. Gran Sport coupe and sedan become model. Anti-lock brakes standard on Limited and Gran Sport, optional on Custom. Price range $16,610-$19,300.

LESABRE SERIES. Completely redesigned. 3800 V-6 engine with tuned port injection and electronically controlled 4-speed automatic transmission with overdrive standard. Air bag, anti-lock brakes and low liftover decklid standard. Price range $18,695-$20,775.

ROADMASTER SERIES. Totally new rear-wheel drive car line in two six-passenger models: sedan and Limited sedan. 5.7-liter V-8 engine with throttle-body fuel injection and four-speed automatic transmission with overdrive standard on sedans. Air bag and anti-lock brakes standard. Price range $21,865-$24,195.

ROADMASTER ESTATE WAGON. 5.7-liter V-8 engine with throttle-body fuel injection and four-speed automatic transmission with overdrive replaces 5.0-liter V-8 engine. Price $23,040.

PARK AVENUE SERIES. Supercharged 3800 V-6 engine standard on Ultra. Price range $25,285-$28,780.

RIVIERA SERIES. Price $25,415.

MODEL YEAR: 1993

SKYLARK SERIES. Custom coupe and sedan models added. Skylark coupe and sedan renamed Limited.

CENTURY SERIES. 2.2-liter MFI engine replaces 2.5-liter engine. Air bag standard (optional on Century Special).

REGAL SERIES. Sedan restyled. Modified 3800 V-6 engine with TPI. New electronically controlled four-speed automatic transmission.

LESABRE SERIES. Anti-lock brakes and traction control standard. Modified 3800 V-6 engine with TPI. Variable effort steering standard on Limited.

ROADMASTER SERIES. Power window lock-out and power mirrors standard.

ROADMASTER ESTATE WAGON. New split folding second seat.

PARK AVENUE SERIES. Vertical grille and tail lamps restyled. Modified 3800 V-6 engine with TPI.

RIVIERA SERIES. New exterior colors.

GENERAL INDEX

INDEX OF ILLUSTRATIONS

NOTE: Boldface indicates illustrations in color.

NOTES & PHOTO CREDITS

In these credits, the following abbreviations for collections have been used. NAHC is the National Automotive History Collection of the Detroit Public Library. MVMA is the Motor Vehicle Manufacturers Association of the United States, Inc. Henry Austin Clark, Jr. of the Long Island Automotive Museum is abbreviated HAC/LIAM. AQ Archives refers to the collections of Automobile Quarterly Publications. Material from the collection of author Terry B. Dunham is abbreviated TBD—and BMD indicates material from the archives of Buick Motor Division.

CHAPTER ONE. 11, 20, 21: MVMA. 12, 13, 18. 19: *The Flint Journal.* 14, 15: Mrs. Edward E. Hays 16: GMI Alumni Archives. 23: AQ Archives.

CHAPTER TWO. 25, 28 above, 35 above: BMD. 26, 27, 28 below, 30, 31: *The Flint Journal.* 33: TBD. 32 above, 35 below: Sloan Museum. 32 below: HAC/LIAM. 34, 36, 37: AQ Archives.

CHAPTER THREE. 39, 53, 58 below: Gerry Fauth. 40, 48, 49, 50, 51, 54, 56: *The Flint Journal.* 41 below, 43, 44 above left, 46 below right: HAC/LIAM. 45 above right, 60: Sloan Museum. 45 below, 52, 58 above: BMD. 55: George Dammann. 58 center: John A. Conde. All other photos: NAHC.

CHAPTER FOUR. 63, 64, 65 left, 81, 82, 93: *The Flint Journal.* 66 below, 73 below left: BMD. 67 right, 72 below right, 76: The Kansas State Historical Society. 68 above: John A. Conde. 69 above, 72 above left, 78: Gerry Fauth. 72 below left: George Dammann. 73 below right, 79 above: AQ Archives. All other photos: BMD.

CHAPTER FIVE. 85, 87 below, 88 above, 90 above left, 92, 93, 95, 96 below: NAHC. 86, 87 above: *The Flint Journal.* 88 below: HAC/LIAM. 90 above right, 102 above: John A. Conde. 91 above, 96 above: Gerry Fauth. 94: TBD. 97 above: The Kansas State Historical Society. 97 below: AQ Archives. 101 above and below left, 102 above: Ray Paszkiewicz. 101 right: Mrs. Edward E. Hays. All other photos: BMD.

CHAPTER SIX. 105, 109, 110, 113 right, 115 below, 118 above: *The Flint Journal.* 106 above, 107 right: John A. Conde. 108, 112, 115 above: Gerry Fauth. 111 above: TBD. 111 below: NAHC. 113 left: C.S. Mott Collection. All other photos: BMD.

CHAPTER SEVEN. 122 above: Jerry Pfafflin. 122 below, 123 below, 129 below: AQ Archives. 123 above: TBD. 124 above and center, 126 above, 128 above: BMD. 124 below, 125, 129 above: NAHC. 126 above and below left, 133 right: Gerry Fauth. 131: *The Flint Journal.* All other photos: HAC/LIAM.

CHAPTER EIGHT. 135: Terry V. Boyce. 136 above: Jerry Pfafflin. 137 center, 145, 148: Gerry Fauth. 138, 139 right, 140, 150 left: HAC/LIAM. 139 left, 150 right: AQ Archives. 141, 142 above and center, 144, 150 above: *The Flint Journal.* 146, 147: TBD. 149: BMD. All other photos: John A Conde.

CHAPTER NINE. 153, 162-163 center, 166: TBD. 154 left, 157 above, 158, 161, 162 above, 163 above, 167: *The Flint Journal.* 157 below: John A. Conde. 164 above left: AQ Archives. 164 right, 165: HAC/LIAM.

CHAPTER TEN. 196 above, 197: *The Flint Journal.* 199 above left, 206 below, 208: BMD. 199 above right, 201 below: Applegate and Applegate. 199 below: AQ Archives. 201 above: John A. Conde. 201 center, 203 above, 206 above: HAC/LIAM. 205, 209: NAHC. All other photos: TBD.

CHAPTER ELEVEN. 212 below right: HAC/LIAM. 214 above right: TBD. All other photos: Hermann C. Brunn.

CHAPTER TWELVE. 219, 220 above left, 225: HAC/LIAM. 220 above right, 226 above: TBD. 220 below left, and center, 223: *The Flint Journal.* 220 below right: Carol Hays. 224: John A. Conde. 226 below, 227 above and below: Terry V. Boyce. 228, 229 below: BMD. 229 above: AQ Archives.

CHAPTER THIRTEEN. 232 above: Applegate and Applegate. 237 below left: AQ Archives. 241 above: HAC/LIAM. All other photos: BMD.

CHAPTER FOURTEEN. 243, 253, 255: AQ Archives. 244 below: William Browning. 245 above: GM Technical Center. 246 above, 247 below, 252 below: BMD. 247 center below, 249 above right, 252 above and center above: NAHC. 249 above left: HAC/LIAM. 249 below, 251 below: TBD. 251 center below, 254 above and below: Applegate and Applegate. All other photos: John A. Conde.

CHAPTER FIFTEEN. 257, 265 above and below: Terry V. Boyce. 258 above, 259 above, 266 below, 270 above left: William Browning. 258 below, 259 left and center, 270 below left and right: BMD. 259 right: TBD. 260 above, 261 above: Applegate and Applegate. 260 center and below, 261 center: HAC/LIAM. 261 right, 263 above center, 264 center, 268 above and center: AQ Archives. 266 right: *The Flint Journal.* 267: Jerry Pfafflin. 272 above: John A. Conde. All other photos: NAHC.

CHAPTER SIXTEEN. 277: AQ Archives. 278 left: *The Flint Journal.* 279 top: Indianapolis Motor Speedway. 279 center and below left: John W. Burnside. 279 below right: Daytona International Speedway. 281, 283 below left: NAHC. 282, 283 right, 284 below and above left, 289 above right, 290 below, 293 below, 296, 297 right, 300 below: William Browning. 286, 287: GM Technical Center. All other photos: BMD.

CHAPTER SEVENTEEN. 306 left, 312, 316: William Browning. 306 below right: Indianapolis Motor Speedway. 308, 309 left, 311 above: *The Flint Journal.* 309 right: Leo Johnson. 313 above and right: Barry Edmonds. 313 left: Bruce Edwards. 315 above and center: GM Technical Center. All other photos: BMD. 323 right: Mike Hayman.

APPENDIX ONE. 353, 355 above: Brad Hindall. 356 above left: AQ Archives. 360, 361: Peter Helck. All other photos: NAHC.

APPENDIX TWO. 363: *The Flint Journal.* 364: Gerry Fauth. 365: TBD. 367, 368: NAHC.

APPENDIX THREE. 371: BMD. 372, 373: W.C. Williams.

APPENDIX FOUR. 377 right, 379 top: HAC/LIAM. 379 center and below, 380 above left and bottom left, 381 right: Leonard J. Peterson. All other photos: TBD.

APPENDIX FIVE. 383: MVMA. 384, 385: TBD. 387: HAC/LIAM. 389: Society of Automotive Engineers.

APPENDIX SIX. 391, 400 center, 401 center right, 407 center right: Nicola Bulgari. 393, 401 below left: AQ Archives. 394, 395, 405 right: General Motors of Canada, Ltd., collection of Vern Bethel. 396 below: Craven Foundation. 397 below left: TBD. 398, 406 above: National Motor Museum at Beaulieu. 401 above and right below, 402, 403, 404, 405 left, 407 above right: David Norton. 407 left: NAHC. 307 below right: BMD. All other photos: Vern Bethel.

ABOUT THE CLUBS

The Buick Club of America, Inc. was founded in 1966 for the preservation and restoration of those vehicles built by the Buick Motor Division of General Motors Corporation. Membership today averages 5000 enthusiasts, including 150 overseas members, and thirty-eight chapters, including a chapter in England. Members receive the club's monthly magazine, *The Buick Bugle*, and advertising privileges therein. Participation in all club events and technical assistance when available are further privileges of membership. It is not necessary to own a Buick to join. Address: P.O. Box 898, Garden Grove, California 92642.

Founded in Oshawa, Ontario in 1971, the McLaughlin Buick Club of Canada is dedicated to preserving McLaughlin and McLaughlin-Buick motorcars, and to maintaining a permanent record of Colonel R.S. McLaughlin's contribution to the automotive industry in North America. Among club activities, annual meets are held in Oshawa and in Langley, British Columbia, and the club's bi-monthly publication is entitled *Accelerator.* Membership at present is over 360 enthusiasts worldwide. Address: 99 Simcoe Street South, Oshawa, Ontario L1H 4G7.